ACCA
STUDY TEXT

Paper 1.2

Financial Information for Management

BPP's NEW STUDY TEXTS FOR ACCA's NEW SYLLABUS

- Targeted to the syllabus and study guide
- Quizzes and questions to check your understanding
- Clear layout and style designed to save you time
- Plenty of exam-style questions
- Chapter Roundups and summaries to help revision
- Mind Maps to integrate the key points

BPP Publishing
February 2001

First edition February 2001

ISBN 0 7517 0726 0

British Library Cataloguing-in-Publication Data
A catalogue record for this book
is available from the British Library

Published by

BPP Publishing Ltd
Aldine House, Aldine Place
London W12 8AW

www.bpp.com

Printed in Great Britain by Ashford Colour Press

We are grateful to the Association of Chartered Certified Accountants for permission to reproduce past examination questions and questions from the pilot paper. The answers have been prepared by BPP Publishing Limited.

Page

THE BPP STUDY TEXT (v)

HELP YOURSELF STUDY FOR YOUR ACCA EXAMS (vii)
The right approach - suggested study sequence - developing your
personal study plan

SYLLABUS (xii)

STUDY GUIDE (xviii)

OXFORD BROOKES DEGREE IN APPLIED ACCOUNTING (xxiv)

THE EXAM PAPER (xxv)

Contents

THE BPP STUDY TEXT

Aims of this Study Text

To provide you with the knowledge and understanding, skills and application techniques that you need if you are to be successful in your exams

This Study Text has been written around the **Financial Information for Management** syllabus.

- It is **comprehensive**. It covers the syllabus content. No more, no less.

- It is written at the **right level**. Each chapter is written with the ACCA's **study guide** in mind.

- It is targeted to the **exam**. We have taken account of the **pilot paper,** questions put to the examiners at the recent ACCA conference and the assessment methodology.

To allow you to study in the way that best suits your learning style and the time you have available, by following your personal Study Plan (see page (ix))

You may be studying at home on your own until the date of the exam, or you may be attending a full-time course. You may like to (and have time to) read every word, or you may prefer to (or only have time to) skim-read and devote the remainder of your time to question practice. Wherever you fall in the spectrum, you will find the BPP Study Text meets your needs in designing and following your personal Study Plan.

To tie in with the other components of the BPP Effective Study Package to ensure you have the best possible chance of passing the exam (see page (vi))

Recommended period of use	Elements of the BPP Effective Study Package
Three to twelve months before the exam	**Study Text** Use the Study Text to acquire knowledge, understanding, skills and the ability to use application techniques.
One to six months before the exam	**Practice & Revision Kit** Attempt the tutorial questions which are provided for each topic area in the Kit. Then try the numerous examination questions, for which there are realistic suggested solutions prepared by BPP's own authors.
From three months before the exam until the last minute	**Passcards** Work through these short, memorable notes which are focused on what is most likely to come up in the exam you will be sitting.
One to six months before the exam	**Success Tapes** These cover the vital elements of your syllabus in less than 90 minutes per subject with these audio cassettes. Each tape also contains exam hints to help you fine tune your strategy.
Three to twelve months before the exam	**Breakthrough Videos** Use a Breakthrough Video to supplement your Study Text. They give you clear tuition on key exam subjects and allow you the luxury of being able to pause or repeat sections until you have fully grasped the topic.

HELP YOURSELF STUDY FOR YOUR ACCA EXAMS

Exams for professional bodies such as ACCA are very different from those you have taken at college or university. You will be under **greater time pressure before** the exam - as you may be combining your study with work as well as in the exam room. There are many different ways of learning and so the BPP Study Text offers you a number of different tools to help you through. Here are some hints and tips: they are not plucked out of the air, but **based on research and experience**. (You don't need to know that long-term memory is in the same part of the brain as emotions and feelings - but it's a fact anyway.)

The right approach

1   **The right attitude**

Believe in yourself	Yes, there is a lot to learn. Yes, it is a challenge. But thousands have succeeded before and you can too.
Remember why you're doing it	Studying might seem a grind at times, but you are doing it for a reason: to advance your career.

2   **The right focus**

Read through the Syllabus and Study guide	These tell you what you are expected to know and are supplemented by Exam Focus Points in the text.
Study the Exam Paper section	The pilot paper is likely to be a reasonable guide of what you should expect in the exam.

3   **The right method**

The big picture	You need to grasp the detail - but keeping in mind how everything fits into the big picture will help you understand better. • The **Introduction** of each chapter puts the material in context. • The **Syllabus content**, **Study guide** and **Exam focus points** show you what you need to **grasp**. • **Mind Maps** show the links and key issues in key topics.
In your own words	To absorb the information (and to practise your written communication skills), it helps **put it into your own words**. • **Take notes.** • Answer the **questions** in each chapter. As well as helping you absorb the information you will practise your written communication skills, which become increasingly important as you progress through your ACCA exams. • Draw **mind maps**. We have some examples. • Try 'teaching' to a colleague or friend.

BPP
PUBLISHING

| Give yourself cues to jog your memory | The BPP Study Text uses **bold** to **highlight key points** and **icons** to identify key features, such as **Exam focus points** and **Key terms.**

• Try **colour coding** with a highlighter pen.

• Write **key points** on cards. |

4   **The right review**

| Review, review, review | It is a **fact** that regularly reviewing a topic in summary form can **fix it in your memory**. Because **review** is so important, the BPP Study Text helps you to do so in many ways.

• **Chapter roundups** summarise the key points in each chapter. Use them to recap each study session.

• The **Quick quiz** is another review technique to ensure that you have grasped the essentials.

• Go through the **Examples** in each chapter a second or third time. |

Suggested study sequence

Tackle the chapters in the order you find them in the Study Text. Taking into account your individual learning style, you could follow this sequence.

Key study steps	Activity
Step 1 **Topic list**	Each numbered topic is a numbered section in the chapter.
Step 2 **Introduction**	This gives you the **big picture** in terms of the **context** of the chapter. The content is referenced to the **Study Guide**, and **Exam Guidance** shows how the topic is likely to be examined. In other words, it sets your **objectives for study.**
Step 3 **Knowledge brought forward boxes**	In these we highlight information and techniques that it is assumed you have 'brought forward' with you from your earlier studies. If there are topics which have changed recently due to legislation for example, these topics are explained in more detail.
Step 4 **Explanations**	Proceed methodically through the chapter, reading each section thoroughly and making sure you understand.
Step 5 **Key terms and Exam focus points**	<ul><li>**Key terms** can often earn you *easy marks* if you state them clearly and correctly in an appropriate exam answer (and they are indexed at the back of the text).</li><li>**Exam focus points** give you a good idea of how we think the examiner intends to examine certain topics.</li></ul>
Step 6 **Note taking**	Take brief notes if you wish, avoiding the temptation to copy out too much.
Step 7 **Examples**	Follow each through to its solution very carefully.
Step 8 **Case examples**	Study each one, and try to add flesh to them from your own experience - they are designed to show how the topics you are studying come alive (and often come unstuck) in the real world.
Step 9 **Questions**	Make a very good attempt at each one.
Step 10 **Answers**	Check yours against ours, and make sure you understand any discrepancies.
Step 11 **Chapter roundup**	Work through it very carefully, to make sure you have grasped the major points it is highlighting.
Step 12 **Quick quiz**	When you are happy that you have covered the chapter, use the **Quick quiz** to check how much you have remembered of the topics covered.

Key study steps	Activity
Step 13 **Question(s) in the Question bank**	Either at this point, or later when you are thinking about revising, make a full attempt at the **Question(s)** suggested at the very end of the chapter. You can find these at the end of the Study Text, along with the **Answers** so you can see how you did. We highlight those that are introductory, and those which are of the standard you would expect to find in an exam.

Developing your personal Study Plan

Preparing a Study Plan (and sticking closely to it) is one of the key elements in learning success.

Step 1. How do you learn?

First you need to be aware of your style of learning. There are four typical learning styles. Consider yourself in the light of the following descriptions and work out which you fit most closely. You can then plan to follow the key study steps in the sequence suggested.

Learning styles	Characteristics	Sequence of key study steps in the BPP Study Text
Theorist	Seeks to understand principles before applying them in practice	1, 2, 3, 4, 7, 8, 5, 9/10, 11, 12, 13 (6 continuous)
Reflector	Seeks to observe phenomena, thinks about them and then chooses to act	
Activist	Prefers to deal with practical, active problems; does not have much patience with theory	1, 2, 9/10 (read through), 7, 8, 5, 11, 3, 4, 9/10 (full attempt), 12, 13 (6 continuous)
Pragmatist	Prefers to study only if a direct link to practical problems can be seen; not interested in theory for its own sake	9/10 (read through), 2, 5, 7, 8, 11, 1, 3, 4, 9/10 (full attempt), 12, 13 (6 continuous)

Step 2. How much time do you have?

Work out the time you have available per week, given the following.

- The standard you have set yourself
- The time you need to set aside later for work on the Practice & Revision Kit and Passcards
- The other exam(s) you are sitting
- Very importantly, practical matters such as work, travel, exercise, sleep and social life

Hours

Note your time available in box A.   A [   ]

Step 3. Allocate your time

- Take the time you have available per week for this Study Text shown in box A, multiply it by the number of weeks available and insert the result in box B.   B [   ]

- Divide the figure in Box B by the number of chapters in this text and insert the result in box C.   C [   ]

Step 4. Implement

Set about studying each chapter in the time shown in box C, following the key study steps in the order suggested by your particular learning style.

This is your personal **Study Plan**.

Short of time: *Skim study technique?*

You may find you simply do not have the time available to follow all the key study steps for each chapter, however you adapt them for your particular learning style. If this is the case, follow the **skim study** technique below (the icons in the Study Text will help you to do this).

- Study the chapters in the order you find them in the Study Text.

- For each chapter, follow the key study steps 1-3, and then skim-read through step 4. Jump to step 11, and then go back to step 5. Follow through steps 7 and 8, and prepare outline answers to questions (steps 9/10). Try the Quick quiz (step 12), following up any items you can't answer, then do a plan for the Question (step 13), comparing it against our answers. You should probably still follow step 6 (note-taking), although you may decide simply to rely on the BPP Passcards for this.

Moving on...

However you study, when you are ready to embark on the practice and revision phase of the BPP Effective Study Package, you should still refer back to this Study Text, both as a source of **reference** (you should find the list of key terms and the index particularly helpful for this) and as a **refresher** (the Chapter roundups and Quick quizzes help you here).

And remember to keep careful hold of this Study Text - you will find it invaluable in your work.

BPP
PUBLISHING

SYLLABUS

Aim

To develop knowledge and understanding of the application of management accounting techniques to support the management processes of planning, control and decision making.

Objectives

On completion of this paper candidates should be able to:

- explain the role of management accounting within an organisation and the requirement for management information

- describe costs by classification and purpose

- identify appropriate material, labour and expense costs

- understand the principles of costing and apply them in straightforward scenarios

- understand and demonstrate the cost factors affecting production and pricing decisions

- understand the basic principles of performance management

- understand the principles of budgeting and apply them in straightforward scenarios

- demonstrate the skills expected in Part 1.

Position of the paper in the overall syllabus

No prior knowledge is required before commencing study for Paper 1.2. Some understanding of the accounting principles and practices from Paper 1.1 Preparing Financing Statements and a basic competence in numeracy are assumed.

This paper provides the basic techniques required to enable the candidate to develop the various methods into more complex problems at later parts. Candidates will, therefore, need a sound understanding of the methods and techniques encountered in this paper to ensure that they can take them further in subsequent papers. The methods introduced in this paper are revisited and extended in Paper 2.4 Financial Management and Control and taken yet further in Papers 3.3 Performance Management and 3.7 Strategic Financial Management.

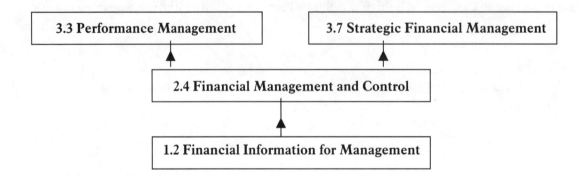

SYLLABUS

1   Accounting for management

(a)   The nature, purpose, scope and interrelations of functions carried out by management in relation to resources, costs, operations, performance

    (i)   setting objectives (long and short-term, strategic and operational, corporate and personal)

    (ii)   planning to meet objectives

    (iii)   implementing objectives

    (iv)   monitoring and controlling against objectives and plans

    (v)   evaluating performance against objectives and plans.

(b)   Nature of internal reporting

    (i)   financial and non-financial information for managers

    (ii)   cost centres, revenue centres, profit centres and investment centres and the impact of these on management information and appraisal

(c)   Management information requirements

    (i)   importance and definition of good information
    (ii)   presentation of information
    (iii)   role of accountants and accounting information
    (iv)   role of IT.

(d)   Maintaining and improving an appropriate system

    (i)   cost units

    (ii)   cost/profit/responsibility centres

    (iii)   methods for recording relevant information

    (iv)   sources of information and recording/processing

    (v)   computer based information, storage and processing

    (vi)   analysis of output information and its dissemination to relevant individuals/ departments.

2   Cost accounting

(a)   Cost accounting versus management accounting

    (i)   purposes of cost and management accounting and financial accounting
    (ii)   role of cost accounting in a management information system
    (iii)   non-financial information

(b)   Nature and purpose of cost classification/definitions.

3   Elements of cost

(a)   Materials

     (i)   standard and actual costs for materials including the use of FIFO, LIFO and weighted average for material valuation and the pricing of material issues

     (ii)   optimal purchase quantities to include discounts

     (iii)   optimal batch quantities

     (iv)   reorder levels

     (v)   material losses.

(b)   Labour

     (i)   direct and indirect labour
     (ii)   different remuneration methods
     (iii)   labour efficiency
     (iv)   labour turnover

(c)   Overheads

     (i)   direct and indirect expenses

     (ii)   principles and processes of overhead cost analysis

     (iii)   allocation and apportionment of overhead costs including reciprocal service centre situations

     (iv)   absorption rates

     (v)   under- and over-absorption

     (vi)   fixed overhead expenditure and volume variances

     (vii)   fixed overhead efficiency and capacity variances where appropriate

     (viii)   changes in the cost structure of a business over time.

4   Cost systems

(a)   Job, batch and contract costing

     (i)   characteristics
     (ii)   direct and indirect costs (including treatment of waste, scrap and rectification costs)
     (iii)   profit on part completed contracts.

(b)   Process costing

     (i)   characteristics

     (ii)   appropriate cost units

     (iii)   valuation of process transfers and work-in-progress using equivalent units of production and based on FIFO and weighted average pricing methods

     (iv)   normal losses and abnormal losses and gains

     (v)   joint and by-products.

(c)   Operation/service costing

    (i)   scope of operation/service costing
    (ii) appropriate cost units
    (iii) collection, classification and ascertainment of costs.

5   Costing methods and techniques

(a)   Standard costing

    (i)   establishment of standard costs
    (ii) variance analysis
    (iii) implications for management
    (iv) operating statements

(b)   Marginal and absorption costing

    (i)   marginal and absorption costing profit and loss accounts
    (ii) reconciliation of the profits under the two methods
    (iii) contrast of absorption and marginal costing
    (iv) activity based costing (in outline only).

6   Decision making

(a)   Cost behaviour

    (i)   fixed, variable and semi-variable costs
    (ii) cost behaviour using an appropriate graph
    (iii) high-low method
    (iv) regression analysis.

(b)   Time series analysis

(c)   CVP analysis

    (i)   break-even point and revenue
    (ii) margin of safety
    (iii) target profit
    (iv) profit/volume ratio
    (v) break-even chart and profit/volume graph

(d)   Limiting factors

    (i)   optimal production plan given a scarce resource
    (ii) linear programming techniques
    (iii) other methods for more than two variable problems

(e)   Preparation of cost estimates for decision making

    (i)   relevant costing techniques to include opportunity/sunk, avoidable/unavoidable, fixed/variable applied to such situations as make or buy, shut down and one-off contracts.

(f)   Decision making with uncertainty

    (i)   concept of expected values
    (ii) decision tree analysis.

(g)   Pricing goods and services

    (i)   price/demand and relationships

     (ii) full cost plus pricing

     (iii) marginal costing

(h)   Price skimming penetration pricing, premium pricing and price discrimination.

(i)   Discounted cash flow techniques

     (i)   simple and compound interest

     (ii) net present values

     (iii) annuities and perpetuities

     (iv) internal rate of return

     (v) future values

     (vi) nominal interest

7   Performance measurement

(a)   Measurement of productivity, activity, profitability and quality of service

(b)   Relationship of measure to type of entity

(c)   Range of measures: monetary and non-monetary

(d)   Indices to allow for price and performance changes through time

(e)   Identification of areas of concern from the information produced

(f)   Difference between business performance and management performance

(g)   Benchmarking.

8   Budgeting

(a)   Budget preparation including fixed and flexible budgets

(b)   Reporting of actual versus budget

Excluded topics

Numerical questions on ABC will not be asked.

Key areas of the syllabus

The key topic areas are:

- cost classification and behaviour
- material, labour and overhead cost
- absorption and marginal costing
- process costing
- standard costing
- budgeting
- discounted cash flow techniques
- CVP analysis
- pricing methods.

Approach to examining the syllabus

The examination is a three hour paper constructed in two sections. Both sections will draw from all parts of the syllabus and will contain both computational and discursive elements.

		Number of Marks
Section A	25 compulsory multiple choice questions	
	(2 marks each)	50
Section B	5 compulsory short-form questions	
	(10 marks each)	50
		100

Additional information

Formulae as required are included in the formulae sheet given in the exam.

BPP
PUBLISHING

Paper 1.2

Financial Information for Management
(United Kingdom)

Study Guide

1 INFORMATION FOR MANAGEMENT

Syllabus reference 1c(i), (ii), d (iii), (iv)

- distinguish between 'data' and 'information'

- describe the sources of information

- identify and explain the attributes of good information

- describe the methods of recording and processing information

- describe the ways in which data could be presented to management

2 MANAGEMENT INFORMATION SYSTEMS

Syllabus reference 1b, c(iii), 2a

- explain what is meant by a management information system

- explain the role of accountants and accounting information within a management information system

- describe the purpose and role of cost and management accounting within a management information system

- compare and contrast financial and cost and management accounting

- outline the managerial processes of planning, decision-making and control

- discuss the management of both financial and non-financial information requirements

- describe the various types of responsibility centres and the impact of these on management information

3 OBJECTIVES, STRATEGY AND PLANNING

Syllabus reference 1a (i), (ii), (iii), (iv)

- define the terms 'objectives' and 'strategy'

- describe the different objectives for different types of organisations

- illustrate the links between strategy and organisational structure

- explain how the objectives and strategy of an organisation impact upon its plans

- describe the planning process

- describe the main techniques used in the planning and decision making process for various types of organisation

- explain the difference between strategic, tactical and operational planning

- describe the basic elements of and purpose of a management control system

- illustrate the need for monitoring and evaluation

- describe methods for monitoring and controlling against objectives and plans

4 THE ROLE OF INFORMATION TECHNOLOGY IN MANAGEMENT INFORMATION

Syllabus reference 1c (iv), d (iv), (v), (vi)

- identify the characteristics and different types of computer hardware and software

- evaluate the potential value of computer systems in handling and processing business data

- describe methods of capturing and processing data by computer

- describe how data is grouped, tabulated, stored and output

- explain the role and features of spreadsheet systems

- describe how output could be analysed and used within an organisation

5 COST CLASSIFICATION

Syllabus reference 1b (ii), d (i), (ii), 2b, 6a (i)

- explain and illustrate classifications used in the analysis of product/service costs including by function, direct and indirect, product and period, fixed and variable, avoidable and unavoidable, controllable and uncontrollable

- explain and illustrate the concept of cost objects, cost units, cost centres, revenue centres, profit centres and investment centres

- describe briefly the process of accounting for input costs and relating them to work done

- describe briefly the different methods of costing final outputs and their appropriateness to different types of business organisation/situation

- describe the nature of control achieved through the comparison of actual costs against plan

6 COST BEHAVIOUR

Syllabus reference 6a

- explain the importance of cost behaviour in relation to business decision-making

- describe factors which influence cost behaviour

- explain how the terms linear, curvilinear and step functions apply to costs

- identify, describe and illustrate graphically different types of cost behaviour

- explain the structure of linear functions and equations

- provide examples of costs which contain both fixed and variable elements

- use high/low analysis to separate the fixed and variable elements of such costs

- construct a scatter graph to establish whether a linear function would be appropriate

- establish a linear function using regression analysis and interpret the results

- calculate and explain the concepts of correlation and coefficient of determination

7 MATERIAL COSTS - 1

Syllabus reference 3a(i), (v)

- describe the different procedures and documents necessary for ordering, receiving and issuing materials from stock

- describe the control procedures used to monitor physical and 'book' stock and to minimise discrepancies and losses

- calculate, explain and evaluate the value of closing stock and material issues using LIFO, FIFO and average methods (weighted and periodic)

- calculate the standard cost of stocks from given information

- prepare ledger entries to record material cost inputs and outputs

- interpret the entries and balances in the material stock account

8 MATERIAL COSTS - 2

Syllabus reference 3a (ii), (iii), (iv)

- explain the reasons for holding stock

- identify and explain the costs of having stocks

- calculate and interpret optimal reorder quantities

- calculate and interpret optimal reorder quantities when discounts apply

- produce and interpret calculations to minimise stock costs when stock is gradually replenished

- describe appropriate methods for establishing reorder levels

9 LABOUR COSTS

Syllabus reference 3b

- explain the difference between, and calculate, direct and indirect labour costs

- explain the methods used to relate input labour costs to work done

- prepare journal and ledger entries to record labour cost inputs and outputs

- describe and illustrate different remuneration methods and incentive schemes

(xix)

- calculate the level, and analyse the costs and causes of, labour turnover

- describe and illustrate measures of labour efficiency and utilisation

- interpret the entries and balances in the labour account

10 OVERHEADS - 1

Syllabus reference 3c (i), (ii), (iii), (iv)

- explain the difference between the treatment of direct and indirect expenses

- describe and justify the process of apportioning manufacturing overhead costs incurred to production

- allocate and apportion factory overheads using an appropriate basis

- re-apportion service centre costs including the use of the reciprocal method

- comment on the use of blanket, department, cost driver, actual and pre-determined absorption rates

- identify, calculate and discuss the appropriate absorption rates using relevant bases

11 OVERHEADS - 2

Syllabus reference 3c (v), (vi), (vii), (viii)

- prepare journal and ledger entries for manufacturing overheads incurred and absorbed

- calculate, explain and account for under - and over-absorbed overheads

- calculate and explain fixed overhead expenditure, volume and, where appropriate, efficiency and capacity variances

- describe and evaluate methods of attributing non-manufacturing overhead costs to units of output

- perform process and cost accounting transactions for selling, distribution and administration overhead in a given business context

- describe how the cost structure of a business has changed over time and the implication of this with regard to overhead analysis

12 MARGINAL AND ABSORPTION COSTING

Syllabus reference 5b

- explain the concept of contribution

- demonstrate and discuss the impact of absorption and marginal costing on stock valuation and profit measurement

- establish the standard cost per unit from given data under absorption and marginal costing

- produce profit and loss accounts using absorption and marginal costing

- reconcile the profits reported under the two methods

- discuss the advantages and disadvantages of absorption and marginal costing

- discuss the use of activity based costing (NB. ABC calculations are not examinable)

- explain and illustrate the concept of cost drivers

13 JOB, BATCH AND CONTRACT COSTING

Syllabus reference 4a

- describe the characteristics of job, batch and contract costing

- describe the situations where the use of job, batch or contract costing would be appropriate

- discuss, and illustrate, the treatment of direct, indirect and abnormal costs

- complete cost records and accounts in job, batch and contract cost accounting situations

- estimate job/contract costs from given information

- explain, and illustrate, measures of profit on uncompleted contracts

14 PROCESS COSTING - 1

Syllabus reference 4b (i), (ii), (iv)

- describe the characteristics of process costing

- describe situations where the use of process costing is appropriate

- describe the key areas of complexity in process costing

- define 'normal' losses and 'abnormal' gains and losses

- state and justify the treatment of normal losses and abnormal gains and losses in process accounts

- account for process scrap

- calculate the cost per unit of process outputs, and prepare simple process accounts, in absorption and marginal costing systems

15 PROCESS COSTING - 2

Syllabus reference 4b (ii), (iii), (v)

- calculate and explain the concept of equivalent units

- allocate process costs between work remaining in process and transfers out of a process using the weighted average cost and FIFO methods

- prepare process accounts in situations where work remains incomplete

- prepare process accounts in situations where losses and gains are identified at different stages of the process

- distinguish between by-products and joint products

- value by-products and joint-products at the point of separation

- prepare process accounts in situations where by-products and/or joint products occur

16 OPERATION/SERVICE COSTING

Syllabus reference 4c

- describe where the use of operation/service costing is appropriate

- illustrate suitable unit cost measures that may be used in a variety of different operations and services

- carry out service cost analysis in internal service situations

- carry out service cost analysis in service industry situations

17 TIME SERIES ANALYSIS

Syllabus reference 6b

- explain the purpose of time series analysis

- explain the components of the additive and multiplicative models

- explain the methods available for establishing the trend

- apply the method of moving averages to isolate the trend for both the multiplicative and additive models

- use the trend and appropriate variations to establish forecast figures

18 COST-VOLUME-PROFIT (CVP) ANALYSIS

Syllabus reference 6c

- explain the objective of CVP analysis

- explain the concept of break-even

- calculate and explain the break-even point and revenue, target profit, profit/volume ratio and margin of safety

- construct break-even, contribution, and profit/volume charts from given data

- apply the CVP model in multi-product situations

19 LIMITING FACTORS

Syllabus reference 6d

- explain and recognise what causes optimisation problems

- identify, formulate and determine the optimal solution when there is a single limiting factor

- formulate a linear programming problem involving two variables

- determine the optimal solution to a linear programming problem using a graph

- determine the optimal solution to a linear programming problem using equations

- explain the methods available for dealing with optimisation problems with more than two variables

- formulate, but do not solve, a linear programming problem involving more than two variables

20 RELEVANT COSTING

Syllabus reference 6e

- explain the concept of relevant costing

- explain the relevance of such terms as opportunity and sunk costs, avoidable and unavoidable costs, fixed and variable costs, historical and replacement costs, controllable and uncontrollable costs, to decision making

- calculate the relevant costs for materials and labour

- calculate and explain the deprival value of an asset

- explain a relevant cost statement and explain the results for such situations as make or buy decisions, shut down decisions and one-off contracts

21 DECISION-MAKING UNDER UNCERTAINTY

Syllabus reference 6f

- explain and calculate expected values

- explain the limitations of the expected value technique

- construct and interpret decision trees including probabilities and expected outcomes and values

- apply the concept of expected value to business decision problems

- distinguish between risk and uncertainty

- explain the concept of risk and how this affects decision making

22 PRICING

Syllabus reference 6g, h

- explain the factors that influence the price of a product

- establish the price/demand relationship of a product

- establish the optimum price/output level when considering profit maximisation and maximisation of revenue

- calculate prices using full cost and marginal cost as the pricing base

- discuss the advantages and disadvantages of these pricing bases

- discuss pricing policy in the context of price skimming, penetration pricing, premium pricing and price discrimination

23 INTEREST

Syllabus reference 6i (i), (iii), (v), (vi)

- explain the difference between simple and compound interest

- explain the difference between nominal and effective interest rates and calculate effective interest rates

- explain what is meant by future values

- calculate future values including the application of the annuity formula

- explain what is meant by discounting

- calculate present values including the application of annuity and perpetuity formulae

24 INVESTMENT APPRAISAL

Syllabus reference 6i (ii), (iv)

- apply discounting principles to calculate the net present value of an investment project and interpret the results

- explain what is meant by the internal rate of return

- estimate the internal rate of return using a graphical approach and the interpolation formula and interpret the results

- identify and discuss the situation where there is conflict between these two methods of investment appraisal

25 BUDGETING

Syllabus reference 8

- explain the functions and purpose of budgeting

- explain the administrative procedures required to ensure an effective budget process

- describe the stages in the budgeting process

- prepare operating budgets including the identification and impact of a principal budget factor

- explain, prepare and evaluate fixed, flexed and flexible budgets

- identify reasons for variances between actual and budgeted information

- describe how the review of actual and budget could be reported to management

26 STANDARD COSTING

Syllabus reference 5a, 3c (vi), (vii)

- explain the purpose of standard costing

- establish the standard cost per unit from given data under absorption and marginal costing

- explain the purpose of the following variances:

  - materials price and usage

  - labour rate, idle time and efficiency

  - variable overhead expenditure and efficiency

  - fixed overhead expenditure, volume and, where appropriate, efficiency and capacity

  - sales volume and price

- calculate and interpret the above variances, using the appropriate costing method

- prepare operating statements to reconcile budgeted to actual profit

- discuss the implications of the results of variance analysis for management

27 INDEX NUMBERS

Syllabus reference 7d

- explain the purpose of index numbers, and calculate and interpret simple index numbers for one or more variables

- deflate time related data using an index

- construct a chained index series

- explain the term 'average index', distinguishing between simple and weighted averages

- calculate Laspeyre and Paasche price and quantity indices

- discuss the relative merits of the Laspeyre and Paasche indices

28 PERFORMANCE MEASUREMENT

Syllabus reference 1a (v), b (ii), 7a, b, c, e, f, g

- outline the essential features of responsibility accounting for various types of entity

- describe the various types of responsibility centre and the impact of these on management appraisal

- describe the range of management performance measures available for various types of entity

- calculate and explain the concepts of return on investment and residual income

- explain and give examples of appropriate non-monetary performance measures

- discuss the potential conflict in the use of a measure for both business and management performance

- analyse the application of financial performance measures including cost, profit, return on capital employed

- assess and illustrate the measurement of profitability, activity and productivity

- discuss the measurement of quality and service

- identify areas of concern from information supplied and performance measures calculated

- describe the features of benchmarking and its application to performance appraisal

OXFORD BROOKES BSc(Hons) IN APPLIED ACCOUNTING

The standard required of candidates completing Part 2 is that required in the final year of a UK degree. Students completing Parts 1 and 2 will have satisfied the examination requirement for an honours degree in Applied Accounting, awarded by Oxford Brookes University.

To achieve the degree, you must also submit two pieces of work based on a **Research and Analysis Project**

- A 5,000 word **Report** on your chosen topic, which demonstrates that you have acquired the necessary research, analytical and IT skills.

- A 1,500 word **Key Skills Statement**, indicating how you have developed your interpersonal and communication skills.

BPP was selected by the ACCA to produce the official text *Success in your Research and Analysis Project* to support students in this task. The book pays particular attention to key skills not covered in the professional examinations.

AN ORDER FORM FOR THE NEW SYLLABUS MATERIAL, INCLUDING THE OXFORD BROOKES PROJECT TEXT, CAN BE FOUND AT THE END OF THIS STUDY TEXT.

THE EXAM PAPER

The examination is a **three hour paper** divided into **two sections**.

		Number of Marks
Section A:	Twenty five multiple choice questions	50
Section B:	Five compulsory questions worth ten marks each	50
		100

Analysis of pilot paper

Section A

1   Twenty five multiple choice questions covering various financial information for management topics

Section B

2   Investment appraisal
3   Absorption costing
4   Linear programming
5   Regression analysis
6   Stock control

BPP
PUBLISHING

Part A
Introduction to financial information for management

Chapter 1

INFORMATION FOR MANAGEMENT

Topic list	Syllabus reference
1 Information	1, 2(a)
2 Planning, control and decision making	1, 2(a)
3 Information systems and management information systems	1, 2(a)
4 Financial accounting and cost and management accounting	1, 2(a)
5 Presentation of information to management	1, 2(a)

Introduction

Welcome to **Financial Information for Management** – Paper 1.2 of the ACCA's new syllabus.

This and the following four chapters provide an introduction to **Financial Information for Management**. This chapter looks at **information** and introduces **cost accounting**. Chapter 2 looks at the role of information technology in management information. Chapters 3-5 provide basic information on how costs are classified and how they behave.

Study guide

Section 1 – Information for management

- Distinguish between data and information
- Describe the sources of information
- Identify and explain the attributes of good information
- Describe the methods of recording and processing information
- Describe the ways in which data could be presented to management

Section 2 – Management information systems

- Explain what is meant by a management information system

- Explain the role of accountants and accounting information within a management information system

- Describe the purpose and role of cost and management accounting within a management information system

- Compare and contrast financial and cost and management accounting

- Outline the managerial processes of planning, decision making and control

- Discuss the management of both financial and non-financial information requirements

Section 3 – Objectives, strategy and planning

- Define the terms 'objectives' and 'strategy'

- Describe the different objectives for different types of organisation

- Illustrate the links between strategy and organisational structure

- Explain how the objectives and strategy of an organisation impact upon its plan

- Describe the planning process

- Describe the main techniques used in the planning and decision making process for various types of organisation

- Explain the difference between strategic, tactical and operational planning

- Describe the basic elements of and purpose of a management control system

- Illustrate the need for monitoring and evaluation

- Describe methods for monitoring and controlling against objectives and plans

Exam guide

The contents of this chapter are mainly to serve as an introduction to the ACCA's **Financial Information for Management** paper. The topics covered here are not classified as key topic areas and are unlikely to be examined in any great depth.

1 INFORMATION

KEY TERMS

- **Data** is the raw material for data processing. Data relates to facts, events and transactions and so forth.

- **Information** is data that has been processed in such a way as to be **meaningful** to the person who receives it. **Information** is anything that is communicated.

1.1 Information is sometimes referred to as processed data. The terms 'information' and 'data' are often used interchangeably. It is important to understand the difference between these two terms.

1.2 Researchers who conduct market research surveys might ask members of the public to complete questionnaires about a product or a service. These completed questionnaires are **data**; they are processed and analysed in order to prepare a report on the survey. This resulting report is **information** and may be used by management for decision-making purposes.

1.3 The qualities of good information are as follows.

- It should be **relevant** for its purpose.
- It should be **complete** for its purpose.
- It should be sufficiently **accurate** for its purpose.
- It should be **clear** to the user.
- The user should have **confidence** in it.
- It should be **communicated** to the right person.
- It should not be excessive - its **volume** should be manageable.
- It should be **timely** - in other words communicated at the most appropriate time.
- It should be communicated by an appropriate **channel** of communication.
- It should be provided at a **cost** which is less than the value of its benefits.

1.4 Let us look at those qualities in more detail.

(a) **Relevance**. Information must be relevant to the purpose for which a manager wants to use it. In practice, far too many reports fail to 'keep to the point' and contain purposeless, irritating paragraphs which only serve to vex the managers reading them.

(b) **Completeness**. An information user should have all the information he needs to do his job properly. If he does not have a complete picture of the situation, he might well make bad decisions.

(c) **Accuracy**. Information should obviously be accurate because using incorrect information could have serious and damaging consequences. However, information should only be accurate enough for its purpose and there is no need to go into unnecessary detail for pointless accuracy.

(d) **Clarity**. Information must be clear to the user. If the user does not understand it properly he cannot use it properly. Lack of clarity is one of the causes of a breakdown in communication. It is therefore important to choose the most appropriate presentation medium or channel of communication.

(e) **Confidence**. Information must be trusted by the managers who are expected to use it. However not all information is certain. Some information has to be certain, especially operating information, for example, related to a production process. Strategic information, especially relating to the environment, is uncertain. However, if the assumptions underlying it are clearly stated, this might enhance the confidence with which the information is perceived.

(f) **Communication**. Within any organisation, individuals are given the authority to do certain tasks, and they must be given the information they need to do them. An office manager might be made responsible for controlling expenditures in his office, and given a budget expenditure limit for the year. As the year progresses, he might try to keep expenditure in check but unless he is told throughout the year what is his current total expenditure to date, he will find it difficult to judge whether he is keeping within budget or not.

(g) **Volume**. There are physical and mental limitations to what a person can read, absorb and understand properly before taking action. An enormous mountain of information, even if it is all relevant, cannot be handled. Reports to management must therefore be **clear** and **concise** and in many systems, control action works basically on the 'exception' principle.

(h) **Timing**. Information which is not available until after a decision is made will be useful only for comparisons and longer-term control, and may serve no purpose even then. Information prepared too frequently can be a serious disadvantage. If, for example, a decision is taken at a monthly meeting about a certain aspect of a company's operations, information to make the decision is only required once a month, and weekly reports would be a time-consuming waste of effort.

(i) **Channel of communication**. There are occasions when using one particular method of communication will be better than others. For example, job vacancies should be announced in a medium where they will be brought to the attention of the people most likely to be interested. The channel of communication might be the company's in-house journal, a national or local newspaper, a professional magazine, a job centre or school careers office. Some internal memoranda may be better sent by 'electronic mail'. Some information is best communicated informally by telephone or word-of-mouth, whereas other information ought to be formally communicated in writing or figures.

(j) **Cost**. Information should have some value, otherwise it would not be worth the cost of collecting and filing it. The benefits obtainable from the information must also exceed the costs of acquiring it, and whenever management is trying to decide whether or not to produce information for a particular purpose (for example whether to computerise an operation or to build a financial planning model) a cost/benefit study ought to be made.

Question 1

The value of information lies in the action taken as a result of receiving it. What questions might you ask in order to make an assessment of the value of information?

Answer

(a)   What information is provided?
(b)   What is it used for?
(c)   Who uses it?
(d)   How often is it used?
(e)   Does the frequency with which it is used coincide with the frequency with which it is provided?
(f)   What is achieved by using it?
(g)   What other relevant information is available which could be used instead?

An assessment of the value of information can be derived in this way, and the cost of obtaining it should then be compared against this value. On the basis of this comparison, it can be decided whether certain items of information are worth having. It should be remembered that there may also be intangible benefits which may be harder to quantify.

Why is information important?

1.5   Consider the following problems and what management needs to solve these problems.

(a)   A company wishes to launch a new product. The company's pricing policy is to charge cost plus 20%. What should the price of the product be?

(b)   An organisation's widget-making machine has a fault. The organisation has to decide whether to repair the machine, buy a new machine or hire a machine. What does the organisation do if its aim is to control costs?

(c)   A firm is considering offering a discount of 2% to those customers who pay an invoice within seven days of the invoice date and a discount of 1% to those customers who pay an invoice within eight to 14 days of the invoice date. How much will this discount offer cost the firm?

1.6   In solving these and a wide variety of other problems, **management need information**.

(a)   In problem (a) of Paragraph 1.5, management would need information about the **cost of the new product**.

(b)   Faced with problem (b), management would need information on the **cost of repairing, buying and hiring the machine**.

(c)   To calculate the cost of the discount offer described in (c), information would be required about **current sales settlement patterns** and **expected changes to the pattern** if discounts were offered.

1.7   The successful management of *any* organisation depends on information: non-profit making organisations such as charities, clubs and local authorities need information for decision making and for reporting the results of their activities just as multi-nationals do. For example a tennis club needs to know the cost of undertaking its various activity so that it can determine the amount of annual subscription it should charge its members.

Sources of information

1.8   Information may be obtained from either an **internal** source or from an **external** source.

Internal sources of information

The financial accounting records

1.9   There is no need for us to give a detailed description of the constituents of the financial accounting records. You are probably familiar with the idea of a system of sales ledgers and purchase ledgers, general ledgers, cash books and so on. These records provide a history of an organisation's monetary transactions. Some of this information is of great value outside the accounts department, for example sales information for the marketing function.

1.10   You will also be aware that to maintain the integrity of its financial accounting records, an organisation of any size will have systems for and controls over transactions. These also give rise to valuable information. A stock control system is the classic example. Besides actually recording the monetary value of purchases and stock in hand for external financial reporting purposes, the system will include purchase orders, goods received notes, goods returned notes and so on, and these can be analysed to provide management information about speed of delivery, say, or the quality of supplies.

Other internal sources

1.11   Much of the information that is not strictly part of the financial accounting records is in fact closely tied in to the accounting system.

(a)   Information relating to **personnel** will be linked to the **payroll system**. Additional information may be obtained from this source if, say, a project is being costed and it is necessary to ascertain the availability and rate of pay of different levels of staff, or the need for and cost of recruiting staff from outside the organisation.

(b)   Much information will be produced by a **production department** about machine capacity, fuel consumption, movement of people, materials, and work in progress, set up times, maintenance requirements and so on. A large part of the traditional work of cost accounting involves ascribing costs to the physical information produced by this source.

(c)   Many service businesses - notably accountants and solicitors - need to keep **detailed records of the time** spent on various activities, both to justify fees to clients and to assess the efficiency of operations.

External sources of information

1.12   We hardly need say that an organisation's files are also full of invoices, letters, advertisements and so on received from customers and suppliers. These documents provide information from an external source. There are many occasions when an active search outside the organisation is necessary.

(a)   A **primary source** of information is, as the term implies, as close as you can get to the origin of an item of information: the eyewitness to an event, the place in question, the document under scrutiny.

(b)   A **secondary source**, again logically enough, provides 'second-hand' information: books, articles, verbal or written reports by someone else.

What type of information is needed?

1.13 Having ascertained that all organisations require information we now need to consider what type of information is needed.

1.14 As you can see, we divided the list into the information requirements for **planning** the club's activities, **controlling** those activities and **making any decisions**. We will go on to look at these processes later in this chapter.

1.15 What should be clear to you is that the information required is not just of a **financial nature** (such as the receipts and payments relating to each activity) but also of a **non-financial nature** (membership details, activities required by members, local community population and so on). Business organisations go through much the same process of planning and controlling as a sports club (though on a larger scale) and therefore require both **financial** and **non-financial information**.

1.16 Financial and non-financial information may be combined to produce a significant third measurement. Suppose that the management of ABC Ltd have decided to provide a canteen for their employees.

   (a) The **financial information** required by management might include canteen staff costs, costs of subsidising meals, capital costs, costs of heat and light and so on.

   (b) The **non-financial information** might include management comment on the effect on employee morale of the provision of canteen facilities, details of the number of meals served each day, meter readings for gas and electricity and attendance records for canteen employees.

1.17 ABC Ltd could now **combine financial and non-financial information** to calculate the average cost to the company of each meal served, thereby enabling them to predict total costs depending on the number of employees in the work force.

1.18 Most people probably consider that management accounting is only concerned with financial information and that people do not matter. This is, nowadays, a long way from the truth. Just as the committee of Dimbledon Tennis Club would want to know whether their members enjoyed the trips to Wimbledon in order to help them to decide whether to run another similar trip, managers of business organisations need to know whether employee morale has increased due to introducing a canteen, whether the bread from particular suppliers is fresh and the reason why the canteen staff are demanding a new dishwasher. This type of non-financial information will play its part in **planning, controlling** and **decision making** and is therefore just as important to management as financial information is.

1.19 **Non-financial information** must therefore be **monitored** as carefully, **recorded** as accurately and **taken into account** as fully as financial information. There is little point in a careful and accurate recording of total canteen costs if the recording of the information on the number of meals eaten in the canteen is uncontrolled and therefore produces inaccurate information.

1.20 While management accounting is mainly concerned with the provision of **financial information** to aid planning, control and decision making, the management accountant cannot ignore **non-financial influences** and should qualify the information he provides with non-financial matters as appropriate.

2 PLANNING, CONTROL AND DECISION MAKING

2.1 When we defined the difference between data and information earlier in this chapter, we said that information is data processed into a form meaningful to the person who receives it. In terms of management accounting, the information is most likely to be for **planning**, **control** or **decision making**.

Planning

2.2 An organisation should never be surprised by developments which occur gradually over an extended period of time because the organisation should have **implemented a planning process**. Planning involves the following.

- Establishing objectives
- Selecting appropriate strategies to achieve those objectives

> **KEY TERMS**
>
> - An **objective** is the aim or **goal** of an organisation (or an individual). Note that in practice, the terms objective, goal and aim are often used interchangeably.
>
> - A **strategy** is a possible course of action that might enable an organisation (or an individual) to achieve its objectives.

Planning therefore forces management to think ahead systematically in both the **short term** and the **long term**.

Objectives of organisations

2.3 The two main types of organisation that you are likely to come across in practice are as follows.

- Profit making
- Non-profit making

2.4 The main objective of profit making organisations is to **maximise profits**. A secondary objective of profit making organisations might be to increase output of its goods/services.

2.5 The main objective of non-profit making organisations is usually to **provide goods and services**. A secondary objective of non-profit making organisations might be to minimise the costs involved in providing the goods/services.

2.6 In conclusion, the objectives of an organisation might include one or more of the following.

- Maximise profits
- Maximise shareholder value
- Minimise costs
- Maximise revenue
- Increase market share

Remember that the type of organisation concerned will have an impact on its objectives.

Strategy and organisational structure

2.7 There are two schools of thought on the link between strategy and organisational structure.

- Structure follows strategy
- Strategy follows structure

2.8 Let's consider the first idea that **structure follows strategy**. What this means is that organisations develop strategies in order that they can cope with changes in the structure of an organisation. Or do they?

2.9 The second school of thought suggests that **strategy follows structure**. This side of the argument suggests that the strategy of an organisation is determined or influenced by the structure of the organisation. The structure of the organisation therefore limits the number of strategies available.

2.10 We could explore these ideas in much more detail, but for the purposes of your **Financial Information for Management** studies, you really just need to be aware that there is a link between **strategy** and the **structure** of an organisation.

Long-term strategic planning

KEY TERM

Long-term planning, also known as **corporate planning**, involves selecting appropriate strategies so as to prepare a long-term plan to attain the objectives.

2.11 The time span covered by a long-term plan depends on the **organisation**, the **industry** in which it operates and the particular **environment** involved. Typical periods are 2, 5, 7 or 10 years although longer periods are frequently encountered.

2.12 **Long-term strategic planning** is a **detailed, lengthy process**, essentially incorporating three stages and ending with a **corporate plan**. The diagram on the next page provides an overview of the process and shows the link between short-term and long-term planning.

Short-term tactical planning

2.13 The **long-term corporate plan** serves as the **long-term framework** for the organisation as a whole but for operational purposes it is necessary to convert the corporate plan into a series of **short-term plans**, usually covering **one year**, which relate to **sections**, **functions** or **departments**. The annual process of short-term planning should be seen as stages in the progressive fulfilment of the corporate plan as each short-term plan steers the organisation towards its long-term objectives. It is therefore vital that, to obtain the maximum advantage from short-term planning, some sort of long-term plan exists.

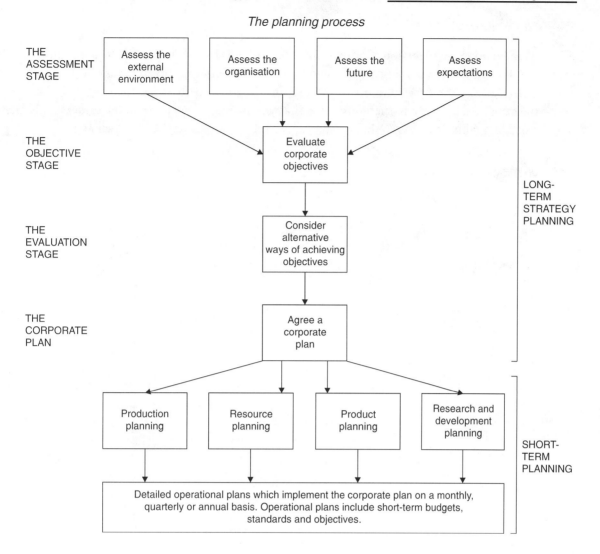

The planning process

Control

2.14 There are two stages in the **control process**.

(a) The **performance of the organisation** as set out in the detailed operational plans is compared with the actual performance of the organisation on a regular and continuous basis. Any deviations from the plans can then be identified and corrective action taken.

(b) **The corporate plan** is reviewed in the light of the comparisons made and any changes in the parameters on which the plan was based (such as new competitors, government instructions and so on) to assess whether the objectives of the plan can be achieved. The plan is modified as necessary before any serious damage to the organisation's future success occurs.

Effective control is therefore not practical without planning, and planning without control is pointless.

2.15 An established organisation should have a system of management reporting that produces control information in a specified format at regular intervals.

Smaller organisations may rely on informal information flows or ad hoc reports produced as required.

BPP
PUBLISHING

Decision making

2.16 **Management is decision taking.** Managers of all levels within an organisation take decisions. Decision making always involves a **choice between alternatives** and it is the role of the management accountant to provide information so that management can reach an informed decision. It is therefore vital that the management accountant understands the decision making process so that he can supply the appropriate type of information.

Decision making process

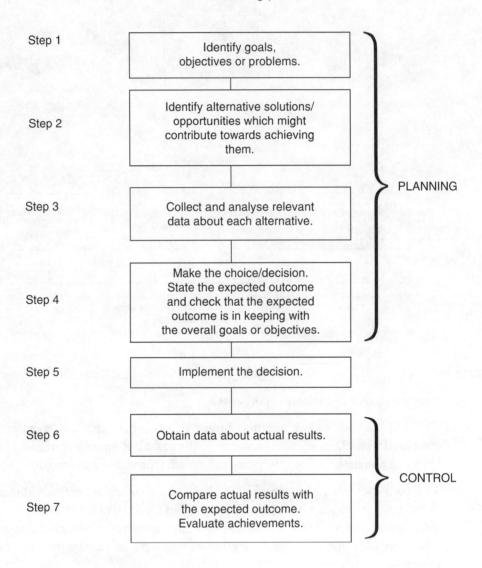

Decision-making process

Anthony's view of management activity

2.17 R N Anthony, a leading writer on organisational control, has suggested that the activities of **planning, control and decision making should not be separated** since all managers make planning and control decisions. He has identified three types of management activity.

(a) **Strategic planning:** 'the process of deciding on objectives of the organisation, on changes in these objectives, on the resources used to attain these objectives, and on the policies that are to govern the acquisition, use and disposition of these resources'.

(b) **Management control:** 'the process by which managers assure that resources are obtained and used effectively and efficiently in the accomplishment of the organisation's objectives'.

(c) **Operational control:** 'the process of assuring that specific tasks are carried out effectively and efficiently'.

Strategic planning

2.18 **Strategic plans** are those which **set or change the objectives,** or strategic targets of an organisation. They would include such matters as the selection of products and markets, the required levels of company profitability, the purchase and disposal of subsidiary companies or major fixed assets and so on.

Management control

2.19 Whilst strategic planning is concerned with setting objectives and strategic targets, **management control** is concerned with **decisions about the efficient and effective use of an organisation's resources** to achieve these objectives or targets.

(a) **Resources,** often referred to as the **'4 Ms'** (men, materials, machines and money).

(b) **Efficiency** in the use of resources means that optimum **output** is achieved from the **input** resources used. It relates to the combinations of men, land and capital (for example how much production work should be automated) and to the productivity of labour, or material usage.

(c) **Effectiveness** in the use of resources means that the **outputs** obtained are in line with the intended **objectives** or targets.

Operational control

2.20 The third, and lowest tier, in Anthony's hierarchy of decision making, consists of **operational control decisions**. As we have seen, operational control is the task of ensuring that **specific tasks** are carried out effectively and efficiently. Just as 'management control' plans are set within the guidelines of strategic plans, so too are 'operational control' plans set within the guidelines of both strategic planning and management control. Consider the following.

(a) Senior management may decide that the company should increase sales by 5% per annum for at least five years - **a strategic plan**.

(b) The sales director and senior sales managers will make plans to increase sales by 5% in the next year, with some provisional planning for future years. This involves planning direct sales resources, advertising, sales promotion and so on. Sales quotas are assigned to each sales territory - **a tactical plan** (management control).

(c) The manager of a sales territory specifies the weekly sales targets for each sales representative. This is **operational planning**: individuals are given tasks which they are expected to achieve.

Although we have used an example of selling tasks to describe operational control, it is important to remember that this level of planning occurs in all aspects of an organisation's activities, even when the activities cannot be scheduled nor properly estimated because they are non-standard activities (such as repair work, answering customer complaints).

2.21 The scheduling of unexpected or 'ad hoc' work must be done at short notice, which is a feature of much **operational planning**. In the repairs department, for example, routine preventive maintenance can be scheduled, but breakdowns occur unexpectedly and repair work must be scheduled and controlled 'on the spot' by a repairs department supervisor.

Management control systems

> **KEY TERM**
>
> A **management control system** is a system which measures and corrects the performance of activities of subordinates in order to make sure that the objectives of an organisation are being met and the plans devised to attain them are being carried out.

2.22 The management function of control is the measurement and correction of the activities of subordinates in order to make sure that the goals of the organisation, or planning targets are achieved.

2.23 The basic elements of a management control system are as follows.

- **Planning:** deciding what to do and identifying the desired results
- **Recording** the plan which should incorporate standards of efficiency or targets
- **Carrying out** the plan and measuring actual results achieved
- **Comparing** actual results against the plans
- **Evaluating** the comparison, and deciding whether further action is necessary
- Where **corrective action** is necessary, this should be implemented

Types of information

2.24 Information within an organisation can be analysed into the three levels assumed in Anthony's hierarchy.

2.25 **Strategic information is used by senior managers** to plan the objectives of their organisation, and to assess whether the objectives are being met in practice. Such information includes **overall** profitability, the profitability of different segments of the business, capital equipment needs and so on.

Strategic information therefore has the following features.

- It is derived from both **internal** and **external** sources.
- It is summarised at a **high level**.
- It is relevant to the **long term**.
- It deals with the **whole organisation** (although it might go into some detail).
- It is often prepared on an **'ad hoc'** basis.
- It is both **quantitative** and **qualitative** (see below).
- It cannot provide complete certainty, given that the future cannot be predicted.

2.26 **Tactical information is used by middle management** to decide how the resources of the business should be employed, and to monitor how they are being and have been employed. Such information includes **productivity measurements** (output per man hour or per machine hour), **budgetary control** or **variance analysis reports**, and **cash flow forecasts** and so on.

2.27 **Tactical information** therefore has the following features.

- It is primarily generated internally.
- It is summarised at a lower level.
- It is relevant to the short and medium term.
- It describes or analyses activities or departments.

- It is prepared routinely and regularly.
- It is based on quantitative measures.

2.28 **Operational information is used by 'front-line' managers** such as foremen or head clerks to ensure that specific tasks are planned and carried out properly within a factory or office and so on. In the payroll office, for example, information at this level will relate to day-rate labour and will include the hours worked each week by each employee, his rate of pay per hour, details of his deductions, and for the purpose of wages analysis, details of the time each man spent on individual jobs during the week. In this example, the information is required weekly, but more urgent operational information, such as the amount of raw materials being input to a production process, may be required daily, hourly, or in the case of automated production, second by second.

Operational information has the following features.

- It is derived almost entirely from internal sources.
- It is highly detailed, being the processing of raw data.
- It relates to the immediate term.
- It is task-specific.
- It is prepared constantly, or very frequently.
- It is largely quantitative.

3 INFORMATION SYSTEMS AND MANAGEMENT INFORMATION SYSTEMS

3.1 An organisation is made up of a series of **information systems**. It is difficult to define an information system since it is really a series of activities or processes.

- Identification of data requirements
- Collection and transcription of data (data capture)
- Data processing
- Communication of processed data to users
- Use of processed data (as information) by users

3.2 Sometimes there are separate information systems for sales, production, personnel, financial and other matters, sometimes there is integration of these sub-systems.

3.3 Information systems can be divided into two broad categories.

- Transaction (or data) processing systems
- Management information systems

Transaction processing systems

3.4 **Transaction processing systems** could be said to represent the **lowest level** in a company's use of information systems. They are used for routine tasks in which data items or transactions must be recorded and processed so that operations can continue. Handling sales orders, purchase orders and stock records are typical examples.

Management information systems

> **KEY TERM**
>
> A **management information system** (MIS) is defined as 'A collective term for the hardware and software used to drive a database system with the outputs, both to screen and print, being designed to provide easily assimilated information for management'.
>
> (CIMA *Computing Terminology*)

3.5 Management information is by no means confined to accounting information, but until relatively recently accounting information systems have been the most formally-constructed and well-developed part of the overall information system of a business enterprise.

3.6 An alternative definition of a management information system is 'an information system making use of available resources to provide managers at all levels in all functions with the information from all relevant sources to enable them to make timely and effective decisions for planning, directing and controlling the activities for which they are responsible.'

3.7 A management information system is therefore **a system of disseminating information which will enable managers to do their job**. Since managers must have information, there will always be a management information system in any organisation.

3.8 Most management information systems are not designed, but grow up informally, with each manager making sure that he or she gets all the information considered necessary to do the job. It is virtually taken for granted that the necessary information flows to the job, and to a certain extent this is so. Much accounting information, for example, is easily obtained, and managers can often get along with frequent face-to-face contact and co-operation with each other. Such an informal system works best in small organisations.

3.9 However, some information systems are specially designed, often because the introduction of computers has forced management to consider its information needs in detail. This is especially the case in large companies.

3.10 Management should try to develop/implement a management information system for their enterprise with care. If they allow the MIS to develop without any formal planning, it will almost certainly be inefficient because data will be obtained and processed in a random and disorganised way and the communication of information will also be random and hit-and-miss.

(a) Some managers will prefer to keep data in their heads and will not commit information to paper. When the manager is absent from work, or is moved to another job, his stand-in or successor will not know as much as he could and should about the work because no information has been recorded to help him.

(b) The organisation will not collect and process all the information that it should, and so valuable information that ought to be available to management will be missing from neglect.

(c) Information may be available but not disseminated to the managers who are in a position of authority and so ought to be given it. The information would go to waste because it would not be used. In other words, the wrong people would have the information.

(d) Information is communicated late because the need to communicate it earlier is not understood and appreciated by the data processors.

3.11 The consequences of a poor MIS might be dissatisfaction amongst employees who believe they should be told more, a lack of understanding about what the targets for achievement are and a lack of information about how well the work is being done. Whether a management information system is formally or informally constructed, it should therefore have certain essential characteristics.

(a) The functions of individuals and their areas of responsibility in achieving company objectives should be defined.

(b) Areas of control within the company (eg cost centres, investment centres) should also be clearly defined.

(c) Information required for an area of control should flow to the manager who is responsible for it.

Cost accounting systems

3.12 **An organisation's cost accounting system will be part of the overall management information system** and, as we shall see in the next section, it will both provide information to assist management with planning, control and decision making as well as accumulating historical costs to establish stock valuations, profits and balance sheet items.

4 FINANCIAL ACCOUNTING AND COST AND MANAGEMENT ACCOUNTING

Financial accounts and management accounts

4.1 Management information provides a common source from which is drawn information for two groups of people.

(a) **Financial accounts** are prepared for individuals **external** to an organisation: shareholders, customers, suppliers, the Inland Revenue, employees.

(b) **Management accounts** are prepared for **internal** managers of an organisation.

4.2 The data used to prepare financial accounts and management accounts are the same. The differences between the financial accounts and the management accounts arise because the data is analysed differently.

Financial accounts	Management accounts
Financial accounts detail the performance of an organisation over a defined period and the state of affairs at the end of that period.	Management accounts are used to aid management record, plan and control the organisation's activities and to help the decision-making process.
Limited companies must, by law, prepare financial accounts.	There is no legal requirement to prepare management accounts.
The format of published financial accounts is determined by law (mainly the Companies Acts), by Statements of Standard Accounting Practice and by Financial Reporting Standards. In	The format of management accounts is entirely at management discretion: no strict rules govern the way they are prepared or presented. Each organisation can devise its own management accounting system and

BPP PUBLISHING

principle the accounts of different organisations can therefore be easily compared.	format of reports.
Financial accounts concentrate on the business as a whole, aggregating revenues and costs from different operations, and are an end in themselves.	Management accounts can focus on specific areas of an organisation's activities. Information may be produced to aid a decision rather than to be an end product of a decision.
Most financial accounting information is of a monetary nature.	Management accounts incorporate non-monetary measures. Management may need to know, for example, tons of aluminium produced, monthly machine hours, or miles travelled by salesmen.
Financial accounts present an essentially historic picture of past operations.	Management accounts are both an historical record and a future planning tool.

Cost accounts

4.3 Cost accounting and management accounting are terms which are often used interchangeably. It is *not* correct to do so.

Cost accounting is concerned with the following.

- Preparing statements (eg budgets, costing)
- Cost data collection
- Applying cots to inventory, products and services

Management accounting is concerned with the following.

- Using financial data and communicating it as information to users

4.4 **Cost accounting is part of management accounting. Cost accounting provides a bank of data for the management accountant to use**. Cost accounts aim to establish the following.

(a) The **cost** of goods produced or services provided.

(b) The **cost** of a department or work section.

(c) What **revenues** have been.

(d) The **profitability** of a product, a service, a department, or the organisation in total.

(e) **Selling prices** with some regard for the costs of sale.

(f) The **value of stocks of goods** (raw materials, work in progress, finished goods) that are still held in store at the end of a period, thereby aiding the preparation of a balance sheet of the company's assets and liabilities.

(g) **Future costs** of goods and services (costing is an integral part of budgeting (planning) for the future).

(h) **How actual costs compare with budgeted costs** (If an organisation plans for its revenues and costs to be a certain amount, but they actually turn out differently, the differences can be measured and reported. Management can use these reports as a guide to whether corrective action (or 'control' action) is needed to sort out a problem revealed by these differences between budgeted and actual results. This system of control is often referred to as budgetary control).

(i) **What information management needs** in order to make sensible decisions about profits and costs.

4.5 It would be wrong to suppose that cost accounting systems are restricted to manufacturing operations, although they are probably more fully developed in this area of work. **Service industries**, **government departments** and **welfare activities** can all make use of cost accounting information. Within a manufacturing organisation, the cost accounting system should be applied not only to **manufacturing** but also to **administration**, **selling and distribution**, **research and development** and all other departments.

5 PRESENTATION OF INFORMATION TO MANAGEMENT

5.1 Most information is likely to be presented to management in the form of a **report**. In small organisations it is possible, however, that information will be communicated less formally (orally or using informal reports/memos).

5.2 Throughout this Study Text, you will come across a number of techniques which allow financial information to be collected. Once it has been collected it is usually analysed and reported back to management in the form of a **report**.

5.3 Main features of a report are as follows.

- **TITLE**

  Most reports are usually given a heading to show that it is a report.

- **WHO IS THE REPORT INTENDED FOR?**

  It is vital that the intended recipients of a report are clearly identified. For example, if you are writing a report for Joe Bloggs, it should be clearly stated at the head of the report.

- **WHO IS THE REPORT FROM?**

  If the recipients of the report have any comments or queries, it is important that they know who to contact.

- **DATE**

  We have already mentioned that information should be communicated at the most appropriate **time**. It is also important to show this timeliness by giving your report a date.

- **SUBJECT**

  What is the report about? Managers are likely to receive a great number of reports that they need to review. It is useful to know what a report is about before you read it!

- **APPENDIX**

  In general, information is summarised in a report and the more detailed calculations and data are included in an appendix at the end of the report.

5.4 We recommend that you should use the following format when writing a report in an examination.

REPORT

To: Board of Directors

From: Cost Accountant   Date:

Subject: Report Format

Body of report

Signed: Cost Accountant

Exam focus point

When producing reports in an examination, remember that they must include the following.

- **Title** – REPORT

- **To** – Who is the report to?

- **From** – Who is the report from?

- **Date** – What is the date of report?

- **Subject** – What is the subject of the report?

Chapter roundup

- **Data** ('raw material') and **information** (data which has been processed into a form meaningful to the recipient and which is of real or perceived value for the intended purpose) are terms which are often used interchangeably – make sure you are aware of the differences.

- Good information should be **relevant, complete, accurate, clear**, it should **inspire confidence**, it should be **appropriately communicated**, its **volume** should be manageable, it should be **timely** and its **cost** should be less than the benefits it provides.

- Information may be obtained from either an **internal** source or an **external** source.

- **Internal** sources of information include the financial accounting records. **External** sources of information include books, reports and documents.

- An **objective** is the aim or goal of an organisation.

- A **strategy** is a possible course of action that might enable an organisation to achieve its objectives.

- The main objectives of an organisation might include the following.

    - Maximise profits
    - Maximise shareholder value
    - Minimise costs
    - Maximise revenue
    - Increase market share

- Information for management accounting is likely to be used for **planning, control** and **decision making**.

- Anthony divides management activities into **strategic planning, management control** and **operational control**.

- A **management control system** is a system which measures and corrects the performance of activities of subordinates in order to make sure that the objectives of an organisation are being met and the plans devised to attain them are being carried out.

- Information within an organisation can be analysed into the three levels assumed in Anthony's hierarchy: **strategic; tactical**; and **operational**.

- An **MIS** is a system of providing and communicating information which will enable managers to do their jobs and as such an MIS is vital to the role of the cost and management accountant.

- **Financial accounting systems** ensure that the assets and liabilities of a business are properly accounted for, and provide information about profits and so on to shareholders and to other interested parties.

- **Management accounting systems** provide information specifically for the use of managers within the organisation.

- The relationship between cost accounting and management accounting maybe summarised as follows: **cost accounting provides a bank of data for the management accountant to use.**

- Data and information are usually presented to management in the form of a report. The main features of a report are as follows.

    - Title
    - To
    - From
    - Date
    - Subject

Quick quiz

1 Define the terms **data** and **information**.

2 The four main qualities of good information are:

- Relevance
- Completeness
- Timely
- Accurate

3 Secondary sources of information include documents or reports written for a specific purpose.

True ☑

False ☐

4 In terms of management accounting, information is most likely to be used for (1) Planning, (2) Control or (3) Decisions .

5 A strategy is the aim or goal of an organisation.

True ☑

False ☐

6

Organisation	Objective
Profit making	Maximise profits
Non-profit making	Provide goals + services

7 What are the three types of management activity identified by R N Anthony?

(1) Stategic Planning
(2) Management Control
(3) Operational Control.

8 A management control system is

A a possible course of action that might enable an organisation to achieve its objectives

B a collective term for the hardware and software used to drive a database system

C a set up that measures and corrects the performance of activities of subordinates in order to make sure that the objectives of an organisation are being met and their associated plans are being carried out

D a system that controls and maximises the profits of an organisation

9 List six differences between financial accounts and management accounts.

10 When preparing reports, what are the five key points to remember.

(1) TITLE
(2) WHO TO
(3) WHO FROM
(4) DATE
(5) Subject.

9) Management Accts   Fin Accts
   Internal.   External

Answers to quick quiz

1   **Data** is the raw material for data processing. **Information** is data that has been processed in such a way as to be meaningful to the person who receives it. **Information** is anything that is communicated.

2   • Relevance
     • Completeness
     • Accuracy
     • Clarity

3   False. Secondary information sources would include items that have not been prepared for a specific purpose (these would be primary information sources).

4   (1) Planning
     (2) Control
     (3) Decision making

5   False. This is the definition of an **objective**. A strategy is a possible course of action that might enable an organisation to **achieve** its objectives.

6   Profit making = maximise profits
     Non-profit making = provide goods and services

7   (1) Strategic planning
     (2) Management control
     (3) Operational control

8   C

9   See paragraph 4.2

10   • Title
     • Who is the report to
     • Who is the report from
     • Date
     • Subject

Now try the question below from the Exam Question Bank

Number	Level	Marks	Time
1	MCQ	n/a	n/a

BPP PUBLISHING

Chapter 2

THE ROLE OF INFORMATION TECHNOLOGY IN MANAGEMENT INFORMATION

Topic list	Syllabus reference
1 The value of computer systems in handling and processing data	1(c), (d)
2 Computer hardware	1(c), (d)
3 Computer software	1(c), (d)
4 Capturing and processing data	1(c), (d)
5 Data output	1(c), (d)
6 Storage devices	1(c), (d)
7 Spreadsheet packages	1(c), (d)
8 Statistical packages	1(c), (d)

Introduction

This Study Text is about financial **information** for management. In the modern business environment the **storage**, **retrieval** and **analysis** of information frequently depends upon **information technology**. In fact, the majority of organisations would cease to function without the support offered by computers since information technology is used for stock control, payroll, sales and purchases, budgeting and a multitude of other tasks. It is therefore vital that you are aware of the terminology used to describe business **information technology**, the elements of a typical business computer system and the principal tasks performed by such a system.

Study guide

Section 4 – The role of information technology in management information

- Identify the characteristics and different types of computer hardware and software
- Evaluate the potential value of computer systems in handling and processing business data
- Describe methods of capturing and processing data by computer
- Describe how data is grouped, tabulated, stored and output
- Explain the role and features of spreadsheet systems
- Describe how output could be analysed and used within an organisation

Exam guide

The role of information technology in management information is not a core syllabus topic in the **Financial Information for Management** syllabus. It is most likely to be examined in the form of objective test questions.

1 THE VALUE OF COMPUTER SYSTEMS IN HANDLING AND PROCESSING DATA

1.1 Here is a very simple example of a data processing model.

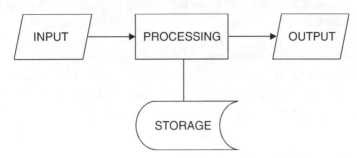

1.2 The processing of business data can be illustrated by a person working at his desk dealing with matters in his in-tray.

(a) A person receives **input from his in-tray**, which he must deal with.

(b) To help him, the person may have a procedures manual or have learned a set of rules telling him how to do the job. He may also use a **calculator** to do computations.

(c) To work on the data from his in-tray, he might need to retrieve some further data/ information from **filing** cabinets.

(d) As a result of doing the work, the person will:

(i) produce some **output**, perhaps a report or a completed routine task;

(ii) probably add to the information held on file in the filing cabinet, or change the information to bring it up to date.

1.3 **Data processing** is essentially the same, no matter whether it is done manually or by computer. Computers use **programs** instead of instruction books, and they store data on **disks** instead of in filing cabinets, but their work still follows the **input, process, output** storage pattern.

Advantages of computers

1.4 Computers are widely used for data processing because they have certain advantages over humans.

(a) **Speed.** Computers can process data much more quickly than a human. This means that a computer has a much higher productivity and so ought to be cheaper for large volumes of data processing than doing the work manually. As computer costs have fallen, this cost advantage of the computer has become more accentuated.

The ability to process data more quickly means that a computer can produce more timely information, when information is needed as soon as possible.

(b) **Accuracy.** Computers are generally accurate, whereas humans are prone to error. The errors in computer data processing are normally human errors (errors in the input of data) although there can be software errors (errors in the programs) and hardware errors (faults or breakdowns in the equipment itself).

(c) **Volume and complexity.** As businesses grow and become more complex, their data processing requirements increase in volume and complexity too. More managers need greater amounts of information. More transactions have to be processed. The volume of DP work is often beyond the capability of even the largest clerical workforce to do

BPP PUBLISHING

manually. Clearing banks, for example, would be unable to function without electronic data processing to ease the demands on their workforce.

(d) **Access to information**. The use of databases and the ability to link a number of users via some form of network improves the distribution of information within and beyond the organisation.

1.5 However the 'manual' or 'human' method of data processing is more suitable when human judgement is involved in the work. For example, the human brain stores a lifetime of experiences and emotions that influence decisions and it is capable of drawing on them and making connections between them at phenomenal speed.

2 COMPUTER HARDWARE

> **KEY TERM**
>
> A **computer** is 'A **device** which will accept input data, process it according to programmed logical and arithmetic rules, store and output data and/or calculate results. The ability to store programmed instructions and to take decisions which vary the way in which a program executes (although within the defined logic of the program) are the principal distinguishing features of a computer. ...' (CIMA *Computing Terminology*)

2.1 Computer hardware components can be classified by their function.

(a) **Input devices** accept input data for processing.

(b) A **processing device**. The computer has a central processor, which performs the data processing, under the control of the stored program(s), by taking in data from input devices and external storage devices, processing them, and then transferring the processed data (information) to an output device or an external storage device. This processing device is called the **central processing unit** (CPU).

(c) **Storage devices** hold data or information on file until they are needed for processing.

(d) **Output devices** accept output from the processing device and convert it into a usable form. The most common output devices are **printers** (which print the output on paper) and **screens** (which display the output).

The input devices, external storage devices and output devices are collectively known as **peripheral devices**. Any unit connected to a computer is a **peripheral**.

The processor or CPU

> **KEY TERM**
>
> The **processor (CPU)** is 'The collection of circuitry and registers that performs the processing in a particular computer and provides that computer with its specific characteristics. In modern computers the CPU comprises a single (albeit increasingly sophisticated) chip device but this is supported by other chips performing specialist functions.' (CIMA *Computing Terminology*)

2.2 The processor (or CPU) is divided into three areas.

- The arithmetic and logic unit
- The control unit
- The main store, or memory

The set of operations that the processor performs is known as the **instruction set**, or **repertoire**, and this determines in part the speed at which processing can be performed.

Computer chips

2.3 In modern computer systems the processing unit may have all its elements - arithmetic and logic unit, control unit, and the input/output interface-on a single 'chip'. A **chip** is a small piece of silicon upon which is etched an integrated circuit, which consists of **transistors** and their interconnecting patterns on an extremely small scale.

2.4 The chip is mounted on a carrier unit which in turn is 'plugged' on to a circuit board - called the **motherboard** - with other chips, each with their own functions.

Arithmetic and logic unit

2.5 The **ALU** is the part of the central processor where the **arithmetic** and **logic** operations are carried out. The **arithmetic** element might be as simple as x + y = z. The **logic** will be something along the lines of '*if* x + y *does not* = z, *then* add 3 to x and try again'.

2.6 The operations are all simple but the significant feature of computer operations is the very rapid speed with which computers can perform vast numbers of simple-step instructions, which combine to represent quite complex processing.

Control unit

2.7 The **control unit** receives program instructions, one at a time, from the main store and decodes them. It then sends out **control signals** to the peripheral devices. The signals are co-ordinated by a clock which sends out a 'pulse' - a sort of tick-tock sequence called a 'cycle' - at regular intervals. The number of cycles produced per second is usually measured in Megahertz (MHz).

1 MHz = one **million** cycles per **second**.

2.8 A typical modern PC might have a specification of 266 MHz. Speeds are improving rapidly. A typical business PC with a specification of 600 MHz was available in early 2001 for around £700.

Memory

2.9 Just as humans can work more quickly if they can remember the rules for doing something rather than having to look them up, a computer's processing is much faster if it has the information it needs readily to hand. The computer's memory is also known as **main store**, **internal store** or **immediate access storage**. This is circuitry which is used to store data within the processing unit whilst the computer is operating.

Bits and bytes

2.10 Each individual storage element in the computer's memory consists of a simple circuit which can be switched on or off. These two states can be conveniently expressed by the

BPP
PUBLISHING

numbers 1 and 0 respectively. Any piece of data or instruction must be coded in these symbols before processing can commence.

2.11 Each 1 or 0 is a **bit**. Bits are grouped together in groups of eight to form **bytes**. A byte may be used to represent a character, for example a letter, a number or another symbol. A byte coding system that is commonly used in microcomputers is ASCII.

2.12 The processing capacity of a computer is in part dictated by the capacity of its memory. Capacity is calculated in **kilobytes** (1 kilobyte = 2^{10} (1,024) bytes) and **megabytes** (1 megabyte = 2^{20} bytes) and **gigabytes** (2^{30}). These are abbreviated to Kb, Mb and Gb.

RAM and ROM

> **KEY TERMS**
>
> - **RAM** (random access memory) is memory that is **directly available** to the processing unit. It holds the data and programs in current use. Data can be written on to or read from random access memory. RAM can be defined as memory with the ability to access any location in the memory in any order with the same speed.
>
> - **ROM** (read-only memory) is a memory chip into which fixed data is written permanently at the time of its manufacture. New data cannot be written into the memory, and so the data on the memory chip is unchangeable and irremovable.

2.13 Random access is an essential requirement for the main memory of a computer. RAM in microcomputers is 'volatile' which means that the contents of the memory are erased when the computer's power is switched off.

2.14 The RAM on a typical business PC is likely to have a capacity of 32 to 128 megabytes. The size of the RAM is *extremely* important. A computer with a 450 MHz clock speed but only 32 Mb of RAM will not be as efficient as a 266 MHz PC with 128 Mb of RAM.

2.15 ROM is 'non-volatile' memory, which means that its contents do not disappear when the computer's power source is switched off. A computer's start-up program, known as a 'bootstrap' program, is always held in a form of a ROM.

Types of computer

2.16 Computers can be classified as follows, although the differences between these categories are becoming increasingly vague.

- Supercomputers
- Mainframe computers, now sometimes called 'enterprise servers'
- Minicomputers, now often called 'mid-range' computers
- Microcomputers, now commonly called PCs

Supercomputers

2.17 **A supercomputer is used to process very large amounts of data very quickly**. They are particularly useful for occasions where high volumes of calculations need to be performed, for example in meteorological or astronomical applications. Manufacturers of supercomputers include Cray and Fujitsu. They are not used commercially.

Mainframes

2.18 **A mainframe computer system is one that has at its heart a very powerful central computer,** linked by cable or telecommunications to hundreds or thousands of terminals, and capable of accepting simultaneous input from all of them. A mainframe has many times more processing power than a PC and offers extensive data storage facilities.

2.19 Older systems are typically very large in terms of size and very sensitive to fluctuations in temperature and air quality, requiring them to be housed in a controlled environment. However, the main modern example (the IBM S/390) uses the same kind of components that are used in PCs, may not be much larger than a fridge-freezer, and has far less need for a specialised environment. The basic IBM S/390 costs around £50,000.

2.20 Mainframes are used by organisations such as banks that have very large volumes of processing to perform and have special security needs. Many organisations have now replaced their old mainframes with networked 'client/server' systems of mid-range computers and PCs because this approach (called **downsizing**) is thought to be cheaper and offer more flexibility.

2.21 Nevertheless, mainframes are considered to offer greater reliability, functionality and data security than networked systems. Proponents claim that for organisations with 200 or more users they are cheaper to run in the medium term than other alternatives.

Medium and small business computers

Minicomputers

2.22 **A minicomputer is a computer whose size, speed and capabilities lie somewhere between those of a mainframe and a PC.** The term was originally used before PCs were developed, to describe computers which were cheaper but less well-equipped than mainframe computers (which had until then been the only type of computer available). The advent of more powerful chips now means that some 'superminis', and even PCs linked in a network, can run more powerfully than some older mainframes.

2.23 With the advent of PCs, and with mainframes now being physically smaller than in the past, the definition of a minicomputer has become rather vague. There is really no definition which distinguishes adequately between a PC and a minicomputer. Price, power and number of users supported have been used to identify distinguishing features, but these differences have tended to erode as microchip technology has progressed. Manufacturers of minicomputers include IBM with its AS400, ICL and DEC.

PCs

2.24 **Personal computers or PCs are now the norm for small to medium-sized business computing and for home computing.** Often they are linked together in a network to enable sharing of information between users.

2.25 A typical PC comprises a keyboard, a screen, a base unit or tower unit (containing the processor and other circuitry and floppy disk drives and CD-ROM drives), a mouse, and sometimes a pair of speakers. A typical modern business PC might have 64Mb of RAM, a 266 Mhz 'Pentium' processor and a 5 Gb hard drive.

BPP
PUBLISHING

File servers

2.26 A **file server** is more powerful than the average desktop PC and it is dedicated to providing additional services for users of networked PCs.

2.27 A very large network is likely to use a 'mainframe' computer as its server, and indeed mainframes are beginning to be referred to as '**enterprise servers**'.

Portables

2.28 The original portable computers were heavy, weighing around five kilograms, and could only be run from the mains electricity supply. Subsequent developments allow true portability.

(a) The **laptop** is powered either from the electricity supply or using a rechargeable battery. It has a hard drive and also uses 3½" floppy disks, CD-ROMs and DVDs, a liquid crystal or gas plasma screen and is fully compatible with desktop PCs.

(b) The **notebook** is about the size of an A4 pad of paper. Some portables are now marketed as '**sub-notebooks**'.

(c) The **pocket computer** or handheld, may or may not be compatible with true PCs. They range from machines which are little more than electronic organisers to relatively powerful processors running 'cut-down' versions of Windows 98 and communications features.

2.29 While portable PCs are becoming more popular (even in the office, as they save precious space on crowded desks), disadvantages include the following.

- **Keyboard ergonomics** (ie keys which are too close together for easy, quick typing).
- **Battery power** (although manufacturers are trying to reduce power consumption).
- The **relative expense** of having to use the telecommunications network to send data.

Question 1

Which of the following is **not** hardware?

A   Printer
B   CPU
C   Word for Windows
D   Keyboard

Answer

C   Word for Windows is a word processing software.

3   COMPUTER SOFTWARE

3.1 **Software refers to computer programs.** Hardware cannot operate without software and software is needed to make the hardware process data in the ways required.

3.2 **Software has to be 'written' by a programmer, and program writing is a labour-intensive operation,** so that although hardware costs have fallen in recent years with the development of integrated circuit technology, the costs of software have tended to rise (because salaries and wages have risen). Software costs can now be much higher than the costs of the hardware for a computer system. The two main categories of software are as follows.

- Operating software
- Application software

KEY TERM

Operating software is software that controls the basic operation of a computer system. It is software that makes the hardware perform its functions, such as bringing data input into store and outputting information to an output device.

3.3   An operating system will typically perform the following tasks.

- Initial set-up of the computer, when it is switched on.
- Checking that the hardware (including printers) is functioning properly.
- Calling up of program files and data files from external storage into memory.
- Opening and closing of files, checking of file labels etc.
- Maintenance of directories in external storage.
- Controlling input and output devices, including the interaction with the user.
- Controlling system security (for example monitoring the use of passwords).
- Handling of interruptions (for example program abnormalities or machine failure).
- Managing multitasking.

3.4   **Multi-tasking** means doing lots of tasks at once, eg printing out a document you have just finished while working on the next one.

3.5   The best-known operating system is Windows 98.

KEY TERM

Applications are ready made programs written to perform a particular job for the user rather than operate the computer. The job will be common to many potential users, so that the package could be adopted by all of them for their data processing operations.

3.6   Examples of **applications** for commercial users which are available in software packages include the following.

- Payroll
- Production control
- Sales accounting (sales ledger system)
- Purchase accounting (purchase ledger system)
- Nominal ledger system and cost book system
- General bookkeeping system
- Audit packages (for internal and external audit use)
- Network analysis (or critical path analysis) programs

3.7   A distinction is sometimes made between application packages and more general purpose packages. A **general purpose package** is an off-the-shelf program that can be used for processing of a general type, but the computer user can apply the package to a variety of specific uses of his own choice.

3.8   Examples of general purpose packages are as follows.

(a)   **Database systems**. This is a package of programs that allows the user to work with a large collection of data held on file (that is, a data base). With most commercial database packages, the user will key the data on to file to create the database records,

BPP
PUBLISHING

but with some packages the database is already provided. The data on file can then be extracted and processed in different ways, according to the nature of the information that the user wants to obtain.

(b) **Expert systems**. This is similar to a database package, in which the file holds a large amount of specialised data, eg legal, engineering or medical information. The user keys in certain facts and the program uses its information on file to produce a decision about something on which an expert's decision would normally be required - for example a user without a legal background can obtain guidance on the law without having to consult a solicitor; or a non-medical user can obtain a medical diagnosis about a patient without having to consult a doctor or surgeon.

(c) **Word processing packages**. These give the user the facility of altering and re-organising large blocks of text on a terminal screen (correcting errors, inserting extra text and so on), and keeping files of standard text for repetitive use.

(d) **Spreadsheet packages**. These are used extensively in financial planning for budgeting, forecasting and other financial modelling.

Integrated software

3.9 **Integrated software** refers to programs, or packages of programs, that perform a variety of different processing operations, using data which is compatible with whatever operation is being carried out.

3.10 Accounts packages often consist of program 'modules' that can be integrated into a larger accounting system. There will be a module each for the sales ledger, the purchase ledger, the nominal ledger, and so on. Output from one 'module' can be used as input to another. The master file in one module can also be used in another module. For example the purchase ledger and sales ledger files could be used to provide input to the nominal ledger system.

4 CAPTURING AND PROCESSING DATA

4.1 The collection of data and its subsequent input to the computer are often problematical areas of data processing. The computer will only accept data which is in machine-sensible form, and if data is captured on a source document that is not in machine-sensible form it must be transcribed into a different form for input to computer processing.

4.2 Because of this, data collection and preparation for input can be lengthy and expensive operations. **The stages of data input are as follows**.

(a) **Origination** of data (transactions giving rise to data which needs to be recorded and processed).

(b) **Transcription** of data into a machine-sensible form, if this is necessary.

(c) Data **input**.

4.3 The ideal methods of data collection and input are those which do the following.

(a) Minimise the time needed to record the original data, and transmit, prepare and input the data to the computer.

(b) Minimise costs.

(c) Minimise errors.

(d) Minimise the 'turnround time' between submitting data for input and getting the processed information back.

Direct data entry with VDU and keyboard

4.4 The principal method of direct data entry is by means of a terminal comprising a VDU with keyboard. **VDU** and **keyboard** can be used as media for **direct data entry** as terminals connected to a mainframe or minicomputer or as an integral part of a microcomputer installation.

Keyboard layout and functions

4.5 A basic keyboard includes the following.

- **Ordinary typing keys** used to enter data or text.
- A **numeric key pad** for use with the built-in calculator.
- **Cursor control keys** (basically up/down/left/right keys to move the cursor).
- A number of **function keys** for use by the system and application software.

4.6 In addition to the function keys, there are special keys that are used to communicate with the operating programs, to let the computer know that you have finished entering a command, that you wish to correct a command and so on. Nothing appears at the cursor point when these keys are used, but they affect operations on screen.

The VDU

4.7 A **VDU** (or monitor) **displays text** and **graphics** and serves a number of purposes.

- It allows the operator to carry out a visual check on what he or she has keyed in.
- It helps the operator to input data by providing 'forms' on the screen for filling in.
- It displays output such as answers to file enquiries.
- It gives messages to the operator.

Character-based systems

4.8 Older systems offer two ways of using a keyboard with VDU to input data. Screen displays typically show white characters on a black background.

(a) **By selecting options from a menu.** A menu is a display of a series of options, and the operator selects which option he or she wants by keying in an appropriate letter or number. A VDU screen might list a number of different options, from which the computer user must choose what he or she wants to do next. For example, a main menu for purchase and sales ledger functions might include:

A - Define codes
B - Set up standing orders
C - Purchase ledger entries
D - Sales ledger entries
E - Supplier details
F - Client details

By selecting D, the operator will be specifying that he or she wants to do some processing of sales ledger entries. When D has been keyed in, another menu may be displayed, calling for the operator to narrow down still further the specification of what he or she wants to do next. A menu-system is thus a hierarchical list of options.

BPP PUBLISHING

(b) **Using commands**. Command codes or instructions are keyed in, to indicate to the program what it should do with the data that follow. The data are then keyed in and processed by the program.

Graphical user interfaces

4.9 Modern systems are more user-friendly than character-based ones, especially for people who have little experience of using computers and/or who have difficulty using a keyboard. They are based on divisions of the screen into sections and coloured images of various kinds: hence the name graphical user interface (**GUI**).

4.10 **Graphical user interfaces** have become the principal means by which humans communicate with machines. Features include the following.

(a) **Windows**. This basically means that the screen can be divided into sections or 'windows' of flexible size which can be opened and closed. This enables two or more documents to be viewed and edited together, and sections of one to be inserted into another. This is particularly useful for word processed documents and spreadsheets, which are too large for the VDU screen.

(b) **Icons**. An icon is an image of an object used to represent an abstract idea or process. In software design, icons may be used instead of numbers, letters or words to identify and describe the various functions available for selection, or files to access. A common icon is a waste paper bin to indicate the deletion of a document.

(c) **Mouse**. This is a device used with on-screen graphics and sometimes as an alternative to using the keyboard to input instructions. It can be used to pick out the appropriate icon (or other option), to mark out the area of a new window, mark the beginning and end of a block for deletion/insertion and so on. It also has a button to execute the current command.

(d) **Pull-down menu**. An initial menu (or 'menu-bar') will be shown across the top of the VDU screen. Using the mouse to move the pointer to the required item in the menu, the pointer 'pulls down' a subsidiary menu, somewhat similar to pulling down a window blind in a room of a house. The pointer and mouse can then be used to select the required item on the pulled-down menu.

(e) Many GUIs (such as Microsoft Windows) also display dialogue boxes, buttons, sliders, check boxes, and a plethora of other graphical widgets that let you tell the computer what to do and how to do it.

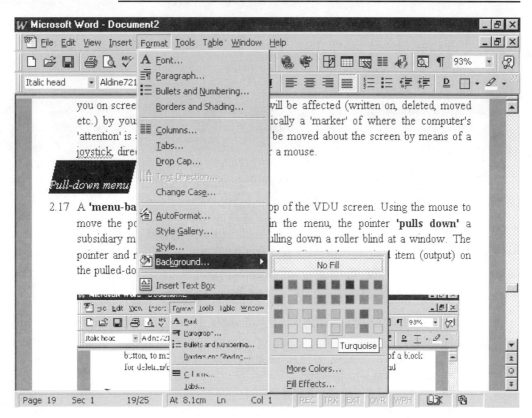

Document reading methods

4.11 Transcribing manually-prepared data into a computer-sensible form such as disk or tape is costly in manpower, time and accuracy. **Document reading methods of data collection involve the use of a source document that both humans and computers can read.** The data on the source document might be pre-printed, or added later by manual processing, but in either case the source document itself is fed in to the computer. Data transcription and verification become unnecessary.

Magnetic ink character recognition (MICR)

4.12 **MICR** is the **recognition of characters** by a machine that reads special formatted characters printed in magnetic ink. Using ink which contains a metallic powder, highly stylised characters are encoded on to documents by means of special typewriters. The document must be passed through a magnetic field before the characters can be detected by a suitable reading device.

4.13 The largest application of MICR is the banking system. Cheques are **pre-encoded** with the customer account number, branch code and cheque number and, after use, **post-encoded** with the amount of the cheque. The cheques are then passed through the reading device and details stored on magnetic disk or tape.

4.14 The main advantage of MICR is its accuracy, but MICR documents are expensive to produce, and so MICR has only limited application in practice.

BPP PUBLISHING

Optical character recognition (OCR)

> **KEY TERM**
>
> **OCR** is 'a method of input which involves a machine that is able to read characters by optical detection of the shape of those characters'.   (CIMA *Computing Terminology*)

4.15   Optical (or laser) scanners can read printed or typed documents at up to 300 pages per hour. They recognise the characters, convert them into machine code and record them on to the magnetic medium being used (or directly input the data to the CPU). The advantage of OCR over MICR is that the computer can read ordinary typed or printed text, provided that the quality of the input document is satisfactory.

Optical mark reading (OMR)

4.16   You use **optical mark reading** when you enter the National Lottery or do a multiple choice exam. Values are denoted by a line or cross in an appropriate box on a preprinted source document. The document is then read by a device which senses the mark in each box and translates it into machine code.

4.17   A business application in which OMR is used is the recording of gas and electricity meter readings by meter readers onto preprinted documents. Once the readings are made, the documents are input to the computer using an OMR reading system.

Bar coding

4.18   A **bar code reader** is a device which reads documents which contain bar codes. These are groups of marks which, by their spacing and thickness, indicate specific codes or values. Such devices are now commonly seen as an input medium for point of sale systems in supermarkets. Many products now carry bar coding on their labels.

Turnround documents

4.19   A **turnround document** is a document that is initially produced by computer. It is then used to collect more data and then re-input to the computer for processing. Examples of turnround documents are as follows.

(a)   Credit card companies include a payment counterfoil with their computer-produced bill which will then be used for inputting payment data to a computer.

(b)   An examining body that stores multiple choice questions on a computer file can produce examination papers by computer. Candidates are then asked to tick the correct answer, and the position of the answer mark will be detectable by OMR reader, and so the examination paper can be marked by computer.

Card reading devices

Magnetic stripe cards

4.20   **Magnetic stripe cards** have been widely distributed over the past decade, so that almost every person with a bank or building society account can use one. None of the information on the surface of the card is strictly necessary for data input to a computer system. All the machine-sensible data is contained on the back, on a magnetic stripe, which is a thin strip of typical magnetic recording tape, about 1.2cm wide stuck to the back of the card. The magnetic card reader converts the information on the tape into computer-sensible form.

Electronic point of sale (EPOS) devices

4.21 More and more large retail stores are introducing **electronic point of sale devices** which act both as cash registers and as terminals connected to a main computer. This enables the computer to produce useful management information such as sales details and analysis and stock control information very quickly. Many use bar coding, as described earlier, or direct keyboard entry. A fully itemised, accurate and descriptive receipt can be produced for the customer, who will also feel the benefit of faster moving queues at the checkout. Management will obtain more information more quickly than was ever possible before, in the following ways.

- Immediate updating of stock levels.
- Identification of fast-moving items for reordering, hence avoidance of stock-outs.
- Sales information.

4.22 The provision of immediate sales information (such as which products sell quickly), perhaps analysed on a branch basis, permits great speed and flexibility in decision-making (certainly of a short-term nature), as consumer wishes can be responded to quickly.

Question 2

As we have seen, there is a wide range of input methods, each one having its own advantages and disadvantages. From the descriptions given in this chapter you should be able to formulate your own ideas on the advantages and disadvantages of each method and you may be required in your examination to select the most suitable data input method in a particular situation. What factors should you consider in selecting an input method?

Answer

(a) **Suitability** for the application
(b) The **timing requirements** of the system (response times required)
(c) The **volume** of data
(d) The **accuracy** required
(e) The **cost** of the method chosen as compared with the benefits to be derived
(f) The use of **turnround** documents for data capture and the benefit of OCR methods

Question 3

Which of the following is an input device?

A   Screen
B   Keyboard
C   Printer
D   CPU

Answer

B   The keyboard is an input device. The screen and the printer are output devices, while the CPU performs the processing function.

BPP PUBLISHING

5 DATA OUTPUT

Printers

5.1 A **line printer** prints a complete line in a single operation, usually printing between 600 and 1,000 lines per minutes. They offer the operational speeds necessary for the **bulk printing requirements** of many systems.

5.2 **Character printers** print a single character at a time. Examples include daisy-wheel printers, dot matrix printers.

    (a) Daisy wheel printers are **slow and noisy**, but produce print of a **high quality**. Companies are unlikely to buy new daisy wheel printers today because other types of printers are more versatile.

    (b) Dot matrix printers are quite widely used in accounting departments. Their main drawback is the **low-resolution** of their printed characters, which is unsuitable for many forms of printed output. They are also relatively **slow** and rather **noisy.** Prices start at under £100.

5.3 **Bubblejet** and **inkjet** printers are small and prices start at under £100, making them popular where a 'private'; output device is required, for example in a director's office. They work by sending a jet of ink on to the paper to produce the required characters. They are fairly **quiet and fast,** but they may produce **smudged** output if the paper is not handled carefully.

5.4 **Laser printers** print a whole page at a time, rather than line by line. Unlike daisywheel and dot matrix printers, they print on to individual **sheets of paper** (in the same way as photocopiers do) and so they do not user 'tractor fed' continuous computer stationery.

5.5 The resolution of printed characters and diagrams with laser printers is **very high** - up to 600 dots per inch - and this high-quality resolution makes laser printing output good enough to be used for commercial printing.

5.6 Typically, a desk-top laser printer will print about 4 to 24 A4 pages per minute. **High speed** lasers print up to 500 pages per minute. Laser printers are a microprocessor in their own right, with **RAM memory for storing data prior to printing.**

5.7 Laser printers are **more expensive** than other types - a good one will cost about £700 - but it is quite possible that several users will be able to **share** a single laser printer.

The choice of output medium

5.8 As with choosing an input medium, choosing a suitable output medium depends on a number of factors, which you should bear in mind when we go on to consider each type of output in turn. These factors are as follows.

    (a) **Is a 'hard' copy of the output required**; in other words, is a printed version of the output needed? If so, what quality must the output be?

        (i) If the output includes documents that are going to be used as OCR turnround documents, the quality of printing must be good.

        (ii) If the information will be used as a working document with a short life or limited use (eg a copy of text for type-checking) then a low quality output on a dot matrix printer might be sufficient.

(b) **The volume of information produced**. For example, a VDU screen can hold a certain amount of data, but it becomes more difficult to read when information goes 'off-screen' and can only be read a bit at a time.

(c) **The speed at which output is required**. For example, to print a large volume of data, a high speed printer might be most suitable to finish the work more quickly (and release the CPU for other jobs).

(d) **The suitability of the output medium to the application** - ie the purpose for which the output is needed.

   (i) A VDU is well-suited to interactive processing with a computer.

   (ii) A graph plotter would be well-suited to output in the form of graphs.

   (iii) Output on to a magnetic disk or tape would be well-suited if the data is for further processing.

   (iv) Large volumes of reference data for human users to hold in a library might be held on microfilm or microfiche, and so output in these forms would be appropriate.

(e) **Cost**: some output devices would not be worth having because their advantages would not justify their cost, and so another output medium should be chosen as 'second best'.

6 STORAGE DEVICES

Disks

6.1 **Disks** are the predominant form of backing storage medium nowadays because they offer direct access to data, an extremely important feature.

6.2 **Disks are covered on both sides with a magnetic material**. Data is held on a number of circular, concentric tracks on the surfaces of the disk, and is read or written by rotating the disk past read/write heads, which can write data from the CPU's memory on to disk, or can read data from the disk for input to the CPU's memory. The mechanism that causes the disk to rotate is called a **disk drive**. The data on a disk is located by its sector, as each track and sector has a unique identification number.

Hard disks

6.3 A modern business PC invariably has an **internal hard disk**, but external disks may be used too. External disks sit alongside the computer in an extra 'box', with its own power supply and plug socket. Internal disks are incorporated inside the microcomputer itself. At the time of writing the average new PC has a hard disk size of around 4 Gigabytes, but 15 Gb disks are not uncommon. The standard size has increased dramatically over recent years as ever more Windows-based software which is hungry for hard disk space is released.

6.4 In larger computer systems **removable disk packs** are commonly used. Several flat disks are mounted on a spindle. There is one read/write head for each surface, and the heads are moved in a synchronised manner across the disk surfaces. The disks rotate at about one thousandth of a millimetre from the heads; the disks need a very clean atmosphere to prevent dirt or dust coming between them. With the growth of minicomputer systems it became necessary to develop a magnetic disk storage medium which was less expensive than the exchangeable disk pack, but which still offered substantial storage capacity. The Winchester disk is a number of flat disks sealed into an airtight pack. They have a very high recording density.

BPP PUBLISHING

Floppy disks

> **KEY TERM**
>
> A **floppy disk** is an exchangeable circular, flexible disk (typically $3^1/_2$ inches in diameter) which is held permanently in a plastic case. The case can bear an identification label for recognising the disk. A $3^1/_2$" disk can hold up to 1.44 Mb of data.

6.5 Modern PCs will also have one or two **floppy disk** drives. The floppy disk provides a cost-effective means of on-line storage for small business computer systems. Floppy disks are used in the smallest microcomputer systems as well as with minicomputers, and are particularly useful in providing a means of decentralised processing.

6.6 **Floppy disks do not require special storage conditions**, and indeed, they are often stored or filed in open trays. However, data on them can be easily corrupted. In particular, they are subject to physical wear, because the read/write head actually comes into contact with the disk surface during operation. This is not the case with other types of disk. Because they can be left lying around an office, they are also prone to physical damage, such as having cups of coffee spilled over them. As the disks tend to be less reliable than hard disks administrative procedures should be instituted to protect them (for example the use of steel filing cabinets and careful handling).

Tape storage

6.7 Like an audio or video cassette, data has to be recorded **along the length** of a computer tape and so it is more difficult to access. In using tapes, it is not practical to read from and then write on to a single piece of tape. Reading and writing are separate operations, using separate heads, and so two drives are necessary for the two operations.

6.8 It follows that magnetic tape as a file storage medium is only practical when every record on the file will be processed in turn. For example a supermarket's stock records might have movements in every item of stock every day, and so tape would be a suitable for backing up at the end of the day.

6.9 Tape cartridges have a **larger capacity** than floppy disks and they are still widely used as a **backing storage** medium.

6.10 Like any other storage medium tapes can get lost, or the data on them can get corrupted. Since tapes can only be updated by producing a completely new carried forward tape this provides an automatic means of data security. The brought forward tapes can be kept for two or three 'generations' to safeguard against the loss of data on a current file. This 'grandfather-father-son' technique allows for files to be reconstructed if a disaster should occur.

CD-ROM

6.11 **Optical disks**, which use similar technology to the laser-based compact disc audio system, are being used increasingly for data storage. Optical disks have very high capacity compared with other media and they are **more difficult to damage**: these advantages suggest that they are likely to develop into the main form of removable storage in the future. The latest PCs are now automatically supplied with a **CD-ROM** drive and some software packages are now only available on CD-ROM.

6.12   The initials **ROM** stand for **read-only memory**. This means that all data is implanted onto the disc when it is made, and subsequent users can only retrieve information, they cannot alter or overwrite or delete what is already on the disk. The **speed** of a CD-ROM drive is relevant to how fast data can be retrieved: an **eight speed** drive is quicker than a **four speed** drive.

6.13   **CD recorders** are now available for general business use with blank CDs (CD-R), but this does not alter the fact that until recently, CDs have not been reusable in the way that floppy disks are. This is why PCs invariably have floppy disk drives as well as CD-ROM drives. However, a **rewritable disk** (CD-RW) is now available. A CD-R can hold up to **650 Mb** of data.

DVD-ROM

6.14   The CD format has started to be superseded by DVD. CD-ROMs hold 650 megabytes of data, which only a few years ago was considered enough for any application. However, the advent of Multimedia files with video graphics and sound encouraged the development of a new storage technology.

6.15   **Digital Versatile Disk (DVD)** ROM technology can store almost 5 gigabytes of data. Access speed are improved as is sound and video quality.

6.16   DVD is some times referred to as **Digital Video Disk**. Many commentators believe DVD will not only replace CD-ROMs, but also VHS cassettes, audio CDs and laser discs.

7   SPREADSHEET PACKAGES

Exam focus point
Section 4 of the study guide for Paper 1.2 states 'explain the role and features of spreadsheet systems'. Remember that you can also draw on your own practical experience at work when answering examination questions.

7.1   As you may already have realised, a large amount of accounting work entails drawing up tables and adding up rows and columns of numbers. A **spreadsheet** is a software package designed to do just that.

BPP
PUBLISHING

The following is a representation of the spreadsheet shown:

	A	B	C	D
1		Cost	Depreciation	NBV
2		£	£	£
3	Fixed assets			
4	Tangible assets			
5	Buildings	12,000	400	11,600
6	Plant and equipment	12,000	1,200	10,800
7	Motor vehicles	7,200	1,800	5,400
8		31,200	3,400	27,800

Cell reference: A10. Sheets: Sheet1, Sheet2, Sheet3, Sheet4.

7.2 A **spreadsheet** consists of a large number of **boxes** or **cells**, each identified by a reference such as A4, D16, AA20 etc. AA20 is immediately to the right of Z20 and to the left of AB20. The screen cursor will highlight any particular cell - in the example above, it is placed over cell A10. At the top or bottom of the screen, the spreadsheet program will give you such information as:

(a) The **reference** of the cell where the cursor lies

(b) The **width** of the column where the cursor lies

(c) The **contents** of the cell where the cursor lies, if there is anything there

7.3 The contents of the cell can be any one of the following.

(a) **Text**. Text contains words or numbers not used in computation.

(b) **Values**. A value is a number used in a computation, or a formula.

(c) **Formulae**. These refer to other cells in the spreadsheet and perform computations with them.

(d) **Automated commands** or **macros**.

How is a spreadsheet used?

7.4 The idea behind a spreadsheet is that the model builder should construct a model, in rows and columns format as follows.

(a) Identifying what data goes into each row and column, by inserting text - eg column headings and row identifications.

(b) Specifying how the numerical data in the model should be derived. Numerical data might be treated as follows.

(i) Inserted into the model via keyboard input.

(ii) Calculated from other data in the model by means of a formula specified within the model itself. The model builder must insert these formulae into the spreadsheet model when it is first constructed.

(iii) Occasionally, imported from data from another computer application program or module.

Commands and facilities

7.5 Spreadsheets are versatile tools. Different spreadsheets will offer different facilities, but some of the more basic ones which should feature in all spreadsheet programs are as follows.

(a) **Print commands.** You should be able to print the contents of the spreadsheet in total or in part, with or without the spreadsheet row and column labels.

(b) **File commands.** You should be able to save the spreadsheet data on your disk, so that you can use the data again, and so the facility to save data is an essential one. A spreadsheet is saved as a file of data.

(c) **Cell editing facilities.** The program should allow alteration of anything shown on the spreadsheet. This is particularly useful for 'what if?' calculations. For instance, suppose you had prepared a forecast balance sheet and you wanted to know what net current assets would be if taxation was £500,000 higher. Using editing facilities, you just have to change the taxation figure, then ask the computer to recalculate the entire spreadsheet on the basis of the new figures. This 'what if' manipulation of data is probably the most important facility in a spreadsheet package, and we shall return to it again later.

(d) **Facilities to rearrange the spreadsheet.** You can **insert** a column or row at a desired spot. The insert command facilitates this, and the formulae in the spreadsheet are adjusted automatically. You can **move** or **copy** a cell, row or column (or range of cells) elsewhere. You can **delete** a cell row or column.

(e) **Format.** This command controls the way in which headings and data are shown, for example by altering column widths, 'justifying' text and numbers (to indent or have a right-hand justification, etc), changing the number of decimal places displayed etc. You can format the whole spreadsheet, or, in certain cases, a specified **range** of cells.

(f) **Copy a formula.** For example, suppose you wanted to have a cumulative list of numbers as follows.

	A	B	C
1	Operation	Cost per operation	Cumulative cost
2	No.	£	£
3	1	9.00	9.00
4	2	10.00	19.00
5	3	14.00	33.00
6	4	3.00	36.00
7	5	86.00	122.00
8	6	9.00	131.00
9		131.00	

The cumulative numbers in the B column are calculated as follows.

BPP PUBLISHING

	A	B	C
1	Operation	Cost per operation	Cumulative cost
2	No.	£	£
3	1	9	=B3
4	2	10	=C3+B4
5	3	14	=C4+B5
6	4	3	=C5+B6
7	5	86	=C6+B7
8	6	9	=C7+B8
9		=SUM(B3:B8)	

To save time it is possible to input = C3+B4 in the C4 cell and then to copy the formula down the column. The spreadsheet package will generate all the other formulae needed automatically, making the necessary changes each time. It is possible to 'replicate' formulae in this way, downwards or sideways throughout the spreadsheet.

(g) **Database** facility. A spreadsheet package will usually provide a facility for sorting data (alphabetically or numerically).

(h) Most spreadsheets also contain a **graphics** facility which enables the presentation of data as graphs or flowcharts for example.

(i) Some spreadsheets offer a **search and replace** facility to highlight and alter individual formulae.

(j) **Macros**. Many spreadsheet commands are provided as **options** in a menu. Some procedures require a number of commands to be executed. This is often time consuming. For example, if you wish to 'print' some or all of your spreadsheet, you will first execute the print command. You may then see a menu which asks you to specify:

(i) What **range** of the spreadsheet you wish to print.

(ii) What **print 'options'** you wish to use. This will lead to a submenu, which will ask you to specify the length of the pages you are using in the printer, what you wish the size of the margins to be and so forth.

Several commands must be executed before the spreadsheet is printed, and you will have to repeat them each time you wish to print your spreadsheet. Many spreadsheets provide a macro facility. This allows the user to automate a sequence of commands, executing them with the depression of two keys.

(k) Some spreadsheets offer a **'protect' facility** to ensure that the contents of a specified range of cells (for example the text titles, or a column of base data) cannot be tampered with.

Using spreadsheet models: sensitivity analysis

7.6 Whenever a forecast or budget is made, management should consider asking **'what if'** questions, and so carry out a form of **sensitivity analysis**. Suppose a forecast profit and loss account has been prepared using a spreadsheet. The accountant might ask a number of questions about it such as the following.

- What if sales were higher?
- What if administrative expenses were reduced by 25%?
- What if closing stock was reduced by £1 million?

7.7 Using the spreadsheet model, the answers to these questions, and others like them, can be obtained simply and quickly, using the editing facility in the program. A great number of such 'what if' questions can be asked and answered quickly, such as what if sales growth per month is nil, ½%, 1%, 1½%, 2½% or minus 1% etc? The information obtained should provide management with a better understanding of what the cash flow position in the future might be, and what factors are critical to ensuring that the cash position remains reasonable.

8 STATISTICAL PACKAGES

8.1 Before the widespread use of computers and microcomputers, accountants wishing to use certain statistical and mathematical techniques had to be arithmetic wizards. Often endless calculations had to be performed and then re-performed before a conclusion could be reached.

8.2 Fortunately computers have changed that. **Computers will perform any necessary calculations speedily and accurately**, leaving the accountant free to analyse and conclude. Familiarity with computers is therefore vital for any accountant wishing to use mathematical and statistical techniques.

8.3 Accountants could, of course, write their own programs each time they wished to use a mathematical or statistical technique. There are, however, a number of suitable packages on the market which, if used, leave the accountant free to analyse and conclude instead of being involved in computer technicalities.

Spreadsheets and statistics

8.4 Modern spreadsheet packages such as **Microsoft Excel** and **Lotus 1-2-3** include statistical functions that probably go well beyond the need of most accountants.

8.5 Besides financial maths techniques like Discounted Cash Flow and statistical techniques like Normal distributions, spreadsheets can calculate medians, modes, and so on, perform tests such as chi-squared tests, do linear programming, regression and so on. All of the techniques, in fact, that you will learn to do **manually** for Paper 1.2, and in your later studies, can be done easily with a spreadsheet.

Statistical software packages

8.6 There are also a variety of packages available that are dedicated to statistical work. Some of these are specially designed to make the work easy for people who are not adept at the techniques. Here are just two examples.

SPSS

8.7 SPSS is the market leader in statistical software for desktop computers. It offers an extensive set of statistics, graphs and reports and a user-friendly interface that enables the user to enter data in a spreadsheet like format (or import data directly from an existing spreadsheet, accounting package or database) and perform a large number of statistical tests. The results can then be exported into packages such as Word or Excel and incorporated into reports

8.8 It is designed to help with tasks like market research, sales forecasting, process control. It does so by identifying patterns in data, and visualising them in the form of bar charts, scattergraphs and so on. Over 60 statistical functions are offered: far more than you will learn about in this book.

BPP PUBLISHING

8.9 The **advantage** of statistical software packages is that they take all the agony out of analysing figures. Instead of hours of number-crunching an analysis can be obtained at the click of a button by selecting the rows and columns of data you want to analyse.

8.10 The **disadvantage** is that it is too easy: if users do not understand what the statistic calculated actually means in the first place, they will not be able to draw any conclusions from the results produced. Worse, they may set up the data wrongly and then draw incorrect conclusions because they cannot see that the results do not make sense.

WinForecast

8.11 In practice, more advanced statistical techniques are relatively little used by many businesses, not least because accountants that should be using them do not feel confident about them. More familiar will be simple management accounting techniques such as cash flow forecasting, and projected profit and loss accounts.

8.12 WinForecast is a package designed to help with this sort of work. Its manufacturer claims that it is 5 to 10 times faster than using a spreadsheet to produce a variety of familiar management accounting reports, because it is designed to remove as much of the mechanics of producing projections as possible.

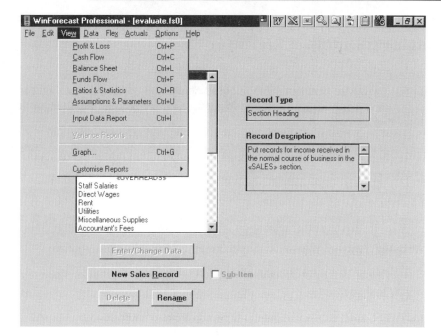

8.13 WinForecast offers What If? facilities to evaluate the effect of changes in variables such as price or demand. It can generate graphs and charts of various types for visual presentation and analysis of data, and it can incorporate formulae to manipulate or compare different scenarios.

Exam focus point

Remember that the contents of this chapter are not core syllabus topics and are therefore most likely to be examined in the objective test section of the exam paper.

BPP PUBLISHING

Chapter roundup

- Manual and electronic data processing are essentially the same. When compared with human beings, however, computers can process data much more **quickly**, are generally **accurate** (whereas human beings are prone to error) and can process both **larger volumes of data** and **more complex data.**

- Computers can be classified as mainframe computers, minicomputers or PCs.

- **Hardware** means the physical devices and components that make up a computer system, such as the CPU, disk drives, VDUs and so on. **Software** refers to the computer programs.

- **Operating software** controls the basic operation of a computer system. **Applications software** enables a computer to do the data processing for the various processing applications the user wishes to computerise (such as a sales ledger system or a payroll system).

- The principal method of direct data input to the computer is by means of a terminal comprising a **VDU** and **keyboard**.

- Instead of direct data entry, data may be copied from source documents and be written on to a magnetic disk or a magnetic tape from a keyboard or terminal. This process is called **encoding**.

- **Document reading methods** of data collection involve the use of a source document that both human beings and computers can read. Such method include **MICR**, **OCR**, **OMR**, **mark sensing**, **bar coding** and **turnround documents**.

- Data can also be collected by **card reading devices**, **magnetic stripe cards** and **EPOS devices**.

- **Output devices** include the VDU and **printers** such as **dot matrix** printers and **laser** printers. The choice of output medium will depend on factors such as the volume of information produced, whether a hard copy is required and the speed at which output is required.

- **External storage devices** are used to store data in computer-sensible form. The most commonly used backing storage medium is **magnetic disk**. Other storage media include **magnetic tape** and **CDs**.

- A **spreadsheet** is a software application which allows you to define a problem logically in terms of text, data and formulae, and then lets the computer bear the brunt of the complicated and tedious calculations. It can be used whenever the problem can be set out in logical stages. Spreadsheets are one of the principal means by which computers are used in cost accounting.

- **Statistical packages** are available to carry out a huge range of techniques. Modern spreadsheets incorporate a wider range of statistical functions than most accountants would ever need.

Quick quiz

1. What are the advantages of computerised data processing over manual data processing? *Speed less errors*

2. What is a CPU? *Central Processing units*

3. What are the disadvantages of portable PCs?

4. What is an application? *Programme Software.*

5. Explain the following terms. *Magnetic Ink Character Recognition, Optical Character Recognition, Optical Mark Recognition*
   MICR, OCR, OMR

6. Which gives better quality output: a dot matrix printer or a laser printer? *Laser*

7. What is the disadvantage of tape storage?

8. List five features of a spreadsheet package. *What if, Calculations, speed*

9. What are the disadvantages of statistical packages? *Include functions that are unlikely to be needed.*

Answers to quick quiz

1. • Speed
   • Accuracy
   • Volume and complexity
   • Access to information

2. The **CPU** is the collection of circuitry and registers that performs the processing in a particular computer and provides that computer with its specific characteristics. It is divided into three areas.

   • The arithmetic and logic unit
   • The control unit
   • The main store, or memory

3. • Keyboard ergonomics
   • Battery power
   • Relative expense

4. An **application** is a ready-made program written to perform a particular job for the user rather than operate the computer.

5. **MICR** (magnetic ink character recognition) is the recognition of characters by a machine that reads special formatted characters printed in magnetic ink.

   OCR (optical character recognition) is a method of input which involves a machine that is able to read characters by optical detection of the shape of those characters.

   OMR (optical mark reading). Values are denoted by a line or cross in an appropriate box on a pre-printed source document. The document is then read by a device which senses the mark in each box and translates it into machine code. Eg, you use OMR when you do multiple choice questions in an exam.

6. Laser printer.

7. It is only practical when every record on the file will be processed in turn.

8. • Print commands
   • File commands
   • Cell editing facilities
   • Facilities to rearrange the spreadsheet
   • Copy a formula

   (see paragraph 7.5 for full listing)

9. • Users must understand what the calculated statistics mean before they can draw any conclusions from the results calculated.

   • As it is easy to use, data must be set up incorrectly and therefore the wrong conclusions may be drawn.

Now try the question below from the Exam Question Bank

Number	Level	Marks	Time
2	MCQ	n/a	n/a

BPP PUBLISHING

Chapter 3

COST CLASSIFICATION

Topic list	Syllabus reference
1 Total product/service costs	1(b), (d)
2 Direct costs and indirect costs	1(b), (d), 3(d)
3 Functional costs	1(b), (d)
4 Fixed costs and variable costs	1(b), (d)
5 Product costs and period costs	1(b), (d)
6 Other cost classifications	1(b), (d)
7 Cost centres, cost units, cost objects, profit centres, revenue centres and investment centres	1(b), (d)

Introduction

The **classification of costs** as either **direct** or **indirect**, for example, is essential in the costing method used by an organisation to determine the cost of a unit of product or service.

The **fixed** and **variable cost classifications**, on the other hand, are important in **absorption** and **marginal costing**, **cost behaviour** and **cost-volume-profit analysis**. You will meet all of these topics as we progress through the Study Text.

This chapter therefore acts as a foundation stone for a number of other chapters in the text and hence an understanding of the concepts covered in it is vital before you move on.

Study guide

Section 5 – Cost classification

- Describe the various types of responsibility centre and the impact of these on management information

- Explain and illustrate classifications used in the analysis of product/service costs including by function, direct and indirect, product and period, fixed and variable, avoidable and unavoidable, controllable and uncontrollable

- Explain and illustrate the concept of cost objects, cost units, cost centres, revenue centres, profit centres and investment centres

- Describe briefly the process of accounting for input costs and relating them to work done

- Explain the difference between the treatment of direct and indirect expenses

Exam guide

Cost classification is one of the key areas of the syllabus and you can therefore expect to see it examined in both Section A and Section B.

1 TOTAL PRODUCT/SERVICE COSTS

1.1 The total cost of making a product or providing a service consists of the following.

(a) Cost of **materials**

(b) Cost of the **wages** and **salaries** (labour costs)

(c) Cost of **other expenses**

- Rent and rates
- Electricity and gas bills
- Depreciation

2 DIRECT COSTS AND INDIRECT COSTS

2.1 Materials, labour costs and other expenses can be classified as either **direct costs** or **indirect costs**.

> **KEY TERMS**
>
> - A **direct cost** is a cost that can be traced in full to the product, service, or department that is being costed.
>
> - An **indirect cost** or **overhead** is a cost that is incurred in the course of making a product, providing a service or running a department, but which cannot be traced directly and in full to the product, service or department.

2.2 (a) **Direct material costs** are the costs of materials that are known to have been used in making and selling a product (or even providing a service).

(b) **Direct labour costs** are the specific costs of the workforce used to make a product or provide a service. Direct labour costs are established by measuring the time taken for a job, or the time taken in 'direct production work'.

(c) **Other direct expenses** are those expenses that have been incurred in full as a direct consequence of making a product, or providing a service, or running a department.

2.3 Examples of indirect costs include supervisors' wages, cleaning materials and buildings insurance.

2.4 Total expenditure may therefore be analysed as follows.

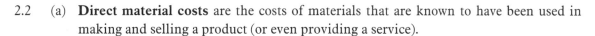

Materials	=	Direct materials	+	Indirect materials
+		+		+
Labour	=	Direct labour	+	Indirect labour
+		+		+
Expenses	=	Direct expenses	+	Indirect expenses
Total cost	=	Direct cost		Overhead

Direct material

KEY TERM

Direct material is all material becoming part of the product (unless used in negligible amounts and/or having negligible cost).

2.5 Direct material costs are charged to the product as part of the **prime cost**. Examples of direct material are as follows.

(a) **Component parts,** specially purchased for a particular job, order or process.

(b) **Part-finished work** which is transferred from department 1 to department 2 becomes finished work of department 1 and a direct material cost in department 2.

(c) **Primary packing materials** like cartons and boxes.

Direct labour

Exam focus point

The study guide for **Financial Information for Management** states that candidates must be able to 'explain the difference between, and calculate, direct and indirect labour costs'.

The pilot paper included a multiple choice question which required the analysis of wages into direct and indirect costs.

KEY TERM

Direct wages are all wages paid for labour (either as basic hours or as overtime) expended on work on the product itself.

2.6 **Direct wages** costs are charged to the product as part of the **prime cost**.

Examples of groups of labour receiving payment as direct wages are as follows.

(a) Workers engaged in **altering** the condition or composition of the product.

(b) Inspectors, analysts and testers **specifically required** for such production.

(c) Foremen, shop clerks and anyone else whose wages are **specifically identified.**

2.7 Two **trends** may be identified in **direct labour costs.**

• The ratio of direct labour costs to total product cost is falling as the use of machinery increases, and hence depreciation charges increase.

• Skilled labour costs and sub-contractors' costs are increasing as direct labour costs decrease.

Question 1

Classify the following labour costs as either direct or indirect.

(a) The basic pay of direct workers (cash paid, tax and other deductions)
(b) The basic pay of indirect workers
(c) Overtime premium
(d) Bonus payments

✓ (e)   Employer's National Insurance contributions
✗ (f)   Idle time of direct workers
(g)   Work on installation of equipment

Answer

(a)   The basic pay of direct workers is a direct cost to the unit, job or process.

(b)   The basic pay of indirect workers is an indirect cost, unless a customer asks for an order to be carried out which involves the dedicated use of indirect workers' time, when the cost of this time would be a direct labour cost of the order.

(c)   Overtime premium paid to both direct and indirect workers is an indirect cost, except in two particular circumstances.

   (i)   If overtime is worked at the specific request of a customer to get his order completed, the overtime premium paid is a direct cost of the order.

   (ii)   If overtime is worked regularly by a production department in the normal course of operations, the overtime premium paid to direct workers could be incorporated into the (average) direct labour hourly rate.

(d)   Bonus payments are generally an indirect cost.

(e)   Employer's national insurance contributions (which are added to employees' total pay as a wages cost) are normally treated as an indirect labour cost.

(f)   Idle time is an overhead cost, that is an indirect labour cost.

(g)   The cost of work on capital equipment is incorporated into the capital cost of the equipment.

Direct expenses

> **KEY TERM**
>
> **Direct expenses** are any expenses which are incurred on a specific product other than direct material cost and direct wages

2.8   **Direct expenses** are charged to the product as part of the **prime** cost. Examples of direct expenses are as follows.

- The **hire of tools** or equipment for a particular job
- **Maintenance costs** of tools, jigs, fixtures and so on

Direct expenses are also referred to as **chargeable expenses.**

Production overhead

> **KEY TERM**
>
> **Production (or factory) overhead** includes all indirect material cost, indirect wages and indirect expenses incurred in the factory from receipt of the order until its completion.

2.9   Production overhead includes the following.

(a)   **Indirect materials** which cannot be traced in the finished product.

- Consumable stores, eg material used in negligible amounts

(b) **Indirect wages**, meaning all wages not charged directly to a product.

  • Wages of non-productive personnel in the production department, eg foremen

(c) **Indirect expenses** (other than material and labour) not charged directly to production.

  • Rent, rates and insurance of a factory
  • Depreciation, fuel, power, maintenance of plant, machinery and buildings

Administration overhead

> **KEY TERM**
>
> **Administration overhead** is all indirect material costs, wages and expenses incurred in the direction, control and administration of an undertaking.

2.10 Examples of administration overhead are as follows.

  • **Depreciation** of office administration overhead, buildings and machinery.
  • **Office salaries**, including salaries of directors, secretaries and accountants.
  • Rent, rates, insurance, lighting, cleaning, telephone charges and so on.

Selling overhead

> **KEY TERM**
>
> **Selling overhead** is all indirect materials costs, wages and expenses incurred in promoting sales and retaining customers.

2.11 Examples of selling overhead are as follows.

  • **Printing** and **stationery**, such as catalogues and price lists.
  • **Salaries** and **commission** of salesmen, representatives and sales department staff.
  • **Advertising** and **sales promotion**, market research.
  • Rent, rates and insurance of sales offices and showrooms, bad debts and so on.

Distribution overhead

> **KEY TERM**
>
> **Distribution overhead** is all indirect material costs, wages and expenses incurred in making the packed product ready for despatch and delivering it to the customer.

2.12 Examples of distribution overhead are as follows.

  • Cost of packing cases.
  • Wages of packers, drivers and despatch clerks.
  • Insurance charges, rent, rates, depreciation of warehouses and so on.

Costs which are both direct and indirect

2.13 A cost may be a **direct cost** in one part of a cost analysis and an **indirect cost** in another part. This point is perhaps best illustrated with a simple example.

2.14 The Donkey Oater Racing Stables trains and races two horses, Sancho Panza and Rosinante. Costs for the recent month are as follows.

		£
Salary of the stable manager		1,000
Wages:		
Special groom to Sancho Panza		80
General stable boy		80
Jockey for both horses:	retainer	200
	race fees	200
Race entrance fees:	Sancho Panza (three races)	150
	Rosinante (two races)	100
Hay, straw and so on		600
Depreciation on stable and riding equipment		200
		£
Rent and rates		300
Heating and lighting		100

2.15 All of the costs listed are direct costs of operating the training and racing stable, with the exception of the various race fees (which are only incurred as and when horses are entered for races).

The direct costs of keeping one of the horses, Sancho Panza, in the month are the costs of the special groom and race fees. All other costs are one of the following.

(a) Costs shared with Rosinante (stable manager's salary, wages of stable boy, jockey's retainer, hay and straw, depreciation, rent, rates, heating and lighting). Some of these costs could be charged directly (for example hay and straw consumed, stable boy's time) if a system for recording the material issued to each horse or time spent with each horse were in operation.

(b) Direct costs of the other horse (race fees).

The direct costs of a race are the entrance fee (£50) and the jockey's fees (£40). Indirect costs would be not only the jockey's retainer, but also the other costs of running the stable.

In conclusion, when classifying a cost as direct or indirect (an overhead), the cost accountant must consider the product or service whose cost is being established.

Question 2

A direct labour employee's wage in week 5 consists of the following.

		£
(a)	Basic pay for normal hours worked, 36 hours at £4 per hour =	144
(b)	Pay at the basic rate for overtime, 6 hours at £4 per hour =	24
(c)	Overtime shift premium, with overtime paid at time-and-a-quarter	
	¼ × 6 hours × £4 per hour =	6
(d)	A bonus payment under a group bonus (or 'incentive') scheme -	
	bonus for the month =	30
	Total gross wages in week 5 for 42 hours of work	204

BPP PUBLISHING

What is the direct labour cost for this employee in week 5?

A £144   B £168   C £198   D £204

Answer

Let's start by considering a general approach to answering multiple choice questions (MCQs). In a numerical question like this, the best way to begin is to ignore the available options and work out your own answer from the available data. If your solution corresponds to one of the four options then mark this as your chosen answer and move on. Don't waste time working out whether any of the other options might be correct. If your answer does not appear among the available options then check your workings. If it still does not correspond to any of the options then you need to take a calculated guess.

Do not make the common error of simply selecting the answer which is closest to yours. The best thing to do is to first eliminate any answers which you know or suspect are incorrect. For example you could eliminate C and D because you know that group bonus schemes are usually indirect costs. You are then left with a choice between A and B, and at least you have now improved your chances if you really are guessing.

The correct answer is B because the basic rate for overtime is a part of direct wages cost. It is only the overtime premium that is usually regarded as an overhead or indirect cost.

3 FUNCTIONAL COSTS

Production, administration and marketing costs

3.1 In a 'traditional' costing system for a manufacturing organisation, costs are classified as follows.

(a) **Production** or **manufacturing costs.** These are costs associated with the factory.

(b) **Administration costs.** These are costs associated with general office departments.

(c) **Marketing,** or **selling** and **distribution costs.** These are costs associated with sales, marketing, warehousing and transport departments.

Classification in this way is known as **classification by function**. Expenses that do not fall fully into one of these classifications might be categorised as **general overheads** or even listed as a classification on their own (for example research and development costs).

3.2 In costing a small product made by a manufacturing organisation, direct costs are usually restricted to some of the production costs. A commonly found build-up of costs is therefore as follows.

	£
Production costs	
Direct materials	A
Direct wages	B
Direct expenses	C
Prime cost	A+B+C
Production overheads	D
Full factory cost	A+B+C+D
Administration costs	E
Selling and distribution costs	F
Full cost of sales	A+B+C+D+E+F

Classification by function in more detail

3.3 Functional costs include the following.

(a) **Production costs** are the costs which are incurred by the sequence of operations beginning with the supply of raw materials, and ending with the completion of the product ready for warehousing as a finished goods item. Packaging costs are production costs where they relate to 'primary' packing (boxes, wrappers and so on).

(b) **Administration costs** are the costs of managing an organisation, that is, planning and controlling its operations, but only insofar as such administration costs are not related to the production, sales, distribution or research and development functions.

(c) **Selling costs,** sometimes known as marketing costs, are the costs of creating demand for products and securing firm orders from customers.

(d) **Distribution costs** are the costs of the sequence of operations with the receipt of finished goods from the production department and making them ready for despatch and ending with the reconditioning for reuse of empty containers.

(e) **Research costs** are the costs of searching for new or improved products, whereas **development costs** are the costs incurred between the decision to produce a new or improved product and the commencement of full manufacture of the product.

(f) **Financing costs** are costs incurred to finance the business such as loan interest.

Question 3

Within the costing system of a manufacturing company the following types of expense are incurred.

Reference number

1	Cost of oils used to lubricate production machinery
2	Motor vehicle licences for lorries
3	Depreciation of factory plant and equipment
4	Cost of chemicals used in the laboratory
5	Commission paid to sales representatives
6	Salary of the secretary to the finance director
7	Trade discount given to customers
8	Holiday pay of machine operatives
9	Salary of security guard in raw material warehouse
10	Fees to advertising agency
11	Rent of finished goods warehouse
12	Salary of scientist in laboratory
13	Insurance of the company's premises
14	Salary of supervisor working in the factory
15	Cost of typewriter ribbons in the general office
16	Protective clothing for machine operatives

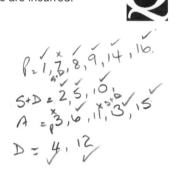

Required

Place each expense within the following classifications.

(a) Production costs
(b) Selling and distribution costs
(c) Administration costs
(d) Research and development costs

Each type of expense should appear only once in your answer. You may use the reference numbers in your answer.

Answer

The reference number for each expense can be classified as follows.

		Reference numbers
(a)	Production costs	1, 3, 8, 9, 14, 16
(b)	Selling and distribution costs	2, 5, 7, 10,11
(c)	Administration costs	6, 13, 15
(d)	Research and development costs	4, 12

4 FIXED COSTS AND VARIABLE COSTS

4.1 A different way of analysing and classifying costs is into **fixed costs** and **variable costs.** Some items of expenditure are part-fixed and part-variable or 'semi-fixed' costs but, in cost accounting, **semi-fixed** or **semi-variable costs** are divided into their fixed and variable elements.

> **KEY TERMS**
>
> - A **fixed cost** is a cost which is incurred for a particular period of time and which, within certain activity levels, is unaffected by changes in the level of activity.
>
> - A **variable cost** is a cost which tends to vary with the level of activity.

4.2 Some examples are as follows.

(a) Direct material costs are **variable costs** because they rise as more units of a product are manufactured.

(b) Sales commission is often a fixed percentage of sales turnover, and so is a **variable cost** that varies with the level of sales.

(c) Telephone call charges are likely to increase if the volume of business expands, and so they are a **variable overhead cost.**

(d) The rental cost of business premises is a constant amount, at least within a stated time period, and so it is a **fixed cost.**

4.3 Costs can be classified as follows.

- Direct costs
- Indirect costs
- Fixed costs
- Variable costs

5 PRODUCT COSTS AND PERIOD COSTS

> **KEY TERMS**
>
> - **Product costs** are costs identified with a finished product. Such costs are initially identified as part of the value of stock. They become expenses (in the form of cost of goods sold) only when the stock is sold.
>
> - **Period costs** are costs that are deducted as expenses during the current period without ever being included in the value of stock held.

5.1 When preparing financial statements (a profit and loss account and balance sheet), accountants frequently distinguish between **product costs** and **period costs.**

6   OTHER COST CLASSIFICATIONS

> **KEY TERMS**
>
> - **Avoidable costs** are specific costs of an activity or business which would be avoided if the activity or business did not exist.
>
> - **Unavoidable costs** are costs which would be incurred whether or not an activity or sector existed.
>
> - A **controllable cost** is a cost which can be influenced by management decisions and actions.
>
> - An **uncontrollable cost** is any cost that cannot be affected by management within a given time span.
>
> - **Discretionary costs** are costs which are likely to arise from decisions made during the budgeting process. They are likely to be fixed amounts of money over fixed periods of time.

6.1   Examples of discretionary costs are as follows.

- Advertising
- Research and Development
- Training

7   COST CENTRES, COST UNITS, COST OBJECTS, PROFIT CENTRES, REVENUE CENTRES AND INVESTMENT CENTRES

Allocation of costs to cost centres

7.1   Costs consist of the costs of the following.

- Direct materials
- Direct labour
- Direct expenses
- Production overheads
- Administration overheads
- General overheads

7.2   When costs are incurred, they are generally allocated to a **cost centre.** A cost centre acts as a **collecting place** for certain costs before they are analysed further. Cost centres may include the following.

- A department
- A machine, or group of machines
- A project (eg the installation of a new computer system)
- Overhead costs eg rent, rates, electricity (which may then be allocated to departments or projects)

7.3   Cost centres are an essential 'building block' of a costing system. They are the starting point for the following.

(a)   The classification of actual costs incurred.
(b)   The preparation of budgets of planned costs.

(c)   The comparison of actual costs and budgeted costs (management control).

Cost units

7.4   Once costs have been traced to cost centres, they can be further analysed in order to establish a **cost per cost unit**. Alternatively, some items of cost may be charged directly to a cost unit, for example direct materials and direct labour costs.

KEY TERM

A **cost unit** is a unit of product or service to which costs can be related. The cost unit is the basic control unit for costing purposes.

7.5   Examples of cost unit include the following.

- Patient episode (in a hospital)
- Barrel (in the brewing industry)
- Room (in a hotel)

Question 4

Suggest suitable cost units which could be used to aid control within the following organisations.

(a)   A public transport authority   *N° of Passengers   n° Passenger/mile*
(b)   A hotel with 50 double rooms and 10 single rooms   *Beds occupied/night*
(c)   A hospital   *N° of Beds/Night*
(d)   A road haulage business   *Tonne/mile*

Answer

(a)   (i)   Passenger/mile
      (ii)   Mile travelled
      (iii) Passenger journey
      (iv)   Ticket issued

(b)   (i)   Guest/night
      (ii)   Bed occupied/night
      (iii) Meal supplied

(c)   (i)   Patient/night
      (ii)   Operation
      (iii) Outpatient visit

(d)   (i)   Tonne/mile
      (ii)   Mile

Cost objects

KEY TERM

A **cost object (or objective)** is any activity for which a separate measurement of costs is desired.

7.6   If the users of management information wish to know the cost of something, this something is called a **cost object**. Examples include the following.

- The cost of a product
- The cost of a service
- The cost of operating a department

Profit centres

7.7 We have seen that a cost centre is where costs are collected. Some organisations, however, work on a profit centre basis. A **profit centre** is similar to a cost centre but is accountable for **costs** *and* **revenues**.

7.8 Profit centre managers should normally have control over how revenue is raised and how costs are incurred. Often, several cost centres will comprise one profit centre.

Revenue centres

7.9 A **revenue centre** is similar to a cost centre and a profit centre but is accountable for **revenues only**.

7.10 Revenue centre managers should normally have control over how revenues are raised.

Investment centres

> **KEY TERM**
>
> An **investment centre** is 'A profit centre with additional responsibilities for capital investment and possibly for financing, and whose performance is measured by its return on investment'. (CIMA *Official Terminology*)

7.11 We shall study investment centres further in Part E of this Study Text when we look at performance measurement.

Responsibility centres

7.12 Cost centres, revenue centres, profit centres and investment centres are also known as **responsibility centres**.

> **KEY TERM**
>
> A **responsibility centre** is a department or organisational function whose performance is the direct responsibility of a specific manager.

> **Exam focus point**
>
> This chapter has introduced a number of new terms and definitions. The topics covered in this chapter are core syllabus topics and could be examined in both Sections A and B of the **Financial Information for Management** examination.
>
> In Section A questions candidates might be asked to choose the correct definition of a cost accounting term from four provided.

Chapter roundup

- A **direct cost** is a cost that can be traced in full to the product, service or department being costed. An **indirect cost** (or overhead) is a cost that is incurred in the course of making a product, providing a service or running a department, but which cannot be traced directly and in full to the product, service or department.

- **Classification by function** involves classifying costs as production/manufacturing costs, administration costs or marketing/selling and distribution costs.

- A different way of analysing and classifying costs is into **fixed costs** and **variable costs**. Many items of expenditure are part-fixed and part-variable and hence are termed **semi-fixed** or **semi-variable**.

- For the preparation of financial statements, costs are often classified as **product costs** and **period costs**. Product costs are costs identified with goods produced or purchased for resale. Period costs are costs deducted as expenses during the current period.

- **Cost centres** are collecting places for costs before they are further analysed. Costs are further analysed into cost units once they have been traced to cost centres.

- A **cost unit** is a unit of product or service to which costs can be related.

- A **cost object** is any activity for which a separate measure of costs is desired.

- **Profit centres** are similar to cost centres but are accountable for both costs and revenues.

- **Revenue centres** are similar to cost centres and profit centres but are accountable for revenues only.

- An **investment centre** is a profit centre with additional responsibilities for capital investment and possibly financing.

- A **responsibility centre** is a department or organisational function whose performance is the direct responsibility of a specific manager.

Quick quiz

1   Give two examples of direct expenses. *Rent Rates*

2   Give an example of an administration overhead, a selling overhead and a distribution overhead. *Salaries, Advertising, Fuel*

3   What are functional costs? *Classifying costs by function*

4   What is the distinction between fixed and variable costs? *Fixed remains constant. Variable - vary*

5   What are product costs and period costs? *Cost identified with products. Costs deducted as expenses during current period.*

6   What is a cost centre? *Where cost are gathered by further analysis*

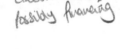

7   What is a cost unit? → *Unit to which costs can be related*

8   What is a profit centre? → *accountable for cost + revenue*

9   What is an investment centre? → *accountable for costs, revenues + capital investment, possibly financing*

Answers to quick quiz

1. • The hire of tools or equipment for a particular job
    • Maintenance costs of tools, fixtures and so on

2. • **Administration overhead** = Depreciation of office administration overhead, buildings and machinery

    • **Selling overhead** = Printing and stationery (catalogues, price lists)

    • **Distribution overhead** = Wages of packers, drivers and despatch clerks

3. Functional costs are classified as follows.

    • **Production** or **manufacturing costs**
    • **Administration costs**
    • **Marketing** or **selling and distribution costs**

4. A **fixed cost** is a cost which is incurred for a particular period of time and which, within certain activity levels, is unaffected by changes in the level of activity.

    A **variable cost** is a cost which tends to vary with the level of activity.

5. **Product costs** are costs identified with a finished product. Such costs are initially identified as part of the value of stock. They become expenses only when the stock is sold.

    Period costs are costs that are deducted as expenses during the current period without ever being included in the value of stock held.

6. A **cost centre** acts as a collecting place for certain costs before they are analysed further.

7. A **cost unit** is a unit of product or service to which costs can be related. The cost unit is the basic control unit for costing purposes.

8. A **profit centre** is similar to a cost centre but is accountable for **costs** and **revenues**.

9. An **investment centre** is a profit centre with additional responsibilities for capital investment and possibly financing.

Now try the question below from the Exam Question Bank

Number	Level	Marks	Time
3	MCQ	n/a	n/a

Chapter 4

COST BEHAVIOUR

Topic list	Syllabus reference
1 The importance of understanding cost behaviour	6(a)
2 Cost behaviour and levels of activity	6(a)
3 Cost behaviour patterns	6(a)
4 Determining the fixed and variable elements of semi-variable costs	6(a)
5 The linear assumption of cost behaviour	6(a)
6 Factors affecting the influence of activity level	6(a)

Introduction

So far in this text we have introduced you to the subject of management information and explained in general terms what it is and what is does. In Chapter 3 we considered the principal methods of classifying costs. In particular, we introduced the concept of the division of costs into those that vary directly with changes in activity levels (**variable costs**) and those that do not (**fixed costs**). This chapter examines further this two-way split of **cost behaviour** and explains one method of splitting total costs into these two elements, the **high-low** method.

Study guide

Section 6 – Cost behaviour

- Explain the importance of cost behaviour in relation to business decision making
- Describe factors which influence cost behaviour
- Explain how the terms linear, curvilinear and step functions apply to costs
- Identify, describe and illustrate graphically different types of cost behaviour
- Provide examples of costs which contain both fixed and variable elements
- Use high/low analysis to separate the fixed and variable elements of such costs

Exam guide

Cost behaviour is a key area of the **Financial Information for Management** syllabus and could be examined in detail either in Section A or Section B (or both).

1 THE IMPORTANCE OF UNDERSTANDING COST BEHAVIOUR

Cost behaviour and decision making

> **KEY TERM**
>
> **Cost behaviour** is the way in which costs are affected by changes in the volume of output.

1.1 Management decisions will often be based on how costs and revenues vary at different activity levels. Examples of such decisions are as follows.

- What should the **planned activity level** be for the next period?
- Should the **selling price** be reduced in order to sell more units?
- Should a particular component be **manufactured internally** or **bought in**?
- Should a **contract** be undertaken?

Cost behaviour and cost control

1.2 If the accountant does not know the level of costs which should have been incurred as a result of an organisation's activities, how can he or she hope to control costs?

Cost behaviour and budgeting

1.3 Knowledge of cost behaviour is obviously essential for the tasks of **budgeting, decision making** and **control accounting**.

1.4 EXAMPLE: COST BEHAVIOUR AND PRODUCTION LEVEL

Fixed and variable cost analysis enables management to decide whether an incentive scheme would be attractive to both employers and employees.

Suppose that Given Hann Hoffa Ltd is a company which manufactures a single product which sells for £20. The costs of production have been estimated to be as follows.

Fixed costs per month	£1,000
Variable costs	£12 per unit

The variable costs have been analysed further.

(a) Labour costs (2 hours at £2 per hour) = £4
(b) Material and other costs = £8

Demand for the product varies from 400 units to 800 units per month. The maximum output which can be achieved is currently only 600 units per month, because the available labour hours are restricted to 1,200 hours per month. The nature of the product is such that stocks of work-in-progress or finished goods cannot be stored.

An incentive scheme has been proposed whereby the payment to employees will be increased from £2 to £3 per hour, provided that the time taken to produce each unit is reduced from 2 hours to 1½ hours.

Required

(a) Ascertain the effect of the incentive scheme on employees' wages and company profits at the following output levels.

    (i) At the minimum level of output per month
    (ii) At the current maximum level of output per month

(b) Show by how much the company would profit if output and sales were increased to the new maximum level.

(c) Draw conclusions from these figures about the effects of the incentive scheme.

1.5 SOLUTION

(a) (i) **400 units per month**

	With the incentive scheme		Without the incentive scheme	
	£	£	£	£
Sales (400 × £20)		8,000		8,000
Materials etc costs (400 × £8)	3,200		3,200	
Labour costs (400 × £3 × 1½ hrs)	1,800		(400 × £2 × 2hrs) 1,600	
Total variable costs		5,000		4,800
Contribution		3,000		3,200
Fixed costs		1,000		1,000
Profit		2,000		2,200

The labour force would work fewer hours (600 instead of 800) but would receive £200 more in pay. Company profits would fall by £200 if the scheme is introduced and demand is 400 units.

(ii) **600 units per month**

	With the incentive scheme		Without the incentive scheme	
	£	£	£	£
Sales (600 × £20)		12,000		12,000
Materials etc costs (600 × £8)	4,800		4,800	
Labour costs (600 × £3 × 1½ hrs)	2,700		(600 × £2 × 2hrs) 2,400	
Total variable costs		7,500		7,200
		4,500		4,800
Fixed costs		1,000		1,000
Profit		3,500		3,800

The labour force would again work fewer hours (900 instead of 1,200) but would receive £300 more in pay. With the introduction of the scheme, company profits would be £300 lower if demand is only 600 units.

(b) Maximum output   = 1,200 hrs ÷ 1½ hrs per unit
                    = 800 units per month

This is also the maximum demand per month.

	With the incentive scheme		
		£	£
Sales	(800 × £20)		16,000
Materials etc costs	(800 × £8)	6,400	
Labour costs	(800 × 1½ hrs × £3)	3,600	
Total variable costs			10,000
			6,000
Fixed costs			1,000
Profit			5,000

Employees would receive higher wages, and company profits would be capable of reaching £5,000 per month if maximum demand is achieved.

(c) The particular incentive scheme under review does not benefit the company unless actual output and sales exceed the current maximum levels, that is unless the improved productivity results in improved sales volumes.

1.6 EXAMPLE: COST BEHAVIOUR AND ACTIVITY LEVEL

Hans Bratch Ltd has a fleet of company cars for sales representatives. Running costs have been estimated as follows.

(a) Cars cost £12,000 when new, and have a guaranteed trade-in value of £6,000 at the end of two years. Depreciation is charged on a straight-line basis.

(b) Petrol and oil cost 15 pence per mile.

(c) Tyres cost £300 per set to replace; replacement occurs after 30,000 miles.

(d) Routine maintenance costs £200 per car (on average) in the first year and £450 in the second year.

(e) Repairs average £400 per car over two years and are thought to vary with mileage. The average car travels 25,000 miles per annum.

(f) Tax, insurance, membership of motoring organisations and so on cost £400 per annum per car.

Required

Calculate the average cost per annum of cars which travel 20,000 miles per annum and 30,000 miles per annum.

1.7 SOLUTION

Costs may be analysed into fixed, variable and stepped cost items, a stepped cost being a cost which is fixed in nature but only within certain levels of activity.

(a) **Fixed costs**

	£ per annum
Depreciation £(12,000 – 6,000) ÷ 2	3,000
Routine maintenance £(200 + 450) ÷ 2	325
Tax, insurance etc	400
	3,725

(b) **Variable costs**

	Pence per mile
Petrol and oil	15.0
Repairs (£400 ÷ 50,000 miles)	0.8
	15.8

(c) Step costs are tyre replacement costs, which are £300 at the end of every 30,000 miles.

  (i) If the car travels less than or exactly 30,000 miles in two years, the tyres will not be changed. Average cost of tyres per annum = £0.

  (ii) If a car travels more than 30,000 miles and up to (and including) 60,000 miles in two years, there will be one change of tyres in the period. Average cost of tyres per annum = £150 (£300 ÷ 2).

  (iii) If a car exceeds 60,000 miles in two years (up to 90,000 miles) there will be two tyre changes. Average cost of tyres per annum = £300. (£600 ÷ 2).

The estimated costs per annum of cars travelling 20,000 miles per annum and 30,000 miles per annum would therefore be as follows.

	20,000 miles per annum £	*30,000 miles per annum* £
Fixed costs	3,725	3,725
Variable costs (15.8p per mile)	3,160	4,740
Tyres	150	150
Cost per annum	7,035	8,615

Exam focus point

Remember that the behavioural analysis of costs is important for planning, control and decision-making.

2 COST BEHAVIOUR AND LEVELS OF ACTIVITY

2.1 There are many factors which may influence costs. The major influence is **volume of output,** or the **level of activity**. The level of activity may refer to one of the following.

- Value of items sold
- Number of items sold
- Number of invoices issued
- Number of units of electricity consumed

Basic principles of cost behaviour

2.2 The basic principle of cost behaviour is that **as the level of activity rises, costs will usually rise**. It will cost more to produce 2,000 units of output than it will cost to produce 1,000 units.

2.3 This principle is common sense. The problem for the accountant, however, is to determine, for each item of cost, the way in which costs rise and by how much as the level of activity increases. For our purposes here, the level of activity for measuring cost will generally be taken to be the **volume of production**.

3 COST BEHAVIOUR PATTERNS

Fixed costs

KEY TERM

A **fixed cost** is a cost which tends to be unaffected by increases or decreases in the volume of output.

3.1 Fixed costs are a **period charge**, in that they relate to a span of time; as the time span increases, so too will the fixed costs (which are sometimes referred to as period costs for this reason). It is important to understand that **fixed costs always have a variable element**, since an increase or decrease in production may also bring about an increase or decrease in fixed costs.

3.2 A sketch graph of a fixed cost would look like this.

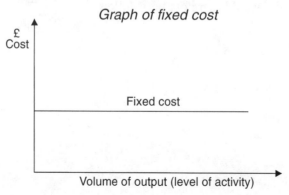

Graph of fixed cost

Examples of a fixed cost would be as follows.

- The salary of the managing director (per month or per annum)
- The rent of a single factory building (per month or per annum)
- Straight line depreciation of a single machine (per month or per annum)

Step costs

> **KEY TERM**
>
> A **step cost** is a cost which is fixed in nature but only within certain levels of activity.

3.3 Consider the depreciation of a machine which may be fixed if production remains below 1,000 units per month. If production exceeds 1,000 units, a second machine may be required, and the cost of depreciation (on two machines) would go up a step. A sketch graph of a step cost could look like this.

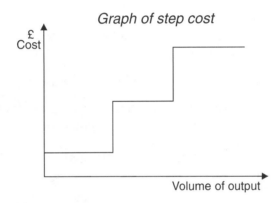

Other examples of step costs are as follows.

(a) Rent is a step cost in situations where accommodation requirements increase as output levels get higher.

(b) Basic pay of employees is nowadays usually fixed, but as output rises, more employees (direct workers, supervisors, managers and so on) are required.

(c) Royalties.

Variable costs

> **KEY TERM**
>
> A **variable cost** is a cost which tends to vary directly with the volume of output. The variable cost per unit is the same amount for each unit produced.

3.4

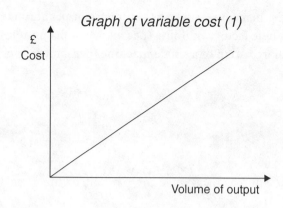

Graph of variable cost (1)

3.5 A constant variable cost per unit implies that the price per unit of say, material purchased is constant, and that the rate of material usage is also constant.

(a) The most important variable cost is the **cost of raw materials** (where there is no discount for bulk purchasing since bulk purchase discounts reduce the cost of purchases).

(b) **Direct labour costs** are, for very important reasons, classed as a variable cost even though basic wages are usually fixed.

(c) **Sales commission** is variable in relation to the volume or value of sales.

(d) **Bonus payments** for productivity to employees might be variable once a certain level of output is achieved, as the following diagram illustrates.

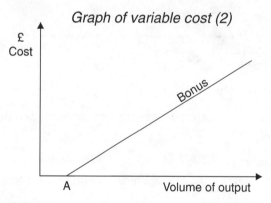

Graph of variable cost (2)

Up to output A, no bonus is earned.

Non-linear or curvilinear variable costs

KEY TERM

If the relationship between total variable cost and volume of output can be shown as a curved line on a graph, the relationship is said to be **curvilinear**.

3.6 Two typical relationships are as follows.

(a)

(b)

£
Cost

Volume of output

£
Cost

Volume of output

Each extra unit of output in graph (a) causes a **less than proportionate** increase in cost whereas in graph (b), each extra unit of output causes **a more than proportionate** increase in cost.

3.7 The cost of a piecework scheme for individual workers with differential rates could behave in a **curvilinear** fashion if the rates increase by small amounts at progressively higher output levels.

Semi-variable costs (or semi-fixed costs or mixed costs)

KEY TERM

A **semi-variable/semi-fixed/mixed cost** is a cost which contains both fixed and variable components and so is partly affected by changes in the level of activity.

3.8 Examples of these costs include the following.

(a) **Electricity and gas bills**

- Fixed cost = standing charge
- Variable cost = charge per unit of electricity used

(b) **Salesman's salary**

- Fixed cost = basic salary
- Variable cost = commission on sales made

(c) **Costs of running a car**

- Fixed cost = road tax, insurance
- Variable costs = petrol, oil, repairs (which vary with miles travelled)

Other cost behaviour patterns

3.9 Other cost behaviour patterns may be appropriate to certain cost items. The cost of materials after deduction of a bulk purchase is shown as follows.

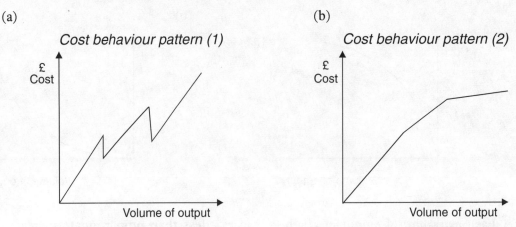

(a)

Cost behaviour pattern (1)

(b)

Cost behaviour pattern (2)

(i)   Graph (a) shows a bulk purchase discount which applies retrospectively to all units purchased.

(ii)   Graph (b) shows a discount which applies only to units purchased in excess of a certain quantity.

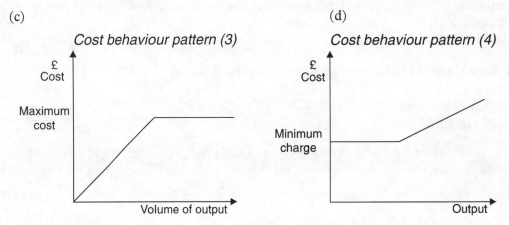

(c)

Cost behaviour pattern (3)

(d)

Cost behaviour pattern (4)

(i)   Graph (c) represents an item of cost which is variable with output up to a certain maximum level of cost.

(ii)   Graph (d) represents a cost which is variable with output, subject to a minimum (fixed) charge.

Cost behaviour and total and unit costs

3.10   The following table relates to different levels of production of the zed. The variable cost of producing a zed is £5. Fixed costs are £5,000.

	1 zed £	10 zeds £	50 zeds £
Total variable cost	5	50	250
Variable cost per unit	5	5	5
Total fixed cost	5,000	5,000	5,000
Fixed cost per unit	5,000	500	100
Total cost (fixed and variable)	5,005	5,050	5,250
Total cost per unit	5,005	505	105

What happens when activity levels rise can be summarised as follows.

- The variable cost per unit remains constant
- The fixed cost per unit falls
- The total cost per unit falls

This may be illustrated graphically as follows.

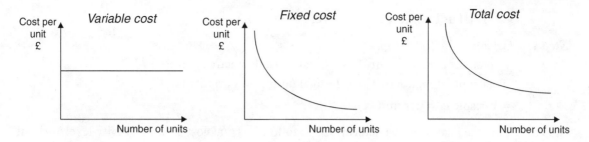

Question 1

Are the following likely to be fixed, variable or mixed costs?

- (a) Telephone bill
- (b) Annual salary of the chief accountant
- (c) The management accountant's annual membership fee to CIMA (paid by the company)
- (d) Cost of materials used to pack 20 units of product X into a box
- (e) Wages of warehousemen

Answer

- (a) Mixed
- (b) Fixed
- (c) Fixed
- (d) Variable
- (e) Variable

4 DETERMINING THE FIXED AND VARIABLE ELEMENTS OF SEMI-VARIABLE COSTS

4.1 It is generally assumed that costs are one of the following.

- Variable
- Fixed
- Semi-variable

Cost accountants tend to separate semi-variable costs into their variable and fixed elements. They therefore generally tend to treat costs as either **fixed** or **variable**.

4.2 There are several methods for identifying the fixed and variable elements of semi-variable costs. Each method is only an estimate, and each will produce different results. One of the principal methods is the **high-low method.**

High-low method

4.3 Follow the steps below to estimate the fixed and variable elements of semi-variable costs.

Step 1. Review records of costs in previous periods.

- Select the period with the **highest** activity level.
- Select the period with the **lowest** activity level.

Step 2. If inflation makes it difficult to compare costs, adjust by indexing up or down.

Step 3. Determine the following.

- Total cost at high activity level
- Total costs at low activity level
- Total units at high activity level

BPP PUBLISHING

• Total units at low activity level

Step 4. Calculate the following.

$$\frac{\text{Total cost at high activity level} - \text{total cost at low activity level}}{\text{Total units at high activity level} - \text{total units at low activity level}}$$

= variable cost per unit (v)

Step 5. The fixed costs can be determined as follows. (Total cost at high activity level) –(total units at high activity level × variable cost per unit)

4.4 The following graph demonstrates the high-low method.

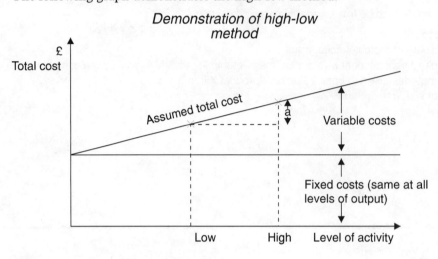

Demonstration of high-low method

4.5 EXAMPLE: THE HIGH-LOW METHOD WITH INFLATION

TS Ltd has recorded the following total costs during the last five years.

Year	Output volume Units	Total cost £	Average price level index
20X0	65,000	145,000	100
20X1	80,000	179,200	112
20X2	90,000	209,100	123
20X3	60,000	201,600	144
20X4	75,000	248,000	160

Required

Calculate the total cost that should be expected in 20X5 if output is 85,000 units and the average price level index is 180.

4.6 SOLUTION

Step 1.

• Period with highest activity = 20X2
• Period with lowest activity = 20X3

Step 2.

• Adjust costs so that they can be compared.

$$20X2 \text{ indexed cost} = £209,100 \times \frac{100}{123} = £170,000$$

$$20X0 \text{ indexed cost} = £201,600 \times \frac{100}{144} = £140,000$$

Step 3.
- Total cost at high activity level = 170,000
- Total cost at low activity level = 140,000
- Total units at high activity level = 90,000
- Total units at low activity level =– 60,000

Step 4. Variable cost per unit

$$= \frac{\text{total cost at high activity level} - \text{total cost at low activity level}}{\text{total units at high activity level} - \text{total units at low activity level}}$$

$$= \frac{170,000 - 140,000}{90,000 - 60,000} = \frac{30,000}{30,000} = £1 \text{ per unit}$$

Step 5. Fixed costs = (total cost at high activity level) – (total units at high activity level $\times$ variable cost per unit)

= 170,000 – (90,000 $\times$ 1) = 170,000 – 90,000 = £80,000

Therefore the costs in 20X5 for output of 85,000 units are as follows.

		£
Variable costs =	85,000 × £1 =	85,000
Fixed costs =		80,000
		165,000

However, we must now index up the 20X5 costs to reflect 20X5 price levels.

$$£165,000 \times \frac{180}{100} = £297,000$$

4.7 The step-by-step guide has been covered in order that you fully understand the process involved.

Question 2

The Valuation Department of a large firm of surveyors wishes to develop a method of predicting its total costs in a period. The following past costs have been recorded at two activity levels.

	Number of valuations (V)	Total cost (TC)
Period 1	420	82,200
Period 2	515	90,275

The total cost model for a period could be represented as follows.

A TC = £46,500 + 85V
B TC = £42,000 + 95V
C TC = £46,500 – 85V
D TC = £51,500 – 95V

Answer

Although we only have two activity levels in this question we can still apply the high-low method.

	Valuations V	Total cost £
Period 2	515	90,275
Period 1	420	82,200
Change due to variable cost	95	8,075

∴ Variable cost per valuation = £8,075/95 = £85.

Period 2: fixed cost = £90,275 – (515 × £85)

= £46,500

Using good MCQ technique, you should have managed to eliminate C and D as incorrect options straightaway. The variable cost must be added to the fixed cost, rather than subtracted from it. Once you had calculated the variable cost as £85 per valuation (as shown above), you should have been able to select option A without going on to calculate the fixed cost (we have shown this calculation above for completeness).

---

5 THE LINEAR ASSUMPTION OF COST BEHAVIOUR

5.1 It is usual for the cost accountant to make the following assumptions.

(a) Costs are generally considered to be fixed, variable or mixed (semi-fixed, semi-variable) within a normal range of output.

(b) Departmental costs are assumed to be mixed costs, with a fixed element and a variable element. The fixed costs and variable costs per unit may be estimated, with varying degrees of probable accuracy, by a variety of methods, of which the high-low method is perhaps the simplest to use (but the least accurate in its estimations).

(c) Departmental costs are therefore assumed to rise in a straight line (linear) fashion as the volume of activity increases.

5.2 A worthwhile question to answer at this stage is: are the assumptions in (b) and (c) above correct? In other words, is it true to say that costs may be divided into a fixed element and a variable cost per unit which is the same for every unit produced? There is a good argument that the variable cost per unit, (or the marginal cost per unit in the language of economics), changes with the level of output. Due to growing economies of scale (in other words, cost savings as activity levels increase) up to a certain level, a view put forward in basic economics is that the variable cost per unit could be graphed as follows.

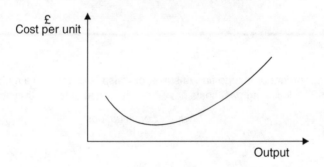

Total costs would therefore appear as a curved line, as follows.

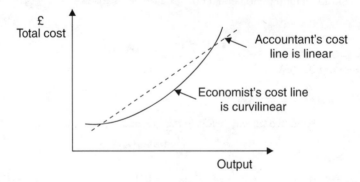

5.3 It is sufficient at this stage to be aware of the difference of views between the 'accountant' and the 'economist', and to understand that the accountant justifies the linear assumption of cost behaviour for the following reasons.

(a) It is easier to understand than curvilinear cost behaviour.

(b) Fixed and variable costs are easier to estimate, and easier to use.

(c) The assumption of linear costs is only used in practice within normal ranges of output, ie within a **relevant range of activity**.

(d) Within this relevant range of activity, the cost estimates of the economist and the accountant would not differ greatly, if at all; therefore linear costs should be used because sufficient accuracy is achieved with less effort (and for less cost).

6 FACTORS AFFECTING THE INFLUENCE OF ACTIVITY LEVEL

6.1 You are by now aware that it is not possible to say that a certain type of cost is always a fixed cost, or that another type is always variable. There are several factors which affect the extent to which a cost is influenced by a change in activity.

(a) **The make-up of the labour force**. The company's activities will determine whether there is a large production workforce. Where this is the case, a large increase in activity may necessitate hiring extra workers. In a non-labour intensive industry, increased output may result in a very low increase in costs.

(b) **The attitude of management to the change in activity**. This will depend on the nature of the cost and the management's objectives in the long and short term. Management may have the power to control the amount by which the cost rises in the case of some indirect costs such as administration and advertising charges.

(c) **The length of time the change in activity is observed**. Changes in cost behaviour may not be noticeable or even occur at all unless a change in activity is sustained.

(d) **The extent to which the company is operating at full capacity**. Where machines were lying idle prior to an increase in activity, the extra demand may be met with a minimal rise in costs.

(e) **The general economic climate**. This may affect the availability of suitable resources and thereby the firm's ability to respond to a change of activity.

(f) **The particular environment of the firm**. This includes the quality of the workforce and industrial relations, and the motivation of the staff.

6.2 It is important to establish the **time span under consideration** in determining cost behaviour patterns. For instance, some fixed costs may become variable in the long run, and, in the very short term, costs which are normally considered to be variable may in fact be fixed.

Chapter roundup

- Costs which are not affected by the level of activity are **fixed** costs or **period** costs.

- Even though fixed costs in total remain constant over a range of activity, the cost per unit will tend to reduce as the level of activity rises because the same fixed cost is being spread over a greater number of units.

- **Step costs** are fixed within a certain range of activity.

- **Variable costs** increase or decrease with the level of activity, and although they can behave in a **curvilinear** fashion, it is usually assumed that there is a linear relationship between cost and activity.

- **Semi-fixed**, **semi-variable** or **mixed costs** are costs which are part fixed and part variable.

- It is often possible to assume that, within the normal range of output, costs are either variable, fixed or semi-variable.

- The fixed and variable elements of semi-variable costs can be determined by the **high-low method**.

Quick quiz

1   Cost behaviour is ...Variability of input costs with activity undertakin...

2   The basic principle of cost behaviour is that as the level of activity rises, costs will usually rise/~~fall~~.

3   Fill in the gaps for each of the graph titles below.

(a)

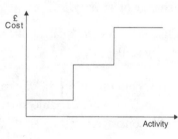

Graph of a ......STEP............cost

Example: Rent

(b)

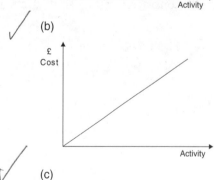

Graph of a ......VARIABLE............cost

Example: Raw Materials

(c)

Graph of a ......Semi Variable............cost

Example: Electric bill

(d)

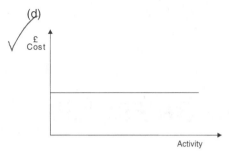

£ Cost

Activity

Graph of a .... Fixed Cost .....cost

Example: Rent

4   Costs are assumed to be either fixed, variable or semi-variable within the normal or relevant range of output.

True   ☑

False   ☐

5   The costs of operating the canteen at 'Eat a lot Company' for the past three months is as follows.

Month	Cost £	Employees
1	72,500	1,250
2	75,000	1,300
3	68,750	1,175

Variable cost (per employee per month) = £50

Fixed cost per month = £10,000

Answers to quick quiz

1   The variability of input costs with activity undertaken.

2   Rise

3   (a)   Step cost. Example: rent, supervisors' salaries
     (b)   Variable cost. Example: raw materials, direct labour
     (c)   Semi-variable cost. Example: electricity and telephone
     (d)   Fixed. Example: rent, depreciation (straight-line)

4   True

5   Variable cost = £50 per employee per month
     Fixed costs = £10,000 per month

	Activity	Cost £
High	1,300	75,000
Low	1,175	68,750
	125	6,250

Variable cost per employee = £6,250/125 = £50

For 1,175 employees, total cost = £68,750

Total cost	= variable cost + fixed cost
£68,750	= (1,175 × £50) + fixed cost
∴ Fixed cost	= £68,750 − £58,750
	= £10,000

Now try the questions below from the Exam Question Bank

Number	Level	Marks	Time
4	MCQ	n/a	n/a
5	Examination	10	18 mins

BPP
PUBLISHING

Chapter 5

CORRELATION AND REGRESSION

Topic list	Syllabus reference
1 Correlation	6(a)
2 The correlation coefficient and the coefficient of determination	6(a)
3 Lines of best fit	6(a)
4 The scattergraph method	6(a)
5 Least squares method of linear regression analysis	6(a)
6 The reliability of regression analysis forecasts	6(a)

Introduction

In chapter 4, we looked at how costs behave and how total costs can be split into fixed and variable costs using the **high-low method**. In this chapter, we shall be looking at another method which is used to split total costs, the **scattergraph method** (line of best fit). This method is used to determine whether there is a linear relationship between two variables. If a **linear function** is considered to be appropriate, **regression analysis** is used to establish the equation (this equation can then be used to make forecasts or predictions).

Study guide

Section 6 – Cost behaviour

- Explain the structure of linear functions and equations
- Construct a scattergraph to establish whether a linear function would be appropriate
- Establish a linear function using regression analysis and interpret the results
- Calculate and explain the concepts of correlation and coefficient of determination

Exam guide

This is a very important topic (forming part of the cost behaviour section of the syllabus) and it is vital that you are able to establish linear equations using regression analysis. This topic might appear in both Section A and Section B of the examination you'll be facing.

1 CORRELATION

KEY TERM

Two variables are said to be correlated if a change in the value of one variable is accompanied by a change in the value of another variable. This is what is meant by **correlation**.

1.1 Examples of variables which might be correlated are as follows.

- A person's height and weight
- The distance of a journey and the time it takes to make it

1.2 One way of showing the correlation between two related variables is on a **scattergraph** or **scatter diagram**, plotting a number of pairs of data on the graph. For example, a scattergraph showing monthly selling costs against the volume of sales for a 12-month period might be as follows.

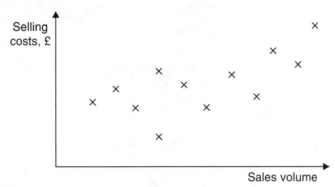

This scattergraph suggests that there is some correlation between selling costs and sales volume, so that as sales volume rises, selling costs tend to rise as well.

Degrees of correlation

1.3 Two variables can be one of the following.

- Perfectly correlated
- Partly correlated
- Uncorrelated

These differing degrees of correlation can be illustrated by scatter diagrams.

Perfect correlation

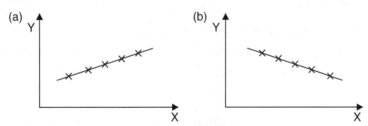

All the pairs of values lie on a straight line. An exact **linear relationship** exists between the two variables.

Partial correlation

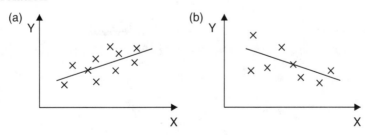

In (a), although there is no exact relationship, low values of X tend to be associated with low values of Y, and high values of X with high values of Y.

In (b) again, there is no exact relationship, but low values of X tend to be associated with high values of Y and vice versa.

No correlation

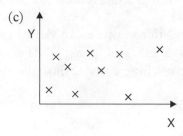

The values of these two variables are not correlated with each other.

Positive and negative correlation

1.4 Correlation, whether perfect or partial, can be **positive** or **negative**.

> **KEY TERMS**
>
> - **Positive correlation** means that low values of one variable are associated with low values of the other, and high values of one variable are associated with high values of the other.
>
> - **Negative correlation** means that low values of one variable are associated with high values of the other, and high values of one variable with low values of the other.

2 THE CORRELATION COEFFICIENT AND THE COEFFICIENT OF DETERMINATION

The correlation coefficient

2.1 The degree of correlation between two variables can be measured, and we can decide, using actual results in the form of pairs of data, whether two variables are perfectly or partially correlated, and if they are partially correlated, whether there is a **high** or **low degree of partial correlation**.

2.2 This degree of correlation is measured by the **Pearsonian correlation coefficient** (the coefficient of correlation), r (also called the 'product moment correlation coefficient').

> **EXAM FORMULA**
>
> **Correlation coefficient**, $r = \dfrac{n\Sigma XY - \Sigma X\Sigma Y}{\sqrt{[n\Sigma X^2 - (\Sigma X)^2][n\Sigma Y^2 - (\Sigma Y)^2]}}$
>
> where X and Y represent pairs of data for two variables X and Y
>
> n = the number of pairs of data used in the analysis

2.3 The correlation coefficient, r must always fall between −1 and +1. If you get a value outside this range you have made a mistake.

- **r = +1** means that the variables are **perfectly positively correlated**
- **r = –1** means that the variables are **perfectly negatively correlated**
- **r = 0** means that the variables are **uncorrelated**

2.4 EXAMPLE: THE CORRELATION COEFFICIENT

The cost of output at a factory is thought to depend on the number of units produced. Data have been collected for the number of units produced each month in the last six months, and the associated costs, as follows.

Month	Output '000s of units	Cost £'000
	X	Y
1	2	9
2	3	11
3	1	7
4	4	13
5	3	11
6	5	15

Handwritten annotations: ×4, 18, 33, 7, 52, 33, 75; $\Sigma x \ 18^2 = 324 = \Sigma x^2$; $\Sigma y \ 66^2 = 4353 =$; Σy^2

Required

Assess whether there is there any correlation between output and cost.

2.5 SOLUTION

$$r = \frac{n\Sigma XY - \Sigma X \Sigma Y}{\sqrt{[n\Sigma X^2 - (\Sigma X)^2][n\Sigma Y^2 - (\Sigma Y)^2]}}$$

We need to find the values for the following.

(a) ΣXY Multiply each value of X by its corresponding Y value, so that there are six values for XY. Add up the six values to get the total.

(b) ΣX Add up the six values of X to get a total. $(\Sigma X)^2$ will be the square of this total.

(c) ΣY Add up the six values of Y to get a total. $(\Sigma Y)^2$ will be the square of this total.

(d) ΣX^2 Find the square of each value of X, so that there are six values for X^2. Add up these values to get a total.

(e) ΣY^2 Find the square of each value of Y, so that there are six values for Y^2. Add up these values to get a total.

Workings

X	Y	XY	X^2	Y^2
2	9	18	4	81
3	11	33	9	121
1	7	7	1	49
4	13	52	16	169
3	11	33	9	121
5	15	75	25	225
$\Sigma X = 18$	$\Sigma Y = 66$	$\Sigma XY = 218$	$\Sigma X^2 = 64$	$\Sigma Y^2 = 766$

$(\Sigma X)^2 = 18^2 = 324$ $(\Sigma Y)^2 = 66^2 = 4,356$

n = 6

BPP PUBLISHING

$$r = \frac{(6 \times 218) - (18 \times 66)}{\sqrt{(6 \times 64 - 324) \times (6 \times 766 - 4{,}356)}}$$

$$= \frac{1{,}308 - 1{,}188}{\sqrt{(384 - 324) \times (4{,}596 - 4{,}356)}}$$

$$= \frac{120}{\sqrt{60 \times 240}} = \frac{120}{\sqrt{14{,}400}} = \frac{120}{120} = 1$$

2.6 There is **perfect positive correlation** between the volume of output at the factory and costs which means that there is a perfect linear relationship between output and costs.

Correlation in a time series

2.7 Correlation exists in a time series if there is a relationship between the period of time and the recorded value for that period of time. The correlation coefficient is calculated with time as the X variable although it is convenient to use simplified values for X instead of year numbers.

For example, instead of having a series of years 20X1 to 20X5, we could have values for X from 0 (20X1) to 4 (20X5).

Note that whatever starting value you use for X (be it 0, 1, 2 ... 721, ... 953), the value of r will always be the same.

Question 1

Sales of product A between 20X7 and 20Y1 were as follows.

Year	Units sold ('000s)
20X7	20
20X8	18
20X9	15
20Y0	14
20Y1	11

Required

Determine whether there is a trend in sales. In other words, decide whether there is any correlation between the year and the number of units sold.

Answer

Workings

Let 20X7 to 20Y1 be years 0 to 4.

X	Y	XY	X^2	Y^2
0	20	0	0	400
1	18	18	1	324
2	15	30	4	225
3	14	42	9	196
4	11	44	16	121
$\Sigma X = 10$	$\Sigma Y = 78$	$\Sigma XY = 134$	$\Sigma X^2 = 30$	$\Sigma Y^2 = 1{,}266$

$(\Sigma X)^2 = 100 \qquad (\Sigma Y)^2 = 6{,}084$

$n = 5$

$$r = \frac{(5 \times 134) - (10 \times 78)}{\sqrt{(5 \times 30 - 100) \times (5 \times 1{,}266 - 6{,}084)}}$$

$$= \frac{670 - 780}{\sqrt{(150 - 100) \times (6,330 - 6,084)}} = \frac{-110}{\sqrt{50 \times 246}}$$

$$= \frac{-110}{\sqrt{12,300}} = \frac{-110}{110.90537} = -0.992$$

There is **partial negative correlation** between the year of sale and units sold. The value of r is close to −1, therefore a **high degree of correlation exists**, although it is not quite perfect correlation. This means that there is a **clear downward trend** in sales.

The coefficient of determination, r^2

2.8 Unless the correlation coefficient r is exactly or very nearly +1, −1 or 0, its meaning or significance is a little unclear. For example, if the correlation coefficient for two variables is +0.8, this would tell us that the variables are positively correlated, but the correlation is not perfect. It would not really tell us much else. A more meaningful analysis is available from **the square of the correlation coefficient, r**, which is called the **coefficient of determination, r^2**

> **KEY TERM**
>
> The **coefficient of determination**, r^2 (alternatively R^2) measures the proportion of the total variation in the value of one variable that can be explained by variations in the value of the other variable.

2.9 In Question 1 above, r = −0.992, therefore r^2 = 0.984. This means that over 98% of variations in sales can be explained by the passage of time, leaving 0.016 (less than 2%) of variations to be explained by other factors.

2.10 Similarly, if the correlation coefficient between a company's output volume and maintenance costs was 0.9, r^2 would be 0.81, meaning that 81% of variations in maintenance costs could be explained by variations in output volume, leaving only 19% of variations to be explained by other factors (such as the age of the equipment).

2.11 Note, however, that if r^2 = 0.81, we would say that 81% of **the variations in y can be explained by variations in x**. We do not necessarily conclude that 81% of variations in y are *caused* by the variations in x. We must beware of reading too much significance into our statistical analysis.

Correlation and causation

2.12 If two variables are well correlated, either positively or negatively, this may be due to **pure chance** or there may be a **reason** for it. The larger the number of pairs of data collected, the less likely it is that the correlation is due to chance, though that possibility should never be ignored entirely.

2.13 If there is a reason, it may not be causal. For example, monthly net income is well correlated with monthly credit to a person's bank account, for the logical (rather than causal) reason that for most people the one equals the other.

2.14 Even if there is a causal explanation for a correlation, it does not follow that variations in the value of one variable cause variations in the value of the other. For example, sales of ice cream and of sunglasses are well correlated, not because of a direct causal link but because the weather influences both variables.

3 LINES OF BEST FIT

3.1 **Correlation enables us to determine the strength of any relationship between two variables but it does not offer us any method of forecasting values for one variable, Y, given values of another variable, X.**

3.2 If we assume that there is a **linear relationship** between the two variables, however, and we determine the **equation of a straight line (Y = a + bX)** which is a good fit for the available data plotted on a scattergraph, we can use the equation for forecasting: we can substitute values for X into the equation and derive values for Y. If you need reminding about linear equations and graphs, refer to your Basic Maths supplement.

3.3 There are a number of techniques for estimating the equation of a line of best fit. We will be looking at the **scattergraph method** and **simple linear regression analysis**. Both provide a technique for estimating values for a and b in the equation

Y = a + bX

where   X and Y are the related variables and
a and b are estimated using pairs of data for X and Y.

4 THE SCATTERGRAPH METHOD

KEY TERM

The **scattergraph method** is to plot pairs of data for two related variables on a graph, to produce a scattergraph, and then to **use judgement** to draw what seems to be a line of best fit through the data.

4.1 EXAMPLE: THE SCATTERGRAPH METHOD

Suppose we have the following pairs of data about output and costs.

Month	Output	Costs
	'000 units	£'000
1	20	82
2	16	70
3	24	90
4	22	85
5	18	73

(a) These pairs of data can be plotted on a **scattergraph** (the **horizontal** axis representing the **independent** variable and the **vertical** axis the **dependent**) and a line of best fit might be judged as the one shown below. It is drawn to pass through the middle of the data points, thereby having as many data points below the line as above it.

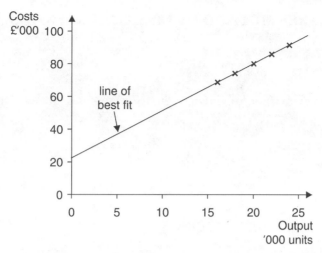

(b) A **formula for the line of best fit** can be found. In our example, suppose that we read the following data from the graph.

  (i)   When X = 0, Y = 22,000. This must be the value of a in the formula Y = a + bX.

  (ii) When X = 20,000, Y = 81,000. Since Y = a + bX, and a = 22,000, this gives us a value for b of

$$\frac{81,000 - 22,000}{20,000} = 2.95$$

(c) In this example the estimated equation from the scattergraph is Y = 22,000 + 2.95X.

Forecasting and scattergraphs

4.2 If the company to which the data in Paragraph 4.1 relates wanted to predict costs at a certain level of output (say 13,000 units), the value of 13,000 could be substituted into the equation Y = 22,000 + 2.95X and an estimate of costs made.

  If X = 13, Y = 22,000 + (2.95 × 13,000)

  ∴ Y = £60,350

4.3 Of course, predictions can be made directly from the scattergraph on the following page.

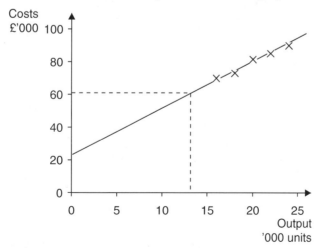

The prediction of the cost of producing 13,000 units from the scattergraph is £61,000.

BPP
PUBLISHING

5 LEAST SQUARES METHOD OF LINEAR REGRESSION ANALYSIS

EXAM FORMULA

The **least squares method of linear regression analysis** involves using the following formulae for a and b in $Y = a + bX$.

$$b = \frac{n\Sigma XY - \Sigma X \Sigma Y}{n\Sigma X^2 - (\Sigma X)^2}$$

$$a = \overline{Y} - b\overline{X}$$

where n   is the number of pairs of data

         $\overline{X}$ is the average X value of all the pairs of data

         $\overline{Y}$ is the average Y value of all the pairs of data

5.1 There are some points to note about these formulae.

(a) The line of best fit that is derived represents the **regression of Y upon X**.

A different line of best fit could be obtained by interchange in X and Y in the formulae. This would then represent the regression of X upon Y ($X = a + bY$) and it would have a slightly different slope. For examination purposes, always use the regression of Y upon X, where X is the independent variable, and Y is the dependent variable whose value we wish to forecast for given values of X. In a time series, X will represent time.

(b) Since $a = \overline{Y} - b\overline{X}$, it follows that the line of best fit must *always* pass through the point ($\overline{X}, \overline{Y}$).

5.2 EXAMPLE: THE LEAST SQUARES METHOD

(a) Given that there is a fairly high degree of correlation between the output and the costs detailed in Paragraph 4.1 (so that a linear relationship can be assumed), calculate an equation to determine the expected level of costs, for any given volume of output, using the least squares method.

(b) Prepare a budget for total costs if output is 22,000 units.

(c) Confirm that the degree of correlation between output and costs is high by calculating the correlation coefficient.

5.3 SOLUTION

(a) *Workings*

	X	Y	XY	X^2	Y^2
	20	82	1,640	400	6,724
	16	70	1,120	256	4,900
	24	90	2,160	576	8,100
	22	85	1,870	484	7,225
	18	73	1,314	324	5,329
$\Sigma X =$	100	$\Sigma Y =$ 400	$\Sigma XY =$ 8,104	$\Sigma X^2 =$ 2,040	$\Sigma Y^2 =$ 32,278

n   =   5 (There are five pairs of data for x and y values)

$$b = \frac{n\Sigma XY - \Sigma X\Sigma Y}{n\Sigma X^2 - (\Sigma X)^2} = \frac{(5 \times 8{,}104) - (100 \times 400)}{(5 \times 2{,}040) - 100^2}$$

$$= \frac{40{,}520 - 40{,}000}{10{,}200 - 10{,}000} = \frac{520}{200} = 2.6$$

$$a = \overline{Y} - b\overline{X} = \frac{400}{5} - 2.6 \times \left(\frac{100}{5}\right) = 28$$

$$Y = 28 + 2.6X$$

where Y = total cost, in thousands of pounds
X = output, in thousands of units.

Note that the fixed costs are £28,000 (when $X = 0$ costs are £28,000) and the variable cost per unit is £2.60.

(b) If the output is 22,000 units, we would expect costs to be

$28 + 2.6 \times 22 = 85.2 = £85{,}200.$

(c) $r = \dfrac{520}{\sqrt{200 \times (5 \times 32{,}278 - 400^2)}} = \dfrac{520}{\sqrt{200 \times 1{,}390}} = \dfrac{520}{527.3} = +0.99$

Regression lines and time series

5.4 The same technique can be applied to calculate a **regression line** (a **trend line**) for a time series. This is particularly useful for purposes of forecasting. As with correlation, years can be numbered from 0 upwards.

Question 2

Using the data in Question 1, calculate the trend line of sales and forecast sales in 20Y2 and 20Y3.

Answer

Using workings from Question 1:

$$b = \frac{(5 \times 134) - (10 \times 78)}{(5 \times 30) - (10)^2} = \frac{670 - 780}{150 - 100} = -2.2$$

$$a = \overline{Y} + b\overline{X} = \frac{78}{5} - \frac{(-2.2 \times 10)}{5} = 20$$

$\therefore Y = 20 - 2.2X$ where $X = 0$ in 20X7, $X = 1$ in 20X8 and so on.

Using the trend line, predicted sales in 20Y2 (year 5) would be:

$20 - (2.2 \times 5) = 9$ ie 9,000 units

and predicated sales in 20Y3 (year 6) would be:

$20 - (2.2 \times 6) = 6.8$ ie 6,800 units.

5.5 In some instances you may have to adjust your regression line forecasts by **seasonal variations**.

Exam focus point

There was a ten mark question in the pilot paper for **Financial Information for Management** which required candidates to use regression analysis to calculate a total cost equation and then to use the equation to forecast total costs at given levels of activity.

BPP
PUBLISHING

Question 3

Suppose that a trend line, found using linear regression analysis, is Y = 300 – 4.7X where X is time (in quarters) and Y = sales level in thousands of units. Given that X = 0 represents 20X0 quarter 1 and that the seasonal variations are as set out below forecast the sales level for 20X5 quarter 4.

	Q_1	Q_2	Q_3	Q_4
Seasonal variations ('000 units)	–20	–8	+4	+15

Answer

X = 0 corresponds to 20X0 quarter 1

∴ X = 23 corresponds to 20X5 quarter 4

Trend sales level = 300 – (4.7 × 23) = 191.9 ie 191,900 units

Seasonally-adjusted sales level = 191.9 + 15 = 206.9 ie 206,900 units

Question 4

Over a 36-month period, sales have been found to have an underlying linear trend of Y = 14.224 + 7.898X, where Y is the number of items sold and X represents the month. Monthly deviations from trend have been calculated and month 37 is expected to be 1.28 times the trend value.

The forecast number of items to be sold in month 37 is approximately

A 389   B 390   C 391   D 392

Answer

This is typical of multiple choice questions that you must work through fully if you are to get the right answer.

Y = 14.224 + 7.898X

If X = 37, trend in sales for month 37 = 14.224 + (7.898 × 37)
                                        = 306.45

∴ Seasonally-adjusted trend value = 306.45 × 1.28
                                    = 392.256

∴ The correct answer is 392, option D.

6 THE RELIABILITY OF REGRESSION ANALYSIS FORECASTS

6.1 As with all forecasting techniques, the results from regression analysis will not be wholly reliable. There are a number of factors which affect the reliability of forecasts made using regression analysis.

(a) **It assumes a linear relationship exists between the two variables** (since linear regression analysis produces an equation in the linear format) whereas a non-linear relationship might exist.

(b) It **assumes that the value of one variable, Y, can be predicted or estimated from the value of one other variable, X**. In reality the value of Y might depend on several other variables, not just X.

(c) When it is used for forecasting, **it assumes that what has happened in the past will provide a reliable guide to the future**.

(d) When calculating a line of best fit, there will be a range of values for X. In the example in Paragraph 5.2 and 5.3, the line Y = 28 + 2.6X was predicted from data with output values ranging from X = 16 to X = 24. Depending on the degree of correlation between X and Y, we might safely use the estimated line of best fit to predict values for Y in the future, provided that the value of X remains within the range 16 to 24. We would be on less safe ground if we used the formula to predict a value for Y when X = 10, or 30, or any other value outside the range 16 to 24, because we would have to **assume that the trend line applies outside the range of X values used to establish the line in the first place**.

(i) **Interpolation** means using a line of best fit to predict a value within the two extreme points of the observed range.

(ii) **Extrapolation** means using a line of best fit to predict a value outside the two extreme points.

When linear regression analysis is used for forecasting a time series (when the X values represent time) it **assumes that the trend line can be extrapolated into the future**. This might not necessarily be a good assumption to make.

(e) As with any forecasting process, **the amount of data available is very important**. Even if correlation is high, if we have fewer than about ten pairs of values, we must regard any forecast as being somewhat unreliable. (It is likely to provide more reliable forecasts than the scattergraph method, however, since it uses all of the available data.)

(f) **The reliability of a forecast will depend on the reliability of the data collected to determine the regression analysis equation**. If the data is not collected accurately or if data used is false, forecasts are unlikely to be acceptable.

6.2 A check on the reliability of the estimated line Y = 28 + 2.6X can be made, however, by calculating the coefficient of correlation. From Paragraph 5.3, we know that r = 0.99. This is a high positive correlation, and r^2 = 0.9801, indicating that 98.01% of the variation in cost can be explained by the variation in volume. This would suggest that a **fairly large degree of reliance** can probably be placed on estimates .

6.3 If there is a **perfect linear relationship** between X and Y (r = ±1) then we can predict Y from any given value of X with **great confidence**.

6.4 If correlation is high (for example r = 0.9) the actual values will all lie quite close to the regression line and so predictions should not be far out. If correlation is below about 0.7, predictions will only give a very rough guide as to the likely value of Y.

Chapter roundup

- When the value of one variable is related to the value of another, they are said to be **correlated**.

- Two variables might be **perfectly correlated**, **partly correlated** or **uncorrelated**. Correlation can be **positive** or **negative**.

- The **degree of correlation** between two variables is measured by the **Pearsonian** (product moment) **correlation coefficient, r**. The nearer r is to +1 or -1, the stronger the relationship.

- The **coefficient of determination, r^2**, measures the proportion of the total variation in the value of one variable that can be explained by the variation in the value of the other variable.

- The **scattergraph method** involves the use of judgement to draw what seems to be a line of best fit through plotted data.

- **Linear regression analysis** (the **least squares method**) is one technique for estimating a line of best fit.

- Once an equation for a line of best fit has been determined, forecasts can be made.

- Like all forecasting techniques, the results obtained will not be wholly reliable. There are a number of factors which affect the reliability of forecasts made using regression analysis.

Quick quiz

1 ~~Positive Correlation~~ .... means that low values of one variable are associated with low values of the other, and high values of one variable are associated with high values of the other.

2 ~~Negative Correlation~~ .... means that low values of one variable are associated with high values of the other, and high values of one variable with low values of the other.

3 • Perfect positive correlation, r = ...+1...........
 • Perfect negative correlation, r = ...−1.............
 • No correlation, r = ...0...............

 The correlation coefficient, r, must always fall within the range ....1............ to ....−1.......... .

4 If the correlation coefficient of a set of data is 0.9, what is the coefficient of determination and how is it interpreted? · 81 81% of Correlation can be determined

5 (a) The equation of a straight line is given as Y = a + bX. Give two methods used for estimating the above equation.

 (b) If Y = a + bX, it is best to use the regression of Y upon X where X is the dependent variable and Y is the independent variable.

 True ☑

 False ☐

6 List five factors affecting the reliability of regression analysis forecasts.

Answers to quick quiz

1 Positive correlation

2 Negative correlation

3 • $r = +1$
 • $r = -1$
 • $r = 0$

 The correlation coefficient, r, must always fall within the range -1 to $+1$.

4 Correlation coefficient = r = 0.9

 Coefficient of determination = $r^2 = 0.9^2 = 0.9025$ or 90.25%

 This tells us that over 90% of the variations in the dependent variable (Y) can be explained by variations in the independent variable, X.

5 (a) • Scattergraph method (line of best fit)
 • Simple linear regression analysis

 (b) False. When using the regression of Y upon X, X is the independent variable and Y is the dependent variable (the value of Y will depend upon the value of X).

6 (a) It assumes a linear relationship exists between the two variables.

 (b) It assumes that the value of one variable, Y, can be predicted or estimated from the value of another variable, X.

 (c) It assumes that what happened in the past will provide a reliable guide to the future.

 (d) It assumes that the trend line can be extrapolated into the future.

 (e) The amount of data available.

Now try the questions below from the Exam Question Bank

Number	Level	Marks	Time
6	MCQ	n/a	n/a
7	Examination	10	18 mins

Part B
Elements of cost

Chapter 6

MATERIAL COSTS

Topic list	Syllabus reference
1 What is stock control?	3(a)
2 The ordering, receipt and issue of raw materials	3(a)
3 The storage of raw materials	3(a)
4 Stock control levels	3(a)
5 Stock valuation	3(a)
6 FIFO (first in, first out)	3(a)
7 LIFO (last in, first out)	3(a)
8 Cumulative weighted average pricing	3(a)
9 Other methods of pricing and valuation	3(a)
10 Stock valuation and profitability	3(a)
11 Ledger entries relating to materials	3(a)

Introduction

The investment in stock is a very important one for most businesses, both in terms of monetary value and relationships with customers (no stock, no sale, loss of customer goodwill). It is therefore vital that management establish and maintain an **effective stock control system** and that they are aware of the major costing problem relating to materials, that of pricing materials issues and valuing stock at the end of each period.

The first half of this chapter will concentrate on a **stock control system** for materials, but similar problems and considerations apply to all forms of stock. In the second half of the chapter we will consider the methods for **pricing materials issues/valuing stock**. We will look at the various methods, their advantages and disadvantages and their impact on profitability.

Since this is a very long chapter, we recommend that you study it in two parts. Firstly, Sections 1-5 and then sections 6-11.

Study guide

Sections 7 and 8 – Material costs

- Describe the different procedures and documents necessary for ordering, receiving and issuing materials from stock

- Describe the control procedures used to monitor physical and 'book' stock and to minimise discrepancies and losses

- Calculate, explain and evaluate the value of closing stock and material issues using LIFO, FIFO and average methods (weighted and periodic)

- Prepare ledger entries to record material cost inputs and outputs

- Interpret the entries and balances in the material stock account

- Explain the reasons for holding stock

- Identify and explain the costs of having stock

- Calculate and interpret optimal reorder quantities

- Calculate the interpret optimal reorder quantities when discounts apply

- Produce and interpret calculations to minimise stock costs when stock is gradually replenished

- Describe appropriate methods for establishing reorder levels

Exam guide

Material costs is another key area of the syllabus so look out for questions on this topic in both sections of the examination.

1 WHAT IS STOCK CONTROL?

1.1 The stocks held in any organisation can generally be classified under four main headings.

- Raw materials
- Work in progress
- Spare parts/consumables
- Finished goods

Not all organisations will have stock of all four general categories.

1.2 This chapter will concentrate on a **stock control system** for materials, but similar problems and considerations apply to all forms of stock. Controls should cover the following functions.

- The **ordering** of stock
- The **purchase** of stock
- The **receipt** of goods into store
- **Storage**
- The **issue** of stock and maintenance of stock at the most appropriate level

Qualitative aspects of stock control

1.3 We may wish to **control stock** for the following reasons.

- Holding costs of stock may be expensive.
- Production will be disrupted if we run out of raw materials.
- Unused stock with a short shelf life may incur unnecessary expenses.

1.4 If manufactured goods are made out of low quality materials, the end product will be of low quality also. It may therefore be necessary to control the quality of stock, in order to maintain a good reputation with consumers.

2 THE ORDERING, RECEIPT AND ISSUE OF RAW MATERIALS

Ordering and receiving materials

2.1 Proper records must be kept of the physical procedures for ordering and receiving a consignment of materials to ensure the following.

- That enough stock is held
- That there is no duplication of ordering
- That quality is maintained
- That there is adequate record keeping for accounts purposes

A typical series of procedures might be as follows.

(a) Current stocks run down to the level where a reorder is required. The stores department issues a **purchase requisition** which is sent to the purchasing department, authorising the department to order further stock. An example of a purchase requisition is shown below.

```
┌─────────────────────────────────────────────────────────────┐
│              PURCHASE REQUISITION   Req. No.                  │
│                                                               │
│  Department/job number:                 Date                  │
│  Suggested Supplier:                                          │
│                                                               │
│                              Requested by:                    │
│                              Latest date required:            │
│                                                               │
├──────────┬──────────┬───────────────────┬───────────────────┤
│          │  Code    │                   │  Estimated Cost    │
│ Quantity │  number  │   Description     ├──────────┬────────┤
│          │          │                   │   Unit   │   £    │
│          │          │                   │          │        │
│          │          │                   │          │        │
│          │          │                   │          │        │
│          │          │                   │          │        │
├──────────┴──────────┴───────────────────┴──────────┴────────┤
│  Authorised signature:                                       │
└─────────────────────────────────────────────────────────────┘
```

(b) The purchasing department draws a **purchase order** which is sent to the supplier. (The supplier may be asked to return an acknowledgement copy as confirmation of his acceptance of the order.) Copies of the purchase order must be sent to the accounts department and the storekeeper (or receiving department).

```
┌─────────────────────────────────────────────────────────────┐
│  Purchase Order/Confirmation                                 │
│                                                               │
│                                                               │
│  Our Order Ref:              Date                            │
│  To                                                           │
│  ⌐(Address)              ⌐  Please deliver to the above address│
│                             Ordered by:                       │
│                             Passed and checked by:            │
│                             Total Order Value £               │
│  └                      ┘                                     │
├──────┬──────┬─────────────────────┬──────────┬──────────────┤
│      │      │                     │          │              │
│      │      │                     │          │              │
│      │      │                     │          │              │
│      │      │                     │          │              │
│      │      │                     │          │              │
│      │      │                     │          │              │
│      │      │              Subtotal│          │              │
│      │      │                     │          │              │
│      │      │       VAT           │          │              │
│      │      │       ( @ 17.5%)    │          │              │
│      │      │         Total       │          │              │
└──────┴──────┴─────────────────────┴──────────┴──────────────┘
```

(c) The purchasing department may have to obtain a number of quotations if either a new stock line is required, the existing supplier's costs are too high or the existing supplier no longer stocks the goods needed. Trade discounts (reduction in the price per unit given to some customers) should be negotiated where possible.

(d) The supplier delivers the consignment of materials, and the storekeeper signs a **delivery note** for the carrier. The packages must then be checked against the copy of the purchase order, to ensure that the supplier has delivered the types and quantities of materials which were ordered. (Discrepancies would be referred to the purchasing department.)

(e) If the delivery is acceptable, the storekeeper prepares a **goods received note (GRN)**, an example of which is shown below.

GOODS RECEIVED NOTE	WAREHOUSE COPY
	NO 5565

DATE: _ _ _ _ _ _ _ _ _ _ _ _ _ TIME: _ _ _ _ _ _ _ _ _ _ _ _

OUR ORDER NO: _   WAREHOUSE A

SUPPLIER AND SUPPLIER'S ADVICE NOTE NO: _ _ _ _ _ _ _ _ _ _ _ _ _ _ _ _ _ _.

QUANTITY	CAT NO	DESCRIPTION

RECEIVED IN GOOD CONDITION:	(INITIALS)

(f) A copy of the **GRN** is sent to the accounts department, where it is matched with the copy of the purchase order. The supplier's invoice is checked against the purchase order and GRN, and the necessary steps are taken to pay the supplier. The invoice may contain details relating to discounts such as trade discounts, quantity discounts (order in excess of a specified amount) and settlement discounts (payment received within a specified number of days).

Question 1

What are the possible consequences of a failure of control over ordering and receipt of materials?

Answer

(a) Incorrect materials being delivered, disrupting operations
(b) Incorrect prices being paid
(c) Deliveries other than at the specified time (causing disruption)
(d) Insufficient control over quality
(e) Invoiced amounts differing from quantities of goods actually received or prices agreed

You may, of course, have thought of equally valid consequences.

Issue of materials

2.2 Materials can only be issued against a **materials/stores requisition**. This document must record not only the quantity of goods issued, but also the cost centre or the job number for which the requisition is being made. The materials requisition note may also have a column, to be filled in by the cost department, for recording the cost or value of the materials issued to the cost centre or job.

Materials requisition note			
Date required _ _ _ _ _ _ _ _ .		Cost centre No/ Job No _ _ _ _ _ _ _ _ _ _ _ .	
Quantity	Item code	Description	£
Signature of requisitioning Manager/ Foreman _ .			Date _ _ _ _ _ _

Materials transfers and returns

2.3 Where materials, having been issued to one job or cost centre, are later transferred to a different job or cost centre, without first being returned to stores, a **materials transfer note** should be raised. Such a note must show not only the job receiving the transfer, but also the job from which it is transferred. This enables the appropriate charges to be made to jobs or cost centres.

2.4 Material returns must also be documented on a **materials returned note**. This document is the 'reverse' of a requisition note, and must contain similar information. In fact it will often be almost identical to a requisition note. It will simply have a different title and perhaps be a distinctive colour, such as red, to highlight the fact that materials are being returned.

Impact of computerisation

2.5 Many stock control systems these days are computerised. Computerised stock control systems vary greatly, but most will have the features outlined below.

(a) **Data must be input into the system**. For example, details of goods received may simply be written on to a GRN for later entry into the computer system. Alternatively, this information may be keyed in directly to the computer: a GRN will be printed and then signed as evidence of the transaction, so that both the warehouse and the supplier can have a hard copy record in case of dispute. Some systems may incorporate the use of devices such as bar code readers.

Other types of transaction which will need to be recorded include the following.

(i) **Transfers** between different categories of stock (for example from work in progress to finished goods)

(ii) **Despatch**, resulting from a sale, of items of finished goods to customers

(iii) **Adjustments** to stock records if the amount of stock revealed in a physical stock count differs from the amount appearing on the stock records

(b) **A stock master file is maintained**. This file will contain details for every category of stock and will be updated for new stock lines. A database file may be maintained.

Question 2

What type of information do you think should be held on a stock master file?

Answer

Here are some examples.

(a) Stock code number, for reference
(b) Brief description of stock item
(c) Reorder level
(d) Reorder quantity
(e) Cost per unit
(f) Selling price per unit (if finished goods)
(g) Amount in stock
(h) Frequency of usage

The file may also hold details of stock movements over a period, but this will depend on the type of system in operation. In a **batch system**, transactions will be grouped and input in one operation and details of the movements may be held in a separate transactions file, the master file updated in total only. In an **on-line system**, transactions may be input directly to the master file, where the record of movements is thus likely to be found. Such a system will mean that the stock records are constantly up to date, which will help in monitoring and controlling stock.

The system may generate orders automatically once the amount in stock has fallen to the reorder level.

(c) **The system will generate outputs**. These may include, depending on the type of system, any of the following.

    (i) **Hard copy** records, for example a printed GRN, of transactions entered into the system.

    (ii) Output on a **VDU** screen in response to an enquiry (for example the current level of a particular line of stock, or details of a particular transaction).

    (iii) Various **printed reports**, devised to fit in with the needs of the organisation. These may include stock movement reports, detailing over a period the movements on all stock lines, listings of GRNs, despatch notes and so forth.

2.6 A computerised stock control system is usually able to give more up to date information and more flexible reporting than a manual system but remember that both manual and computer based stock control systems need the same types of data to function properly.

3 THE STORAGE OF RAW MATERIALS

3.1 Storekeeping involves storing materials to achieve the following objectives.

- Speedy **issue** and **receipt** of materials
- Full **identification** of all materials at all times
- Correct **location** of all materials at all times
- **Protection** of materials from damage and deterioration
- Provision of **secure stores** to avoid pilferage, theft and fire
- **Efficient** use of storage space
- **Maintenance** of correct stock levels
- Keeping correct and up-to-date **records** of receipts, issues and stock levels

Recording stock levels

3.2 One of the objectives of storekeeping is to maintain accurate records of current stock levels. This involves the accurate recording of stock movements (issues from and receipts into

100

stores). The most frequently encountered system for recording stock movements is the use of bin cards and stores ledger accounts.

Bin cards

3.3 A **bin card** shows the level of stock of an item at a particular stores location. It is kept with the actual stock and is updated by the storekeeper as stocks are received and issued. A typical bin card is shown below.

Bin card

Part code no			Location			
Bin number			Stores ledger no			
Receipts			Issues			Stock balance
Date	Quantity	G.R.N. No.	Date	Quantity	Req. No.	

The use of bin cards is decreasing, partly due to the difficulty in keeping them updated and partly due to the merging of stock recording and control procedures, frequently using computers.

Stores ledger accounts

3.4 A typical stores ledger account is shown below. Note that it shows the value of stock.

Stores ledger account

Material				Maximum Quantity						
Code				Minimum Quantity						
Date	Receipts				Issues				Stock		
	G.R.N. No.	Quantity	Unit Price £	Amount £	Stores Req. No.	Quantity	Unit Price £	Amount £	Quantity	Unit Price £	Amount £

3.5 The above illustration shows a card for a manual system, but even when the stock records are computerised, the same type of information is normally included in the computer file. The running balance on the stores ledger account allows stock levels and valuation to be monitored.

Free stock

3.6 Managers need to know the **free stock balance** in order to obtain a full picture of the current stock position of an item. Free stock represents what is really **available for future use** and is calculated as follows.

	Materials in stock	X
+	Materials on order from suppliers	X
–	Materials requisitioned, not yet issued	(X)
	Free stock balance	X

3.7 Knowledge of the level of physical stock assists stock issuing, stocktaking and controlling maximum and minimum stock levels: knowledge of the level of free stock assists ordering.

Question 3

A wholesaler has 8,450 units outstanding for Part X100 on existing customers' orders; there are 3,925 units in stock and the calculated free stock is 5,525 units.

How many units does the wholesaler have on order with his supplier?

A 9,450   ✓B 10,050   C 13,975   D 17,900

Answer

Free stock balance = units in stock + units on order – units ordered, but not yet issued

5,525 = 3,925 + units on order – 8,450

Units on order = 10,050

The correct answer is B.

Identification of materials: stock codes (materials codes)

3.8 Materials held in stores are **coded** and **classified**. Advantages of using code numbers to identify materials are as follows.

(a) Ambiguity is avoided.

(b) Time is saved. Descriptions can be lengthy and time-consuming.

(c) Production efficiency is improved. The correct material can be accurately identified from a code number.

(d) Computerised processing is made easier.

(e) Numbered code systems can be designed to be flexible, and can be expanded to include more stock items as necessary.

The digits in a code can stand for the type of stock, supplier, department and so forth.

Stocktaking

3.9 Stocktaking involves counting the physical stock on hand at a certain date, and then checking this against the balance shown in the stock records. There are two methods of carrying out this process, **periodic stocktaking** and **continuous stocktaking**.

KEY TERMS

- **Periodic stocktaking** is a 'process whereby all stock items are physically counted and valued at a set point in time, usually at the end of an accounting period' (CIMA *Official Terminology*).

- **Continuous stocktaking** is 'the process of counting and valuing selected items at different times on a rotating basis' (CIMA *Official Terminology*). This involves a specialist team counting and checking a number of stock items each day, so that each item is checked at least once a year. Valuable items or items with a high turnover could be checked more frequently.

3.10 The **advantages of continuous stocktaking compared to periodic stocktaking** are as follows.

    (a) The annual stocktaking is unnecessary and the disruption it causes is avoided.

    (b) Regular skilled stocktakers can be employed, reducing likely errors.

    (c) More time is available, reducing errors and allowing investigation.

    (d) Deficiencies and losses are revealed sooner than they would be if stocktaking were limited to an annual check.

    (e) Production hold-ups are eliminated because the stores staff are at no time so busy as to be unable to deal with material issues to production departments.

    (f) Staff morale is improved and standards raised.

    (g) Control over stock levels is improved, and there is less likelihood of overstocking or running out of stock.

Stock discrepancies

3.11 There will be occasions when stock checks disclose discrepancies between the physical amount of an item in stock and the amount shown in the stock records. When this occurs, the cause of the discrepancy should be investigated, and appropriate action taken to ensure that it does not happen again.

Perpetual inventory

3.12 **A perpetual inventory system involves recording every receipt and issue of stock as it occurs on bin cards and stores ledger accounts.** This means that there is a continuous record of the balance of each item of stock. The balance on the stores ledger account therefore represents the stock on hand and this balance is used in the calculation of closing stock in monthly and annual accounts. In practice, physical stocks may not agree with recorded stocks and therefore continuous stocktaking is necessary to ensure that the perpetual inventory system is functioning correctly and that minor stock discrepancies are corrected.

Obsolete, deteriorating and slow-moving stocks and wastage

3.13 **Obsolete stocks are those items which have become out-of-date and are no longer required.** Obsolete items are written off to the profit and loss account and disposed of.

3.14 Stock items may be wasted because, for example, they get broken. All **wastage** should be noted on the stock records immediately so that physical stock equals the stock balance on records and the cost of the wastage written off to the profit and loss account.

3.15 **Slow-moving stocks are stock items which are likely to take a long time to be used up**. For example, 5,000 units are in stock, and only 20 are being used each year. This is often caused by overstocking. Managers should investigate such stock items and, if it is felt that the usage rate is unlikely to increase, excess stock should be written off as for obsolete stock, leaving perhaps four or five years' supply in stock.

4 STOCK CONTROL LEVELS

Why hold stock?

4.1 The costs of purchasing stock are usually one of the largest costs faced by an organisation and, once obtained, stock has to be carefully controlled and checked.

4.2 The main reasons for holding stocks can be summarised as follows.

- To ensure sufficient goods are available to meet expected demand
- To provide a buffer between processes
- To meet any future shortages
- To take advantage of bulk purchasing discounts
- To absorb seasonal fluctuations and any variations in usage and demand
- To allow production processes to flow smoothly and efficiently
- As a necessary part of the production process (such as when maturing cheese)
- As a deliberate investment policy, especially in times of inflation or possible shortages

Holding costs

4.3 If stocks are too high, **holding costs** will be incurred unnecessarily. Such costs occur for a number of reasons.

(a) **Costs of storage and stores operations.** Larger stocks require more storage space and possibly extra staff and equipment to control and handle them.

(b) **Interest charges.** Holding stocks involves the tying up of capital (cash) on which interest must be paid.

(c) **Insurance costs.** The larger the value of stocks held, the greater insurance premiums are likely to be.

(d) **Risk of obsolescence.** The longer a stock item is held, the greater is the risk of obsolescence.

(e) **Deterioration.** When materials in store deteriorate to the extent that they are unusable, they must be thrown away with the likelihood that disposal costs would be incurred.

Costs of obtaining stock

4.4 On the other hand, if stocks are kept low, small quantities of stock will have to be ordered more frequently, thereby increasing the following **ordering or procurement costs**.

(a) **Clerical and administrative costs** associated with purchasing, accounting for and receiving goods

(b) **Transport costs**

(c) **Production run costs**, for stock which is manufactured internally rather than purchased from external sources

Stockout costs

4.5 An additional type of cost which may arise if stocks are kept too low is the type associated with running out of stock. There are a number of causes of **stockout costs**.

- Lost contribution from lost sales
- Loss of future sales due to disgruntled customers

- Loss of customer goodwill
- Cost of production stoppages
- Labour frustration over stoppages
- Extra costs of urgent, small quantity, replenishment orders

Objective of stock control

4.6 The overall objective of stock control is, therefore, to maintain stock levels so that the total of the following costs is minimised.

- Holding costs
- Ordering costs
- Stockout costs

Stock control levels

4.7 Based on an analysis of past stock usage and delivery times, a series of control levels can be calculated and used to maintain stocks at their optimum level (in other words, a level which minimises costs). These levels will determine 'when to order' and 'how many to order'.

(a) **Reorder level**. When stocks reach this level, an order should be placed to replenish stocks. The reorder level is determined by consideration of the following.

- The maximum rate of consumption
- The maximum lead time

The maximum lead time is the time between placing an order with a supplier, and the stock becoming available for use

FORMULA TO LEARN

Reorder level = maximum usage × maximum lead time

(b) **Minimum level**. This is a warning level to draw management attention to the fact that stocks are approaching a dangerously low level and that stockouts are possible.

FORMULA TO LEARN

Minimum level = reorder level – (average usage × average lead time)

(c) **Maximum level**. This also acts as a warning level to signal to management that stocks are reaching a potentially wasteful level.

FORMULA TO LEARN

Maximum level = reorder level + reorder quantity – (minimum usage × minimum lead time)

Question 4

A large retailer with multiple outlets maintains a central warehouse from which the outlets are supplied. The following information is available for Part Number SF525.

Average usage	350 per day
Minimum usage	180 per day
Maximum usage	420 per day
Lead time for replenishment	11-15 days
Re-order quantity	6,500 units
Re-order level	6,300 units

(a) Based on the data above, what is the maximum level of stock?

    A 5,250   B 6,500   √ C 10,820   D 12,800

(b) Based on the data above, what is the approximate number of Part Number SF525 carried as buffer stock?

    A 200   B 720   C 1,680   √ D 1,750

Answer

(a) Maximum stock level   = reorder level + reorder quantity – (min usage × min lead time)
                                  = 6,300 + 6,500 – (180 × 11)
                                  = 10,820

The correct answer is C.

Using good MCQ technique, if you were resorting to a guess you should have eliminated option A. The maximum stock level cannot be less than the reorder quantity.

(b) Buffer stock   = minimum level

Minimum level   = reorder level – (average usage × average lead time)
                   = 6,300 – (350 × 13) = 1,750.

The correct answer is D.

Option A could again be easily eliminated. With minimum usage of 180 per day, a buffer stock of only 200 would not be much of a buffer!

(d) **Reorder quantity**. This is the quantity of stock which is to be ordered when stock reaches the reorder level. If it is set so as to minimise the total costs associated with holding and ordering stock, then it is known as the economic order quantity.

(e) **Average stock**. The formula for the average stock level assumes that stock levels fluctuate evenly between the minimum (or safety) stock level and the highest possible stock level (the amount of stock immediately after an order is received, ie safety stock + reorder quantity).

FORMULA TO LEARN

Average stock = safety stock + ½ reorder quantity

Question 5

A component has a safety stock of 500, a re-order quantity of 3,000 and a rate of demand which varies between 200 and 700 per week. The average stock is approximately

    √ A 2,000   B 2,300   C 2,500   D 3,500

Answer

Average stock	= safety stock + ½ reorder quantity
	= 500 + (0.5 × 3,000)
	= 2,000

The correct answer is A.

Economic order quantity (EOQ)

4.8 **Economic order theory assumes that the average stock held is equal to one half of the reorder quantity** (although as we saw in the last section, if an organisation maintains some sort of buffer or safety stock then average stock = buffer stock + half of the reorder quantity). We have seen that there are certain costs associated with holding stock. These costs tend to increase with the level of stocks, and so could be reduced by ordering smaller amounts from suppliers each time.

4.9 On the other hand, as we have seen, there are costs associated with ordering from suppliers: documentation, telephone calls, payment of invoices, receiving goods into stores and so on. These costs tend to increase if small orders are placed, because a larger number of orders would then be needed for a given annual demand.

4.10 Suppose a company purchases raw material at a cost of £16 per unit. The annual demand for the raw material is 25,000 units. The holding cost per unit is £6.40 and the cost of placing an order is £32.

4.11 We can tabulate the annual relevant costs for various order quantities as follows.

Order quantity (units)		100	200	300	400	500	600	800	1,000
Average stock (units)	(a)	50	100	150	200	250	300	400	500
Number of orders	(b)	250	125	83	63	50	42	31	25
		£	£	£	£	£	£	£	£
Annual holding cost	(c)	320	640	960	1,280	1,600	1,920	2,560	3,200
Annual order cost	(d)	8,000	4,000	2,656	2,016	1,600	1,344	992	800
Total relevant cost		8,320	4,640	3,616	3,296	3,200	3,264	3,552	4,000

Notes

(a) Average stock = Order quantity ÷ 2 (ie assuming no safety stock)
(b) Number of orders = annual demand ÷ order quantity
(c) Annual holding cost = Average stock × £6.40
(d) Annual order cost = Number of orders × £32

4.12 You will see that the economic order quantity is 500 units. At this point the total annual relevant costs are at a minimum.

4.13 We can present the information tabulated in Paragraph 4.11 in graphical form. The vertical axis represents the relevant annual costs for the investment in stocks, and the horizontal axis can be used to represent either the various order quantities or the average stock levels; two scales are actually shown on the horizontal axis so that both items can be incorporated. The graph shows that, as the average stock level and order quantity increase, the holding cost increases. On the other hand, the ordering costs decline as stock levels and order quantities increase. The total cost line represents the sum of both the holding and the ordering costs.

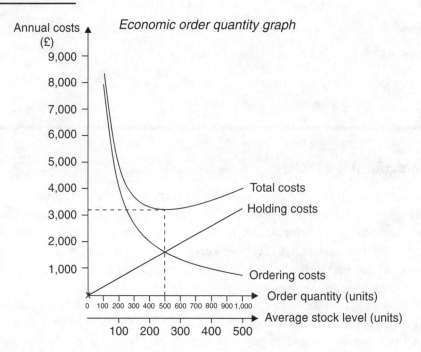

Economic order quantity graph

4.14 Note that the total cost line is at a minimum for an order quantity of 500 units and occurs at the point where the ordering cost curve and holding cost curve intersect. **The EOQ is therefore found at the point where holding costs equal ordering costs.**

4.15 There is also a formula for the EOQ and this will be provided in your examination.

EXAM FORMULA

$$EOQ = \sqrt{\frac{2C_0D}{C_H}}$$

where C_H = cost of holding one unit of stock for one time period
             C_0 = cost of ordering a consignment from a supplier
             D = demand during the time period

Question 6

Calculate the EOQ using the formula and the information in Paragraph 4.10.

Answer

$$EOQ = \sqrt{\frac{2 \times £32 \times 25,000}{£6.40}}$$

$$= \sqrt{250,000}$$

$$= 500 \text{ units}$$

Economic batch quantity (EBQ)

4.16 You may come across a problem in which the **basic EOQ formula requires modification because re-supply is gradual, instead of instantaneous.** Typically, a manufacturing company might hold stocks of a finished item, which is produced in batches. Once the order for a new batch has been placed, and the production run has started, finished output might be used before the batch run has been completed.

4.17 If the daily demand for an item of stock is ten units, and the storekeeper orders 100 units in a batch. The rate of production is 50 units a day.

(a) On the first day of the batch production run, the stores will run out of its previous stocks, and re-supply will begin. 50 units will be produced during the day, and ten units will be consumed. The closing stock at the end of day 1 will be 50 – 10 = 40 units.

(b) On day 2, the final 50 units will be produced and a further ten units will be consumed. Closing stock at the end of day 2 will be (40 + 50 –10) = 80 units.

(c) In eight more days, stocks will fall to zero.

4.18 The minimum stock in this example is zero, and the maximum stock is 80 units. The maximum stock is the quantity ordered (Q = 100) minus demand during the period of the batch production run which is Q × D/R, where

    D   is the rate of demand
    R   is the rate of production
    Q   is the quantity ordered.

In our example, the maximum stock is $(100 - \dfrac{10}{50} \times 100) = 100 - 20 = 80$ units.

The maximum stock level, given gradual re-supply, is thus $Q - \dfrac{QD}{R} = Q(1 - D/R)$.

4.19 The position can be represented graphically as follows.

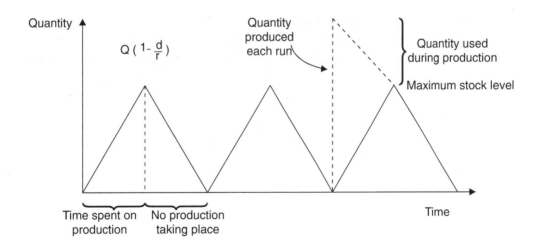

4.20 An amended EOQ (economic batch quantity, or EBQ) formula is required because average stocks are not Q/2 but Q(1 – D/R)/2.

FORMULA TO LEARN

The **EBQ** is $\sqrt{\dfrac{2C_oD}{C_H(1-D/R)}}$

where R = the production rate per time period (which must exceed the stock usage)
Q = the amount produced in each batch
D = the usage per time period
C_o = the set up cost per batch
C_H = the holding cost per unit of stock per time period

Question 7

A company is able to manufacture its own components for stock at the rate of 4,000 units a week. Demand for the component is at the rate of 2,000 units a week. Set up costs for each production run are £50. The cost of holding one unit of stock is £0.001 a week.

Required

Calculate the economic production run.

Answer

$$Q = \sqrt{\dfrac{2 \times 50 \times 2,000}{0.001(1 - 2,000 / 4,000)}} = 20,000 \text{ units (giving a stock cycle of 10 weeks)}$$

Bulk discounts

4.21 The solution obtained from using the simple EOQ formula may need to be modified if bulk discounts (also called quantity discounts) are available. The following graph shows the effect that discounts granted for orders of certain sizes may have on total costs.

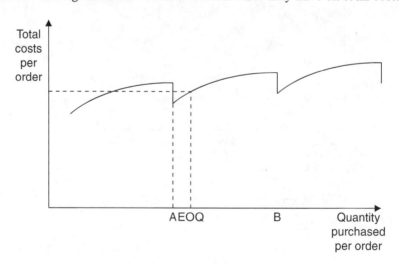

The graph above shows the following.

- Differing bulk discounts are given when the order quantity exceeds A, B and C
- The minimum total cost (ie when quantity B is ordered rather than the EOQ)

4.22 To decide mathematically whether it would be worthwhile taking a discount and ordering larger quantities, it is necessary to **minimise** the total of the following.

110

- Total material costs
- Ordering costs
- Stock holding costs

4.23 The **total cost** will be **minimised** at one of the following.

- At the **pre-discount EOQ level,** so that a discount is not worthwhile
- At the **minimum order size** necessary to earn the discount

4.24 EXAMPLE: BULK DISCOUNTS

The annual demand for an item of stock is 45 units. The item costs £200 a unit to purchase, the holding cost for one unit for one year is 15% of the unit cost and ordering costs are £300 an order.

The supplier offers a 3% discount for orders of 60 units or more, and a discount of 5% for orders of 90 units or more.

Required

Calculate the cost-minimising order size.

4.25 SOLUTION

(a) The EOQ ignoring discounts is $\sqrt{\dfrac{2 \times 300 \times 45}{15\% \text{ of } 200}} = 30$

	£
Purchases (no discount) 45 × £200	9,000
Holding costs 15 (30 ÷ 2) units × £30	450
Ordering costs 1.5 orders × £300	450
Total annual costs	9,900

(b) With a discount of 3% and an order quantity of 60 units costs are as follows.

	£
Purchases £9,000 × 97%	8,730
Holding costs 30 units × 15% of 97% of £200	873
Ordering costs 0.75 orders × £300	225
Total annual costs	9,828

(c) With a discount of 5% and an order quantity of 90 units costs are as follows.

	£
Purchases £9,000 × 95%	8,550.0
Holding costs 45 units × 15% of 95% of £200	1,282.5
Ordering costs 0.5 orders × £300	150.0
Total annual costs	9,982.5

The cheapest option is to order 60 units at a time.

4.26 Note that the value of C_H varied according to the size of the discount, because C_H was a percentage of the purchase cost. This means that **total holding costs are reduced because of a discount**. This could easily happen if, for example, most of C_H was the cost of insurance, based on the cost of stock held.

Question 8

A company uses an item of stock as follows.

Purchase price: £96 per unit
Annual demand: 4,000 units
Ordering cost: £300
Annual holding cost: 10% of purchase price
Economic order quantity: 500 units

Required

Ascertain whether the company should order 1,000 units at a time in order to secure an 8% discount.

Answer

The total annual cost at the economic order quantity of 500 units is as follows.

	£
Purchases 4,000 × £96	384,000
Ordering costs £300 × (4,000/500)	2,400
Holding costs £96 × 10% × (500/2)	2,400
	388,800

The total annual cost at an order quantity of 1,000 units would be as follows.

	£
Purchases £384,000 × 92%	353,280
Ordering costs £300 × (4,000/1,000)	1,200
Holding costs £96 × 92% × 10% × (1,000/2)	4,416
	358,896

The company should order the item 1,000 units at a time, saving £(388,800 − 358,896) = £29,904 a year.

Other systems of stores control and reordering

4.27 (a) **Under the order cycling method, quantities on hand of each stores item are reviewed periodically** (every 1, 2 or 3 months). For low-cost items, a technique called the 90-60-30 day technique can be used, so that when stocks fall to 60 days' supply, a fresh order is placed for a 30 days' supply so as to boost stocks to 90 days' supply. For high-cost items, a more stringent stores control procedure is advisable so as to keep down the costs of stock holding.

(b) **The two-bin system of stores control (or visual method of control) is one whereby each stores item is kept in two storage bins.** When the first bin is emptied, an order must be placed for re-supply; the second bin will contain sufficient quantities to last until the fresh delivery is received. This is a simple system which is not costly to operate but it is not based on any formal analysis of stock usage and may result in the holding of too much or too little stock.

(c) **Materials items may be classified as expensive, inexpensive or in a middle-cost range.** Because of the practical advantages of simplifying stores control procedures without incurring unnecessary high costs, it may be possible to segregate materials for selective stores control.

 (i) Expensive and medium-cost materials are subject to careful stores control procedures to minimise cost.

 (ii) Inexpensive materials can be stored in large quantities because the cost savings from careful stores control do not justify the administrative effort required to implement the control.

This selective approach to stores control is sometimes called the **ABC method** whereby materials are classified A, B or C according to their expense-group A being the expensive, group B the medium-cost and group C the inexpensive materials.

(d)   A similar selective approach to stores control is the **Pareto (80/20) distribution** is based on the finding that in many stores, 80% of the value of stores is accounted for by only 20% of the stores items, and stocks of these more expensive items should be controlled more closely.

5   STOCK VALUATION

5.1   You may be aware from your studies for Paper 1.1 **Preparing Financial Statements** that, for financial accounting purposes, stocks are valued at the **lower of cost and net realisable value**. In practice, stocks will probably be valued at cost in the stores records throughout the course of an accounting period. Only when the period ends will the value of the stock in hand be reconsidered so that items with a net realisable value below their original cost will be revalued downwards, and the stock records altered accordingly.

Charging units of stock to cost of production or cost of sales

5.2   It is important to be able to distinguish between the way in which the physical items in stock are actually issued. In practice a storekeeper may issue goods in the following way.

- The oldest goods first
- The latest goods received first
- Randomly
- Those which are easiest to reach

5.3   By comparison the cost of the goods issued must be determined on a **consistently applied basis**, and must ignore the likelihood that the materials issued will be costed at a price different to the amount paid for them.

5.4   This may seem a little confusing at first, and it may be helpful to explain the point further. Suppose that there are three units of a particular material in stock.

Units	Date received	Purchase cost
A	June 20X1	£100
B	July 20X1	£106
C	August 20X1	£109

In September, one unit is issued to production. As it happened, the physical unit actually issued was B. The accounting department must put a value or cost on the material issued, but the value would not be the cost of B, £106. The principles used to value the materials issued are not concerned with the actual unit issued, A, B, or C. Nevertheless, the accountant may choose to make one of the following assumptions.

(a)   The unit issued is valued as though it were the earliest unit in stock, ie at the purchase cost of A, £100. This valuation principle is called **FIFO**, or **first in, first out**.

(b)   The unit issued is valued as though it were the most recent unit received into stock, ie at the purchase cost of C, £109. This method of valuation is **LIFO**, or **last in, first out**.

(c)   The unit issued is valued at an average price of A, B and C, ie £105.

5.5   In the following sections we will consider each of the pricing methods detailed above (and a few more), using the following transactions to illustrate the principles in each case.

TRANSACTIONS DURING MAY 20X3

	Quantity	Unit cost	Total cost	Market value per unit on date of transaction
	Units	£	£	£
Opening balance, 1 May	100	2.00	200	
Receipts, 3 May	400	2.10	840	2.11
Issues, 4 May	200			2.11
Receipts, 9 May	300	2.12	636	2.15
Issues, 11 May	400			2.20
Receipts, 18 May	100	2.40	240	2.35
Issues, 20 May	100			2.35
Closing balance, 31 May	200			2.38
			1,916	

6 FIFO (FIRST IN, FIRST OUT)

6.1 **FIFO assumes that materials are issued out of stock in the order in which they were delivered into stock:** issues are priced at the cost of the earliest delivery remaining in stock.

Using **FIFO**, the cost of issues and the closing stock value in the example would be as follows.

Date of issue	Quantity issued	Value		
	Units		£	£
4 May	200	100 o/s at £2	200	
		100 at £2.10	210	
				410
11 May	400	300 at £2.10	630	
		100 at £2.12	212	
				842
20 May	100	100 at £2.12		212
Cost of issues				1,464
Closing stock value	200	100 at £2.12	212	
		100 at £2.40	240	
				452
				1,916

Notes

(a) The cost of materials issued plus the value of closing stock equals the cost of purchases plus the value of opening stock (£1,916).

(b) The market price of purchased materials is rising dramatically. In a period of inflation, there is a tendency with FIFO for materials to be issued at a cost lower than the current market value, although closing stocks tend to be valued at a cost approximating to current market value.

6.2 The advantages and disadvantages of the **FIFO** method are as follows.

Advantages	Disadvantages
It is a logical pricing method which probably represents what is physically happening: in practice the oldest stock is likely to be used first.	FIFO can be cumbersome to operate because of the need to identify each batch of material separately.
It is easy to understand and explain to managers.	Managers may find it difficult to compare costs and make decisions when they are charged with varying prices for the same materials.
The stock valuation can be near to a valuation based on replacement cost.	In a period of high inflation, stock issue prices will lag behind current market value.

Question 9

Draw up an extract from a stores ledger account using the columns shown below. Complete the columns in as much details as possible using the information in Paragraphs 5.5 and 6.1.

		STORES LEDGER ACCOUNT									
Date	Receipts				Issues				Stock		
	GRN No	Quantity	Unit price £	Amount £	Stores Req No	Quantity	Unit price £	Amount £	Quantity	Unit price £	Amount £

Answer

	STORES LEDGER ACCOUNT (extract)										
Date	Receipts				Issues				Stock		
	GRN No.	Quantity	Unit price £	Amount £	Stores Req. No.	Quantity	Unit price £	Amount £	Quantity	Unit price £	Amount £
1.5.X3									100	2.00	200.00
3.5.X3		400	2.10	840.00					100	2.00	200.00
									400	2.10	840.00
									500		1,040.00
4.5.X3						100	2.00	200.00			
						100	2.10	210.00	300	2.10	630.00
9.5.X3		300	2.12	636.00					300	2.10	630.00
									300	2.12	636.00
									600		1,266.00
11.5.X3						300	2.10	630.00			
						100	2.12	212.00	200	2.12	424.00
18.5.X3		100	2.40	240.00					200	2.12	424.00
									100	2.40	240.00
									300		664.00
20.5.X3						100	2.12	212.00	100	2.12	212.00
									100	2.40	240.00
31.5.X3									200		452.00

7 LIFO (LAST IN, FIRST OUT)

7.1 **LIFO assumes that materials are issued out of stock in the reverse order to which they were delivered:** the most recent deliveries are issued before earlier ones, and are priced accordingly.

Using LIFO, the cost of issues and the closing stock value in the example above would be as follows.

Date of issue	Quantity issued Units	Valuation	£	£
4 May	200	200 at £2.10		420
11 May	400	300 at £2.12	636	
		100 at £2.10	210	
				846
20 May	100	100 at £2.40		240
Cost of issues				1,506
Closing stock value	200	100 at £2.10	210	
		100 at £2.00	200	
				410
				1,916

Notes

(a) The cost of materials issued plus the value of closing stock equals the cost of purchases plus the value of opening stock (£1,916).

(b) In a period of inflation there is a tendency with **LIFO** for the following to occur.

(i) Materials are issued at a price which approximates to current market value.

(ii) Closing stocks become undervalued when compared to market value.

7.2 The advantages and disadvantages of the **LIFO** method are as follows.

Advantages	Disadvantages
Stocks are issued at a price which is close to current market value.	The method can be cumbersome to operate because it sometimes results in several batches being only part-used in the stock records before another batch is received.
Managers are continually aware of recent costs when making decisions, because the costs being charged to their department or products will be current costs.	LIFO is often the opposite to what is physically happening and can therefore be difficult to explain to managers.
	As with FIFO, decision making can be difficult because of the variations in prices.

8 CUMULATIVE WEIGHTED AVERAGE PRICING

8.1 The cumulative weighted average pricing method calculates a **weighted average price** for all units in stock. Issues are priced at this average cost, and the balance of stock remaining would have the same unit valuation. The average price is determined by dividing the total cost by the total number of units.

A new weighted average price is calculated whenever a new delivery of materials into store is received. This is the key feature of cumulative weighted average pricing.

8.2 In our example, issue costs and closing stock values would be as follows.

Date	Received Units	Issued Units	Balance Units	Total stock value £	Unit cost £	£
Opening stock			100	200	2.00	
3 May	400			840	2.10	
			* 500	1,040	2.08	
4 May		200		(416)	2.08	416
			300	624	2.08	
9 May	300			636	2.12	
			* 600	1,260	2.10	
11 May		400		(840)	2.10	840
			200	420	2.10	
18 May	100			240	2.40	
			* 300	660	2.20	
20 May		100		(220)	2.20	220
						1,476
Closing stock value			200	440	2.20	440
						1,916

* A new stock value per unit is calculated whenever a new receipt of materials occurs.

Notes

(a) The cost of materials issued plus the value of closing stock equals the cost of purchases plus the value of opening stock (£1,916).

(b) In a period of inflation, using the cumulative weighted average pricing system, the value of material issues will rise gradually, but will tend to lag a little behind the

BPP PUBLISHING

current market value at the date of issue. Closing stock values will also be a little below current market value.

8.3 The advantages and disadvantages of **cumulative weighted average pricing** are these.

Advantages	Disadvantages
Fluctuations in prices are smoothed out, making it easier to use the data for decision making.	The resulting issue price is rarely an actual price that has been paid, and can run to several decimal places.
It is easier to administer than FIFO and LIFO, because there is no need to identify each batch separately.	Prices tend to lag a little behind current market values when there is gradual inflation.

9 OTHER METHODS OF PRICING AND VALUATION

Periodic weighted average pricing

9.1 Under the periodic weighted average pricing method, a retrospective average price is calculated for *all* materials issued during the period. The average issue price is calculated for our example as follows.

$$\frac{\text{Cost of all receipts in the period} + \text{Cost of opening stock}}{\text{Number of units received in the period} + \text{Number of units of opening stock}} = \frac{£1,716 + £200}{800 + 100}$$

Issue price = £2.129 per unit

Closing stock values are a balancing figure.

9.2 The issue costs and closing stock values are calculated as follows.

Date of issue	*Quantity issued* Units	*Valuation* £
4 May	200 × £2.129	426
11 May	400 × £2.129	852
20 May	100 × £2.129	213
Cost of issues		1,491
Value of opening stock plus purchases		1,916
Value of 200 units of closing stock (at £2.129)		425

9.3 The periodic weighted average pricing method is easier to calculate than the cumulative weighted average method, and therefore requires less effort, but it must be applied retrospectively since the costs of materials used cannot be calculated until the end of the period.

Standard cost pricing

9.4 **Under the standard cost pricing method, all issues are at predetermined standard price.** Such a method is used with a system of standard costing, which will be covered later in this text when we study standard costing (in Chapter 24).

Replacement cost pricing

9.5 Arguments for **replacement cost pricing** include the following.

(a) When materials are issued out of stores, they will be replaced with a new delivery; issues should therefore be priced at the current cost to the business of replacing them in stores.

(b) Closing stocks should be valued at current replacement cost in the balance sheet to show the true value of the assets of the business.

9.6 The advantages and disadvantages of **replacement costing** are as follows.

Advantages	Disadvantages
Issues are at up-to-date costs so that managers can take recent trends into account when making decisions based on their knowledge of the costs being incurred.	The price may not be an actual price paid, and a difference will then arise on issues.
It is recommended as a method of accounting for inflation.	It can be difficult to determine the replacement cost.
It is easy to operate once the replacement cost has been determined.	The method is not acceptable to the Inland Revenue or for SSAP 9, although this should not be a major consideration in internal cost accounts.

Question 10

Which pricing method can be used as a practical alternative to replacement cost pricing?

Answer

LIFO is a reasonably accurate method of accounting for inflation provided that closing stock values are periodically reviewed and revalued.

Highest in, first out (HIFO)

9.7 This method values issues at the highest price of the items in stock at the time of issue. Although prudent it is an approach which does not follow any particular chronological order.

Next in, first out (NIFO)

9.8 This method values issues at the price to be paid for the next delivery, which may or may not be the same as replacement cost. This method does value issues at the most up-to-date price but it is administratively difficult.

Specific price

9.9 This method values issues at their individual price and the stock balance is made up of individual items valued at individual prices. It is only really suitable for expensive stock lines where stock holdings and usage rates are low.

10   STOCK VALUATION AND PROFITABILITY

10.1   In the previous descriptions of FIFO, LIFO, average costing and so on, the example used raw materials as an illustration. Each method produced different figures for both the value of closing stocks and also the cost of material issues. Since raw materials costs affect the cost of production, and the cost of production works through eventually into the cost of sales, it follows that different methods of stock valuation will provide different profit figures. The following example will help to illustrate the point.

10.2   EXAMPLE: STOCK VALUATION AND PROFITABILITY

On 1 November 20X2, Delilah's Dresses (Haute Couture Emporium) held 3 pink satin dresses with orange sashes, designed by Freda Swoggs. These were valued at £120 each. During November 20X2, 12 more of the dresses were delivered as follows.

Date	Units received	Purchase cost per dress
10 November	4	£125
20 November	4	£140
25 November	4	£150

A number of the pink satin dresses with orange sashes were sold during November as follows.

Date	Dresses sold	Sales price per dress
14 November	5	£200
21 November	5	£200
28 November	1	£200

Required

Calculate the gross profit (sales – (opening stock + purchases – closing stock)) from selling the pink satin dresses with orange sashes in November 20X2, applying the following principles of stock valuation.

(a)   FIFO
(b)   LIFO
(c)   Cumulative weighted average pricing

10.3   SOLUTION

(a) **FIFO** Date	Cost of sales	Total £	Closing stock £
14 November	3 units × £120 + 2 units × £125		
		610	
21 November	2 units × £125 + 3 units × £140		
		670	
28 November	1 unit × £140	140	
Closing stock	4 units × £150		600
		1,420	600

(b) **LIFO**

Date	Cost of sales	Total £	Closing stock £
14 November	4 units × £125 + 1 unit × £120	620	
21 November	4 units × £140 + 1 unit × £120	680	
28 November	1 unit × £150	150	
Closing stock	3 units × £150 + 1 unit × £120		570
		1,450	570

(c) **Cumulative weighted average pricing**

		Unit cost £	Balance in stock £	Cost of sales £	Closing stock £
1 November	3	120.00	360		
10 November	4	125.00	500		
	7	122.86	860		
14 November	5	122.86	614	614	
	2		246		
20 November	4	140.00	560		
	6	134.33	806		
21 November	5	134.33	672	672	
	1		134		
25 November	4	150.00	600		
	5	146.80	734		
28 November	1	146.80	147	147	
30 November	4	146.80	587	1,433	587

Profitability

	FIFO £	LIFO £	Weighted average £
Opening stock	360	360	360
Purchases	1,660	1,660	1,660
	2,020	2,020	2,020
Closing stock	600	570	587
Cost of sales	1,420	1,450	1,433
Sales (11 × £200)	2,200	2,200	2,200
Gross profit	780	750	767

10.4 In the example above, **different stock valuation methods produced different costs of sale and hence different profits. As opening stock values and purchase costs are the same for each method, the different costs of sale are due to different closing stock valuations. The differences in profits therefore equal the differences in closing stock valuations.**

10.5 The profit differences are only **temporary**. In the example, the opening stock in December 20X2 will be £600, £570 or £587, depending on the stock valuation method used. Different opening stock values will affect the cost of sales and profits in December, so that in the long run, inequalities in costs of sales each month will even themselves out.

11 LEDGER ENTRIES RELATING TO MATERIALS

11.1 In cost accounting, we are concerned not only with the cost of individual items of stock, but with the total costs of all raw material stocks used, and the total costs of all finished goods sold during an accounting period. These total costs, which are the sum of all the costs on individual stores ledger records, are recorded as follows.

(a)   In a **raw material stores account,** or stores ledger control account, for raw materials stocks.
(b)   In a **finished goods stock (control) account,** for finished goods stocks.

The cost of stocks manufactured in the production department is recorded in the **work in progress control account.**

11.2   EXAMPLE: LEDGER ENTRIES FOR MATERIALS

At 1 July 20X6, the total value of items held in store was £50,000. During July the following transactions occurred.

	£
Materials purchased from suppliers, on credit	120,000
Materials returned to suppliers, because they were of unsatisfactory quality	3,000
Materials purchased for cash	8,000
Direct materials issued to the production department	110,000
Indirect materials issued as production overhead costs	25,000
Value of materials written off after a discrepancy was found in a stock check	1,000
Direct materials returned to store from production	4,000

Required

Draw up a stores ledger account and stock adjustment account for July 20X6.

11.3   SOLUTION

(a)   The opening balance of stocks brought forward is a debit balance in the stores account.

(b)   When materials are received which are bought on credit, the accounting entry is to:

DEBIT   Stores account
CREDIT   Trade creditor's (supplier's) account

(c)   When materials are returned to suppliers, the reduction of items in stock and the reduction in the amounts owed to the suppliers is shown by the double entry:

CREDIT   Stores account
DEBIT   Creditor's account

(d)   When materials are purchased for cash, the entry is:

DEBIT   Stores account
CREDIT   Cash (or bank) account

when the goods are received and the cash paid.

(e)   When materials are issued from stores, the reduction in stocks is shown as a credit entry in the stores account. The corresponding debit entry is to work in progress account (for direct materials) or production overhead account (for indirect production materials).

CREDIT   Stores account
DEBIT   Work in progress account or production overhead account

(f)   The entries are reversed when materials are returned to store unused by the department which requisitioned them.

(g)   The accounting entries for stock credit notes or debit notes have already been described, ie for a loss of stocks:

CREDIT   Stores account
DEBIT   Stock adjustment account

(h) The balance on the account at the end of the period will be closing stocks, carried forward as opening stocks at 1 August 20X6.

In our example, the stores account for July 20X6 will be as follows.

STORES ACCOUNT

	£		£
Opening stock b/f	50,000	Returns to suppliers (creditors a/c)	3,000
Purchases (creditors a/c)	120,000		
Purchases (cash a/c)	8,000	Work in progress account - issues	110,000
Returns from WIP (WIP a/c)	4,000	Production overhead a/c -issues	25,000
		Loss of stock - adjustment a/c	1,000
		Closing stock c/f	43,000
	182,000		182,000
Opening stock b/f	43,000		

STOCK ADJUSTMENT ACCOUNT

	£		£
Stores account	1,000	Profit and loss account	1,000

Exam focus point

The pilot paper for **Financial Information for Management** included three multiple choice questions on topics covered in this chapter (worth a total of 6%).

There was also an entire ten mark question covering optimal reorder levels and discounts.

Remember that all questions in this paper are compulsory and it is therefore vital that you are happy with the contents of this chapter.

BPP
PUBLISHING

Chapter roundup

- **Stock control** includes the functions of stock ordering and purchasing, receiving goods into store, storing and issuing stock and controlling the level of stocks.

- Every movement of material in a business should be documented using the following as appropriate: purchase requisition, purchase order, GRN, materials requisition note, materials transfer note and materials returned note.

- **Perpetual inventory** refers to a stock recording system whereby the records (bin cards and stores ledger accounts) are updated for each receipt and issue of stock as it occurs.

- Stocktaking can be carried out on a **continuous** or **periodic** basis.

- **Free stock balance** calculations take account of stock on order from suppliers, and of stock which has been requisitioned but not yet delivered.

- **Stock costs** include purchase costs, holding costs, ordering costs and stockout costs.

- **Stock control levels** can be calculated in order to maintain stocks at the optimum level. The three critical control levels are reorder level, minimum level and maximum level.

- The **economic order quantity** (EOQ) is the order quantity which minimises stock costs. The EOQ can be calculated using a table, graph or formula.

$$EOQ = \sqrt{\frac{2C_o D}{C_H}}$$

- The **economic batch quantity (EBQ)** is a modification of the EOQ and is used when resupply is gradual instead of instantaneous.

$$EBQ = \sqrt{\frac{2C_o D}{C_H(1-D/R)}}$$

- The correct pricing of issues and valuation of stock are of the utmost importance because they have a direct effect on the calculation of profit. Several different methods can be used in practice.

- **FIFO** assumes that materials are issued out of stock in the order in which they were delivered into stock: issues are priced at the cost of the earliest delivery remaining in stock. **LIFO** assumes that materials are issued out of stock in the reverse order to which they were delivered: the most recent deliveries are issued before earlier ones and issues are priced accordingly.

- There are two weighted average methods of pricing: **cumulative weighted average** and **periodic weighted average**.

- Under the **standard costing method**, all issues are at a predetermined standard price.

- Although **replacement costing** is recommended as a method of accounting for inflation, in many instances it is impractical because of the difficulty of maintaining records of replacement market values.

- The total costs of all raw materials stocks used during an accounting period are recorded in a **raw materials stores account**.

- The total costs of all finished goods sold in an accounting period are recorded in a **finished goods (stock) control account**.

- The cost of stocks manufactured in the production department is recorded in the **work in progress control account**.

Quick quiz

1   List six objectives of storekeeping.

   * ....
   * ....
   * ....
   * ....
   * ....
   * ....

2   Free stock represents...

3   Free stock is calculated as follows. (Delete as appropriate)

   (a)   + –   Materials in stock   X
   (b)   + –   Materials in order   X
   (c)   + –   Materials requisitioned (not yet issued)   X
              Free stock balance   X

4   How does periodic stocktaking differ from continuous stocktaking?

5   Match up the following.

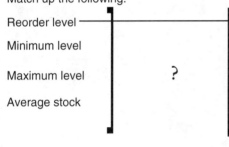

   Reorder level ──────────────▶ Maximum usage × maximum lead time

   Minimum level   Safety stock + $^1/_2$ reorder level

   Maximum level   **?**   Reorder level – (average usage × average lead time)

   Average stock   Reorder level + reorder quantity – (minimum usage × minimum lead time)

6    $$EOQ = \sqrt{\frac{2C_o D}{C_H}}$$

   Where

   (a) C_H = ...

   (b) C_o = ...

   (c)   D = ...

7   When is the economic batch quantity used?

8   Which of the following are true?

   I   With FIFO, the stock valuation will be very close to replacement cost.

   II   With LIFO, stocks are issued at a price which is close to the current market value.

   III   Decision making can be difficult with both FIFO and LIFO because of the variations in prices.

   IV   A disadvantage of the weighted average method of stock valuation is that the resulting issue price is rarely an actual price that has been paid and it may be calculated to several decimal places.

   A   I and II only
   B   I, II and III only
   C   I and III only
   D   I, II, III and IV

9   In which ledger account is the cost of stocks manufactured in the production department recorded?

BPP PUBLISHING

Answers to quick quiz

1   •   Speedy **issue** and **receipt** of materials
    •   Full **identification** of all materials at all times
    •   Correct **location** of all materials at all times
    •   **Protection** of materials from damage and deterioration
    •   Provision of **secure stores** to avoid pilferage, theft and fire
    •   **Efficient** use of storage space
    •   **Maintenance** of correct stock levels
    •   Keeping correct and up-to-date **records** of receipts, issues and stock levels

2   Stock that is readily available for future use.

3   (a)   +
    (b)   +
    (c)   −

4   **Periodic stocktaking.** All stock items physically counted and valued, usually annually.

    Continuous stocktaking. Counting and valuing selected items at different times of the year (at least once a year).

5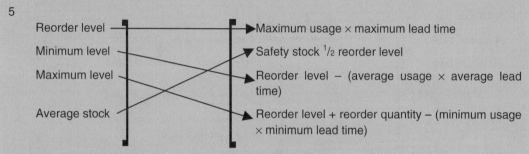

   Reorder level ———→ Maximum usage × maximum lead time

   Minimum level ——→ Safety stock $^1/_2$ reorder level

   Maximum level ——→ Reorder level − (average usage × average lead time)

   Average stock ——→ Reorder level + reorder quantity − (minimum usage × minimum lead time)

6   (a)   Cost of holding one unit of stock for one time period
    (b)   Cost of ordering a consignment from a supplier
    (c)   Demand during the time period

7   When resupply of a product is gradual instead of instantaneous.

8   D

9   Work in progress control account

Now try the questions below from the Exam Question Bank

Number	Level	Marks	Time
8	MCQ	n/a	n/a
9	Examination	10	18 mins

Chapter 7

LABOUR COSTS

Topic list	Syllabus reference
1 Measuring labour activity	3(b)
2 Remuneration methods	3(b)
3 Recording labour costs	3(b)
4 Labour turnover	3(b)
5 Accounting for labour costs	3(b)

Introduction

Just as management need to control stocks and operate an appropriate valuation policy in an attempt to control material costs, so too must they be aware of the most suitable **remuneration policy** for their organisation. We will be looking at a number of methods of remuneration and will consider the various types of **incentive scheme** that exist. We will also examine the procedures and documents required for the accurate **recording of labour costs**. **Labour turnover** will be studied too.

Study guide

Section 9 – Labour costs

- Explain the difference between, and calculate direct and indirect labour costs
- Explain the methods used to relate input labour costs to work done
- Prepare journal and ledger entries to record labour cost inputs and outputs
- Describe and illustrate different remuneration methods and incentive schemes
- Calculate the level and analyse the costs and causes of, labour turnover
- Describe and illustrate measures of labour efficiency and utilisation
- Interpret the entries and balances in the labour account

Exam guide

Labour costs is a key area of the syllabus. You can expect to see questions on this topic in both sections of the examination.

BPP PUBLISHING

1   MEASURING LABOUR ACTIVITY

> **KEY TERMS**
>
> - **Production** is the quantity or volume of output produced.
>
> - **Standard hour of production** is a concept used in standard costing, and means the number of units that can be produced by one worker working in the standard way at the standard rate for one hour.
>
> - **Productivity** is a measure of the efficiency with which output has been produced.

1.1   Suppose that an employee is expected to produce three units in every hour that he works. The standard rate of productivity is three units per hour, and one unit is valued at $\frac{1}{3}$ of a standard hour of output. If, during one week, the employee makes 126 units in 40 hours of work the following comments can be made.

(a)   **Production** in the week is 126 units.

(b)   **Productivity** is a relative measure of the hours actually taken and the hours that should have been taken to make the output.

(i)	**Either,** 126 units should take	42 hours
	But did take	40 hours
	Productivity ratio = 42/40 × 100% =	105%
(ii)	**Or alternatively,** in 40 hours, he should make (× 3)	120 units
	But did make	126 units
	Productivity ratio = 126/120 × 100% =	105%

A productivity ratio greater than 100% indicates that actual efficiency is better than the expected or 'standard' level of efficiency.

1.2   Management will wish to **plan** and **control** both production levels and labour productivity.

(a)   **Production levels can be raised** as follows.

- Working overtime
- Hiring extra staff
- Sub-contracting some work to an outside firm
- Managing the work force so as to achieve more output.

(b)   **Production levels can be reduced as follows**.

- Cancelling overtime
- Laying off staff

(c)   **Productivity,** if improved, will enable a company to achieve its production targets in fewer hours of work, and therefore at a lower cost.

Productivity and its effect on cost

1.3   **Improved productivity** is an important means of reducing total unit costs. In order to make this point clear, a simple example will be used.

1.4   Clooney Ltd has a production department in its factory consisting of a work team of just two men, Doug and George. Doug and George each work a 40 hour week and refuse to do any overtime. They are each paid £100 per week and production overheads of £400 per week are charged to their work.

(a) In week one, they produce 160 units of output between them. Productivity is measured in units of output per man hour.

Production	160 units
Productivity (80 man hours)	2 units per man hour
Total cost	£600 (labour plus overhead)
Cost per man hour	£7.50
Cost per unit	£3.75

(b) In week two, management pressure is exerted on Doug and George to increase output and they produce 200 units in normal time.

Production	200 units (up by 25%)
Productivity	2.5 units per man hour (up by 25%)
Total cost	£600
Cost per man hour	£7.50 (no change)
Cost per unit	£3.00 (a saving of 20% on the previous cost; 25% on the new cost)

(c) In week three, Doug and George agree to work a total of 20 hours of overtime for an additional £50 wages. Output is again 200 units and overhead charges are increased by £100.

Production	200 units (up 25% on week one)
Productivity (100 man hours)	2 units per hour (no change on week one)
Total cost (£600 + £50 + £100)	£750
Cost per unit	£3.75

(d) Conclusions

  (i) An increase in production without an increase in productivity will not reduce unit costs (week one compared with week three).

  (ii) An **increase in productivity will reduce unit costs** (week one compared with week two).

1.5 **Labour cost control** is largely concerned with **productivity**. Rising wage rates have increased automation, which in turn has improved productivity and reduced costs.

1.6 Where **automation** is introduced, productivity is often, but misleadingly, measured in terms of **output per man-hour**.

Suppose, for example, that a work-team of six men (240 hours per week) is replaced by one machine (40 hours per week) and a team of four men (160 hours per week), and as a result output is increased from 1,200 units per week to 1,600 units.

	Production	*Man hours*	*Productivity*
Before the machine	1,200 units	240	5 units per man hour
After the machine	1,600 units	160	10 units per man hour

Labour productivity has doubled because of the machine, and employees would probably expect extra pay for this success. For control purposes, however, it is likely that a new measure of productivity is required, **output per machine hour**, which may then be measured against a standard output for performance reporting.

Efficiency, capacity and production volume ratios

1.7 Other measures of labour activity include the following.

- Production volume ratio, or activity ratio
- Efficiency ratio (or productivity ratio)
- Capacity ratio

Efficiency ratio	$\times$ **Capacity ratio**	$=$ **Production volume ratio**
$\dfrac{\text{Expected hours to make output}}{\text{Actual hours taken}}$	$\times \quad \dfrac{\text{Actual hours worked}}{\text{Hours budgeted}}$	$= \dfrac{\text{Output measured in expected or standard hours}}{\text{Hours budgeted}}$

These ratios are usually expressed as percentages.

1.8 EXAMPLE: RATIOS

Rush and Fluster Ltd budgets to make 25,000 standard units of output (in four hours each) during a budget period of 100,000 hours.

Actual output during the period was 27,000 units which took 120,000 hours to make.

Required

Calculate the efficiency, capacity and production volume ratios.

1.9 SOLUTION

(a) Efficiency ratio $\quad \dfrac{(27{,}000 \times 4) \text{ hours}}{120{,}000} \times 100\% = 90\%$

(b) Capacity ratio $\quad \dfrac{120{,}000 \text{ hours}}{100{,}000 \text{ hours}} \times 100\% = 120\%$

(c) Production volume ratio $\quad \dfrac{(27{,}000 \times 4) \text{ hours}}{100{,}000} \times 100\% = 108\%$

(d) The production volume ratio of 108% (more output than budgeted) is explained by the 120% capacity working, offset to a certain extent by the poor efficiency ($90\% \times 120\% = 108\%$).

1.10 Where efficiency standards are associated with remuneration schemes they generally allow 'normal time' (that is, time required by the average person to do the work under normal conditions) plus an allowance for rest periods and possible delays. There should therefore be a readily achievable standard of efficiency (otherwise any remuneration scheme will fail to motivate employees), but without being so lax that it makes no difference to the rate at which work is done.

2 REMUNERATION METHODS

2.1 Labour remuneration methods have an effect on the following.

- The cost of finished products and services.
- The morale and efficiency of employees.

2.2 There are three basic groups of remuneration method.

- Time work
- Piecework schemes
- Bonus/incentive schemes

Time work

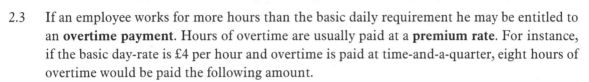

FORMULA TO LEARN

The most common form of **time work** is a **day-rate system** in which wages are calculated by the following formula.

Wages = Hours worked × rate of pay per hour

2.3 If an employee works for more hours than the basic daily requirement he may be entitled to an **overtime payment**. Hours of overtime are usually paid at a **premium rate**. For instance, if the basic day-rate is £4 per hour and overtime is paid at time-and-a-quarter, eight hours of overtime would be paid the following amount.

	£
Basic pay (8 × £4)	32
Overtime premium (8 × £1)	8
Total (8 × £5)	40

2.4 The **overtime premium** is the extra rate per hour which is paid, not the whole of the payment for the overtime hours.

2.5 If employees work unsocial hours, for instance overnight, they may be entitled to a **shift premium**. The extra amount paid per hour, above the basic hourly rate, is the **shift premium**.

2.6 **Day-rate systems** may be summarised as follows.

(a) They are easy to understand.

(b) They do not lead to very complex negotiations when they are being revised.

(c) They are most appropriate when the quality of output is more important than the quantity, or where there is no basis for payment by performance.

(d) There is no incentive for employees who are paid on a day-rate basis to improve their performance.

Piecework schemes

FORMULA TO LEARN

In a **piecework scheme**, wages are calculated by the following formula.

Wages = Units produced × Rate of pay per unit

2.7 Suppose for example, an employee is paid £1 for each unit produced and works a 40 hour week. Production overhead is added at the rate of £2 per direct labour hour.

Weekly production Units	Pay (40 hours) £	Overhead £	Conversion cost £	Conversion cost per unit £
40	40	80	120	3.00
50	50	80	130	2.60
60	60	80	140	2.33
70	70	80	150	2.14

As his output increases, his wage increases and at the same time unit costs of output are reduced.

2.8 It is normal for pieceworkers to be offered a **guaranteed minimum wage,** so that they do not suffer loss of earnings when production is low through no fault of their own.

Question 1

Penny Pincher is paid 50p for each towel she weaves, but she is guaranteed a minimum wage of £60 for a 40 hour week. In a series of four weeks, she makes 100, 120, 140 and 160 towels.

Required

Calculate her pay each week, and the conversion cost per towel if production overhead is added at the rate of £2.50 per direct labour hour.

Answer

Week	Output		Pay	Production overhead	Conversion cost	Unit conversion cost
	Units		£	£	£	£
1	100	(minimum)	60	100	160	1.60
2	120		60	100	160	1.33
3	140		70	100	170	1.21
4	160		80	100	180	1.13

There is no incentive to Penny Pincher to produce more output unless she can exceed 120 units in a week. The guaranteed minimum wage in this case is too high to provide an incentive.

2.9 If employee makes several different types of product, it may not be possible to add up the units for payment purposes. Instead, a **standard time allowance** is given for each unit to arrive at a total of piecework hours for payment.

2.10 EXAMPLE: PIECEWORK

An employee is paid £5 per piecework hour produced. In a 35 hour week he produces the following output.

	Piecework time allowed per unit
3 units of product A	2.5 hours
5 units of product B	8.0 hours

Required

Calculate the employee's pay for the week.

2.11 SOLUTION

Piecework hours produced are as follows.

Product A	3 × 2.5 hours	7.5 hours
Product B	5 × 8 hours	40.0 hours
Total piecework hours		47.5 hours

Therefore employee's pay = 47.5 × £5 = £237.50 for the week.

Differential piecework schemes

2.12 **Differential piecework schemes** offer an incentive to employees to increase their output by paying higher rates for increased levels of production. For example:

up to 80 units per week, rate of pay per unit	=	£1.00
80 to 90 units per week, rate of pay per unit	=	£1.20
above 90 units per week, rate of pay per unit	=	£1.30

Employers should obviously be careful to make it clear whether they intend to pay the increased rate on all units produced, or on the extra output only.

Piecework schemes generally

2.13 **Piecework schemes** may be summarised as follows.

- They enjoy fluctuating popularity.
- They are occasionally used by employers as a means of increasing pay levels.
- They are often seen to drive employees to work too hard to earn a satisfactory wage.

Careful inspection of output is necessary to ensure that quality doesn't fall as production increases.

Bonus/incentive schemes

2.14 In general, **bonus schemes** were introduced to compensate workers paid under a time-based system for their inability to increase earnings by working more efficiently. Various types of incentive and bonus schemes have been devised which encourage greater productivity. The characteristics of such schemes are as follows.

(a) Employees are paid more for their efficiency.

(b) The profits arising from productivity improvements are shared between employer and employee.

(c) Morale of employees is likely to improve since they are seen to receive extra reward for extra effort.

2.15 A bonus scheme must satisfy certain conditions to operate successfully.

(a) Its **objectives** should be **clearly stated** and **attainable** by the employees.

(b) The **rules** and conditions of the scheme should be **easy to understand**.

(c) It must **win** the full **acceptance** of everyone concerned.

(d) It should be seen to be **fair to employees and employers**..

(e) The bonus should ideally be **paid soon after the extra effort has been made** by the employees.

(f) **Allowances** should be made for external factors outside the employees' control which reduce their productivity (machine breakdowns, material shortages).

(g) Only those employees who make the extra effort should be rewarded.

(h) The scheme must be **properly communicated** to employees.

2.16 We shall be looking at the following types of incentive schemes in detail.

- High day rate system
- Individual bonus schemes

- Group bonus schemes
- Profit sharing schemes
- Incentive schemes involving shares
- Value added incentive schemes

Some organisations employ a variety of incentive schemes. A scheme for a production labour force may not necessarily be appropriate for white-collar workers. An organisation's incentive schemes may be regularly reviewed, and altered as circumstances dictate.

High day-rate system

KEY TERM

A **high day-rate system** is a system where employees are paid a high hourly wage rate in the expectation that they will work more efficiently than similar employees on a lower hourly rate in a different company.

2.17 For example if an employee would make 100 units in a 40 hour week if he were paid £2 per hour, but 120 units if he were paid £2.50 per hour, and if production overhead is added to cost at the rate of £2 per direct labour hour, costs per unit of output would be as follows.

(a) Costs per unit of output on the low day-rate scheme would be:

$$\frac{(40 \times £4)}{100} = £1.60 \text{ per unit}$$

(b) Costs per unit of output on the high day-rate scheme would be:

$$\frac{(40 \times £4.50)}{120} = £1.50 \text{ per unit}$$

(c) Note that in this example the labour cost per unit is lower in the first scheme (80p) than in the second (83.3p), but the unit conversion cost (labour plus production overhead) is higher because overhead costs per unit are higher at 80p than with the high day-rate scheme (66.7p).

(d) In this example, the high day-rate scheme would reward both employer (a lower unit cost by 10p) and employee (an extra 50p earned per hour).

2.18 There are two **advantages** of a high day-rate scheme over other incentive schemes.

(a) It is **simple** to calculate and **easy** to understand.
(b) It **guarantees** the employee a consistently **high wage**.

2.19 The **disadvantages** of such schemes are as follows.

(a) **Employees cannot earn more than the fixed hourly rate for their extra effort**. In the previous example, if the employee makes 180 units instead of 120 units in a 40 hour week on a high day-rate pay scheme, the cost per unit would fall to £1 but his wage would be the same - 40 hours at £4.50. All the savings would go to benefit the company and none would go to the employee.

(b) **There is no guarantee that the scheme will work consistently**. The high wages may become the accepted level of pay for normal working, and supervision may be necessary to ensure that a high level of productivity is maintained. Unit costs would rise.

(c) **Employees may prefer to work at a normal rate of output**, even if this entails accepting the lower wage paid by comparable employers.

Individual bonus schemes

> **KEY TERM**
>
> An **individual bonus scheme** is a remuneration scheme whereby **individual** employees qualify for a bonus on top of their basic wage, with each person's bonus being calculated separately.

2.20 (a) The bonus is **unique** to the individual. It is not a share of a group bonus.

(b) The individual can earn a bonus by working at an **above-target** standard of efficiency.

(c) The individual earns a **bigger bonus the greater his efficiency**, although the bonus scheme might incorporate quality safeguards, to prevent individuals from sacrificing quality standards for the sake of speed and more pay.

2.21 To be successful, however, an **individual bonus scheme** must take account of the following factors.

(a) Each individual should be rewarded for the **work done by that individual**. This means that each person's output and time must be measured separately. Each person must therefore work without the assistance of anyone else.

(b) Work should be **fairly routine**, so that standard times can be set for jobs.

(c) The bonus should be **paid soon after the work is done**, to provide the individual with the incentive to try harder.

Group bonus schemes

> **KEY TERM**
>
> A **group bonus scheme** is an incentive plan which is related to the output performance of an entire group of workers, a department, or even the whole factory.

2.22 Where individual effort cannot be measured, and employees work as a team, an individual incentive scheme is impracticable but a **group bonus scheme** would be feasible.

2.23 The other **advantages** of group bonus schemes are as follows.

(a) They are **easier to administer** because they reduce the clerical effort required to measure output and calculate individual bonuses.

(b) They **increase co-operation** between fellow workers.

(c) They have been found to **reduce** accidents, spoilage, waste and absenteeism.

2.24 Serious **disadvantages** would occur in the following circumstances.

(a) The employee groups demand **low efficiency standards** as a condition of accepting the scheme.

(b) Individual employees are browbeaten by their fellow workers for working too slowly.

Profit-sharing schemes

> **KEY TERM**
>
> A **profit sharing scheme** is a scheme in which employees receive a certain proportion of their company's year-end profits (the size of their bonus being related to their position in the company and the length of their employment to date).

2.25 The advantage of these schemes is that the company will only pay what it can afford out of actual profits and the bonus can be paid also to non-production personnel.

The disadvantages of profit sharing are as follows.

(a) Employees must **wait until the year end** for a bonus. The company is therefore expecting a long-term commitment to greater efforts and productivity from its workers without the incentive of immediate reward.

(b) **Factors** affecting profit may be **outside the control** of employees, in spite of their greater efforts.

(c) **Too many employees** are involved in a single scheme for the scheme to have a great motivating effect on individuals.

Incentive schemes involving shares

2.26 It is becoming increasingly common for companies to use their shares, or the right to acquire them, as a form of incentive.

> **KEY TERMS**
>
> • A **share option scheme** is a scheme in which gives its members the right to buy shares in the company for which they work at a set date in the future and at a price usually determined when the scheme is set up.
>
> • An **employee share ownership plan (ESOP)** is a scheme which acquires shares on behalf of a number of employees, and it must distribute these shares within 20 years of acquisition.

The Government has encouraged companies to set up schemes of this nature in the hope that workers will feel they have a stake in the company which employs them. The **disadvantages** of these schemes are as follows.

(a) As the benefits are not certain, as the market value of shares at a future date cannot realistically be predicted in advance.

(b) The benefits are not immediate, as a scheme must be in existence for a number of years before members can exercise their rights.

Value added incentive schemes

2.27 **Value added is an alternative to profit as a business performance measure** and it can be used as the basis of an incentive scheme. It is calculated as follows.

> **KEY TERM**
>
> **Value added** = sales − cost of bought-in materials and services

The advantage of value added over profit as the basis for an incentive scheme is that it excludes any bought-in costs, and is affected only by costs incurred internally, such as labour.

A basic value added figure would be agreed as the target for a business, and some of any excess value added earned would be paid out as a bonus. For example, it could be agreed that value added should be, say, treble the payroll costs and a proportion of any excess earned, say one third, would be paid as bonus.

Payroll costs for month	£40,000
Therefore, value added target (× 3)	£120,000
Value added achieved	£150,000
Therefore, excess value added	£30,000
Employee share to be paid as bonus	£10,000

2.28 EXAMPLE: INCENTIVE SCHEMES

Swetton Tyres Ltd manufactures a single product. Its work force consists of 10 employees, who work a 36-hour week exclusive of lunch and tea breaks. The standard time required to make one unit of the product is two hours, but the current efficiency (or productivity) ratio being achieved is 80%. No overtime is worked, and the work force is paid £4 per attendance hour.

Because of agreements with the work force about work procedures, there is some unavoidable idle time due to bottlenecks in production, and about four hours per week per person are lost in this way.

The company can sell all the output it manufactures, and makes a 'cash profit' of £20 per unit sold, deducting currently achievable costs of production but *before* deducting labour costs.

An incentive scheme is proposed whereby the work force would be paid £5 per hour in exchange for agreeing to new work procedures that would reduce idle time per employee per week to two hours and also raise the efficiency ratio to 90%.

Required

Evaluate the incentive scheme from the point of view of profitability.

2.29 SOLUTION

The current situation

Hours in attendance	10 × 36	=	360 hours
Hours spent working	10 × 32	=	320 hours
Units produced, at 80% efficiency	$\dfrac{320}{2} \times \dfrac{80}{100}$	=	128 units

	£
Cash profits before deducting labour costs (128 × £20)	2,560
Less labour costs (£4 × 360 hours)	1,440
Net profit	1,120

BPP
PUBLISHING

The incentive scheme

Hours spent working	10×34	$=$	340 hours
Units produced, at 90% efficiency	$\dfrac{340}{2} \times \dfrac{90}{100}$	$=$	153 units

	£
Cash profits before deducting labour costs ($153 \times £20$)	3,060
Less labour costs ($£5 \times 360$)	1,800
Net profit	1,260

In spite of a 25% increase in labour costs, profits would rise by £140 per week. The company and the workforce would both benefit provided, of course, that management can hold the work force to their promise of work reorganisation and improved productivity.

Question 2

The following data relate to work at a certain factory.

Normal working day	8 hours
Basic rate of pay per hour	£6
Standard time allowed to produce 1 unit	2 minutes
Premium bonus	75% of time saved at basic rate

What will be the labour cost in a day when 340 units are made?

A £48	B £51	C £63	D £68

Answer

Standard time for 340 units ($\times$ 2 minutes)	680 minutes
Actual time (8 hours per day)	480 minutes
Time saved	200 minutes

	£
Bonus = 75% $\times$ 200 minutes $\times$ £6 per hour	15
Basic pay = 8 hours $\times$ £6	48
Total labour cost	63

Therefore the correct answer is C.

Using basic MCQ technique you can eliminate option A because this is simply the basic pay without consideration of any bonus. You can also eliminate option D, which is based on the standard time allowance without considering the basic pay for the eight-hour day. Hopefully your were not forced to guess, but had you been you would have had a 50% chance of selecting the correct answer (B or C) instead of a 25% chance because you were able to eliminate two of the options straightaway.

3 RECORDING LABOUR COSTS

Organisation for controlling and measuring labour costs

3.1 Several departments and management groups are involved in the collection, recording and costing of labour. These include the following.

- Personnel
- Production planning
- Timekeeping
- Wages
- Cost accounting

Personnel department

3.2 The **personnel department** is responsible for the following.

- Engagement, transfer and discharge of employees.
- Classification and method of remuneration.

The department is headed by a **professional personnel officer** trained in personnel management, labour laws, company personnel policy and industry conditions who should have an understanding of the needs and problems of the employees.

3.3 Additional labour maybe found as follows.

- Contacting recruitment agencies
- Placing advertisements in newspapers and journals (trade)
- Contacting local schools and technical colleges
- Review any CVs held on file of persons known to be available for work

All potential employees/interviewees should complete an application form.

3.4 When a person is engaged a **personnel record card** should be prepared showing full personal particulars, previous employment, medical category and wage rate. Other details to be included are National Insurance number, address, telephone number, transfers, promotions, changes in wage rates, sickness and accidents and, when an employee leaves, the reason for leaving.

3.5 Personnel departments sometimes **maintain records of overtime and shift working**. Overtime has to be sanctioned by the works manager or personnel office who advise the time-keepers who control the time booked.

3.6 The personnel department is responsible for issuing **reports to management** on normal and overtime hours worked, absenteeism and sickness, lateness, labour turnover and disciplinary action.

Production planning department

3.7 This department is responsible for the following.

- Scheduling work
- Issuing job orders to production departments
- Chasing up jobs when they run late

Timekeeping department

3.8 The **timekeeping department** is responsible for recording the attendance time and job time of the following.

- The time spent in the factory by each worker
- The time spent by each worker on each job

Such timekeeping provides basic data for statutory records, payroll preparation, labour costs of an operation or overhead distribution (where based on wages or labour hours) and statistical analysis of labour records for determining productivity and control of labour costs.

Attendance time

3.9 The bare minimum record of employees' time is a simple **attendance record** showing days absent because of holiday, sickness or other reason. A typical record of attendance is shown as follows.

NAME: A.N. OTHER								DEPT: 072						NI REF: WD 4847 41C								LEAVE ENTITLEMENT: 20								
	1	2	3	4	5	6	7	8	9	10	11	12	13	14	15	16	17	18	19	20	21	22	23	24	25	26	27	28	29	30	31
JAN																															
FEB																															
MAR																															
APR																															
MAY																															
JUNE																															
JULY																															
AUG																															
SEPT																															
OCT																															
NOV																															
DEC																															

Illness: I	Leave: L	Training: T	*Note overleaf:* (1) The reasons for special leave (eg bereavement).
Industrial Accident: IA	Unpaid Leave: UL	Jury Service: J	
Maternity: M	Special Leave: SL		(2) Ensure training is noted on personnel card.

RECORD OF ATTENDANCE

3.10 It is also necessary to have a record of the following.

- Time of arrival
- Time of breaks
- Time of departure

These may be recorded as follows.

- In a signing-in book
- By using a time recording clock which stamps the time on a clock card
- By using swipe cards (which made a computer record)

An example of a clock card is shown as follows.

No	Ending
Name	

HOURS	RATE	AMOUNT	DEDUCTIONS	
Basic			Income Tax	
O/T			NI	
Others			Other	
			Total deduction	

Total	
Less deductions	
Net due	

Time	Day	Basic time	Overtime
1230	T		
0803	T		
1700	M		
1305	M		
1234	M		
0750	M		

Signature _ _ _ _ _ _ _ _ _ _ _

Job time

3.11 **Continuous production.** Where **routine, repetitive** work is carried out it might not be practical to record the precise details. For example if a worker stands at a conveyor belt for seven hours his work can be measured by keeping a note of the number of units that pass through his part of the process during that time.

3.12 **Job costing.** When the work is not of a repetitive nature the records required might be one or several of the following.

(a) **Daily time sheets.** A time sheet is filled in by the employee as a record of how their time has been spent. The total time on the time sheet should correspond with time shown on the attendance record.

(b) **Weekly time sheets.** These are similar to daily time sheets but are passed to the cost office at the end of the week. An example of a weekly timesheet is shown below.

Time Sheet No. _ _ _ _ _ _ _ _ _ _ _ _							
Employee Name _ _ _ _ _ _ _ _ Clock Code _ _ _ _ _ _ _ _ Dept _ _ _ _ _ _ _							
Date _ _ _ _ _ _ _ _ _ _ _ _ _ _ _ Week No. _ _ _ _ _ _ _ _ _ _ _							
Job No.	Start Time	Finish Time	Qty	Checker	Hrs	Rate	Extension

(c) **Job cards.** Cards are prepared for each job or batch. When an employee works on a job he or she records on the job card the time spent on that job. Job cards are therefore likely to contain entries relating to numerous employees. On completion of the job it will contain a full record of the times and quantities involved in the job or batch. A typical job card is shown as follows.

JOB CARD			
Department _ _ _ _ _ _ _ _ _ _ _ _ _ _ _ _ _ _ _ Job no _ .			
Date _ . Operation no. _ _ _ _ _ _ _ _ _ _ _ _ _ _ _ _ _ _ _			
Time allowance _ _ _ _ _ _ _ _ _ _ _ _ _ _ _ _ _ Time started _ Time finished _ _ _ _ _ _ _ _ _ _ _ _ _ _ _ _ _ _ _ Hours on the job _ _ _ _ _ _ _ _ _ _ _ _ _ _ _ _ _ _ .			
Description of job	Hours	Rate	Cost
Employee no _ Certified by _ Signature _			

A job card will be given to the employee, showing the work to be done and the expected time it should take. The employee will record the time started and time finished for each job. Breaks for tea and lunch may be noted on the card, as standard times, by the production planning department. The hours actually taken and the cost of those hours will be calculated by the accounting department.

3.13 **Piecework.** The wages of pieceworkers and the labour cost of work done by them is determined from what is known as a **piecework ticket** or an **operation card**. The card records the total number of items (or 'pieces') produced and the number of rejects. Payment is only made for 'good' production.

OPERATION CARD				
Operator's Name _____		Total Batch Quantity _____		
Clock No _____		Start Time _____		
Pay week No _____ Date _____		Stop Time _____		
Part No _____		Works Order No _____		
Operation _____		Special Instructions _____		
Quantity Produced	No Rejected	Good Production	Rate	£
Inspector _____		Operative _____		
Foreman _____		Date _____		
PRODUCTION CANNOT BE CLAIMED WITHOUT A PROPERLY SIGNED CARD				

Note that the attendance record of a pieceworker is required for calculations of holidays, sick pay and so on.

3.14 **Other types of work.** Casual workers are paid from job cards or time sheets. Time sheets are also used where outworkers are concerned.

3.15 Office work can be measured in a similar way, provided that the work can be divided into distinct jobs. Firms of accountants and advertising agencies, for example, book their staff time to individual clients and so make use of time sheets for salaried staff.

Salaried labour

3.16 Even though salaried staff are paid a flat rate monthly, they may be required to prepare timesheets. The reasons are as follows.

(a) Timesheets provide management with information (eg product costs).

(b) Timesheet information may provide a basis for billing for services provided (eg service firms where clients are billed based on the number of hours work done).

(c) Timesheets are used to record hours spent and so support claims for overtime payments by salaried staff.

3.17 An example of a timesheet (as used in the service sector) is shown as follows.

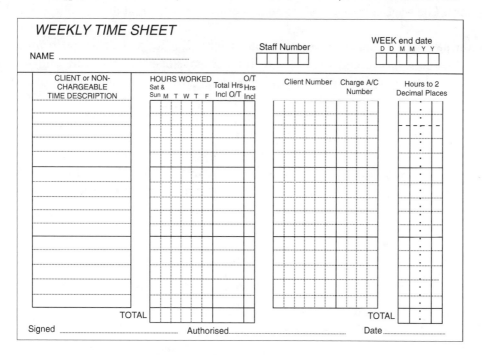

Idle time

3.18 **Idle time** occurs when employees cannot get on with their work, through no fault of their own. Examples are as follows.

- Machine breakdowns
- Shortage of work

3.19 **Idle time** has a cost because employees will still be paid their basic wage or salary for these unproductive hours and so there should be a record of idle time. This may simply comprise an entry on time sheets coded to 'idle time' generally, or separate idle time cards may be prepared. A supervisor might enter the time of a stoppage, its cause, its duration and the employees made idle on an idle time record card. Each stoppage should have a reference number which can be entered on time sheets or job cards.

Wages department

3.20 Responsibilities of the payroll department include the following.

- Preparation of the payroll and payment of wages.
- Maintenance of employee records.
- Summarising wages cost for each cost centre.
- Summarising the hours worked for each cost centre.
- Summarising other payroll information eg bonus payment, pensions etc.
- Providing an internal check for the preparation and payout of wages.

3.21 **Attendance cards** are the basis for payroll preparation. For **time workers,** the gross wage is the product of time attended and rate of pay. To this is added any overtime premium or bonus. For **piece workers,** gross wages are normally obtained by the product of the number of good units produced and the unit rate, with any premiums, bonuses and allowances for incomplete jobs added.

3.22 After calculation of net pay, a pay slip is prepared showing all details of earnings and deductions. The wage envelope or the attendance card may be used for this purpose.

3.23 When the payroll is complete, a coin and note analysis is made and a cheque drawn to cover the total amount. On receipt of the cash, the pay envelopes are made up and sealed. A receipt is usually obtained on payout (the attendance card can be used). Wages of absentees are retained until claimed by an authorised person.

3.24 **Internal checks** are necessary to prevent fraud. One method is to distribute the payroll work so that no person deals completely with any transaction. All calculations should be checked on an adding machine where possible. Makeup of envelopes should not be done by persons who prepare the payroll. The cashier should reconcile his analysis with the payroll summary.

Cost accounting department

3.25 The cost accounting department has the following responsibilities.

- The accumulation and classification of all cost data (which includes labour costs).
- Preparation of cost data reports for management.
- Analysing labour information on time cards and payroll.

3.26 In order to establish the labour cost involved in products, operations, jobs and cost centres, the following documents are used.

- Clock cards
- Job cards
- Idle time cards
- Payroll

3.27 Analyses of labour costs are used for the following.

(a) Charging wages directly attributable to production to the appropriate job or operation.

(b) Charging wages which are not directly attributable to production as follows.

   (i) Idle time of production workers is charged to indirect costs as part of the overheads.

   (ii) Wages costs of supervisors, or store assistants are charged to the overhead costs of the relevant department.

(c) Producing idle time reports which show a summary of the hours lost through idle time, and the cause of the idletime. Idle time may be analysed as follows.

   (i) Controllable eg lack of materials.
   (ii) Uncontrollable eg power failure.

FORMULA TO LEARN

$$\text{Idle time ratio} = \frac{\text{Idle hours}}{\text{Total hours}} \times 100\%$$

3.28 The idle time ratio is useful because it shows the proportion of available hours which were lost as a result of idle time.

4 LABOUR TURNOVER

The reasons for labour turnover

4.1 Some employees will leave their job and go to work for another company or organisation. Sometimes the reasons are unavoidable.

- Illness or accidents
- A family move away from the locality
- Marriage, pregnancy or difficulties with child care provision
- Retirement or death

4.2 Other causes of labour turnover are to some extent controllable.

- Paying a lower wage rate than is available elsewhere.
- Requiring employees to work in unsafe or highly stressful conditions.
- Requiring employees to work uncongenial hours.
- Poor relationships between management and staff.
- Lack of opportunity for career enhancement.
- Requiring employees to work in inaccessible places (eg no public transport).
- Discharging employees for misconduct, bad timekeeping or unsuitability.

Measuring labour turnover

KEY TERM

Labour turnover is a measure of the number of employees leaving/being recruited in a period of time expressed as a percentage of the total labour force.

FORMULA TO LEARN

$$\text{Labour turnover rate} = \frac{\text{Replacements}}{\text{Average number of employees in period}} \times 100\%$$

4.3 EXAMPLE : LABOUR TURNOVER RATE

Revolving Doors plc had a staff of 2,000 at the beginning of 20X1 and, owing to a series of redundancies caused by the recession, 1,000 at the end of the year. Voluntary redundancy was taken by 1,500 staff at the end of June, 500 more than the company had anticipated, and these excess redundancies were immediately replaced by new joiners.

The labour turnover rate is calculated as follows.

$$\text{Rate} = \frac{500}{(2,000 + 1,000) \div 2} \times 100\% = 33\%$$

The costs of labour turnover

4.4 The costs of labour turnover can be large and management should attempt to keep labour turnover as low as possible so as to minimise these costs. The **cost of labour turnover** may be divided into the following.

- Preventative costs
- Replacement costs

4.5 **Replacement costs**. These are the costs incurred as a result of hiring new employees. and they include the following.

- Cost of selection and placement
- Inefficiency of new labour; productivity will be lower
- Costs of training
- Loss of output due to delay in new labour becoming available
- Increased wastage and spoilage due to lack of expertise among new staff
- The possibility of more frequent accidents at work
- Cost of tool and machine breakages

4.6 **Preventative costs** are costs incurred in order to prevent employees leaving and they include the following.
- Cost of personnel administration incurred in maintaining good relationships
- Cost of medical services including check-ups, nursing staff and so on
- Cost of welfare services, including sports facilities and canteen meals
- Pension schemes providing security to employees

The prevention of high labour turnover

4.7 Labour turnover will be reduced by the following actions.
- Paying satisfactory wages
- Offering satisfactory hours and conditions of work
- Creating a good informal relationship between members of the workforce
- Offering good training schemes and a well-understood career or promotion ladder
- Improving the content of jobs to create job satisfaction
- Proper planning so as to avoid redundancies
- Investigating the cause of an apparently high labour turnover

5 ACCOUNTING FOR LABOUR COSTS

5.1 We will use an example to briefly review the principal bookkeeping entries for wages.

5.2 EXAMPLE: THE WAGES CONTROL ACCOUNT

The following details were extracted from a weekly payroll for 750 employees at a factory.

Analysis of gross pay

	Direct workers £	Indirect workers £	Total £
Ordinary time	36,000	22,000	58,000
Overtime: basic wage	8,700	5,430	14,130
premium	4,350	2,715	7,065
Shift allowance	3,465	1,830	5,295
Sick pay	950	500	1,450
Idle time	3,200	-	3,200
	56,665	32,475	89,140
Net wages paid to employees	£45,605	£24,220	£69,825

Required

Prepare the wages control account for the week.

5.3 SOLUTION

(a) **The wages control account** acts as a sort of 'collecting place' for net wages paid and deductions made from gross pay. The gross pay is then analysed between direct and indirect wages.

(b) The first step is to determine which wage costs are **direct** and which are **indirect**. The direct wages will be debited to the work in progress account and the indirect wages will be debited to the production overhead account.

(c) There are in fact only two items of direct wages cost in this example, the ordinary time (£36,000) and the basic overtime wage (£8,700) paid to direct workers. All other payments (including the overtime premium) are indirect wages.

(d) The net wages paid are debited to the control account, and the balance then represents the deductions which have been made for income tax, national insurance, and so on.

WAGES CONTROL ACCOUNT

	£		£
Bank: net wages paid	69,825	Work in progress - direct labour	44,700
Deductions control accounts*		Production overhead control:	
(£89,140 – £69,825)	19,315	Indirect labour	27,430
		Overtime premium	7,065
		Shift allowance	5,295
		Sick pay	1,450
		Idle time	3,200
	89,140		89,140

* In practice there would be a separate deductions control account for each type of deduction made (for example, PAYE and National Insurance).

Direct and indirect labour costs

5.4 We had a brief look at direct and indirect labour costs in Chapter 3. Have a go at the following questions to remind yourself about the classification of labour costs.

Question 3

A direct labour employee's wage in week 5 consists of the following.

		£
(a)	Basic pay for normal hours worked, 36 hours at £4 per hour =	144
(b)	Pay at the basic rate for overtime, 6 hours at £4 per hour =	24
(c)	Overtime shift premium, with overtime paid at time-and-a-quarter ¼ × 6 hours × £4 per hour =	6
(d)	A bonus payment under a group bonus (or 'incentive') scheme - bonus for the month =	30
	Total gross wages in week 5 for 42 hours of work	204

Required

Establish which costs are direct costs and which are indirect costs.

Answer

Items (a) and (b) are direct labour costs of the items produced in the 42 hours worked in week 5.

Overtime premium, item (c), is usually regarded as an overhead expense, because it is 'unfair' to charge the items produced in overtime hours with the premium. Why should an item made in overtime be more costly just because, by chance, it was made after the employee normally clocks off for the day?

Group bonus scheme payments, item (d), are usually overhead costs, because they cannot normally be traced directly to individual products or jobs.

In this example, the direct labour employee costs were £168 in direct costs and £36 in indirect costs.

Question 4

Jaffa plc employs two types of labour: skilled workers, considered to be direct workers, and semi-skilled workers considered to be indirect workers. Skilled workers are paid £8 per hour and semi-skilled £5 per hour.

The skilled workers have worked 20 hours overtime this week, 12 hours on specific orders and 8 hours on general overtime. Overtime is paid at a rate of time and a quarter.

The semi-skilled workers have worked 30 hours overtime, 20 hours for a specific order at a customer's request and the rest for general purposes. Overtime again is paid at time and a quarter.

What would be the total overtime pay considered to be a direct cost for this week?

A   £245
B   £325
C   £345
D   £407.50

Answer

		Direct cost £	Indirect cost £
Skilled workers			
Specific overtime	(12 hours × £8 × 1.25)	120	
General overtime	(8 hours × £10 × 1)	80	
	(8 hours × £10 × 0.25)		20
Semi-skilled workers			
Specific overtime	(20 hours × £5 × 1.25)	125	
General overtime	(10 hours × £5 × 1.25)		62.50
		325	82.50

The correct answer is therefore B.

If you selected option A, you forgot to include the direct cost of the general overtime of £80 for the skilled workers.

If you selected option C, you included the overtime premium for skilled workers' general overtime of £20.

If you selected option D, you calculated the total of direct cost + indirect cost instead of the direct cost.

Exam focus point

Question 4 is very similar to one of the multiple choice questions from the pilot paper for **Financial Information for Management**. The study guide for this paper states that candidates should be able to explain the difference between and calculate direct and indirect labour costs.

Chapter roundup

- **Labour** is a major cost in many businesses and it is therefore vital that you have understood this chapter's topics, a summary of them being set out below.

- **Production** is the quantity or volume of output produced. **Productivity** is a measure of the efficiency with which output has been produced. An increase in production without an increase in productivity will not reduce unit costs.

- There are three basic groups of **remuneration** method, **time work**, **piecework** schemes and **bonus/incentive** schemes.

- Labour attendance time is recorded on, for example, an attendance record or clock card. Job time may be recorded on daily time sheets, weekly time sheets or job cards depending on the circumstances. The manual recording of times on time sheets or job cards, is however, liable to error or even deliberate deception and may be unreliable.

- The labour cost of pieceworkers is recorded on a piecework ticket/operation card.

- **Idle time** has a cost and must, therefore, be recorded.

- **Labour turnover** is the rate at which employees leave a company and this rate should be kept as low as possible. The cost of labour turnover can be divided into **preventative** and **replacement** costs.

- The **wages control account** acts as a collecting place for wages before they are analysed to work in progress and production overhead control accounts.

Quick quiz

1   Distinguish between the terms production and productivity.

2   List five types of incentive scheme.

3   What are the requirements for a successful individual bonus scheme?

4   What is a value added incentive scheme?

5   When does idle time occur?

6   What are the responsibilities of a typical wages department?

7   Define the idle time ratio.

8   List six methods of reducing labour turnover.

BPP
PUBLISHING

Answers to quick quiz

1   •   **Production** is the quantity or volume of output produced
    •   **Productivity** is a measure of the efficiency with which output has been produced

2   •   High day rate system
    •   Individual bonus schemes
    •   Group bonus schemes
    •   Profit sharing schemes
    •   Incentive schemes involving shares
    •   Value added incentive schemes

3   •   Each individual should be rewarded for the work done by that individual
    •   Work should be fairly routine, so that standard times can be set for jobs
    •   The bonus should be paid soon after the work is done

4   **Value added** is an alternative to profit as a business performance measure and it can be used as the basis of an incentive scheme

    Value added = Sales – cost of bought-in materials and services

5   **Idle time** occurs when employees cannot get on with their work, through no fault of their own, for example when machines break down or there is a shortage of work.

6   •   Preparation of the payroll and payment of wages
    •   Maintenance of employee records
    •   Summarising wages cost for each cost centre
    •   Summarising the hours worked for each cost centre
    •   Summarising other payroll information, eg bonus payment, pensions etc
    •   Providing an internal check for the preparation and payout of wages

7   Idle time ratio $= \dfrac{\text{Idle hours}}{\text{Total hours}} \times 100\%$

8   •   Paying satisfactory wages
    •   Offering satisfactory hours and conditions of work
    •   Creating a good informal relationship between members of the workforce
    •   Offering good training schemes and a well-understood career or promotion ladder
    •   Improving the content of jobs to create job satisfaction
    •   Proper planning so as to avoid redundancies
    •   Investigating the cause of an apparently high labour turnover

Now try the questions below from the Exam Question Bank

Number	Level	Marks	Time
10	MCQ	n/a	n/a
11	Examination	10	18 mins

Chapter 8

OVERHEADS AND ABSORPTION COSTING

Introduction

Absorption costing is a method of accounting for overheads. It basically a method of sharing out overheads incurred amongst units produced.

This chapter begins by explaining why absorption costing might be necessary and then provides an overview of how the cost of a unit of product is built up under a system of absorption costing. A detailed analysis of this costing method is then provided, covering the three stages of absorption costing: **allocation**, **apportionment** and **absorption**. You will also see how to account for using absorption costing when it comes to preparing the profit and loss account.

The chapter ends with a brief look at a costing method that might be more appropriate than absorption costing in the current industrial environment, **activity based costing**.

Study guide

Section 10 – Overheads 1

- Describe and justify the process of apportioning manufacturing overhead costs incurred to production

- Allocate and apportion factory overheads using an appropriate basis

- Reapportion service centre costs including the use of the reciprocal method

- Comment on the use of blanket, department, cost driver, actual and predetermined absorption rates

- Identify, calculate and discuss the appropriate absorption rates using relevant bases

BPP
PUBLISHING

- Calculate, explain and account for under- and over-absorbed overheads
- Describe and evaluate methods of attributing non-manufacturing overhead costs to units of output
- Discuss the use of activity based costing (NB ABC calculations are not examinable)
- Explain and illustrate the concept of cost drivers

Section 11 – Overheads 2

- Prepare journal and ledger entries for manufacturing overheads incurred and absorbed

Exam guide

Overhead apportionment and absorption is one of the most important topics in your **Financial Information for Management** studies and is almost certain to appear in the exam you will be facing. Make sure that you study the contents of this chapter and work through the calculations very carefully.

1 OVERHEADS

KEY TERM

Overhead is the cost incurred in the course of making a product, providing a service or running a department, but which cannot be traced directly and in full to the product, service or department.

1.1 Overhead is actually the total of the following.

- Indirect materials
- Indirect labour
- Indirect expenses

1.2 The total of these indirect costs is usually split into the following.

- **Production** overhead
- **Administration** overhead
- **Selling and distribution** overhead

1.3 In cost accounting there are two schools of thought as to the correct method of dealing with overheads.

- Absorption costing
- Marginal costing

2 ABSORPTION COSTING: AN INTRODUCTION

2.1 **The objective of absorption costing is to include in the total cost of a product** (unit, job, process and so on) **an appropriate share of the organisation's total overhead.** An appropriate share is generally taken to mean an amount which reflects the amount of time and effort that has gone into producing a unit or completing a job.

2.2 An organisation with one production department that produces identical units will divide the total overheads among the total units produced. **Absorption costing is a method for sharing overheads between different products on a fair basis.**

Is absorption costing necessary?

2.3 Suppose that a company makes and sells 100 units of a product each week. The prime cost per unit is £6 and the unit sales price is £10. Production overhead costs £200 per week and administration, selling and distribution overhead costs £150 per week. The weekly profit could be calculated as follows.

	£	£
Sales (100 units × £10)		1,000
Prime costs (100 × £6)	600	
Production overheads	200	
Administration, selling and distribution costs	150	
		950
Profit		50

2.4 In absorption costing, overhead costs will be added to each unit of product manufactured and sold.

	£ per unit
Prime cost per unit	6
Production overhead (£200 per week for 100 units)	2
Full factory cost	8

The weekly profit would be calculated as follows.

	£
Sales	1,000
Less factory cost of sales	800
Gross profit	200
Less administration, selling and distribution costs	150
Net profit	50

2.5 Sometimes, but not always, the overhead costs of administration, selling and distribution are also added to unit costs, to obtain a full cost of sales.

	£ per unit
Prime cost per unit	6.00
Factory overhead cost per unit	2.00
Administration etc costs per unit	1.50
Full cost of sales	9.50

The weekly profit would be calculated as follows.

	£
Sales	1,000
Less full cost of sales	950
Profit	50

2.6 It may already be apparent that the weekly profit is £50 no matter how the figures have been presented. So, how does absorption costing serve any useful purpose in accounting?

2.7 The **theoretical justification** for using absorption costing is that all production overheads are incurred in the production of the organisation's output and so each unit of the product receives some benefit from these costs. Each unit of output should therefore be charged with some of the overhead costs.

2.8 The **practical reasons** for using absorption costing are as follows.

   (a) **Stock valuations**. Stock in hand must be valued for two reasons.

      (i) For the closing stock figure in the balance sheet

      (ii) For the cost of sales figure in the profit and loss account

The valuation of stocks will affect profitability during a period because of the way in which the cost of sales is calculated.

> The cost of goods produced
> + the value of opening stocks
> − the value of closing stocks
> = the cost of goods sold.

In our example, closing stocks might be valued at prime cost (£6), but in absorption costing, they would be valued at a fully absorbed factory cost, £8 per unit. (They would not be valued at £9.50, the full cost of sales, because the only costs incurred in producing goods for finished stock are factory costs.)

(b) **Pricing decisions**. Many companies attempt to fix selling prices by calculating the full cost of production or sales of each product, and then adding a margin for profit. In our example, the company might have fixed a gross profit margin at 25% on factory cost, or 20% of the sales price, in order to establish the unit sales price of £10. 'Full cost plus pricing' can be particularly useful for companies which do jobbing or contract work, where each job or contract is different, so that a standard unit sales price cannot be fixed. Without using absorption costing, a full cost is difficult to ascertain.

(c) **Establishing the profitability of different products**. This argument in favour of absorption costing is more contentious, but is worthy of mention here. If a company sells more than one product, it will be difficult to judge how profitable each individual product is, unless overhead costs are shared on a fair basis and charged to the cost of sales of each product.

Statement of standard accounting practice 9 (SSAP 9)

2.9 Of these three arguments, the problem of valuing stocks is perhaps the most significant. **Absorption costing is recommended in financial accounting** by the *Statement of standard accounting practice* on stocks and long-term contracts (SSAP 9). SSAP 9 deals with **financial accounting systems**. The cost accountant is (in theory) free to value stocks by whatever method seems best, but where companies integrate their financial accounting and cost accounting systems into a single system of accounting records, the valuation of closing stocks will be determined by SSAP 9.

2.10 SSAP 9 states that costs of all stocks should comprise those costs which have been incurred in the normal course of business in **bringing the product to its 'present location and condition'**. These costs incurred will include all related production overheads, even though these overheads may accrue on a time basis. In other words, in financial accounting, closing stocks should be valued at full factory cost, and it may therefore be convenient and appropriate to value stocks by the same method in the cost accounting system.

3 PRODUCT COST BUILD-UP USING ABSORPTION COSTING

3.1 The procedure of building up the cost of a unit of production (cost unit) under a system of absorption costing is as follows.

(a) **Direct costs** are **allocated** directly to cost units.

(b) **Indirect costs** which are clearly identifiable with particular administration cost centres, production cost centres, service/backup departments or selling and distribution cost centres are **allocated** to those cost centres. Frequently it is not possible to identify a discrete item of cost with one particular cost centre and so the cost is allocated to an overhead cost centre for the overhead.

(c) The **overheads** within the general overhead cost centre have to be split over several cost centres on an agreed basis. Let us consider rates for example. The cost of rates would first be allocated to the rent and rates cost centre. Although rates are levied upon the premises as a whole, for internal costing purposes they need to be **apportioned** between various cost centres. The basis used for apportioning rates is usually the floor area occupied by the various cost centres. The basis upon which the apportionment is made varies from cost to cost but the basis chosen should produce as fair and equitable a division as possible.

(d) The general overheads apportioned to service/backup departments and the overheads directly allocated to those departments then have to be **apportioned** to production departments.

(e) Costs apportioned to administration cost centres, marketing cost centres, distribution cost centres and so on are not usually included as part of the product cost and are deducted from the full cost of production to arrive at the cost of sales.

(f) The overheads both allocated to the production cost centres and apportioned directly and via the service departments cannot be related directly to cost units but do form part of the total product cost. These overheads must therefore be shared out in some equitable fashion among all the cost units produced. The process by which this is done is known as **overhead absorption**.

(g) Product costs (and non-production and non-service department overheads) are then charged to cost of sales.

The above procedures are set out in the following diagram. Don't worry if the process is not totally clear to you, we will be covering it in greater detail as we work through this chapter.

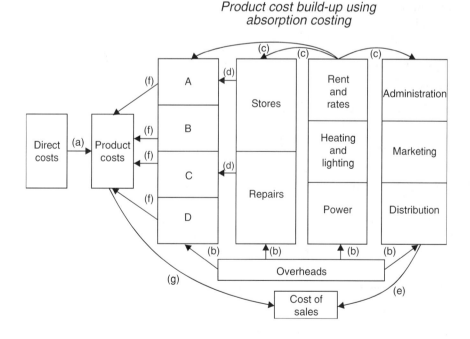

Product cost build-up using absorption costing

4 OVERHEAD ALLOCATION

> **KEY TERM**
>
> **Allocation** is the process by which whole cost items are charged direct to a cost unit or cost centre.

4.1 Cost centres may be one of the following types.

(a) A **production department**, to which production overheads are charged

(b) A **production area service department**, to which production overheads are charged

(c) An **administrative department**, to which administration overheads are charged

(d) A **selling** or a **distribution department**, to which sales and distribution overheads are charged

(e) An **overhead cost centre**, to which items of expense which are shared by a number of departments, such as rent and rates, heat and light and the canteen, are charged

4.2 The following costs would therefore be charged to the following cost centres via the process of allocation.

• Direct labour will be charged to a production cost centre.
• The cost of a warehouse security guard will be charged to the warehouse cost centre.
• Paper (recording computer output) will be charged to the computer department.
• Costs such as the canteen are charged direct to various overhead cost centres.

4.3 As an example of overhead allocation, consider the following costs of a company.

Wages of the foreman of department A	£200
Wages of the foreman of department B	£150
Indirect materials consumed in department A	£50
Rent of the premises shared by departments A and B	£300

The cost accounting system might include three overhead cost centres.

Cost centre:	101	Department A
	102	Department B
	201	Rent

Overhead costs would be allocated directly to each cost centre, ie £200 + £50 to cost centre 101, £150 to cost centre 102 and £300 to cost centre 201. The rent of the factory will be subsequently shared between the two production departments, but for the purpose of day to day cost recording, the rent will first of all be charged in full to a separate cost centre.

5 OVERHEAD APPORTIONMENT

First stage: apportioning general overheads

5.1 **Overhead apportionment** follows on from overhead allocation. The first stage of overhead apportionment is to identify all overhead costs as production department, production service department, administration or selling and distribution overhead. The costs for heat and light, rent and rates, the canteen and so on (ie costs allocated to general overhead cost centres) must therefore be shared out between the other cost centres.

Bases of apportionment

5.2 It is considered important that overhead costs should be shared out on a **fair basis**. You will appreciate that because of the complexity of items of cost it is rarely possible to use only one method of apportioning costs to the various departments of an organisation. The bases of apportionment for the most usual cases are given below.

Overhead to which the basis applies	Basis
Rent, rates, heating and light, repairs and depreciation of buildings	Floor area occupied by each cost centre
Depreciation, insurance of equipment	Cost or book value of equipment
Personnel office, canteen, welfare, wages and cost offices, first aid	Number of employees, or labour hours worked in each cost centre
Heating, lighting (see above)	Volume of space occupied by each cost centre

Exam focus point

If an examination question calls for the apportionment of overhead items, the basis to be used will be obvious in the majority of cases. But you may encounter one or two items for which two (or more) bases may appear to be equally acceptable. In such circumstances, do not take too much time trying to weigh up the merits of each: use the method you prefer. Always indicate the basis of apportionment you have chosen, and in any case of doubt explain why you chose one basis in preference to another.

5.3 EXAMPLE: OVERHEAD APPORTIONMENT

Fire Bases Ltd has incurred the following overhead costs.

	£
Depreciation of factory	1,000
Factory repairs and maintenance	600
Factory office costs (treat as production overhead)	1,500
Depreciation of equipment	800
Insurance of equipment	200
Heating	390
Lighting	100
Canteen	900
	5,490

Information relating to the production and service departments in the factory is as follows.

	Department			
	Production A	*Production B*	*Service X*	*Service Y*
Floor space (square metres)	1,200	1,600	800	400
Volume (cubic metres)	3,000	6,000	2,400	1,600
Number of employees	30	30	15	15
Book value of equipment	£30,000	£20,000	£10,000	£20,000

Required

Determine how the overhead costs should be apportioned between the four departments.

5.4 SOLUTION

Item of cost	Basis of apportionment	Total cost	To Department A	B	X	Y
		£	£	£	£	£
Factory depreciation	(floor area)	1,000	300	400	200	100
Factory repairs	(floor area)	600	180	240	120	60
Factory office costs	(number of employees)	1,500	500	500	250	250
Equipment depreciation	(book value)	800	300	200	100	200
Equipment insurance	(book value)	200	75	50	25	50
Heating	(volume)	390	90	180	72	48
Lighting	(floor area)	100	30	40	20	10
Canteen	(number of employees)	900	300	300	150	150
Total		5,490	1,775	1,910	937	868

Second stage: service department cost apportionment

5.5 The second stage of overhead apportionment concerns the **treatment of service departments**. A factory is divided into a number of production and service departments, but only the production departments are directly involved in the manufacture of the units. In order to be able to add production overheads to unit costs, it is necessary to have all the overheads charged to the production departments. The next stage in absorption costing is, therefore, to **apportion the costs of service departments to the production departments**. One method by which service department costs can be apportioned is known as the **reciprocal method (repeated distribution method)**.

The reciprocal method (repeated distribution method) of service department cost apportionment

KEY TERM

Apportionment is a procedure whereby indirect costs are spread fairly between departments.

5.6 It could therefore be argued that a fair sharing of service department costs is not possible unless recognition is given to the work done by each service department for other service departments. A stores department may, for example, use a maintenance department and the maintenance department may in turn use the stores department. The reciprocal method of apportionment, is best explained by means of an example.

5.7 EXAMPLE: RECIPROCAL METHOD OF APPORTIONMENT

A company has two production and two service departments (stores and maintenance). The following information about activity in the recent costing period is available.

	Production departments A	B	Stores department	Maintenance department
Overhead costs	£10,030	£8,970	£10,000	£8,000
Cost of material acquisitions	£30,000	£50,000	-	£20,000
Maintenance hours needed	8,000	1,000	1,000	-

Required

Apportion the overheads of the service departments to the two production departments.

5.8 SOLUTION

If we give consideration to the work done by the stores and maintenance departments for each other, service department costs should be apportioned as follows.

	Dept A	Dept B	Stores	Maintenance
Stores (100%)	30%	50%	-	20%
Maintenance (100%)	80%	10%	10%	-

5.9

	Production Dept A £	Production Dept B £	Stores £	Maintenance £
Overhead costs	10,030	8,970	10,000	8,000
Apportion stores costs (note (a))	3,000	5,000	(10,000)	2,000
			0	10,000
Apportion maintenance costs	8,000	1,000	1,000	(10,000)
			1,000	0
Repeat: Apportion stores	300	500	(1,000)	200
Repeat: Apportion maintenance	160	20	20	(200)
Repeat: Apportion stores	6	10	(20)	4
Repeat: Apportion maintenance (note (b))	4	-	-	(4)
	21,500	15,500	0	0

Notes

(a) The first apportionment could have been the costs of maintenance, rather than stores; there is no difference to the final results.

(b) When the repeated distributions bring service department costs down to small numbers (here £4) the final apportionment to production departments is an approximate rounding.

Using algebra

5.10 A quicker way, perhaps, of arriving at your conclusions in the example above is to use **algebra** and **simultaneous equations**.

5.11 Let us use the same data as the example above.

(a) Let S be the total stores department overhead for apportionment, after it has been apportioned overhead from Maintenance.

(b) Let M be the total of maintenance department overhead after it has been apportioned overhead from Stores.

5.12 We can set up our equations as follows.

$$S = 0.1M + £10,000 \quad (1)$$
$$M = 0.2S + £8,000 \quad (2)$$

5.13 Multiplying (2) by 5 gives us

$$5M = S + £40,000 \quad (3), \text{ which can be rearranged so that}$$
$$S = 5M - £40,000 \quad (4)$$

Subtracting (1) from (4)

$$S = 5M - £40,000 \quad (4)$$
$$S = 0.1M + £10,000 \quad (1)$$

$$0 = 4.9M - £50,000$$

$$M = \frac{£50,000}{4.9} = £10,204$$

Substituting in (1)

$$S = 0.1 \times (£10,204) + £10,000$$
$$S = £11,020$$

5.14 These overheads can be apportioned as follows, using the percentages in Paragraph 5.8. Note that the result is the same as that obtained when using the reciprocal (repeated distribution) method.

	Production dept A £	Production dept B £	Stores £	Maintenance £
Overhead costs	10,030	8,970	10,000	8,000
Apportion stores total	3,306	5,510	(11,020)	2,204
Apportion maintenance total	8,164	1,020	1,020	(10,204)
	21,500	15,500	-	-

Exam focus point

You must never ignore the existence of reciprocal services unless the question clearly instructs you to do so. The question will usually indicate clearly if you are required to use a specific method of reciprocal apportionment.

Question 1

Sandstorm Ltd is a jobbing engineering concern which has three production departments (forming, machines and assembly) and two service departments (maintenance and general).

The following analysis of overhead costs has been made from the year just ended.

	£	£
Rent and rates		8,000
Power		750
Light, heat		5,000
Repairs, maintenance:		
Forming	800	
Machines	1,800	
Assembly	300	
Maintenance	200	
General	100	
		3,200
Departmental expenses:		
Forming	1,500	
Machines	2,300	
Assembly	1,100	
Maintenance	900	
General	1,500	
		7,300
Depreciation:		
Plant		10,000
Fixtures and fittings		250
Insurance:		
Plant		2,000
Buildings		500

	£	£
Indirect labour:		
Forming	3,000	
Machines	5,000	
Assembly	1,500	
Maintenance	4,000	
General	2,000	
	15,500	
	52,500	

Other available data are as follows.

	Floor area sq. ft	Plant value £	Fixtures & fittings £	Effective horse-power	Direct cost for year £	Labour hours worked	Machine hours worked
Forming	2,000	25,000	1,000	40	20,500	14,400	12,000
Machines	4,000	60,000	500	90	30,300	20,500	21,600
Assembly	3,000	7,500	2,000	15	24,200	20,200	2,000
Maintenance	500	7,500	1,000	5	-	-	-
General	500	-	500	-	-	-	-
	10,000	100,000	5,000	150	75,000	55,100	35,600

Service department costs are apportioned as follows.

	Maintenance %	General %
Forming	20	20
Machines	50	60
Assembly	20	10
General	10	–
Maintenance	–	10
	100	100

Required

Using the data provided prepare an analysis showing the distribution of overhead costs to departments.

Answer

Analysis of distribution of actual overhead costs

	Basis	Forming £	Machines £	Assembly £	Machining £	General £	Total £
Directly allocated overheads:							
Repairs, maintenance		800	1,800	300	200	100	3,200
Departmental expenses		1,500	2,300	1,100	900	1,500	7,300
Indirect labour		3,000	5,000	1,500	4,000	2,000	15,500
Apportionment of other overheads:							
Rent, rates	1	1,600	3,200	2,400	400	400	8,000
Power	2	200	450	75	25	0	750
Light, heat	1	1,000	2,000	1,500	250	250	5,000
Dep'n of plant	3	2,500	6,000	750	750	0	10,000
Dep'n of F and F	4	50	25	100	50	25	250
Insurance of plant	3	500	1,200	150	150	0	2,000
Insurance of buildings	1	100	200	150	25	25	500
		11,250	22,175	8,025	6,750	4,300	52,500

Basis of apportionment:

1   floor area
2   effective horsepower
3   plant value

4   fixtures and fittings value

Apportionment of service department overheads to production departments, using the reciprocal method.

	Forming	Machines	Assembly	Maintenance	General	Total
	£	£	£	£	£	£
Overheads	11,250	22,175	8,025	6,750	4,300	52,500
	1,350	3,375	1,350	(6,750)	675	
					4,975	
	995	2,985	498	497	(4,975)	
	99	249	99	(497)	50	
	10	30	5	5	(50)	
	1	3	1	(5)		
	13,705	28,817	9,978	0	0	52,500

Exam focus point

There were four marks available in one of the compulsory ten-mark questions in Section B of the pilot paper for Paper 1.2 which required the reapportionment of service cost centre costs using the **reciprocal method**.

6   OVERHEAD ABSORPTION

6.1   Having allocated and/or apportioned all overheads, the next stage in absorption costing is to add them to, or **absorb them into,** the cost of production or sales.

(a)   **Production costs** are added to the **prime cost** (direct materials, labour and expenses) to give the **factory cost,** (full cost of production). Production overheads are therefore included in the value of stocks of finished goods.

(b)   **Administration and selling and distribution overheads** are then added, the sum of the factory cost and these overheads being the total cost of sales. These overheads are therefore not included in the value of closing stock.

Use of a predetermined absorption rate

6.2   Overheads are not absorbed on the basis of actual costs but on the basis of **estimated** or **budgeted** figures (calculated prior to the beginning of the period) using what is known as an **absorption rate**. There are a number of reasons for this.

(a)   Goods are produced and sold throughout the year, but many actual overheads are not known until the end of the year. It would be inconvenient to wait until the year end in order to decide what overhead costs should be.

(b)   An attempt to calculate overhead costs more regularly (such as each month) is possible, although estimated costs must be added for occasional expenditures such as rent and rates (incurred once or twice a year). The difficulty with this approach would be that actual overheads from month to month would fluctuate randomly; therefore, overhead costs charged to production would depend to a certain extent on random events and changes.

6.3   EXAMPLE : USE OF A PREDETERMINED ABSORPTION RATE

Suppose that a company budgets to make 1,200 units of a product in the first half of 20X5. Budgeted production overhead costs, all fixed costs, are £12,000. Due to seasonal demand for the company's product, the volume of production varies from month to month. Actual overhead costs are £2,000 per month. Actual monthly production in the first half of 20X5 is listed below, and total actual production in the period is 1,080 units.

The table below shows the production overhead cost per unit using the following.

(a) A predetermined absorption rate of $\dfrac{£12,000}{1,200}$ = £10 per unit

(b) An actual overhead cost per unit each month

(c) An actual overhead cost per unit based on actual six-monthly expenditure of £12,000 and actual six-monthly output of 1,080 units = £11.11 per unit

				Overhead cost per unit	
			(a)	(b)	(c)
			Predetermined	Actual cost	Average actual cost
Month	Expenditure	Output	unit rate	each month	in the six months
	(A)	(B)		(A) ÷ (B)	
	£	Units	£	£	£
Jan	2,000	100	10	20.00	11.11
Feb	2,000	120	10	16.67	11.11
Mar	2,000	140	10	14.29	11.11
April	2,000	160	10	12.50	11.11
May	2,000	320	10	6.25	11.11
June	2,000	240	10	8.33	11.11
	12,000	1,080			

6.4 Points to note

(a) Methods (a) and (c) give a **constant overhead cost per unit** each month, regardless of seasonal variations in output. Method (b) gives **variable unit overhead costs**, depending on the season of the year. For this reason, it is argued that method (a) or (c) would provide more useful (long-term) costing information.

In addition, if prices are based on full cost with a percentage mark-up for profit, method (b) would give seasonal variations in selling prices, with high prices in low-season and low prices in high-season. Methods (a) and (c) would give a constant price based on 'cost plus'.

(b) With method (a), overhead costs per unit are known throughout the period, and cost statements can be prepared at any time. This is because **predetermined overhead rates are known in advance**. With method (c), overhead costs cannot be established until after the end of an accounting period. For example, overhead costs of output in January 20X5 cannot be established until actual costs and output for the period are known, which will be not until after the end of June 20X5.

(c) For the reasons given above, predetermined overhead rates are preferable to rates based on actual overhead costs, in spite of being based on estimates of costs.

6.5 Overhead absorption rates are therefore calculated as follows.

(a) The overhead likely to be incurred during the coming year is estimated.

(b) The total hours, units, or direct costs on which the overhead absorption rates are to be based (activity level) are estimated.

(c) The estimated overhead is divided by the budgeted activity level to arrive at an absorption rate.

6.6 The activity level can be based on a number of measures.

Full capacity   Output (expressed in standard hours) that could be achieved if sales orders, supplies and workforce were available for all installed workplaces.

Practical capacity   Full capacity less an allowance for known unavoidable volume losses.

Budgeted capacity   Standard hours planned for the period, taking into account budgeted sales, supplies, workforce availability and efficiency expected.

The examiner might try to confuse you by referring to '**full practical capacity**'. This simply means **100% of practical capacity**.

Choosing the appropriate absorption base

6.7   The different **bases of absorption** (or 'overhead recovery rates') are as follows.

- A percentage of direct materials cost
- A percentage of direct labour cost
- A percentage of prime cost
- A rate per machine hour
- A rate per direct labour hour
- A rate per unit
- A percentage of factory cost (for administration overhead)
- A percentage of sales or factory cost (for selling and distribution overhead)

6.8   The choice of an absorption basis is a matter of judgement and common sense, what is required is an **absorption basis** which realistically reflects the characteristics of a given cost centre and which avoids undue anomalies.

6.9   Many factories use a **direct labour hour rate** or **machine hour rate** in preference to a rate based on a percentage of direct materials cost, wages or prime cost.

(a)   A **direct labour** hour basis is most appropriate in a **labour intensive** environment.

(b)   A **machine hour** rate would be used in departments where production is controlled or dictated by machines.

(c)   A **rate per unit** would be effective only if all units were identical.

6.10 EXAMPLE: OVERHEAD ABSORPTION

The budgeted production overheads and other budget data of Hairy Mammoth Ltd are as follows.

Budget	*Production dept A*	*Production dept B*
Overhead cost	£36,000	£5,000
Direct materials cost	£32,000	
Direct labour cost	£40,000	
Machine hours	10,000	
Direct labour hours	18,000	
Units of production		1,000

Required

Calculate the absorption rate using the various bases of apportionment.

6.11 SOLUTION

(a) Department A

    (i)   Percentage of direct materials cost $\dfrac{£36,000}{£32,000} \times 100\% = 112.5\%$

    (ii)   Percentage of direct labour cost $\dfrac{£36,000}{£40,000} \times 100\% = 90\%$

    (iii)   Percentage of prime cost $\dfrac{£36,000}{£72,000} \times 100\% = 50\%$

    (iv)   Rate per machine hour $\dfrac{£36,000}{10,000\text{hrs}} = £3.60$ per machine hour

    (v)   Rate per direct labour hour $\dfrac{£36,000}{18,000\text{hrs}} = £2$ per direct labour hour

(b) The department B absorption rate will be based on units of output.

$$\frac{£5,000}{1,000\text{units}} = £5 \text{ per unit produced}$$

6.12 The choice of the basis of absorption is significant in determining the cost of individual units, or jobs, produced. Using the previous example, suppose that an individual product has a material cost of £80, a labour cost of £85, and requires 36 labour hours and 23 machine hours to complete. The overhead cost of the product would vary, depending on the basis of absorption used by the company for overhead recovery.

(a) As a percentage of direct material cost, the overhead cost would be
    112.5% × £80   = £90.00

(b) As a percentage of direct labour cost, the overhead cost would be
    90% × £85   = £76.50

(c) As a percentage of prime cost, the overhead cost would be 50% × £165   = £82.50

(d) Using a machine hour basis of absorption, the overhead cost would be
    23 hrs × £3.60   = £82.80

(e) Using a labour hour basis, the overhead cost would be 36 hrs × £2   = £72.00

6.13 In theory, each basis of absorption would be possible, but the company should choose a basis for its own costs which seems to be '**fairest**'. In our example, this choice will be significant in determining the cost of individual products, as the following summary shows, but the total cost of production overheads is the budgeted overhead expenditure, no matter what basis of absorption is selected. It is the relative share of overhead costs borne by individual products and jobs which is affected by the choice of overhead absorption basis. A summary of the product costs in the previous example is shown as follows.

	Percentage of materials cost	*Percentage of labour cost*	*Percentage of prime cost*	*Machine hours*	*Direct labour hours*
	Basis of overhead recovery				
	£	£	£	£	£
Direct material	80	80.00	80.00	80.00	80
Direct labour	85	85.00	85.00	85.00	85
Production overhead	90	76.50	82.50	82.80	72
Full factory cost	255	241.50	247.50	247.80	237

7 BLANKET ABSORPTION RATES AND DEPARTMENTAL ABSORPTION RATES

KEY TERM

A **blanket overhead absorption rate** is an absorption rate used throughout a factory and for all jobs and units of output irrespective of the department in which they were produced.

7.1 For example, if total overheads were £500,000 and there were 250,000 direct machine hours during the period, the **blanket overhead rate** would be £2 per direct machine hour and all jobs passing through the factory would be charged at that rate. Such a rate is not appropriate, however, if there are a number of departments, and jobs do not spend an equal amount of time in each department.

7.2 It is argued that if a single factory overhead absorption rate is used, some products will receive a higher overhead charge than they ought 'fairly' to bear, whereas other products will be under-charged. By using **a separate absorption rate** for each department, charging of overheads will be equitable and the full cost of production of items will be representative of the cost of the efforts and resources put into making them.

7.3 EXAMPLE: SEPARATE ABSORPTION RATES

Fire Dragon Ltd has two production departments, for which the following budgeted information is available.

	Department A	Department B	Total
Budgeted overheads	£360,000	£200,000	£560,000
Budgeted direct labour hours	200,000 hrs	40,000 hrs	240,000 hrs

If a single factory overhead absorption rate is applied, the rate of overhead recovery would be:

$$\frac{£560,000}{240,000 \text{hours}} = £2.33 \text{ per direct labour hour}$$

If separate departmental rates are applied, these would be:

$$Department\ A = \frac{£360,000}{200,000 \text{hours}} \qquad Department\ B = \frac{£200,000}{40,000 \text{hours}}$$

$$= £1.80 \text{ per direct labour hour} \qquad = £5 \text{ per direct labour hour}$$

Department B has a higher overhead rate of cost per hour worked than department A.

Now let us consider two separate jobs.

Job X has a prime cost of £100, takes 30 hours in department B and does not involve any work in department A.

Job Y has a prime cost of £100, takes 28 hours in department A and 2 hours in department B.

What would be the factory cost of each job, using the following rates of overhead recovery?

(a) A single factory rate of overhead recovery
(b) Separate departmental rates of overhead recovery

7.4 SOLUTION

		Job X		Job Y
(a)	**Single factory rate**	£		£
	Prime cost	100		100
	Factory overhead (30 × £2.33)	70		70
	Factory cost	170		170
(b)	**Separate departmental rates**	£		£
	Prime cost	100		100.00
	Factory overhead: department A	0	(28 × £1.80)	50.40
	department B	(30 × £5) 150	(2 × £5)	10.00
	Factory cost	250		160.40

7.5 Using a single factory overhead absorption rate, both jobs would cost the same. However, since job X is done entirely within department B where overhead costs are relatively higher, whereas job Y is done mostly within department A, where overhead costs are relatively lower, it is arguable that job X should cost more than job Y. This will occur if separate departmental overhead recovery rates are used to reflect the work done on each job in each department separately.

7.6 If all jobs do not spend approximately the same time in each department then, to ensure that all jobs are charged with their fair share of overheads, it is necessary to establish **separate overhead rates for each department**.

Question 2

The following data relate to one year in department A.

Budgeted machine hours	25,000
Actual machine hours	21,875
Budgeted overheads	£350,000
Actual overheads	£350,000

Based on the data above, what is the machine hour absorption rate as conventionally calculated?

A £12   B £14   C £16   D £18

Answer

Don't forget, if your calculations produce a solution which does not correspond with any of the options available, then eliminate the unlikely options and make a guess from the remainder. Never leave out a multiple choice question.

A common pitfall is to think 'we haven't had answer A for a while, so I'll guess that'. The examiner is *not* required to produce an even spread of A, B, C and D answers in the examination. There is no reason why the answer to *every* question cannot be D!

The correct answer in this case is B.

$$\text{Overhead absorption rate} = \frac{\text{Budgeted overheads}}{\text{Budgeted machine hours}} = \frac{£350,000}{25,000} = £14 \text{ per machine hour}$$

---

8 NORMAL COSTING

8.1 We know that the **overhead absorption rate is predetermined** using figures from the **annual budget**. If overheads are to be absorbed on the basis of direct labour hours, the overhead absorption rate will be calculated using the total overheads and the number of direct labour hours included in the annual budget.

8.2   Using the predetermined absorption rate, the *actual* cost of production can be established as follows.

> Direct materials
plus: direct labour
plus: direct expenses
plus: overheads (based on the predetermined recovery rate)
equals: actual cost of production

This is known as **normal costing**.

8.3   Many students become seriously confused about what can appear a very unusual method of costing. The following example should help clarify this costing method.

8.4   EXAMPLE: NORMAL COSTING

Normal Ltd budgeted to make 100 units of product Z at a cost of £3 per unit in direct materials and £4 per unit in direct labour. The sales price would be £12 per unit, and production overheads were budgeted to amount to £200. A unit basis of overhead recovery is in operation. During the period 120 units were actually produced and sold (for £12 each) and the actual cost of direct materials was £380 and of direct labour, £450. Overheads incurred came to £210.

Required

Determine the cost of sales of product Z, and the profit. Ignore administration, selling and distribution overheads.

8.5   SOLUTION

In normal costing, the cost of production and sales is the actual direct cost plus the cost of overheads, absorbed at a predetermined rate as established in the budget. In our example, the overhead recovery rate would be £2 per unit produced (£200 ÷100 units).

The actual cost of sales is calculated as follows.

	£
Direct materials (actual)	380
Direct labour (actual)	450
Overheads absorbed (120 units × £2)	240
Full cost of sales, product Z	1,070
Sales of product Z (120 units × £12)	1,440
Profit, product Z	370

Notice that the actual overheads **incurred**, £210, are not the same as the overheads **absorbed** into the cost of production, £240. In normal absorption costing £240 is the 'correct' cost. This discrepancy between actual overheads incurred and the overheads absorbed, which is an inevitable feature of normal costing, is only reconciled at the end of an accounting period, as the '**under-absorption**' or '**over-absorption**' of **overhead**.

9   OVER AND UNDER ABSORPTION OF OVERHEADS

9.1   **The rate of overhead absorption is based on estimates** (of both numerator and denominator) and it is quite likely that either one or both of the estimates will not agree with what actually occurs.

(a)   **Over-absorption** means that the overheads charged to the cost of sales are greater then the overheads actually incurred.

(b) **Under-absorption** means that insufficient overheads have been included in the cost of sales.

It is almost inevitable that at the end of the accounting year there will have been an over absorption or under absorption of the overhead actually incurred.

9.2 Suppose that the budgeted overhead in a production department is £80,000 and the budgeted activity is 40,000 direct labour hours. The overhead recovery rate (using a direct labour hour basis) would be £2 per direct labour hour.

Actual overheads in the period are, say £84,000 and 45,000 direct labour hours are worked.

	£
Overhead incurred (actual)	84,000
Overhead absorbed (45,000 × £2)	90,000
Over-absorption of overhead	6,000

In this example, the cost of produced units or jobs has been charged with £6,000 more than was actually spent. An adjustment to reconcile the overheads charged to the actual overhead is necessary and the over-absorbed overhead will be written as an adjustment to the profit and loss account at the end of the accounting period.

The reasons for under-/over-absorbed overhead

9.3 **The overhead absorption rate is predetermined from budget estimates of overhead cost and the expected volume of activity.** Under- or over-recovery of overhead will occur in the following circumstances.

- Actual overhead costs are different from budgeted overheads
- The actual activity level is different from the budgeted activity level
- Actual overhead costs *and* actual activity level differ from the budgeted costs and level

9.4 EXAMPLE: REASONS FOR UNDER-/OVER-ABSORBED OVERHEAD

Big Lizards Ltd has a budgeted production overhead of £50,000 and a budgeted activity of 25,000 direct labour hours and therefore a recovery rate of £2 per direct labour hour.

Required

Calculate the under-/over-absorbed overhead, and the reasons for the under-/over-absorption, in the following circumstances.

(a) Actual overheads cost £47,000 and 25,000 direct labour hours are worked.
(b) Actual overheads cost £50,000 and 21,500 direct labour hours are worked.
(c) Actual overheads cost £47,000 and 21,500 direct labour hours are worked.

9.5 SOLUTION

(a)	£
Actual overhead	47,000
Absorbed overhead (25,000 × £2)	50,000
Over-absorbed overhead	3,000

The reason for the over-absorption is that although the actual and budgeted direct labour hours are the same, actual overheads cost less than expected.

(b)

	£
Actual overhead	50,000
Absorbed overhead (21,500 × £2)	43,000
Under-absorbed overhead	7,000

The reason for the under-absorption is that although budgeted and actual overhead costs were the same, fewer direct labour hours were worked than expected.

(c)

	£
Actual overhead	47,000
Absorbed overhead (21,500 × £2)	43,000
Under-absorbed overhead	4,000

The reason for the under absorption is a combination of the reasons in (a) and (b).

9.6 EXAMPLE: UNDER AND OVER ABSORPTION OF OVERHEADS

Rioch Havery Ltd is a small company which manufactures two products, A and B, in two production departments, machining and assembly. A canteen is operated as a separate production service department.

The budgeted production, sales and overheads in the year to 31 March 20X3 are as follows.

	Product A	Product B
Sales price per unit	£50	£70
Sales (units)	2,200	1,400
Production (units)	2,000	1,500
Material cost per unit	£14	£12

Direct labour:

	Product A *Hours per unit*	Product B *Hours per unit*
Machining department (£4 per hour)	2	3
Assembly department (£3 per hour)	1	2

Machine hours per unit:		
Machining department	$3\frac{1}{2}$	4
Assembly department		

Budgeted production overheads:

	Machining department £	*Assembly department* £	*Canteen* £	*Total* £
Allocated costs	10,000	25,000	12,000	47,000
Apportionment of other general production overheads	26,000	12,000	8,000	46,000
	36,000	37,000	20,000	93,000
Number of employees	30	20	1	51
Floor area (square metres)	5,000	2,000	500	5,500

Required

(a) Calculate an absorption rate for overheads in each production department for the year to 31 March 20X3 and the budgeted cost per unit of products A and B.

(b) Suppose that actual results in the year to 31 March 20X3 are as follows.

	Product A	Product B	
Sales (units)	2,400	1,400	
Production (units)	2,200	1,500	
Sales price per unit	£50	£70	
Direct materials cost per unit	£14	£12	
Direct labour hours per unit:			
Machining department	2 hrs	3 hrs	(actual cost £4 per hour)
Assembly department	1 hr	2 hrs	(actual cost £3 per hour)
Machining hours:			
Machining department	3 hrs	4 hrs	
Assembly department	½ hr		

	Machining department £	Assembly department £	Canteen £	Total £
Actual production overheads:				
Allocated costs	30,700	27,600	10,000	68,300
Apportioned share of general production overheads	17,000	8,000	5,000	30,000
	47,700	35,600	15,000	98,300

Calculate the 'actual' cost of product A and product B.

9.7 SOLUTION

Step 1. **Choose absorption rates**

Since machine time appears to be more significant than labour time in the machining department, a machine hour rate of absorption will be used for overhead recovery in this department. In the assembly department, machining is insignificant and a direct labour hour rate of absorption would seem to be the basis which will give the fairest method of overhead recovery.

Step 2. **Apportion budgeted overheads**

Next we need to apportion **budgeted** overheads to the two production departments. Canteen costs will be apportioned on the basis of the number of employees in each department. (Direct labour hours in each department are an alternative basis of apportionment, but the number of employees seems to be more directly relevant to canteen costs).

	Machining department £	Assembly department £	Total £
Budgeted allocated costs	10,000	25,000	35,000
Share of general overheads	26,000	12,000	38,000
Apportioned canteen costs (30:20)	12,000	8,000	20,000
	48,000	45,000	93,000

Step 3. **Calculate overhead absorption rates**

The overhead absorption rates are predetermined, using budgeted estimates. Since the overheads are production overheads, the budgeted activity relates to the volume of production, in units (the production hours required for volume of sales being irrelevant).

	Product A	Product B	Total
Budgeted production (units)	2,000	1,500	
Machining department: machine hours	6,000 hrs	6,000 hrs	12,000 hrs
Assembly department: direct labour hours	2,000 hrs	3,000 hrs	5,000 hrs

The overhead absorption rates will be as follows.

171

	Machining department	*Assembly department*
Budgeted overheads	£48,000	£45,000
Budgeted activity	12,000 hrs	5,000 hrs
Absorption rate	£4 per machine hour	£9 per direct labour hour

Step 4. Determine a budgeted cost per unit

The budgeted cost per unit would be as follows.

	Product A		*Product B*	
	£	£	£	£
Direct materials		14		12
Direct labour:				
Machining department	8		12	
Assembly department	3		6	
	11		18	
Prime cost		25		30
Production overhead:				
Machining department	12		16	
Assembly department	9		18	
	21		34	
Full cost		46		64

Step 5. **Apportion actual service department overhead to production departments**

When the actual costs are analysed, the 'actual' overhead of the canteen department (£15,000) would be split between the machining and assembly departments.

	Machining department	*Assembly department*	*Total*
	£	£	£
Allocated cost	30,700	27,600	58,300
Apportioned general overhead	17,000	8,000	25,000
Canteen (30:20)	9,000	6,000	15,000
	56,700	41,600	98,300

Step 6. **Determine an actual cost per unit**

The overhead absorption rate remains as budgeted, £4 per machine hour in the machining department and £9 per direct labour hour in the assembly department.

	Product A	*Product B*
	£	£
Prime cost per unit (same as budgeted)	25	30
Overhead cost per unit (same as budgeted)	21	34
'Actual' cost per unit	46	64

The actual cost per unit is the same as the budgeted unit cost for the following reasons.

(a) Actual unit costs for direct materials and direct labour were the same as in the budget.

(b) The actual machine hours (machining department) and direct labour hours (assembly department) per unit were the same as in the budget.

Step 7. **Establish the over- or under-absorption of overheads**

There would be an over- or under-absorption of overheads as follows.

		Machining department £		Assembly department £	Total £
Overheads absorbed					
Product A (2,200 units)	(× 12)	26,400	(× 9)	19,800	46,200
Product B (1,500 units)	(× 16)	24,000	(× 18)	27,000	51,000
		50,400		46,800	97,200
Overheads incurred		56,700		41,600	98,300
(Under)/over-absorbed overhead		(6,300)		5,200	(1,100)

The total under-absorbed overhead of £1,100 will be written off to the profit and loss account at the end of the year, to compensate for the fact that overheads charged to production (£97,200) were less than the overheads actually incurred (£98,300).

9.8 The distinction between **overheads incurred** (actual overheads) and **overheads absorbed** is an important one which you must learn and understand. The difference between them is known as under- or over-absorbed overheads.

Question 3

The budgeted and actual data for Tecpointer Ltd for the year to 31 March 20X5 are as follows.

	Budgeted	Actual
Direct labour hours	9,000	9,900
Direct wages	£34,000	£35,500
Machine hours	10,100	9,750
Direct materials	£55,000	£53,900
Units produced	120,000	122,970
Overheads	£63,000	£61,500

The cost accountant of Tecpointer Ltd has decided that overheads should be absorbed on the basis of labour hours.

Required

Calculate the amount of under- or over-absorbed overheads for Tecpointer Ltd for the year to 31 March 20X5.

Answer

$$\text{Overhead absorption rate} = \frac{£63,000}{9,000} = £7 \text{ per hour}$$

Overheads absorbed by production = 9,900 × £7 = £69,300

	£
Actual overheads	61,500
Overheads absorbed	69,300
Over-absorbed overheads	7,800

Exam focus point

You can always work out whether overheads are under- or over-absorbed by using the following rule.

- If **Actual** overhead incurred – **Absorbed** overhead = **NEGATIVE** (N), then overheads are **over-absorbed** (O) (NO)

- If **Actual** overhead incurred – **Absorbed** overhead = **POSITIVE** (P), then overheads are **under-absorbed** (U) (PU)

So, remember the **NOPU** rule when you go into your examination and you won't have any trouble in deciding whether overheads are under- or over-absorbed!

Question 4

A management consultancy recovers overheads on chargeable consulting hours. Budgeted overheads were £615,000 and actual consulting hours were 32,150. Overheads were under-recovered by £35,000.

If actual overheads were £694,075 what was the budgeted overhead absorption rate per hour?

A £19.13   B £20.50   C £21.59   D £22.68

Answer

	£
Actual overheads	694,075
Under-recoverable overheads	35,000
Overheads recovered for 32,150 hours at budgeted overhead absorption rate (x)	659,075

$$32,150x = 659,075$$

$$x = \frac{659,075}{32,150} = £20.50$$

The correct option is B.

10 LEDGER ENTRIES RELATING TO OVERHEADS

10.1 The bookkeeping entries for overheads are not as straight forward as those for materials and labour. We shall now consider the way in which overheads are dealt with in a cost accounting system.

10.2 When an absorption costing system is in use we now know that the amount of overhead included in the cost of an item is absorbed at a predetermined rate. The entries made in the cash book and the nominal ledger, however, are the actual amounts.

10.3 You will remember that it is highly unlikely that the actual amount and the predetermined amount will be the same. The difference is called **under- or over-absorbed overhead**. To deal with this in the cost accounting books, therefore, we need to have an account to collect under- or over-absorbed amounts for each type of overhead.

10.4 EXAMPLE: THE UNDER-/OVER-ABSORBED OVERHEAD ACCOUNT

Gnocci Ltd absorbs production overheads at the rate of £0.50 per operating hour and administration overheads at 20% of the production cost of sales. Actual data for one month was as follows.

Administration overheads	£32,000
Production overheads	£46,500
Operating hours	90,000
Production cost of sales	£180,000

What entries need to be made for overheads in the ledgers?

10.5 SOLUTION

PRODUCTION OVERHEADS

	DR		CR
	£		£
Cash	46,500	Absorbed into WIP (90,000 × £0.50)	45,000
		Under absorbed overhead	1,500
	46,500		46,500

ADMINISTRATION OVERHEADS

	DR		CR
	£		£
Cash	32,000	To cost of sales (180,000 × 0.2)	36,000
Over-absorbed overhead	4,000		
	36,000		36,000

UNDER-/OVER-ABSORBED OVERHEADS

	DR		CR
	£		£
Production overhead	1,500	Administration overhead	4,000
Balance to profit and loss account	2,500		
	4,000		4,000

Less production overhead has been absorbed than has been spent so there is under-absorbed overhead of £1,500. More administration overhead has been absorbed (into cost of sales, note, not into WIP) and so there is over-absorbed overhead of £4,000. The net over-absorbed overhead of £2,500 is a credit in the profit and loss account.

11 NON-MANUFACTURING OVERHEADS

11.1 For **external reporting** (eg statutory accounts) it is not necessary to allocate non-manufacturing overheads to products. This is because many for the overheads are non-manufacturing, and are regarded as **period costs**.

11.2 For **internal reporting** purposes and for a number of industries which base the selling price of their product on estimates of **total** cost or even actual cost, a total cost per unit of output may be required. Builders, law firms and garages often charge for their services by adding a percentage profit margin to actual cost. For product pricing purposes and for internal management reports it may therefore be appropriate to allocate non-manufacturing overheads to units of output.

Bases for apportioning non-manufacturing overheads

11.3 A number of non-manufacturing overheads such as delivery costs or salespersons' salaries are clearly identified with particular products and can therefore be classified as direct costs. The majority of non-manufacturing overheads, however cannot be directly allocated to particular units of output. Two possible methods of allocating such non-manufacturing overheads are as follows.

11.4 **Method 1: Choose a basis for the overhead absorption rate** which most closely matches the non-manufacturing overhead such as direct labour hours, direct machine hours and so on. The problem with such a method is that most non-manufacturing overheads are unaffected in the short term by changes in the level of output and tend to be fixed costs.

11.5 **Method 2 : Allocate non-manufacturing overheads on the ability of the products to bear such costs**. One possible approach is to use the manufacturing cost as the basis for allocating non-manufacturing costs to products.

BPP PUBLISHING

> ### FORMULA TO LEARN
>
> The **overhead absorption rate** is calculated as follows.
>
> $$\text{Overhead absorption rate} = \frac{\text{Estimated non-manufacturing overheads}}{\text{Estimated manufacturing costs}}$$

11.6 If, for example, budgeted distribution overheads are £200,000 and budgeted manufacturing costs are £800,000, the predetermined distribution overhead absorption rate will be 25% of manufacturing cost. Other bases for absorbing overheads are as follows.

Types of overhead	Possible absorption base
Selling and marketing	Sales value
Research and development	Consumer cost (= production cost minus cost of direct materials) or added value (= sales value of product minus cost of bought in materials and services)
Distribution	Sales values
Administration	Consumer cost or added value

Administration overheads

11.7 The administration overhead usually consists of the following.

- Executive salaries
- Office rent and rates
- Lighting
- Heating and cleaning the offices

In cost accounting, administration overheads are regarded as periodic charges which are charged against the gross costing profit for the year (as in financial accounting).

Selling and distribution overheads

11.8 **Selling and distribution overheads** are often considered collectively as one type of overhead but they are actually quite different forms of expense.

(a) **Selling costs** are incurred in order to obtain sales

(b) **Distribution costs** begin as soon as the finished goods are put into the warehouse and continue until the goods are despatched or delivered to the customer

11.9 **Selling overhead** is therefore often absorbed on the basis of sales value so that the more profitable product lines take a large proportion of overhead. The normal cost accounting entry for selling overhead is as follows.

DR   Cost of goods sold
CR   Selling overhead control account

11.10 **Distribution overhead** is more closely linked to production than sales and from one point of view could be regarded as an extra cost of production. It is, however, more usual to regard production cost as ending on the factory floor and to deal with distribution overhead separately. It is generally absorbed on a percentage of production cost but special circumstances, such as size and weight of products affecting the delivery charges, may cause a different basis of absorption to be used. The cost accounting entry is as follows.

DR   Cost of goods sold
CR   Distribution overhead control account

12   ACTIVITY BASED COSTING

12.1   **Absorption costing** appears to be a relatively straightforward way of adding overhead costs to units of production using, more often than not, a **volume related absorption basis** (such as direct labour hours or direct machine hours). **Absorption costing assumes that all overheads are related primarily to production volume**. In reality, however, direct labour or direct machine hours may account for only 5% of a product's cost. However, a product may cause the overheads of service support functions (data processing, production scheduling and first item inspection) to increase. Are such overheads affected by the production volume? No – these overheads tend to be affected by the **range** and **complexity** of the products manufactured.

12.2   Because absorption costing tends to allocate too great a proportion of overheads to high volume products (which cause relatively little diversity), and too small a proportion of overheads to low volume products (which cause greater diversity and therefore use more support services), alternative methods of costing have been developed. **Activity based costing (ABC)** is one such development.

12.3   The major ideas behind **activity based costing** are as follows.

(a)   **Activities cause costs**. Activities include ordering, materials handling, machining, assembly, production scheduling and despatching.

(b)   Products create demand for the activities.

(c)   Costs are assigned to products on the basis of a product's consumption of the activities.

Outline of an ABC system

12.4   An ABC costing system operates as follows.

Step 1.   Identify an organisation's major activities.

Step 2.   Identify the factors which determine the size of the costs of an activity/cause the costs of an activity. These are known as **cost drivers**.

Activity	Cost driver
Ordering	Number of orders
Materials handling	Number of production runs
Production scheduling	Number of production runs
Despatching	Number of despatches

For those costs that vary with production levels in the short term, ABC uses **volume-related cost drivers** such as labour or machine hours. The cost of oil used as a lubricant on the machines would therefore be added to products on the basis of the number of machine hours since oil would have to be used for each hour **the machine** ran.

Step 3.   Collect the costs of each activity into what are known as **cost pools** (equivalent to cost centres under more traditional costing methods).

Step 4. Charge support overheads to products on the basis of their usage of the activity. A product's usage of an activity is measured by the number of the activity's cost driver it generates.

Suppose, for example, that the cost pool for the ordering activity totalled £100,000 and that there were 10,000 orders (the cost driver). Each product would therefore be charged with £10 for each order it required. A batch requiring five orders would therefore be charged with £50.

12.5 **Absorption costing** and **ABC** have many similarities. In both systems, **direct costs go straight to the product and overheads are allocated to production cost centres/cost pools.** The main difference is as follows.

(a) **Absorption costing** uses usually two **absorption bases** (labour hours and/or machine hours) to charge overheads to products.

(b) **ABC** uses many **cost drivers** as absorption bases (number of orders, number of dispatches and so on) to charge overheads to products.

12.6 In summary, ABC has absorption rates which are more closely linked to the cause of the overheads.

12.7 A **cost driver** is an activity which generates costs. Examples of cost drivers include the following.

- Sales levels as these **drive** the costs of sales commission
- Miles travelled as these **drive** the fuel costs
- Hours worked as these **drive** the costs of labour

The principal idea of ABC is to identify cost drivers.

12.8 Consider the following.

(a) **Overheads which vary with output** should be traced to products using volume-related cost drivers eg direct labour hours or direct machine hours.

(b) **Overheads which do not vary with output** should be traced to products using transaction based cost drivers eg number of production runs, or number of orders received and so on.

Chapter roundup

- Product costs are built up using absorption costing by a process of **allocation**, **apportionment** and **absorption**.

- In absorption costing, it is usual to add overheads into product costs by applying a **predetermined overhead absorption rate**. (This is set annually, in the budget).

- To work out the **absorption rate**, budgeted overheads are allocated to production cost centres, service department cost centres or general overhead cost centres. General overheads are then apportioned to production and service department cost centres using an appropriate basis. The service department cost centre overheads are then apportioned to production cost centres. All production overhead is thus identified with cost centres engaged directly in production.

- The **absorption rate** is calculated by dividing the budgeted overhead by the budgeted level of activity (budgeted direct labour hours or budgeted machine hours).

- Management should try to establish an absorption rate that provides a reasonably 'accurate' estimate of overhead costs for jobs, products or services. This means that when a predetermined overhead rate is used the bases for apportioning overhead costs between departments should be 'fair' and separate departmental absorption rates should be used.

- The **overhead absorption rate** is predetermined using figures from the budget. Actual costs of production include overheads based on this predetermined recovery rate. This is known as **normal costing**.

- **If overheads absorbed exceed overheads incurred**, the cost of production (or sales) will have been too high. The amount of **overabsorption** will be written as a 'favourable' adjustment to the profit and loss account. **If overheads absorbed are lower than the amount of overheads incurred**, the cost of production (or sales) will have been too low. The amount of **under-absorption** will be written as an 'adverse' adjustment to the profit and loss account.

- Under- or over-absorbed overhead is inevitable in normal absorption costing because the predetermined overhead absorption rates are based on forecasts (guesses) about overhead expenditure and the level, or volume, of activity.

- **Activity based costing (ABC)** is an alternative to the more traditional absorption costing. ABC involves the identification of the factors **(cost drivers)** which cause the costs of an organisation's major activities. **Support overheads** are charged to products on the basis of their usage of an activity.

Quick quiz

1 What is allocation? *The process of determining which costs go with which Product or Service*

2 Name the three stages in charging overheads to units of output. *Allocation Apportionment + Absorption*

3 Match the following overheads with the most appropriate basis of apportionment.

Overhead		Basis of apportionment	
(a)	Depreciation of equipment *3*	(1)	Direct machine hours
(b)	Heat and light costs *4*	(2)	Number of employees
(c)	Canteen *2*	(3)	Book value of equipment
(d)	Insurance of equipment *1*	(4)	Floor area

4 A direct labour hour basis is most appropriate in which of the following environments?

 A Machine-intensive
 B Labour-intensive
 C When all units produced are identical
 D None of the above

5 What is the problem with using a single factory overhead absorption rate?
It tends to allocate high costs to low activity Products and low costs to high activity products

179

6   How is under-/over-absorbed overhead accounted for? *It is allocated to the P+L at year end*

7   Why does under- or over-absorbed overhead occur? *Costs are either higher or lower than anticipated*

8   What are the major ideas of activity based costing? *That is based on cost drivers such no of orders thereby allocating cost more fairly*

9   What is the advantage of using cost drivers instead of traditional absorption bases? *Cost are allocated are more closely linked with the product*

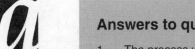

Answers to quick quiz

1   The process whereby whole cost items are charged direct to a cost unit or cost centre.

2   • Allocation
     • Apportionment
     • Absorption

3   (a)   (3)
     (b)   (4)
     (c)   (2)
     (d)   (3)

4   B

5   Because some products will receive a higher overhead charge than they ought 'fairly' to bear and other products will be undercharged.

6   Under-/over-absorbed overhead is written as an adjustment to the profit and loss account at the end of an accounting period.

     • Over-absorbed overhead → credit in profit and loss account
     • Under-absorbed overhead → debit in profit and loss account

7   • Actual overhead costs are different from budgeted overheads
     • The actual activity level is different from the budgeted activity level
     • Actual overhead costs *and* actual activity level differ from the budgeted costs and level

8   • Activities cause costs
     • Products create demand for the activities
     • Costs are assigned to products on the basis of a product's consumption of the activities

9   ABC has absorption rates which are more closely linked to the cause of the overheads

Now try the questions below from the Exam Question Bank

Number	Level	Marks	Time
12	MCQ	n/a	n/a
13	Examination	10	18 mins

Chapter 9

MARGINAL AND ABSORPTION COSTING

Topic list	Syllabus reference
1 Marginal cost and marginal costing	3(c)
2 Contribution	3(c)
3 The principles of marginal costing	3(c)
4 Marginal costing and absorption costing and the calculation of profit	3(c)
5 Reconciling the profit figures given by the two methods	3(c)
6 Marginal costing versus absorption costing - which is better?	3(c)
7 Introduction to decision making	3(c)

Introduction

This chapter defines **marginal costing** and compares it with absorption costing. Whereas absorption costing recognises fixed costs (usually fixed production costs) as part of the cost of a unit of output and hence as product costs, marginal costing treats all fixed costs as period costs. Two such different costing methods obviously each have their supporters and we will be looking at the arguments both in favour of and against each method, as well as their comparative usefulness for reporting to management, for reporting profits and stock values in externally published accounts and for providing decision-making information. Each costing method, because of the different stock valuation used, produces a different profit figure and we will be looking at this particular point in detail.

Study guide

Section 12 – Marginal and absorption costing

- Explain the concept of contribution

- Demonstrate and discuss the impact of absorption and marginal costing on stock valuation and profit measurement

- Produce profit and loss accounts using absorption and marginal costing

- Reconcile the profits reported under the two methods

- Discuss the advantages and disadvantages of absorption and marginal costing

Exam guide

Look out for Section B questions in your examination which require you to produce profit and loss accounts using absorption and marginal costing and then to reconcile the profits reported under the two methods.

1   MARGINAL COST AND MARGINAL COSTING

> **KEY TERMS**
>
> - **Marginal costing** is an alternative method of costing to absorption costing. In marginal costing, only variable costs are charged as a cost of sale and a contribution is calculated (sales revenue minus variable cost of sales). Closing stocks of work in progress or finished goods are valued at marginal (variable) production cost. Fixed costs are treated as a period cost, and are charged in full to the profit and loss account of the accounting period in which they are incurred.
>
> - **Marginal cost** is the cost of a unit of a product or service which would be avoided if that unit were not produced or provided.

1.1   The marginal production cost per unit of an item usually consists of the following.

- Direct materials
- Direct labour
- Variable production overheads

1.2   Direct labour costs might be excluded from marginal costs when the work force is a given number of employees on a fixed wage or salary. Even so, it is not uncommon for direct labour to be treated as a variable cost, even when employees are paid a basic wage for a fixed working week. If in doubt, you should treat direct labour as a variable cost unless given clear indications to the contrary. Direct labour is often a step cost, with sufficiently short steps to make labour costs act in a variable fashion.

1.3   The **marginal cost of sales** usually consists of the marginal cost of production adjusted for stock movements plus the variable selling costs, which would include items such as sales commission, and possibly some variable distribution costs.

2   CONTRIBUTION

> **KEY TERM**
>
> **Contribution** is the difference between sales value and the marginal cost of sales.

2.1   **Contribution** is of fundamental importance in marginal costing, and the term 'contribution' is really short for 'contribution towards covering fixed overheads and making a profit'.

3   THE PRINCIPLES OF MARGINAL COSTING

3.1   The principles of marginal costing are as follows.

(a)   Period fixed costs are the same, for any volume of sales and production (provided that the level of activity is within the 'relevant range'). Therefore, by selling an extra item of product or service the following will happen.

- Revenue will increase by the sales value of the item sold.
- Costs will increase by the variable cost per unit.
- Profit will increase by the amount of contribution earned from the extra item.

182

(b)   Similarly, if the volume of sales falls by one item, the profit will fall by the amount of contribution earned from the item.

(c)   **Profit measurement should therefore be based on an analysis of total contribution**. Since fixed costs relate to a period of time, and do not change with increases or decreases in sales volume, it is misleading to charge units of sale with a share of fixed costs. Absorption costing is therefore misleading, and it is more appropriate to deduct fixed costs from total contribution for the period to derive a profit figure.

(d)   When a unit of product is made, the extra costs incurred in its manufacture are the **variable production costs**. Fixed costs are unaffected, and no extra fixed costs are incurred when output is increased. It is therefore argued that the valuation of closing stocks should be at variable production cost (direct materials, direct labour, direct expenses (if any) and variable production overhead) because these are the only costs properly attributable to the product.

3.2   EXAMPLE: MARGINAL COSTING PRINCIPLES

Rain Until September Ltd makes a product, the Splash, which has a variable production cost of £6 per unit and a sales price of £10 per unit. At the beginning of September 20X0, there were no opening stocks and production during the month was 20,000 units. Fixed costs for the month were £45,000 (production, administration, sales and distribution). There were no variable marketing costs.

Required

Calculate the contribution and profit for September 20X0, using marginal costing principles, if sales were as follows.

(a)   10,000 Splashes
(b)   15,000 Splashes
(c)   20,000 Splashes

3.3   SOLUTION

The first stage in the profit calculation must be to identify the variable cost of sales, and then the contribution. Fixed costs are deducted from the total contribution to derive the profit. All closing stocks are valued at marginal production cost (£6 per unit).

	10,000 Splashes		15,000 Splashes		20,000 Splashes	
	£	£	£	£	£	£
Sales (at £10)		100,000		150,000		200,000
Opening stock	0		0		0	
Variable production cost	120,000		120,000		120,000	
	120,000		120,000		120,000	
Less value of closing						
stock (at marginal cost)	60,000		30,000		-	
Variable cost of sales		60,000		90,000		120,000
Contribution		40,000		60,000		80,000
Less fixed costs		45,000		45,000		45,000
Profit/(loss)		(5,000)		15,000		35,000
Profit (loss) per unit		£(0.50)		£1		£1.75
Contribution per unit		£4		£4		£4

3.4   The conclusions which may be drawn from this example are as follows.

(a) The **profit per unit varies** at differing levels of sales, because the average fixed overhead cost per unit changes with the volume of output and sales.

(b) The **contribution per unit is constant** at all levels of output and sales. Total contribution, which is the contribution per unit multiplied by the number of units sold, increases in direct proportion to the volume of sales.

(c) Since the **contribution per unit does not change**, the most effective way of calculating the expected profit at any level of output and sales would be as follows.

  (i) First calculate the total contribution.
  (ii) Then deduct fixed costs as a period charge in order to find the profit.

(d) In our example the expected profit from the sale of 17,000 Splashes would be as follows.

	£
Total contribution (17,000 × £4)	68,000
Less fixed costs	45,000
Profit	23,000

3.5 (a) If total contribution **exceeds fixed costs**, a profit is made

  (b) If total contribution **exactly equals fixed costs**, no profit or loss is made (**breakeven point**)

  (c) If total contribution is **less than fixed costs**, there will be a loss

Question 1

Argot Slang Ltd makes two products, the Drawl and the Twang. Information relating to each of these products for April 20X1 is as follows.

	Drawl	Twang
Opening stock	nil	nil
Production (units)	15,000	6,000
Sales (units)	10,000	5,000
Sales price per unit	£20	£30
Unit costs	£	£
Direct materials	8	14
Direct labour	4	2
Variable production overhead	2	1
Variable sales overhead	2	3

Fixed costs for the month	£
Production costs	40,000
Administration costs	15,000
Sales and distribution costs	25,000

Required

(a) Using marginal costing principles and the method in 3.4(d) above, calculate the profit in April 20X1.

(b) Calculate the profit if sales had been 15,000 units of Drawl and 6,000 units of Twang.

Answer

(a)

	£
Contribution from Drawls (unit contribution = £20 − £16 = £4 × 10,000)	40,000
Contribution from Twangs (unit contribution = £30 − £20 = £10 × 5,000)	50,000
Total contribution	90,000
Fixed costs for the period	80,000
Profit	10,000

(b)   At a higher volume of sales, profit would be as follows.

	£
Contribution from sales of 15,000 Drawls (× £4)	60,000
Contribution from sales of 6,000 Twangs (× £10)	60,000
Total contribution	120,000
Less fixed costs	80,000
Profit	40,000

Profit or contribution information

3.6   The main advantage of **contribution information** (rather than profit information) is that it allows an easy calculation of profit if sales increase or decrease from a certain level. By comparing total contribution with fixed overheads, it is possible to determine whether profits or losses will be made at certain sales levels. **Profit information,** on the other hand, does not lend itself to easy manipulation but note how easy it was to calculate profits using contribution information in Question 1. **Contribution information** is more useful for **decision making** than profit information, as we shall see in Section 7 of this chapter.

4   MARGINAL COSTING AND ABSORPTION COSTING AND THE CALCULATION OF PROFIT

4.1   **Marginal costing** as a cost accounting system is significantly different from absorption costing. It is an **alternative method** of accounting for costs and profit, which rejects the principles of absorbing fixed overheads into unit costs.

(a)   **In marginal costing**

   (i)   Closing stocks are valued at marginal production cost.

   (ii)   Fixed costs are charged in full against the profit of the period in which they are incurred.

(b)   **In absorption costing** (sometimes referred to as **full costing**)

   (i)   Closing stocks are valued at full production cost, and include a share of fixed production costs.

   (ii)   This means that the cost of sales in a period will include some fixed overhead incurred in a previous period (in opening stock values) and will exclude some fixed overhead incurred in the current period but carried forward in closing stock values as a charge to a subsequent accounting period.

4.2   In **marginal costing**, it is necessary to identify the following.

*   Variable costs
*   Contribution
*   Fixed costs

In **absorption costing** it is not necessary to distinguish variable costs from fixed costs.

4.3   EXAMPLE: MARGINAL AND ABSORPTION COSTING COMPARED

Look back at the information contained in Question 1. Suppose that the budgeted production for April 20X1 was 15,000 units of Drawl and 6,000 units of Twang, and production overhead is absorbed on the basis of budgeted direct labour costs.

BPP
PUBLISHING

Required

Calculate the profit if production was as budgeted, and sales were as follows.

(a)   10,000 units of Drawl and 5,000 units of Twang
(b)   15,000 units of Drawl and 6,000 units of Twang

Administration, sales and distribution costs should be charged as a period cost.

4.4   SOLUTION

Budgeted production overhead is calculated as follows.

		£
Fixed		40,000
Variable:	Drawls (15,000 × £2)	30,000
	Twangs (6,000 × £1)	6,000
Total		76,000

The **production overhead absorption rate** would be calculated as follows.

$$\frac{\text{Budgeted production overhead}}{\text{Budgeted direct labour cost}} = \frac{£76,000}{(15,000 \times £4) + (6,000 \times £2)} \times 100\%$$

$$= 105.56\% \text{ of direct labour cost}$$

(a)   If sales are 10,000 units of Drawl and 5,000 units of Twang, profit would be as follows.

	Absorption costing		
	Drawls	*Twangs*	*Total*
	£	£	£
Costs of production			
Direct materials	120,000	84,000	204,000
Direct labour	60,000	12,000	72,000
Overhead (105.56% of labour)	63,333	12,667	76,000
	243,333	108,667	352,000
Less closing stocks	(1/3) 81,111	(1/6) 18,111	99,222
Production cost of sales	162,222	90,556	252,778
Administration costs			15,000
Sales and distribution costs			
Variable			35,000
Fixed			25,000
Total cost of sales			327,778
Sales	200,000	150,000	350,000
Profit			22,222

Note. There is no under-/over-absorption of overhead, since actual production is the same as budgeted production.

The profit derived using absorption costing techniques is different from the profit (£10,000) using marginal costing techniques at this volume of sales (see earlier question).

(b)   If production and sales are exactly the same, (15,000 units of Drawl and 6,000 units of Twang) profit would be £40,000.

	£
Sales (300,000 + 180,000)	480,000
Cost of sales (352,000* + 15,000 + 48,000 + 25,000)	440,000
Profit	40,000

* No closing stock if sales and production are equal.

This is the same as the profit calculated by marginal costing techniques in the earlier question.

4.5 We can draw a number of conclusions from this example.

(a) Marginal costing and absorption costing are different techniques for assessing profit in a period.

(b) If there are **changes in stocks during a period,** so that opening stock or closing stock values are different, **marginal costing and absorption costing give different results** for profit obtained.

(c) **If the opening and closing stock volumes and values are the same, marginal costing and absorption costing will give the same profit figure.** This is because the total cost of sales during the period would be the same, no matter how calculated.

The long-run effect on profit

4.6 **In the long run, total profit for a company will be the same whether marginal costing or absorption costing is used.** Different accounting conventions merely affect the profit of individual accounting periods.

4.7 EXAMPLE: COMPARISON OF TOTAL PROFITS

To illustrate this point, let us suppose that a company makes and sells a single product. At the beginning of period 1, there are no opening stocks of the product, for which the variable production cost is £4 and the sales price £6 per unit. Fixed costs are £2,000 per period, of which £1,500 are fixed production costs.

	Period 1	Period 2
Sales	1,200 units	1,800 units
Production	1,500 units	1,500 units

Required

Determine the profit in each period using the following methods of costing.

(a) Absorption costing. Assume normal output is 1,500 units per period.
(b) Marginal costing.

4.8 SOLUTION

(a) **Absorption costing:** the absorption rate for fixed production overhead is

$$\frac{£1,500}{1,500\,\text{units}} = £1 \text{ per unit}$$

	Period 1		Period 2		Total	
	£	£	£	£	£	£
Sales		7,200		10,800		18,000
Production costs						
Variable	6,000		6,000		12,000	
Fixed	1,500		1,500		3,000	
	7,500		7,500		15,000	
Add opening stock b/f	-		1,500			
	7,500		9,000			
Less closing stock c/f	1,500		-		-	
Production cost of sales	6,000		9,000		15,000	
Other costs	500		500		1,000	
Total cost of sales		6,500		9,500		16,000
Unadjusted profit		700		1,300		2,000
(Under-)/over-absorbed overhead		-		-		-
Profit		700		1,300		2,000

(b) **Marginal costing**

	Period 1		Period 2		Total	
	£	£	£	£	£	£
Sales		7,200		10,800		18,000
Variable production cost	6,000		6,000		12,000	
Add opening stock b/f	-		1,200			
	6,000		7,200			
Less closing stock c/f	1,200		-		-	
Variable production cost of sales		4,800		7,200		12,000
Contribution		2,400		3,600		6,000
Fixed costs		2,000		2,000		4,000
Profit		400		1,600		2,000

Notes

(a) **The total profit over the two periods is the same for each method of costing, but the profit in each period is different.**

(b) In absorption costing, fixed production overhead of £300 is carried forward from period 1 into period 2 in stock values, and becomes a charge to profit in period 2. In marginal costing all fixed costs are charged in the period they are incurred, therefore the profit in period 1 is £300 lower and in period 2 is £300 higher than the absorption costing profit.

Question 2

The overhead absorption rate for product X is £10 per machine hour. Each unit of product X requires five machine hours. Stock of product X on 1.1.X1 was 150 units and on 31.12.X1 it was 100 units. What is the difference in profit between results reported using absorption costing and results reported using marginal costing?

A   The absorption costing profit would be £2,500 less
B   The absorption costing profit would be £2,500 greater
C   The absorption costing profit would be £5,000 less
D   The absorption costing profit would be £5,000 greater

Answer

Difference in profit = **change** in stock levels × fixed overhead absorption per unit = (150 – 100) × £10 × 5 = £2,500 **lower** profit, because stock levels **decreased**. The correct answer is therefore option A.

The key is the change in the volume of stock. Stock levels have **decreased** therefore absorption costing will report a **lower** profit. This eliminates options B and D.

Option C is incorrect because it is based on the closing stock only (100 units × £10 × 5 hours).

5 RECONCILING THE PROFIT FIGURES GIVEN BY THE TWO METHODS

5.1 **The difference in profits reported under the two costing systems is due to the different stock valuation methods used.**

5.2 **If stock levels increase between the beginning and end of a period, absorption costing will report the higher profit.** This is because some of the fixed production overhead incurred during the period will be carried forward in closing stock (which reduces cost of sales) to be set against sales revenue in the following period instead of being written off in full against profit in the period concerned.

5.3 **If stock levels decrease, absorption costing will report the lower profit** because as well as the fixed overhead incurred, fixed production overhead which had been carried forward in opening stock is released and is also included in cost of sales.

5.4 EXAMPLE: RECONCILING PROFITS

The profits reported under absorption costing and marginal costing for period 1 in the example in Paragraph 4.7 would be reconciled as follows.

	£
Marginal costing profit	400
Adjust for fixed overhead in stock:	
Stock increase of 300 units × £1 per unit	300
Absorption costing profit	700

Question 3

When opening stocks were 8,500 litres and closing stocks 6,750 litres, a firm had a profit of £62,100 using marginal costing.

Assuming that the fixed overhead absorption rate was £3 per litre, what would be the profit using absorption costing?

A £41,850　　　　—B £56,850　　　　C £67,350　　　　D £82,350

Answer

Difference in profit = (8,500 – 6,750) × £3 = £5,250

Absorption costing profit = £62,100 – £5,250 = £56,850

The correct answer is B.

Since stock levels reduced, the absorption costing profit will be lower than the marginal costing profit. You can therefore eliminate options C and D.

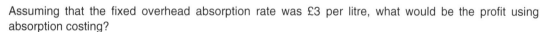

189

6 MARGINAL COSTING VERSUS ABSORPTION COSTING - WHICH IS BETTER?

6.1 There are accountants who favour each costing method.

(a) **Arguments in favour of absorption costing are as follows**.

(i) Fixed production costs are incurred in order to make output; it is therefore 'fair' to charge all output with a share of these costs.

(ii) Closing stock values, by including a share of fixed production overhead, will be valued on the principle required for the financial accounting valuation of stocks by SSAP 9.

(iii) A problem with calculating the contribution of various products made by a company is that it may not be clear whether the contribution earned by each product is enough to cover fixed costs, whereas by charging fixed overhead to a product we can decide whether it is profitable or not.

(iv) Where stock building is necessary, such as in fireworks manufacture, fixed costs should be included in stock valuations otherwise a series of losses will be shown in earlier periods, to be offset eventually by excessive profits when the goods are sold.

(b) **Arguments in favour of marginal costing are as follows**.

(i) It is simple to operate.

(ii) There are no apportionments, which are frequently done on an arbitrary basis, of fixed costs. Many costs, such as the managing director's salary, are indivisible by nature.

(iii) Fixed costs will be the same regardless of the volume of output, because they are period costs. It makes sense, therefore, to charge them in full as a cost to the period.

(iv) The cost to produce an extra unit is the variable production cost. It is realistic to value closing stock items at this directly attributable cost.

(v) As we have seen, the size of total contribution varies directly with sales volume at a constant rate per unit. For management purposes, better information about expected profit is obtained from the use of variable costs and contribution in the accounting system.

(vi) It is also argued that absorption costing gives managers the wrong signals. Goods are produced, not to meet market demand, but to absorb allocated overheads. Production in excess of demand in fact increases the overheads (for example warehousing) the organisation must bear.

(vii) Under- or over-absorption of overheads is avoided.

(viii) **It is a great aid to decision making, especially when a particular resource is limited,** as we shall see in Section 7. **Absorption costing information is not really appropriate for decision making.**

7 INTRODUCTION TO DECISION MAKING

7.1 There is one particular situation where marginal costing principles are used as opposed to absorption costing principles. This is when we are dealing with a **scarce resource**.

7.2 What is a scarce resource? We are all affected by scarce resources in our lives. Everyday examples include the following: time; money; and sleep.

We are more likely to say that we don't have enough money, rather than say 'for me, money is a scarce resource'.

7.3 The scarce resource is known as a **limiting factor** or a **key factor** since it limits how we pass our time, or how we spend our money. We all have to make decisions regarding how best to use any scarce resource.

7.4 A manufacturing company, may have a number of possible limiting factors.

- Sales, if there is a limit to sales demand.
- Labour hours, if these are insufficient to meet the level of production demanded.
- Materials, if these are insufficient to meet the level of production demanded.

7.5 If there are insufficient resources to make everything, management is faced with the problem of deciding which products to produce by considering the limiting factors.

7.6 **In limiting factor analysis, it is assumed that management wishes to maximise profit. Profit will be maximised when contribution is maximised** (given that fixed cost do not change). This is where marginal costing principles are applied.

7.7 If materials are the limiting factor, contribution will be maximised by earning the biggest contribution from each kg of material. Similarly, if labour hours are the limiting factor, contribution will be maximised by earning the biggest contribution from each labour hour worked.

7.8 Therefore the **limiting factor decision** involves calculating the contribution earned from each unit of the limiting factor, for each different product.

7.9 EXAMPLE: LIMITING FACTOR

ER Ltd makes two products, the Greene and the Ross. Unit variable costs are as follows.

	Greene £	Ross £
Direct materials	1	3
Direct labour (£3 per hour)	6	3
Variable overhead	1	1
	8	7

The sales price per unit is £14 per Greene and £11 per Ross. During July 20X6 the available direct labour is limited to 8,000 hours. Sales demand in July is expected to be 3,000 units for Greenes and 5,000 units for Rosses.

Required

Determine the profit-maximising production mix, assuming that monthly fixed costs are £20,000, and that opening stocks of finished goods and work in progress are nil.

7.10 SOLUTION

(a) The first step in the solution is to confirm that the limiting factor is something other than sales demand.

	Greene	Ross	Total
Labour hours per unit	2 hrs	1 hr	
Sales demand	3,000 units	5,000 units	
Labour hours needed	6,000 hrs	5,000 hrs	11,000 hrs
Labour hours available			8,000 hrs
Shortfall			3,000 hrs

Labour is the limiting factor on production.

(b) The second step is to identify the contribution earned by each product per unit of limiting factor, that is per labour hour worked.

	Greene	Ross
	£	£
Sales price	14	11
Variable cost	8	7
Unit contribution	6	4
Labour hours per unit	2 hrs	1 hr
Contribution per labour hour (= unit of limiting factor)	£3	£4

Although Greenes have a higher unit contribution than Rosses, two Rosses can be made in the time it takes to make one Greene. Because labour is in short supply it is more profitable to make Rosses than Greenes.

(c) The final stage in the solution is to work out the budgeted production and sales mix. Sufficient Rosses will be made to meet the full sales demand, and the remaining labour hours available will then be used to make Greenes.

Product	Demand	Hours required	Hours available	Priority of manufacture
Ross	5,000	5,000	5,000	1st
Greene	3,000	6,000	3,000 (bal)	2nd
		11,000	8,000	

Product	Units	Hours needed	Contribution per unit	Total
			£	£
Ross	5,000	5,000	4	20,000
Greene	1,500	3,000	6	9,000
		8,000		29,000
Less fixed costs				20,000
Profit				9,000

7.11 In conclusion.

(a) Unit contribution is *not* the correct way to decide priorities.

(b) Labour hours are the scarce resource, and therefore **contribution per labour hour** is the correct way to decide priorities.

(c) The Ross earns £4 contribution per labour hour, and the Greene earns £3 contribution per labour hour. Rosses therefore make more profitable use of the scarce resource, and should be manufactured first.

Other considerations regarding limiting factors

7.12 The following points should also be borne in mind when making a decision which involves limiting factors.

(a) In the long run management should seek to remove the limiting factor.

(b) In the short term management may be able to find ways around the limiting factor (such as overtime working and sub-contracting).

(c) It may not be easy to identify the limiting factor.

7.13 We will be studying **decision making** in detail in Section D of this Study Text.

Chapter roundup

- In your examination you may be asked to calculate the profit for an accounting period using either of the two methods of accounting. **Absorption costing** is most often used for routine profit reporting and must be used for financial accounting purposes. **Marginal costing** provides better management information for planning and decision making.

- **Marginal cost** is the variable cost of one unit of product or service.

- **Contribution** is an important measure in marginal costing, and it is calculated as the difference between sales value and marginal or variable cost.

- In **marginal costing**, fixed production costs are treated as **period costs** and are written off as they are incurred. In **absorption costing**, fixed production costs are absorbed into the cost of units and are carried forward in stock to be charged against sales for the next period. Stock values using absorption costing are therefore greater than those calculated using marginal costing.

- **Reported profit figures using marginal costing or absorption costing will differ if there is any change in the level of stocks in the period**. If production is equal to sales, there will be no difference in calculated profits using these costing methods.

- **SSAP 9** recommends the use of absorption costing for the valuation of stocks in financial accounts.

- There are a number of arguments both for and against each of the costing systems.

- The distinction between marginal costing and absorption costing is very important and it is vital that you now understand the contrast between the two systems.

Quick quiz

1 What is marginal costing? *Contribution Per Unit*

2 What is a period cost in marginal costing? *Fixed Cost*

3 Sales value – marginal cost of sales = ... *Contribution.*

4 What is a breakeven point? *Where Sales + Contribution are the same.*

5 Marginal costing and absorption costing are different techniques for assessing profit in a period. If there are changes in stock during a period, marginal costing and absorption costing give different results for profit obtained.

Which of the following statements are true?

I If stock levels increase, marginal costing will report the higher profit.

II If stock levels decrease, marginal costing will report the lower profit.

III If stock levels decrease, marginal costing will report the higher profit.

IV If the opening and closing stock volumes are the same, marginal costing and absorption costing will give the same profit figure.

A All of the above
B I, II and IV
C I and IV
D III and IV

6 Which of the following are arguments in favour of marginal costing?

   (a) Closing stock is valued in accordance with SSAP 9.
   (b) It is simple to operate.
   (c) There is no under or over absorption of overheads.
   (d) Fixed costs are the same regardless of activity levels.
   (e) The information from this costing method may be used for decision making.

7 What is a limiting factor? A scale rescale

Answers to quick quiz

1 Marginal costing is an alternative method of costing to absorption costing. In marginal costing, only variable costs are charged as a cost of sale and a contribution is calculated (sales revenue – variable cost of sales).

2 A fixed cost

3 Contribution

4 The point at which total contribution exactly equals fixed costs (no profit or loss is made)

5 D

6 (b), (c), (d), (e)

7 A scarce resource (which is in **limited** supply)

Now try the questions below from the Exam Question Bank

Number	Level	Marks	Time
14	MCQ	n/a	n/a
15	Examination	10	18 mins

Part C
Costing systems

Chapter 10

JOB, BATCH AND CONTRACT COSTING

Topic list	Syllabus reference
1 Job costing	4(a)
2 Job costing for internal services	4(a)
3 Job costing example	4(a)
4 Batch costing	4(a)
5 Introduction to contract costing	4(a)
6 Recording contract costs	4(a)
7 Contract accounts	4(a)
8 Progress payments	4(a)
9 Profits on contracts	4(a)
10 Losses on incomplete contracts	4(a)
11 Disclosure of long-term contracts in financial accounts	4(a)

Introduction

A **costing system** is designed to suit the way goods are processed or manufactured or the way services are provided. Each organisation's costing system will therefore have unique features but costing systems of firms in the same line of business will more than likely have common aspects. On the other hand, organisations involved in completely different activities, such as hospitals and car part manufacturers, will use very different methods.

This chapter begins by covering **job costing**. We will see the circumstances in which job costing should be used and how the costs of jobs are calculated. We will look at how the **costing of individual jobs** fits in with the recording of total costs in control accounts. The chapter then moves on to **batch costing**, the procedure for which is similar to job costing.

The final costing method considered in this chapter is **contract costing**. Contract costing is similar to job costing but the job is of such importance that a formal contract is made between the supplier and the customer. We will see how to record contract costs, how to account for any profits and losses arising on contracts at the end of an accounting period and we will look briefly at how contract balances are disclosed in financial accounts.

Study guide

Section 5 – Cost classification

- Describe briefly the different methods of costing final outputs and their appropriateness to different types of business organisation/situation

Section 13 – Job, batch and contract costing

- Describe the characteristics of job, batch and contract costing
- Describe the situations where the use of job, batch or contract costing would be appropriate
- Discuss and illustrate the treatment of direct, indirect and abnormal costs
- Complete cost records and accounts in job, batch and contract cost accounting situations
- Estimate job/contract costs from given information

- Explain, and illustrate, measures of profit on uncompleted contracts

Exam guide

Job, batch and contract costing are not included in the list of key areas of the syllabus. Make sure that you are able to deal with basic calculations which may be tested in either section of your examination.

1   JOB COSTING

KEY TERMS

- A **job** is a cost unit which consists of a single order or contract.

- **Job costing** is a costing method applied where work is undertaken to customers' special requirements and each order is of comparatively short duration.

1.1   The work relating to a job is usually carried out within a factory or workshop and moves through processes and operations as a **continuously identifiable unit**.

Procedure for the performance of jobs

1.2   The normal procedure which is adopted in jobbing concerns involves the following.

(a)   The prospective customer approaches the supplier and indicates the requirements of the job.

(b)   A responsible official sees the prospective customer and agrees with him the precise details of the items to be supplied, for example the quantity, quality, size and colour of the goods, the date of delivery and any special requirements.

(c)   The estimating department of the organisation then prepares an estimate for the job. This will include the cost of the materials to be used, the wages expected to be paid, the appropriate amount for factory, administration, selling and distribution overhead, the cost where appropriate of additional equipment needed specially for the job, and finally the supplier's **profit margin**. The total of these items will represent the quoted **selling price**.

(d)   At the appropriate time, the job will be 'loaded' on to the factory floor. This means that as soon as all materials, labour and equipment are available and subject to the scheduling of other orders, the job will be started. In an efficient organisation, the start of the job will be timed to ensure that while it will be ready for the customer by the promised date of delivery it will not be loaded too early, otherwise storage space will have to be found for the product until the date it is required by (and was promised to) the customer.

Collection of job costs

1.3   A separate record must be maintained to show the details of individual jobs. The process of collecting job costs may be outlined as follows.

(a)   **Materials requisitions are sent to stores.** Where a perpetual inventory system is maintained, an advance copy of the requisition is used to appropriate from free stock the relevant quantities of materials. The second copy of the requisition is sent as and when the materials are needed.

(b) **The material requisition note will be used to cost the materials issued to the job** concerned, and this cost may then be recorded on a **job cost sheet**. The cost may include items already in stock and/or items specially purchased.

(c) **The job ticket is passed to the worker who is to perform the first operation**. The times of his starting and finishing the operation are recorded on the ticket, which is then passed to the person who is to carry out the second operation, where a similar record of the times of starting and finishing is made.

(d) When the job is completed, the **job ticket is sent to the cost office**, where the time spent will be costed and recorded on the job cost sheet.

(e) The **relevant costs** of materials issued, direct labour performed and direct expenses incurred as recorded on the job cost sheet **are charged to the job account** in the work in progress ledger.

(f) **The job account is debited with the job's share of the factory overhead,** based on the absorption rate(s) in operation. If the job is incomplete at the end of an accounting period, it is valued at factory cost in the closing balance sheet (where a system of absorption costing is in operation).

(g) **On completion of the job,** the job account is charged with the appropriate administration, selling and distribution overhead, after which **the total cost of the job can be ascertained.**

(h) The difference between the agreed selling price and the total actual cost will be the supplier's profit (or loss).

Job cost sheet (or card)

1.4 An example of a job cost sheet is shown on page 200. Job cost sheets show the following.

- Detail of relatively small jobs.
- A summary of direct materials, direct labour and so on for larger jobs.

1.5 When jobs are completed, **job cost sheets** are transferred from the **work in progress** category to **finished goods**. When delivery is made to the customer, the costs become a **cost of sale**. If the completed job was carried out in order to build up finished goods stocks (rather than to meet a specific order) the quantity of items produced and their value are recorded on **finished goods stores ledger cards**.

Rectification costs

> **KEY TERM**
>
> **Rectification cost** is the cost incurred in rectifying sub-standard output.

1.6 If the finished output is found to be sub-standard, it may be possible to rectify the fault. The sub-standard output will then be returned to the department or cost centre where the fault arose. You should know how to deal with such costs in a job costing system.

| JOB COST CARD | | | | | Job No. B641 | |

Customer	Mr J White		Customer's Order No.		Vehicle make	Peugot 205 GTE
Job Description	Repair damage to offside front door				Vehicle reg. no.	G 614 SOX
Estimate Ref. 2599			Invoice No.			
Quoted price	£338.68		Invoice price	£355.05	Date to collect	14.6.XO

Material						Labour								Overheads			
Date	Req. No.	Qty.	Price	Cost		Date	Emp-loyee	Cost Ctre	Hrs.	Rate	Bonus	Cost		Hrs	OAR	Cost	
				£	p							£	p			£	p
12.6	36815	1	75.49	75	49	12.6	018	B	1.98	6.50	-	12	87	7.9	2.50	19	75
12.6	36816	1	33.19	33	19	13.6	018	B	5.92	6.50	-	38	48				
12.6	36842	5	6.01	30	05						13.65	13	65				
13.6	36881	5	3.99	19	95												
Total C/F				158	68	Total C/F						65	00	Total C/F		19	75

Expenses						Job Cost Summary		Actual		Estimate	
			Cost					£	p	£	p
Date	Ref.	Description	£	p							
						Direct Materials B/F		158	68	158	68
						Direct Expenses B/F		50	00		
						Direct Labour B/F		65	00	180	00
12.6	-	N. Jolley Panel-beating	50	-		Direct Cost		273	68		
						Overheads B/F		19	75		
								293	43		
						Admin overhead (add 10%)		29	34		
						= Total Cost		322	77	338	68
						Invoice Price		355	05		
Total C/F			50	-		Job Profit/Loss		32	28		

Comments

Job Cost Card Completed by _

1.7 **Rectification costs** can be treated in two ways.

(a) If rectification work is not a frequent occurrence, but arises on occasions with specific jobs to which it can be traced directly, then the rectification costs should be **charged as a direct cost to the jobs concerned.**

(b) If rectification is regarded as a normal part of the work carried out generally in the department, then the rectification costs should be **treated as production overheads.**

This means that they would be included in the total of production overheads for the department and absorbed into the cost of all jobs for the period, using the overhead absorption rate.

Job costing and computerisation

1.8 **Job costing cards** exist in **manual** systems, but it is increasingly likely that in large organisations the job costing system will be **computerised**, using accounting software specifically designed to deal with job costing requirements. A computerised job accounting system is likely to contain the following features.

(a) Every job will be given a job code number, which will determine how the data relating to the job is stored.

(b) A separate set of codes will be given for the type of costs that any job is likely to incur. Thus, 'direct wages', say, will have the same code whichever job they are allocated to.

(c) In a sophisticated system, costs can be analysed both by job (for example all costs related to Job 456), but also by type (for example direct wages incurred on all jobs). It is thus easy to perform variance analysis and to make comparisons between jobs.

(d) A job costing system might have facilities built into it which incorporate other factors relating to the performance of the job. In complex jobs, sophisticated planning techniques might be employed to ensure that the job is performed in the minimum time possible. Time management features therefore may be incorporated into job costing software.

Cost plus pricing

1.9 The usual method of fixing selling prices within a jobbing concern is known as **cost plus pricing** where a desired profit margin is added to total costs to arrive at the selling price.

1.10 The **disadvantages** of cost plus pricing are as follows.

(a) There are no incentives to **control costs** as a profit is guaranteed.

(b) There is no motive to tackle **inefficiencies** or **waste**.

(c) It doesn't take into account any significant differences in actual and estimated volumes of activity. Since the overhead absorption rate is based upon estimated volumes, there may be **under-/over-absorbed overheads** not taken into account.

(d) Because overheads are apportioned in an arbitrary way, this may lead to **under and over pricing**.

1.11 The **cost plus system** is often adopted where **one-off jobs** are carried out to **customers' specifications**.

Exam focus point

An exam question about job costing may ask you to accumulate costs to arrive at a job cost, and then to determine a job price by adding a certain amount of profit. To do this, you need to remember the following crucial formula.

	%
Cost of job	100
+ profit	25
= price	125

Profit may be expressed either as a percentage of job cost (such as 25% 25/100 mark up) or as a percentage of price (such as 20% (25/125) margin).

2 JOB COSTING FOR INTERNAL SERVICES

2.1 **Job costing systems** may be used to control the costs of **internal service departments**, eg the maintenance department. A job costing system enables the cost of a specific job to be charged to a user department. Therefore instead of apportioning the total costs of service departments, each job done is charged to the individual user department.

2.2 An **internal job costing system** for service departments will have the following advantages.

(a) **Realistic apportionment**. The identification of expenses with jobs and the subsequent charging of these to the department(s) responsible means that costs are borne by those who incurred them.

(b) **Increased responsibility and awareness**. User departments will be aware that they are charged for the specific services used and may be more careful to use the facility more efficiently. They will also appreciate the true cost of the facilities that they are using and can take decisions accordingly.

(c) **Control of service department costs**. The service department may be restricted to charging a standard cost to user departments for specific jobs carried out. It will then be possible to measure the efficiency or inefficiency of the service department by recording the difference between the standard charges and the actual expenditure.

(d) **Budget information**. This information will ease the budgeting process, as the purpose and cost of service department expenditure can be separately identified.

Question 1

Twist and Tern Ltd is a company that carries out jobbing work. One of the jobs carried out in February was job 1357, to which the following information relates.

Direct material Y:	400 kilos were issued from stores at a cost of £5 per kilo.
Direct material Z:	800 kilos were issued from stores at a cost of £6 per kilo. 60 kilos were returned.
Department P:	300 labour hours were worked, of which 100 hours were done in overtime.
Department Q:	200 labour hours were worked, of which 100 hours were done in overtime.

Overtime work is not normal in Department P, where basic pay is £4 per hour plus an overtime premium of £1 per hour. Overtime work was done in Department Q in February because of a request by the customer of another job to complete his job quickly. Basic pay in Department Q is £5 per hour and overtime premium is £1.50 per hour.

Department P had to carry out rectification work which took 20 hours in normal time. These 20 hours are additional to the 300 hours above. This rectification work is normal for a job such as job 1357, and since it was expected, it is included in the direct cost of the job.

Overhead is absorbed at the rate of £3 per direct labour hour in both departments.

Required

Calculate the following.

(a)   The direct materials cost of job 1357
(b)   The direct labour cost of job 1357
(c)   The full production cost of job 1357

Answer

(a)   £
Direct material Y (400 kilos × £5)   2,000
Direct material Z (800 − 60 kilos × £6)   4,440
Total direct material cost   6,440

(b)   £
Department P (320 hours × £4)   1,280
Department Q (200 hours × £5)   1,000
Total direct labour cost   2,280

Rectification work, being normal and expected, is included in the direct labour cost of Department P. In Department P, overtime premium will be charged to overhead. In Department Q, overtime premium will be charged to the job of the customer who asked for overtime to be worked.

(c)   £
Direct material cost   6,440
Direct labour cost   2,280
Production overhead (520 hours × £3)   1,560
                                                                      10,280

3   JOB COSTING EXAMPLE

3.1   An example may help to illustrate the principles of job costing, and the way in which the costing of individual jobs fits in with the recording of total costs in control accounts.

3.2   Fateful Morn Ltd is a jobbing company. On 1 June 20X2, there was one uncompleted job in the factory. The job card for this work is summarised as follows.

Job Card, Job No 6832

Costs to date	£
Direct materials	630
Direct labour (120 hours)	350
Factory overhead (£2 per direct labour hour)	240
Factory cost to date	1,220

During June, three new jobs were started in the factory, and costs of production were as follows.

Direct materials		£
Issued to:	Job 6832	2,390
	Job 6833	1,680
	Job 6834	3,950
	Job 6835	4,420
Damaged stock written off from stores		2,300

Material transfers	£
Job 6834 to Job 6833	250
Job 6832 to 6834	620

Materials returned to store	£
From Job 6832	870
From Job 6835	170

Direct labour hours recorded	
Job 6832	430 hrs
Job 6833	650 hrs
Job 6834	280 hrs
Job 6835	410 hrs

The cost of labour hours during June 20X2 was £3 per hour, and production overhead is absorbed at the rate of £2 per direct labour hour. Production overheads incurred during the month amounted to £3,800. Completed jobs were delivered to customers as soon as they were completed, and the invoiced amounts were as follows.

Job 6832	£5,500
Job 6834	£8,000
Job 6835	£7,500

Administration and marketing overheads are added to the cost of sales at the rate of 20% of factory cost. Actual costs incurred during June 20X2 amounted to £3,200.

Required

(a) Prepare the job accounts for each individual job during June 20X2; (the accounts should only show the cost of production, and not the full cost of sale).

(b) Prepare the summarised job cost cards for each job, and calculate the profit on each completed job.

(c) Show how the costs would be shown in the company's cost control accounts.

3.3 SOLUTION

(a) **Job accounts**

JOB 6832

	£		£
Balance b/f	1,220	Job 6834 a/c	620
Materials (stores a/c)	2,390	(materials transfer)	
Labour (wages a/c)	1,290	Stores a/c (materials returned)	870
Production overhead (o'hd a/c)	860	Cost of sales a/c (balance)	4,270
	5,760		5,760

JOB 6833

	£		£
Materials (stores a/c)	1,680	Balance c/f	5,180
Labour (wages a/c)	1,950		
Production overhead (o'hd a/c)	1,300		
Job 6834 a/c (materials transfer)	250		
	5,180		5,180

JOB 6834

	£		£
Materials (stores a/c)	3,950	Job 6833 a/c (materials transfer)	250
Labour (wages a/c)	840		
Production overhead (o'hd a/c)	560	Cost of sales a/c (balance)	5,720
Job 6832 a/c (materials transfer)	620		
	5,970		5,970

JOB 6835

	£		£
Materials (stores a/c)	4,420	Stores a/c (materials returned)	170
Labour (wages a/c)	1,230		
Production overhead (o'hd a/c)	820	Cost of sales a/c (balance)	6,300
	6,470		6,470

(b) Job cards, summarised

	Job 6832	*Job 6833*	*Job 6834*	*Job 6835*
	£	£	£	
Materials	1,530*	1,930	4,320 **	4,250
Labour	1,640	1,950	840	1,230
Production overhead	1,100	1,300	560	820
Factory cost	4,270	5,180	(c/f) 5,720	6,300
Admin & marketing o'hd (20%)	854		1,144	1,260
Cost of sale	5,124		6,864	7,560
Invoice value	5,500		8,000	7,500
Profit/(loss) on job	376		1,136	(60)

* £(630 + 2,390 − 620 − 870) ** £(3,950 + 620 − 250)

(c) Control accounts

STORES CONTROL (incomplete)

	£		£
WIP a/c (returns)	1,040	WIP a/c	
		(2,390 + 1,680 + 3,950 + 4,420)	12,440
		Profit and loss a/c:	
		stock written off	2,300

WORK IN PROGRESS CONTROL

	£		£
Balance b/f	1,220	Stores control a/c (returns)	1,040
Stores control a/c	12,440	Cost of sales a/c	
Wages control a/c	5,310	*(4,270 + 5,720 + 6,300)	16,290
Production o'hd control a/c	3,540	Balance c/f (Job No 6833)	5,180
	22,510		22,510

* 1,770 hours at £3 per hour

COST OF SALES CONTROL

	£		£
WIP control a/c	16,290	Profit and loss	19,548
Admin & marketing o'hd a/c			
(854 + 1,144 + 1,260)	3,258		
	19,548		19,548

SALES

	£		£
Profit and loss	21,000	CLC	21,000
		(5,500 + 8,000 + 7,500)	
	21,000		21,000

PRODUCTION OVERHEAD CONTROL

	£		£
CLC	3,800	WIP a/c	3,540
(overhead incurred)		Under-absorbed o'hd a/c	260
	3,800		3,800

UNDER-/OVER-ABSORBED OVERHEADS

	£		£
Production o'hd control a/c	260	Admin & marketing o'hd a/c	58
		Profit and loss a/c	202
	260		260

ADMIN & MARKETING OVERHEAD CONTROL

	£		£
CLC	3,200	Cost of sales a/c	3,258
(overhead incurred)			
Over absorbed o'hd a/c	58		
	3,258		3,258

PROFIT AND LOSS

	£		£
Cost of sales a/c	19,548	Sales a/c	21,000
Stores a/c (stock written off)	2,300		
Under-absorbed overhead a/c	202	Loss (CLC) - balance	1,050
	22,050		22,050

FINANCIAL LEDGER CONTROL (CLC) (incomplete)

	£		£
Sales a/c	21,000	Production overhead a/c	3,800
P & L a/c (loss)	1,050	Admin and marketing o'hd a/c	3,200

The loss of £1,050 is the sum of the profits/losses on each completed job £(376 + 1,136 − 60) = £1,452, minus the total of under-absorbed overhead (£202) and the stock write-off (£2,300).

Question 2

A furniture-making business manufactures quality furniture to customers' orders. It has three production departments (A, B and C) which have overhead absorption rates (per direct labour hour) of £12.86, £12.40 and £14.03 respectively.

Two pieces of furniture are to be manufactured for customers. Direct costs are as follows.

	Job XYZ	Job MNO
Direct material	£154	£108
Direct labour	20 hours dept A	16 hours dept A
	12 hours dept B	10 hours dept B
	10 hours dept C	14 hours dept C

Labour rates are as follows: £3.80(A); £3.50 (B); £3.40 (C)

The firm quotes prices to customers that reflect a required profit of 25% on selling price. Calculate the total cost and selling price of each job.

Answer

		Job XYZ		Job MNO
		£		£
Direct material		154.00		108.00
Direct labour: dept A	(20 × 3.80)	76.00	(16 × 3.80)	60.80
dept B	(12 × 3.50)	42.00	(10 × 3.50)	35.00
dept C	(10 × 3.40)	34.00	(14 × 3.40)	47.60
Total direct cost		306.00		251.40
Overhead: dept A	(20 × 12.86)	257.20	(16 × 12.86)	205.76
dept B	(12 × 12.40)	148.80	(10 × 12.40)	124.00
dept C	(10 × 14.03)	140.30	(14 × 14.03)	196.42
Total cost		852.30		777.58
Profit (note)		284.10		259.19
Quoted selling price		1,136.40		1,036.77

(*Note.* If profit is 25% on selling price, this is the same as $33^1/3\%$ (25/75) on cost.)

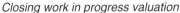

Question 3

A firm uses job costing and recovers overheads on direct labour.

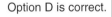

Three jobs were worked on during a period, the details of which are as follows.

	Job 1	Job 2	Job 3
	£	£	£
Opening work in progress	8,500	0	46,000
Material in period	17,150	29,025	0
Labour for period	12,500	23,000	4,500

The overheads for the period were exactly as budgeted, £140,000.

Jobs 1 and 2 were the only incomplete jobs.

What was the value of closing work in progress?

A £81,900　　　　B £90,175　　　　C £140,675　　　　D £214,425

Answer

Total labour cost = £12,500 + £23,000 + £4,500 = £40,000

$$\text{Overhead absorption rate} = \frac{£140,000}{£40,000} \times 100\% = 350\% \text{ of direct labour cost}$$

Closing work in progress valuation

		Job 1		Job 2	Total
		£		£	£
Costs given in question		38,150		52,025	90,175
Overhead absorbed	(12,500 × 350%)	43,750	(23,000 × 350%)	80,500	124,250
					214,425

Option D is correct.

We can eliminate option B because £90,175 is simply the total of the costs allocated to Jobs 1 and 2, with no absorption of overheads. Option A is an even lower cost figure, therefore it can also be eliminated.

Option C is wrong because it is a simple total of all allocated costs, including Job 3 which is not incomplete.

4　BATCH COSTING

4.1　The procedures for **costing batches** are very similar to those for costing jobs.

(a) The batch is treated as a **job** during production and the costs are collected in the manner already described in this chapter.

(b) Once the batch has been completed, the **cost per unit** can be calculated as the **total batch cost divided by the number of units in the batch.**

4.2 EXAMPLE: BATCH COSTING

A company manufactures widgets to order and has the following budgeted overheads for the year, based on normal activity levels.

Department	Budgeted overheads £	Budgeted activity
Welding	6,000	1,500 labour hours
Assembly	10,000	1,000 labour hours

Selling and administrative overheads are 20% of factory cost. An order for 250 widgets type X128, made as Batch 5997, incurred the following costs.

Materials   £12,000
Labour   100 hours welding shop at £2.50/hour
            200 hours assembly shop at £1/hour

£500 was paid for the hire of special X-ray equipment for testing the welds.

Required

Calculate the cost per unit for Batch 5997.

4.3 SOLUTION

The first step is to calculate the overhead absorption rate for the production departments.

Welding $= \dfrac{£6,000}{1,500} = £4$ per labour hour

Assembly $= \dfrac{£10,000}{1,000} = £10$ per labour hour

Total cost - Batch no 5997

	£	£
Direct material		12,000
Direct expense		500
Direct labour 100 × 2.50 =	250	
200 × 1.00 =	200	
		450
Prime cost		12,950
Overheads 100 × 4 =	400	
200 × 10 =	2,000	
		2,400
Factory cost		15,350
Selling and administrative cost (20% of factory cost)		3,070
Total cost		18,420

Cost per unit $= \dfrac{£18,420}{250} = £73.68$

5 INTRODUCTION TO CONTRACT COSTING

> **KEY TERMS**
>
> - A **contract** is a cost unit or cost centre which is charged with the direct costs of production and an apportionment of head office overheads.
>
> - **Contract costing** is a method of job costing where the job to be carried out is of such magnitude that a formal contract is made between the customer and supplier. It applies where work is undertaken to customers' special requirements and each order is of long duration (as compared with job costing). The work is usually constructional and in general the method is similar to job costing.

5.1 In industries such as building and construction work, civil engineering and shipbuilding, job costing is not usually appropriate. **Contract costing** is.

Features of contract costing

5.2 - A **formal contract** is made between customer and supplier.
- Work is undertaken to **customers' special requirements.**
- The work is for a **relatively long duration.**
- The work is frequently **constructional in nature.**
- The method of costing is **similar to job costing.**
- The work is frequently **based on site.**
- It is not unusual for a site to have its own cashier and time-keeper.

5.3 The problems which may arise in contract costing are as follows.

(a) **Identifying direct costs**: because of the large size of the job, many cost items which are usually thought of as production overhead are charged as direct costs of the contract (for example supervision, hire of plant, depreciation and so on).

(b) **Low indirect costs**: because many costs normally classed as overheads are charged as direct costs of a contract, the absorption rate for overheads should only apply a share of the cost of those cost items which are not already direct costs.

(c) **Difficulties of cost control**: because of the size of some contracts and some sites, there are often cost control problems (material usage and losses, pilferage, labour supervision, damage to and loss of plant and tools and so on).

(d) **Dividing the profit between different accounting periods**: when a contract covers two or more accounting periods, how should the profit (or loss) on the contract be divided between the periods?

6 RECORDING CONTRACT COSTS

Direct materials

6.1 The **direct materials** used on a contract may be obtained as follows.

- From the company's central stores
- From the company's suppliers (direct)

6.2 The following points concern **materials obtained from the company's central stores.**

(a)   A material requisition note must be sent to the store keeper from the contract site.

(b)   The contract manager or foreman must sign all material requisition notes, authorising the issue of materials.

(c)   The requisition note provides a record of the cost of the materials issued to the contract.

(d)   Contract foreman prefer to have too much material, rather than run out. This means that they will often requisition more material than actually needed. The surplus material will need to be returned to stores via a **material returns note**.

(e)   The material returns note must be signed by the foreman and checked by the storekeeper. The accounting entry when materials are returned is as follows.

CREDIT   Contract account (work in progress or 'job' account)
DEBIT   Stores account

(f)   Materials on site which relate to an incomplete contract should be carried forward as **'closing stock of materials on site'**.

6.3   When materials are delivered directly from the company's suppliers:

(a)   a copy of the goods received note will be sent from the site to the accounting department, and checked against the invoice received from the supplier;

(b)   the entire invoice cost will then be charged directly to the contract.

Direct labour

6.4   It is usual for **direct labour** on a contract site to be paid on an hourly basis.

- On a **small site**, the foreman will log the hours worked by each employee.
- On a **large site** there will probably be a resident timekeeper.

Since all the work done is spent exclusively on a single contract, the direct labour cost of the contract should be easily identified from the wages sheets.

6.5   Employees who work on several contracts at the same time, will have to record the time spent on each contract on **time sheets**. Each contract will then be charged with the cost of these recorded hours. Any revenue earned from other small jobs done whilst working on a contract should be treated as follows.

DEBIT   Cash (cash received)
CREDIT   Contract account

6.6   **Payment of wages** depends on the following.

(a)   If the **site is nearby**, the wages will be calculated in the head office accounting department, and wage packets made up by the head office cashier. The wages may then be transported from head office to the site by security van, and distributed by the site foreman. Unclaimed wages will be returned to the head office cashier.

(b)   If the **site is a long way** from head office, the wages may still be calculated by the accounting department at head office, but the job of distributing wage packets might be given to a site cashier. A local bank will be authorised by head office to issue the appropriate amount of wages to the site cashier.

6.7   The **cost of supervision**, which is usually a production overhead in unit costing, job costing and so on, will be a direct cost of a contract.

Subcontractors

6.8 On large contracts, much work may be done by **subcontractors**. The invoices of subcontractors will be treated as a **direct expense to the contract.**

The cost of plant

6.9 A feature of most contract work is the amount of plant used. Plant used on a contract may be **owned** by the company, or **hired** from a plant hire firm.

(a) If the plant is **hired**, the cost will be a direct expense of the contract.
(b) If the plant is **owned**, a variety of accounting methods may be employed.

Method one: charging depreciation

6.10 **The contract may be charged depreciation on the plant, on a straight line or reducing balance basis.** For example if a company has some plant which cost £10,000 and is depreciated at 10% per annum straight line (to a residual value of nil) and a contract makes use of the plant for six months, a depreciation charge of £500 would be made against the contract. The disadvantage of this method of costing for plant is that the contract site foreman is not made directly responsible and accountable for the actual plant in his charge. The foreman must be responsible for receipt of the plant, returning the plant after it has been used and proper care of the plant whilst it is being used.

Method two: charging the contract with current book value

6.11 **A more common method of costing for plant is to charge the contract with the current book value of the plant.**

CREDIT   Plant account (fixed asset account) - with the value of the plant net of depreciation

DEBIT   Contract account

At the end of an accounting period, the contract account is credited with the written down value of the equipment.

CREDIT   Contract account (plant written down value) carried forward as an opening balance at the start of the next period.

When plant is returned from the site to head office (or transferred to another contract site), the contract account is credited with the written down value of the plant.

CREDIT   Contract account (written down value)
DEBIT   Plant account (or another contract account)

6.12 EXAMPLE : CHARGING THE CONTRACT WITH CURRENT BOOK VALUE

Contract number 123 obtained some plant and loose tools from central store on 1 January 20X2. The book value of the plant was £100,000 and the book value of the loose tools was £8,000. On 1 October 20X2, some plant was removed from the site: this plant had a written down value on 1 October of £20,000. At 31 December 20X2, the plant remaining on site had a written down value of £60,000 and the loose tools had a written down value of £5,000.

CONTRACT 123 ACCOUNT

	£		£
1 January 20X2		*1 October 20X2*	
Plant issued to site	100,000	Plant transferred	20,000
Loose tools issued to site	8,000	*31 December 20X2*	
		Plant value c/f	60,000
		Loose tools value c/f	5,000
		Depreciation (bal fig)	23,000
	108,000		108,000

The difference between the values on the debit and the credit sides of the account (£20,000 for plant and £3,000 for loose tools) is the depreciation cost of the equipment for the year.

Method three: using a plant account

6.13 A third method of accounting for plant costs is to **open a plant account, which is debited with the depreciation costs and the running costs** (repairs, fuel and so on) **of the equipment**. A notional hire charge is then made to contracts using the plant. For example suppose that a company owns some equipment which is depreciated at the rate of £100 per month. Running costs in May 20X3 are £300. The plant is used on 20 days in the month, 12 days on Contract X and 8 days on Contract Y. The accounting entries would be as follows.

PLANT ACCOUNT

	£		£
Depreciation (cost ledger control account)	100	Contract X (hire for 12 days)	240
Running costs (cost ledger control a/c, wages a/c and stores a/c)	300	Contract Y (hire for 8 days)	160
	400		400

CONTRACT X

	£		£
Plant account (notional hire)	240		

CONTRACT Y

	£		£
Plant account (notional hire)	160		

Overhead costs

6.14 **Overhead costs** are added periodically (for example at the end of an accounting period) and are based on predetermined overhead absorption rates for the period. You may come across examples where a share of head office general costs is absorbed as an overhead cost to the contract, but this should not happen if the contract is unfinished at the end of the period, because only production overheads should be included in the value of any closing work in progress.

7 CONTRACT ACCOUNTS

7.1 The account for a contract is a **job account**, or **work in progress account**, and is a record of the direct materials, direct labour, direct expenses and overhead charges on the contract. If we ignore, for the moment, profits on a part-finished contract, a typical contract account might appear as shown below. Check the items in the account carefully, and notice how the cost (or value) of the work done emerges as work in progress. On an unfinished contract, where no profits are taken mid-way through the contract, this cost of work in progress is carried forward as a closing stock balance.

7.2 EXAMPLE: A CONTRACT ACCOUNT

CONTRACT 794 - LUTTERBINS HOLIDAY CAMP

	£		£
Materials requisition from stores	15,247	Materials returned to stores or	
Materials and equipment purchased	36,300	transferred to other sites	2,100
Maintenance and operating costs		Proceeds from sale of materials	
of plant and vehicles	14,444	on site and jobbing work for	
Hire charges for plant and		other customers	600
vehicles not owned	6,500	Book value of plant transferred	4,800
Tools and consumables	8,570	Materials on site c/d	7,194
Book value of plant on site b/d	14,300	Book value of plant on site c/d	6,640
Direct wages	23,890		21,334
Supervisors' and engineers' salaries			
(proportion relating to time spent		Cost of work done c/d	
on the contract)	13,000	(balancing item)	139,917
Other site expenses	12,000		
Overheads (apportioned perhaps on			
the basis of direct labour hours)	17,000		
	161,251		161,251
Materials on site b/d	7,194		
Book value of plant on site b/d	6,640		
Cost of work done b/d	139,917		

8 PROGRESS PAYMENTS

8.1 A customer is likely to be required under the terms of the contract to make **progress payments** to the contractor throughout the course of the work. The amount of the payments will be based on the **value of work done** (as a proportion of the contract price) as assessed by the architect or surveyor (for a building contract) or qualified engineer in his certificate. A **certificate** provides confirmation that work to a certain value has been completed, and that some payment to the contractor is now due. The amount of the payment will be calculated as follows.

> **The value of work done and certified by the architect or engineer**
> minus **a retention (commonly 10%)**
> minus **the payments made to date**
> equals **payment due.**

8.2 Thus, if an architect's certificate assesses the value of work done on a contract to be £125,000 and if the retention is 10%, and if £92,000 has already been paid in progress payments the current payment = £125,000 – £12,500 – £92,000 = £20,500

8.3 When **progress payments** are received from the customer, the accounting entry is as follows.

DEBIT Bank (or financial ledger control account)
CREDIT Cash received on account, or contractee account.

8.4 **Retention monies** are released when the contract is completed and accepted by the customer.

9 PROFITS ON CONTRACTS

9.1 You may have noticed that the progress payments do not necessarily give rise to profit immediately because of **retentions. So how are profits calculated on contracts?**

9.2 EXAMPLE: PROFITS ON CONTRACTS COMPLETED IN ONE ACCOUNTING PERIOD

If a contract is started and completed in the same accounting period, the calculation of the profit is straightforward, sales minus the cost of the contract. Suppose that a contract, No 6548, has the following costs.

	£
Direct materials (less returns)	40,000
Direct labour	35,000
Direct expenses	8,000
Plant costs	6,000
Overhead	11,000
	100,000

The work began on 1 February 20X3 and was completed on 15 November 20X3 in the contractor's same accounting year.

The contract price was £120,000 and on 20 November the inspecting engineer issued the final certificate of work done. At that date the customer had already paid £90,000 and the remaining £30,000 was still outstanding at the end of the contractor's accounting period. The accounts would appear as follows.

CONTRACT 6548 ACCOUNT

	£		£
Materials less returns	40,000	Cost of sales (P&L)	100,000
Labour	35,000		
Expenses	8,000		
Plant cost	6,000		
Overhead	11,000		
	100,000		100,000

WORK CERTIFIED ACCOUNT

	£		£
Turnover (P&L)	120,000	Contractee account	120,000
	120,000		120,000

CONTRACTEE (CUSTOMER) ACCOUNT

	£		£
Work certified a/c - value of work certified	120,000	Cash	90,000
		Balance c/f (debtor in balance sheet)	30,000
	120,000		120,000

The profit on the contract will be treated in the profit and loss account as follows.

	£
Turnover	120,000
Cost of sales	100,000
	20,000

Taking profits on incomplete contracts

9.3 A more difficult problem emerges when a contract is **incomplete** at the end of an accounting period. The contractor may have spent considerable sums of money on the work, and received substantial progress payments, and even if the work is not finished, the contractor will want to claim some profit on the work done so far.

9.4 Suppose that a company starts four new contracts in its accounting year to 31 December 20X1, but at the end of the year, none of them has been completed. All of the contracts are eventually completed in the first few months of 20X2 and they make profits of £40,000, £50,000, £60,000 and £70,000 respectively, £220,000 in total. If profits are not taken until the contracts are finished, the company would make no profits at all in 20X1, when most of the work was done, and £220,000 in 20X2. Such violent fluctuations in profitability would be confusing not only to the company's management, but also to shareholders and the investing public at large.

9.5 The problem arises because **contracts are for long-term work**, and it is a well-established practice that some profits should be taken in an accounting period, even if the contract is incomplete.

9.6 EXAMPLE: PROFITS ON INCOMPLETE CONTRACTS

Suppose that contract 246 is started on 1 July 20X2. Costs to 31 December 20X2, when the company's accounting year ends, are derived from the following information.

	£
Direct materials issued from store	18,000
Materials returned to store	400
Direct labour	15,500
Plant issued, at book value 1 July 20X2	32,000
Written-down value of plant 31 December 20X2	24,000
Materials on site, 31 December 20X2	1,600
Overhead costs	2,000

As at 31 December, certificates had been issued for work valued at £50,000 and the contractee had made progress payments of £45,000. The company has calculated that more work has been done since the last certificates were issued, and that the cost of work done but not yet certified is £8,000.

9.7 SOLUTION

The contract account would be prepared as follows.

CONTRACT 246 ACCOUNT

	£	£		£
Materials	18,000		Value of plant c/d	24,000
Less returns	400		Materials on site c/d	1,600
		17,600	Cost of work done not	
Labour		15,500	certified c/d	8,000
Plant issued at book value		32,000	Cost of sales (P&L)	33,500
Overheads		2,000		
		67,100		67,100

WORK CERTIFIED ACCOUNT

	£		£
Turnover (P&L)	50,000	Contractee account	50,000
	50,000		50,000

CONTRACTEE ACCOUNT

	£		£
Work certified account	50,000	Cash (progress payment)	45,000
		Balance c/f	5,000
	50,000		50,000

Points to note

(a) **The work done, but not yet certified, must be valued at cost,** and not at the value of the unissued certificates. It would be imprudent to suppose that the work has been done to the complete satisfaction of the architect or engineer, who may not issue certificates until further work is done.

(b) It would appear that £50,000 should be recognised as turnover and £33,500 as cost of sales leaving £16,500 as net profit. However it is often considered imprudent to claim this full amount of profit, and it is commonly argued that the profit taken should be a more conservative figure (in our example, less than £16,500, so that amounts taken to turnover and cost of sales relating to the contract should be less than £50,000 and £33,500 respectively).

(c) We have ignored retentions here.

Estimating the size of the profit

Exam focus point

The method of calculating profit on an incomplete contract may vary, and you should check any examination question carefully to find out whether a specific method is stated in the text of the question.

9.8 The **concept of prudence** should be applied when estimating the size of the profit on an incomplete contract and the following guidelines should be noted.

(a) **If the contract is in its early stages, no profit should be taken**. Profit should only be taken when the outcome of the contract can be assessed with reasonable accuracy.

(b) **For a contract on which substantial costs have been incurred, but which is not yet near completion** (that is, it is in the region of 35% to 85% complete) a formula which has often been used in the past is as follows.

Profit taken = $^2/_3$ (or $^3/_4$) of the notional profit

where notional profit = (the value of work certified to date) – (the cost of the work certified).

In the example above, the notional profit for contract 246 is £16,500 (£(50,000 - 33,500)) and the profit taken for the period using the above formula would be calculated as follows.

$^2/_3$ of £16,500 = £11,000 (or $^3/_4$ of £16,500 = £12,375)

(c) **Where the contractee withholds a retention, or where progress payments are not made as soon as work certificates are issued**, it would be more prudent to reduce the profit taken by the proportion of retentions to the value of work certified.

Profit taken = $^2/_3$ (or $^3/_4$) × notional profit × $\dfrac{\text{cash received on account}}{\text{value of work certified}}$

In our example of contract 246, this would be:

$^2/_3 \times £16,500 \times \dfrac{£45,000}{£50,000} = £9,900$

(d) **If the contract is nearing completion, the size of the eventual profit should be foreseeable with reasonable certainty and there is no need to be excessively prudent.** The profit taken may be calculated by one of three methods.

(i) **Work certified to date minus the cost of work certified.** In our example, this would be the full £16,500.

(ii) $\dfrac{\text{Cost of work done}}{\text{Estimated total cost of contract}} \times$ **estimated total profit on contract**

In our example, if the estimated total cost of the contract 246 is £64,000 and the estimated total profit on the contract is £18,000, the profit taken would be:

$$\frac{£(33,500 + 8,000)}{£64,000} \times £18,000 = £11,672$$

(iii) **Profit taken** $= \dfrac{\textbf{Value of work certified}}{\textbf{contract price}} \times \textbf{estimated total profit}$

This is perhaps the most-favoured of the three methods. In our example of contract 246, if the final contract price is £82,000 and the estimated total profit is £18,000 the profit taken would be:

$$\frac{£50,000}{£82,000} \times £18,000 = £10,976$$

Some companies may feel that it is prudent to reduce the profit attributed to the current accounting period still further, to allow for retentions of cash by the contractee. In our example, the profit taken would now be:

$$\frac{£50,000}{£82,000} \times £18,000 \times \frac{£45,000}{£50,000} = £9,878$$

This formula simplifies to:

$$\frac{\text{cash received to date}}{\text{contract price}} \times \text{estimated total profit from the contract}$$

(e) **A loss on the contract may be foreseen.** The method of dealing with losses is covered in the next section.

9.9 It should be apparent from these different formulae that the profit taken on an incomplete contract will depend on two things.

- The degree of completion
- The choice of formula

Question 4

Landy Stroyers plc is a construction company. Data relating to one of its contracts, XYZ, for the year to 31 December 20X2, are as follows.

	£'000
Value of work certified to 31 December 20X1	500
Cost of work certified to 31 December 20X1	360
Plant on site b/f at 1 January 20X2	30
Materials on site b/f at 1 January 20X2	10
Cost of contract to 1 January 20X2 b/f	370
Materials issued from store	190
Sub-contractors' costs	200
Wages and salaries	200
Overheads absorbed by contract in 20X2	100
Plant on site c/f at 31 December 20X2	15
Materials on site c/f at 31 December 20X2	5
Value of work certified to 31 December 20X2	1,200
Cost of work certified to 31 December 20X2	950

No profit has been taken on the contract prior to 20X2. There are no retentions.

Required

(a) Calculate the total cumulative cost of contract XYZ to the end of December 20X2.

(b) Turnover on the contract is taken as the value of work certified. Calculate the gross profit for the contract for the year to 31 December 20X2.

Answer

(a)

CONTRACT ACCOUNT

	£'000		£'000
Cost of contract b/f	370	Plant on site c/f	15
Plant on site b/f	30✓	Materials on site c/f	5
Materials on site b/f	10✓	Cost of contract c/f (balance)	1,080
Materials from stores	190✓		
Sub-contractors' costs	200✓		
Wages and salaries	200✓		
Overheads	100✓		
	1,100		1,100

(b) No profit had been taken on the contract prior to 20X2, and so profit is quite simply calculated as follows.

	£'000
Value of work certified to 31.12.X2	1,200
Cost of work certified to 31.12.X2	950
Gross profit to 31.12.X2	250

10 LOSSES ON INCOMPLETE CONTRACTS

10.1 At the end of an accounting period, it may be that instead of finding that the contract is profitable, a loss is expected. When this occurs, the **total expected loss should be taken into account as soon as it is recognised, even though the contract is not yet complete.** The contract account should be debited with the **anticipated future loss** (final cost of contract – full contract price – (cost of work at present – value of work certified at present)) and the profit and loss account debited with the total expected loss (final cost of contract – full contract price).

The same accounting procedure would be followed on completed contracts, as well as incomplete contracts, but it is essential that the full amount of the loss on the total contract, if foreseeable, should be charged against company profits at the earliest opportunity, even if a contract is incomplete. This means that in the next accounting period, the contract should break even, making neither a profit nor a loss, because the full loss has already been charged to the profit and loss account.

10.2 EXAMPLE: LOSS ON CONTRACT

Contract 257 was begun on 22 March 20X3. By 31 December 20X3, the end of the contractor's accounting year, costs incurred were as follows.

	£
Materials issued	24,000
Materials on site, 31 December	2,000
Labour	36,000
Plant issued to site 22 March	40,000
Written-down value of plant, 31 December	28,000
Overheads	6,000

The contract is expected to end in February 20X4 and at 31 December 20X3, the cost accountant estimated that the final cost of the contract would be £95,000. The full contract price is £90,000. Work certified at 31 December was valued at £72,000. The contractee has made progress payments up to 31 December of £63,000.

Required

Prepare the contract account.

10.3 SOLUTION

CONTRACT 257 ACCOUNT

	£		£
Materials issued	24,000	Materials on site c/f	2,000
Labour	36,000	Plant at written-down value, c/f	28,000
Plant issued, written-down value	40,000	Cost of work c/d (balancing figure)	76,000
Overheads	6,000		
	106,000		106,000
Cost of work done, b/d	76,000	Cost of sales (P&L)	77,000
Anticipated future loss*	1,000		
	77,000		77,000

* The total estimated loss on the contract is £5,000 (£90,000 – £95,000). Of this amount £4,000 has been lost in the current period (£76,000 – £72,000) and so £1,000 is anticipated as arising in the future: the company will invoice £18,000 (£90,000 – £72,000) and will incur costs of £19,000 (£95,000 – £76,000). This is taken as a loss in the current period.

The loss is posted £72,000 to turnover and £77,000 to cost of sales (£5,000 net).

Question 5

Jibby Ltd's year end is 30 April. At 30 April 20X4 costs of £43,750 have been incurred on contract N53. The value of work certified at the period end is £38,615. The contract price is £57,500 but it is anticipated that the final costs at 30 September 20X4, when the contract is expected to end, will be £63,111.

Required

(a)   Prepare the contract account.
(b)   Calculate the figures for turnover and cost of sales for the period to 30 April 20X4.

Answer

(a)

CONTRACT N53

	£		£
Cost of work done b/d	43,750	Cost of sales (P&L)	44,226
Anticipated future loss*	476		
	44,226		44,226

*£[(63,111 – 57,500) – (43,750 – 38,615)] = £476.

(b)   Turnover = £38,615

Cost of sales = £44,226

---

11   DISCLOSURE OF LONG-TERM CONTRACTS IN FINANCIAL ACCOUNTS

11.1   **SSAP 9** defines how **stocks** and **work in progress** should be valued in the financial accounts, and makes particular reference to long-term contract work in progress and profits. Although there is no requirement that cost accounting procedures should be the same as financial accounting procedures and standards, it is generally thought that conformity between the financial and cost accounts is desirable in contract costing.

11.2   SSAP 9 makes the following requirements with relation to the profit and loss account.

(a) The profit and loss account will contain turnover and related costs deemed to accrue to the contract over the period, so that the profit and loss account reflects the net profit on the contract taken in the period.

(b) The profit taken needs to reflect the proportion of the work carried out at the accounting date, and to take account of any known inequalities of profitability at the various stages of a contract.

(c) Where the outcome of a contract cannot be reasonably assessed before its completion, no profits should be taken on the incomplete contract.

(d) The amount of profit taken to the profit and loss account for an incomplete contract should be judged with prudence.

(e) If it is expected that there will be a loss on the contract as a whole, provision needs to be made for the whole of the loss as soon as it is recognised (in accordance with the prudence concept). The amount of the loss should be deducted from the amounts for long-term contracts included under stocks, and where a credit balance results, it should be disclosed separately under creditors or provisions for liabilities and charges.

11.3 **SSAP 9** requires the following **disclosures** in the balance sheet.

Balances relating to long-term contracts are split into two elements.

(a) Work done on long-term contracts not yet recognised in the profit and loss account is disclosed under 'stocks' as 'long-term contract balances'.

(b) The difference between

(i)	amounts recognised as turnover	X
(ii)	progress payments received	(X)
		X

will be recognised in debtors as 'amounts recoverable on long-term contracts' if (i) is greater than (ii), or will be offset against the balances in (a) above if (ii) is greater than (i).

Chapter roundup

- **Job costing** is the costing method used where each cost unit is separately identifiable.

- Each job is given a **number** to distinguish it from other jobs.

- Costs for each job are collected on a **job cost sheet** or **job card.**

- Material costs for each job are determined from **material requisition notes**.

- Labour times on each job are recorded on a **job ticket**, which is then costed and recorded on the job cost sheet. Some labour costs, such as overtime premium or the cost of rectifying sub-standard output, might be charged either directly to a job or else as an overhead cost, depending on the circumstances in which the costs have arisen.

- **Overhead** is absorbed into the cost of jobs using the predetermined overhead absorption rates.

- The usual method of fixing prices within a jobbing concern is **cost plus pricing**.

- An **internal job costing system** can be used for costing the work of service departments.

- **Batch costing** is similar to job costing in that each batch of similar articles is separately identifiable. The **cost per unit** manufactured in a batch is the total batch cost divided by the number of units in the batch.

- **Contract costing** is a form of job costing which applies where the job is on a large scale and for a long duration. The majority of costs relating to a contact are direct costs.

- Contract costs are collected in a **contract account**.

- A customer is likely to be required to make **progress payments** which are calculated as the value of work done and certified by the architect or engineer minus a retention minus the payments made to date.

- The long duration of a contract usually means that an estimate must be made of the profit earned on each incomplete contract at the end of the accounting period. There are several different ways of calculating contract profits, but the overriding consideration must be the application of the prudence concept. **If a loss is expected on a contract, the total expected loss should be taken into account as soon as it is recognised, even if the contract is not complete.**

- The loss should be deducted from the amounts for long-term contracts included under stocks in the balance sheet. If the resulting balance is a credit, it should be disclosed separately under creditors or provisions for liabilities and charges.

- **SSAP 9** requires the following disclosures in the balance sheet.

  o Work done on long-term contracts which has yet to be recognised in the profit and loss account in disclosed under 'stocks' as 'long-term contract balances'.

  o The difference between (a) 'amounts recognised as turnover' and (b) 'progress payments received' will be recognised in debtors as 'amounts recoverable on long-term contracts' if (a) > (b), but will be offset against the stock balance mentioned above if (b) > (a).

Quick quiz

1   Which of the following are not characteristics of job costing?

     I   Customer driven production
     II   Complete production possible within a single accounting period
     III   Homogeneous products

     A   I and II only
     B   I and III only
     C   II and III only
     D   III only

2   The cost of a job is £100,000

    (a)   If profit is 25% of the job cost, the price of the job = £ *125,000* ✓

    (b)   If there is a 25% margin, the price of the job = £ *133333* ✓

3   List six features of contract costing

- ✓ *May extend over accounting period*
- ✗ *All cost are gathered together on a contract sheet*
- ✓ *A formal agreement maybe made*
- ✓ *Work undertaken to customers special requirements*
- ....
- ....

4   When progress payments are received from a customer for a contract, what is the accounting entry?

✓ DEBIT *Bank Acct*

✓ CREDIT *Contractee acct*

5   What are the three methods of calculating profit on a contract which is nearing completion?

6   How would you account for a loss on an incomplete contract?

Answers to quick quiz

1   D

2   (a)   £100,000 + (25% × £100,000) = £100,000 + £25,000 = £125,000

    (b)   Let price of job = x

$$\therefore \text{Profit} = 25\% \times x \text{ (selling price)}$$

$$\text{If profit} = 0.25x$$

$$x - 0.25x = \text{cost of job}$$

$$0.75x = £100,000$$

$$x = \frac{£100,000}{0.75}$$

$$= £133,333$$

3
- A formal contract is made between customer and supplier
- Work is undertaken to customers' special requirements
- The work is for a relatively long duration
- The work is frequently constructional in nature
- The method of costing is similar to job costing
- The work is frequently based on site

4   DEBIT   BANK/CASH

    CREDIT   CASH RECEIVED ON ACCOUNT/CONTRACTEE ACCOUNT

5   (a)   Work certified to date – cost of work certified

    (b) $\dfrac{\text{Cost of work done}}{\text{Estimated total cost of contract}} \times \text{estimated total profit on contract}$

    (c) $\dfrac{\text{Value of work certified}}{\text{Contract price}} \times \text{estimated total profit}$

6   If a loss is expected on an incomplete contract, the total expected loss should be taken into account as soon as it is recognised, even though the contract is not yet complete.

Now try the questions below from the Exam Question Bank

Number	Level	Marks	Time
16	MCQ	n/a	n/a
17	Examination	10	18 mins

Chapter 11

PROCESS COSTING

Topic list		Syllabus reference
1	Introduction to process costing	4(b)
2	The basics of process costing	4(b)
3	Dealing with losses in process	4(b)
4	Accounting for scrap	4(b)
5	Losses with a disposal cost	4(b)
6	Valuing closing work in progress	4(b)
7	Valuing opening work in progress: FIFO method	4(b)
8	Valuing opening work in progress: weighted average cost method	4(b)

Introduction

We have already looked at three costing methods, **job costing**, **batch costing** and **contract costing**. In this chapter we will consider a fourth, **process costing**. The chapter will consider the topic from basics, looking at how to account for the most simple of processes. We then move on to how to account for any **losses** which might occur, as well as what to do with any **scrapped units** which are sold. We also consider how to deal with any **closing work in progress** and then look at two methods of valuing **opening work in progress**. Valuation of both opening and closing work in progress hinges on the concept of **equivalent units**, which will be explained in detail.

Study guide

Section 5 – Cost classification

- Describe briefly the different methods of costing final outputs and their appropriateness to different types of business organisation/situation

Section 14 – Process costing 1

- Describe the characteristics of process costing

- Describe situations where the use of process costing is appropriate

- Describe the key areas of complexity in process costing

- Define 'normal' loses and 'abnormal' gains and losses

- State and justify the treatment of normal losses and abnormal gains and losses in process accounts

- Account for process scrap

- Calculate the cost per unit of process outputs, and prepare simple process accounts, in absorption and marginal costing systems

---

Section 15 – Process costing 2

- Calculate and explain the concept of equivalent units

- Allocate process costs between work remaining in process and transfer out of a process using the weighted average cost and FIFO methods

- Prepare process accounts in situations where work remains incomplete

- Prepare process accounts in situations where losses and gains are identified at different stages of the process

Exam guide

Process costing is one of the key areas of the syllabus and a common Section B examination question might require you to prepare a process account for a period. Make sure that you can deal with losses, gains, scrap and work in progress.

---

1 INTRODUCTION TO PROCESS COSTING

KEY TERM

Process costing is a costing method used where it is not possible to identify separate units of production, or jobs, usually because of the continuous nature of the production processes involved.

1.1 It is common to identify process costing with **continuous production** such as the following.

- Oil refining
- Paper
- Foods and drinks
- Chemicals

Process costing may also be associated with the continuous production of large volumes of low-cost items, such as **cans** or **tins**.

1.2 The following are features of process costing which make it different from job or batch costing.

(a) The **output** of one process becomes the **input** to the next until the finished product is made in the final process.

(b) The continuous nature of production in many processes means that there will usually be **closing work in progress which must be valued**. In process costing it is not possible to build up cost records of the cost per unit of output or the cost per unit of closing stock because production in progress is an **indistinguishable homogeneous mass**.

(c) There is often a **loss in process** due to spoilage, wastage, evaporation and so on.

(d) Output from production may be a single product, but there may also be a **by-product** (or by-products) and/or **joint products.**

1.3 The aim of this chapter is to describe how cost accountants keep a set of accounts to record the costs of production in a processing industry. The aim of the set of accounts is to derive a cost, or valuation, for output and closing stock.

2   THE BASICS OF PROCESS COSTING

2.1   Where a series of separate processes is required to manufacture the finished product, the output of one process becomes the input to the next until the final output is made in the final process. If two processes are required the accounts would look like this.

PROCESS 1 ACCOUNT

	Units	£		Units	£
Direct materials	1,000	50,000	Output to process 2	1,000	90,000
Direct labour		20,000			
Production overhead		20,000			
	1,000	90,000		1,000	90,000

PROCESS 2 ACCOUNT

	Units	£		Units	£
Materials from process 1	1,000	90,000	Output to finished goods	1,000	150,000
Added materials		30,000			
Direct labour		15,000			
Production overhead		15,000			
	1,000	150,000		1,000	150,000

2.2   Note that direct labour and production overhead may be treated together in an examination question as **conversion cost**.

2.3   **Added** materials, labour and overhead in process 2 are added gradually throughout the process. Materials from process 1, in contrast, will often be introduced in full at the start of process 2.

2.4   The 'units' columns in the process accounts are for **memorandum purposes** only and help you to ensure that you do not miss out any entries.

Framework for dealing with process costing

2.5   Process costing is centred around **four key steps**. The exact work done at each step will depend on whether there are normal losses, scrap, opening and closing stock and so on.

Step 1.   **Determine output and losses.** This step involves the following.

- Determining expected output
- Calculating normal loss and abnormal loss and gain
- Calculating equivalent units if there is closing or opening work in progress

Step 2.   **Calculate cost per unit of output, losses and WIP**. This step involves calculating cost per unit or cost per equivalent unit.

Step 3.   **Calculate total cost of output, losses and WIP**. In some examples this will be straightforward; however in cases where there is closing and/or opening work-in-progress a **statement of evaluation** will have to be prepared.

Step 4.   **Complete accounts**. This step involves the following.

- Completing the process account
- Writing up the other accounts required by the question

3   DEALING WITH LOSSES IN PROCESS

3.1   Losses during processing can happen when liquids evaporate, when there is wastage and if completed units are rejected.

A **loss** therefore occurs when the quantity of materials output from a process is less than the quantities input. How would any losses be costed?

Three different ways of costing losses

3.2   Suppose that input to a process consists of 100 litres of material. Total process costs are £85,652. What is the cost per litre if output is as follows?

(a)   92 litres
(b)   98 litres

Base cost per unit on output

3.3   One way of costing the output is to say that **the cost per unit should be based on actual units produced (output), so that any lost units have no cost at all.**

		Cost per unit		
(a)	If output is 92 litres	$\dfrac{£85,652}{92}$	=	£931 per litre
(b)	If output is 98 litres	$\dfrac{£85,652}{98}$	=	£874 per litre

You should see that the **cost per litre varies** according to the actual loss in the period. Therefore, if some loss in process is unavoidable, and if the amount of loss varies from period to period, this approach to costing will result in **fluctuations** in unit costs.

3.4   It might be more satisfactory to take a **longer-term view of loss**, and calculate **average unit costs** on the basis of **average loss** over a longer period of time. This would give **greater stability** and **consistency** to unit costs of production between one period (such as one month) and the next.

Base cost per unit on input

3.5   A second way of costing the output is to say that **lost units have a cost, which should be charged to the P & L account** whenever they occur. The cost per unit would then be based on units of **input** rather than units of output.

		Cost per unit £	Cost of output £	Cost of loss £
(a)	If output is 92 litres	$\dfrac{£85,652}{100}$ 856.52	(× 92) 78,799.84	(× 8) 6,852.16
(b)	If output is 98 litres	$\dfrac{£85,652}{100}$ 856.52	(× 98) 83,938.96	(× 2) 1,713.04

The cost of the loss would be written off directly to the P & L account.

The main drawback to this method of costing is that if some loss in processing is unavoidable and to be expected, there would be some cost of production unavoidably written off to the P & L account in every period, and this is an unsatisfactory method of costing.

Differentiate between expected and unexpected losses

3.6 The third method of costing loss (described below) is a **compromise system**, which is based on the following view.

- If some loss is to be expected, it should not be given a cost.
- If there is some loss that 'shouldn't happen', it ought to be given a cost.

Normal loss and abnormal loss/gain

> **KEY TERMS**
>
> - **Normal loss** is the loss expected during a process. It is not given a cost.
>
> - **Abnormal loss** is the loss resulting when actual loss is greater than normal or expected loss, and it is given a cost.
>
> - **Abnormal gain** is the gain resulting when actual loss is less than the normal or expected loss, and it is given a 'negative cost'.

3.7 Normal loss, abnormal loss and abnormal gain can be illustrated using the information in Paragraph 3.2. The cost per unit should be based on **expected output**, which is **input minus normal loss**. Let's suppose that normal loss is 5% of input.

3.8 If actual output is 92 litres, the steps are as follows.

Step 1. **Determine output and losses**
Normal output is 95 litres, and so there is an abnormal loss of 3 litres.

Step 2. **Calculate cost per unit of output, losses and WIP**
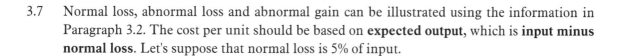
$$\text{Cost per unit} = \frac{£85,652}{(100-5)\text{litres}} = \frac{£85,652}{95} = £901.60 \text{ per litre}$$

Step 3. **Calculate total cost of output and losses**

	£
Cost of output (92 × £901.60)	82,947.20
Normal loss	0.00
Abnormal loss (3 litres × £901.60)	2,704.80
	85,652.00

Step 4. **Complete accounts**
The process account and abnormal loss account would be:

BPP PUBLISHING

PROCESS ACCOUNT

	Units	£		Units	£
Cost of materials,			Finished goods	92	82,947.20
labour and overhead	100	85,652	Normal loss	5	0.00
			Abnormal loss	3	2,704.80
	100	85,652		100	85,652.00

ABNORMAL LOSS A/C

	£		£
Process a/c	2704.80	P & L account	2704.80

3.9 If actual output is 98 litres, the steps are as follows.

Step 1. Determine output and losses

Normal output is 95 litres, and normal loss is 5 litres, therefore there is an abnormal gain of (98 – 95) = 3 litres.

Step 2. Calculate cost per unit of output and losses

This will be £901.60 as above.

Step 3. Calculate total cost of output and losses

	£
Cost of output (98 × £901.60)	88,356.80
Normal loss	0.00
	88,356.80
Abnormal gain (3 litres × £901.60)	(2,704.80)
	85,652.00

Step 4. Complete accounts

The process account and abnormal gain account would be as follows.

PROCESS ACCOUNT

	Units	£		Units	£
Cost of materials, labour			Finished goods	98	88,356.80
and overhead	100	85,652.00	Normal loss	5	0.00
Abnormal gain	3	2,704.80			
	103	88,356.80		103	88,356.80

ABNORMAL GAIN A/C

	£		£
P & L account	2704.80	Process a/c	2704.80

3.10 EXAMPLE: NORMAL AND ABNORMAL LOSS

Gunner Ltd operates a manufacturing process, and during March 20X3 the following processing took place.

Opening stock	nil	Closing stock	nil
Units introduced	1,000 units	Output	900 units
Costs incurred	£4,500	Loss	100 units

Required

Determine the cost of output in the following circumstances.

(a) Expected or normal loss is 10% of input.
(b) There is no expected loss, so that the entire loss of 100 units was unexpected.

3.11 SOLUTION

(a) If loss is expected, and is an unavoidable feature of processing, it is argued by cost accountants that there is no point in charging a cost to the loss. It is more sensible to accept that the loss will occur, and spread the costs of production over the expected units of output.

Step 1. **Determine output and losses**

Normal output is 90% of 1,000 units which is 900 units. Normal loss is therefore 100 units (1,000 – 900).

Step 2. **Calculate cost per unit of output, losses and WIP**

$$\text{Cost per unit of output} = \frac{\text{Costs}}{\text{Expected output}} = \frac{£4,500}{900} = £5$$

Step 3. **Calculate total cost of output and losses**

	£
Cost of output (900 × £5)	4,500
Normal loss (100 × £0)	-
	4,500

Step 4. **Complete accounts**

Normal loss is not given any cost, so that the process account would appear as follows.

PROCESS ACCOUNT

	Units	£		Units	£
Costs incurred	1,000	4,500	Normal loss	100	0
			Output units	900	4,500
	1,000	4,500		1,000	4,500

It helps to enter normal loss into the process 'T' account, just to make sure that your memorandum columns for units are the same on the debit and the credit sides of the account.

(b) If loss is unexpected and occurred perhaps as a result of poor workmanship, poor quality materials and so on, it is argued that it would be reasonable to charge a cost to the units of loss. The cost would then be transferred to an 'abnormal loss' account, and eventually written off to the profit and loss account as an item of loss in the period. Units of 'good output' would not be burdened with the cost of the loss, so that the cost per unit remains unaltered.

Step 1. **Determine output and losses**

Normal output is 1,000 units as stated in the question. Therefore abnormal loss is 100 units.

Step 2. **Calculate cost per unit of output, losses and WIP**

$$\text{Cost per unit of output} = \frac{£4,500}{1,000\,\text{units}} = £4.50$$

Step 3. **Calculate total cost of output and losses**

	£
Cost of output (900 × £4.50)	4,050
Abnormal loss (100 × £4.50)	450
	4,500

Step 4. **Complete accounts**

The process account and abnormal loss account would look like this.

PROCESS ACCOUNT

	Units	£		Units	£
Costs incurred	1,000	4,500	Abnormal loss	100	450
			Output units	900	4,050
	1,000	4,500		1,000	4,500

ABNORMAL LOSS ACCOUNT

	Units	£		Units	£
Process account	100	450	Profit and loss account	100	450

3.12 EXAMPLE: ABNORMAL LOSSES AND GAINS

Suppose that input to a process is 1,000 units at a cost of £4,500. Normal loss is 10% and there are no opening or closing stocks. What would be the accounting entries for the cost of output and the cost of the loss if actual output were as follows.

(a) 860 units (so that actual loss is 140 units).
(b) 920 units (so that actual loss is 80 units).

3.13 SOLUTION

The same principles described earlier for evaluating normal and abnormal loss may be applied to situations where normal loss and abnormal loss/gain occur together.

(a) Normal loss is given no share of cost.

(b) The cost of output is based on the **expected units of output**, which in our example amount to 90% of 1,000 = 900 units.

(c) Abnormal loss is given a cost, which is written off to the profit and loss account via an abnormal loss/gain account.

(d) Abnormal gain is treated in the same way, except that being a gain rather than a loss, it appears as a **debit** entry in the process account (whereas a loss appears as a **credit** entry in this account).

(a) *Step 1.* **Determine output and losses**

If actual output is 860 units, the actual loss is 140 units.

	Units
Actual loss	140
Normal loss (10% of 1,000)	100
Abnormal loss	40

Step 2. **Calculate cost per unit of output, losses and WIP**

The cost per unit of output and the cost per unit of abnormal loss are based on expected output.

$$\frac{\text{Costs incurred}}{\text{Expected output}} = \frac{£4,500}{900 \text{ units}}$$

Cost per unit   £5

Normal loss is not assigned any cost.

Step 3. **Calculate total cost of output and losses**

	£
Cost of output (860 × £5)	4,300
Normal loss (100 × £0)	-
Abnormal loss (40 × £5)	200
	4,500

Step 4. **Complete accounts**

PROCESS ACCOUNT

	Units	£		Units		£
Cost incurred	1,000	4,500	Normal loss	100		0
			Output (finished goods a/c)	860	(× £5)	4,300
			Abnormal loss	40	(× £5)	200
	1,000	4,500		1,000		4,500

ABNORMAL LOSS ACCOUNT

	Units	£		Units	£
Process a/c	40	200	Profit and loss a/c	40	200

(b) *Step 1.* **Determine output and losses**

If actual output is 920 units, the actual loss is 80 units.

	Units
Actual loss	80
Normal loss (10% of 1,000)	100
Abnormal gain	20

Step 2. **Calculate cost per unit of output, losses and WIP**

The cost per unit of output and the cost per unit of abnormal gain are based on expected output.

$$\frac{\text{Costs incurred}}{\text{Expected output}} = \frac{£4,500}{900 \text{units}} = £5 \text{ per unit}$$

Step 3. **Calculate total cost of output and losses**

	£
Cost of output (920 × £5)	4,600
Normal loss (100 × £0)	-
Abnormal gain (20 × £5)	(100)
	4,500

(Whether there is abnormal loss or gain does not affect the valuation of units of output. The figure of £5 per unit is exactly the same as when there were 40 units of abnormal loss.)

Step 4. **Complete accounts**

PROCESS ACCOUNT

	Units	£		Units		£
Cost incurred	1,000	4,500	Normal loss	100		0
Abnormal gain a/c	20(× £5)	100	Output (finished goods a/c)	920	(× £5)	4,600
	1,020	4,600		1,020		4,600

ABNORMAL GAIN

	Units	£		Units	£
Profit and loss a/c	20	100	Process a/c	20	100

3.14 EXAMPLE: ABNORMAL LOSSES AND GAINS AGAIN

During a four week period, period 3, costs of input to a process were £29,070. Input was 1,000 units, output was 850 units and normal loss is 10%.

During the next period, period 4, costs of input were again £29,070. Input was again 1,000 units, but output was 950 units.

There were no units of opening or closing stock.

Required

Prepare the process account and abnormal loss or gain account for each period.

3.15 SOLUTION

Step 1. **Determine output and losses**

If normal output is 900 units (90% × 1,000 units), and actual output in period 3 is 850 units, then there is an abnormal loss of 50 units (900 – 850). If actual output is 950 units in period 4, there is an abnormal gain of 50 units (900 – 950).

Step 2. **Calculate cost per unit of output, losses and WIP**

For each period the cost per unit is based on expected output.

$$\frac{\text{Cost of input}}{\text{Expected units of output}} = \frac{£29,070}{900} = £32.30 \text{ per unit}$$

Step 3. **Calculate total cost of output and losses**

Period 3	£
Output (850 × £32.30)	27,455
Normal loss (100 × £0)	-
Abnormal loss (50 × £32.30)	1,615
	29,070

Period 4	£
Output (950 × £32.30)	30,685
Normal loss (100 × £0)	-
Abnormal gain (50 × £32.30)	(1,615)
	29,070

Step 4. **Complete accounts**

PROCESS ACCOUNT

	Units	£		Units	£
Period 3					
Cost of input	1,000	29,070	Normal loss	100	0
			Finished goods a/c	850	27,455
			(× £32.30)		
			Abnormal loss a/c	50	1,615
			(× £32.30)		
	1,000	29,070		1,000	29,070
Period 4					
Cost of input	1,000	29,070	Normal loss	100	0
Abnormal gain a/c	50	1,615	Finished goods a/c	950	30,685
(× £32.30)			(× £32.30)		
	1,050	30,685		1,050	30,685

ABNORMAL LOSS OR GAIN ACCOUNT

	£		£
Period 3		*Period 4*	
Abnormal loss in process a/c	1,615	Abnormal gain in process a/c	1,615

A nil balance on this account will be carried forward into period 5.

(*Note.* It is considered more appropriate to value all units of output at a value based on expected loss (£32.30 per unit) rather than to have random fluctuations in the cost per unit each period due to variations in the loss.

3.16 If there is a closing balance in the abnormal loss or gain account when the profit for the period is calculated, this balance is taken to the profit and loss account: an abnormal gain will adjust profit upwards and an abnormal loss will adjust profit downwards.

Question 1

3,000 units of material are input to a process. Process costs are as follows.

Material	£11,700
Conversion costs	£6,300

Output is 2,000 units. Normal loss is 20% of input.

Required

Prepare a process account and the appropriate abnormal loss/gain account.

Answer

Step 1. Determine output and losses

We are told that output is 2,000 units.

Normal loss = 20% × 3,000 = 600 units

Abnormal loss = (3,000 – 600) – 2,000 = 400 units

Step 2. Calculate cost per unit of output and losses

$$\text{Cost per unit} = \frac{£(11,700 + 6,300)}{2,400} = £7.50$$

Step 3. Calculate total cost of output and losses

		£
Output	(2,000 × £7.50)	15,000
Normal loss		0
Abnormal loss	(400 × £7.50)	3,000
		18,000

Step 4. Complete accounts

PROCESS ACCOUNT

	Units	£		Units	£
Material	3,000	11,700	Output	2,000	15,000
Conversion costs		6,300	Normal loss	600	
			Abnormal loss	400	3,000
	3,000	18,000		3,000	18,000

ABNORMAL LOSS ACCOUNT

	£		£
Process a/c	3,000	P&L account	3,000

Question 2

Charlton Ltd manufactures a product in a single process operation. Normal loss is 10% of input. Loss occurs at the end of the process. Data for June are as follows.

Opening and closing stocks of work in progress	Nil
Cost of input materials (3,300 units)	£59,100
Direct labour and production overhead	£30,000
Output to finished goods	2,750 units

The full cost of finished output in June was

A £74,250   B £81,000   C £82,500   D £89,100

Answer

Step 1. **Determine output and losses**

	Units
Actual output	2,750
Normal loss (10% × 3,300)	330
Abnormal loss	220
	3,300

Step 2. **Calculate cost per unit of output and losses**

$$\frac{\text{Cost of input}}{\text{Expected units of output}} = \frac{£89,100}{3,300-330} = £30 \text{ per unit}$$

Step 3. **Calculate total cost of output and losses**

	£
Cost of output (2,750 × £30)	82,500 **(The correct answer is C)**
Normal loss	0
Abnormal loss (220 × £30)	6,600
	89,100

If you were reduced to making a calculated guess, you could have eliminated option D. This is simply the total input cost, with no attempt to apportion some of the cost to the abnormal loss.

Option A is incorrect because it results from allocating a full unit cost to the normal loss: remember that normal loss does not carry any of the process cost.

Option B is incorrect because it results from calculating a 10% normal loss based on *output* of 2,750 units (275 units normal loss), rather than on *input* of 3,300 units.

4 ACCOUNTING FOR SCRAP

4.1 **Loss or spoilage may have a scrap value.** When loss or spoilage is sold as scrap, there are two ways of accounting for the income.

(a) **Add** the revenue from the scrap sales to total sales revenue in the period.

(b) **Subtract** the sales revenue from the scrap from the costs of production and the cost of abnormal loss in the period. This is the more usual method to adopt.

4.2 If a distinction is made between normal loss and abnormal loss/gain the accounting treatment of scrap in process costing is as follows.

(a) The scrap value of normal loss will probably be deducted from the cost of materials in the process. This is done in the cost accounts themselves by crediting the scrap value of normal loss to the process account.

(b) The scrap value of **abnormal loss (or abnormal gain)** will probably be set off against its cost, in an abnormal loss (abnormal gain) account, and only the balance on the account will be written to the P & L account at the end of the period.

4.3 Accounting for scrap fits into our process costing framework as follows.

Step 1. Determine output and losses

This stage is important, as the scrap value of normal losses will be accounted for differently.

Steps 2 and 3. **Calculate costs of output and losses**

To do this we must first **separate** the scrap value of normal loss from abnormal loss. Then we will subtract the scrap value of normal loss from the cost of the process and divide by the expected output to determine cost per unit, and subsequently total costs.

Step 4. Complete accounts

In the process account the units of **normal loss** will be costed at their **scrap value**. The units of **abnormal loss/gain** will be costed at the cost per unit calculated in Steps 2 and 3.

The other relevant accounting entries are as follows.

- For **normal losses**

  DEBIT   Scrap account
  CREDIT   Process account

  with the scrap value of normal loss.

- For **abnormal losses**

  DEBIT   Scrap account
  CREDIT   Abnormal loss account

  with the scrap value of abnormal loss.

- For **abnormal gains**

  DEBIT   Abnormal gain account
  CREDIT   Scrap account

  with the scrap value of abnormal gain.

- **Complete scrap account**

  DEBIT   Cash received
  CREDIT   Scrap account

  with cash received from sale of actual scrap.

4.4 EXAMPLE: SCRAP AND NORMAL LOSS

Suppose that input to a process costs £1,370, normal loss is 10% and units scrapped sell for £2 each. 100 units are input and 90 units output.

Required

Show the process account and the scrap account.

4.5 SOLUTION

Step 1. Determine output and losses

Normal loss is 10% of 100 units, ie 10 units. Normal output is therefore 90 units (100 – 10). There is therefore no abnormal loss or gain.

Step 2. **Calculate costs of output and losses**

The total value of scrap is $10 \times £2 = £20$. The scrap value of normal loss is deducted from the materials cost, in order to calculate the output cost per unit, before it is credited to the process account as a value for normal loss.

The cost per unit of output would be calculated as follows.

	£
Cost of input	1,370
Less scrap value of normal loss	
(10 units × £2)	(20)
	1,350
Expected units of output	90 units
Cost per unit (£1,350 ÷ 90)	£15 per unit

Step 3. **Calculate total costs of output and losses**

	£
Output (90 × £15)	1,350
Normal loss (100 × £0)	-
	1,350

Step 4. **Complete accounts**

The accounting entries would be as follows.

PROCESS ACCOUNT

	Units	£		Units	£
Input costs	100	1,370	Normal loss ** (scrap a/c)	10	20
			Output (finished goods a/c)	90	1,350
	100	1,370		100	1,370

SCRAP ACCOUNT

	£		£
Scrap value of normal loss in process **	20	Cash a/c or financial ledger control = actual cash received for scrap	20
	20		20

4.6 If there is abnormal loss or abnormal gain, the scrap value of actual loss will differ from the normal loss scrap value. This discrepancy is ignored in the process account and is dealt with instead in the abnormal loss or gain account and the scrap account.

Question 3

Nan Ltd has a factory which operates two production processes. Normal spoilage in each process is 10%, and scrapped units out of process 1 sell for 50p per unit whereas scrapped units out of process 2 sell for £3. Output from process 1 is transferred to process 2: output from process 2 is finished output ready for sale.

Relevant information about costs for period 5 are as follows.

	Process 1		Process 2	
	Units	£	Units	£
Input materials	2,000	£8,100		
Transferred to process 2	1,750			
Materials from process 1			1,750	
Added materials			1,250	£1,900
Labour and overheads		£10,000		£22,000
Output to finished goods			2,800	

Required

Prepare the following cost accounts.

(a)   Process 1
(b)   Process 2
(c)   Abnormal loss
(d)   Abnormal gain
(e)   Scrap

Answer

(a)   *Process 1*

Step 1.   Determine output and losses

The normal loss is 10% of 2000 units = 200 units, and the actual loss is (2000 - 1750) = 250 units. This means that there is abnormal loss of 50 units.

Actual output	1,750 units
Abnormal loss	50 units
Expected output (90% of 2,000)	1,800 units

Step 2.   Calculate cost per unit of output and losses

(i)   The total value of scrap is 250 units at 50p per unit = £125. We must split this between the scrap value of normal loss and the scrap value of abnormal loss.

	£
Normal loss	100
Abnormal loss	25
Total scrap (250 units × 50p)	125

(ii)   The scrap value of normal loss is first deducted from the materials cost in the process, in order to calculate the output cost per unit and then credited to the process account as a 'value' for normal loss. The cost per unit in process 1 is calculated as follows.

	Total cost		Cost per expected unit of output
	£		£
Materials	8,100		
Less normal loss scrap value *	100		
	8,000	(÷ 1,800)	4.44
Labour and overhead	10,000	(÷ 1,800)	5.56
Total	18,000	(÷ 1,800)	10.00

* It is usual to set this scrap value of normal loss against the cost of materials.

Step 3.   Calculate total cost of output and losses

		£
Output	(1,750 units × £10.00)	17,500
Normal loss	(200 units × £0.50)	100
Abnormal loss	(50 units × £10.00)	500
		18,100

Step 4.   Complete accounts

Now we can put the process 1 account together.

PROCESS 1 ACCOUNT

	Units	£		Units	£
Materials	2,000	8,100	Output to process 2*	1,750	17,500
Labour and			Normal loss		
overhead		10,000	(scrap a/c)	200	100
			Abnormal loss a/c*	50	500
	2,000	18,100		2,000	18,100

* At £10 per unit.

(b) *Process 2*

Step 1. Determine output and losses

The normal loss is 10% of the units processed = 10% of (1,750 (from process 1) + 1,250) = 300 units. The actual loss is (3,000 - 2,800) = 200 units, so that there is abnormal gain of 100 units. These are *deducted* from actual output in arriving at the number of expected units (normal output) in the period.

Expected units of output

	Units
Actual output	2,800
Abnormal gain	(100)
Expected output (90% of 3,000)	2,700

Step 2. Calculate cost per unit of output and losses

(i) The total value of scrap is 200 units at £3 per unit = £600. We must split this between the scrap value of normal loss and the scrap value of abnormal gain. Abnormal gain's scrap value is 'negative'.

		£
Normal loss scrap value	300 units × £3	900
Abnormal gain scrap value	100 units × £3	(300)
Scrap value of actual loss	200 units × £3	600

(ii) The scrap value of normal loss is first deducted from the cost of materials in the process, in order to calculate a cost per unit of output, and then credited to the process account as a 'value' for normal loss. The cost per unit in process 2 is calculated as follows.

	Total cost £		Cost per expected unit of output £
Materials:			
Transferred from process 1	17,500		
Added in process 2	1,900		
	19,400		
Less scrap value of normal loss	900		
	18,500	(÷ 2,700)	6.85
Labour and overhead	22,000	(÷ 2,700)	8.15
	40,500	(÷ 2,700)	15.00

Step 3. Calculate total cost of output and losses

		£
Output	(2,800 × £15.00)	42,000
Normal loss	(300 units × £3.00)	900
		42,900
Abnormal gain	(100 units × £15.00)	(1,500)
		41,400

Step 4. Complete accounts

PROCESS 2 ACCOUNT

	Units	£		Units	£
From process 1	1,750	17,500	Finished output	2,800	42,000
Added materials	1,250	1,900			
Labour and			Normal loss	300	900
overhead		22,000	(scrap a/c)		
	3,000	41,400			
Abnormal gain a/c	100	1,500			
	3,100	42,900		3,100	42,900

(c) and (d)

Abnormal loss and abnormal gain accounts

For each process, one or the other of these accounts will record three items.

(i) The cost/value of the abnormal loss/gain. This is the corresponding entry to the entry in the process account.

(ii) The scrap value of the abnormal loss or gain, to set off against it.

(iii) A balancing figure, which is written to the P&L account as an adjustment to the profit figure.

ABNORMAL LOSS ACCOUNT

	£		£
Process 1	500	Scrap a/c (scrap value of abnormal loss)	25
		Profit and Loss a/c (balance)	475
	500		500

ABNORMAL GAIN ACCOUNT

	£		£
Scrap a/c (scrap value of abnormal gain units)	300	Process 2	1,500
Profit & Loss a/c (balance)	1,200		
	1,500		1,500

(e) *Scrap account*

This is credited with the cash value of actual units scrapped. The other entries in the account should all be identifiable as corresponding entries to those in the process accounts, and abnormal loss and abnormal gain accounts.

SCRAP ACCOUNT

	£		£
Normal loss:		Cash: sale of	
Process 1 (200 × 50p)	100	process 1 scrap (250 × 50p)	125
Process 2 (300 × £3)	900	Cash: sale of	
Abnormal loss a/c	25	process 2 scrap (200 × £3)	600
		Abnormal gain a/c	300
	1,025		1,025

Question 4

Look back at Question 1. Suppose the units of loss could be sold for £1 each. Prepare appropriate accounts.

Answer

Step 1. **Determine output and losses**

Actual output	2,000 units
Abnormal loss	400 units
Expected output	2,400 units

Step 2. **Calculate cost per unit of output and losses**

	£
Scrap value of normal loss	600
Scrap value of abnormal loss	400
Total scrap (1,000 units × £1)	1,000

Step 3. **Calculate total cost of output and losses**

		£
Output	(2,000 × £7.25)	14,500
Normal loss	(600 × £1.00)	600
Abnormal loss	(400 × £7.25)	2,900
		18,000

$$\text{Cost per expected unit} = \frac{£\big((11,700 - 600) + 6,300\big)}{2,400} = £7.25$$

Step 4. **Complete accounts**

PROCESS ACCOUNT

	Units	£		Units	£
Material	3,000	11,700	Output	2,000	14,500
Conversion costs		6,300	Normal loss	600	600
			Abnormal loss	400	2,900
	3,000	18,000		3,000	18,000

ABNORMAL LOSS ACCOUNT

	£		£
Process a/c	2,900	Scrap a/c	400
		P&L a/c	2,500
	2,900		2,900

SCRAP ACCOUNT

	£		£
Normal loss	600	Cash	1,000
Abnormal loss	400		
	1,000		1,000

5 LOSSES WITH A DISPOSAL COST

5.1 As well as being able to deal with questions in which scrap or loss units are **worthless** or have a **scrap value**, you must also be able to deal with losses which have a **disposal cost**.

5.2 The basic calculations required in such circumstances are as follows.

(a) Increase the process costs by the cost of disposing of the units of normal loss and use the resulting cost per unit to value good output and abnormal loss/gain.

(b) The normal loss is given no value in the process account.

(c) Include the disposal costs of normal loss on the debit side of the process account.

(d) Include the disposal costs of abnormal loss in the abnormal loss account and hence in the transfer of the cost of abnormal loss to the profit and loss account.

5.3 Suppose that input to a process was 1,000 units at a cost of £4,500. Normal loss is 10% and there are no opening and closing stocks. Actual output was 860 units and loss units had to be disposed of at a cost of £0.90 per unit.

Normal loss = 10% × 1,000 = 100 units. ∴ Abnormal loss = 900 – 860 = 40 units

$$\text{Cost per unit} = \frac{£4,500 + (100 \times £0.90)}{900} = £5.10$$

5.4 The relevant accounts would be as follows.

PROCESS ACCOUNT

	Units	£		Units	£
Cost of input	1,000	4,500	Output	860	4,386
Disposal cost of			Normal loss	100	-
normal loss		90	Abnormal loss	40	204
	1,000	4,590		1,000	4,590

ABNORMAL LOSS ACCOUNT

	£		£
Process a/c	204	Profit and loss a/c	240
Disposal cost (40 × £0.90)	36		
	240		240

6   VALUING CLOSING WORK IN PROGRESS

6.1   In the examples we have looked at so far we have assumed that opening and closing stocks of work in process have been nil. We must now look at more realistic examples and consider how to allocate the costs incurred in a period between completed output (that is, finished units) and partly completed closing stock.

6.2   Some examples will help to illustrate the problem, and the techniques used to share out (apportion) costs between finished output and closing stocks.

6.3   Suppose that we have the following account for Process 2 for period 9.

PROCESS ACCOUNT

	Units	£			£
Materials	1,000	6,200	Finished goods	800	?
Labour and overhead		2,850	Closing WIP	200	?
	1,000	9,050		1,000	9,050

How do we value the finished goods and closing work in process?

6.4   With any form of process costing involving closing WIP, we have to apportion costs between output and closing WIP. To apportion costs 'fairly' we make use of the concept of **equivalent units of production**.

Equivalent units

> **KEY TERM**
>
> **Equivalent units** are notional whole units which represent incomplete work, and which are used to apportion costs between work in process and completed output.

6.5   We will assume that in the example above the degree of completion is as follows.

(a)   **Direct materials**. These are added in full at the start of processing, and so any closing WIP will have 100% of their direct material content. (This is not always the case in practice. Materials might be added gradually throughout the process, in which case closing stock will only be a certain percentage complete as to material content. We will look at this later in the chapter.)

(b)   **Direct labour and production overhead**. These are usually assumed to be incurred at an even rate through the production process, so that when we refer to a unit that is 50% complete, we mean that it is half complete for labour and overhead, although it might be 100% complete for materials.

6.6   Let us also assume that the closing WIP is 100% complete for materials and 25% complete for labour and overhead.

6.7   How would we now put a value to the finished output and the closing WIP?

In **Step 1** of our framework, we have been told what output and losses are. However we also need to calculate **equivalent units**.

STATEMENT OF EQUIVALENT UNITS

| | | Materials | | Labour and overhead | |
	Total units	Degree of completion	Equivalent units	Degree of completion	Equivalent units
Finished output	800	100%	800	100%	800
Closing WIP	200	100%	200	25%	50
	1,000		1,000		850

6.8 In **Step 2** the important figure is **average cost per equivalent unit**. This can be calculated as follows.

STATEMENT OF COSTS PER EQUIVALENT UNIT

	Materials	Labour and overhead
Costs incurred in the period	£6,200	£2,850
Equivalent units of work done	1,000	850
Cost per equivalent unit (approx)	£6.20	£3.3529

6.9 To calculate total costs for **Step 3**, we prepare a statement of evaluation to show how the costs should be apportioned between finished output and closing WIP.

STATEMENT OF EVALUATION

		Materials			Labour and overheads		
		Cost per			Cost per		
Item	Equivalent units	equivalent units	Cost	Equivalent units	equivalent units	Cost	Total cost
		£	£		£	£	£
Finished output	800	6.20	4,960	800	3.3529	2,682	7,642
Closing WIP	200	6.20	1,240	50	3.3529	168	1,408
	1,000		6,200	850		2,850	9,050

6.10 The process account (work in progress, or work in process account) would be shown as follows.

PROCESS ACCOUNT

	Units	£		Units	£
Materials	1,000	6,200	Finished goods	800	7,642
Labour overhead		2,850	Closing WIP	200	1,408
	1,000	9,050		1,000	9,050

Different rates of input

6.11 In many industries, materials, labour and overhead may be **added at different rates** during the course of production.

(a) Output from a previous process (for example the output from process 1 to process 2) may be introduced into the subsequent process all at once, so that closing stock is 100% complete in respect of these materials.

(b) Further materials may be added gradually during the process, so that closing stock is only partially complete in respect of these added materials.

(c) Labour and overhead may be 'added' at yet another different rate. When production overhead is absorbed on a labour hour basis, however, we should expect the degree of completion on overhead to be the same as the degree of completion on labour.

242

When this situation occurs, **equivalent units**, and a **cost per equivalent unit**, should be calculated separately for each type of material, and also for conversion costs.

6.12 EXAMPLE: EQUIVALENT UNITS AND DIFFERENT DEGREES OF COMPLETION

Suppose that Columbine Ltd is a manufacturer of processed goods, and that results in process 2 for April 20X3 were as follows.

Opening stock	nil
Material input from process 1	4,000 units
Costs of input:	£
material from process 1	6,000
added materials in process 2	1,080
conversion costs	1,720

Output is transferred into the next process, process 3.

Closing work in process amounted to 800 units, complete as to:

process 1 material	100%
added materials	50%
conversion costs	30%

Required

Prepare the account for process 2 for April 20X3.

6.13 SOLUTION

(a)   STATEMENT OF EQUIVALENT UNITS (OF PRODUCTION IN THE PERIOD)

			Equivalent units of production					
			Process 1		*Added*		*Labour and*	
Input	*Output*	*Total*	*material*		*materials*		*overhead*	
Units		Units	Units	%	Units	%	Units	%
4,000	Completed production	3,200	3,200	100	3,200	100	3,200	100
	Closing stock	800	800	100	400	50	240	30
4,000		4,000	4,000		3,600		3,440	

(b)   STATEMENT OF COST (PER EQUIVALENT UNIT)

Input	*Cost*	*Equivalent production in units*	*Cost per unit*
	£		£
Process 1 material	6,000	4,000	1.50
Added materials	1,080	3,600	0.30
Labour and overhead	1,720	3,440	0.50
	8,800		2.30

(c)   STATEMENT OF EVALUATION (OF FINISHED WORK AND CLOSING STOCKS)

Production	Cost element	Number of equivalent units	Cost per equivalent unit £	Total £	Cost £
Completed production		3,200	2.30		7,360
Closing stock:	process 1 material	800	1.50	1,200	
	added material	400	0.30	120	
	labour and overhead	240	0.50	120	
					1,440
					8,800

(d)   PROCESS ACCOUNT

	Units	£		Units	£
(ex process 1 a/c)					
Process 1 material	4,000	6,000	Process 3 a/c	3,200	7,360
(Stores a/c)			(finished output)		
Added material		1,080			
(Wages a/c and o'h a/c)					
Conversion costs		1,720	Closing stock c/f	800	1,440
	4,000	8,800		4,000	8,800

7   VALUING OPENING WORK IN PROGRESS: FIFO METHOD

7.1   Opening work in progress is partly complete at the beginning of a period and is valued at the cost incurred to date. In the example in Paragraph 6.12, closing work in progress of 800 units at the end of April 20X3 would be carried forward as opening stock, value £1,440, at the beginning of May 20X3.

7.2   It therefore follows that the work required to complete units of opening stock is 100% minus the work in progress done in the previous period. For example, if 100 units of opening stock are 70% complete at the beginning of June 20X2, the equivalent units of production would be as follows.

Equivalent units in previous period	(May 20X2) (70%)	=	70
Equivalent units to complete work in current period	(June 20X2) (30%)	=	30
Total work done			100

7.3   **The FIFO method of valuation** deals with production on a first in, first out basis. The assumption is that the first units completed in any period are the units of opening stock that were held at the beginning of the period.

7.4   EXAMPLE: WIP AND FIFO

Suppose that information relating to process 1 of a two-stage production process is as follows, for August 20X2.

Opening stock 500 units: degree of completion	60%
cost to date	£2,800

Costs incurred in August 20X2	£
Direct materials (2,500 units introduced)	13,200
Direct labour	6,600
Production overhead	6,600
	26,400

Closing stock 300 units: degree of completion	80%

There was no loss in the process.

Required

Prepare the process 1 account for August 20X2.

7.5 SOLUTION

As the term implies, first in, first out means that in August 20X2 the first units completed were the units of opening stock.

Opening stocks:	work done to date =	60%
	plus work done in August 20X2 =	40%

The cost of the work done up to 1 August 20X2 is known to be £2,800, so that the cost of the units completed will be £2,800 plus the cost of completing the final 40% of the work on the units in August 20X2.

Once the opening stock has been completed, all other finished output in August 20X2 will be work started as well as finished in the month.

	Units
Total output in August 20X2 ★	2,700
Less opening stock, completed first	500
Work started and finished in August 20X2	2,200

(★ Opening stock plus units introduced minus closing stock = 500 + 2,500 – 300)

What we are doing here is taking the total output of 2,700 units, and saying that we must divide it into two parts as follows.

(a) The opening stock, which was first in and so must be first out.
(b) The rest of the units, which were 100% worked in the period.

Dividing finished output into two parts in this way is a necessary feature of the FIFO valuation method.

Continuing the example, closing stock of 300 units will be started in August 20X2, but not yet completed.

The total cost of output to process 2 during 20X2 will be as follows.

		£	
Opening stock	cost brought forward	2,800	(60%)
	plus cost incurred during August 20X2,		
	to complete	x	(40%)
		2,800 + x	
Fully worked 2,200 units		y	
Total cost of output to process 2, FIFO basis		2,800 + x + y	

Equivalent units will again be used as the basis for apportioning **costs incurred during August 20X2**. Be sure that you understand the treatment of 'opening stock units completed', and can relate the calculations to the principles of FIFO valuation.

Step 1. **Determine output and losses**

STATEMENT OF EQUIVALENT UNITS

	Total units		Equivalent units of production in August 20X2
Opening stock units completed	500	(40%)	200
Fully worked units	2,200	(100%)	2,200
Output to process 2	2,700		2,400
Closing stock	300	(80%)	240
	3,000		2,640

Step 2. **Calculate cost per unit of output and losses**

The cost per equivalent unit in August 20X2 can now be calculated.

STATEMENT OF COST PER EQUIVALENT UNIT

$$\frac{\text{Cost incurred}}{\text{Equivalent units}} = \frac{£26,400}{2,640}$$

Cost per equivalent unit = £10

Step 3. **Calculate total costs of output, losses and WIP**

STATEMENT OF EVALUATION

	Equivalent units	Valuation £
Opening stock, work done in August 20X2	200	2,000
Fully worked units	2,200	22,000
Closing stock	240	2,400
	2,640	26,400

The total value of the completed opening stock will be £2,800 (brought forward) plus £2,000 added in August before completion = £4,800.

Step 4. **Complete accounts**

PROCESS 1 ACCOUNT

	Units	£		Units	£
Opening stock	500	2,800	Output to process 2:		
Direct materials	2,500	13,200	Opening stock completed	500	4,800
Direct labour		6,600	Fully worked units	2,200	22,000
Production o'hd		6,600		2,700	26,800
			Closing stock	300	2,400
	3,000	29,200		3,000	29,200

We now know that the value of x is £(4,800 – 2,800) = £2,000 and the value of y is £22,000.

Question 5

The following information relates to process 3 of a three-stage production process for the month of January 20X4.

Opening stock

300 units complete as to:		£
materials from process 2	100%	4,400
added materials	90%	1,150
labour	80%	540
production overhead	80%	810
		6,900

In January 20X4, a further 1,800 units were transferred from process 2 at a valuation of £27,000. Added materials amounted to £6,600 and direct labour to £3,270. Production overhead is absorbed at the rate of 150% of direct labour cost. Closing stock at 31 January 20X4 amounted to 450 units, complete as to:

process 2 materials	100%
added materials	60%
labour and overhead	50%

Required

Prepare the process 3 account for January 20X4 using FIFO valuation principles.

Answer

Step 1. STATEMENT OF EQUIVALENT UNITS

	Total units	Process 2 materials		Added materials		Conversion costs
Opening stock	300	0	(10%)	30	(20%)	60
Fully worked units *	1,350	1,350		1,350		1,350
Output to finished goods	1,650	1,350		1,380		1,410
Closing stock	450	450	(60%)	270	(50%)	225
	2,100	1,800		1,650		1,635

    * Transfers from process 2, minus closing stock.

Step 2. STATEMENT OF COSTS PER EQUIVALENT UNIT

	Total cost £	Equivalent units	Cost per equivalent unit £
Process 2 materials	27,000	1,800	15.00
Added materials	6,600	1,650	4.00
Direct labour	3,270	1,635	2.00
Production overhead (150% of £3,270)	4,905	1,635	3.00
			24.00

Step 3. STATEMENT OF EVALUATION

	Process 2 materials £		Additional materials £		Labour £		Overhead £	Total £
Opening stock cost b/f	4,400		1,150		540		810	6,900
Added in Jan 20X4	-	(30x£4)	120	(60x£2)	120	(60x£3)	180	420
	4,400		1,270		660		990	7,320
Fully worked units	20,250		5,400		2,700		4,050	32,400
Output to finished Goods	24,650		6,670		3,360		5,040	39,720
Closing stock (450x£15)	6,750	(270x£4)	1,080	(225x£2)	450	(225x£3)	675	8,955
	31,400		7,750		3,810		5,715	48,675

Step 4. **COMPLETE ACCOUNTS**

PROCESS 3 ACCOUNT

	Units	£		Units	£
Opening stock b/f	300	6,900	Finished goods a/c	1,650	39,720
Process 2 a/c	1,800	27,000			
Stores a/c		6,600			
Wages a/c		3,270			
Production o'hd a/c		4,905	Closing stock c/f	450	8,955
	2,100	48,675		2,100	48,675

8 VALUING OPENING WORK IN PROGRESS: WEIGHTED AVERAGE COST METHOD

8.1 An alternative to FIFO is the **weighted average cost method of stock valuation** which calculates a weighted average cost of units produced from both opening stock and units introduced in the current period.

By this method **no distinction is made between units of opening stock and new units introduced** to the process during the accounting period. The cost of opening stock is added to costs incurred during the period, and completed units of opening stock are each given a value of one full equivalent unit of production.

8.2 EXAMPLE: WEIGHTED AVERAGE COST METHOD

Magpie Ltd produces an item which is manufactured in two consecutive processes. Information relating to process 2 during September 20X3 is as follows.

Opening stock 800 units

Degree of completion:		£
process 1 materials	100%	4,700
added materials	40%	600
conversion costs	30%	1,000
		6,300

During September 20X3, 3,000 units were transferred from process 1 at a valuation of £18,100. Added materials cost £9,600 and conversion costs were £11,800.

Closing stock at 30 September 20X3 amounted to 1,000 units which were 100% complete with respect to process 1 materials and 60% complete with respect to added materials. Conversion cost work was 40% complete.

Magpie Ltd uses a weighted average cost system for the valuation of output and closing stock.

Required

Prepare the process 2 account for September 20X3.

8.3 SOLUTION

Step 1. Opening stock units count as a full equivalent unit of production when the weighted average cost system is applied. Closing stock equivalent units are assessed in the usual way.

STATEMENT OF EQUIVALENT UNITS

	Total units		Process 1 material	Equivalent units Added material		Conversion costs
Opening stock	800	(100%)	800	800		800
Fully worked units *	2,000	(100%)	2,000	2,000		2,000
Output to finished goods	2,800		2,800	2,800		2,800
Closing stock	1,000	(100%)	1,000	(60%) 600	(40%)	400
	3,800		3,800	3,400		3,200

(* 3,000 units from process 1 minus closing stock of 1,000 units)

Step 2. The cost of opening stock is added to costs incurred in September 20X3, and a cost per equivalent unit is then calculated.

STATEMENT OF COSTS PER EQUIVALENT UNIT

	Process 1 material £	Added materials £	Conversion costs £
Opening stock	4,700	600	1,000
Added in September 20X3	18,100	9,600	11,800
Total cost	22,800	10,200	12,800
Equivalent units	3,800 units	3,400 units	3,200 units
Cost per equivalent unit	£6	£3	£4

Step 3. STATEMENT OF EVALUATION

	Process 1 material £	Added materials £	Conversion costs £	Total cost £
Output to finished goods (2,800 units)	16,800	8,400	11,200	36,400
Closing stock	6,000	1,800	1,600	9,400
				45,800

Step 4.

PROCESS 2 ACCOUNT

	Units	£		Units	£
Opening stock b/f	800	6,300	Finished goods a/c	2,800	36,400
Process 1 a/c	3,000	18,100			
Added materials		9,600			
Conversion costs		11,800	Closing stock c/f	1,000	9,400
	3,800	45,800		3,800	45,800

Which method should be used?

8.4 **FIFO stock valuation is more common than the weighted average method, and should be used unless an indication is given to the contrary.** You may find that you are presented with limited information about the opening stock, which forces you to use either the FIFO or the weighted average method. The rules are as follows.

(a) If you are told the degree of completion of each element in opening stock, but not the value of each cost element, then you must use the **FIFO method**.

(b) If you are not given the degree of completion of each cost element in opening stock, but you are given the value of each cost element, then you must use the **weighted average method**.

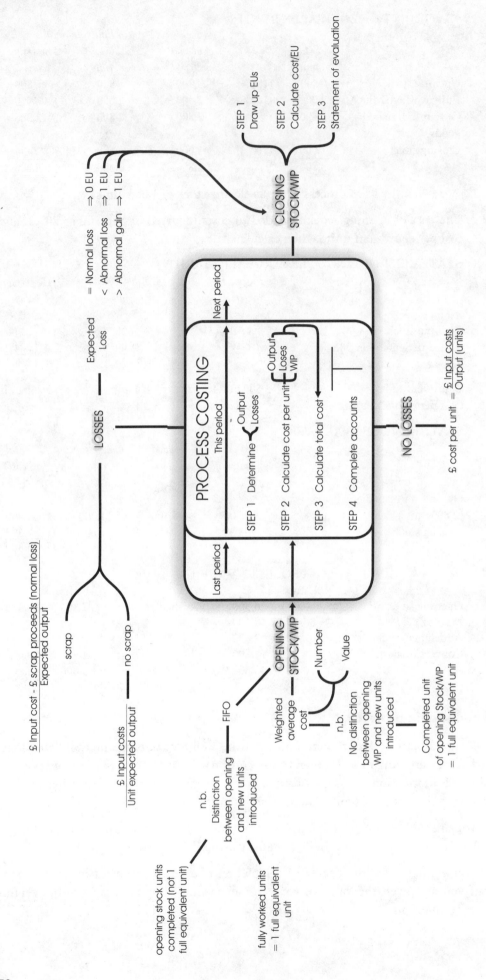

Chapter roundup

- Many students find process costing daunting. It shouldn't be. Use our suggested four-step approach to dealing with questions and you should find the topic quite straightforward.

  Step 1. Determine output and losses

  Step 2. Calculate cost per unit of output, losses and WIP

  Step 3. Calculate total cost of output, losses and WIP

  Step 4. Complete accounts

- **Process costing** is used where there is a continuous flow of identical units.

- Losses may occur in process. If a certain level of loss is expected, this is known as **normal loss**. If losses are greater than expected, the extra loss is **abnormal loss**. If losses are less than expected, the difference is known as **abnormal gain**.

- It is conventional for the **scrap value** of normal loss to be deducted from the cost of materials before a cost per equivalent unit is calculated.

- Abnormal losses and gains never affect the cost of good units of production. The scrap value of abnormal losses is not credited to the process account, and abnormal loss and gain units carry the same full cost as a good unit of production.

- When units are partly completed at the end of a period (and hence there is closing work in progress), it is necessary to calculate the **equivalent units of production** in order to determine the cost of a completed unit.

- Account can be taken of opening work in progress using either the **FIFO** method or the **weighted average cost method.**

Quick quiz

1 Define process costing. *Used when Continuous flow of identical units*

2 Process costing is centred around four key steps.

   Step 1. *Identify output + losses.*

   Step 2. *Calculate Cost per unit Output + WIP*

   Step 3. *" total Cost of Output + WIP*

   Step 4. *Complete Process accounts*

3 Abnormal gains result when actual loss is less than normal or expected loss.

   True ☑

   False ☐

4 Normal loss (no scrap value)   Same value as good output (positive cost)

   Abnormal loss   ?   No value

   Abnormal gain   Same value as good output (negative cost)

5 How is revenue from scrap treated?

   A As an addition to sales revenue
   B As a reduction in costs of processing
   C As a bonus to employees
   D Any of the above

6 What is an equivalent unit? *The Cost calculated. of goods not Completed ie WIP*

7 When there is closing WIP at the end of a process, what is the first step in the four-step approach to process costing questions and why must it be done? *Calculate Equivalent units as stock calculated differently.*

8 What is the weighted average cost method of stock valuation? *opens stock Stock treated as fully complete.*

9   Unless given an indication to the contrary, the weighted average cost method of stock valuation should be used to value opening WIP.

True   ☐✓

False   ☑

Answers to quick quiz

1   **Process costing** is a costing method used where it is not possible to identify separate units of production, or jobs, usually because of the continuous nature of the production processes involved.

2   *Step 1.*   Determine output and losses
      Step 2.   Calculate cost per unit of output, losses and WIP
      Step 3.   Calculate total cost of output, losses and WIP
      Step 4.   Complete accounts

3   True

4   Normal loss (no scrap value) → Same value as good output (positive cost)

     Abnormal loss → No value

     Abnormal gain → Same value as good output (negative cost)

5   B

6   An **equivalent unit** is a notional whole unit which represents incomplete work, and which is used to apportion costs between work in process and completed output.

7   *Step 1.*   It is necessary to calculate the equivalent units of production (by drawing up a statement of equivalent units). Equivalent units of production are notional whole units which represent incomplete work and which are used to apportion costs between work in progress and completed output.

8   A method where no distinction is made between units of opening stock and new units introduced to the process during the current period.

9   False. FIFO stock valuation is more common than the weighted average method and should be used unless an indication is given to the contrary.

Now try the questions below from the Exam Question Bank

Number	Level	Marks	Time
18	MCQ	n/a	n/a
19	Examination	10	18 mins

Chapter 12

PROCESS COSTING, JOINT PRODUCTS AND BY-PRODUCTS

Topic list	Syllabus reference
1 Contrasting joint products and by-products	4(b)
2 Problems in accounting for joint products	4(b)
3 Dealing with common costs	4(b)
4 Joint products in process accounts	4(b)
5 Accounting for by-products	4(b)

Introduction

You should now be aware of the most simple and the more complex areas of process costing. In this chapter we are going to turn our attention to the methods of accounting for **joint products** and **by-products** which arise as a result of a **continuous process**.

Study guide

Section 15 – Process costing 2

- Distinguish between by-products and joint products
- Value by-products and joint products at the point of separation
- Prepare process accounts in situations where by-products and/or joint products occur

Exam guide

Even though this is part of the topic **process costing**, which is a key area of the syllabus, you are unlikely to be examined on **joint products** and **by-products** in Section B of your examination. Be prepared to answer multiple choice questions, however, on the contents of this chapter.

1   CONTRASTING JOINT PRODUCTS AND BY-PRODUCTS

> ### KEY TERMS
>
> - **Joint products** are two or more products which are output from the same processing operation, but which are indistinguishable from each other up to their point of separation.
>
> - A **by-product** is a supplementary or secondary product (arising as the result of a process) whose value is small relative to that of the principal product.

1.1 (a) Joint products have a **substantial sales value**. Often they require further processing before they are ready for sale. Joint products arise, for example, in the oil refining industry where diesel fuel, petrol, paraffin and lubricants are all produced from the same process.

(b) The distinguishing feature of a by-product is its **relatively low sales value** in comparison to the main product. In the timber industry, for example, by-products include sawdust, small offcuts and bark.

1.2 **What exactly separates a joint product from a by-product?**

(a) A **joint product** is regarded as an important saleable item, and so it should be **separately costed**. The profitability of each joint product should be assessed in the cost accounts.

(b) A **by-product** is not important as a saleable item, and whatever revenue it earns is a 'bonus' for the organisation. Because of their relative insignificance, by-products are **not separately costed**.

Exam focus point
The study guide for Paper 1.2 states that you must be able to 'distinguish between by-products and joint products'.

2 PROBLEMS IN ACCOUNTING FOR JOINT PRODUCTS

2.1 Joint products are not separately identifiable until a certain stage is reached in the processing operations. This stage is the **'split-off point'**, sometimes referred to as the **separation point**. Costs incurred prior to this point of separation are **common** or **joint costs**, and these need to be allocated (apportioned) in some manner to each of the joint products. In the following sketched example, there are two different split-off points.

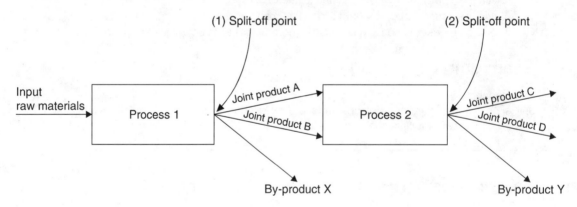

2.2 The **problems in accounting for joint products** are basically of two different sorts.

(a) How common costs should be apportioned between products, in order to put a value to closing stocks and to the cost of sale (and profit) for each product.

(b) Whether it is more profitable to sell a joint product at one stage of processing, or to process the product further and sell it at a later stage.

3 DEALING WITH COMMON COSTS

3.1 The problem of costing for joint products concerns **common costs**, that is those common processing costs shared between the units of eventual output up to their 'split-off point'.

Some method needs to be devised for sharing the common costs between the individual joint products for the following reasons.

(a) To put a value to closing stocks of each joint product.
(b) To record the costs and therefore the profit from each joint product.
(c) Perhaps to assist in pricing decisions.

3.2 Here are some examples of the common costs problem.

(a) How to spread the common costs of oil refining between the joint products made (petrol, naphtha, kerosene and so on).

(b) How to spread the common costs of running the telephone network between telephone calls in peak and cheap rate times, or between local and long distance calls.

3.3 Various methods that might be used to establish a basis for apportioning or allocating common costs to each product are as follows.

- Physical measurement
- Relative sales value apportionment method; sales value at split-off point

Dealing with common costs: physical measurement

3.4 With physical measurement, **the common cost is apportioned to the joint products on the basis of the proportion that the output of each product bears by weight or volume to the total output.** An example of this would be the case where two products, product 1 and product 2, incur common costs to the point of separation of £3,000 and the output of each product is 600 tons and 1,200 tons respectively.

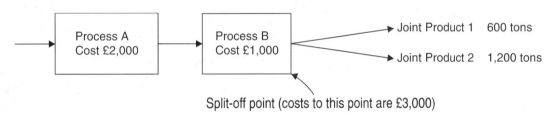

Product 1 sells for £4 per ton and product 2 for £2 per ton.

The division of the common costs (£3,000) between product 1 and product 2 could be based on the tonnage of output.

	Product 1		*Product 2*	*Total*
Output	600 tons	+	1,200 tons	1,800 tons
Proportion of common cost	$\dfrac{600}{1,800}$	+	$\dfrac{1,200}{1,800}$	
	£		£	£
Apportioned cost	1,000		2,000	3,000
Sales	2,400		2,400	4,800
Profit	1,400		400	1,800
Profit/sales ratio	58.3%		16.7%	37.5%

3.5 Physical measurement has the following limitations.

(a) Where the products separate during the processes into different states, for example where one product is a gas and another is a liquid, this method is unsuitable.

(b) This method does not take into account the relative income-earning potentials of the individual products, with the result that one product might appear very profitable and another appear to be incurring losses.

Dealing with common costs: sales value at split-off point

3.6 With relative sales value apportionment of common cost, **the cost is allocated according to the product's ability to produce income**. This method is most widely used because the assumption that some profit margin should be attained for all products under normal marketing conditions is satisfied. The common cost is apportioned to each product in the proportion that the sales (market) value of that product bears to the sales value of the total output from the particular processes concerned. Using the previous example where the sales price per unit is £4 for product 1 and £2 for product 2.

(a) Common costs of processes to split-off point	£3,000
(b) Sales value of product 1 at £4 per ton	£2,400
(c) Sales value of product 2 at £2 per ton	£2,400

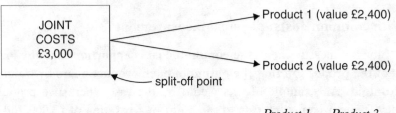

	Product 1	Product 2	Total
Sales	£2,400	£2,400	£4,800
Proportion of common cost apportioned	$\left(\dfrac{2,400}{4,800}\right)$	$\left(\dfrac{2,400}{4,800}\right)$	
	£	£	£
Apportioned cost	1,500	1,500	3,000
Sales	2,400	2,400	4,800
Profit	900	900	1,800
Profit/sales ratio	37.5%	37.5%	37.5%

3.7 A comparison of the gross profit margin resulting from the application of the above methods for allocating common costs will illustrate the greater acceptability of the relative sales value apportionment method. Physical measurement gives a higher profit margin to product 1, not necessarily because product 1 is highly profitable, but because it has been given a smaller share of common costs.

Question 1

In process costing, a joint product is

A   A product which is produced simultaneously with other products but which is of lesser value than at least one of the other products

B   A product which is produced simultaneously with other products and is of similar value to at least one of the other products

C   A product which is produced simultaneously with other products but which is of greater value than any of the other products

D   A product produced jointly with another organisation

Answer

The correct answer is B, a product which is of similar value to at least one of the other products.

---

4   JOINT PRODUCTS IN PROCESS ACCOUNTS

4.1   This example illustrates how joint products are incorporated into process accounts.

EXAMPLE: JOINT PRODUCTS AND PROCESS ACCOUNTS

Three joint products are manufactured in a common process, which consists of two consecutive stages. Output from process 1 is transferred to process 2, and output from process 2 consists of the three joint products, Hans, Nils and Bumpsydaisies. All joint products are sold as soon as they are produced.

Data for period 2 of 20X6 are as follows.

	Process 1	Process 2
Opening and closing stock	None	None
Direct material		
(30,000 units at £2 per unit)	£60,000	-
Conversion costs	£76,500	£226,200
Normal loss	10% of input	10% of input
Scrap value of normal loss	£0.50 per unit	£2 per unit
Output	26,000 units	10,000 units of Han
		7,000 units of Nil
		6,000 units of Bumpsydaisy

Selling prices are £18 per unit of Han, £20 per unit of Nil and £30 per unit of Bumpsydaisy.

Required

(a)   Prepare the Process 1 account.
(b)   Prepare the Process 2 account using the sales value method of apportionment.
(c)   Prepare a profit statement for the joint products.

4.2   SOLUTION

(a)   **Process 1 equivalent units**

	Total units	Equivalent units
Output to process 2	26,000	26,000
Normal loss	3,000	0
Abnormal loss (balance)	1,000	1,000
	30,000	27,000

Costs of process 1

	£
Direct materials	60,000
Conversion costs	76,500
	136,500
Less scrap value of normal loss (3,000 × £0.50)	1,500
	135,000

Cost per equivalent unit $\dfrac{£135,000}{27,000} = £5$

PROCESS 1 ACCOUNT

	£		£
Direct materials	60,000	Output to process 2	
Conversion costs	76,500	(26,000 × £5)	130,000
		Normal loss (scrap value)	1,500
		Abnormal loss a/c	
		(1,000 × £5)	5,000
	136,500		136,500

(b) **Process 2 equivalent units**

	Total units	Equivalent units
Units of Hans produced	10,000	10,000
Units of Nils produced	7,000	7,000
Units of Bumpsydaisies produced	6,000	6,000
Normal loss (10% of 26,000)	2,600	0
Abnormal loss (balance)	400	400
	26,000	23,400

Costs of process 2

	£
Material costs - from process 1	130,000
Conversion costs	226,200
	356,200
Less scrap value of normal loss (2,600 × £2)	5,200
	351,000

Cost per equivalent unit $\dfrac{£351,000}{23,400} = £15$

Cost of good output (10,000 + 7,000 + 6,000) = 23,000 units × £15 = £345,000

The sales value of joint products, and the apportionment of the output costs of £345,000, is as follows.

	Sales value £	%	Costs (process 2) £
Hans (10,000 × £18)	180,000	36	124,200
Nils (7,000 × £20)	140,000	28	96,600
Bumpsydaisy (6,000 × £30)	180,000	36	124,200
	500,000	100	345,000

PROCESS 2 ACCOUNT

	£		£
Process 1 materials	130,000	Finished goods accounts	
Conversion costs	226,200	- Hans	124,200
		- Nils	96,600
		- Bumpsydaisies	124,200
		Normal loss (scrap value)	5,200
		Abnormal loss a/c	6,000
	356,200		356,200

(c) PROFIT STATEMENT

	Hans £'000	Nils £'000	Bumpsydaisies £'000
Sales	180.0	140.0	180.0
Costs	124.2	96.6	124.2
Profit	55.8	43.4	55.8
Profit/ sales ratio	31%	31%	31%

Question 2

Prepare the Process 2 account and a profit statement for the joint products in the above example using the units basis of apportionment.

Answer

PROCESS 2 ACCOUNT

	£		£
Process 1 materials	130,000	Finished goods accounts	
Conversion costs	226,200	- Hans (10,000 × £15)	150,000
		- Nils (7,000 × £15)	105,000
		- Bumpsydaisies (6,000 × £15)	90,000
		Normal loss (scrap value)	5,200
		Abnormal loss a/c (400 × £15)	6,000
	356,200		356,200

PROFIT STATEMENT

	Hans £'000	Nils £'000	Bumpsydaisies £'000
Sales	180	140	180
Costs	150	105	90
Profit	30	35	90
Profit/ sales ratio	16.7%	25%	50%

5 ACCOUNTING FOR BY-PRODUCTS

5.1 The by-product has some commercial value and its accounting treatment of income may be as follows.

(a) Income (minus any post-separation further processing or selling costs) from the sale of the by-product may be **added to sales of the main product**, thereby increasing sales turnover for the period.

(b) The sales of the by-product may be **treated as a separate, incidental source of income** against which are set only post-separation costs (if any) of the by-product. The revenue would be recorded in the profit and loss account as 'other income'.

(c) The sales income of the by-product may be **deducted from the cost of production** or cost of sales of the main product.

(d) The **net realisable value of the by-product may be deducted from the cost of production of the main product**. The net realisable value is the final saleable value of the by-product minus any post-separation costs. Any closing stock valuation of the main product or joint products would therefore be reduced.

The choice of method (a), (b), (c) or (d) will be influenced by the circumstances of production and ease of calculation, as much as by conceptual correctness. The method you are most likely to come across in examinations is method (d). An example will help to clarify the distinction between the different methods.

5.2 EXAMPLE: METHODS OF ACCOUNTING FOR BY-PRODUCTS

During November 20X3, Splatter Ltd recorded the following results.

Opening stock	main product P, nil
	by-product Z, nil
Cost of production	£120,000

Sales of the main product amounted to 90% of output during the period, and 10% of production was held as closing stock at 30 November.

Sales revenue from the main product during November 20X2 was £150,000.

A by-product Z is produced, and output had a net sales value of £1,000. Of this output, £700 was sold during the month, and £300 was still in stock at 30 November.

Required

Calculate the profit for November using the four methods of accounting for by-products.

5.3 SOLUTION

The four methods of accounting for by-products are shown below.

(a)   Income from by-product added to sales of the main product

	£	£
Sales of main product (£150,000 + £700)		150,700
Opening stock	0	
Cost of production	120,000	
	120,000	
Less closing stock (10%)	12,000	
Cost of sales		108,000
Profit, main product		42,700

The closing stock of the by-product has no recorded value in the cost accounts.

(b)   **By-product income treated as a separate source of income**

	£	£
Sales, main product		150,000
Opening stock	0	
Cost of production	120,000	
	120,000	
Closing stock (10%)	12,000	
Cost of sales, main product		108,000
Profit, main product		42,000
Other income		700
Total profit		42,700

The closing stock of the by-product again has no value in the cost accounts.

(c)   **Sales income of the by-product deducted from the cost of production in the period**

	£	£
Sales, main product		150,000
Opening stock	0	
Cost of production (120,000 – 700)	119,300	
	119,300	
Less closing stock (10%)	11,930	
Cost of sales		107,370
Profit, main product		42,630

Although the profit is different from the figure in (a) and (b), the by-product closing stock again has no value.

(d) **Net realisable value of the by-product deducted from the cost of production in the period**

	£	£
Sales, main product		150,000
Opening stock	0	
Cost of production (120,000 – 1,000)	119,000	
	119,000	
Less closing stock (10%)	11,900	
Cost of sales		107,100
Profit, main product		42,900

As with the other three methods, closing stock of the by-product has no value in the books of accounting, but the value of the closing stock (£300) has been used to reduce the cost of production, and in this respect it has been allowed for in deriving the cost of sales and the profit for the period.

Question 3

Randolph Ltd manufactures two joint products, J and K, in a common process. A by-product X is also produced. Data for the month of December 20X2 were as follows.

Opening stocks	nil	
Costs of processing	direct materials	£25,500
	direct labour	£10,000

Production overheads are absorbed at the rate of 300% of direct labour costs.

		Production Units	Sales Units
Output and sales consisted of:	product J	8,000	7,000
	product K	8,000	6,000
	by-product X	1,000	1,000

The sales value per unit of J, K and X is £4, £6 and £0.50 respectively. The saleable value of the by-product is deducted from process costs before apportioning costs to each joint product. Costs of the common processing are apportioned between product J and product K on the basis of sales value of production.

The individual profits for December 20X2 are:

	Product J £	Product K £
A	5,250	6,750
B	6,750	5,250
C	22,750	29,250
D	29,250	22,750

Answer

The sales value of production was £80,000.

	£	
Product J (8,000 × £4)	32,000	(40%)
Product K (8,000 × £6)	48,000	(60%)
	80,000	

The costs of production were as follows.	£
Direct materials	25,500
Direct labour	10,000
Overhead (300% of £10,000)	30,000
	65,500
Less sales value of by-product (1,000 × 50p)	500
Net production costs	65,000

The profit statement would appear as follows (nil opening stocks).

	Product J	£	Product K	£	Total £
Production costs	(40%)	26,000	(60%)	39,000	65,000
Less closing stock	(1,000 units)	3,250	(2,000 units)	9,750	13,000
Cost of sales		22,750		29,250	52,000
Sales	(7,000 units)	28,000	(6,000 units)	36,000	64,000
Profit		5,250		6,750	12,000

The correct answer is therefore A.

If you selected option B, you got the profits for each product mixed up.

If you selected option C or D, you calculated the cost of sales instead of the profit.

Chapter roundup

- **Joint products** are two or more products separated in a process, each of which has a **significant value** compared to the other. A **by-product** is an incidental product from a process which has an **insignificant value** compared to the main product.

- The point at which joint and by-products become separately identifiable is known as the **split-off point** or **separation point**. Costs incurred up to this point are called common costs or joint costs.

- There are four methods of apportioning joint costs, each of which can produce significantly different results. These methods are as follows.

    o Physical measurement

    o Relative sales value apportionment method; sales value at split-off point

    o Relative sales value apportionment method; sales value of end product less further processing costs after split-off point

    o Weighted average method

- The **relative sales value method** is most widely used because (ignoring the effect of further processing costs) it assumes that all products achieve the same profit margin.

- The most common method of accounting for by-products is to deduct the **net realisable value** of the by-product from the cost of the main products.

Quick quiz

1   What is the difference between a joint product and a by-product? *Joint Product is separated by a Process, by product is material.*

2   What is meant by the term 'split-off' point? *Point at which Products separate*

3   Name two methods of apportioning common costs to joint products. *Physical measurement, weighted average*

4   Describe the four methods of accounting for by-products.

Answers to quick quiz

1   A **joint product** is regarded as an important saleable item whereas a **by-product** is not.

2   The **split-off point** (or the **separation point**) is the point at which joint products become separately identifiable in a processing operation.

3   Physical measurement and sales value at split-off point.

4   See paragraph 5.1.

Now try the questions below from the Exam Question Bank

Number	Level	Marks	Time
20	MCQ	n/a	n/a
21	Examination	10	18 mins

Chapter 13

SERVICE COSTING

Topic list	Syllabus reference
1 What is service costing?	4(c)
2 Unit cost measures	4(c)
3 Service cost analysis	4(c)
4 Service cost analysis in internal service situations	4(c)
5 The usefulness of costing services that do not earn revenue	4(c)
6 Service cost analysis in service industry situations	4(c)

Introduction

Having covered job, batch, contract and process costing, we will now turn our attention to **service costing**, the service being a **specialist service** provided to third parties or an **internal service** provided within an organisation. The chapter looks at the calculation of a cost per unit of service and at methods of cost accounting in both types of situation.

Study guide

Section 16 – Operation/service costing

- Describe situations where the use of operation/service costing is appropriate

- Illustrate suitable unit cost measures that may be used in a variety of different operations and services

- Carry out service cost analysis in internal service situations

- Carry out service cost analysis in service industry situations

Exam guide

Service costing is not one of the key areas of the syllabus and is most likely to be examined in the form of multiple choice questions (in Section A of your examination).

1   WHAT IS SERVICE COSTING?

KEY TERM

Service costing (or **function costing**) is a costing method concerned with establishing the costs, not of items of production, but of services rendered.

1.1   Service costing is used in the following circumstances.

(a) A company operating in a service industry will cost its services, for which sales revenue will be earned; examples are electricians, car hire services, road, rail or air transport services and hotels.

(b) A company may wish to establish the cost of services carried out by some of its departments; for example the costs of the vans or lorries used in distribution, the costs of the computer department, or the staff canteen.

1.2 Service costing differs from product costing (such as job or process costing) in the following ways.

(a) With many services, the cost of direct materials consumed will be relatively small compared to the labour, direct expenses and overheads cost. In product costing the direct materials are often a greater proportion of the total cost.

(b) Although many services are revenue-earning, others are not (such as the distribution facility or the staff canteen). This means that the purpose of service costing may not be to establish a profit or loss (nor to value closing stocks for the balance sheet) but may rather be to provide management information about the comparative costs or efficiency of the services, with a view to helping managers to budget for their costs using historical data as a basis for estimating costs in the future and to control the costs in the service departments.

(c) The procedures for recording material costs, labour hours and other expenses will vary according to the nature of the service.

1.3 Specific characteristics of services are **intangibility, simultaneity, perishability** and **heterogeneity.** Consider the service of providing a haircut.

(a) A haircut is **intangible** in itself, and the performance of the service comprises many other intangible factors, like the music in the salon, the personality of the hairdresser, the quality of the coffee.

(b) The production and consumption of a haircut are **simultaneous,** and therefore it cannot be inspected for quality in advance, nor can it be returned if it is not what was required.

(c) Haircuts are **perishable,** that is, they cannot be stored. You cannot buy them in bulk, and the hairdresser cannot do them in advance and keep them stocked away in case of heavy demand. The incidence of work in progress in service organisations is less frequent than in other types of organisation.

(d) A haircut is **heterogeneous** and so the exact service received will vary each time: not only will two hairdressers cut hair differently, but a hairdresser will not consistently deliver the same standard of haircut.

2 UNIT COST MEASURES

2.1 One particular problem with service costing is the **difficulty in defining a realistic cost unit** that represents a suitable measure of the service provided. Frequently, a composite cost unit may be deemed more appropriate. Hotels, for example, may use the 'occupied bed-night' as an appropriate unit for cost ascertainment and control.

2.2 Typical cost units used by companies operating in a service industry are shown below.

Service	Cost unit
Road, rail and air transport services	Passenger/mile or kilometre, ton/mile, tonne/ kilometre
Hotels	Occupied bed-night
Education	Full-time student
Hospitals	Patient
Catering establishment	Meal served

Question 1

Can you think of examples of cost units for internal services such as canteens, distribution and maintenance?

Answer

Service	*Cost unit*
Canteen	Meal served
Vans and lorries used in distribution	Mile or kilometre, ton/mile, tonne/kilometre
Maintenance	Man hour

2.3 Each organisation will need to ascertain the **cost unit** most appropriate to its activities. If a number of organisations within an industry use a common cost unit, then valuable comparisons can be made between similar establishments. This is particularly applicable to hospitals, educational establishments and local authorities. Whatever cost unit is decided upon, the calculation of a cost per unit is as follows.

FORMULA TO LEARN

$$\text{Cost per service unit} = \frac{\text{Total costs for period}}{\text{Number of service units in the period}}$$

---

3 SERVICE COST ANALYSIS

3.1 **Service cost analysis** should be performed in a manner which ensures that the following objectives are attained.

(a) Planned costs should be compared with actual costs.

Differences should be investigated and corrective action taken as necessary.

(b) A cost per unit of service should be calculated.

If each service has a number of variations (such as maintenance services provided by plumbers, electricians and carpenters) then the calculation of a cost per unit of each service may be necessary.

(c) The cost per unit of service should be used as part of the control function.

For example, costs per unit of service can be compared, month by month, period by period, year by year and so on and any unusual trends can be investigated.

(d) Prices should be calculated for services being sold to third parties.

The procedure is similar to job costing. A mark-up is added to the cost per unit of service to arrive at a selling price.

(e) Costs should be analysed into fixed, variable and semi-variable costs to help assist management with planning, control and decision making.

4   SERVICE COST ANALYSIS IN INTERNAL SERVICE SITUATIONS

Exam focus point

The study guide for Paper 1.2 specifically mentions that candidates must be able to 'carry out service cost analysis in **internal service** situations'.

Transport costs

4.1   '**Transport costs**' is a term used here to refer to the costs of the transport services used by a company, rather than the costs of a transport organisation, such as British Rail.

4.2   If a company has a fleet of lorries or vans which it uses to distribute its goods, it is useful to know how much the department is costing for a number of reasons.

(a)   Management should be able to budget for expected costs, and to control actual expenditure on transport by comparing actual costs with budgeted costs.

(b)   The company may charge customers for delivery or 'carriage outwards' costs, and a charge based on the cost of the transport service might be appropriate.

(c)   If management knows how much its own transport is costing, a comparison can be made with alternative forms of transport (independent transport companies, British Rail) to decide whether a cheaper or better method of delivery can be found.

(d)   Similarly, if a company uses, say, a fleet of lorries, knowledge of how much transport by lorry costs should help management to decide whether another type of vehicle, say vans, would be cheaper to use.

4.3   Transport costs may be analysed to provide the cost of operating one van or lorry each year, but it is more informative to analyse costs as follows.

(a)   The cost per mile or kilometre travelled.

(b)   The cost per ton/mile or tonne/kilometre (the cost of carrying one tonne of goods for one kilometre distance) or the cost per kilogram/metre.

4.4   For example, suppose that a company lorry makes five deliveries in a week.

Delivery	Tonnes carried	Distance (one way) Kilometres	Tonne/kilometres carried
1	0.4	180	72
2	0.3	360	108
3	1.2	100	120
4	0.8	250	200
5	1.0	60	60
			560

If the costs of operating the lorry during the week are known to be £840, the cost per tonne/kilometre would be:

$$\frac{£840}{560 \text{tonne/kilometre}} = £1.50 \text{ per tonne/kilometre}$$

4.5 Transport costs might be collected under five broad headings.

(a) **Running costs** such as petrol, oil, drivers' wages
(b) **Loading costs** (the labour costs of loading the lorries with goods for delivery)
(c) **Servicing, repairs,** spare parts and tyre usage
(d) **Annual direct expenses** such as road tax, insurance and depreciation
(e) **Indirect costs of the distribution department** such as the wages of managers

4.6 The role of the cost accountant is to provide a system for **recording and analysing costs**. Just as production costs are recorded by means of material requisition notes, labour time sheets and so on, so too must transport costs be recorded by means of log sheets or time sheets, and material supply notes.

The purpose of a lorry driver's log sheet is to record distance travelled, or the number of tonne/kilometres and the drivers' time.

Canteen costs

4.7 Another example of service costing is the cost of a company's **canteen services**. A feature of canteen costing is that some revenue is earned when employees pay for their meals, but the prices paid will be insufficient to cover the costs of the canteen service. The company will subsidise the canteen and a major purpose of canteen costing is to establish the size of the subsidy.

4.8 If the costs of the canteen service are recorded by a system of service cost accounting, the likely headings of expense would be as follows.

(a) **Food and drink**: separate canteen stores records may be kept, and the consumption of food and drink recorded by means of 'materials issues' notes.

(b) **Labour costs of the canteen staff**: hourly paid staff will record their time at work on a time card or time sheet. Salaried staff will be 'fixed' cost each month.

(c) **Consumable stores** such as crockery, cutlery, glassware, table linen and cleaning materials will also be recorded in some form of stock control system.

(d) **The cost of gas and electricity** may be separately metered; otherwise an apportionment of the total cost of such utilities for the building as a whole will be made to the canteen department.

(e) Asset records will be kept and **depreciation charges** made for major items of equipment like ovens and furniture.

(f) An apportionment of other **overhead costs** of the building (rent and rates, building insurance and maintenance and so on) may be charged against the canteen.

Cash income from canteen sales will also be recorded.

4.9 Suppose that a canteen recorded the following costs and revenue during the month.

	£
Food and drink	11,250
Labour	11,250
Heating and lighting	1,875
Repairs and consumable stores	1,125
Financing costs	1,000
Depreciation	750
Other apportioned costs	875
Revenue	22,500

The canteen served 37,500 meals in the month.

The size of the subsidy could be easily identified as follows:

	£
The total costs of the canteen	28,125
Revenue	22,500
Loss, to be covered by the company	5,625

The cost per meal averages 75p and the revenue per meal 60p. If the company decided that the canteen should pay its own way, without a subsidy, the average price of a meal would have to be raised by 15 pence.

5 THE USEFULNESS OF COSTING SERVICES THAT DO NOT EARN REVENUE

5.1 The techniques for costing services are similar to the techniques for costing products, but why should we want to establish a cost for 'internal' services, services that are provided by one department for another, rather than sold externally to customers? In other words, what is the purpose of service costing for non-revenue-earning services?

5.2 Service costing has two basic purposes.

(a) **To control the costs in the service department**. If we establish a distribution cost per tonne kilometre, a canteen cost per employee, or job costs of repairs, we can establish control measures in the following ways.

    (i)   Comparing actual costs against a target or standard

    (ii)   Comparing current actual costs against actual costs in previous periods

(b) **To control the costs of the user departments**, and prevent the unnecessary use of services. If the costs of services are charged to the user departments in such a way that the charges reflect the use actually made by each department of the service department's services then the following will occur.

    (i)   The overhead costs of user departments will be established more accurately; indeed some service department variable costs might be identified as directly attributable costs of the user department.

    (ii)   If the service department's charges for a user department are high, the user department might be encouraged to consider whether it is making an excessively costly and wasteful use of the service department's service.

    (iii) The user department might decide that it can obtain a similar service at a lower cost from an external service company.

5.3 EXAMPLE: COSTING INTERNAL SERVICES

(a) If maintenance costs in a factory are costed as jobs (that is, if each bit of repair work is given a job number and costed accordingly) repair costs can be charged to the departments on the basis of repair jobs actually undertaken, instead of on a more generalised basis, such as apportionment according to machine hour capacity in each department. Departments with high repair costs could then consider their high incidence of repairs, the age and reliability of their machines, or the skills of the machine operatives.

(b) If mainframe computer costs are charged to a user department on the basis of a cost per hour, the user department would assess whether it was getting good value from its use of the mainframe computer and whether it might be better to hire the service of a

6 SERVICE COST ANALYSIS IN SERVICE INDUSTRY SITUATIONS

Distribution costs

6.1 EXAMPLE: SERVICE COST ANALYSIS IN THE SERVICE INDUSTRY

This example shows how a rate per tonne/kilometre can be calculated for a distribution service.

Rick Shaw Ltd operates a small fleet of delivery vehicles. Standard costs have been established as follows.

Loading	1 hour per tonne loaded
Loading costs:	
Labour (casual)	£2 per hour
Equipment depreciation	£80 per week
Supervision	£80 per week
Drivers' wages (fixed)	£100 per man per week
Petrol	10p per kilometre
Repairs	5p per kilometre
Depreciation	£80 per week per vehicle
Supervision	£120 per week
Other general expenses (fixed)	£200 per week

There are two drivers and two vehicles in the fleet.

During a slack week, only six journeys were made.

Journey	Tonnes carried (one way)	One-way distance of journey Kilometres
1	5	100
2	8	20
3	2	60
4	4	50
5	6	200
6	5	300

Required

Calculate the expected average full cost per tonne/kilometre for the week.

6.2 SOLUTION

Variable costs	*Journey*	1	2	3	4	5	6
		£	£	£	£	£	£
Loading labour		10	16	4	8	12	10
Petrol (both ways)		20	4	12	10	40	60
Repairs (both ways)		10	2	6	5	20	30
		40	22	22	23	72	100

Total costs

	£
Variable costs (total for journeys 1 to 6)	279
Loading equipment depreciation	80
Loading supervision	80
Drivers' wages	200
Vehicles depreciation	160
Drivers' supervision	120
Other costs	200
	1,119

Journey	Tonnes	*One way distance* Kilometres	Tonne/kilometres
1	5	100	500
2	8	20	160
3	2	60	120
4	4	50	200
5	6	200	1,200
6	5	300	1,500
			3,680

Cost per tonne/kilometre $\frac{£1,119}{3,680} = £0.304$

Note that the large element of fixed costs may distort this measure but that a variable cost per tonne/kilometre of £279/3,680 = £0.076 may be useful for budgetary control.

Education

6.3 The techniques described in the preceding paragraphs can be applied, in general, to any service industry situation. Attempt the following question about education.

Question 2

A university with annual running costs of £3 million has the following students.

Classification	*Number*	*Attendance weeks per annum*	*Hours per week*
3 year	2,700	30	28
4 year	1,500	30	25
Sandwich	1,900	35	20

Required

Calculate a cost per suitable cost unit for the university to the nearest penny.

Answer

We need to begin by establishing a cost unit for the university. Since there are three different categories of students we cannot use 'a student' as the cost unit. Attendance hours would seem to be the most appropriate cost unit. The next step is to calculate the number of units.

Number of students	*Weeks*	*Hours*	*Total hours per annum*
2,700	× 30	× 28	= 2,268,000
1,500	× 30	× 25	= 1,125,000
1,900	× 35	× 20	= 1,330,000
			4,723,000

The cost per unit is calculated as follows.

$$\text{Cost per unit} = \frac{\text{Total cost}}{\text{Number of units}} = £(\frac{3,000,000}{4,723,000}) = \underline{\underline{£0.64}}$$

Question 3

State which of the following are characteristics of service costing.

(i)   High levels of indirect costs as a proportion of total costs
(ii)   Use of composite cost units
(iii) Use of equivalent units

A   (i) only
B   (i) and (ii) only
C   (ii) only
D   (ii) and (iii) only

Answer

B   In service costing it is difficult to identify many attributable direct costs. Many costs must be shared over several cost units, therefore characteristic (i) does apply. Composite cost units such as tonne-mile or room-night are often used, therefore characteristic (ii) does apply. Equivalent units are more often used in costing for tangible products, therefore characteristic (iii) does not apply. The correct answer is therefore B.

Chapter roundup

- **Service costing** can be used by companies operating in a **service industry** or by companies wishing to establish the **cost of services carried out by some of their departments**.

- Service organisations do not make or sell tangible goods.

- **Specific characteristics of services**

    o   Intangibility
    o   Simultaneity
    o   Perishability
    o   Heterogeneity

- One main problem with service costing is being able to define a realistic **cost unit** that represents a suitable measure of the service provided. If the service is a function of two activity variables, a **composite cost unit** may be more appropriate.

- **Cost per service unit** = $\dfrac{\text{Total costs for period}}{\text{Number of service units in the period}}$

  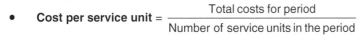

- Service department costing is also used to establish a specific cost for an **internal service** which is a service provided by one department for another, rather than sold externally to customers eg canteen, maintenance.

Quick quiz

1 Define service costing *Cost accounting for services provided eg canteen transport etc.*

2 Match up the following services with their typical cost units

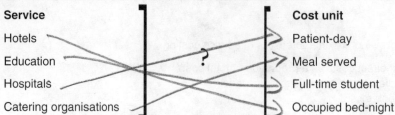

Service		Cost unit
Hotels		Patient-day
Education	?	Meal served
Hospitals		Full-time student
Catering organisations		Occupied bed-night

3 What is the advantage of organisations within an industry using a common cost unit? *Ability to compare*

4 Cost per service unit = $\dfrac{TOTAL\ COST}{TOTAL\ UNITS}$

5 Service department costing is used to establish a specific cost for an 'internal service' which is a service provided by one department for another.

True ☑

False ☐

Answers to quick quiz

1 Cost accounting for services or functions eg canteens, maintenance, personnel (service centres/functions).

2

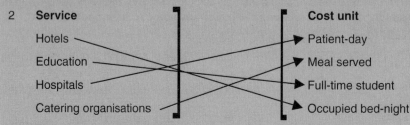

Service		Cost unit
Hotels		Patient-day
Education		Meal served
Hospitals		Full-time student
Catering organisations		Occupied bed-night

3 It is easier to make comparisons.

4 Cost per service unit = $\dfrac{\text{Total costs for period}}{\text{Number of service units in the period}}$

5 True

Now try the questions below from the Exam Question Bank

Number	Level	Marks	Time
22	MCQ	n/a	n/a
23	Examination	10	18 mins

Part D
Decision making

Chapter 14

TIME SERIES ANALYSIS

Topic list	Syllabus reference
1 The components of time series	6(b)
2 Finding the trend	6(b)
3 Finding the seasonal variations	6(b)
4 Forecasting and time series analysis	6(b)

Introduction

In this chapter we will be looking at a technique called **time series analysis**. With this method we look at **past data** about the variable which we want to forecast (such as sales levels) to see if there are **any patterns**. We then assume that these patterns will continue into the future. We are then able to forecast what we believe will be the value of a variable at some particular point of time in the future.

Study guide

Section 17 – Time series analysis

- Explain the purpose of time series analysis

- Explain the components of the additive and multiplicative models

- Explain the methods available for establishing the trend

- Apply the method of moving averages to isolate the trend for both the multiplicative and additive models

- Use the trend and appropriate variations to establish forecast figures

Exam guide

Time series analysis is not one of the key areas of the syllabus for Paper 1.2. Make sure that you are able to isolate the trend using both the multiplicative and additive models as this is the type of question you might face in your examination.

1   THE COMPONENTS OF TIME SERIES

> **KEY TERM**
>
> A **time series** is a series of figures or values recorded over time. The graph of a time series is called a **historigram**.

1.1   The following are examples of time series.

- Output at a factory each day for the last month
- Monthly sales over the last two years
- Total annual costs for the last ten years
- The Retail Prices Index each month for the last ten years
- The number of people employed by a company each year for the last 20 years

1.2   The main features of a time series are as follows.

- A trend
- Seasonal variations or fluctuations
- Cycles, or cyclical variations
- Non-recurring, random variations

The trend

KEY TERM

The **trend** is the underlying long-term movement over time in the values of the data recorded.

1.3   EXAMPLE: PREPARING TIME SERIES GRAPHS AND IDENTIFYING TRENDS

	Output per labour hour Units	Cost per unit £	Number of employees
20X4	30	1.00	100
20X5	24	1.08	103
20X6	26	1.20	96
20X7	22	1.15	102
20X8	21	1.18	103
20X9	17	1.25	98
	(A)	(B)	(C)

(a)   In time series (A) there is a **downward trend** in the output per labour hour. Output per labour hour did not fall every year, because it went up between 20X5 and 20X6, but the long-term movement is clearly a downward one.

Graph showing trend of output per labour hour in years 20X4-X9

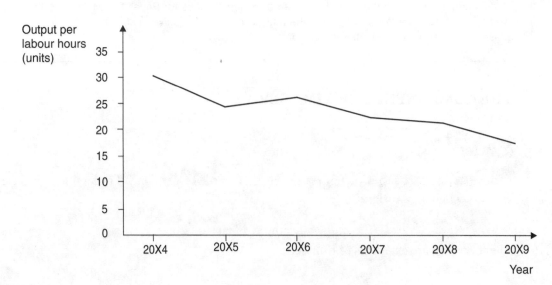

(b) In time series (B) there is an **upward trend** in the cost per unit. Although unit costs went down in 20X7 from a higher level in 20X6, the basic movement over time is one of rising costs.

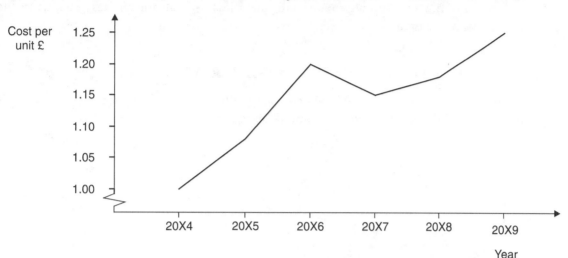

Graph showing trend of costs per unit in years 20X4-X9

(c) In time series (C) there is no clear movement up or down, and the number of employees remained fairly constant around 100. The trend is therefore a **static**, or **level one**.

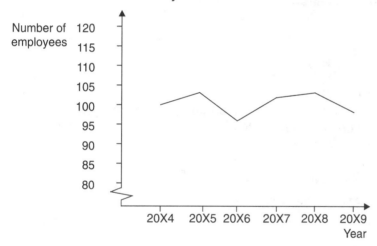

Graph showing trend of number of employees in year 20X4-X9

Seasonal variations

KEY TERM

Seasonal variations are short-term fluctuations in recorded values, due to different circumstances which affect results at different times of the year, on different days of the week, at different times of day, or whatever.

1.4 Examples of seasonable variations are as follows.

(a) Sales of ice cream will be higher in summer than in winter, and sales of overcoats will be higher in autumn than in spring.

(b) Shops might expect higher sales shortly before Christmas, or in their winter and summer sales.

(c) Sales might be higher on Friday and Saturday than on Monday.

(d) The telephone network may be heavily used at certain times of the day (such as mid-morning and mid-afternoon) and much less used at other times (such as in the middle of the night).

1.5 EXAMPLE: A TREND AND SEASONAL VARIATIONS

The number of customers served by a company of travel agents over the past four years is shown in the following **historigram** (time series graph).

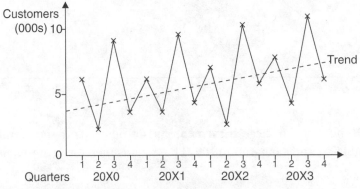

In this example, there would appear to be large seasonal fluctuations in demand, but there is also a basic upward trend.

Cyclical variations

1.6 **Cyclical variations** are medium-term changes in results caused by circumstances which repeat in cycles. In business, cyclical variations are commonly associated with **economic cycles, successive booms** and **slumps** in the economy. Economic cycles may last a few years. **Cyclical variations are longer term than seasonal variations.**

Summarising the components

1.7 The components of a time series can be summarised by the following equation.

$$Y = T + S + C + I$$

where   Y = the actual time series
       T = the trend series
       S = the seasonal component
       C = the cyclical component
       I = the random or irregular component

1.8 Though you should be aware of the cyclical component, you will not be expected to carry out any calculation connected with isolating it. The mathematical model which we will use, the **additive model**, therefore excludes any reference to C.

FORMULA TO LEARN

Additive model: Series = Trend + Seasonal + Random

$$Y = T + S + I$$

2 FINDING THE TREND

2.1 **The main problem we are concerned with in time series analysis is how to identify the trend and seasonal variations.**

2.2 There are three main methods of finding a trend.

    (a) A **line of best fit** (the **trend line**) can be drawn by eye on a graph. (We will cover this in Section 4 of this chapter.)

    (b) A statistical technique known as **linear regression by the least squares method** can be used. (We covered this in Chapter 5.)

    (c) A technique known as **moving averages** can be used.

Finding the trend by moving averages

> **KEY TERMS**
>
> • A **moving average** is an average of the results of a fixed number of periods.
>
> • The **moving averages method** is a technique used to find the trend. This method attempts to remove seasonal variations from actual data by a process of averaging.

2.3 EXAMPLE: MOVING AVERAGES OF AN ODD NUMBER OF RESULTS

Year	Sales
	Units
20X0	390
20X1	380
20X2	460
20X3	450
20X4	470
20X5	440
20X6	500

Required

Take a moving average of the annual sales over a period of three years.

2.4 SOLUTION

    (a) Average sales in the three year period 20X0 – 20X2 were

$$\left(\frac{390 + 380 + 460}{3}\right) = \frac{1,230}{3} = 410$$

        This average relates to the middle year of the period, 20X1.

    (b) Similarly, average sales in the three year period 20X1 – 20X3 were

$$\left(\frac{380 + 460 + 450}{3}\right) = \frac{1,290}{3} = 430$$

        This average relates to the middle year of the period, 20X2.

    (c) The average sales can also be found for the periods 20X2 - 20X4, 20X3 - 20X5 and 20X4 - 20X6, to give the following.

Year	Sales	Moving total of 3 years' sales	Moving average of 3 years' sales (÷ 3)
20X0	390		
20X1	380	1,230	410
20X2	460	1,290	430
20X3	450	1,380	460
20X4	470	1,360	453
20X5	440	1,410	470
20X6	500		

Note the following points.

(i) The moving average series has five figures relating to the years from 20X1 to 20X5. The original series had seven figures for the years from 20X0 to 20X6.

(ii) There is an upward trend in sales, which is more noticeable from the series of moving averages than from the original series of actual sales each year.

2.5 The above example averaged over a three-year period. Over what period should a moving average be taken? The answer to this question is that **the moving average which is most appropriate will depend on the circumstances and the nature of the time series**. Note the following points.

(a) A moving average which takes an average of the results in many time periods will represent results over a longer term than a moving average of two or three periods.

(b) On the other hand, with a moving average of results in many time periods, the last figure in the series will be out of date by several periods. In our example, the most recent average related to 20X5. With a moving average of five years' results, the final figure in the series would relate to 20X4.

(c) When there is a known cycle over which seasonal variations occur, such as all the days in the week or all the seasons in the year, the most suitable moving average would be one which covers one full cycle.

Question 1

Using the following data, what is the three-month moving average for the period January-June?

Month	No of new houses finished
January	500
February	450
March	700
April	900
May	1,250
June	1,000

Answer

Month	No of new houses finished	Moving total 3 months new houses finished	Moving average of 3 months new houses finished (÷ 3)
January	500		
February	450	1,650	550
March	700	2,050	683.33
April	900	2,850	950
May	1,250	3,150	1,050
June	1,000		

Moving averages of an even number of results

2.6 In the previous example, moving averages were taken of the results in an **odd number of time periods**, and the average then related to the **mid-point of the overall period**. If a moving average were taken of results in an **even number of time periods**, the basic technique would be the same, but **the mid-point of the overall period would not relate to a single period**. For example, suppose an average were taken of the following four results.

Spring	120	
Summer	90	average 115
Autumn	180	
Winter	70	

The average would relate to the mid-point of the period, between summer and autumn. The trend line average figures need to relate to a particular time period; otherwise, seasonal variations cannot be calculated. To overcome this difficulty, we take a **moving average of the moving average**. An example will illustrate this technique.

2.7 EXAMPLE: MOVING AVERAGES OVER AN EVEN NUMBER OF PERIODS

Calculate a moving average trend line of the following results.

Year	Quarter	Volume of sales '000 units
20X5	1	600
	2	840
	3	420
	4	720
20X6	1	640
	2	860
	3	420
	4	740
20X7	1	670
	2	900
	3	430
	4	760

2.8 SOLUTION

A moving average of four will be used, since the volume of sales would appear to depend on the season of the year, and each year has four quarterly results.

The moving average of four does not relate to any specific period of time; therefore a second moving average of two will be calculated on the first moving average trend line.

Year	Quarter	Actual volume of sales '000 units (A)	Moving total of 4 quarters' sales '000 units (B)	Moving average of 4 quarters' sales '000 units (B ÷ 4)	Mid-point of 2 moving averages Trend line '000 units (C)
20X5	1	600			
	2	840			
	3	420	2,580	645.0	650.00
	4	720	2,620	655.0	657.50
20X6	1	640	2,640	660.0	660.00
	2	860	2,640	660.0	662.50
	3	420	2,660	665.0	668.75
	4	740	2,690	672.5	677.50
20X7	1	670	2,730	682.5	683.75
	2	900	2,740	685.0	687.50
	3	430	2,760	690.0	
	4	760			

By taking a mid point (a moving average of two) **of the original moving averages, we can relate the results to specific quarters** (from the third quarter of 20X5 to the second quarter of 20X7).

3 FINDING THE SEASONAL VARIATIONS

3.1 Once a trend has been established, by whatever method, we can find the **seasonal variations**.

3.2 How do we go about finding the seasonal component?

Step 1. The additive model for time series analysis is $Y = T + S + I$.

Step 2. If we deduct the trend from the additive model, we get $Y - T = S + I$.

Step 3. If we assume that I, the random, or irregular component of the time series is relatively small and therefore negligible, then $S = Y - T$.

Therefore, the seasonal component, $S = Y - T$ (the de-trended series).

3.3 EXAMPLE: THE TREND AND SEASONAL VARIATIONS

Output at a factory appears to vary with the day of the week. Output over the last three weeks has been as follows.

	Week 1 '000 units	Week 2 '000 units	Week 3 '000 units
Monday	80	82	84
Tuesday	104	110	116
Wednesday	94	97	100
Thursday	120	125	130
Friday	62	64	66

Required

Find the seasonal variation for each of the 15 days, and the average seasonal variation for each day of the week using the moving averages method.

3.4 SOLUTION

Actual results fluctuate up and down according to the day of the week and so a **moving average of five** will be used. **The difference between the actual result on any one day (Y) and the trend figure for that day (T) will be the seasonal variation (S) for the day.** The seasonal variations for the 15 days are as follows.

		Actual (Y)	Moving total of five days' output	Trend (T)	Seasonal variation (Y–T)
Week 1	Monday	80			
	Tuesday	104			
	Wednesday	94	460	92.0	+2.0
	Thursday	120	462	92.4	+27.6
	Friday	62	468	93.6	−31.6
Week 2	Monday	82	471	94.2	−12.2
	Tuesday	110	476	95.2	+14.8
	Wednesday	97	478	95.6	+1.4
	Thursday	125	480	96.0	+29.0
	Friday	64	486	97.2	−33.2
Week 3	Monday	84	489	97.8	−13.8
	Tuesday	116	494	98.8	+17.2
	Wednesday	100	496	99.2	+0.8
	Thursday	130			
	Friday	66			

You will notice that the variation between the actual results on any one particular day and the trend line average is not the same from week to week. This is because **Y – T contains not only seasonal variations but random variations,** but **an average of these variations can be taken.**

	Monday	Tuesday	Wednesday	Thursday	Friday
Week 1			+2.0	+27.6	−31.6
Week 2	−12.2	+14.8	+1.4	+29.0	−33.2
Week 3	−13.8	+17.2	+0.8		
Average	−13.0	+16.0	+1.4	+28.3	−32.4

Variations around the basic trend line should cancel each other out, and add up to 0. At the moment they do not. **The average seasonal estimates must therefore be corrected so that they add up to zero** and so we spread the total of the daily variations (0.30) across the five days (0.3 ÷ 5) so that the final total of the daily variations goes to zero.

	Monday	Tuesday	Wednesday	Thursday	Friday	Total
Estimated average daily variation	−13.00	+16.00	+1.40	+28.30	−32.40	0.30
Adjustment to reduce total variation to 0	−0.06	−0.06	−0.06	−0.06	−0.06	−0.30
Final estimate of average daily variation	−13.06	+15.94	+1.34	+28.24	−32.46	0.00

These might be rounded up or down as follows.

Monday −13; Tuesday +16; Wednesday +1; Thursday +28; Friday −32; Total 0.

Question 2

Calculate a four-quarter moving average trend centred on actual quarters and then find seasonal variations from the following.

	Spring	Summer	Autumn	Winter
		Sales in £'000		
20X7	200	120	160	280
20X8	220	140	140	300
20X9	200	120	180	320

Answer

		Sales (Y)	4-quarter total	8-quarter total	Moving average (T)	Seasonal variation (Y-T)
20X7	Spring	200				
	Summer	120				
			760			
	Autumn	160		1,540	192.5	−32.5
			780			
	Winter	280		1,580	197.5	+82.5
			800			
20X8	Spring	220		1,580	197.5	+22.5
			780			
	Summer	140		1,580	197.5	−57.5
			800			
	Autumn	140		1,580	197.5	−57.5
			780			
	Winter	300		1,540	192.5	+107.5
			760			
20X9	Spring	200		1,560	195.0	+5.0
			800			
	Summer	120		1,620	202.5	−82.5
			820			
	Autumn	180				
	Winter	320				

We can now average the seasonal variations.

	Spring	Summer	Autumn	Winter	Total
20X7			−32.5	+82.5	
20X8	+22.5	−57.5	−57.5	+107.5	
20X9	+5.0	−82.5			
	+27.5	−140.0	−90.0	+190.0	
Average variations (in £'000)	+13.75	−70.00	−45.00	+95.00	−6.25
Adjustment so sum is zero	+1.5625	+1.5625	+1.5625	+1.5625	+6.25
Adjusted average variations	+15.3125	−68.4375	−43.4375	+96.5625	0

These might be rounded up or down to:

Spring £15,000, Summer −£68,000, Autumn −£43,000, Winter £96,000

Seasonal variations using the multiplicative model

3.5 The method of estimating the seasonal variations in the additive model is to use the differences between the trend and actual data. **The additive model assumes that the components of the series are independent of each other,** an increasing trend not affecting the seasonal variations for example.

The alternative is to use the **multiplicative model** whereby **each actual figure is expressed as a proportion of the trend.** Sometimes this method is called the **proportional model.**

> **FORMULA TO LEARN**
>
> **Multiplicative model:**   Series =   Trend × Seasonal × Random
>
> Y   =   T × S × I

3.6 The additive model example above can be reworked on this alternative basis. The trend is calculated in exactly the same way as before but we need a different approach for the seasonal variations.

The multiplicative model is Y = T × S × I and, just as we calculated S = Y – T for the additive model we can calculate **S = Y/T for the multiplicative model.**

		Actual (Y)	Trend (T)	Seasonal variation (Y/T)
Week 1	Monday	80		
	Tuesday	104		
	Wednesday	94	92.0	1.022
	Thursday	120	92.4	1.299
	Friday	62	93.6	0.662
Week 2	Monday	82	94.2	0.870
	Tuesday	110	95.2	1.155
	Wednesday	97	95.6	1.015
	Thursday	125	96.0	1.302
	Friday	64	97.2	0.658
Week 3	Monday	84	97.8	0.859
	Tuesday	116	98.8	1.174
	Wednesday	100	99.2	1.008
	Thursday	130		
	Friday	66		

3.7 The summary of the seasonal variations expressed in **proportional terms** is as follows.

	Monday	Tuesday	Wednesday	Thursday	Friday
Week 1			1.022	1.299	0.662
Week 2	0.870	1.155	1.015	1.302	0.658
Week 3	0.859	1.174	1.008		
Total	1.729	2.329	3.045	2.601	1.320
Average	0.8645	1.1645	1.0150	1.3005	0.6600

Instead of summing to zero, as with the absolute approach, these should sum (in this case) to 5 (an average of 1).

They actually sum to 5.0045 so 0.0009 has to be deducted from each one. This is too small to make a difference to the figures above, so we should deduct 0.002 and 0.0025 to each of two seasonal variations. We could arbitrarily decrease Monday's variation to 0.8625 and Tuesday's to 1.162.

3.8 **The multiplicative model is better than the additive model for forecasting when the trend is increasing or decreasing over time.** In such circumstances, seasonal variations are likely to be increasing or decreasing too. The additive model simply adds absolute and unchanging seasonal variations to the trend figures whereas the multiplicative model, by multiplying increasing or decreasing trend values by a constant seasonal variation factor, takes account of changing seasonal variations.

3.9 We can summarise the steps to be carried out when calculating the seasonal variation as follows.

Step 1. Calculate the moving total for an appropriate period.

Step 2. Calculate the moving average (the trend) for the period. (Calculate the mid-point of two moving averages if there are an even number of periods.)

Step 3. Calculate the seasonal variation. For an additive model, this is Y – T. For a multiplicative model, this is Y/T.

Step 4. Calculate an average of the seasonal variations.

Step 5. Adjust the average seasonal variations so that they add up to **zero** for an **additive model**. When using the **multiplicative model**, the average seasonal variations should add up to an **average of 1**.

Question 3

Find the average seasonal variations for the sales data in Question 2 using the multiplicative model.

Answer

	Spring	Summer	Autumn	Winter	Total
20X7			0.83	1.42	
20X8	1.11	0.71	0.71	1.56	
20X9	1.03	0.59			
	2.14	1.30	1.54	2.98	

	Spring	Summer	Autumn	Winter	Total
Average variations	1.070	0.650	0.770	1.490	3.980
Adjustment to sum to 4	+ 0.005	– 0.005	– 0.005	+ 0.005	0.020
Adjusted average variations	1.075	0.655	0.775	1.495	4.000

Seasonally-adjusted data

> **KEY TERM**
>
> **Seasonally-adjusted data (deseasonalised)** are data which have had any seasonal variations taken out, so leaving a figure which might indicate the trend. Seasonally-adjusted data should indicate whether the overall trend is rising, falling or stationary.

3.10 EXAMPLE: SEASONALLY-ADJUSTED DATA

Actual sales figures for four quarters, together with appropriate seasonal adjustment factors derived from previous data, are as follows.

		Seasonal adjustments	
	Actual	*Additive*	*Multiplicative*
Quarter	*sales*	*model*	*model*
	£'000	£'000	
1	150	+3	1.02
2	160	+4	1.05
3	164	–2	0.98
4	170	–5	0.95

Required

Deseasonalise these data.

3.11 SOLUTION

We are reversing the normal process of applying seasonal variations to trend figures.

The rules for deseasonalising data are as follows.

- **Additive model** - subtract positive seasonal variations from and add negative seasonal variations to actual results.

- **Multiplicative model** - divide the actual results by the seasonal variation factors.

		Deseasonalised sales	
Quarter	*Actual sales* £'000	*Additive model* £'000	*Multiplicative model* £'000
1	150	147	147
2	160	156	152
3	164	166	167
4	170	175	179

4 FORECASTING AND TIME SERIES ANALYSIS

Making a forecast

4.1 Time series analysis data can be used to make forecasts as follows.

Step 1. **Plot a trend line**: use the line of best fit method or the moving averages method.

Step 2. **Extrapolate the trend line**. This means extending the trend line outside the range of known data and forecasting future results from historical data.

Step 3. **Adjust forecast trends** by the applicable average seasonal variation to obtain the actual forecast.

   (a) **Additive model** - add positive variations to and subtract negative variations from the forecast trends.

   (b) **Multiplicative model** - multiply the forecast trends by the seasonal variation.

4.2 EXAMPLE: FORECASTING

Use the trend values and the estimates of seasonal variations calculated in Paragraph 3.4 to forecast sales in week 4.

4.3 SOLUTION

We begin by plotting the trend values on a graph and extrapolating the trend line.

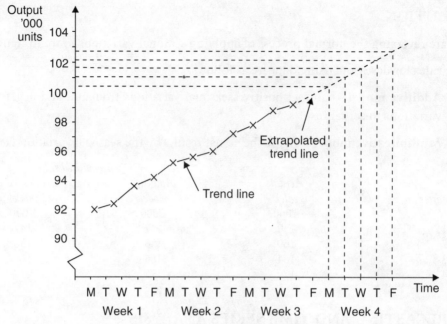

From the extrapolated trend line we can take the following readings and adjust them by the seasonal variations.

Week 4	*Trend line readings*	*Seasonal variations*	*Forecast*
Monday	100.5	−13	87.5
Tuesday	101.5	+16	117.1
Wednesday	101.7	+1	102.7
Thursday	102.2	+28	130.2
Friday	102.8	−32	70.8

4.4 If we had been using the multiplicative model the forecast for Tuesday, for example, would be $101.1 \times 1.1645 = 117.7$ (from Paragraph 3.7).

4.5 You may be asked to forecast sales of a particular product in a given year by using an equation which calculates the trend.

4.6 EXAMPLE: FORECASTING USING AN EQUATION TO CALCULATE THE TREND

In a time series analysis, the trend equation for product Z is given by

$TREND = 0.0002 {\star} YEAR^2 + 0.1 {\star} YEAR + 40.1$

Due to the cyclical factor, it is estimated that the forecast sales for 1997 is estimated at 1.92 times trend. Calculate the forecast sales for 1997.

4.7 SOLUTION

YEAR	= 1997
TREND	= $(0.0002 \times 1997^2) + (0.1 \times 1997) + 40.1$
	= 1,037
FORECAST	= $1,037 \times 1.92$
	= 1,992

Question 4

Unemployment numbers actually recorded in a town for the first quarter of 1999 were 4,700. The underlying trend at this point was 4,400 people and the seasonal factor is 0.85. Using the multiplicative model for seasonal adjustment, the seasonally-adjusted figure (in whole numbers) for the quarter is

A 5,529   B 5,176   C 3,995   D 3,740

Answer

The correct answer is A.

If you remembered the ruling that you need to **divide** by the seasonal variation factor to obtain seasonally-adjusted figures (using the multiplicative model), then you should have been able to eliminate options C and D. This might have been what you did if you weren't sure whether you divided the **actual results** or the **trend** by the seasonal variation factor.

$$\text{Seasonally adjusted data} = \frac{\text{Actual results}}{\text{Seasonal factor}} = \frac{4,700}{0.85} = 5,529$$

Residuals

> **KEY TERM**
>
> A **residual** is the difference between the results which would have been predicted (for a past period for which we already have data) by the trend line adjusted for the average seasonal variation and the actual results.

4.8   **The residual is therefore the difference which is not explained by the trend line and the average seasonal variation**. The residual gives some indication of how much actual results were affected by other factors. Large residuals suggest that any forecast is likely to be unreliable.

4.9   In the example in Paragraph 3.4, the 'prediction' for Wednesday of week 2 would have been 95.6 + 1 = 96.6. As the actual value was 97, the residual was only 97 – 96.6 = 0.4.

The reliability of time series analysis forecasts

4.10   All forecasts are subject to error, but the likely errors vary from case to case.

(a)   The further into the future the forecast is for, the more unreliable it is likely to be.

(b)   The less data available on which to base the forecast, the less reliable the forecast.

(c)   The pattern of trend and seasonal variations cannot be guaranteed to continue in the future.

(d)   There is always the danger of random variations upsetting the pattern of trend and seasonal variation.

(e)   The extrapolation of the trend line is done by judgement and can introduce error.

The following information is to be used for questions 5 and 6 below

In a time series analysis, the multiplicative model is used to forecast sales and the following seasonal variations apply.

Quarter	1	2	3	4
Seasonal variation	0.8	1.9	0.75	?

The actual sales value for the last two quarters of 20X1 were:

Quarter 3: £250,000
Quarter 4: £260,000

Question 5

The seasonal variation for the fourth quarter is:

A 0.55
B −3.45
C 1.00
D 1.45

Answer

The correct answer is A.

As this is a multiplicative model, the seasonal variations should sum (in this case) to 4 (an average of 1) as there are four quarters.

Let x = seasonal variation in quarter 4.

$0.8 + 1.9 + 0.75 + x = 4$

$$\therefore 3.45 + x = 4$$
$$x = 4 - 3.45$$
$$x = 0.55$$

Question 6

The trend line for sales:

A remained constant between quarter 3 and quarter 4
B increased between quarter 3 and quarter 4
C decreased between quarter 3 and quarter 4
D cannot be determined from the information given

Answer

The correct answer is C.

For a multiplicative model, the seasonal component is as follows.

$S = Y/T$

$\therefore T = Y/S$

	Quarter	
	3	*4*
Seasonal component(s)	0.8	0.9
Actual series (Y)	£250,000	£260,000
Trend (T) (= Y/S)	£312,500	£288,889

The trend line for sales has therefore decreased between quarter 3 and quarter 4.

Chapter roundup

- A **time series** is a series of figures or values recorded over time. A graph of a time series is called a **historigram**.

- There are four components of a time series: **trend**, **seasonal variations**, **cyclical variations** and **random variations**.

- The **trend** is the underlying long-term movement over time in the values of the data recorded. **Seasonal variations** are short-term fluctuations due to different circumstances which affect results at different points in time. **Cyclical variations** are medium-term changes in results caused by circumstances which repeat in cycles.

- One method of finding the trend is by the use of **moving averages**.

- Remember that when finding the moving average of an **even number of results**, a second moving average has to be calculated so that trend values can relate to specific actual figures.

- **Seasonal variations are the difference between actual and trend figures**. An average of the seasonal variations for each time period within the cycle must be determined and then adjusted so that the total of the seasonal variations sums to zero.

- Seasonal variations can be estimated using the **additive model ($Y = T + S + I$, with seasonal variations = $Y - T$)** or the **proportional (multiplicative) model ($Y = T \times S \times I$, with seasonal variations = Y/T)**.

- **Forecasts** can be made by **extrapolating the trend** and **adjusting for seasonal variations**. Remember, however, that all forecasts are subject to error.

Quick quiz

1 What are the four main components of a time series? *Trend. Seasonal variation, Random Cyclical.*

2 **Additive model**

$Y = T + S + I$

where Y = *Actual Time Series*
  T = *TREND*
  S = *Seasonal Variation*
  I = *Random.*

3 What is the formula for the multiplicative model? *$Y = T \times S \times I$.*

4 If the trend is increasing or decreasing over time, it is better to use the additive model for forecasting.

True ☐

False ☑

5 List three methods for finding trend lines. *Histogram, Additive Model, Multiplicative Model.*

6

Results		Method
Odd number of time periods	] → [**?**	Calculate 1 moving average
Even number of time periods	] → [	Calculate 2 moving averages

  BPP PUBLISHING

7   A = Y – T
     B = Y/T

Seasonal variation

Multiplicative model = *B*
Additive model = *A*

8   When calculating seasonal variations, adjust the average seasonal variations so that they add up to zero for a(n) additive/multiplicative model. When using the ~~additive~~/multiplicative model, the average seasonal variations should add up to an average of 1.

9   When deseasonalising data, the following rules apply to the additive model.

     I   Add positive seasonal variations
     II   Subtract positive seasonal variations
     III   Add negative seasonal variations
     IV   Subtract negative seasonal variations

     A   I and II
     B   II and III
     C   II and IV
     D   I only

10   Time series analysis data can be used to make forecasts by **extrapolating** the trend line. What does extrapolation mean? Extending the trend line after data has be Plotted on a graph.

11   Cyclical variation is the term used for the difference which is not explained by the trend line and the average seasonal variation.

     True   ☐

     False   ☑

12   List the factors that might explain why time series analysis forecasts may not be 100% reliable.

Further into the future the forecast the less reliable the data

The less data available " " ` ` `

Trend + Seasonal Variations defined maynot carry on into the future.

Random Variations May upset the pattern in seasonal variations.

The extrapolation of the line is done by judgement and May not be accurate

Answers to quick quiz

1. - Trend
    - Seasonal variation (fluctuation)
    - Cyclical variations
    - Random variations

2. Y = the actual time series
    T = the trend series
    S = the seasonal component
    I = the random/irregular component

3. $Y = T \times S \times I$

4. False

5. - Line of best fit
    - Linear regression
    - Moving averages

6. Odd number of time periods = calculate 1 moving average
    Even number of time periods = calculate 2 moving averages.

7. Multiplicative model   = B = Y/T
    Additive model   = A = Y – T

8. When calculating seasonal variations, adjust the average seasonal variations so that they add up to **zero** for an **additive model**. When using the **multiplicative model**, the average seasonal variations should add up to an average of **1**.

9. B

10. Extending the trend line outside the range of known data and forecasting future results from historical data.

11. False. The residual is the term used to explain the difference which is not explained by the trend line and the average seasonal variation.

12. (a) The further into the future a forecast is made, the more unreliable it is likely to be.
    (b) The less data available for forecasting, the less reliable the forecast.
    (c) The trend and seasonal variation patterns identified may not continue in the future.
    (d) Random variations may upset the pattern of trend and seasonal variation.
    (e) The extrapolation of the trend line is done by judgement and may not be accurate.

Now try the questions below from the Exam Question Bank

Number	Level	Marks	Time
24	MCQ	n/a	n/a
25	Examination	10	18 mins

Chapter 15

COST-VOLUME-PROFIT (CVP) ANALYSIS

Topic list	Syllabus reference
1 CVP analysis and breakeven point	6(c)
2 The profit/volume (P/V) ratio	6(c)
3 The margin of safety	6(c)
4 Breakeven arithmetic and profit targets	6(c)
5 Breakeven charts, contribution charts and profit/volume charts	6(c)
6 Limitations of CVP analysis	6(c)

Introduction

You should by now realise that the cost accountant needs estimates of **fixed** and **variable costs**, and **revenues**, at various output levels. The cost accountant, must also be fully aware of **cost behaviour** because, to be able to estimate costs, he must know what a particular cost will do given particular conditions.

An understanding of cost behaviour is not all that you may need to know, however. The application of **cost-volume-profit analysis**, which is based on the cost behaviour principles and marginal costing ideas, is sometimes necessary so that the appropriate decision-making information can be provided. As you may have guessed, this chapter is going to look at that very topic, **cost-volume-profit analysis** or **breakeven analysis.**

Study guide

Section 18 – Cost-volume-profit (CVP) analysis

- Explain the objective of CVP analysis

- Explain the concept of breakeven

- Calculate and explain the break-even point and revenue, target profit, profit/volume ratio and margin of safety

- Construct breakeven, contribution and profit/volume charts from given data

- Apply the CVP model in multi-product situations

Exam guide

CVP analysis is one of the key areas of the syllabus. Most examination questions will require that you can recall the formulae included in this chapter – make sure that you learn them so that you can apply them when you need to.

1 CVP ANALYSIS AND BREAKEVEN POINT

> **KEY TERM**
>
> **Cost-volume-profit (CVP)/breakeven analysis** is the study of the interrelationships between costs, volume and profit at various levels of activity

1.1 The management of an organisation usually wishes to know the profit likely to be made if the aimed-for production and sales for the year are achieved. Management may also be interested to know the following.

(a) The **breakeven** point which is the activity levels at which there is neither profit nor loss.

(b) The **amount** by which actual **sales can fall** below anticipated sales, **without** a **loss** being incurred.

1.2 The breakeven point (BEP) can be calculated arithmetically.

> **FORMULA TO LEARN**
>
> $$\text{Breakeven point} = \frac{\text{Total fixed costs}}{\text{Contribution per unit}} = \frac{\text{Contribution required to break even}}{\text{Contribution per unit}}$$
>
> $$= \text{Number of units of sale required to break even.}$$

1.3 EXAMPLE: BREAKEVEN POINT

Expected sales	10,000 units at £8 = £80,000
Variable cost	£5 per unit
Fixed costs	£21,000

Required

Compute the breakeven point.

1.4 SOLUTION

The contribution per unit is £(8–5)	=	£3
Contribution required to break even	=	fixed costs = £21,000
Breakeven point (BEP)	=	21,000 ÷ 3
	=	7,000 units
In revenue, BEP	=	(7,000 × £8) = £56,000

Sales above £56,000 will result in profit of £3 per unit of additional sales and sales below £56,000 will mean a loss of £3 per unit for each unit by which sales fall short of 7,000 units. In other words, profit will improve or worsen by the amount of contribution per unit.

	7,000 units		7,001 units
	£		£
Revenue	56,000		56,008
Less variable costs	35,000		35,005
Contribution	21,000		21,003
Less fixed costs	21,000		21,000
Profit	0	(= breakeven)	3

2 THE PROFIT/VOLUME (P/V) RATIO

2.1 An alternative way of calculating the breakeven point to give an answer in terms of sales revenue is as follows.

FORMULA TO LEARN

$$\frac{\text{Required contribution} + \text{Fixed costs}}{\text{P/V ratio}} = \textbf{Sales revenue at breakeven point}$$

(The **profit/volume** or **P/V ratio** is also sometimes called a C/S (contribution/sales) ratio).

2.2 In the example in Paragraph 1.3 the P/V ratio is $\dfrac{£3}{£8} = 37.5\%$

Breakeven is where sales revenue equals $\dfrac{£21,000}{37.5\%} = £56,000$

At a price of £8 per unit, this represents 7,000 units of sales.

The P/V ratio is a measure of how much contribution is earned from each £1 of sales. The P/V ratio of 37.5% in the above example means that for every £1 of sales, a contribution of 37.5p is earned. Thus, in order to earn a total contribution of £21,000 and if contribution increases by 37.5p per £1 of sales, sales must be:

$$\frac{£1}{37.5\text{p}} \times £21,000 = £56,000$$

Question 1

The P/V ratio of product W is 20%. IB Ltd, the manufacturer of product W, wishes to make a contribution of £50,000 towards fixed costs. How many units of product W must be sold if the selling price is £10 per unit?

Answer

$$\frac{\text{Required contribution}}{\text{P/V ratio}} = \frac{£\,50,000}{20\%} = £250,000$$

∴ Number of units = £250,000 ÷ £10 = 25,000.

3   THE MARGIN OF SAFETY

> **KEY TERM**
>
> The **margin of safety** is the difference in units between the budgeted sales volume and the breakeven sales volume and it is sometimes expressed as a percentage of the budgeted sales volume.

3.1   The margin of safety may also be expressed as the difference between the budgeted sales revenue and breakeven sales revenue, expressed as a percentage of the budgeted sales revenue.

3.2   EXAMPLE: MARGIN OF SAFETY

Mal de Mer Ltd makes and sells a product which has a variable cost of £30 and which sells for £40. Budgeted fixed costs are £70,000 and budgeted sales are 8,000 units.

Required

Calculate the breakeven point and the margin of safety.

3.3   SOLUTION

(a)   Breakeven point $= \dfrac{\text{Total fixed costs}}{\text{Contribution per unit}} = \dfrac{£70,000}{£(40-30)}$

$= 7,000$ units

(b)   Margin of safety $= 8,000 - 7,000$ units $= 1,000$ units

which may be expressed as $\dfrac{1,000 \, \text{units}}{8,000 \, \text{units}} \times 100\% = 12\frac{1}{2}\%$ of budget

(c)   The margin of safety indicates to management that actual sales can fall short of budget by 1,000 units or 12½% before the breakeven point is reached and no profit at all is made.

4   BREAKEVEN ARITHMETIC AND PROFIT TARGETS

> **FORMULA TO LEARN**
>
> At the **breakeven point**, sales revenue equals total costs and there is no profit.
>
> $\qquad$ S $\qquad$ = V + F
> where $\quad$ S $\qquad$ = Sales revenue
> $\qquad$ V $\qquad$ = Total variable costs
> $\qquad$ F $\qquad$ = Total fixed costs
>
> Subtracting V from each side of the equation, we get:
> $\qquad$ S − V = F, that is, **total contribution = fixed costs**

4.1   EXAMPLE: BREAKEVEN ARITHMETIC

Butterfingers Ltd makes a product which has a variable cost of £7 per unit.

Required

If fixed costs are £63,000 per annum, calculate the selling price per unit if the company wishes to break even with a sales volume of 12,000 units.

4.2 SOLUTION

			£
Contribution required to break even (= Fixed costs)	=	£63,000	
Volume of sales	=	12,000 units	
Required contribution per unit (S – V)	=	£63,000 ÷ 12,000 =	5.25
Variable cost per unit (V)	=		7.00
Required sales price per unit (S)	=		12.25

Target profits

4.3 A similar formula may be applied where a company wishes to achieve a certain profit during a period. To achieve this profit, sales must cover all costs and leave the required profit.

> ### FORMULA TO LEARN
>
> The **target profit** is achieved when: S = V + F + P,
>
> where   P = required profit
>
> Subtracting V from each side of the equation, we get:
>
> $$S - V = F + P, \text{ so}$$
> $$\text{Total contribution required} = F + P$$

4.4 EXAMPLE: TARGET PROFITS

Riding Breeches Ltd makes and sells a single product, for which variable costs are as follows.

	£
Direct materials	10
Direct labour	8
Variable production overhead	6
	24

The sales price is £30 per unit, and fixed costs per annum are £68,000. The company wishes to make a profit of £16,000 per annum.

Required

Determine the sales required to achieve this profit.

4.5 SOLUTION

Required contribution   =   fixed costs + profit = £68,000 + £16,000 = £84,000

Required sales can be calculated in one of two ways.

(a) $\dfrac{\text{Required contribution}}{\text{Contribution per unit}} = \dfrac{£84,000}{£(30 - 24)} = 14,000$ units, or £420,000 in revenue

(b) $\dfrac{\text{Required contribution}}{\text{P/V ratio}} = \dfrac{£84,000}{20\% \star} = £420,000$ of revenue, or 14,000 units.

$\star$ P/V ratio $= \dfrac{£30 - £24}{£30} = \dfrac{£6}{£30} = 0.2 = 20\%.$

Question 2

Seven League Boots Ltd wishes to sell 14,000 units of its product, which has a variable cost of £15 to make and sell. Fixed costs are £47,000 and the required profit is £23,000.

Required

Calculate the sales price per unit.

Answer

Required contribution	=	fixed costs plus profit
	=	£47,000 + £23,000
	=	£70,000
Required sales		14,000 units

	£
Required contribution per unit sold	5
Variable cost per unit	15
Required sales price per unit	20

Decisions to change sales price or costs

4.6 You may come across a problem in which you will be expected to offer advice as to the effect of altering the selling price, variable cost per unit or fixed cost. Such problems are slight variations on basic breakeven arithmetic.

4.7 EXAMPLE: CHANGE IN SELLING PRICE

Stomer Cakes Ltd bake and sell a single type of cake. The variable cost of production is 15p and the current sales price is 25p. Fixed costs are £2,600 per month, and the annual profit for the company at current sales volume is £36,000. The volume of sales demand is constant throughout the year.

The sales manager, Ian Digestion, wishes to raise the sales price to 29p per cake, but considers that a price rise will result in some loss of sales.

Required

Ascertain the minimum volume of sales required each month to raise the price to 29p.

4.8 SOLUTION

The minimum volume of demand which would justify a price of 29p is one which would leave total profit at least the same as before, ie £3,000 per month. Required profit should be converted into required contribution, as follows.

	£
Monthly fixed costs	2,600
Monthly profit, minimum required	3,000
Current monthly contribution	5,600
Contribution per unit (25p – 15p)	10p
Current monthly sales	56,000 cakes

The minimum volume of sales required after the price rise will be an amount which earns a contribution of £5,600 per month, no worse than at the moment. The contribution per cake at a sales price of 29p would be 14p.

$$\text{Required sales} = \frac{\text{required contribution}}{\text{contribution per unit}} = \frac{\pounds 5,600}{14p} = 40,000 \text{ cakes per month.}$$

4.9 EXAMPLE: CHANGE IN PRODUCTION COSTS

Close Brickett Ltd makes a product which has a variable production cost of £8 and a variable sales cost of £2 per unit. Fixed costs are £40,000 per annum, the sales price per unit is £18, and the current volume of output and sales is 6,000 units.

The company is considering whether to have an improved machine for production. Annual hire costs would be £10,000 and it is expected that the variable cost of production would fall to £6 per unit.

Required

(a) Determine the number of units that must be produced and sold to achieve the same profit as is currently earned, if the machine is hired.

(b) Calculate the annual profit with the machine if output and sales remain at 6,000 units per annum.

4.10 SOLUTION

The current unit contribution is $\pounds(18 - (8+2)) = \pounds 8$

(a)

	£
Current contribution (6,000 × £8)	48,000
Less current fixed costs	40,000
Current profit	8,000

With the new machine fixed costs will go up by £10,000 to £50,000 per annum. The variable cost per unit will fall to $\pounds(6 + 2) = \pounds 8$, and the contribution per unit will be £10.

	£
Required profit (as currently earned)	8,000
Fixed costs	50,000
Required contribution	58,000
Contribution per unit	£10
Sales required to earn £8,000 profit	5,800 units

(b) **If sales are 6,000 units**

	£	£
Sales (6,000 × £18)		108,000
Variable costs: production (6,000 × £6)	36,000	
sales (6,000 × £2)	12,000	
		48,000
Contribution (6,000 × £10)		60,000
Less fixed costs		50,000
Profit		10,000

Alternative calculation

	£
Profit at 5,800 units of sale (see (a))	8,000
Contribution from sale of extra 200 units (× £10)	2,000
Profit at 6,000 units of sale	10,000

Sales price and sales volume

4.11 It may be clear by now that, given no change in fixed costs, **total profit is maximised when the total contribution is at its maximum**. Total contribution in turn depends on the unit contribution and on the sales volume.

4.12 An increase in the sales price will increase unit contribution, but sales volume is likely to fall because fewer customers will be prepared to pay the higher price. A decrease in sales price will reduce the unit contribution, but sales volume may increase because the goods on offer are now cheaper. The **optimum combination** of sales price and sales volume is arguably the one which **maximises total contribution**.

 4.13 **EXAMPLE: PROFIT MAXIMISATION**

C Ltd has developed a new product which is about to be launched on to the market. The variable cost of selling the product is £12 per unit. The marketing department has estimated that at a sales price of £20, annual demand would be 10,000 units.

However, if the sales price is set above £20, sales demand would fall by 500 units for each 50p increase above £20. Similarly, if the price is set below £20, demand would increase by 500 units for each 50p stepped reduction in price below £20.

Required

Determine the price which would maximise C Ltd's profit in the next year.

4.14 SOLUTION

At a price of £20 per unit, the unit contribution would be £(20 – 12) = £8. Each 50p increase (or decrease) in price would raise (or lower) the unit contribution by 50p. The total contribution is calculated at each sales price by multiplying the unit contribution by the expected sales volume.

	Unit price £	Unit contribution £	Sales volume Units	Total contribution £
	20.00	8.00	10,000	80,000
(a) **Reduce price**				
	19.50	7.50	10,500	78,750
	19.00	7.00	11,000	77,000
(b) **Increase price**				
	20.50	8.50	9,500	80,750
	21.00	9.00	9,000	81,000
	21.50	9.50	8,500	80,750
	22.00	10.00	8,000	80,000
	22.50	10.50	7,500	78,750

The total contribution would be maximised, and therefore profit maximised, at a sales price of £21 per unit, and sales demand of 9,000 units.

Quadratic equations and breakeven points

4.15 In the problems that we have looked at so far, the relationships have all been linear. We shall now look at relationships which are expressed as quadratic equations. If you need reminding about quadratic equations, study the Basic Maths supplement which comes with this Study Text.

4.16 EXAMPLE: QUADRATICS AND BREAKEVEN ANALYSIS

A company manufactures a product. Total fixed costs are £75 and the variable cost per unit is £5x, where x is the quantity of the product produced and sold. The total revenue function is given by $R = (25 - x)x$.

Required

Find the breakeven point.

4.17 SOLUTION

Total costs (C) $\quad$ = fixed costs + variable costs
$\quad\quad\quad\quad\quad\quad$ = £(75 + 5x)

Total revenue (R) $\quad$ = $25x - x^2$

Breakeven point occurs when C = R

$\quad$ ie when $75 + 5x = 25x - x^2$

$\quad$ ie when $0 = x^2 - 20x + 75$

$$x = \frac{20 \pm \sqrt{400 - (4 \times 1 \times 75)}}{2} = \frac{20 \pm 10}{2} = 5 \text{ or } 15$$

Therefore the company will breakeven when it produces either 5 or 15 units.

Question 3

Betty Battle Ltd manufactures a product which has a selling price of £20 and a variable cost of £10 per unit. The company incurs annual fixed costs of £29,000. Annual sales demand is 9,000 units.

New production methods are under consideration, which would cause a £1,000 increase in fixed costs and a reduction in variable cost to £9 per unit. The new production methods would result in a superior product and would enable sales to be increased to 9,750 units per annum at a price of £21 each.

If the change in production methods were to take place, the breakeven output level would be:

A   400 units higher
B   400 units lower
C   100 units higher
D   100 units lower

Answer

	Current £	Revised £	Difference
Selling price	20	21	
Variable costs	10	9	
Contribution per unit	10	12	
Fixed costs	£29,000	£30,000	
Breakeven point (units)	2,900	2,500	**400 lower**

$$\text{Breakeven point} = \frac{\text{Total fixed costs}}{\text{Contribution per unit}}$$

$$\text{Current BEP} = \frac{£29,000}{£10} = 2,900 \text{ units}$$

$$\text{Revised BEP} = \frac{£30,000}{£12} = 2,500 \text{ units}$$

The correct answer is therefore B.

5 BREAKEVEN CHARTS, CONTRIBUTION CHARTS AND PROFIT/VOLUME CHARTS

> **Exam focus point**
>
> Remember that you can pick up easy marks in an examination for drawing graphs neatly and accurately. Always use a ruler, label your axes and use an appropriate scale.

Breakeven charts

5.1 **The breakeven point can also be determined graphically using a breakeven chart.** This is a chart which shows approximate levels of profit or loss at different sales volume levels within a limited range.

5.2 A breakeven chart has the following axes.

- A **horizontal** axis showing the **sales/output** (in value or units)
- A **vertical axis** showing £ for **sales revenues** and **costs**

5.3 The following lines are drawn on the breakeven chart.

(a) The **sales line**

- Starts at the origin
- Ends at the point signifying expected sales

(b) The **fixed costs line**

- Runs parallel to the horizontal axis
- Meets the vertical axis at a point which represents total fixed costs

(c) The **total costs line**

- Starts where the fixed costs line meets the vertical axis
- Ends at the point which represents anticipated sales on the horizontal axis and total costs of anticipated sales on the vertical axis

5.4 The **breakeven point** is the **intersection** of the **sales line** and the **total costs line**.

5.5 The distance between the **breakeven point** and the **expected (or budgeted) sales**, in units, indicates the **margin of safety**.

5.6 EXAMPLE: A BREAKEVEN CHART

The budgeted annual output of a factory is 120,000 units. The fixed overheads amount to £40,000 and the variable costs are 50p per unit. The sales price is £1 per unit.

Required

Construct a breakeven chart showing the current breakeven point and profit earned up to the present maximum capacity.

5.7 SOLUTION

We begin by calculating the profit at the budgeted annual output.

	£
Sales (120,000 units)	120,000
Variable costs	60,000
Contribution	60,000
Fixed costs	40,000
Profit	20,000

Breakeven chart (1) is shown on the following page.

The chart is drawn as follows.

(a) The **vertical axis** represents **money** (costs and revenue) and the **horizontal axis** represents the **level of activity** (production and sales).

(b) The fixed costs are represented by a **straight line parallel to the horizontal axis** (in our example, at £40,000).

(c) The **variable costs** are added 'on top of' fixed costs, to give **total costs**. It is assumed that fixed costs are the same in total and variable costs are the same per unit at all levels of output.

The line of costs is therefore a straight line and only two points need to be plotted and joined up. Perhaps the two most convenient points to plot are total costs at zero output, and total costs at the budgeted output and sales.

- At zero output, costs are equal to the amount of fixed costs only, £40,000, since there are no variable costs.

- At the budgeted output of 120,000 units, costs are £100,000.

	£
Fixed costs	40,000
Variable costs 120,000 × 50p	60,000
Total costs	100,000

(d) The sales line is also drawn by plotting two points and joining them up.

- At zero sales, revenue is nil.
- At the budgeted output and sales of 120,000 units, revenue is £120,000.

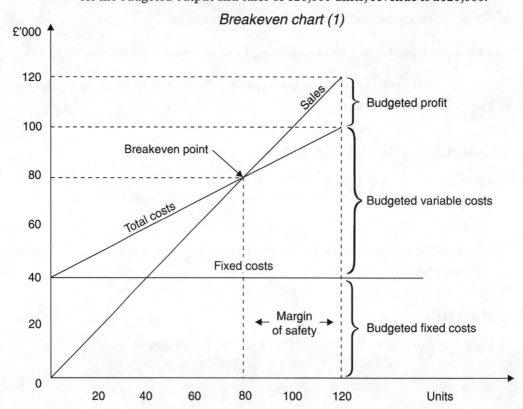

Breakeven chart (1)

5.8 **The breakeven point is where total costs are matched exactly by total revenue.** From the chart, this can be seen to occur at output and sales of 80,000 units, when revenue and costs are both £80,000. This breakeven point can be proved mathematically as:

$$\frac{\text{Required contribution}(=\text{fixed costs})}{\text{Contribution per unit}} = \frac{£40,000}{50\text{p per unit}} = 80,000 \text{ units}$$

5.9 The margin of safety can be seen on the chart as the difference between the budgeted level of activity and the breakeven level.

The value of breakeven charts

5.10 Breakeven charts are used as follows.

- To **plan** the production of a company's products
- To **market** a company's products
- To give a **visual display** of breakeven arithmetic

5.11 EXAMPLE: VARIATIONS IN THE USE OF BREAKEVEN CHARTS

Breakeven charts can be used to **show variations** in the possible **sales price, variable costs** or **fixed costs**. Suppose that a company sells a product which has a variable cost of £2 per unit. Fixed costs are £15,000. It has been estimated that if the sales price is set at £4.40 per unit, the expected sales volume would be 7,500 units; whereas if the sales price is lower, at £4 per unit, the expected sales volume would be 10,000 units.

Required

Draw a breakeven chart to show the budgeted profit, the breakeven point and the margin of safety at each of the possible sales prices.

5.12 SOLUTION

Workings	*Sales price £4.40 per unit* £		*Sales price £4 per unit* £
Fixed costs	15,000		15,000
Variable costs (7,500 × £2.00)	15,000	(10,000 × £2.00)	20,000
Total costs	30,000		35,000
Budgeted revenue (7,500 × £4.40)	33,000	(10,000 × £4.00)	40,000

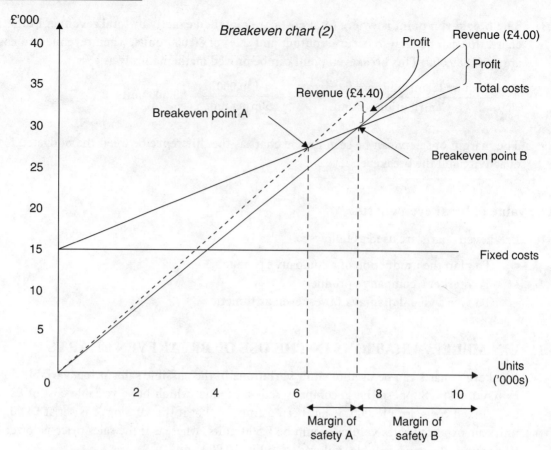

Breakeven chart (2)

(a) **Breakeven point A** is the breakeven point at a sales price of £4.40 per unit, which is 6,250 units or £27,500 in costs and revenues.

(check: $\dfrac{\text{Required contribution to breakeven}}{\text{Contribution per unit}} \quad \dfrac{£15,000}{£2.40 \text{ per unit}} = 6,250 \text{ units})$

The margin of safety (A) is 7,500 units – 6,250 units = 1,250 units or 16.7% of expected sales.

(b) **Breakeven point B** is the breakeven point at a sales price of £4 per unit which is 7,500 units or £30,000 in costs and revenues.

(check: $\dfrac{\text{Required contribution to breakeven}}{\text{Contribution per unit}} \quad \dfrac{£15,000}{£2 \text{ per unit}} = 7,500 \text{ units})$

The margin of safety (B) = 10,000 units – 7,500 units = 2,500 units or 25% of expected sales.

5.13 Since a price of £4 per unit gives a higher expected profit and a wider margin of safety, this price will probably be preferred even though the breakeven point is higher than at a sales price of £4.40 per unit.

Contribution (or contribution breakeven) charts

5.14 As an alternative to drawing the fixed cost line first, it is possible to start with that for variable costs. This is known as a **contribution chart**. An example is shown below using the example in Paragraphs 5.6 and 5.7.

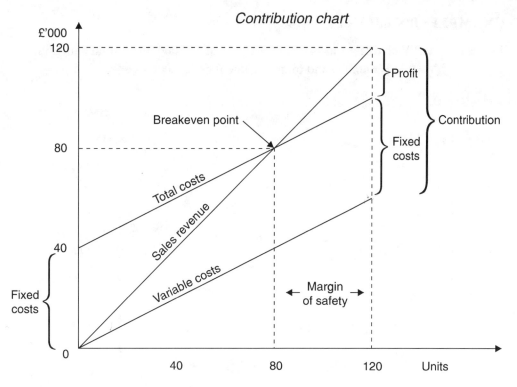

Contribution chart

5.15 One of the **advantages** of the contribution chart is that is shows clearly the **contribution** for **different levels of production** (indicated here at 120,000 units, the budgeted level of output) as the 'wedge' shape between the sales revenue line and the variable costs line. At the **breakeven point**, the **contribution equals fixed costs** exactly. At levels of output **above** the **breakeven** point, the **contribution** is **larger**, and not only covers fixed costs, but also leaves a profit. **Below** the **breakeven** point, the **loss** is the amount by which contribution fails to cover fixed costs.

The Profit/Volume (P/V) chart

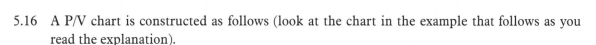

KEY TERM

The **profit/volume (P/V) chart** is a variation of the breakeven chart which illustrates the relationship of costs and profit to sales, and the margin of safety.

5.16 A P/V chart is constructed as follows (look at the chart in the example that follows as you read the explanation).

(a) 'P' is on the y axis and actually comprises not only 'profit' but contribution to profit (in monetary value), extending above and below the x axis with a zero point at the intersection of the two axes, and the negative section below the x axis representing fixed costs. This means that at zero production, the firm is incurring a loss equal to the fixed costs.

(b) 'V' is on the x axis and comprises either volume of sales or value of sales (revenue).

(c) The profit-volume line is a straight line drawn with its starting point (at zero production) at the intercept on the y axis representing the level of fixed costs, and with a gradient of contribution/unit (or the P/V ratio if sales value is used rather than units). The P/V line will cut the x axis at the breakeven point of sales volume. Any point on the P/V line above the x axis represents the profit to the firm (as measured on the vertical axis) for that particular level of sales.

5.17 EXAMPLE: P/V CHART

Let us draw a P/V chart for our example. At sales of 120,000 units, total contribution will be 120,000 × £(1 – 0.5) = £60,000 and total profit will be £20,000.

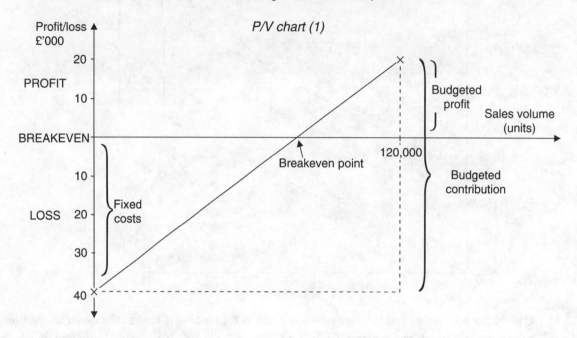

The advantage of the P/V chart

5.18 **The P/V chart shows clearly the effect on profit and breakeven point of any changes in selling price, variable cost, fixed cost and/or sales demand.** If the budgeted selling price of the product in our example is increased to £1.20, with the result that demand drops to 105,000 units despite additional fixed costs of £10,000 being spent on advertising, we could add a line representing this situation to our P/V chart.

5.19 At sales of 105,000 units, contribution will be 105,000 × £(1.20 – 0.50) = £73,500 and total profit will be £23,500 (fixed costs being £50,000).

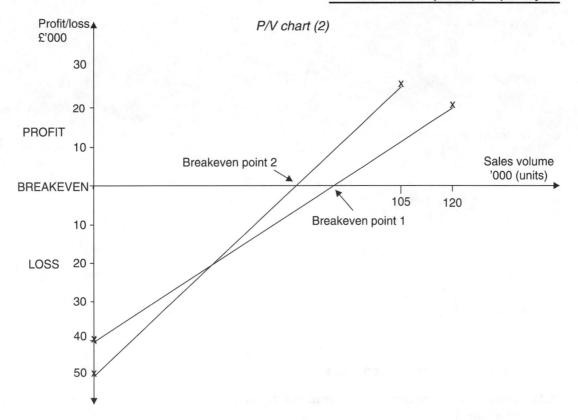

P/V chart (2)

5.20 The diagram shows that if the selling price is increased, the breakeven point occurs at a lower level of sales revenue (71,429 units instead of 80,000 units), although this is not a particularly large increase when viewed in the context of the projected sales volume. It is also possible to see that for sales above 50,000 units, the profit achieved will be higher (and the loss achieved lower) if the price is £1.20. For sales volumes below 50,000 units the first option will yield lower losses.

5.21 The P/V chart is the clearest way of presenting such information; two conventional breakeven charts on one set of axes would be very confusing.

5.22 Changes in the variable cost per unit or in fixed costs at certain activity levels can also be easily incorporated into a P/V chart. The profit or loss at each point where the cost structure changes should be calculated and plotted on the graph so that the profit/volume line becomes a series of straight lines.

5.23 For example, suppose that in our example, at sales levels in excess of 120,000 units the variable cost per unit increases to £0.60 (perhaps because of overtime premiums that are incurred when production exceeds a certain level). At sales of 130,000 units, contribution would therefore be $130,000 \times £(1 - 0.60) = £52,000$ and total profit would be £12,000.

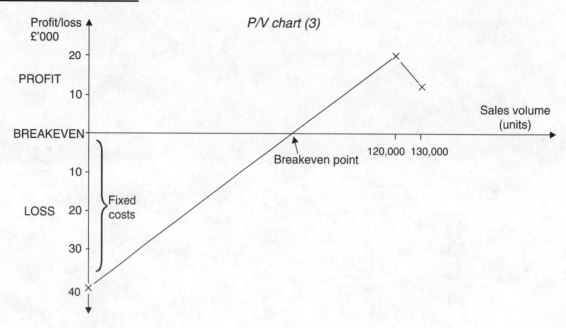

The multi-product breakeven and P/V chart

5.24 Since most companies sell more than one product, a multi-product chart of some type might be required.

5.25 **A very serious limitation of breakeven charts is that they can show the costs, revenues, profits and margins of safety for a single product only**, or for a single 'sales mix' of products.

5.26 For example suppose that Farmyard Ltd sells three products, X, Y and Z, which have variable unit costs of £3, £4 and £5 respectively. The sales price of X is £8, the price of Y is £6 and the price of Z is £6. Fixed costs per annum are £10,000.

5.27 A breakeven chart cannot be drawn, because we do not know the proportions of X, Y and Z in the sales mix. (If you are not sure about this point, you should try to draw a breakeven chart with the information given. It should not be possible.)

5.28 If, however, we now assume that budgeted sales are as follows:

      X   2,000 units
      Y   4,000 units
      Z   3,000 units

a breakeven chart can be drawn. The chart would make the assumption that output and sales of X, Y and Z are in the proportions 2,000 : 4,000 : 3,000 at all levels of activity, in other words that the sales mix is 'fixed' in these proportions.

(a) *Workings*

Budgeted costs		*Costs*	*Budgeted revenue*	*Revenue*
		£		£
Variable costs of X	(2,000 × £3)	6,000	X (2,000 × £8)	16,000
Variable costs of Y	(4,000 × £4)	16,000	Y (4,000 × £6)	24,000
Variable costs of Z	(3,000 × £5)	15,000	Z (3,000 × £6)	18,000
Total variable costs		37,000		58,000
Fixed costs		10,000		
Total budgeted costs		47,000		

(b)   The breakeven chart can now be drawn.

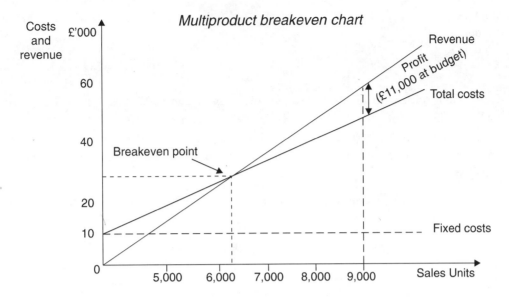

Multiproduct breakeven chart

5.29   The same information could be shown on a P/V chart, as follows.

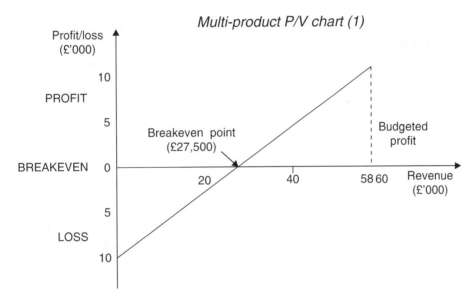

Multi-product P/V chart (1)

5.30   The breakeven point is approximately £27,500. This may either be read from the breakeven chart or computed mathematically. The budgeted P/V ratio for all three products together is

$$\frac{\text{contribution}}{\text{sales}} = \frac{£(58,000 - 37,000)}{£58,000} = 36.21\%$$

The required contribution to break even is £10,000, the amount of fixed costs. The breakeven point is

$$\frac{£10,000}{36.21\%} = £27,500 \text{ (approx) in sales revenue}$$

5.31   An addition to the P/V chart would now be made to show further information about the contribution earned by each product individually, so that their performance and profitability can be compared.

	Contribution £	Sales £	C/S ratio %
Product X	10,000	16,000	62.50
Product Y	8,000	24,000	33.33
Product Z	3,000	18,000	16.67
Total	21,000	58,000	36.21

5.32 By convention, the products are shown individually on a P/V chart from left to right, in order of the size of their P/V ratio. In this example, product X will be plotted first, then product Y and finally product Z. A dotted line is used to show the cumulative profit/loss and the cumulative sales as each product's sales and contribution in turn are added to the sales mix.

Product	Cumulative sales £		Cumulative profit £
X	16,000	(£10,000 – £10,000)	-
X and Y	40,000		8,000
X, Y and Z	58,000		11,000

You will see on the graph which follows that these three pairs of data are used to plot the dotted line, to indicate the contribution from each product. The solid line which joins the two ends of this dotted line indicates the average profit which will be earned from sales of the three products in this mix.

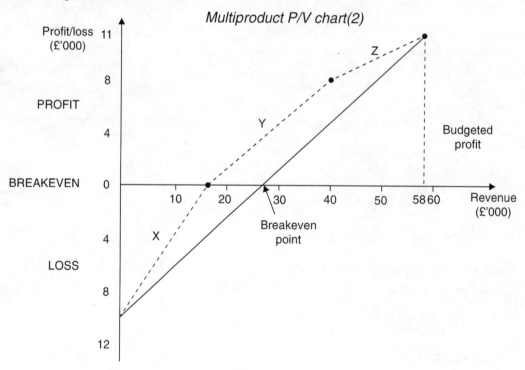

5.33 From this diagram, it may be apparent that since X is the most profitable in terms of P/V ratio, it might be worth considering an increase in the sales of X, even if there is a consequent fall in the sales of Z. Alternatively, the pricing structure of the products should be reviewed and a decision made as to whether the price of product Z should be raised so as to increase its P/V ratio (although an increase is likely to result in some fall in sales volume).

5.34 The **multi-product P/V chart** is therefore **helpful** in identifying the following.

(a) The overall company breakeven point.

(b) Which products should be expanded in output and which should be discontinued.

(c) How changes in selling price/sales volume will effect the company's breakeven point/profit.

6 LIMITATIONS OF CVP ANALYSIS

6.1 Breakeven analysis is a useful technique for managers. Breakeven arithmetic can provide **simple** and **quick** estimates. **Breakeven charts** provide a **graphical representation** of breakeven arithmetic. Breakeven analysis has a number of limitations.

- It **can only apply to a single product** or a single mix of a group of products.
- A breakeven chart may be **time-consuming** to prepare.
- It **assumes** fixed costs are constant at all levels of output.
- It **assumes** that **variable costs** are the **same** per unit at all levels of output.
- It **assumes** that **sales prices** are **constant** at all levels of output.
- It assumes **production** and **sales** are the **same** (stock levels are ignored).
- It **ignores** the **uncertainty** in the estimates of fixed costs and variable cost per unit.

BPP
PUBLISHING

Chapter roundup

- **Cost-volume- profit (CVP)/breakeven analysis** is the study of the interrelationships between costs, volume and profits at various levels of activity.

- **Breakeven point** = **Number of units of sale** required to breakeven

  $$= \frac{\text{Fixed costs}}{\text{Contribution per unit}}$$

  $$= \frac{\text{Contribution required to break even}}{\text{Contribution per unit}}$$

- **Breakeven point** = **Sales revenue** required to break even

  $$= \frac{\text{Contribution required to break even}}{\text{P/V ratio}}$$

  $$= \frac{\text{Fixed costs}}{\text{P/V ratio}}$$

- The **P/V ratio** (or **C/S ratio**) is a measure of how much contribution is earned form each £1 of sales.

- The **margin of safety** is the difference in units between the **budgeted sales volume** and the **breakeven sales volume.** It is sometimes expressed as a percentage of the budgeted sales volume.

- Alternatively, the **margin of safety** can be expressed as the difference between the **budgeted sales revenue** and the **breakeven sales revenue** expressed as a percentage of the budgeted sales revenue.

- At the **breakeven point**, sales revenue = total costs and there is no profit. At the breakeven point **total contribution = fixed costs.**

- The **target profit** is achieved when S = V + F + P. Therefore the **total contribution required** for a target profit = **fixed costs + required profit.**

- The breakeven point can also be determined graphically using a **breakeven chart** or a **contribution breakeven chart**.

- The **profit/volume (PV) chart** is a variation of the breakeven chart which illustrates the relationship of costs and profits to sales and the margin of safety.

- The **P/V chart** shows clearly the effect on profit and breakeven point of any changes in selling price, variable cost, fixed cost and/or sales demand.

- Since most companies sell more than one product, a **multi-product breakeven** or **P/V chart** might be useful in determining the breakeven point.

- **Breakeven analysis** is a useful technique for managers as it can provide simple and quick estimates. **Breakeven charts** provide a graphical representation of breakeven arithmetic. Breakeven analysis does, however, have a number of **limitations.**

Quick quiz

1 What does CVP analysis study? ~~Interrelationships between. Costs, volume + Profit @ various levels of activity~~

2 The **breakeven point** is the .... ~~N° of units of Sale~~ or ..... ~~Sales Revenue~~ ....
    ....

3 Use the following to make up three formulae which can be used to calculate the breakeven point.

Contribution per unit
Contribution per unit
Fixed costs
Fixed costs
Contribution required to breakeven
Contribution required to breakeven
P/V ratio
P/V ratio

(a) Breakeven points (sales units) $= \dfrac{\text{Fixed Costs}}{\text{Contribution Per unit}}$

or $\dfrac{\text{Contribution Required to Breakeven}}{\text{Contribution Per unit}}$

(b) Breakeven point (sales revenue) $= \dfrac{\text{Contribution Required to breakeven}}{\text{P/V ratio}}$

or $\dfrac{\text{Fixed Costs}}{\text{P/V Ratio}}$

4 The P/V ratio is a measure of how much profit is earned from each £1 of sales.

True ☑

False ☐

5 The **margin of safety** is the difference in units between the budgeted sales volume and the breakeven sales volume. How is it sometimes expressed? *Percentage of budgeted Sales revenue*

6 Profits are maximised at the breakeven point.

True ☑

False ☐

7 At the breakeven point, total contribution = ... *Fixed Costs* ....

8 The total contribution required for a **target profit** = ... *Fixed Costs + Required Profit* ...

9 Give three uses of breakeven charts. *Visualise Breakeven figures, Effect on Profit*

10 Breakeven charts show approximate levels of profit or loss at different sales volume levels within a limited range. Which of the following are true?

I The sales line starts at the origin
II The fixed costs line runs parallel to the vertical axis
III Breakeven charts have a horizontal axis showing the sales/output (in value or units)
IV Breakeven charts have a vertical axis showing £ for revenues and costs
V The breakeven point is the intersection of the sales line and the fixed cost line

A I and II
B I and III
C I, III and IV
D I, III, IV, and V

11 On a breakeven chart, the distance between the breakeven point and the expected (or budgeted) sales, in units, indicates the ....

12 Give seven limitations of CVP analysis.

- ...*Assume Sales remain Constant*...
- ...*Assume fixed costs remain constant*...

- Time Consuming to prepare.
- Only applies to a single product
- Variable cost are the same per unit at all levels of output
- It Assumes production + sales are the same.
- It Ignores the uncertainty in the estimates of fixed costs + variable cost per unit

Answers to quick quiz

1   The interrelations between **costs, volume** and **profits** of a product at various activity levels.

2   The **breakeven point** is the number of units of sale required to breakeven or the sales revenue required to breakeven.

3   (a)   Breakeven points (sales units) $= \dfrac{\text{Fixed costs}}{\text{Contribution per unit}}$

   or $\dfrac{\text{Contribution required to break even}}{\text{Contribution per unit}}$

   (b)   Breakeven point (sales revenue) $= \dfrac{\text{Fixed costs}}{\text{P/V ratio}}$

   or $\dfrac{\text{Contribution required to break even}}{\text{P/V ratio}}$

4   False. The P/V ratio is a measure of how much **contribution** is earned from each £1 of sales.

5   As a **percentage** of the budgeted sales volume.

6   False. At the breakeven point there is no profit.

7   At the breakeven point, total contribution = fixed costs

8   Fixed costs + required profit

9   - To plan the production of a company's products
   - To market a company's products
   - To give a visual display of breakeven arithmetic

10   B

11   Margin of safety

12   - It **can only apply to a single product** or a single mix of a group of products.
   - A breakeven chart may be **time-consuming** to prepare.
   - It **assumes** fixed costs are constant at all levels of output.
   - It **assumes** that **variable costs** are the **same** per unit at all levels of output.
   - It **assumes** that **sales prices** are **constant** at all levels of output.
   - It assumes **production** and **sales** are the **same** (stock levels are ignored).
   - It **ignores** the **uncertainty** in the estimates of fixed costs and variable cost per unit.

Now try the questions below from the Exam Question Bank

Number	Level	Marks	Time
26	MCQ	n/a	n/a
27	Examination	10	18 mins

Chapter 16

RELEVANT COSTING AND DECISION MAKING

Topic list	Syllabus reference
1 Relevant costs	6(c)
2 Choice of product (product mix) decisions	6(c)
3 Make or buy decisions	6(c)
4 Shut down decisions	6(c)
5 One-off contracts	6(c)

Introduction

Management at all levels within an organisation take decisions. The overriding requirement of the information that should be supplied by the cost accountant to aid decision making is that of **relevance.** This chapter therefore begins by looking at the costing technique required in decision-making situations, that of **relevant costing**, and explains how to decide which costs need taking into account when a decision is being made and which costs do not.

We then go on to see how to apply relevant costing to some specific decision-making scenarios.

Study guide

- Explain the concept of relevant costing

- Explain the relevance of such terms as opportunity and sunk costs, avoidable and unavoidable costs, fixed and variable costs, historical and replacement costs, controllable and uncontrollable costs, to decision making

- Calculate the relevant costs for materials and labour

- Calculate and explain the deprival value of an asset

- Construct a relevant cost statement and explain the results for such situations as make or buy decisions, shut down decisions and one-off contracts

Exam guide

Relevant costing is not one of the key syllabus topics for Paper 1.2. However, make sure that you can calculate relevant costs for materials and labour and the deprival value of an asset. Multiple choice questions are a good way of testing your understanding of this subject.

1   RELEVANT COSTS

Relevant costs

> ### KEY TERM
>
> A **relevant cost** is a future cash flow arising as a direct consequence of a decision.

1.1   Decision making should be based on relevant costs.

(a)   **Relevant costs are future costs**.

    (i)   A decision is about the future; it cannot alter what has been done already. Costs that have been incurred in the past are totally irrelevant to any decision that is being made 'now'. Such costs are **past costs** or **sunk costs**.

    (ii)   Costs that have been incurred include not only costs that have already been paid, but also **committed costs** (a future cash flow that will be incurred anyway, regardless of the decision taken now).

(b)   **Relevant costs are cash flows**. Only cash flow information is required. This means that costs or charges which do not reflect additional cash spending (such as depreciation and notional costs) should be ignored for the purpose of decision making.

(c)   **Relevant costs are incremental costs**. For example, if an employee is expected to have no other work to do during the next week, but will be paid his basic wage (of, say, £100 per week) for attending work and doing nothing, his manager might decide to give him a job which earns the organisation £40. The net gain is £40 and the £100 is irrelevant to the decision because although it is a future cash flow, it will be incurred anyway whether the employee is given work or not.

1.2   Other terms are sometimes used to describe relevant costs.

> ### KEY TERM
>
> **Avoidable costs** are costs which would not be incurred if the activity to which they relate did not exist.

1.3   One of the situations in which it is necessary to identify the avoidable costs is in deciding whether or not to discontinue a product. The only costs which would be saved are the avoidable costs which are usually the variable costs and sometimes some specific costs. Costs which would be incurred whether or not the product is discontinued are known as **unavoidable costs**.

> ### KEY TERM
>
> **Differential cost** is 'the difference in total cost between alternatives.'
>
> CIMA *Official Terminology*

1.4   For example, if decision option A costs £300 and decision option B costs £360, the differential cost is £60.

> ### KEY TERM
>
> An **opportunity cost** is 'The value of the benefit sacrificed when one course of action is chosen, in preference to an alternative'.
>
> CIMA *Official Terminology*

1.5   Suppose for example that there are three options, A, B and C, only one of which can be chosen. The net profit from each would be £80, £100 and £70 respectively.

Since only one option can be selected option B would be chosen because it offers the biggest benefit.

	£
Profit from option B	100
Less opportunity cost (ie the benefit from the most profitable alternative, A)	80
Differential benefit of option B	20

The decision to choose option B would not be taken simply because it offers a profit of £100, but because it offers a differential profit of £20 in excess of the next best alternative.

Controllable and uncontrollable costs

1.6   We came across the term **controllable costs** at the beginning of this study text. **Controllable costs** are items of expenditure which can be directly influenced by a given manager within a given time span.

1.7   As a general rule, **committed fixed costs** such as those costs arising from the possession of plant, equipment and buildings (giving rise to depreciation and rent) are largely **uncontrollable** in the short term because they have been committed by longer-term decisions affecting longer-term needs.

1.8   **Discretionary fixed costs**, for example, advertising and research and development costs can be thought of as being **controllable** because they are incurred as a result of decisions made by management and can be raised or lowered at fairly short notice.

Sunk costs

> ### KEY TERM
>
> A **sunk cost** is a past cost which is not directly relevant in decision making.

1.9   The principle underlying decision accounting is that **management decisions can only affect the future.** In decision making, managers therefore require information about **future costs and revenues** which would be affected by the decision under review, and they must not be misled by events, costs and revenues in the past, about which they can do nothing. Therefore **sunk costs**, which have been charged already as a cost of sales in a previous accounting period or will be charged in a future accounting period although the expenditure has already been incurred (or the expenditure decision irrevocably taken), are irrelevant to decision making.

An example of this type of cost is **depreciation**. If a fixed asset has been purchased, depreciation may be charged for several years but the cost is a **sunk cost**, about which nothing can now be done.

1.10 Another example of sunk costs are development costs which have already been incurred. Suppose that a company has spent £250,000 in developing a new service for customers, but the marketing department's most recent findings are that the service might not gain customer acceptance and could be a commercial failure. The decision whether or not to abandon the development of the new service would have to be taken, but the £250,000 spent so far should be ignored by the decision makers because it is a **sunk cost**.

Fixed and variable costs

Exam focus point

Unless you are given an indication to the contrary, you should assume the following.

- Variable costs will be relevant costs.
- Fixed costs are irrelevant to a decision.

This need not be the case, however, and you should analyse variable and fixed cost data carefully. Do not forget that 'fixed' costs may only be fixed in the short term.

Non-relevant variable costs

1.11 There might be occasions when a variable cost is in fact a sunk cost. For example, suppose that a company has some units of raw material in stock. They have been paid for already, and originally cost £2,000. They are now obsolete and are no longer used in regular production, and they have no scrap value. However, they could be used in a special job which the company is trying to decide whether to undertake. The special job is a 'one-off' customer order, and would use up all these materials in stock.

In deciding whether the job should be undertaken, the relevant cost of the materials to the special job is nil. Their original cost of £2,000 is a **sunk cost**, and should be ignored in the decision.

However, if the materials did have a scrap value of, say, £300, then their relevant cost to the job would be the **opportunity cost** of being unable to sell them for scrap, ie £300.

Attributable fixed costs

1.12 There might be occasions when a fixed cost is a relevant cost, and you must be aware of the distinction between 'specific' or 'directly attributable' fixed costs, and general fixed overheads.

   (a) **Directly attributable fixed costs** are those costs which, although fixed within a relevant range of activity level are relevant to a decision for either of the following reasons.

      (i) They could increase if certain extra activities were undertaken. For example, it may be necessary to employ an extra supervisor if a particular order is accepted. The extra salary would be an attributable fixed cost.

      (ii) They would decrease or be eliminated entirely if a decision were taken either to reduce the scale of operations or shut down entirely.

(b) **General fixed overheads** are those fixed overheads which will be unaffected by decisions to increase or decrease the scale of operations, perhaps because they are an apportioned share of the fixed costs of items which would be completely unaffected by the decisions. An apportioned share of head office charges is an example of general fixed overheads for a local office or department. General fixed overheads are not relevant in decision making.

Absorbed overhead

1.13 **Absorbed overhead** is a **notional** accounting cost and hence should be ignored for decision-making purposes. It is overhead *incurred* which *may* be relevant to a decision.

The relevant cost of materials

1.14 The relevant cost of raw materials is generally their **current replacement cost,** *unless* the materials have already been purchased and would not be replaced once used. In this case the relevant cost of using them is the **higher** of the following.

- Their current resale value
- The value they would obtain if they were put to an alternative use

If the materials have no resale value and no other possible use, then the relevant cost of using them for the opportunity under consideration would be nil.

You should test your knowledge of the relevant cost of materials by attempting the following question.

Question 1

O'Reilly Ltd has been approached by a customer who would like a special job to be done for him, and who is willing to pay £22,000 for it. The job would require the following materials.

Material	Total units required	Units already in stock	Book value of units in stock £/unit	Realisable value £/unit	Replacement cost £/unit
A	1,000	0	-	-	6
B	1,000	600	2	2.50	5
C	1,000	700	3	2.50	4
D	200	200	4	6.00	9

Material B is used regularly by O'Reilly Ltd, and if units of B are required for this job, they would need to be replaced to meet other production demand.

Materials C and D are in stock as the result of previous over-buying, and they have a restricted use. No other use could be found for material C, but the units of material D could be used in another job as substitute for 300 units of material E, which currently costs £5 per unit (of which the company has no units in stock at the moment).

Required

Calculate the relevant costs of material for deciding whether or not to accept the contract.

Answer

(a) **Material A** is not yet owned. It would have to be bought in full at the replacement cost of £6 per unit.

(b) **Material B** is used regularly by the company. There are existing stocks (600 units) but if these are used on the contract under review a further 600 units would be bought to replace them. Relevant costs are therefore 1,000 units at the replacement cost of £5 per unit.

(c)   1,000 units of **material C** are needed and 700 are already in stock. If used for the contract, a further 300 units must be bought at £4 each. The existing stocks of 700 will not be replaced. If they are used for the contract, they could not be sold at £2.50 each. The realisable value of these 700 units is an opportunity cost of sales revenue forgone.

(d)   The required units of **material D** are already in stock and will not be replaced. There is an opportunity cost of using D in the contract because there are alternative opportunities either to sell the existing stocks for £6 per unit (£1,200 in total) or avoid other purchases (of material E), which would cost 300 x £5 = £1,500. Since substitution for E is more beneficial, £1,500 is the opportunity cost.

(e)   **Summary of relevant costs**

	£
Material A (1,000 × £6)	6,000
Material B (1,000 × £5)	5,000
Material C (300 × £4) plus (700 × £2.50)	2,950
Material D	1,500
Total	15,450

The relevant cost of labour

1.15   In situations where labour is in short supply, the relevant cost of labour is best explained by means of an example.

1.16 EXAMPLE: RELEVANT COST OF LABOUR

LW plc is currently deciding whether to undertake a new contract.

15 hours of labour are required for the contract. Labour is currently at full capacity producing product L.

STANDARD COST CARD
PRODUCT L

	£/unit
Direct materials (10kg @ £2)	20
Direct labour (5 hrs @ £6)	30
	50
Selling price	72
Contribution	22

What is the relevant cost of using 15 hours of labour for the contract?

1.17 SOLUTION

Contribution earned per unit of Product L produced = £22

If it requires 5 hours of labour to make one unit of product L, the contribution earned per labour hour = £22/5 = £4.40.

Relevant cost of 15 hours of labour

	£
Direct labour (15 hours @ £6)	90
Contribution lost by not making product L (£4.40 × 15 hours)	66
	154

1.18   It is important that you should be able to identify the relevant costs which are appropriate to a decision. In many cases, this is a fairly straightforward problem, but there are cases where great care should be taken. Attempt the following question.

Question 2

A company has been making a machine to order for a customer, but the customer has since gone into liquidation, and there is no prospect that any money will be obtained from the winding up of the company.

Costs incurred to date in manufacturing the machine are £50,000 and progress payments of £15,000 had been received from the customer prior to the liquidation.

The sales department has found another company willing to buy the machine for £34,000 once it has been completed.

To complete the work, the following costs would be incurred.

(a)   Materials: these have been bought at a cost of £6,000. They have no other use, and if the machine is not finished, they would be sold for scrap for £2,000.

(b)   Further labour costs would be £8,000. Labour is in short supply, and if the machine is not finished, the work force would be switched to another job, which would earn £30,000 in revenue, and incur direct costs of £12,000 and absorbed (fixed) overhead of £8,000.

(c)   Consultancy fees £4,000. If the work is not completed, the consultant's contract would be cancelled at a cost of £1,500.

(d)   General overheads of £8,000 would be added to the cost of the additional work.

Required

Assess whether the new customer's offer should be accepted.

Answer

(a)   Costs incurred in the past, or revenue received in the past are not relevant because they cannot affect a decision about what is best for the future. Costs incurred to date of £50,000 and revenue received of £15,000 are 'water under the bridge' and should be ignored.

(b)   Similarly, the price paid in the past for the materials is irrelevant. The only relevant cost of materials affecting the decision is the opportunity cost of the revenue from scrap which would be forgone - £2,000.

(c)   **Labour costs**

	£
Labour costs required to complete work	8,000
Opportunity costs: contribution forgone by losing	
other work £(30,000 – 12,000)	18,000
Relevant cost of labour	26,000

(d)   The incremental cost of consultancy from completing the work is £2,500.

	£
Cost of completing work	4,000
Cost of cancelling contract	1,500
Incremental cost of completing work	2,500

(e)   Absorbed overhead is a notional accounting cost and should be ignored. Actual overhead incurred is the only overhead cost to consider. General overhead costs (and the absorbed overhead of the alternative work for the labour force) should be ignored.

(f)   Relevant costs may be summarised as follows.

		£	£
Revenue from completing work			34,000
Relevant costs			
Materials:	opportunity cost	2,000	
Labour:	basic pay	8,000	
	opportunity cost	18,000	
Incremental cost of consultant		2,500	
			30,500
Extra profit to be earned by accepting the order			3,500

The deprival value of an asset

1.19 In simple terms, the deprival value of an asset represents the amount of money that a company would have to receive if it were deprived of an asset in order to be no worse off than it already is. The deprival value of an asset is best demonstrated by means of an example.

1.20 EXAMPLE: DEPRIVAL VALUE OF AN ASSET

A machine cost £14,000 ten years ago. It is expected that the machine will generate future revenues of £10,000. Alternatively, the machine could be scrapped for £8,000. An equivalent machine in the same condition would cost £9,000 to buy now. What is the deprival value of the machine?

1.21 SOLUTION

Firstly, let us think about the relevance of the costs given to us in the question.

Cost of machine = £14,000 = past/sunk cost
Future revenues = £10,000 = revenue expected to be generated
Net realisable value = £8,000 = scrap proceeds
Replacement cost = £9,000

When calculating the deprival value of an asset, use the following diagram.

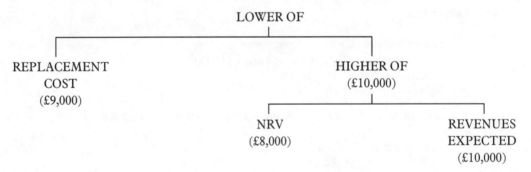

Therefore, the deprival value of the machine is the lower of the replacement cost and £10,000. The deprival value is therefore £9,000.

2 CHOICE OF PRODUCT (PRODUCT MIX) DECISIONS

2.1 One of the more common decision-making problems is a situation where there are not enough resources to meet the potential sales demand, and so a decision has to be made about what mix of products to produce, using what resources there are as effectively as possible.

KEY TERM

A **limiting factor** is a factor which limits the organisation's activities.

2.2 A **limiting factor** could be sales if there is a limit to sales demand but any one of the organisation's resources (labour, materials and so on) may be insufficient to meet the level of production demanded.

2.3 It is assumed in limiting factor accounting that management wishes to maximise profit and that **profit will be maximised when contribution is maximised** (given no change in fixed cost expenditure incurred). In other words, **marginal costing ideas are applied**.

2.4 **Contribution will be maximised by earning the biggest possible contribution from each unit of limiting factor.** For example if grade A labour is the limiting factor, contribution will be maximised by earning the biggest contribution from each hour of grade A labour worked.

2.5 The limiting factor decision therefore involves the determination of the contribution earned by each different product from each unit of the limiting factor.

2.6 EXAMPLE: LIMITING FACTOR

AB Ltd makes two products, the Ay and the Be. Unit variable costs are as follows.

	Ay £	Be £
Direct materials	1	3
Direct labour (£3 per hour)	6	3
Variable overhead	1	1
	8	7

The sales price per unit is £14 per Ay and £11 per Be. During July 20X2 the available direct labour is limited to 8,000 hours. Sales demand in July is expected to be 3,000 units for Ays and 5,000 units for Bes.

Required

Determine the profit-maximising production mix, assuming that monthly fixed costs are £20,000, and that opening stocks of finished goods and work in progress are nil.

2.7 SOLUTION

Step 1. Confirm that the limiting factor is something other than sales demand.

	Ays	Bes	Total
Labour hours per unit	2 hrs	1 hr	
Sales demand	3,000 units	5,000 units	
Labour hours needed	6,000 hrs	5,000 hrs	11,000 hrs
Labour hours available			8,000 hrs
Shortfall			3,000 hrs

Labour is the limiting factor on production.

Step 2. Identify the contribution earned by each product per unit of limiting factor, that is per labour hour worked.

	Ays £	Bes £
Sales price	14	11
Variable cost	8	7
Unit contribution	6	4
Labour hours per unit	2 hrs	1 hr
Contribution per labour hour (= unit of limiting factor)	£3	£4

Although Ays have a higher unit contribution than Bes, two Bes can be made in the time it takes to make one Ay. Because labour is in short supply it is more profitable to make Bes than Ays.

Step 3. Determine the **optimum production plan**. Sufficient Bes will be made to meet the full sales demand, and the remaining labour hours available will then be used to make Ays.

(a)

Product	Demand	Hours required	Hours available	Priority of manufacture
Bes	5,000	5,000	5,000	1st
Ays	3,000	6,000	3,000 (bal)	2nd
		11,000	8,000	

(b)

Product	Units	Hours needed	Contribution per unit £	Total £
Bes	5,000	5,000	4	20,000
Ays	1,500	3,000	6	9,000
		8,000		29,000
Less fixed costs				20,000
Profit				9,000

2.8 In conclusion.

(a) Unit contribution is *not* the correct way to decide priorities.

(b) Labour hours are the scarce resource, and therefore contribution **per labour hour** is the correct way to decide priorities.

(c) The Be earns £4 contribution per labour hour, and the Ay earns £3 contribution per labour hour. Bes therefore make more profitable use of the scarce resource, and should be manufactured first.

Exam focus point

If an examination question asks you to determine the optimum production plan, follow the five-step approach shown below.

Step 1. Identify the limiting factor
Step 2. Calculate contribution per unit for each product
Step 3. Calculate contribution per unit of limiting factor
Step 4. Rank products (make product with highest contribution per unit of limiting factor first)
Step 5. Make products in rank order until scare resource is used up **(optimal production plan)**

3 MAKE OR BUY DECISIONS

3.1 A **make or buy problem** involves a decision by an organisation about whether it should make a product/carry out an activity with its own internal resources, or whether it should pay another organisation to make the product/carry out the activity. Examples of make or buy decisions would be as follows.

(a) Whether a company should manufacture its own components, or buy the components from an outside supplier.

(b) Whether a construction company should do some work with its own employees, or whether it should subcontract the work to another company.

(c) Whether the design and development of a new computer system should be entrusted to in-house data processing staff or whether an external software house should be hired to do the work.

3.2 The 'make' option should give management more direct control over the work, but the 'buy' option often has the benefit that the external organisation has a specialist skill and expertise in the work. Make or buy decisions should certainly not be based exclusively on cost considerations.

3.3 If an organisation has the freedom of choice about whether to make internally or buy externally and has no scarce resources that put a restriction on what it can do itself, the relevant costs for the decision will be the **differential costs** between the two options.

3.4 EXAMPLE: MAKE OR BUY

Buster Ltd makes four components, W, X, Y and Z, for which costs in the forthcoming year are expected to be as follows.

	W	*X*	*Y*	*Z*
Production (units)	1,000	2,000	4,000	3,000
Unit marginal costs	£	£	£	£
Direct materials	4	5	2	4
Direct labour	8	9	4	6
Variable production overheads	2	3	1	2
	14	17	7	12

Directly attributable fixed costs per annum and committed fixed costs are as follows.

	£
Incurred as a direct consequence of making W	1,000
Incurred as a direct consequence of making X	5,000
Incurred as a direct consequence of making Y	6,000
Incurred as a direct consequence of making Z	8,000
Other fixed costs (committed)	30,000
	50,000

A subcontractor has offered to supply units of W, X, Y and Z for £12, £21, £10 and £14 respectively.

Required

Decide whether Buster Ltd should make or buy the components.

3.5 SOLUTION

(a) The relevant costs are the differential costs between making and buying, and they consist of differences in unit variable costs plus differences in directly attributable fixed costs. Subcontracting will result in some fixed cost savings.

	W	X	Y	Z
	£	£	£	£
Unit variable cost of making	14	17	7	12
Unit variable cost of buying	12	21	10	14
	(2)	4	3	2
Annual requirements (units)	1,000	2,000	4,000	3,000
Extra variable cost of buying (per annum)	(2,000)	8,000	12,000	6,000
Fixed costs saved by buying	1,000	5,000	6,000	8,000
Extra total cost of buying	(3,000)	3,000	6,000	(2,000)

(b) The company would save £3,000 pa by subcontracting component W (where the purchase cost would be less than the marginal cost per unit to make internally) and would save £2,000 pa by subcontracting component Z (because of the saving in fixed costs of £8,000).

(c) In this example, relevant costs are the variable costs of in-house manufacture, the variable costs of subcontracted units, and the saving in fixed costs.

(d) Important further considerations would be as follows.

   (i)   If components W and Z are subcontracted, the company will have spare capacity. How should that spare capacity be profitably used? Are there hidden benefits to be obtained from subcontracting? Would the company's workforce resent the loss of work to an outside subcontractor, and might such a decision cause an industrial dispute?

   (ii) Would the subcontractor be reliable with delivery times, and would he supply components of the same quality as those manufactured internally?

   (iii) Does the company wish to be flexible and maintain better control over operations by making everything itself?

   (iv) Are the estimates of fixed cost savings reliable? In the case of Product W, buying is clearly cheaper than making in-house. In the case of product Z, the decision to buy rather than make would only be financially beneficial if the fixed cost savings of £8,000 could really be 'delivered' by management. All too often in practice, promised savings fail to materialise!

Question 3

BB Limited makes three components - S, T and W. The following costs have been recorded.

	Component S Unit cost	Component T Unit cost	Component W Unit cost
	£	£	£
Variable cost	2.50	8.00	5.00
Fixed cost	2.00	8.30	3.75
Total cost	4.50	16.30	8.75

Another company has offered to supply the components to BB Limited at the following prices.

	Component S	Component T	Component W
Price each	£4	£7	£5.50

Which component(s), if any, should BB Limited consider buying in?

A   Buy in all three components
B   Do not buy any
C   Buy in S and W
D   Buy in T only

Answer

BB Ltd should buy the component if the variable cost of making the component is more than the variable cost of buying the component.

	Component S	Component T	Component W
	£	£	£
Variable cost of making	2.50	8.00	5.00
Variable cost of buying	4.00	7.00	5.50
	(1.50)	1.00	(0.50)

The variable cost of making component T is greater than the variable cost of buying it.

∴ BB Ltd should consider buying in component T only.

The correct answer is D.

Make or buy decisions and limiting factors

3.6   In a situation where a company must subcontract work to make up a shortfall in its own production capability, its total costs are minimised if those components/products subcontracted are those with the lowest extra variable cost of buying per unit of limiting factor saved by buying.

3.7   EXAMPLE: MAKE OR BUY AND LIMITING FACTORS

Green Ltd manufactures two components, the Alpha and the Beta, using the same machines for each. The budget for the next year calls for the production and assembly of 4,000 of each component. The variable production cost per unit of the final product, the gamma, is as follows.

	Machine hours	Variable cost
		£
1 unit of Alpha	3	20
1 unit of Beta	2	36
Assembly		20
		76

Only 16,000 hours of machine time will be available during the year, and a sub-contractor has quoted the following unit prices for supplying components: Alpha £29; Beta £40. Advise Green Ltd.

3.8   SOLUTION

(a)   There is a shortfall in machine hours available, and some products must be sub-contracted.

Product	Units		Machine hours
Alpha	4,000		12,000
Beta	4,000		8,000
		Required	20,000
		Available	16,000
		Shortfall	4,000

(b)   The assembly costs are not relevant costs because they are unaffected by the make or buy decision. The units subcontracted should be those which will add least to the costs of Green Ltd. Since 4,000 hours of work must be sub-contracted, the cheapest policy is to subcontract work which adds the least extra costs (the least extra variable costs) per hour of own-time saved.

BPP
PUBLISHING

(c)

	Alpha £	Beta £
Variable cost of making	20	36
Variable cost of buying	29	40
Extra variable cost of buying	9	4
Machine hours saved by buying	3 hrs	2 hrs
Extra variable cost of buying, per hour saved	£3	£2

It is cheaper to buy Betas than to buy Alphas and so the priority for making the components in-house will be in the reverse order to the preference for buying them from a subcontractor.

(d)

Component	Hrs per unit to make in-house	Hrs required in total	Cumulative hours
Alpha	3 hrs	12,000	12,000
Beta	2 hrs	8,000	20,000
		20,000	
Hours available		16,000	
Shortfall		4,000	

There are enough machine hours to make all 4,000 units of Alpha and 2,000 units of Beta. 4,000 hours production of Beta must be sub-contracted. This will be the cheapest production policy available

(e)

Component	Machine hours	Number of units	Unit variable cost	Total variable cost
Make			£	£
Alpha	12,000	4,000	20	80,000
Beta (balance)	4,000	2,000	36	72,000
	16,000			152,000
Buy	Hours saved			
Beta (balance)	4,000	2,000	40	80,000
		Total variable costs of components		232,000
		Assembly costs (4,000 × £20)		80,000
		Total variable costs		312,000

4 SHUT DOWN DECISIONS

4.1 **Shut down decisions** involve the following.

(a) Whether or not to shut down a factory, department, or product line either because it is making a loss or it is too expensive to run.

(b) If the decision is to shut down, whether the closure should be permanent or temporary.

4.2 Let us demonstrate the decision of whether or not to shut down a product line and make more or less of another product line by studying the following example.

4.3 Suppose that a company manufactures three products, Corfus, Cretes and Zantes. The present net profit from these is as follows.

	Corfus £	Cretes £	Zantes £	Total £
Sales	50,000	40,000	60,000	150,000
Variable costs	30,000	25,000	35,000	90,000
Contribution	20,000	15,000	25,000	60,000
Fixed costs	17,000	18,000	20,000	55,000
Profit/loss	3,000	(3,000)	5,000	5,000

The company is concerned about its poor profit performance, and is considering whether or not to cease selling Cretes. It is felt that selling prices cannot be raised or lowered without adversely affecting net income. £5,000 of the fixed costs of Cretes are attributable fixed costs which would be saved if production ceased. All other fixed costs would remain the same.

4.4 By stopping production of Cretes, the consequences would be a £10,000 fall in profits.

	£
Loss of contribution	(15,000)
Savings in fixed costs	5,000
Incremental loss	(10,000)

4.5 Suppose, however, it were possible to use the resources realised by stopping production of Cretes and switch to producing a new item, Rhodes, which would sell for £50,000 and incur variable costs of £30,000 and extra direct fixed costs of £6,000. A new decision is now required.

	Cretes	Rhodes
	£	£
Sales	40,000	50,000
Less variable costs	25,000	30,000
Contribution	15,000	20,000
Less direct fixed costs	5,000	6,000
Contribution to shared fixed costs and profit	10,000	14,000

It would be more profitable to shut down production of Cretes and switch resources to making Rhodes, in order to boost profits to £9,000.

5 ONE-OFF CONTRACTS

5.1 This type of decision-making situation will concern a contract which would utilise an organisation's spare capacity but which would have to be accepted at a price lower than that normally required by the organisation. In general you can assume that a contract will probably be accepted if it increases contribution and hence profit, and rejected if it reduces profit. Let us consider an example.

5.2 EXAMPLE: ONE-OFF CONTRACTS

Belt and Braces Ltd makes a single product which sells for £20. It has a full cost of £15 which is made up as follows.

	£
Direct material	4
Direct labour (2 hours)	6
Variable overhead	2
General fixed overhead	3
	15

The labour force is currently working at 90% of capacity and so there is a spare capacity for 2,000 units. A customer has approached the company with a request for the manufacture of a special order of 2,000 units for which he is willing to pay £25,000. Assess whether the contract should be accepted.

5.3 SOLUTION

	£	£
Value of order		25,000
Cost of order		
Direct materials (£4 × 2,000)	8,000	
Direct labour (£6 × 2,000)	12,000	
Variable overhead (£2 × 2,000)	4,000	
Relevant cost of order		24,000
Profit from order acceptance		1,000

Fixed costs will be incurred regardless of whether the contract is accepted and so are not relevant to the decision. The contract should be accepted since it increases contribution to profit by £1,000.

5.4 There are, however, several other factors which would need to be considered before a final decision is taken.

(a) The acceptance of the contract at a lower price may lead other customers to demand lower prices as well.

(b) There may be more profitable ways of using the spare capacity.

(c) Accepting the contract may lock up capacity that could be used for future full-price business.

(d) Fixed costs may, in fact, alter if the contract is accepted.

Chapter roundup

- **Relevant costs** are future cash flows arising as a direct consequence of a decision.

  - Relevant costs are **future costs**
  - Relevant costs are **cashflows**
  - Relevant costs are **incremental costs**

- Relevant costs are also **differential costs** and **opportunity costs.**

  - **Differential cost** is the difference in total cost between alternatives.

  - An **opportunity cost** is the value of the benefit sacrificed when one course of action is chosen in preference to an alternative.

- A **sunk cost** is a past cost which is not directly relevant in decision making.

- The principle underlying decision accounting is that management decisions can only affect the **future**. Management therefore require information about **future costs and revenues.**

- **In general**, variable costs will be relevant costs and fixed costs will be irrelevant to a decision.

- The **deprival value** of an asset represents the amount of money that a company would have to receive if it were deprived of an asset in order to be no worse off than it already is.

- A **limiting factor** is a factor which limits the organisation's activities.

- In a **limiting factor situation,** contribution will be maximised by earning the biggest possible contribution per unit of limiting factor.

- In a **make or buy** situation with no limiting factors, the relevant costs for the decision are the **differential costs** between the two options.

- **Shutdown decisions** involve deciding whether or not to shut down a factory, department or product line.

- The decision to accept or reject a contract should be made on the basis of whether or not the contract **increases contribution and profit**.

Quick quiz

1 Relevant costs are:

(a) Differential costs
(b) Future costs
(c) Cash flows.
(d) Incremental costs.
(e) Opportunity cost

2 Sunk costs are directly relevant in decision making.

True ☐

False ☑

3 The following information relates to machine Z.

Purchase price = £7,000
Expected future revenues = £5,000
Scrap value = £4,000
Replacement cost = £4,500

Complete the following diagram in order to calculate the deprival value of machine Z.

LOWER OF   [4500]

REPLACEMENT COST   [4500]

HIGHER OF   [5000]

NRV   [4000]

REVENUES   [5000]

The deprival value of machine Z is ...... 1000 ....

4 A limiting factor is a factor which ... limits the amount of production i.e. labour hours

5 When determining the optimum production plan, what five steps are involved?

Step 1. Determine limiting factor
Step 2 Calculate Contribution
Step 3. Calculate Contribution per limiting factor
Step 4. Rank in order of highest Contribution
Step 5. Calculate

6 A sunk cost is:

A a cost committed to be spent in the current period
B a cost which is irrelevant for decision making
C a cost connected with oil exploration in the North Sea
D a cost unaffected by fluctuations in the level of activity

333

Answers to quick quiz

1   (a)   Future costs
    (b)   Cash flows
    (c)   Incremental costs
    (d)   Differential costs
    (e)   Opportunity costs

2   False

3

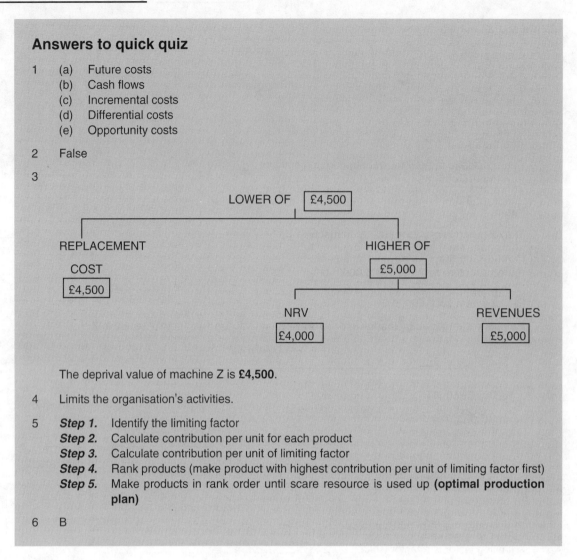

The deprival value of machine Z is **£4,500**.

4   Limits the organisation's activities.

5   ***Step 1.***   Identify the limiting factor
    Step 2.   Calculate contribution per unit for each product
    Step 3.   Calculate contribution per unit of limiting factor
    Step 4.   Rank products (make product with highest contribution per unit of limiting factor first)
    Step 5.   Make products in rank order until scare resource is used up **(optimal production plan)**

6   B

Now try the questions below from the Exam Question Bank

Number	Level	Marks	Time
28	MCQ	n/a	n/a
29	Examination	10	18 mins

Chapter 17

DECISION MAKING WITH UNCERTAINTY

Topic list	Syllabus reference
1 Expected values	6(f)
2 Decision making with expected values	6(f)
3 Decision trees	6(f)
4 Risk and uncertainty in decision making	6(f)

Introduction

If you have not studied the topic of probability before, we recommend that you have a look at the Basic Maths supplement which comes with this Study Text. Once you have done that we are ready to examine the related topic of **expected values** and we will see how the concept can be used to assist decision making.

Although simple decisions can be made using expected values, more complex problems, although solvable using the basic principles, require a clear logical approach to ensure that all possible choices and outcomes of a decision are taken into consideration. **Decision trees**, the topic of the third section of this chapter, are a useful way of interpreting such problems.

Study guide

Section 21 – Decision making under uncertainty

- Explain and calculate expected values

- Explain the limitations of the expected value technique

- Construct and interpret decision trees including probabilities and expected outcomes and values

- Apply the concept of expected value to business decision problems

- Distinguish between risk and uncertainty

- Explain the concept of risk and how this affects decision making

1   EXPECTED VALUES

> **KEY TERM**
>
> An **expected value** (or EV) is a weighted average value, based on probabilities.

1.1   If the probability of an outcome of an event is p, then the expected number of times that this outcome will occur in n events (the expected value) is equal to n × p. For example, suppose that the probability that a transistor is defective is 0.02. How many defectives would we expect to find in a batch of 4,000 transistors?

$$
\begin{aligned}
EV &= 4,000 \times 0.02 \\
&= 80 \text{ defectives would be expected.}
\end{aligned}
$$

1.2 EXAMPLE: EXPECTED VALUES

The daily sales of Product T may be as follows.

Units	Probability
1,000	0.2
2,000	0.3
3,000	0.4
4,000	0.1
	1.0

Required

Calculate the expected daily sales.

1.3 SOLUTION

The EV of daily sales may be calculated by multiplying each possible outcome (volume of daily sales) by the probability that this outcome will occur.

Units	Probability	Expected value Units
1,000	0.2	200
2,000	0.3	600
3,000	0.4	1,200
4,000	0.1	400
	EV of daily sales	2,400

In the long run the expected value should be approximately the actual average, if the event occurs many times over. In the example above, we do not expect sales on any one day to equal 2,400 units, but in the long run, over a large number of days, average sales should equal 2,400 units a day.

Expected values and single events

1.4 The point made in the preceding paragraph is an important one. An **expected value** can be calculated when the **event will only occur once or twice**, but it will not be a true long-run average of what will actually happen, because there is no long run.

1.5 Suppose, for example, that a businessman is trying to decide whether to invest in a project. He estimates that there are three possible outcomes.

Outcome	Profit/(loss) £	Probability
Success	10,000	0.2
Moderate success	2,000	0.7
Failure	(4,000)	0.1

The expected value of profit may be calculated as follows.

Profit/(loss) £	Probability	Expected value £
10,000	0.2	2,000
2,000	0.7	1,400
(4,000)	0.1	(400)
	Expected value of profit	3,000

1.6 In this example, the project is a one-off event, and as far as we are aware, it will not be repeated. The actual profit or loss will be £10,000, £2,000 or £(4,000), and the average value of £3,000 will not actually happen. There is no long-run average of a single event.

1.7 Nevertheless, the expected value can be used to help the manager decide whether or not to invest in the project. Generally the following rules apply.

- A project with a **positive EV** (EV is a profit) should be **accepted**
- A project with a **negative EV** (EV is a loss) should be **rejected**

1.8 Provided that we understand the limitations of using expected values for single events, they can offer a helpful guide for management decisions, and suggest to managers whether any particular decision is worth the risk of taking (subject, of course, to reasonable accuracy in the estimates of the probabilities themselves).

Question 1

A company manufactures and sells product D. The selling price of the product is £6 per unit, and estimates of demand and variable costs of sales are as follows.

Probability	Demand	Probability	Variable cost per unit
	Units		£
0.3	5,000 *500*	0.1	3.00 *.30*
0.6	6,000 *3600*	0.3	3.50 *1.05*
0.1	8,000 *800*	0.5	4.00 *2.00*
	5900	0.1	4.50 *.45*
			3.80

The unit variable costs do not depend on the volume of sales.

Fixed costs will be £10,000.

The expected profit will be:

SALES 5900 units × 6.2   35400
VARIABLE 5900 " × .38   (22 420)
FIXED Costs   (10 000)
*   2980*

A £13,749
B £12,980
C £5,900
(D) £2,980

Answer

The EV of demand is as follows.

Demand	Probability	Expected value
Units		Units
5,000	0.3	1,500
6,000	0.6	3,600
8,000	0.1	800
	EV of demand	5,900

The EV of the variable cost per unit is as follows.

Variable costs	Probability	Expected value
£		£
3.00	0.1	0.30
3.50	0.3	1.05
4.00	0.5	2.00
4.50	0.1	0.45
	EV of unit variable costs	3.80

		£
Sales	5,900 units × £6.00	35,400
Less variable costs	5,900 units × £3.80	22,420
Contribution		12,980
Less fixed costs		10,000
Expected profit		2,980

The correct answer is therefore D.

If you selected option A, you calculated the average demand (6,333 units) and the average variable cost per unit (£3.75) and deducted fixed costs of £10,000. This is not the correct method to use.

If you selected option B, you calculated the expected contribution instead of the expected profit.

If you selected option C, you calculated the expected value of demand (5,900 units) and expressed this as a financial amount, £5,900.

The expected value of a probability

1.9 You might be required to calculate a **weighted average probability** of an event occurring: an EV of a probability. Consider the following example.

1.10 EXAMPLE: THE EXPECTED VALUE OF A PROBABILITY

A salesman has three small areas to cover, areas A, B and C. He never sells more than one item per day, and the probabilities of making a sale when he visits each area are as follows.

Area	Probability
A	30%
B	25%
C	10%

He visits only one area each day. He visits Area A as often as he visits Area B, but he only visits Area C half as often as he visits Area A.

Required

(a) Calculate the probability that on any one day he will visit Area C.
(b) Calculate the probability that he will make a sale on any one day.
(c) Calculate the probability that if he does make a sale, it will be in Area A.

1.11 SOLUTION

(a) The probabilities of visiting each area are obtained from the ratios in which he visits them.

Area	Ratio	Probability
A	2	0.4
B	2	0.4
C	1	0.2
	5	1.0

The probability that he will visit Area C is 0.2.

(b) The probability of making a sale on any one day is found as follows.

Area	Probability of a sale	Probability of visiting area	EV of probability of a sale
	x	*p*	*px*
A	0.30	0.4	0.12
B	0.25	0.4	0.10
C	0.10	0.2	0.02
			0.24

The probability of making a sale is 0.24 or 24%.

(c) The probability of making a sale is 0.24 and the probability that the sale will be in Area A rather than B or C can be established as follows.

$$\frac{\text{EV of probability of sale in A}}{\text{EV of probability of sale in A, B or C}} = \frac{0.12}{0.24} = 0.5.$$

One half of all sales will be made in Area A.

> **FORMULA TO LEARN**
>
> $E(x) = \Sigma x P(x)$
>
> This is read as '**the expected value of** "**x**" is equal to the sum of the products of each value of x and the corresponding probability of that value of x occurring'.

2   DECISION MAKING WITH EXPECTED VALUES

2.1   The **expected values** for single events can offer a helpful guide for management decisions: a project with a positive EV should be accepted; a project with a negative EV should be rejected.

2.2   Another decision rule involving expected values that you are likely to come across is the choice of an option which has the **highest EV of profit** (or the lowest EV of cost).

2.3   Choosing the option with the highest EV of profit is a decision rule that has both merits and drawbacks, as the following example will show.

2.4   EXAMPLE: THE EXPECTED VALUE CRITERION

Suppose that there are two mutually exclusive projects with the following possible profits.

Project A		*Project B*	
Probability	*Profit*	*Probability*	*Profit/(loss)*
	£		£
0.8	5,000	0.1	(2,000)
0.2	6,000	0.2	5,000
		0.6	7,000
		0.1	8,000

Required

Determine which project should be chosen.

Solution

2.5   The EV of profit for each project is as follows.   £

(a) Project A $(0.8 \times 5,000) + (0.2 \times 6,000) =$ 5,200

(b) Project B $(0.1 \times (2,000)) + (0.2 \times 5,000) + (0.6 \times 7,000) + (0.1 \times 8,000) = 5,800$

Project B has a higher EV of profit. This means that on the balance of probabilities, it could offer a better return than A, and so is arguably a better choice.

On the other hand, the minimum return from project A would be £5,000 whereas with B there is a 0.1 chance of a loss of £2,000. So project A might be a safer choice.

Limitations of expected values

2.6 Evaluating decisions by using expected values have a number of limitations.

(a) The **probabilities** used when calculating expected values are likely to be estimates. They may therefore be **unreliable** or **inaccurate**.

(b) Expected values are **long-term averages** and may not be suitable for use in situations involving **one-off decisions**. They may therefore be useful as a guide to decision making.

(c) Expected values do not consider the **attitudes to risk** of the people involved in the decision making process. They do not, therefore, take into account all of the factors involved in the decision.

(d) The **time value of money** may not be taken into account: £100 now is worth more than £100 in ten years' time. We shall study the time value of money in Chapters 19 and 20 in this Study Text.

Question 2

In a decision problem, option A will give payoffs of £5 and £2 both with probabilities of 0.5, whereas option B gives payoffs of £6 with probability 0.6 and £1 with probability 0.4. What is the expected value of the optimal decision?

A £6.00
B £3.50
C £4.00
D £7.00

Answer

Expected value of option A = (5 × 0.5) + (2 × 0.5) = 2.5 + 1.0
= 3.5

Expected value of option B = (6 × 0.6) + (1 × 0.4) = 3.6 + 0.4
= 4.0

The expected value of option B is greater than that of option A, therefore the expected value of the optimal decision is £4.00. Option C is therefore correct.

If you selected option A, you calculated the highest possible payoff and did not take any of the associated probabilities into account.

If you selected B, you incorrectly chose the expected value of option A instead of option B.

If you selected option D, you calculated the total of the possible payoffs in either case but have taken no account of probabilities.

3 DECISION TREES

KEY TERM

A **decision tree** is an analytical tool to assist in decision making. It ensures that all possible choices and outcomes are taken into consideration.

3.1 **Expected values** are generally used for making **simple decisions**. More **complex problems** are best solved with the use of **decision trees**.

3.2 Exactly how does the use of a decision tree permit a clear and logical approach?

- All possible choices that can be made are shown as **branches** on the tree.
- All possible outcomes of each choice are shown as **subsidiary branches** on the tree.

3.3 There are two stages to preparing a decision tree.

- Drawing the tree itself, to show all the choices and outcomes
- Putting in the numbers (the probabilities, outcome values and EVs)

Drawing a decision tree: the basic rules

3.4 Every decision tree starts from a **decision point** with the **decision options** that are being considered.

(a) There should be a line, or branch, for each option or alternative.

(b) It helps to identify the decision point, and any subsequent decision point in the tree, with a symbol. Here, we shall use a square shape.

(c) There is no accepted convention on the shapes used at the points of a decision tree. If you have to investigate a ready-drawn tree, remember that the very first (leftmost) point will always be a decision point.

3.5 It is conventional to draw decision trees from left to right, and so a decision tree will start as follows.

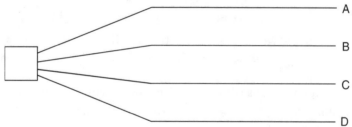

The square is the decision point, and A, B, C and D represent four alternatives from which a choice must now be made.

3.6 If the outcome from any choice or alternative is **100% certain**, the branch of the decision tree for that alternative is **complete**.

3.7 If the outcome of a particular alternative is **uncertain**, the various possible outcomes must be shown. We show this on a decision tree by inserting an **outcome or event point** on the branch of the tree. Each possible outcome is then shown as a subsidiary branch, coming out from the outcome point. The probability of each outcome occurring should be written on to the branch of the tree which represents that outcome.

3.8 To distinguish decision points from outcome points, a circle will be used as a symbol for an outcome or event point.

In the example above, there are two choices facing the decision maker, A and B. The outcome if A is chosen is known with certainty, but if B is chosen, there are two possible outcomes, high sales (0.6 probability) or low sales (0.4 probability).

3.9 Clarity becomes an issue when the options are more complex. For example a company might be considering three options.

- Launch a new product, and advertise nationally.
- Launch a new product, and do not advertise.
- Don't launch the product.

This could be shown in either of two ways, as shown below. Usually, the first method will be clearer than the second method.

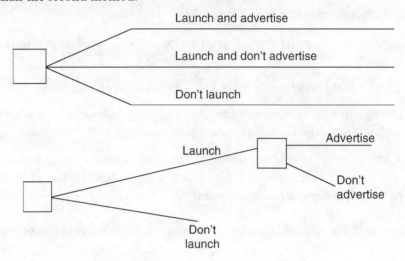

3.10 When several outcomes are uncertain, it is usually simpler to show two or more stages of outcome points on the decision tree.

3.11 For example suppose that a company can choose to launch a new product XYZ or not. If the product is launched, expected sales and expected unit costs might be as follows.

Sales		Unit costs	
Units	Probability	£	Probability
10,000	0.8	6	0.7
15,000	0.2	8	0.3

(a) The decision tree could be drawn as follows.

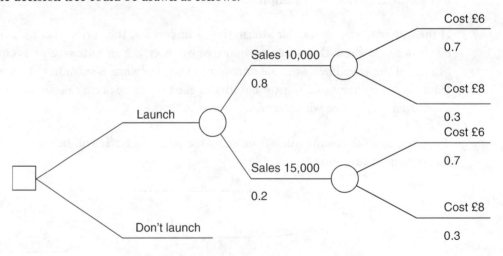

(b) The layout shown above will usually be less complex than working out the alternative way of drawing the tree, which is shown below.

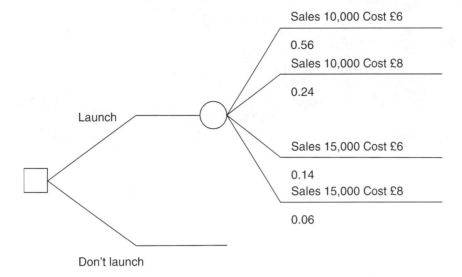

3.12 Occasionally, a decision taken now will influence another decision which might then have to be taken at some time in the future, depending on how results turn out. When this situation arises, the decision tree can be drawn as a **two-stage tree**, as follows.

In this tree, either decision A or B or else decision C or D is dependent on the outcome which occurs as a consequence of choosing decision X.

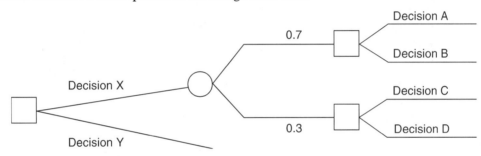

Exam focus point

Remember to use a sharp pencil and a ruler when drawing decision trees – marks are usually awarded for presentation in an examination.

Evaluating the decision with a decision tree: rollback analysis

3.13 The EV of each decision option can be evaluated, using the decision tree to help keep the logic properly sorted out. The basic rules are as follows.

(a) We start on the right hand side of the tree and work back towards the left hand side and the current decision under consideration.

(b) It helps if we label each decision point and outcome point on the tree, to give it an identification.

(c) Working from right to left, we calculate the EV of revenue, cost, contribution or profit at each outcome point on the tree.

3.14 Suppose that the following decision tree represents a decision under consideration.

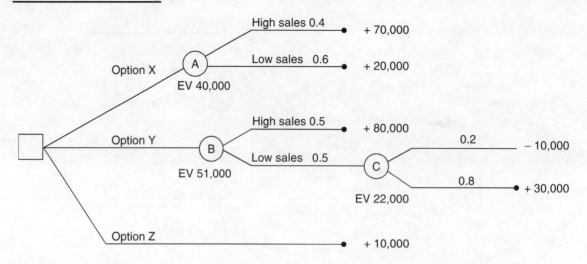

3.15 At outcome point C (the right-most outcome point) the EV is calculated as follows.

Profit	*Probability*	
x	*p*	*px*
(10,000)	0.2	(2,000)
30,000	0.8	24,000
	EV =	22,000

At outcome point B therefore, the EV is as follows.

Profit	*Probability*	
x	*p*	*px*
80,000	0.5	40,000
22,000	0.5	11,000
	EV =	51,000

It remains to calculate the EV at outcome point A.

Profit	*Probability*	
x	*p*	*px*
70,000	0.4	28,000
20,000	0.6	12,000
	EV =	40,000

The calculation of EVs, first at outcome points A and C and then at outcome point B, brings us back to the initial decision, where the choices can now be compared, as follows.

Option
X: EV = EV at A = £40,000
Y: EV = EV at B = £51,000
Z: Certain value £10,000.

If the decision is to select the option with the highest EV of profit, the evaluation of the decision tree would then point to option Y.

3.16 The decision tree should be drawn in '**chronological order**' from **left to right**. When there are two-stage decision trees, the first decision in time should be drawn on the left. This is the decision of immediate concern to management.

3.17 When there are two decision stages in the decision tree, the second stage decision must be evaluated first so that we can evaluate the part of the decision tree to the left of it.

3.18 EXAMPLE: DRAWING AND EVALUATING A DECISION TREE

These rules for drawing decision trees might seem quite simple when you look at an example.

Beethoven Ltd has a new wonder product, the vylin, of which it expects great things. At the moment the company has two courses of action open to it, to test market the product or abandon it. If they test it, it will cost £100,000 and the market response could be positive or negative with probabilities of 0.60 and 0.40. If the response is positive the company could either abandon the product or market it full scale. If it markets the vylin full scale, the outcome might be low, medium or high demand, and the respective net pay offs would be (200), 200 or 1,000 in units of £1,000 (ie the result could range from a net loss of £200,000 to a gain of £1,000,000). These outcomes have probabilities of 0.20, 0.50 and 0.30 respectively.

If the result of the test marketing is negative and the company goes ahead and markets the product, estimated losses would be £600,000. If, at any point, the company abandons the product, there would be a net gain of £50,000 from the sale of scrap. All the financial values have been discounted to the present.

Required

(a) Draw a decision tree.
(b) Include figures for cost, loss or profit on the appropriate branches of the tree.
(c) Evaluate the options and state what option you think should be chosen.

3.19 SOLUTION

(a) The starting point for the tree is to establish what decision has to be made now. What are the alternative options? In this case, they are to test market or to abandon.

(b) The outcome of the 'abandon' option is known with certainty. There are two possible outcomes of the option to test market, positive response and negative response.

(c) Depending on the outcome of the test market, another decision will then be made, to abandon the product or to go ahead with the market launch.

(d) This is the logical structure on which the decision tree should be drawn, as follows.

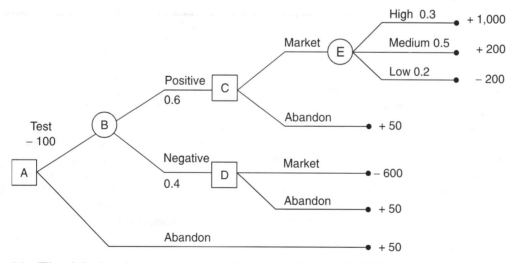

(e) The right-hand-most outcome point is point E, and the EV is as follows.

	Profit (£'000)	Probability	
	x	p	px
High	1,000	0.3	300
Medium	200	0.5	100
Low	(200)	0.2	(40)
			EV 360

This is the EV of the decision to market the product if the test market shows a positive response.

(f) (i) At decision point C, the choices are as follows.

- Market, EV + 360 (the EV at point E)
- Abandon, value + 50

The choice would be to market the product, and so the EV at decision point C is +360.

(ii) At decision point D, the choices are as follows.

- Market, value – 600
- Abandon, value +50

The choice would be to abandon, and so the EV at decision point D is +50.

The second stage decisions have therefore been made. If the original decision is to test market, the company will market the product if the test shows positive customer response, and will abandon the product if the test results are negative.

(g) The evaluation of the decision tree is completed as follows.

(i) Calculate the EV at outcome point B.

0.6×360 (EV at C) + 0.4×50 (EV at D) = 216 + 20 = 236

(ii) Compare the options at point A.

- Test: EV = EV at B minus test marketing cost = 236 – 100 = 136
- Abandon: value 50

The choice would be to test market the product, because it has a higher EV of profit.

Question 3

A software company has just won a contract worth £80,000 if it delivers a successful product on time, but only £40,000 if it is late. It faces the problem now of whether to produce the work in-house or to sub-contract it. To sub-contract the work would cost £30,000, but the local sub-contractor is so fast and reliable as to make it certain that successful software is produced on time.

If the work is produced in-house the cost would be only £20,000 but, based on past experience, would have only a 90% chance of being successful. In the event of the software *not* being successful, there would be insufficient time to rewrite the whole package internally, but there would still be the options of either a 'late rejection' of the contract (at a further cost of £10,000) or of 'late sub-contracting' the work on the same terms as before. With this late start the local sub-contractor is estimated to have only a 50/50 chance of producing the work on time or of producing it late. In this case the sub-contractor still has to be paid £30,000, regardless of whether he meets the deadline or not.

Required

(a) Draw a decision tree for the software company, using squares for decision points and circles for outcome (chance) points, including all relevant data on the diagram.

(b) Calculate expected values as appropriate and recommend a course of action to the software company with reasons.

Answer

(a)   *All values in £'000*

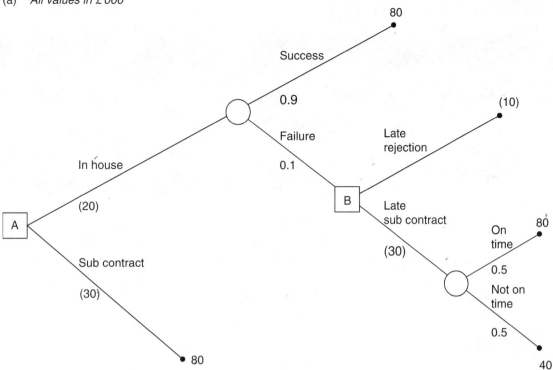

(b)   *At decision point B*

EV of late rejection = −10
EV of late sub-contract = (80 × 0.5) + (40 × 0.5) − 30 = 30
The optimum strategy at B is therefore to subcontract with EV = 30.

At decision point A

EV of sub-contract = 80 − 30 = 50
EV of in-house = (80 × 0.9) + (30* × 0.1) − 20 = 55
The optimum strategy at A is therefore to produce in-house with EV = 55.
*This is the optimum EV at decision point B.

Conclusions

The decisions which will maximise expected profits are to attempt initially to produce in-house and if this fails to sub-contract. The expected profit is £55,000.

Assuming that the probabilities have been correctly estimated, the company has a 90% chance of making a profit of £60,000, a 5% chance of making £30,000 and a 5% chance of making a £10,000 loss. If the company is not willing to risk making a loss, the initial option of subcontracting should be taken since this offers a guaranteed profit of £50,000.

4 RISK AND UNCERTAINTY IN DECISION MAKING

What are risk and uncertainty?

> **KEY TERMS**
>
> - **Risk** involves situations or events which may or may not occur, but whose probability of occurrence can be calculated statistically and the frequency of their occurrence predicted from past records. Thus insurance deals with risk.
>
> - **Uncertain events** are those whose outcome **cannot** be predicted with statistical confidence.

4.1 In everyday usage the terms risk and uncertainty are not clearly distinguished. If you are asked for a definition, do not make the **mistake of believing that the latter** is a more **extreme version of the former**. It is not a question of degree, it is a question of whether or **not sufficient information is available to allow the lack of certainty to be quantified**. As a rule, however, the terms are used interchangeably.

Risk preference

> **KEY TERMS**
>
> - A **risk seeker** is a decision maker who is interested in the best outcomes no matter how small the chance that they may occur.
>
> - A decision maker is **risk neutral** if he is concerned with what will be the most likely outcome.
>
> - A **risk averse** decision maker acts on the assumption that the worst outcome might occur.

4.2 This has clear implications for managers and organisations. A **risk seeking manager** working for an **organisation** that is characteristically **risk averse** is likely to make decisions that are **not in line with the goals of the organisation**. There may be a role for the management accountant here, who could be instructed to present decision-making information in such a way as to ensure that the manager considers *all* the possibilities, including the worst.

Allowing for uncertainty

Conservatism

4.3 This approach simply involves **estimating outcomes in a conservative manner in order to provide a built-in safety factor**. However, the method **fails to consider explicitly a range** of outcomes and, by concentrating only on conservative figures, may also fail to consider **the expected or most likely outcomes**.

4.4 Conservatism is **associated with risk aversion** and prudence (in the general sense of the word). In spite of its shortcomings it is probably the most widely used method in practice.

Worst possible, most likely and best possible outcomes

4.5   A more scientific version of conservatism is to measure the most likely outcome (or profit) from a decision, the worst possible outcome, and the best that can happen. This will show the **full range of possible outcomes** from a decision, and might help managers to reject certain alternatives because the worst possible outcome might involve an unacceptable amount of loss.

Chapter roundup

- An **expected value** is a weighted average value based on probabilities. The expected value of a probability is equal to the sum of the products of each value of x and the corresponding probability of that value of x occurring

- **Decision trees** ensure that all possible choices and outcomes of a decision are taken into account by the adoption of a clear and logical approach.

- The steps in **rollback analysis**, which evaluates the EV of each decision option, are as follows.

  o   Work from right to left, to the particular decision under consideration.
  o   Label each decision point and outcome point.
  o   Work from left to right and calculate EVs at each outcome point.

- **Risk** involves situations or events which may or may not occur, but whose probability of occurrence can be calculated statistically and the frequency of their occurrence predicted from past records.

- **Uncertain events** are those whose outcome **cannot** be predicted with statistical confidence.

Quick quiz

1   An expected value is calculated as E(x) = $\Sigma x P(x)$.

2   Give four limitations of expected values.

   - Not long Term.
   - Good for 1 off project.
   - ~~Do not take~~ really money terms into Acct
   - ....

3   How does a decision tree aid the answering of complex probability questions?   *Ensures all possible outcomes + decisions taken into acct*

4   The decision tree should be drawn in chronological order from left to right/~~right to left~~ (delete as appropriate).

5   **Uncertain events** are those whose outcome can be predicted with statistical confidence.

   True   [ ]
   False [✓]

Answers to quick quiz

1    $E(x) = \Sigma x P(x)$

2
   - Probabilities used are estimates. Expected values may be unreliable therefore.
   - Expected values are long-term averages and may not be suitable for one-off decisions.
   - Expected values do not take into account all factors involved in decisions.
   - The time value of money may not be taken into account.

3
   - All possible choices that can be made are shown as **branches** on the tree.
   - All possible outcomes of each choice are shown as **subsidiary branches** on the tree.

4   The decision tree should be drawn in chronological order from **left to right**.

5   False. Uncertain events are those whose outcome **cannot** be predicted with statistical confidence.

Now try the questions below from the Exam Question Bank

Number	Level	Marks	Time
30	MCQ	n/a	n/a
31	Examination	10	18 mins

Chapter 18

LINEAR PROGRAMMING

Topic list	Syllabus reference
1 The problem	6(d)
2 Formulating the problem	6(d)
3 Graphing the model	6(d)
4 Finding the best solution	6(d)
5 Two-plus variable models	6(d)

Introduction

We are now going to look at a decision-making technique which involves **allocating resources in order to achieve the best results**. The name '**linear programming**' sounds rather formidable and the technique *can* get very complicated. Don't worry though: you are only expected to be able to analyse the simplest examples, using a graphical technique (ie draw lines!). Get a ruler and sharpen your pencil!

Study guide

Section 19 – Limiting factors

- Explain and recognise what causes optimisation problems

- Identify, formulate and determine the optimal solution when there is a single limiting factor

- Formulate a linear programming problem involving two variables

- Determine the optimal solution to a linear programming problem using a graph

- Determine the optimal solution to a linear programming problem using equations

- Explain the methods available for dealing with optimisation problems with more than two variables

- Formulate, but do not solve, a linear programming problem involving more than two variables

Exam guide

The contents of this chapter are not one of the key areas of the syllabus. However, there was a compulsory ten-mark question in the pilot paper so you can expect to be examined on this topic in both Section A and Section B of your exam.

1   THE PROBLEM

Exam focus point

The study guide for Paper 1.2 states that candidates should be able to 'explain and recognise what causes **optimisation** problems'.

1.1 A typical business problem is to decide how a company should **divide up its production among the various types of product** it manufactures in order to obtain the **maximum possible profit**. A business cannot simply aim to produce as much as possible because there will be **limitations** or **constraints** within which the production must operate. Such constraints could be one or more of the following.

- Limited quantities of raw materials available
- A fixed number of man-hours per week for each type of worker
- Limited machine hours

1.2 Moreover, since the profits generated by different products vary, it may be better not to produce any of a less profitable line, but to concentrate all resources on producing the more profitable ones. On the other hand limitations in market demand could mean that some of the products produced may not be sold.

> **KEY TERM**
>
> **Linear programming** is a technique for solving problems of profit maximisation or cost minimisation and resource allocation. 'Programming' has nothing to do with computers: the word is simply used to denote a series of events.

2 FORMULATING THE PROBLEM

2.1 Let us imagine that B Ltd makes just two models, the Super and the Deluxe, and that the **only constraint** faced by the company is that **monthly machine capacity is restricted to 400 hours**. The Super requires 5 hours of machine time per unit and the Deluxe 1.5 hours. Government restrictions mean that the maximum number of units that can be sold each month is 150, that number being made up of any combination of the Super and the Deluxe.

2.2 Let us now work through the steps involved in setting up a linear programming model.

Step 1. **Define variables**

What are the quantities that the company can vary? Obviously not the number of machine hours or the maximum sales, which are fixed by external circumstances beyond the company's control. The only things which it can determine are the number of each type of unit to manufacture. It is these numbers which have to be determined in such a way as to get the maximum possible profit. Our variables will therefore be as follows.

Let x = the number of units of the Super manufactured.
Let y = the number of units of the Deluxe manufactured.

Step 2. **Establish constraints**

Having defined these two variables we can now translate the two constraints into inequalities involving the variables.

Let us first consider the machine hours constraint. Each Super requires 5 hours of machine time. Producing five Supers therefore requires $5 \times 5 = 25$ hours of machine time and, more generally producing x Supers will require $5x$ hours. Likewise producing y Deluxes will require $1.5y$ hours. The total machine hours needed to make x Supers and y Deluxes is $5x + 1.5y$. We know that this cannot be greater than 400 hours so we arrive at the following inequality.

$5x + 1.5y \leq 400$

We can obtain the other inequality more easily. The total number of Supers and Deluxes made each month is x + y but this has to be less than 150 due to government restrictions. The sales order constraint is therefore as follows.

$$x + y \leq 150$$

Non-negativity

The variables in linear programming models should usually be non-negative in value. In this example, for instance, you cannot make a negative number of units and so we need the following constraints.

$$x \geq 0; \ y \geq 0$$

Do not forget these non-negativity constraints when formulating a linear programming model.

Step 3. **Establish objective function**

We have yet to introduce the question of profits. Let us assume that the profit on each model is as follows.

	£
Super	100
Deluxe	200

The **objective** of B Ltd is to **maximise profit** and so the **function** to be maximised is as follows.

$$\text{Profit (P)} = 100x + 200y$$

The problem has now been reduced to the following four inequalities and one equation.

$$5x + 1.5y \leq 400$$
$$x + y \leq 150$$
$$x \geq 0$$
$$y \geq 0$$
$$P = 100x + 200y$$

Have you noticed that **the inequalities are all linear expressions**? If plotted on a graph, they would all give **straight lines**. This explains why the technique is called **linear programming** and also gives a hint as to how we should proceed with trying to find the solution to the problem.

Question 1

Patel plc manufactures two products, X and Y, in quantities x and y units per week respectively. The contribution is £60 per X and £70 per Y. For practical reasons, no more than 100 Xs can be produced per week. If Patel plc uses linear programming to determine a profit-maximising production policy and on the basis of this information, which one of the following constraints is correct?

A $x \leq 60$
B $y \leq 100$
C $x \leq 100$
D $60x + 70y \leq 100$

Answer

The correct answer is C because the question states that the number of Xs produced cannot exceed 100 and so $x \leq 100$.

BPP
PUBLISHING

Option A has no immediate bearing on the number of units of X produced which must be ≤ 100. (£60 represents the contribution per unit of X).

We have no information on the production volume of Product Y and option B is therefore incorrect.

The contribution earned per week is given by 60x + 70y but we have no reason to suppose that this must be less than or equal to 100. Option D is therefore incorrect.

Exam focus point

Students often have problems with constraints of the style 'the quantity of one type must not exceed twice that of the other'. This can be interpreted as follows: the quantity of one type (say X) must not exceed (must be less than or equal to) twice that of the other (2Y) (ie X ≤ 2Y).

3   GRAPHING THE MODEL

3.1   We have looked at how to **formulate a problem** and in this section we will look at solving a problem using graphs.

3.2   **A graphical solution is only possible when there are two variables in the problem. One variable is represented by the x axis and one by the y axis of the graph. Since non-negative values are not usually allowed, the graph shows only zero and positive values of x and y.**

3.3   A linear equation with one or two variables is shown as a straight line on a graph. Thus y = 6 would be shown as follows.

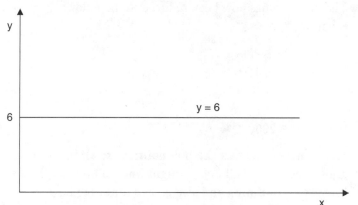

If the problem included a constraint that y could not exceed 6, the **inequality** y ≤ 6 would be represented by the shaded area of the graph below.

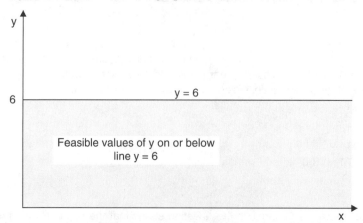

3.4   The equation 4x + 3y = 24 is also a straight line on a graph. To draw any straight line, we need only to plot two points and join them up. The easiest points to plot are the following.

(a) x = 0 (in this example, if x = 0, 3y = 24, y = 8)
(b) y = 0 (in this example, if y = 0, 4x = 24, x = 6)

By plotting the points, (0, 8) and (6, 0) on a graph, and joining them up, we have the line for 4x + 3y = 24.

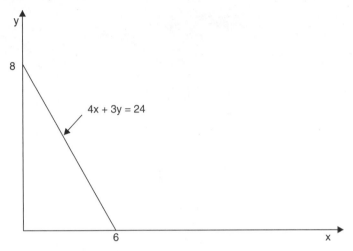

3.5   If we had a constraint 4x + 3y ≤ 24, any combined value of x and y within the shaded area below (on or below the line) would satisfy the constraint.

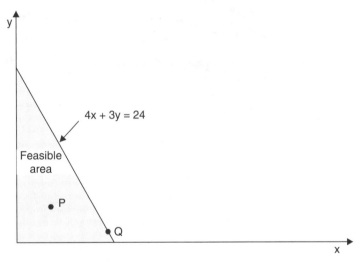

For example, at point P where (x = 2, y = 2) 4x + 3y = 14 which is less than 24; and at point Q where x = 5.5, y = 2/3, 4x + 3y = 24. Both P and Q lie within the **feasible area** (the area where the inequality is satisfied, also called the feasible region). A **feasible area** enclosed on all sides may also be called a **feasible polygon**.

3.6   The inequalities y ≥ 6, x ≥ 6 and 4x + 3y ≥ 24, would be shown graphically as follows.

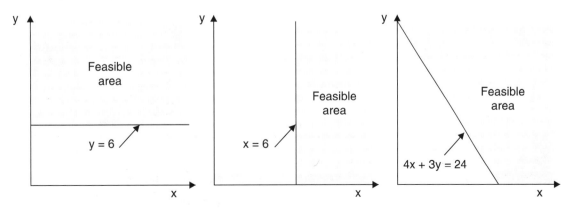

3.7 **When there are several constraints, the feasible area of combinations of values of x and y must be an area where all the inequalities are satisfied.**

Thus, if $y \leq 6$ *and* $4x + 3y \leq 24$ the feasible area would be the shaded area in the graph following

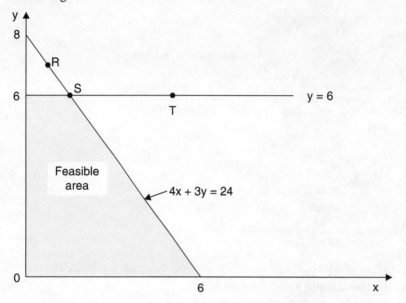

(a) Point R ($x = 0.75$, $y = 7$) is not in the feasible area because although it satisfies the inequality $4x + 3y \leq 24$, it does not satisfy $y \leq 6$.

(b) Point T ($x = 5$, $y = 6$) is not in the feasible area, because although it satisfies the inequality $y \leq 6$, it does not satisfy $4x + 3y \leq 24$.

(c) Point S ($x = 1.5$, $y = 6$) satisfies both inequalities and lies just on the boundary of the feasible area since $y = 6$ exactly, and $4x + 3y = 24$. Point S is thus at the intersection of the two equation lines.

3.8 Similarly, if $y \geq 6$ and $4x + 3y \geq 24$ but $x \leq 6$, the feasible area would be the shaded area in the graph below.

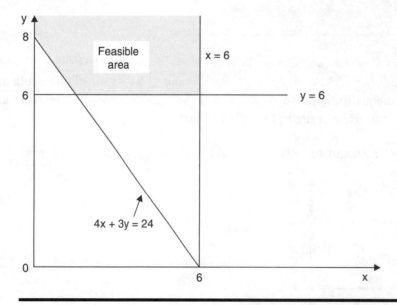

Question 2

Draw the feasible region which arises from the constraints facing B Ltd (see paragraph 2.2).

Answer

If $5x + 1.5y = 400$, then if $x = 0$, $y = 267$ and if $y = 0$, $x = 80$.
If $x + y = 150$, then if $x = 0$, $y = 150$ and if $y = 0$, $x = 150$

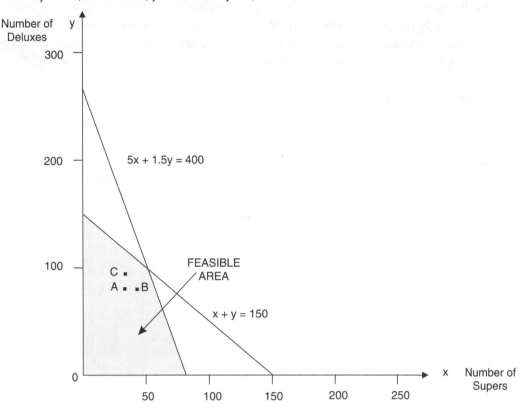

Question 3

In a linear programming problem, one of the constraints is given by $2x \leq 3y$. Which of the following statements about the graphical presentation of this constraint is correct?

I   The constraint line passes through the point $x = 2$, $y = 3$.
II   The constraint line passes through the origin.
III The constraint line passes through the point $x = 3$, $y = 2$.
IV The region below the constraint line is part of the feasible area.

A   I and II only
B   I and III only
C   II and III only
D   II, III and IV only

Answer

When $x = 0$ then y must also equal 0, therefore statement II is correct.

When $x = 3$, $6 = 3y$ and hence $y = 2$, therefore statement III is correct.

Statements II and III are correct and therefore option C is the right answer.

Statement I is incorrect since when $x = 2$, $4 = 3y$ and $y = 1.33$ and y does not equal 3 when $x = 2$.

Statement IV is incorrect since $3y$ is greater than $2x$ above the line, not below it.

---

4   FINDING THE BEST SOLUTION

4.1   Having found the **feasible region** (which includes all the possible solutions to the problem) we need to find which of these possible solutions is **'best'** in the sense that it yields the **maximum possible profit**. We could do this by finding out what profit each of the possible solutions would give, and then choosing as our 'best' combination the one for which the profit is greatest.

4.2 Consider, however, the feasible region of the problem faced by B Ltd (see the solution to Question 2). Even in such a simple problem as this, there are a great many possible solution points within the feasible area. Even to write them all down would be a time consuming process and also an unnecessary one, as we shall see.

4.3 Let us look again at the graph of B Ltd's problem.

Consider, for example, the point A at which 40 Supers and 80 Deluxes are being manufactured. This will yield a profit of $((40 \times 100) + (80 \times 200)) = £20,000$. We would clearly get more profit at point B, where the same number of Deluxes are being manufactured but where the number of Supers being manufactured has increased by five, or from point C where the same number of Supers but 10 more Deluxes are manufactured. This argument suggests that **the 'best' solution is going to be a point on the edge of the feasible area rather than in the middle of it.**

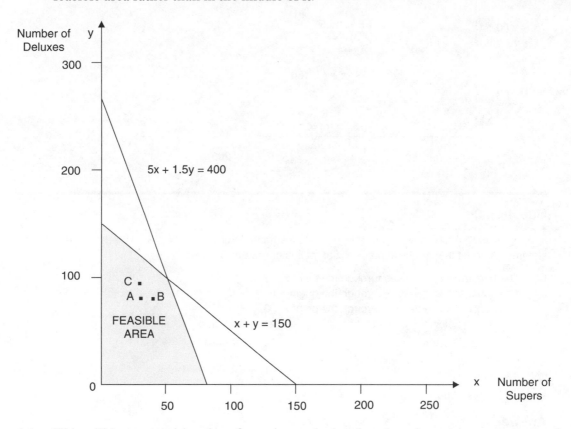

4.4 This still leaves us with quite a few points to look at but there is a way we can narrow down the candidates for the best solution still further. Suppose that B Ltd wish to make a profit of £10,000. The company could sell the following combinations of Supers and Deluxes.

(a) 100 Super, no Deluxe

(b) No Super, 50 Deluxe

(c) A proportionate mix of Super and Deluxe, such as 80 Super and 10 Deluxe or 50 Super and 25 Deluxe

4.5 The possible combinations of Supers and Deluxes required to earn a profit of £10,000 could be shown by the straight line $100x + 200y = 10,000$.

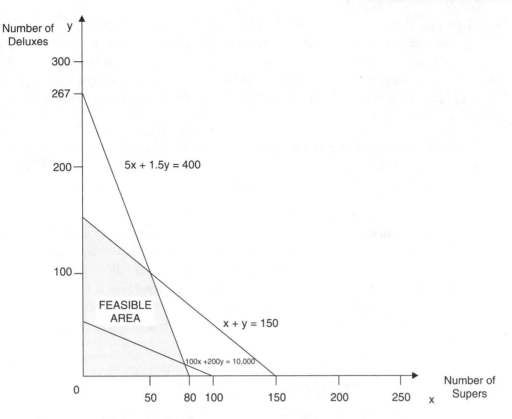

4.6   For a total profit of £15,000, a similar line $100x + 200y = 15,000$ could be drawn to show the various combinations of Supers and Deluxes which would achieve the total of £15,000.

Similarly a line $100x + 200y = 8,000$ would show the various combinations of Supers and Deluxes which would earn a total profit of £8,000.

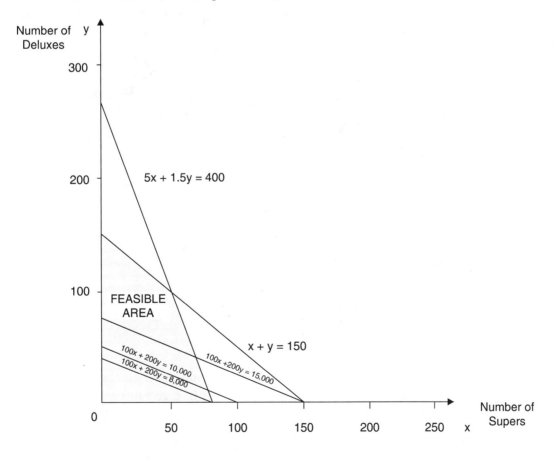

4.7   **These profit lines are all parallel.** (They are called **iso-profit lines,** 'iso' meaning equal.) A similar line drawn for any other total profit would also be parallel to the three lines shown here. This means that if we wish to know the slope or gradient of the profit line, for any value of total profit, we can simply draw one line for any convenient value of profit, and we will know that all the other lines will be parallel to the one drawn: they will have the same slope.

4.8   **Bigger profits are shown by lines further from the origin** $(100x + 200y = 15,000)$, **smaller profits by lines closer to the origin** $(100x + 200y = 8,000)$. As B Ltd try to **increase possible profit** we need to **slide the profit line outwards from the origin**, while always keeping it **parallel** to the other profit lines.

4.9   As we do this there will come a point at which, if we were to move the profit line out any further, it would cease to lie in the feasible region and therefore larger profits could not be achieved in practice because of the constraints. In our example concerning B Ltd this will happen, as you should test for yourself, where the profit line is just passing through the intersection of $x + y = 150$ with the y axis (at $(0, 150)$). The point $(0, 150)$ will therefore give us the best production combination of the Super and the Deluxe, that is, to produce 150 Deluxe models and no Super models.

4.10 EXAMPLE: A MAXIMISATION PROBLEM

Brunel Ltd manufactures plastic-covered steel fencing in two qualities, standard and heavy gauge. Both products pass through the same processes, involving steel-forming and plastic bonding.

Standard gauge fencing sells at £18 a roll and heavy gauge fencing at £24 a roll. Variable costs per roll are £16 and £21 respectively. There is an unlimited market for the standard gauge, but demand for the heavy gauge is limited to 1,300 rolls a year. Factory operations are limited to 2,400 hours a year in each of the two production processes.

	Processing hours per roll	
Gauge	*Steel-forming*	*Plastic-bonding*
Standard	0.6	0.4
Heavy	0.8	1.2

What is the production mix which will maximise total contribution and what would be the total contribution?

4.11 SOLUTION

(a) Let S be the number of standard gauge rolls per year.

Let H be the number of heavy gauge rolls per year.

The objective is to maximise 2S + 3H (contribution) subject to the following constraints.

$$0.6S + 0.8H \leq 2,400 \text{(steel-forming hours)}$$
$$0.4S + 1.2H \leq 2,400 \text{(plastic-bonding hours)}$$
$$H \leq 1,300 \text{(sales demand)}$$
$$S, H \geq 0$$

Note that **the constraints are inequalities,** and are not equations. There is no requirement to use up the total hours available in each process, nor to satisfy all the demand for heavy gauge rolls.

(b) If we take the production constraint of 2,400 hours in the steel-forming process

$$0.6S + 0.8H \leq 2,400$$

it means that since there are only 2,400 hours available in the process, output must be limited to a maximum of:

(i) $\dfrac{2,400}{0.6}$ = 4,000 rolls of standard gauge;

(ii) $\dfrac{2,400}{0.8}$ = 3,000 rolls of heavy gauge; or

(iii) a proportionate combination of each.

This maximum output represents the boundary line of the constraint, where the inequality becomes the equation

$0.6S + 0.8H = 2,400$.

(c) The line for this equation may be drawn on a graph by joining up two points on the line (such as S = 0, H = 3,000; H = 0, S = 4,000).

(d) The other constraints may be drawn in a similar way with lines for the following equations.

$$0.4S + 1.2H = 2,400 \quad \text{(plastic-bonding)}$$
$$H = 1,300 \quad \text{(sales demand)}$$

(e)

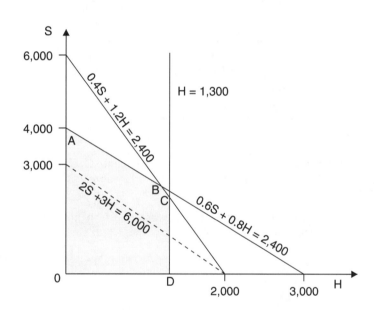

To satisfy all the constraints simultaneously, the values of S and H must lie on or below each constraint line. The outer limits of the **feasible polygon** are the lines, but all combined values of S and H within the shaded area are **feasible solutions**.

(f) The next step is to find the **optimal solution**, which **maximises the objective function**. Since the objective is to **maximise contribution**, the solution to the problem must involve relatively high values (within the feasible polygon) for S, or H or a combination of both.

If, as is likely, there is only one combination of S and H which provides the optimal solution, this combination will be one of the **outer corners of the feasible polygon**. There are four such corners, A, B, C and D. However, it is possible that any combination of values for S and H on the boundary line between two of these corners might provide solutions with the same total contribution.

(g) To solve the problem we establish **the slope of the iso-contribution lines,** by drawing a line for any one level of contribution. In our solution, a line 2S + 3H = 6,000 has

361 **BPP**
PUBLISHING

been drawn. (6,000 was chosen as a convenient multiple of 2 and 3). **This line has no significance except to indicate the slope, or gradient, of every iso-contribution line for 2S + 3H.**

Using a ruler to judge at which corner of the feasible polygon we can draw an **iso-contribution line** which is as far to the right as possible, (away from the origin) but which still touches the **feasible polygon**.

(h)   This occurs at corner B where the constraint line 0.4S + 1.2H = 2,400 crosses with the constraint line 0.6S + 0.8H = 2,400. At this point, there are simultaneous equations, from which the exact values of S and H may be calculated.

$$
\begin{aligned}
0.4S + \quad 1.2H &= 2,400 & (1) \\
0.6S + \quad 0.8H &= 2,400 & (2) \\
1.2S + \quad 3.6H &= 7,200 & (3)\ ((1) \times 3) \\
1.2S + \quad 1.6H &= 4,800 & (4)\ ((2) \times 2) \\
2H &= 2,400 & (5)\ ((3) - (4)) \\
H &= 1,200 & (6)
\end{aligned}
$$

Substituting 1,200 for H in either equation, we can calculate that S = 2,400.

The contribution is maximised where H = 1,200, and S = 2,400.

	Units	Contribution per unit £	Total contribution £
Standard gauge	2,400	2	4,800
Heavy gauge	1,200	3	3,600
			8,400

Question 4

The Dervish Chemical Company operates a small plant. Operating the plant requires two raw materials, A and B, which cost £5 and £8 per litre respectively. The maximum available supply per week is 2,700 litres of A and 2,000 litres of B.

The plant can operate using either of two processes, which have differing contributions and raw materials requirements, as follows.

Process	Raw materials consumed (litres per processing hour)		Contribution per hour £
	A	B	
1	20	10	70
2	30	20	60

The plant can run for 120 hours a week in total, but for safety reasons, process 2 cannot be operated for more than 80 hours a week.

Formulate a linear programming model, and then solve it, to determine how many hours process 1 should be operated each week and how many hours process 2 should be operated each week.

Answer

The decision variables are processing hours in each process. If we let the processing hours per week for process 1 be P_1 and the processing hours per week for process 2 be P_2 we can formulate an objective and constraints as follows.

The objective is to maximise $70P_1 + 60P_2$, subject to the following constraints.

$$
\begin{aligned}
20P_1 + 30P_2 &\leq 2,700 & \text{(material A supply)} \\
10P_1 + 20P_2 &\leq 2,000 & \text{(material B supply)} \\
P_2 &\leq 80 & \text{(maximum time for } P_2 \text{)} \\
P_1 + P_2 &\leq 120 & \text{(total maximum time)} \\
P_1, P_2 &\geq 0 & \text{(non-negativity)}
\end{aligned}
$$

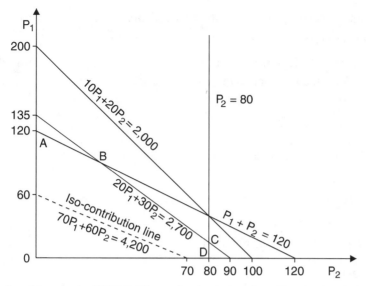

The feasible area is ABCDO. The optimal solution, found by moving the iso-contribution line outwards, is at point A, where P_1 = 120 and P_2 = 0. Total contribution would be 120×70 = £8,400 a week.

Multiple solutions

4.12 **It is possible that the optimum position might lie, not at a particular corner, but all along the length of one of the sides of the feasibility polygon. This will occur if the iso-contribution line is exactly parallel to one of the constraint lines.**

4.13 If this happens then there is no one optimum solution but a **range of optimum solutions**. All of these will maximise the objective function at the same level. However, *any* value of the decision variables that happens to satisfy the constraint between the points where the constraint line forms part of the feasibility region would produce this optimum level of contribution.

Minimisation problems in linear programming

4.14 Although decision problems with limiting factors usually involve the maximisation of contribution, there may be a requirement to **minimise costs**. A graphical solution, involving two variables, is very similar to that for a maximisation problem, with the exception that instead of finding a contribution line touching the feasible area as far away from the origin as possible, we look for a **total cost line touching the feasible area as close to the origin as possible.**

4.15 EXAMPLE: A MINIMISATION PROBLEM

Bilton Sandys Ltd has undertaken a contract to supply a customer with at least 260 units in total of two products, X and Y, during the next month. At least 50% of the total output must be units of X. The products are each made by two grades of labour, as follows.

	X *Hours*	Y *Hours*
Grade A labour	4	6
Grade B labour	4	2
Total	8	8

Although additional labour can be made available at short notice, the company wishes to make use of 1,200 hours of Grade A labour and 800 hours of Grade B labour which has already been assigned to working on the contract next month. The total variable cost per unit is £120 for X and £100 for Y.

Bilton Sandys Ltd wishes to minimise expenditure on the contract next month. How much of X and Y should be supplied in order to meet the terms of the contract?

4.16 SOLUTION

(a) Let the number of units of X supplied be x, and the number of units of Y supplied be y.

The objective is to minimise 120x + 100y (costs), subject to the following constraints.

x + y	≥	260	(supply total)
x	≥	0.5 (x + y)	(proportion of x in total)
4x + 6y	≥	1,200	(Grade A labour)
4x + 2y	≥	800	(Grade B labour)
x, y	≥	0	

The constraint x ≥ 0.5 (x + y) needs simplifying further.

x	≥ 0.5 (x + y)
2x	≥ x + y
x	≥ y

In a graphical solution, the line will be x = y. Check this carefully in the following diagram.

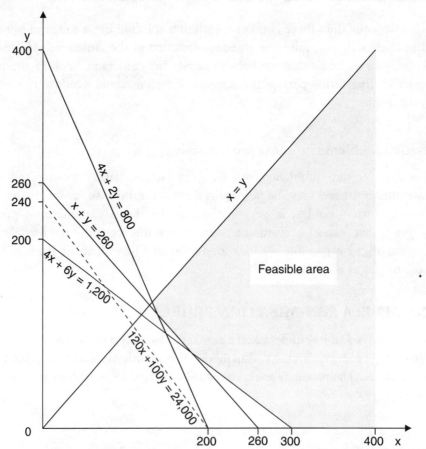

(b) The cost line 120x + 100y = 24,000 has been drawn to show the slope of every cost line 120x + 100 y. **Costs are minimised where a cost line touches the feasible area as close as possible to the origin of the graph.** This occurs where the constraint line 4x + 2y = 800 crosses the constraint line x + y = 260. This point is found as follows.

$$
\begin{array}{rcll}
x + y &=& 260 & (1) \\
4x + 2y &=& 800 & (2) \\
2x + y &=& 400 & (3)\,((2) \div 2) \\
x &=& 140 & (4)\,((3) - (1)) \\
y &=& 120 & (5)
\end{array}
$$

(c) Costs will be minimised by supplying the following.

	Unit cost £	Total cost £
140 units of X	120	16,800
120 units of Y	100	12,000
		28,800

The proportion of units of X in the total would exceed 50%, and demand for Grade A labour would exceed the 1,200 hours minimum.

The use of simultaneous equations

4.17 You might think that a lot of time could be saved if we started by solving the simultaneous equations in a linear programming problem and did not bother to draw the graph. Certainly, this procedure may give the right answer, but in general, it is *not* recommended until you have shown graphically which constraints are effective in determining the optimal solution. (In particular, if a question requires 'the graphical method', you *must* draw a graph). To illustrate this point, consider the following graph.

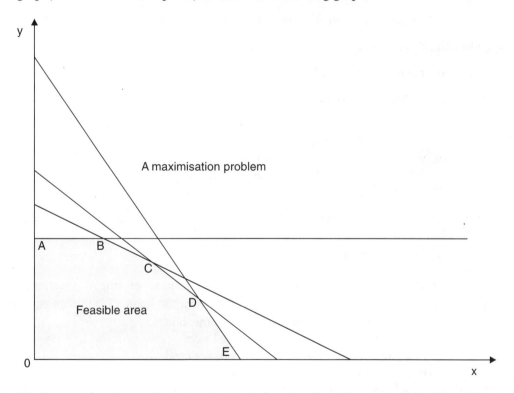

4.18 No figures have been given on the graph but the feasible area is OABCDE. When solving this problem, we would know that the optimum solution would be at one of the corners of the feasible area. We need to work out the profit at each of the corners of the feasible area and pick the one where the profit is greatest.

Once the optimum point has been determined graphically, simultaneous equations can be applied to find the exact values of x and y at this point.

5   TWO-PLUS VARIABLE MODELS

5.1   **The graphical method cannot be used when there are more than two decision variables. A method called the simplex method is available in these circumstances,** but in practice it is much easier to use a computer. You are expected to be able to **formulate problems** for a solution and to interpret the results of a solution, but not actually to work out the solution for yourself.

5.2   TDS Ltd manufactures two products, X and Y, which earn a contribution of £8 and £14 per unit respectively. At current selling prices, there is no limit to sales demand for Y, but maximum demand for X would be 1,200 units. The company aims to maximise its annual profits, and fixed costs are £15,000 per annum. In the year to 30 June 20X2, the company expects to have a limited availability of resources and estimates of availability are:

Skilled labour	maximum 9,000 hours
Machine time	maximum 4,000 hours
Material M	maximum 1,000 tonnes

The usage of these resources per unit of product are:

	X	Y
Skilled labour time	3 hours	4 hours
Machine time	1 hour	2 hours
Material M	½ tonne	¼ tonne

5.3   The linear programming problem would now be formulated as follows:

Let x and y be the number of units made and sold of product X and product Y respectively.

Objective function

Maximise contribution $= 8x + 14y$

Subject to the following constraints

$3x + 4y$	$\leq$	9,000	(skilled labour)*
$x + 2y$	$\leq$	4,000	(machine time)
$0.5x + 0.25y$	$\leq$	1,000	(material M)
x	$\leq$	1,200	(demand for X)
x, y	$\geq$	0	

* This constraint is that skilled labour hours cannot exceed 9,000 hours, and since a unit of X needs 3 hours and a unit of Y needs 4 hours, $3x + 4y$ cannot exceed 9,000. The other constraints are formulated in a similar way.

5.4   The problem can be solved using the simplex technique of linear programming by introducing a **slack variable** into each constraint, to turn the inequality into an equation.

Let	a	=	the number of unused skilled labour hours
	b	=	the number of unused machine hours
	c	=	the number of unused tonnes of material M
	d	=	the amount by which demand for X falls short of 1,200 units.

Then

$3x + 4y + a$	=	9,000	(labour hours)
$x + 2y + b$	=	4,000	(machine hours)
$0.5x + 0.25y + c$	=	1,000	(tonnes of M)
$x + d$	=	1,200	(demand for X)

5.5   The **simplex technique** uses the decision variables (here x and y) and the slack variables to test a number of feasible solutions to the problem until the **optimal solution** is found (here, until the combination of values for x, y, a, b, c and d is found that maximises total contribution).

The technique is a repetitive step-by-step process (and therefore an ideal computer application), that tests a number of **feasible solutions** in turn. If the manual process is used this is done in the form of a tableau (or 'table' or 'matrix') of figures. This is best illustrated by giving the final tableau to the problem here, which shows the **contribution-maximising** solution.

Variables in the solution	x	y	a	b	c	d	Solution column
x	1	0	1	-2	0	0	1,000
y	0	1	-0.5	1.5	0	0	1,500
c	0	0	-0.375	0.625	1	0	125
d	0	0	-1	2	0	1	200
Solution row	0	0	1	5	0	0	29,000

Interpretation of the final tableau

5.6 There is a column in the tableau for every variable, including the slack variables, but the important parts of the tableau are the '**variables in the solution**' column, the **solution row**, and the **solution column**. These tell us a number of things.

5.7 The variables in the solution are x, y, c and d. It follows that a and b have **zero values**. To be the variable in the solution on a particular row of the table, a value of 1 must appear in the **column** for that variable, with **zero values** in every other row of that column. For example, x is the variable in the solution for the row which has 1 in the x column. There are zeros in every other row in the x column.

5.8 **The solution column gives the value of each variable.**

x	1,000	(units made of X)
y	1,500	(units made of Y)
c	125	(unused material M)
d	200	(amount below the 1,200 maximum of demand for X)

This means that contribution will be maximised by making and selling 1,000 units of X and 1,500 units of Y. This will leave 125 unused tonnes of material M, and production and sales of X will be 200 units below the limit of sales demand. Since a and b are both zero, there is no unused labour and machine time; in other words, all the available labour and machine hours will be fully utilised.

5.9 The value of the **objective function** - here, the **total contribution** - is in both the solution row and the solution column. Here it is £29,000.

Shadow prices

5.10 The **solution row** gives the **shadow prices** of each variable. (They might be shown with negative rather than positive values).

> **KEY TERM**
>
> The **shadow price** of a resource is the amount by which the value of the objective function (contribution) will go up (or down) if one unit more (or less) of the resource were made available. The shadow price is also known as the **dual price**.

Here, the shadow prices are:

a £1 per labour hour
b £5 per machine hour

5.11 This means that if more labour hours could be made available **at their normal variable cost per hour** total contribution could be increased by £1 per extra labour hour. Similarly, if more machine time could be made available, **at its normal variable cost**, total contribution could be increased by £5 per extra machine hour.

5.12 **The shadow or dual price is the opportunity cost of the scarce resources, which is the amount of benefit forgone by not having the availability of the extra resources.**

If in this example labour is paid £3 per hour, but extra labour could be made available by paying 20% more per extra hour worked (£3.60 per hour), then it would be beneficial to take on the extra labour, given the objective to maximise short-term profits. The extra labour would cost 60 pence per hour above the normal variable cost, and since the shadow price of labour is £1 per hour, there would be a net gain to the company of 40 pence per hour.

Chapter roundup

- **Linear programming**, at least at this fairly simple level, is a technique that can be carried out in a fairly 'handle-turning' manner once you have got the basic ideas sorted out. The steps involved are as follows.

  o Define variables
  o Establish constraints (including non-negativity)
  o Construct objective function
  o Draw a graph of the constraints
  o Establish the feasible region
  o Add an iso-profit/contribution line
  o Determine optimal solution

- The **graphical method** can only cope with two variables. If there are more than two decision variables a computer software package is likely to be used.

Quick quiz

1 What are the three main steps involved in setting up a linear programming model?

Step 1. ....Define Variables....................................

Step 2. ....Establish Constraints............................

Step 3. ....Establish objective functions................

2 Draw the inequality 4x + 3y ≤ 24 on the graph below.

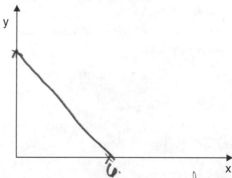

3 A feasible area enclosed on all sides may also be called a ...polygon.................. .

4 How does the graphical solution of minimisation problems differ from that of maximisation problems?

5   The graphical method cannot be used when there are more than two decision variables.

     True   [✓]

     False   [   ]

6   When there are more than two decision variables a method called the ....Simplex............
     method is available in these circumstances.

7   What is a shadow price? Dual Price.

Answers to quick quiz

1   **Step 1.**   Define variables
     Step 2.   Establish constraints
     Step 3.   Establish objective function

2
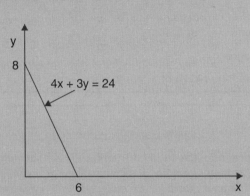

3   Feasible polygon.

4   Instead of finding a contribution line touching the feasible area as far away from the origin as possible, we look for a total cost line touching the feasible area **as close to the origin as possible**.

5   True

6   Simplex

7   The **shadow price** of a resource is the amount by which the value of the objective function (contribution) will go up (or down) if one unit more (or less) of the resource were made available. The shadow price is also known as the **dual price.**

Now try the questions below from the Exam Question Bank

Number	Level	Marks	Time
32	MCQ	n/a	n/a
33	Examination	10	18 mins

Chapter 19

INTEREST

Topic list	Syllabus reference
1 Simple interest	6(i)
2 Compound interest	6(i)
3 Regular savings and sinking funds	6(i)
4 Loans and mortgages	6(i)
5 Annual Percentage Rate (APR) of interest	6(i)

Introduction

We now turn our attention to the topic of **interest**. This chapter (and the next) deal with the problems of **investing money** or **capital**. If a company (or an individual investor) puts some capital into an investment, a **financial return** will be expected. When you invest your savings in a building society account, you expect your money to grow (or **compound**) over time. This chapter shall describe the technique of **compounding** and chapter 20 will describe the technique of **discounting**.

Study guide

Section 23 – Interest

- Explain the difference between simple and compound interest
- Explain the difference between nominal and effective interest rates and calculate effective interest rates
- Explain what is meant by future values

Exam guide

Discounted cash flow techniques is a key topic area of the syllabus for **Financial Information for Management**. Discounted cashflow techniques relevant to this chapter include the following (as per the syllabus).

- Simple and compound interest
- Annuities
- Future values
- Nominal interest

1   SIMPLE INTEREST

> **KEY TERM**
>
> - **Interest** is the amount of money which an investment earns over time.
>
> - **Simple interest** is interest which is earned in equal amounts every year (or month) and which is a given proportion of the original investment (the principal).

1.1 If a sum of money is invested for a period of time, then the amount of simple interest which accrues is equal to the number of periods × the interest rate × the amount invested. We can write this as a formula.

> **FORMULA TO LEARN**
>
> The formula for **simple interest** is as follows.
>
> $S = P + nrP$
>
> where P = the original sum invested
>
> r = the interest rate (expressed as a proportion, so 10% = 0.1)
>
> n = the number of periods (normally years)
>
> S = the sum invested after n periods, consisting of the original capital (X) plus interest earned (future value)

1.2 EXAMPLE: SIMPLE INTEREST

How much will an investor have after five years if he invests £1,000 at 10% simple interest per annum?

1.3 SOLUTION

Using the formula $S = P + nrP$

where P = £1,000
   r = 10%
   n = 5

∴ $S = £1,000 + (5 \times 0.1 \times £1,000) = £1,500$

1.4 If, for example, the sum of money is invested for 3 months and the interest rate is a rate per annum, then $n = {}^3/_{12} = {}^1/_4$. If the investment period is 197 days and the rate is an annual rate, then $n = {}^{197}/_{365}$.

2 COMPOUND INTEREST

Compounding

2.1 Interest is normally calculated by means of **compounding**.

If a sum of money, the principal, is invested at a fixed rate of interest such that the interest is added to the principal and no withdrawals are made, then the amount invested will grow by an increasing number of pounds in each successive time period, because **interest earned in earlier periods will itself earn interest in later periods**.

2.2 EXAMPLE: COMPOUND INTEREST

Suppose that £2,000 is invested at 10% interest. After one year, the original principal plus interest will amount to £2,200.

	£
Original investment	2,000
Interest in the first year (10%)	200
Total investment at the end of one year	2,200

(a) After two years the total investment will be £2,420.

	£
Investment at end of one year	2,200
Interest in the second year (10%)	220
Total investment at the end of two years	2,420

The second year interest of £220 represents 10% of the original investment, and 10% of the interest earned in the first year.

(b) Similarly, after three years, the total investment will be £2,662.

	£
Investment at the end of two years	2,420
Interest in the third year (10%)	242
Total investment at the end of three years	2,662

2.3 Instead of performing the calculations in Paragraph 2.2, we could have used the following formula.

> **EXAM FORMULA**
>
> The basic formula for **compound interest** is $S = P(1 + r)^n$
>
> where P = the original sum invested
>
> r = the interest rate, expressed as a proportion (so 5% = 0.05)
>
> n = the number of periods
>
> S = the sum invested after n periods (future value)

2.4 Using the formula for compound interest, $S = P(1 + r)^n$

where P = £2,000

r = 10% = 0.1

n = 3

S = £2,000 × 1.10^3

= £2,000 × 1.331

= £2,662.

The interest earned over three years is £662, which is the same answer that was calculated in the example above.

Question 1

What would be the total value of £5,000 invested now:

(a) after three years, if the interest rate is 20% per annum;
(b) after four years, if the interest rate is 15% per annum;
(c) after three years, if the interest rate is 6% per annum?

Answer

(a) £5,000 × 1.20^3 = £8,640
(b) £5,000 × 1.15^4 = £8,745.03
(c) £5,000 × 1.06^3 = £5,955.08

Question 2

At what annual rate of compound interest will £2,000 grow to £2,721 after four years?

A 7% B 8% C 9% D 10%

Answer

Using the formula for compound interest, $S = P(1 + r)^n$, we know that P = £2,000, S = £2,721 and n = 4. We need to find r. It is essential that you are able to rearrange equations confidently when faced with this type of multiple choice question - there is not a lot of room for guessing!

$$
\begin{aligned}
2{,}721 &= 2{,}000 \times (1 + r)^4 \\
(1 + r)^4 &= 2{,}721/2{,}000 = 1.3605 \\
1 + r &= \sqrt[4]{1.3605} = 1.08 \\
r &= 0.08 = 8\%
\end{aligned}
$$

The correct answer is B.

Inflation

2.5 The same compounding formula can be used to **predict future prices** after allowing for **inflation**. For example, if we wish to predict the salary of an employee in five years time, given that he earns £8,000 now and wage inflation is expected to be 10% per annum, the compound interest formula would be applied as follows.

$$
\begin{aligned}
S &= P(1 + r)^n \\
&= £8{,}000 \times 1.10^5 \\
&= £12{,}884.08
\end{aligned}
$$

say, £12,900.

Withdrawals of capital or interest

2.6 If an investor takes money out of an investment, it will cease to earn interest. Thus, if an investor puts £3,000 into a bank deposit account which pays interest at 8% per annum, and makes no withdrawals except at the end of year 2, when he takes out £1,000, what would be the balance in his account after four years?

	£
Original investment	3,000.00
Interest in year 1 (8%)	240.00
Investment at end of year 1	3,240.00
Interest in year 2 (8%)	259.20
Investment at end of year 2	3,499.20
Less withdrawal	1,000.00
Net investment at start of year 3	2,499.20
Interest in year 3 (8%)	199.94
Investment at end of year 3	2,699.14
Interest in year 4 (8%)	215.93
Investment at end of year 4	2,915.07

2.7 A quicker approach would be as follows.

	£
£3,000 invested for 2 years at 8% would increase in value to £3,000 $\times 1.08^2 =$	3,499.20
Less withdrawal	1,000.00
	2,499.20

£2,499.20 invested for a further two years at 8% would increase in value to

£2,499.20 × 1.08² = £2,915.07

Reverse compounding

2.8 The basic principle of compounding can be applied in a number of different situations.

Reducing balance depreciation

2.9 The basic compound interest formula can be used to deal with one method of **depreciation** (as you should already know, depreciation is an accounting technique whereby the cost of a capital asset is spread over a number of different accounting periods as a charge against profit in each of the periods).

2.10 The reducing balance method of depreciation is a kind of **reverse compounding** in which **the value of the asset goes down at a certain rate**. The **rate of 'interest'** is therefore **negative**.

2.11 EXAMPLE: REDUCING BALANCE DEPRECIATION

An item of equipment is bought for £1,000 and is to be depreciated at a fixed rate of 40% per annum. What will be its value at the end of four years?

2.12 SOLUTION

A depreciation rate of 40% equates to a **negative rate of interest**, therefore r = –40% = –0.4. We are told that P = £1,000 and that n = 4. Using the formula for compound interest we can calculate the value of S, the value of the equipment at the end of four years.

$$S = P(1 + r)^n = 1,000(1 + (-0.4))^4 = £129.60.$$

Falling prices

2.13 As well as rising at a compound rate, perhaps because of inflation, costs can also **fall at a compound rate**.

2.14 EXAMPLE: FALLING PRICES

Suppose that the cost of product X is currently £10.80. It is estimated that over the next five years its cost will **fall by 10% pa compound**. The cost of product X at the end of five years is therefore calculated as follows, using the formula for compound interest, $S = P(1 + r)^n$.

P = £10.80
r = –10% = –0.1
n = 5
∴ S = £10.80 × $(1 + (-0.1))^5$ = £6.38

Changes in the rate of interest

2.15 It is possible that the rate of interest will change during the period of an investment. When this happens, the compounding formula must be amended slightly.

FORMULA TO LEARN

The formula for **compound interest** when there are **changes in the rate of interest** is as follows.

$$S = P(1 + r_1)^y (1 + r_2)^{n-y}$$

where r_1 = the initial rate of interest

  y = the number of years in which the interest rate r_1 applies

  r_2 = the next rate of interest

  $n - y$ = the (balancing) number of years in which the interest rate r_2 applies.

Question 3

(a) If £8,000 is invested now, to earn 10% interest for three years and 8% thereafter, what would be the size of the total investment at the end of five years?

(b) An investor puts £10,000 into an investment for ten years. The annual rate of interest earned is 15% for the first four years, 12% for the next four years and 9% for the final two years. How much will the investment be worth at the end of ten years?

(c) An item of equipment costs £6,000 now. The annual rates of inflation over the next four years are expected to be 16%, 20%, 15% and 10%. How much would the equipment cost after four years?

Answer

(a) £8,000 $\times 1.10^3 \times 1.08^2$ = £12,419.83

(b) £10,000 $\times 1.15^4 \times 1.12^4 \times 1.09^2$ = £32,697.64

(c) £6,000 $\times 1.16 \times 1.20 \times 1.15 \times 1.10$ = £10,565.28

3 REGULAR SAVINGS AND SINKING FUNDS

3.1 An investor may decide to add to his investment from time to time, and you may be asked to calculate the **future value** (or **terminal value**) of an investment to which equal annual amounts will be added. An example might be an individual or a company making annual payments into a pension fund: we may wish to know the value of the fund after n years.

3.2 EXAMPLE: REGULAR SAVINGS

A person invests £400 now, and a further £400 each year for three more years. How much would the total investment be worth after four years, if interest is earned at the rate of 10% per annum?

3.3 SOLUTION

In problems such as this, we call **now 'Year 0'**, the time **one year from now 'Year 1'** and so on. It is also a good idea to draw a time line in order to establish exactly when payments are made.

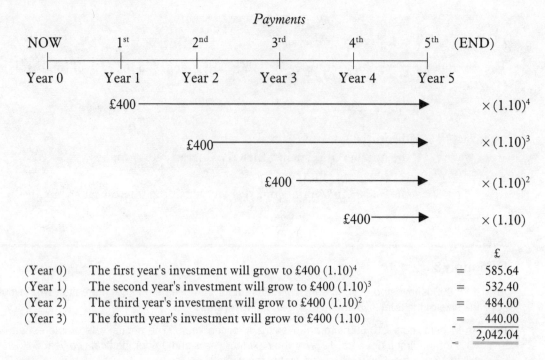

			£
(Year 0)	The first year's investment will grow to £400 (1.10)^4	=	585.64
(Year 1)	The second year's investment will grow to £400 (1.10)^3	=	532.40
(Year 2)	The third year's investment will grow to £400 (1.10)^2	=	484.00
(Year 3)	The fourth year's investment will grow to £400 (1.10)	=	440.00
			2,042.04

3.4   The solution can be written as $(400 \times 1.1) + (400 \times 1.1^2) + (400 \times 1.1^3) + (400 \times 1.1^4)$ with the values placed in reverse order for convenience. This is a **geometric progression** with A (the first term) $= (400 \times 1.1)$, R = 1.1 and n = 4. (Look at the Basic Maths supplement that comes with this Study Text if you are unfamiliar with geometric progressions.)

FORMULA TO LEARN

The sum of a **geometric progression**, $S = \dfrac{A(R^n - 1)}{R - 1}$

where   A = the first term
        R = the common ratio
        n = the number of terms

In our example:

   A = 400 × 1.1
   R = 1.1
   n = 4

If $S = \dfrac{A(R^n - 1)}{R - 1}$

   $S = \dfrac{400 \times 1.1(1.1^4 - 1)}{1.1 - 1}$

   = £2,042.04

3.5   EXAMPLE: INVESTMENTS AT THE ENDS OF YEARS

(a)   If, in the previous example, the investments had been made at the end of each of the first, second, third and fourth years, so that the last £400 invested had no time to earn interest. We can show this situation on the following time line.

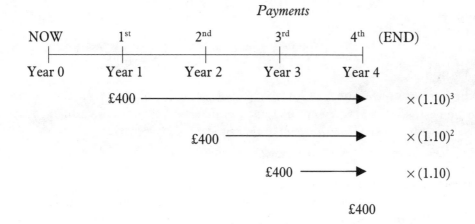

Payments

(Year 0)   No payment
(Year 1)   The first year's investment will grow to £400 × (1.10)³
(Year 2)   The second year's investment will grow to £400 × (1.10)²
(Year 3)   The third year's investment will grow to £400 × (1.10)
(Year 4)   The fourth year's investment remains at £400

The value of the fund at the end of the four years is as follows.

$$400 + (400 \times 1.1) + (400 \times 1.1^2) + (400 \times 1.1^3)$$

This is a **geometric progression** with

$$A = £400$$
$$R = 1.1$$
$$n = 4$$

If $S = \dfrac{A(R^n - 1)}{R - 1}$

$S = \dfrac{400\,(1.1^4 - 1)}{1.1 - 1}$

$= £1,856.40$

(b) If our investor made investments as in (a) above, but also put in a £2,500 lump sum one year from now, the value of the fund after four years would be

$£1,856.40 + £2,500 \times 1.1^3$
$= £1,856.40 + £3,327.50 = £5,183.90$

That is, **we can compound parts of investments separately, and add up the results.**

Question 4

A man invests £1,000 now, and a further £1,000 each year for five more years. How much would the total investment be worth after six years, if interest is earned at the rate of 8% per annum?

Answer

This is a geometric progression with A (the first term) = £1,000 × 1.08, R = 1.08 and n=6.

If $S = \dfrac{A(R^n - 1)}{R - 1}$

$S = \dfrac{1,000 \times 1.08\,(1.08^6 - 1)}{1.08 - 1}$

$= £7,922.80$

Sinking funds

> ### KEY TERM
>
> A **sinking fund** is an investment into which equal annual instalments are paid in order to earn interest, so that by the end of a given number of years, the investment is large enough to pay off a known commitment at that time.

3.6 Repayments against a repayment mortgage can of course be seen as payments into a sinking fund. The total of the constant annual payments (which are usually paid in equal monthly instalments) plus the interest they earn over the term of the mortgage must be sufficient to pay off the initial loan plus accrued interest. We shall be looking at mortgages later on in this chapter.

3.7 Another common known future commitment is the need to **replace an asset at the end of its life**. To ensure that the money is available to buy a replacement a company might decide to invest cash in a sinking fund during the course of the life of the existing asset.

3.8 EXAMPLE: SINKING FUNDS

A company has just bought an asset with a life of four years. At the end of four years, a replacement asset will cost £12,000, and the company has decided to provide for this future commitment by setting up a sinking fund into which equal annual investments will be made, starting at year 1 (one year from now). The fund will earn interest at 12%.

Required

Calculate the annual investment.

3.9 SOLUTION

Let us start by drawing a time line where £A = equal annual investments.

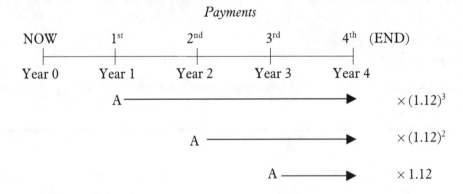

(Year 0)   No payment
(Year 1)   The first year's investment will grow to $£A \times (1.12)^3$
(Year 2)   The second year's investment will grow to $£A \times (1.12)^2$
(Year 3)   The third year's investment will grow to $£A \times (1.12)$
(Year 4)   The fourth year's investment will remain at £A.

The value of the fund at the end of four years is as follows.

$$A + A(1.12) + A(1.12^2) + A(1.12^3)$$

This is a geometric progression with

A = A
R = 1.12
n = 4

The value of the sinking fund at the end of year 4 is £12,000 (given in the question) therefore

$$£12,000 = \frac{A(1.12^4 - 1)}{1.12 - 1}$$

$$£12,000 = 4.779328A$$

$$\therefore A = \frac{£12,000}{4.779328}$$

$$= £2,510.81$$

Therefore, four investments, each of £2,510.81 should therefore be enough to allow the company to replace the asset.

Exam focus point

Section A of the pilot paper for Paper 1.2 included a multiple choice question that was very similar to the example we have shown here. Make sure that you understand the workings clearly and then have a go at Question 5 below.

Question 5

A farmer has just bought a combine harvester which has a life of ten years. At the end of ten years a replacement combine harvester will cost £100,000 and the farmer would like to provide for this future commitment by setting up a sinking fund into which equal annual investments will be made, starting *now*. The fund will earn interest at 10% per annum.

Answer

The value of the fund at the end of ten years is a geometric progression with:

A = £A × 1.1
R = 1.1
n = 10

Therefore the value of the sinking fund at the end of ten years is £100,000.

$$\therefore £100,000 = \frac{A \times 1.1(1.1^{10} - 1)}{1.1 - 1}$$

$$A = \frac{£100,000 \times 0.1}{1.1(1.1^{10} - 1)}$$

$$= \frac{£10,000}{1.75311670611}$$

$$= £5,704.12$$

4   LOANS AND MORTGAGES

Loans

4.1   Most people will be familiar with the repayment of loans. The repayment of loans is best illustrated by means of an example.

4.2   EXAMPLE: LOANS

Timothy Lakeside borrows £50,000 now at an interest rate of 8 percent per annum. The loan has to be repaid through five equal instalments *after* each of the next five years. What is the annual repayment?

4.3   SOLUTION

Let us start by calculating the final value of the loan (at the end of year 5).

Using the formula $S = P(1 + r)^n$

where P = £50,000
       r = 8% = 0.08
       n = 5
       S = the sum invested after 5 years (future value)
∴   S = £50,000 $(1 + 0.08)^5$
          = £73,466.40

The value of the initial loan after 5 years (£73,466.40) must equal the sum of the repayments.

A time line will clarify when each of the repayments are made. Let £A = the annual repayments which start a year from now, ie at year 1.

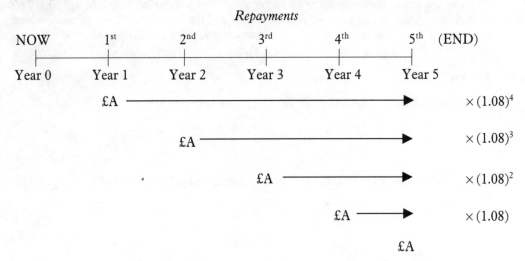

(Year 0)   No payment
(Year 1)   The first year's investment will grow to £A $\times (1.08)^4$
(Year 2)   The second year's investment will grow to £A $\times (1.08)^3$
(Year 3)   The third year's investment will grow to £A $\times (1.08)^2$
(Year 4)   The fourth year's investment will grow to £A $\times (1.08)$
(Year 5)   The fourth year's investment remains at £A.

The value of the repayments at the end of five years is as follows.

$$A + (A \times 1.08) + (A \times 1.08^2) + (A \times 1.08^3) + (A \times 1.08^4)$$

This is a geometric progression with

380

A = A
R = 1.08
n = 5

The sum of this geometric progression, $S = \dfrac{A(R^n - 1)}{R - 1}$ = £73,466.40 since the sum of repayments must **equal** the final value of the loan (ie £73,466.40).

$$S = £73,466.40 = \frac{A(1.08^5 - 1)}{1.08 - 1}$$

£73,466.40 = A × 5.86660096

A $= \dfrac{£73,466.40}{5.86660096}$

         = £12,522.82

The annual repayments are therefore £12,522.82.

Question 6

John Johnstone borrows £120,000 now at an interest rate of 7% per annum. The loan has to be repaid through ten equal instalments after each of the next ten years. What is the annual repayment?

Answer

The final value of the loan (at the end of year 10) is

$$S = £50,000 \, (1 + 0.07)^{10}$$
$$= £98,357.57$$

The value of the initial loan after 10 years (£98,357.57) must equal the sum of the repayments.

The sum of the repayments is a geometric progression with

A = A
R = 1.07
n = 10

The sum of the repayments = £98,357.57

$S = £98,357.57$ $= \dfrac{A(R^n - 1)}{R - 1}$

         $= \dfrac{A(1.07^{10} - 1)}{1.07 - 1}$

         = 13.816448A

∴   A $= \dfrac{£98,837.57}{13.816448}$

         = £7,153.62 per annum

Sinking funds and loans compared

4.4   (a)   **Sinking funds**. The sum of the **regular savings**, £A per period at r% over n periods *must* equal the sinking fund required at the end of n periods.

      (b)   **Loan repayments**. The sum of the **regular repayments** of £A per period at r% over n periods *must* equal the final value of the loan at the end of n periods.

The final value of a loan can therefore be seen to be equivalent to a sinking fund.

Mortgages

4.5 As you are probably aware, when a mortgage is taken out on a property over a number of years, there are several ways in which the loan can be repaid. One such way is the **repayment mortgage** which has the following features.

- A certain amount, S, is borrowed to be paid back over n years.
- Interest, at a rate r, is added to the loan retrospectively at the end of each year.
- A constant amount A is paid back each year.

Income tax relief affects repayments but, for simplicity, we will ignore it here.

4.6 Let us consider the repayments.

(a) At the end of one year A has been repaid.

(b) At the end of two years the initial repayment of A has earned interest and so has a value of $A(1 + r)$ and another A has been repaid. The value of the amount repaid is therefore $A(1 + r) + A$.

(c) At the end of three years, the initial repayment will have a value of $A(1 + r)^2$, the second repayment a value of $A(1 + r)$ and a third repayment of A will have been made. The value of the amount repaid is therefore $A(1 + r)^2 + (1 + r) + A$.

(d) At the end of n years the value of the repayments is therefore $A(1 + r)^{n-1} + A(1 + r)^{n-2} + ... + A(1 + r)^2 + A(1 + r) + A$.

This is a **geometric progression** with 'A' = A, 'R' = (1 + r) and 'n' = n and hence the **sum of the repayments** $= \dfrac{A[(1+r)^n - 1]}{r} = \dfrac{A(R^n - 1)}{R - 1}$

4.7 During the time the repayments have been made, the initial loan has accrued interest and hence has a value of $S(1 + r)^n$.

The repayments must, at the end of n years, repay the initial loan plus the accrued interest and hence, after n years.

Therefore the **sum of the repayments** must equal the **final value of the mortgage**.

Sum of repayments = final value of mortgage

$$\dfrac{A(R^n - 1)}{R - 1} = SR^n$$

$$\therefore A = \dfrac{SR^n \times (R^n - 1)}{R - 1}$$

4.8 EXAMPLE: MORTGAGES

(a) Sam has taken out a £30,000 mortgage over 25 years. Interest is to be charged at 12%. Calculate the monthly repayment.

(b) After nine years, the interest rate changes to 10%. What is the new monthly repayment?

4.9 SOLUTION

(a) **Final value of mortgage** $= £30{,}000 \times (1.12)^{25}$
$\phantom{\text{Final value of mortgage}} = £510{,}002$

Sum of repayments, S, where A = annual repayment
$\phantom{\text{Sum of repayments, S, where }}$ R = 1.12
$\phantom{\text{Sum of repayments, S, where }}$ n = 25

$$\therefore S = \frac{A(1.12^{25} - 1)}{1.12 - 1}$$

$$= 133.334A$$

Sum of repayments = final value of mortgage

$$133.334A = £510{,}002$$

$$A = \frac{£510{,}002}{133.334}$$

$$A = £3{,}825$$

If annual repayment = £3,825

$$\text{Monthly repayment} = \frac{£3{,}825}{12}$$

$$= £318.75$$

(b) After 9 years, the **value of the loan** $= £30{,}000 \times (1.12)^{9}$
$\phantom{\text{After 9 years, the value of the loan }} = £83{,}192$

After 9 years, the **sum of the repayments** $= \dfrac{A(R^{n} - 1)}{R - 1}$

where A = £3,825
$\phantom{\text{where }}$ R = 1.12
$\phantom{\text{where }}$ n = 9

$$\therefore \text{Sum of repayments} = \frac{3{,}825(1.12^{9} - 1)}{1.12 - 1}$$

$$= £56{,}517$$

	£
Value of loan at year 9	83,192
Sum of repayments at year 9	56,517
Loan outstanding at year 9	26,675

A new interest rate of 10% is to be charged on the outstanding loan of £26,675 for 16 years (25 – 9).

Final value of loan $= £26{,}675 \times (1.1)^{16}$
$\phantom{\text{Final value of loan }} = £122{,}571$

Sum of repayments $= \dfrac{A(R^{n} - 1)}{R - 1}$

where R = 1.1
$\phantom{\text{where }}$ n = 16
$\phantom{\text{where }}$ A = annual repayment

$$\therefore \text{Sum of repayments} = \frac{A(1.1^{16} - 1)}{1.1 - 1}$$

$$= 35.94973A$$

Final value of loan = sum of repayments

$$£122,571 = 35.94973A$$

$$\therefore A = \frac{£122,571}{35.94973}$$

$$A = £3,410$$

$$\therefore \text{monthly repayment} = \frac{£3,410}{12}$$

$$= £284$$

4.10 The final value of a loan/mortgage can be likened to a sinking fund also, since the final value must equate to the sum of the periodic repayments (compare this with a sinking fund where the sum of the regular savings must equal the fund required at some point in the future).

Question 7

Nicky Eastlacker has taken out a £200,000 mortgage over 25 years. Interest is to be charged at 9%. Calculate the monthly repayment.

Answer

Final value of mortgage $= £200,000 \times (1.09)^{25}$

$$= £1,724,616$$

Sum of repayments, S $= \dfrac{A(R^n - 1)}{R - 1}$

Where A = Annual repayment
  R = 1.09
  n = 25

$\therefore £1,724,616 = \dfrac{A(1.09^{25} - 1)}{1.09 - 1}$

$\therefore$ A = £20,361.25 per annum

If annual repayment $= £20,361.25$

Monthly repayment $= \dfrac{£20,361.25}{12}$

$$= £1,696.77$$

---

5 ANNUAL PERCENTAGE RATE (APR) OF INTEREST

Effective annual rate of interest

5.1 In the previous examples, interest has been calculated **annually**, but this isn't always the case. Interest may be compounded **daily, weekly, monthly** or **quarterly**.

The **equivalent annual** rate of interest, when interest is compounded at shorter intervals, is known as an **effective annual rate of interest**.

FORMULA TO LEARN

Effective Annual Rate of Interest $= [(1+r)^{\frac{12}{n}} - 1]$ or $[(1+r)^{\frac{365}{y}} - 1]$

where   r is the rate of interest for each time period
         n is the number of months in the time period
         y is the number of days in the time period.

5.2   EXAMPLE: THE EFFECTIVE ANNUAL RATE OF INTEREST

Calculate the effective annual rate of interest of:

(a)   1.5% per month, compound
(b)   4.5% per quarter, compound
(c)   9% per half year, compound

5.3   SOLUTION

(a) $(1.015)^{12} - 1$ $= 0.1956 = 19.56\%$
(b) $(1.045)^{4} - 1$ $= 0.1925 = 19.25\%$
(c) $(1.09)^{2} - 1$ $= 0.1881 = 18.81\%$

Nominal rates of interest and the annual percentage rate

5.4   **Most interest rates are expressed as per annum figures** even when the interest is compounded over periods of less than one year. In such cases, the given interest rate is called a **nominal rate**. We can, however, work out the **effective rate**. It is this effective rate (shortened to one decimal place) which is quoted in advertisements as the **annual percentage rate (APR)**, sometimes called the **compound annual rate (CAR)**.

Exam focus point

Students often become seriously confused about the various rates of interest.

- The **NOMINAL RATE** is the interest rate expressed as a per annum figure, eg 12% pa nominal even though interest may be compounded over periods of less than one year.

- Adjusted nominal rate = **EQUIVALENT ANNUAL RATE**

- Equivalent annual rate (the rate per day or per month adjusted to give an annual rate) = **EFFECTIVE ANNUAL RATE**

- Effective annual rate = **ANNUAL PERCENTAGE RATE (APR)** = **COMPOUND ANNUAL RATE (CAR)**

5.5   EXAMPLE: NOMINAL AND EFFECTIVE RATES OF INTEREST

A building society may offer investors 10% per annum interest payable half-yearly. If the 10% is a nominal rate of interest, the building society would in fact pay 5% every six months, compounded so that the effective annual rate of interest would be

$[(1.05)^{2} - 1] = 0.1025 = 10.25\%$ per annum.

5.6 Similarly, if a bank offers depositors a nominal 12% per annum, with interest payable quarterly, the effective rate of interest would be 3% compound every three months, which is

$[(1.03)^4 - 1] = 0.1255 = 12.55\%$ per annum.

Question 8

Calculate the effective annual rate of interest of:

(a)   15% nominal per annum compounded quarterly;
(b)   24% nominal per annum compounded monthly.

Answer

(a)   15% per annum (nominal rate) is 3.75% per quarter. The effective annual rate of interest is

$[1.0375^4 - 1] = 0.1587 = 15.87\%$

(b)   24% per annum (nominal rate) is 2% per month. The effective annual rate of interest is

$[1.02^{12} - 1] = 0.2682 = 26.82\%$

Question 9

A bank adds interest monthly to investors' accounts even though interest rates are expressed in annual terms. The current rate of interest is 12%. Fred deposits £2,000 on 1 July. How much interest will have been earned by 31 December (to the nearest £)?

A £123.00   B £60.00   C £240.00   D £120.00

Answer

The nominal rate is 12% pa payable monthly.

$\therefore$ The effective rate $= \dfrac{12\%}{12 \text{ months}} = 1\%$ compound monthly.

$\therefore$ In the six months from July to December, the interest earned $= (£2,000 \times (1.01)^6) - £2,000 = £123.04$.

The correct answer is A.

Exam focus point

You will probably find it useful to draw a time line to identify the time periods and interest rates involved when answering questions on financial mathematics. Don't be afraid to include a quick sketch of a time line in an examination – it should help to clarify exactly when investments are made in saving funds or repayments are made on a loan. It will also show the examiner that you know what you are doing!

Chapter roundup

- **Simple interest** is interest which is earned in equal amounts every year (or month) and which is a given proportion of the principal. The simple interest formula is **S = P + nrX**.

- **Compounding** means that, as interest is earned, it is added to the original investment and starts to earn interest itself. The basic formula for compound interest is $S = P(1 + r)^n$.

- If the **rate of interest changes during the period** of an investment, the compounding formula must be amended slightly to $S = P(1+r_1)^y(1 + r_2)^{n-y}$

- The **final value** (or **terminal value**), S, of an investment to which equal annual amounts will be added is found using the formula **S, = A(R^n – 1)/(R – 1)** (the formula for a geometric progression).

- The basic compound interest formula can be used to calculate the net book value of an asset depreciated using the reducing balance method of depreciation by using a negative rate of 'interest' (**reverse compounding**).

- A **sinking fund** is an investment into which equal annual instalments are paid in order to earn interest, so that by the end of a given number of years, the investment is large enough to pay off a known commitment at that time. Commitments include the replacement of an asset and the repayment of a mortgage

$$S = A\frac{(R^n - 1)}{R - 1}$$

    where S = the required value of the fund at the end of n years
    A = the annual payment into the fund
    R = the common ratio

    Note that this is the same formula as that of a geometric progression.

- The **annual repayment (A)** under a repayment mortgage can be calculated as

$$\frac{SR^n \times (R^n - 1)}{R - 1}$$

    Note that this is a rearrangement of the formula for that of a geometric progression.

- An **effective annual rate of interest** is the corresponding annual rate when interest is compounded at intervals shorter than a year.

- A **nominal rate** of interest is an interest rate expressed as a per annum figure although the interest is compounded over a period of less than one year. The corresponding effective rate of interest shortened to one decimal place is the **annual percentage rate (APR)**.

Quick quiz

1   The formula for simple interest is .... $S = P + nrX$ ....

    Where P = *Initial Sum*
           r = *Interest rate*
           n = *Period*
           S = *Total after n. Period*

2   The basic formula for compound interest is ..... $S = P(1 + r)^n$ ....

    Where P = *Initial Sum*
           r = *Interest rate*
           n = *No of Periods*
           S = *Amount after n periods*

3   A depreciation rate of 20% equates to an interest rate of

    A   ± 20%

    B   −20%

    C   +0.2

    D   −0.2

4   If Smita Smitten invests £250 *now* and a further £250 each year for five more years at an interest rate of 20%, which of the following are true if the final investment is calculated using the formula for the sum of a geometric progression?

	A =	n =
A	£250 × 1.2	5
B	£250 × 1.2	4
C	£250	5
D	£250	4

5   A shopkeeper wishes to refurbish his store in five years' time. At the end of five years, the refurbishment will cost £50,000, and the storekeeper has decided to provide for this future refurbishment by setting up a sinking fund into which equal annual investments will be made, starting one year from now. The fund will earn interest at 10%. Using the formula for the sum of a geometric progression, calculate the annual investment. 8189.87

6   What is the formula used for calculating the sum of the repayments of a mortgage? $\dfrac{A(R^n-1)}{(R-1)}$

7   The effective annual rate of interest is the same as the annual percentage rate which is the same as the compound annual rate.

True   ✓

False ☐

8   What is the formula used to calculate the APR? $\left[(1+r)^{12/n}-1\right]$ or $\left[(1+r)^{365/i}-1\right]$

Answer to quick quiz

1   S = P + nrX

    Where P = the original sum invested

               r = the rate of interest (as a proportion)

               n = the number of periods

               S = the sum invested after n periods (future value)

2    $S = P(1 + r)^n$

    Where P = the original sum invested

               r = the rate of interest (as a proportion)

               n = the number of periods

               S = the sum invested after n periods (future value)

3   D   A depreciation rate of 20% equates to a negative rate of interest of −20% where r = −0.2.

4   A $S = \dfrac{A(R^n-1)}{R-1}$

    Where   A = the first term

                        = £250 × 1.2 (as investment is made *now*)

                 n = 5 years (the number of periods)

5   Using $S = \dfrac{A\,(R^n - 1)}{R - 1}$

      Where S = final value of fund = £50,000
                 A = annual investment = ?
                 R = common ratio = 1.1
                 n = number of periods = 5

      $£50,000 = \dfrac{A\,(1.1^5 - 1)}{1.1 - 1}$

      $\therefore\ A\ =\ \dfrac{£50,000 \times (1.1 - 1)}{(1.1^5 - 1)}$

      $= £8,189.87$

6   $S\ =\ \dfrac{A\,(R^n - 1)}{R - 1}$ (the sum of a geometric progression formula)

7   True.   Effective annual rate = APR = CAR

8   $APR = [(1 + r^{12/n}) - 1]$ or $[(1 + r)^{365/y} - 1]$

    where r = the rate of interest for each time period
              n = the number of months in the time period
              y = the number of days in the time period

Now try the questions below from the Exam Question Bank

Number	Level	Marks	Time
34	MCQ	n/a	n/a
35	Examination	10	18 mins

BPP PUBLISHING

Chapter 20

INVESTMENT APPRAISAL

Topic list	Syllabus reference
1 The concept of discounting	6(i)
2 The net present value (NPV) method	6(i)
3 The internal rate of return (IRR) method	6(i)
4 Annuities and perpetuities	6(i)
5 Linking compounding and discounting	6(i)

Introduction

Discounting is the reverse of compounding, the topic of the previous chapter. Its major application in business is in the **evaluation of investments**, to decide whether they offer a satisfactory return to the investor. We will be looking at two methods of using discounting to appraise investments, the **net present value (NPV) method** and the **internal rate of return (IRR) method**.

Study guide

Section 23 – Interest

- Calculate future values including the application of the annuity formula

- Explain what is meant by discounting

- Calculate present values including the application of annuity and perpetuity formulae

Section 24 – Investment appraisal

- Apply discounting principles to calculate the net present value of an investment project and interpret the results

- Explain what is meant by the internal rate of return

- Estimate the internal rate of return using a graphical approach and the interpolation formula and interpret the results

- Identify and discuss the situation where there is conflict between these two methods of investment appraisal

Exam guide

Discounted cash flow techniques is a key topic area of the syllabus for **Financial Information for Management.** Discounted cashflow techniques relevant to this chapter include the following (as per the syllabus)

- Net present values
- Annuities and perpetuities
- Internal rate of return

1 THE CONCEPT OF DISCOUNTING

The basic principles of discounting

1.1 The **basic principle of compounding** is that if we invest £P now for n years at r% interest per annum, we should obtain £P $(1 + r)^n$ in n years time.

1.2 Thus if we invest £10,000 now for four years at 10% interest per annum, we will have a total investment worth £10,000 $\times 1.10^4$ = £14,641 at the end of four years (that is, at year 4 if it is now year 0).

> **KEY TERM**
>
> The basic principle of **discounting** is that if we wish to have £S in n years' time, we need to invest a certain sum *now* (year 0) at an interest rate of r% in order to obtain the required sum of money in the future.

1.3 For example, if we wish to have £14,641 in four years' time, how much money would we need to invest now at 10% interest per annum? This is the reverse of the situation described in Paragraph 1.2.

Using our corresponding formula, S = $P(1 + r)^n$

where   P = the original sum invested
        r = 10%
        n = 4
        S = £14,641

£14,641   = $P(1 + 0.1)^4$

£14,641   = $P \times 1.4641$

∴P   = $\dfrac{£14,641}{1.4641}$ = £10,000

1.4 £10,000 now, with the capacity to earn a return of 10% per annum, is the equivalent in value of £14,641 after four years. We can therefore say that **£10,000 is the present value of £14,641 at year 4, at an interest rate of 10%.**

Present value

> **KEY TERM**
>
> The term '**present value**' simply means the amount of money which must be invested now for n years at an interest rate of r%, to earn a given future sum of money at the time it will be due.

BPP PUBLISHING

The formula for discounting

EXAM FORMULA

The **discounting formula** is

$$P = S \times \frac{1}{(1+r)^n}$$

where S is the sum to be received after n time periods
           P is the present value (PV) of that sum
           r is the rate of return, expressed as a proportion
           n is the number of time periods (usually years).

The rate r is sometimes called a cost of capital.

Note that this equation is just a rearrangement of the compounding formula.

1.5 EXAMPLE: DISCOUNTING

(a) Calculate the present value of £60,000 at year 6, if a return of 15% per annum is obtainable.

(b) Calculate the present value of £100,000 at year 5, if a return of 6% per annum is obtainable.

(c) How much would a person need to invest now at 12% to earn £4,000 at year 2 and £4,000 at year 3?

1.6 SOLUTION

The discounting formula, $X = S \times \dfrac{1}{(1+r)^n}$ is required.

(a) S   = £60,000
      n   = 6
      r   = 0.15

$$PV = 60,000 \times \frac{1}{1.15^6}$$

$$= 60,000 \times 0.432$$
$$= £25,920$$

(b) S   = £100,000
      n   = 5
      r   = 0.06

$$PV = 100,000 \times \frac{1}{1.06^5}$$

$$= 100,000 \times 0.747$$
$$= £74,700$$

(c) S   = £4,000
      n   = 2 or 3
      r   = 0.12

$$PV = (4{,}000 \times \frac{1}{1.12^2}) + (4{,}000 \times \frac{1}{1.12^3})$$

$$= 4{,}000 \times (0.797 + 0.712)$$

$$= £6{,}036$$

This calculation can be checked as follows.

	£
Year 0	6,036.00
Interest for the first year (12%)	724.32
	6,760.32
Interest for the second year (12%)	811.24
	7,571.56
Less withdrawal	(4,000.00)
	3,571.56
Interest for the third year (12%)	428.59
	4,000.15
Less withdrawal	(4,000.00)
Rounding error	0.15

Question 1

What is the present value at 7% interest of £16,000 at year 12?

Answer

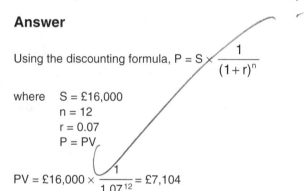

Using the discounting formula, $P = S \times \dfrac{1}{(1+r)^n}$

where
$S = £16{,}000$
$n = 12$
$r = 0.07$
$P = PV$

$$PV = £16{,}000 \times \frac{1}{1.07^{12}} = £7{,}104$$

Capital expenditure appraisal

1.7 **Discounted cash flow techniques can be used to evaluate capital expenditure proposals (investments).**

> **KEY TERM**
>
> **Discounted cash flow (DCF)** involves the application of discounting arithmetic to the estimated future cash flows (receipts and expenditures) from a project in order to decide whether the project is expected to earn a satisfactory rate of return.
>
> There are two methods of using DCF techniques.
>
> - The net present value (NPV) method
> - The internal rate of return (IRR) method

2 THE NET PRESENT VALUE (NPV) METHOD

KEY TERM

The **net present value (NPV) method** works out the present values of all items of income and expenditure related to an investment at a given rate of return, and then works out a net total. If it is positive, the investment is considered to be acceptable. If it is negative, the investment is considered to be unacceptable.

2.1 EXAMPLE: THE NET PRESENT VALUE OF A PROJECT

Dog Ltd is considering whether to spend £5,000 on an item of equipment. The 'cash profits', the excess of income over cash expenditure, from the project would be £3,000 in the first year and £4,000 in the second year.

The company will not invest in any project unless it offers a return in excess of 15% per annum.

Required

Assess whether the investment is worthwhile, or 'viable'.

2.2 SOLUTION

In this example, an outlay of £5,000 now promises a return of £3,000 **during** the first year and £4,000 **during** the second year. It is a convention in DCF, however, that cash flows spread over a year are assumed to occur **at the end of the year**, so that the cash flows of the project are as follows.

	£
Year 0 (now)	(5,000)
Year 1 (at the end of the year)	3,000
Year 2 (at the end of the year)	4,000

2.3 The NPV method takes the following approach.

(a) The project offers £3,000 at year 1 and £4,000 at year 2, for an outlay of £5,000 now.

(b) The company might invest elsewhere to earn a return of 15% per annum.

(c) If the company did invest at exactly 15% per annum, how much would it need to invest now, at 15%, to earn £3,000 at the end of year 1 plus £4,000 at the end of year 2?

(d) Is it cheaper to invest £5,000 in the project, or to invest elsewhere at 15%, in order to obtain these future cash flows?

2.4 If the company did invest elsewhere at 15% per annum, the amount required to earn £3,000 in year 1 and £4,000 in year 2 would be as follows.

Year	Cash flow £	Discount factor 15%	Present value £
1	3,000	$\dfrac{1}{1.15} = 0.870$	2,610
2	4,000	$\dfrac{1}{(1.15)^2} = 0.756$	3,024
			5,634

2.5 The choice is to invest £5,000 in the project, or £5,634 elsewhere at 15%, in order to obtain these future cash flows. We can therefore reach the following conclusion.

- It is cheaper to invest in the project, by £634.
- The project offers a return of over 15% per annum.

2.6 The net present value is the difference between the present value of cash inflows from the project (£5,634) and the present value of future cash outflows (in this example, £5,000 × $1/1.15^0$ = £5,000).

2.7 An NPV statement could be drawn up as follows.

Year	Cash flow £	Discount factor 15%	Present value £
0	(5,000)	1.000	(5,000)
1	3,000	$\dfrac{1}{1.15} = 0.870$	2,610
2	4,000	$\dfrac{1}{(1.15)^2} = 0.756$	3,024
		Net present value	+634

The project has a positive net present value, so it is acceptable.

Question 2

A company is wondering whether to spend £18,000 on an item of equipment, in order to obtain cash profits as follows.

Year	£
1	6,000
2	8,000
3	5,000
4	1,000

The company requires a return of 10% per annum.

Required

Use the NPV method to assess whether the project is viable.

Answer

	Cash flow £	Discount factor 10%	Present value £
0	(18,000)	1.000	(18,000)
1	6,000	$\dfrac{1}{1.10} = 0.909$	5,454
2	8,000	$\dfrac{1}{1.10^2} = 0.826$	6,608
3	5,000	$\dfrac{1}{1.10^3} = 0.751$	3,755
4	1,000	$\dfrac{1}{1.10^4} = 0.683$	683
		Net present value	(1,500)

The NPV is negative. We can therefore draw the following conclusions.

(a) It is cheaper to invest elsewhere at 10% than to invest in the project.
(b) The project would earn a return of less than 10%.
(c) The project is not viable (since the PV of the costs is greater than the PV of the benefits).

Discount tables

2.8 Assuming that money earns, say, 10% per annum:

(a) the PV (present value) of £1 at year 1 is $£1 \times \dfrac{1}{1.10}$ = £1 × 0.909;

(b) similarly, the PV of £1 at year 2 is $£1 \times \dfrac{1}{(1.10)^2}$ = £1 × 0.826;

(c) the PV of £1 at year 3 is $£1 \times \dfrac{1}{(1.10)^3}$ = £1 × 0.751.

Discount tables show the value of $1/(1 + r)^n$ for different values of r and n. The 10% discount factors of 0.909, 0.826 and 0.751 are shown in the discount tables at the end of this Study Text in the column for 10%. (You will be given discount tables in your examination.)

Question 3

Daisy Ltd is considering whether to make an investment costing £28,000 which would earn £8,000 cash per annum for five years. The company expects to make a return of at least 11% per annum.

Required

Assess whether the project is viable.

Answer

Year	Cash flow £	Discount factor 11%	Present value £
0	(28,000)	1.000	(28,000)
1	8,000	0.901	7,208
2	8,000	0.812	6,496
3	8,000	0.731	5,848
4	8,000	0.659	5,272
5	8,000	0.593	4,744
		NPV	1,568

The NPV is positive, therefore the project is viable because it earns more than 11% per annum.

Project comparison

2.9 **The NPV method can also be used to compare two or more investment options.** For example, suppose that Daisy Ltd can choose between the investment outlined in Question 3 above *or* a second investment, which also costs £28,000 but which would earn £6,500 in the first year, £7,500 in the second, £8,500 in the third, £9,500 in the fourth and £10,500 in the fifth. Which one should Daisy Ltd choose?

2.10 **The decision rule is to choose the option with the highest NPV.** We therefore need to calculate the NPV of the second option.

Year	Cash flow £	Discount factor 11%	Present value £
0	(28,000)	1.000	(28,000)
1	6,500	0.901	5,857
2	7,500	0.812	6,090
3	8,500	0.731	6,214
4	9,500	0.659	6,261
5	10,500	0.593	6,227
		NPV =	2,649

Daisy Ltd should therefore invest in the second option since it has the higher NPV.

Expected values and discounting

2.11 Future cash flows cannot be predicted with complete accuracy. To take account of this uncertainty an **expected net present value** can be calculated which is a **weighted average net present value based on the probabilities of different sets of circumstances occurring**. Let us have a look at an example.

2.12 EXAMPLE: EXPECTED NET PRESENT VALUE

An organisation with a cost of capital of 5% is contemplating investing £340,000 in a project which has a 25% chance of being a big success and producing cash inflows of £210,000 after one and two years. There is, however, a 75% change of the project not being quite so successful, in which case the cash inflows will be £162,000 after one year and £174,000 after two years.

Required

Calculate an NPV and hence advise the organisation.

2.13 SOLUTION

	Discount	Success		Failure	
Year	factor	Cash flow	PV	Cash flow	PV
	5%	£'000	£'000	£'000	£'000
0	1.000	(340)	(340.00)	(340)	(340.000)
1	0.952	210	199.92	162	154.224
2	0.907	210	190.47	174	157.818
			50.39		(27.958)

$$\text{NPV} = (25\% \times 50.39) + (75\% \times -27.958) = -8.371$$

The NPV is – £8,371 and hence the organisation should not invest in the project.

3 THE INTERNAL RATE OF RETURN (IRR) METHOD

3.1 The **internal rate of return (IRR) method** of evaluating investments is an alternative to the NPV method. The NPV method of discounted cash flow determines whether an investment earns a **positive or a negative NPV when discounted at a given rate of interest**. If the NPV is zero (that is, the present values of costs and benefits are equal) the return from the project would be exactly the rate used for discounting.

> **KEY TERM**
>
> The **IRR method of discounted cash flow** is a method which determines the rate of interest (the internal rate of return) at which the NPV is 0. The internal rate of return is therefore the rate of return on an investment.

3.2 The IRR method will indicate that a project is viable **if the IRR exceeds the minimum acceptable rate of return**. Thus if the company expects a minimum return of, say, 15%, a project would be viable if its IRR is more than 15%.

3.3 EXAMPLE: THE IRR METHOD OVER ONE YEAR

If £500 is invested today and generates £600 in one year's time, the internal rate of return (r) can be calculated as follows.

PV of cost = PV of benefits

$$500 = \frac{600}{(1+r)}$$

$$500\,(1 + r) = 600$$

$$1 + r = \frac{600}{500} = 1.2$$

$$r = 0.2 = 20\%$$

3.4 The arithmetic for calculating the IRR is more complicated for investments and cash flows extending over a period of time longer than one year. An approximate IRR can be calculated using either a **graphical method** or by a technique known as the **interpolation** method.

Graphical approach

3.5 The easiest way to estimate the IRR of a project is to **find the project's NPV at a number of costs of capital** and **sketch a graph of NPV against discount rate**. You can then use the sketch to estimate the **discount rate at which the NPV is equal to zero (the point where the curve cuts the axis)**.

3.6 EXAMPLE: GRAPHICAL APPROACH

A project might have the following NPVs at the following discount rates.

Discount rate	NPV
%	£
5	5,300
10	2,900
15	(1,700)
20	(3,200)

This could be sketched on a graph as follows.

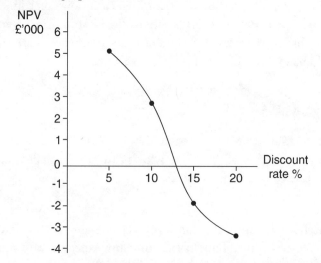

The IRR can be **estimated as 13%**. The NPV should then be **recalculated using this interest rate**. The resulting NPV **should be equal to, or very near, zero. If it is not,**

additional NPVs at different discount rates should be calculated, the graph resketched and a more accurate **IRR** determined.

The interpolation method

3.7 The interpolation method is best explained by means of an example.

3.8 EXAMPLE: INTERPOLATION

A project costing £800 in year 0 is expected to earn £400 in year 1, £300 in year 2 and £200 in year 3.

Required

Calculate the internal rate of return.

3.9 SOLUTION

The IRR is calculated by first of all finding the NPV at each of two interest rates. Ideally, one interest rate should give a small positive NPV and the other a small negative NPV. The IRR would then be somewhere between these two interest rates: above the rate where the NPV is positive, but below the rate where the NPV is negative.

A very rough guideline for estimating at what interest rate the NPV might be close to zero, is to take

$$\tfrac{2}{3} \times \left(\frac{\text{profit}}{\text{cost of the project}} \right)$$

In our example, the total profit over three years is £(400 + 300 + 200 − 800) = £100. An approximate IRR is therefore calculated as:

$$\tfrac{2}{3} \times \frac{100}{800} = 0.08 \text{ approx.}$$

A starting point is to try 8%.

(a) Try 8%

Year	Cash flow £	Discount factor 8%	Present value £
0	(800)	1.000	(800.0)
1	400	0.926	370.4
2	300	0.857	257.1
3	200	0.794	158.8
		NPV	(13.7)

The NPV is negative, therefore the project fails to earn 8% and the IRR must be less than 8%.

(b) Try 6%

Year	Cash flow £	Discount factor 6%	Present value £
0	(800)	1.000	(800.0)
1	400	0.943	377.2
2	300	0.890	267.0
3	200	0.840	168.0
		NPV	12.2

The NPV is positive, therefore the project earns more than 6% and less than 8%.

The **IRR is now calculated by interpolation**. The result will not be exact, but it will be a close approximation. Interpolation assumes that the NPV falls in a straight line from +12.2 at 6% to −13.7 at 8%.

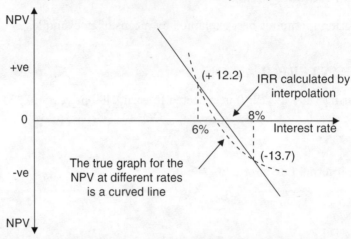

Graph to show IRR calculation by interpolation

FORMULA TO LEARN

The IRR, where the NPV is zero, can be calculated as follows.

$$\text{IRR} = a\% + [\frac{A}{A-B} \times (b-a)]\% \text{ where}$$

       a is one interest rate
       b is the other interest rate
       A is the NPV at rate a
       B is the NPV at rate b

(c)   Thus, in our example, $\text{IRR} = 6\% + \left[\frac{12.2}{(12.2+13.7)} \times (8-6)\right]\%$

                             = 6% + 0.942%

                             = 6.942% approx

(d)   The answer is only an **approximation** because the NPV falls in a slightly curved line and not a straight line between +12.2 and −13.7. Provided that NPVs close to zero are used, the linear assumption used in the interpolation method is nevertheless fairly accurate.

(e)   Note that the formula will still work if A and B are both positive, or both negative, and even if a and b are a long way from the true IRR, but the results will be less accurate.

Question 4

The net present value of an investment at 15% is £50,000 and at 20% is - £10,000. The internal rate of return of this investment (to the nearest whole number) is:

A   16%
B   17%
C   18%
D   19%

Answer

$$IRR = a\% + [\frac{A}{A-B} \times (b-a)]\%$$

Where
a	=	one interest rate = 15%
b	=	other interest rate = 20%
A	=	NPV at rate a = £50,000
B	=	NPV at rate b = £10,000

$$IRR = 15\% + [\frac{£50,000}{£50,000 - (-10,000)} \times (20-15)]\%$$

$$= 15\% + 4.17\%$$
$$= 19.17\%$$
$$= 19\%$$

The correct answer is therefore D.

NPV and IRR compared

3.10 Sometimes there will be conflict between the NPV and IRR methods of investment appraisal. When such a situation arises, it is necessary to look at the relative advantages of each method.

3.11 **Advantages of IRR method**

(a) The main advantage is that the information it provides is more **easily understood** by managers, especially non-financial managers. It is fairly easy to understand the meaning of 'The project will be expected to have an initial capital outlay of £100,000, and to earn a yield of 25%. This is in excess of the target yield of 15% for investments'. It is not so easy to understand the meaning of 'The project will cost £100,000 and have an NPV of £30,000 when discounted at the minimum required rate of 15%'.

(b) A **discount rate does not have to be specified** before the IRR can be calculated. A given cost of capital rate is simply required to which the IRR can be compared.

3.12 **Advantages of NPV method**

(a) The NPV method takes into account the **relative size of investments** (unlike the IRR method). For example, both the following projects have a IRR of 18%.

	Project A £	Project B £
Cost, year 0	350,000	35,000
Annual savings, years 1-6	100,000	10,000

Clearly, project A is bigger (ten times as big) and so more 'profitable' but if the only information on which the projects were judged were to be their IRR of 18%, project B would be made to seem just as beneficial as project A, which is not the case.

(b) **When discount rates are expected to differ over the life of the project, such variations can be incorporated easily into NPV calculations, but not into IRR calculations.**

4 ANNUITIES AND PERPETUITIES

> **KEY TERM**
>
> An **annuity** is a constant sum of money received or paid each year for a given number of years.

4.1 Many individuals nowadays may invest in **annuities** which can be purchased either through a single payment or a number of payments. For example, individuals planning for their retirement might make regular payments into a pension fund over a number of years. Over the years, the pension fund should (hopefully) grow and the final value of the fund can be used to buy an annuity. (There may also be a lump sum payment of up to 25% of the final fund value but don't worry about these details as they are not part of your **Financial Information for Management** syllabus.)

4.2 An **annuity** might run until the recipient's death, or it might run for a guaranteed term of n years.

The formula for the present value of an annuity

4.3 There is a formula which you need to be able to use when calculating the PV of an annuity.

> **EXAM FORMULA**
>
> The **present value of an annuity** of £A per annum receivable or payable for n years commencing in one year, discounted at r% per annum:
>
> $$PV = A \times \frac{1}{r}\left(1 - \frac{1}{(1+r)^n}\right)$$

4.4 EXAMPLE: THE ANNUITY FORMULA

What is the present value of £4,000 per annum for years 1 to 4, at a discount rate of 10% per annum?

4.5 SOLUTION

Using the annuity formula with r = 0.1 and n = 4.

$$PV = 4,000 \times \left(\frac{1}{0.1}\left(1 - \frac{1}{(1+0.1)^4}\right)\right)$$

$$= 4,000 \times 3.170 = £12,680$$

Calculating a required annuity

4.6 If PV of £A $= A\left(\frac{1}{r}\left(1 - \frac{1}{(1+r)^n}\right)\right)$

$$\therefore A = \frac{\text{PV of } \pounds A}{\left(\frac{1}{r}\left(1 - \frac{1}{(1+r)^n}\right)\right)}$$

This enables us to calculate the annuity required to yield a given rate of return (r) on a given investment (P).

4.7 EXAMPLE: REQUIRED ANNUITY

The present value of a ten-year annuity receivable which begins in one year's time at 7% per annum compound is £3,000. What is the annual amount of the annuity?

4.8 SOLUTION

PV of £A = £3,000

     r = 0.07

     t = 10

$$A = \frac{3,000}{\left(\frac{1}{0.07}\left(1 - \frac{1}{(1.07)^{10}}\right)\right)}$$

$$= \frac{\pounds 3,000}{7.024} = 427.11$$

Question 5

(a) It is important to practise using the annuity factor formula. Calculate annuity factors in the following cases.

  (i) n = 4, r = 10%
  (ii) n = 3, r = 9.5%
  (iii) For twenty years at a rate of 25%

(b) What is the present value of £4,000 per annum for four years, **years 2 to 5**, at a discount rate of 10% per annum? Use the annuity formula.

Answer

(a) (i) $\dfrac{1}{0.1}\left(1 - \dfrac{1}{(1+0.1)^4}\right) = 3.170$

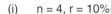

  (ii) $\dfrac{1}{0.095}\left(1 - \dfrac{1}{(1+0.095)^3}\right) = 2.509$

  (iii) $\dfrac{1}{0.25}\left(1 - \dfrac{1}{(1+0.25)^{20}}\right) = 3.954$

(b) The formula will give the value of £4,000 at 10% per annum, not as a year 0 present value, but as a value at the year preceding the first annuity cash flow, that is, at year (2 - 1) = year 1. We must therefore discount our solution in paragraph 4.5 further, from a year 1 to a year 0 value.

  $PV = \pounds 12,680 \times \dfrac{1}{1.10} = \pounds 11,527.27$

Question 6

In the formula

$$PV = \frac{1}{r}\left(1 - \frac{1}{(1+r)^n}\right)$$

$$r = 0.04$$
$$n = 10$$

What is the PV?

A   6.41
B   7.32
C   8.11
D   9.22

Answer

$$PV = \frac{1}{0.04}\left(1 - \frac{1}{(1+0.04)^{10}}\right)$$

$$= 8.11$$

The correct answer is therefore C.

Annuity tables

4.9   To calculate the present value of a constant annual cash flow, or annuity, we can multiply the annual cash flows by the sum of the discount factors for the relevant years. These total factors are known as **cumulative present value factors** or **annuity factors**. As with 'present value factors of £1 in year n', there are tables for annuity factors, which are shown at the end of this text. (For example, the cumulative present value factor of £1 per annum for five years at 11% per annum is in the column for 11% and the year 5 row, and is 3.696).

The use of annuity tables to calculate a required annuity

4.10   Just as the formula can be used to calculate an annuity, so too can the tables. Since the present value of an annuity is PV = A × annuity factor from the tables, we have

> **FORMULA TO LEARN**
>
> $$\text{Annuity (A)} = \frac{\text{Present value of an annuity}}{\text{Annuity factor}}$$

4.11   EXAMPLE: ANNUITY TABLES

A bank grants a loan of £3,000 at 7% per annum. The borrower is to repay the loan in ten annual instalments. How much must she pay each year?

4.12   SOLUTION

Since the bank pays out the loan money *now*, the present value (PV) of the loan is £3,000. The annual repayment on the loan can be thought of as an annuity. We can therefore use the annuity formula

$$\text{Annuity} = \frac{PV}{\text{annuity factor}}$$

in order to calculate the loan repayments. The annuity factor is found by looking in the cumulative present value tables under n = 10 and r = 7%. The corresponding factor = 7.024.

Therefore, annuity $= \dfrac{£3,000}{7.024}$

$= £427.11$

The loan repayments are therefore £427.11 per annum.

Perpetuities

KEY TERMS

- A **perpetuity** is an annuity which lasts for ever, instead of stopping after n years.

- The **present value of a perpetuity** is PV = A/r where r is the cost of capital as a proportion.

EXAM FORMULA

The present value of £A per annum, payable or receivable in perpetuity, commencing in one year, discounted at r% per annum

$$PV = \dfrac{A}{r}$$

4.13 EXAMPLE: A PERPETUITY

How much should be invested *now* (to the nearest £) to receive £35,000 per annum in perpetuity if the annual rate of interest is 9%?

4.14 SOLUTION

$PV = \dfrac{A}{r}$

where A = £35,000
       r = 9%

$\therefore$ PV $= \dfrac{£35,000}{0.09}$

$= £388,889$

4.15 EXAMPLE: A PERPETUITY

Mostly Ltd is considering a project which would cost £50,000 now and yield £9,000 per annum every year in perpetuity, starting a year from now. The cost of capital is 15%.

Required

Assess whether the project is viable.

BPP PUBLISHING

4.16 SOLUTION

Year	Cash flow £	Discount factor 15%	Present value £
0	(50,000)	1.0	(50,000)
1 - ∞	9,000	1/0.15	60,000
		NPV	10,000

The project is viable because it has a positive net present value when discounted at 15%.

The timing of cash flows

4.17 Note that both annuity tables and the formulae assume that the first payment or receipt is a year from now. Always check examination questions for when the first payment falls.

For example, if there are five equal payments starting now, and the interest rate is 8%, we should use a factor of 1 (for today's payment) + 3.312 (for the other four payments) = 4.312.

Question 7

Hilarious Jokes Ltd has arranged a fifteen year lease, at an annual rent of £9,000. The first rental payment is to be paid immediately, and the others are to be paid at the end of each year.

What is the present value of the lease at 9%?

A £79,074   B £72,549   C £81,549   D £70,074

Answer

The correct way to answer this question is to use the cumulative present value tables for r = 9% and n = 14 because the first payment is to be paid immediately (and not in one year's time). A common trap in a question like this would be to look up r = 9% and n = 15 in the tables. If you did this, get out of the habit now, before you sit your exam!

From the cumulative present value tables, when r = 9% and n = 14, the annuity factor is 7.786.

The first payment is made now, and so has a PV of £9,000 (£9,000 × 1.00). Payments 2-15 have a PV of £9,000 × 7.786 = £70,074.

∴ The total PV = £9,000 (1st payment) + £70,074 (Payments 2-15)
= £79,074.

The correct answer is A.

(Alternatively, the annuity factor can be increased by 1 to take account of the fact that the first payment is *now*.

∴ annuity factor = 7.786 + 1 = 8.786

∴ PV = annuity × annuity factor
= £9,000 × 8.786 = £79,074)

Question 8

How much should be, invested now (to the nearest £) to receive £20,000 per annum in perpetuity if the annual rate of interest is 20%?

A   £4,000
B   £24,000
C   £93,500
D   £100,000

Answer

$$PV = \frac{A}{r}$$

Where   A   =   annuity = £20,000
            r   =   cost of capital as a proportion = 0.2

$$PV = \frac{£20,000}{0.2}$$

$$= £100,000$$

The correct answer is therefore D.

---

5   LINKING COMPOUNDING AND DISCOUNTING

Sinking funds

5.1   In the previous chapter we introduced you to **sinking funds**. You will remember that a sinking fund is an investment into which equal annual instalments (an **annuity**) are paid in order to earn interest, so that by the end of a given period, the investment is large enough to pay off a known commitment at that time (**future value**).

5.2   EXAMPLE: A SINKING FUND (1)

Jamie wants to buy a Porsche 911. This will cost him £45,000 in two years' time. He has decided to set aside an equal amount each quarter until he has the amount he needs. Assuming he can earn interest in his building society account at 5% pa how much does he need to set aside each year? Assume the first amount is set aside one period from now.

(a)   Calculate the amounts using the annuity formula.
(b)   Calculate the amounts using annuity tables.

5.3   SOLUTION

If Jamie needs £45,000 in two years' time, the present value that he needs is

$$PV \quad = \frac{£45,000}{(1+0.05)^2}$$

$$= £40,816$$

(a)   **Using the annuity formula**

The annuity factor $= \dfrac{1}{r}\left(1 - \dfrac{1}{(1+r)^n}\right)$

where   r = 0.05
            n = 2

Annuity factor $= \dfrac{1}{0.05}\left(1 - \dfrac{1}{(1+0.05)^2}\right)$

$$= 1.8594$$

The amount to save each quarter is an annuity. We can therefore use the formula

$$\text{Annuity} = \frac{\text{PV}}{\text{Annuity factor}}$$

$$= \frac{£40,816}{1.8594}$$

$$= £21,951$$

Therefore Jamie must set aside £12,951 per annum.

(b) **Using annuity tables**

When n = 2 and r = 5% the annuity factor (from cumulative present value tables) is 1.859.

$$\text{Annuity} = \frac{\text{PV}}{\text{Annuity factor}}$$

$$= \frac{£40,816}{1.859}$$

$$= £21,956$$

The difference of £5 (£21,956 – £21,951) is due to rounding.

5.4 EXAMPLE: A SINKING FUND (2)

At this point it is worth considering the value of the fund that would have built up if we had saved £21,956 pa for two years at an interest rate of 5%, with the first payment at the end of year 1.

5.5 SOLUTION

The situation we are looking at here can be shown on the following time line.

Saving

NOW	1st	2nd	(END)
0	1	2	

£21,956 ⟶ × (1.05)

£21,956 × 1

The value of the fund at the end of year 2 is

21,956 + 21,956(1.05)

This is a geometric progression with

A = £21,956
R = 1.05
n = 2

If $S = \frac{A(R^n - 1)}{R - 1}$

$$= \frac{21,956(1.05^2 - 1)}{1.05 - 1}$$

$$= £45,000 \text{ (to the nearest £100)}$$

Therefore, if we were to save £21,956 for two years at 5% per annum we would achieve a final value of £45,000. Can you see how compounding and discounting really are the reverse of each other? In our first example, we calculated that Jamie needed to save £21,956 pa for two years at a cost of capital of 5%. In the second example, we demonstrated that using the equation for the sum of a geometric progression, saving £21,956 pa for two years would result in a sinking fund of £45,000.

5.6 Work through these two examples again if you are not totally clear: it is vitally important that you understand how compounding and discounting are linked.

Mortgages

5.7 We also considered mortgages in Chapter 19. You will remember that the final value of a mortgage must be equal to the sum of the repayments. If the repayments are regular, they can be treated as an annuity, in which case the annuity formula may be used in mortgage calculations.

5.8 When an individual takes out a mortgage, the present value of the mortgage is the amount of the loan taken out. Most mortgages will be taken out at a given rate of interest for a fixed term.

$$\text{Annuity} = \frac{\text{Present value of annuity (original vaue of mortgage)}}{\text{Annuity factor (from formula or tables)}}$$

The annuity is the regular repayment value.

Let's have a look at an example.

5.9 EXAMPLE: MORTGAGES

Tim has taken out a £30,000 mortgage over 25 years. Interest is to be charged at 12%. Calculate the monthly repayment.

5.10 SOLUTION

Present value of mortgage $= £30,000$

Annuity factor $= \dfrac{1}{0.12}\left(1 - \dfrac{1}{(1+0.12)^{25}}\right)$

$= 7.843$

Annuity (annual repayments) $= \dfrac{\text{PV}}{\text{annuity factor}}$

$= \dfrac{£30,000}{7.843}$

$= £3,825$

Monthly repayment $= £3,825 \div 12 = £318.75$

Did you recognise any of these figures? Look back at Paragraph 4.8 in the previous chapter. We have used the same information but used the annuity formula method rather than the sum of a geometric progression.

5.11 EXAMPLE: INTEREST RATE CHANGES

After nine years, the interest rate on Tim's mortgage changes to 10%. What is the new monthly repayment?

5.12 SOLUTION

In the solution in Paragraph 4.9 in Chapter 19, it was established that the value of the mortgage after 9 years was £26,675.

After 9 years, our annuity factor changes to

Annuity factor $\qquad = \dfrac{1}{0.1}\left(1 - \dfrac{1}{(1+0.1)^{16}}\right)$

$\qquad\qquad\qquad\qquad = 7.8237$

Annuity (annual repayments) $\quad = \dfrac{PV}{\text{annuity factor}}$

$\qquad\qquad\qquad\qquad = \dfrac{£26,675}{7.8237}$

$\qquad\qquad\qquad\qquad = £3,410$

∴ The monthly repayments $\qquad = £3,410 \div 12 = £284$

This is the same as the answer that we calculated in Chapter 19, Paragraph 4.9 when we used the sum of a geometric progression formula.

5.13 Sinking funds are an example of **saving** whilst mortgages are an example of **borrowing**.

Borrowing versus saving

5.14 The chief advantage of borrowing money via a loan or mortgage is that the asset the money is used to purchase can be **owned now** (and therefore be put to use to earn money) rather than waiting. On the other hand, borrowing money **takes some control away from the business's managers** and **makes a business venture more risky**. Because an obligation is owed to the lender the managers may have **less freedom** to do what they like with their assets. If the business is not successful the debt will still be owed, and if the lender demands that it is repaid immediately the business might collapse.

5.15 The advantages of saving up are that **no interest has to be paid** and the business **does not have to surrender any control to a third party**. The savings will **earn** interest. However the money will not be available for other, potentially more profitable, uses. Also, the business cannot be **sure** in advance that it will be able to generate the cash needed over the timescale envisaged.

Exam focus point

Note that both annuity tables and the formulae used in this chapter assume that the first payment or receipt is **a year from now**. Always check examination questions for when the first payment falls. For example, if there are five equal payments starting **now**, and the interest rate is 8% we should use a factor of 1 (for today's payment) + 3.312 (for the other four payments) = 4.312.

Chapter roundup

- **Discounting** is the reverse of compounding.

- The concept of present value can be thought of in two ways.

  ○ It is the value today of an amount to be received some time in the future.

  ○ It is the amount which would have to be invested today to produce a given amount at some future date.

- The **discounting formula** is $P = S \times \dfrac{1}{(1+r)^n}$ which is a rearrangement of the compounding formula.

- **Discounted cash flow techniques** can be used to evaluate capital expenditure projects. There are two methods: the **NPV method** and the **IRR method**.

- The **NPV method** works out the present values of all items of income and expenditure related to an investment at a given rate of return, and then works out a net total. If it is **positive**, the investment is considered to be **acceptable**. If it is **negative**, the investment is considered to be **unacceptable**.

- The **IRR method** is to determine the rate of interest (the IRR) at which the NPV is 0. Interpolation, using the following formula, is often necessary. **The project is viable if the IRR exceeds the minimum acceptable return**.

$$IRR = a\% + \left[\frac{A}{A-B} \times (b-a) \right]\%$$

- It is also possible to calculate the IRR of a project using the **graphical method**.

- When there is conflict between the NPV and IRR methods of investment appraisal, it is necessary to consider the relative **advantages** of each method.

- An **annuity** is a constant sum of money each year for a given number of years. The present value of an annuity can be calculated using the following formula.

$$PV = A \times \frac{1}{r} \left(1 - \frac{1}{(1+r)^t} \right)$$

Alternatively, the present value of an annuity can be calculated by using annuity factors found in annuity tables.

$$Annuity = \frac{PV \text{ of annuity}}{Annuity \text{ factor}}$$

- A **perpetuity** is an annuity which lasts forever, instead of stopping after n years. The present value of a perpetuity = A/r.

- Compounding and discounting are directly linked to each other. Make sure that you understand clearly the relationship between them.

Quick quiz

1   What does the term present value mean?   *Value today of amount to be recieved in future*

2   The discounting formula is $P = S \times \dfrac{1}{(1+r)^n}$

Where

S = *b*
P = *c*
r = *a*
n = *d*

BPP PUBLISHING

(a) the rate of return (as a proportion)
(b) the sum to be received after n time periods
(c) the PV of that sum
(d) the number of time periods

3 What are the two usual methods of capital expenditure appraisal using DCF techniques? *NPV-IRR*

4 What is the formula used to calculate the IRR and what do the symbols used represent?

5 An annuity is a sum of money received every year.

True ☐

False ☑

6 What is a perpetuity? *last brewes.*

7 What is the formula for the present value of a perpetuity? *P = A/r*

8 If Fred were to save £7,000 per annum, and we used the formula for the sum of a geometric progression to calculate the value of the fund that would have built up over ten years at an interest rate of 20%, what is the value of A to be used in the formula if:

(a) the first payment is now   *60342.   5000 × 1.2*
(b) the first payment is in one year's time   *43342.15   5000*

9 What is the main advantages of borrowing as opposed to saving? *Good brought can be. used to stort earning money rather than being money up when it could be used in more profitable ventures*

Answers to quick quiz

1 The amount of money which must be invested now for n years at an interest rate of r% to give a future sum of money at the time it will be due.

2 S = (b)
P = (c)
r = (a)
n = (d)

3 The net present value (NPV) method
The Internal rate of return (IRR) method

4 $$\text{IRR} = a\% + \left[\frac{A}{A-B} \times (b-a)\right]\%$$

Where a = are interest rate
b = another interest rate
A = the NPV at rate a
B = the NPV at rate b

5 False. It is a **constant** sum of money **received** or **paid** each year for a **given number** of years.

6 An annuity which lasts forever.

7 PV = A/r

8 (a) A = £5,000 × 1.2
(b) A = £5,000

9 The money is available **now** to buy the required asset as opposed to at the end of the savings period.

Now try the questions below from the Exam Question Bank

Number	Level	Marks	Time
36	MCQ	n/a	n/a
37	Examination	10	18 mins

Chapter 21

PRICING

Topic list	Syllabus reference
1 Factors influencing the price of a product	6(g), (h)
2 Full cost-plus pricing	6(g), (h)
3 Marginal cost-plus pricing	6(g), (h)
4 Other pricing policies	6(g), (h)
5 The optimal price/output level	6(g), (h)

Introduction

In this chapter we will begin by looking at the factors which influence the price of a product. Perhaps the most important of these is the level of **demand** for an organisation's product and how that demand changes as the price of the product changes (its **elasticity of demand**). We will then turn our attention to specific approaches to pricing with a look at two **cost-based approaches: full cost-plus pricing** and **marginal cost-plus pricing**. The next section of the chapter will discuss the **pricing strategies** to adopt in particular circumstances, such as when a new product is launched.

We will end the chapter by looking at the **optimum price/output level**. This is the point at which a business can maximise its profits.

Study guide

Section 22 - Pricing

- Explain the factors that influence the price of a product

- Establish the price/demand relationship of a product

- Establish the optimum price/output level when considering profit maximisation and maximisation of revenue

- Calculate prices using full cost and marginal cost as the pricing base

- Discuss the advantages and disadvantages of these pricing bases

- Discuss pricing policy in the context of price skimming, penetration pricing, premium pricing and price discrimination

Exam guide

Pricing methods is one of the key areas of the syllabus for Paper 1.2. You can expect to encounter questions in both sections of your examination on this topic.

1   FACTORS INFLUENCING THE PRICE OF A PRODUCT

1.1   In this first section of the chapter you will be learning about the many factors which influence the price which can be charged for a product or service. We will begin by looking at the basic economic analysis of demand.

The economic analysis of demand

1.2   There are two extremes in the relationship between price and demand. A supplier can either **sell a certain quantity, Q, at any price** (as in graph (a)). Demand is totally unresponsive to changes in price and is said to be **completely inelastic**. Alternatively, **demand might be limitless at a certain price** P (as in graph (b)), but there would be no demand above price P and there would be little point in dropping the price below P. In such circumstances demand is said to be **completely elastic**.

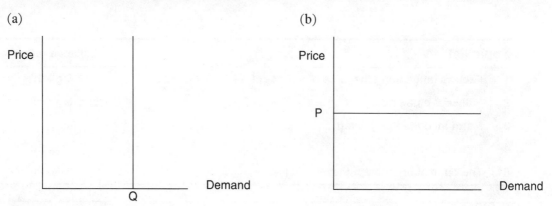

1.3   A more **normal situation** is shown below. The **downward-sloping** demand curve shows that demand will increase as prices are lowered. Demand is therefore **elastic**.

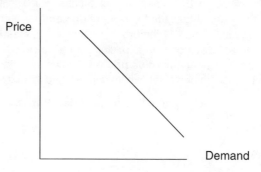

Price elasticity of demand (η)

> **KEY TERM**
>
> **Price elasticity of demand** (η) is a measure of the extent of change in market demand for a good in response to a change in its price. It is measured as:
>
> $$\frac{\text{The change in quantity demanded, as a \% of demand}}{\text{The change in price, as a \% of the price}}$$

1.4   Since the demand goes up when the price falls, and goes down when the price rises, the elasticity has a negative value, but it is usual to ignore the minus sign.

1.5   EXAMPLE: PRICE ELASTICITY OF DEMAND

The price of a good is £1.20 per unit and annual demand is 800,000 units. Market research indicates that an increase in price of 10 pence per unit will result in a fall in annual demand of 75,000 units. What is the price elasticity of demand?

1.6 SOLUTION

Annual demand at £1.20 per unit is 800,000 units.
Annual demand at £1.30 per unit is 725,000 units.

% change in demand = (75,000/800,000) × 100% = 9.375%
% change in price = (10p/120p) × 100% = 8.333%
Price elasticity of demand = (−9.375/8.333) = −1.125
Ignoring the minus sign, price elasticity is 1.125.

The demand for this good, at a price of £1.20 per unit, would be referred to as **elastic** because the **price elasticity of demand is greater than 1**.

Elastic and inelastic demand

1.7 The value of demand elasticity may be anything from zero to infinity.

KEY TERM

Demand is referred to as **inelastic** if the absolute value is less than 1 and **elastic** if the absolute value is greater than 1.

1.8 Think about what this means.

- Where demand is **inelastic**, the **quantity demanded falls by a smaller percentage than the percentage increase in price**.

- Where demand is **elastic, demand falls** by a **larger percentage than the percentage rise in price**.

Question 1

If the price elasticity of demand is zero, which of the following is/are true?

I   Demand is 'perfectly inelastic'
II   There is no change in price regardless of the quantity demanded
III The demand curve is a vertical straight line
IV   There is no change in the quantity demanded, regardless of any change in price

A   I and III only
B   I and IV only
C   I, II and III only
D   I, III and IV only

Answer

Demand is perfectly inelastic when price changes have no impact on demand. The price elasticity of demand will equal zero only if demand remains unchanged. Statement I is therefore correct.

The price elasticity of demand will equal zero only if demand remains unchanged. If the price remains unchanged, the denominator of the price elasticity of demand equation will have an infinite value. Statement II is therefore incorrect.

If the price elasticity of demand is zero it means that demand never changes and so the graph is a vertical straight line. Statement III is therefore correct.

The price elasticity of demand will equal zero only when demand remains unchanged. Statement IV is therefore correct.

The correct answer is therefore D since statements I, III and IV are correct.

Question 2

The price of a good is £1.50 per unit and annual demand is 600,000 units. If an increase in price of 10p per unit results in a fall in demand of 65,000 units per year, what is the price elasticity of demand (to 3 dp)?

A   1.625
B   0.615
C   1.944
D   1.612

Answer

% change in demand = $\dfrac{65}{600} \times 100\% = 10.8333\%$

% change in price = $\dfrac{10}{150} \times 100\% = 6.6667\%$

Price elasticity of demand = $\dfrac{10.8333}{6.6667} = 1.625$ (to 3dp)

Option A is therefore correct.

If you chose option B, you mixed up the denominator and the numerator in the price elasticity of demand equation.

If you selected option C, you based the changes in price and demand on the final values of £1.60 and 535,000 instead of the initial values of £1.50 and 600,000.

If you selected option D, you have rounded the percentage changes to one decimal place only (and cannot therefore calculate the price elasticity of demand correct to three decimal places).

Elasticity and the pricing decision

1.9   In practice, organisations will have only a rough idea of the shape of their demand curve: there will only be a limited amount of data about quantities sold at certain prices over a period of time *and*, of course, factors other than price might affect demand. Because any conclusions drawn from such data can only give an indication of likely future behaviour, management skill and expertise are also needed. Despite this limitation, an **awareness of the concept of elasticity can assist management with pricing decisions**.

(a)   (i)   In circumstances of **inelastic demand, prices should be increased** because revenues will increase and total costs will reduce (because quantities sold will reduce).

(ii)   In circumstances of **elastic demand**, increases in prices will bring decreases in revenue and decreases in price will bring increases in revenue. Management therefore have to **decide** whether the **increase/decrease in costs will be less than/greater than the increases/decreases in revenue**.

(b)   In situations of **very elastic demand**, overpricing can lead to a massive drop in quantity sold and hence a massive drop in profits whereas underpricing can lead to costly stock outs and, again, a significant drop in profits. **Elasticity must therefore be reduced by creating a customer preference which is unrelated to price** (through advertising and promotional activities).

(c)   In situations of **very inelastic demand**, customers are **not sensitive to price**. **Quality, service, product mix and location** are therefore **more important** to a firm's pricing strategy.

Determining factors

1.10 **Factors that determine the degree of elasticity**

(a) **The price of the good.**

(b) **The price of other goods.** For some goods the market demand is interconnected. Such goods are of two types.

    (i) **Substitutes,** so that an increase in demand for one version of a good is likely to cause a decrease in demand for others. Common examples are rival brands of the same commodity (like *Coca-Cola* and *Pepsi-Cola*), bus journeys versus car journeys.

    (ii) **Complements,** so that an increase in demand for one is likely to cause an increase in demand for the other. Examples are cups and saucers, cars and components.

(c) **Income.** A rise in income gives households more to spend and they will want to buy more goods. However this phenomenon does not affect all goods in the same way.

    (i) **Normal goods** are those for which a **rise in income increases the demand**.

    (ii) **Inferior goods** are those for which **demand falls as income rises**, such as cheap wine.

    (iii) For some goods **demand rises up to a certain point and then remains unchanged,** because there is a limit to which consumers can or want to consume. Examples are basic foodstuffs such as salt and bread.

(d) **Tastes and fashions.** A change in fashion will alter the demand for a good, or a particular variety of a good. Changes in taste may stem from psychological, social or economic causes. There is an argument that tastes and fashions are created by the producers of products and services. There is undeniably some truth in this, but the modern focus on responding to customers' needs and wants suggests otherwise.

(e) **Expectations.** Where consumers believe that prices will rise or that shortages will occur they will attempt to stock up on the product, thereby creating excess demand in the short term.

(f) **Obsolescence.** Many products and services have to be replaced periodically.

    (i) Physical goods are literally 'consumed'. Carpets become threadbare, glasses get broken, foodstuffs get eaten, children grow out of clothes.

    (ii) Technological developments render some goods obsolete. Manual office equipment has been largely replaced by electronic equipment, because it does a better job, more quickly, quietly, efficiently and effectively.

Demand and the market

1.11 Economic theory suggests that the volume of **demand** for a good in **the market as a whole** is influenced by a variety of variables.

- The price of the good
- The price of other goods
- The size and distribution of household income
- Expectations
- Obsolescence
- The perceived quality of the product
- Tastes and fashion

Demand and the individual firm

1.12 The **volume of demand for one organisation's goods rather than another's** is influenced by three principal factors: product life cycle, quality and marketing.

Product life cycle

> ### KEY TERM
>
> **Product life cycle** is 'The period which begins with the initial product specification, and ends with the withdrawal from the market of both the product and its support. It is characterised by defined stages including research, development, introduction, maturity, decline and abandonment.'
> (CIMA *Official Terminology*)

1.13 Most products pass through the following phases.

Phase	Description
Introduction	The product is introduced to the market. Heavy capital expenditure will be incurred on product development and perhaps also on the purchase of new fixed assets and building up stocks for sale. On its introduction to the market, the product will begin to earn some revenue, but initially demand is likely to be small. Potential customers will be unaware of the product or service, and the organisation may have to spend further on advertising to bring the product or service to the attention of the market.
Growth	The product gains a bigger market as demand builds up. Sales revenues increase and the product begins to make a profit. The initial costs of the investment in the new product are gradually recovered.
Maturity	Eventually, the growth in demand for the product will slow down and it will enter a period of relative maturity. It will continue to be profitable. The product may be modified or improved, as a means of sustaining its demand.
Saturation and decline	At some stage, the market will have bought enough of the product and it will therefore reach 'saturation point'. Demand will start to fall. For a while, the product will still be profitable in spite of declining sales, but eventually it will become a loss-maker and this is the time when the organisation should decide to stop selling the product or service, and so the product's life cycle should reach its end.

1.14 The life expectancy of a product will influence the pricing decision. **Short-life products** must be quite **highly priced** so as to give the manufacturer a chance to **recover his investment** and **make a worthwhile** return. This is why fashion goods and new high technology goods, for example, tend to have high prices.

1.15 We have already mentioned that the current tendency is towards shorter product life cycles. Notwithstanding this observation, the **life cycles** of different products may **vary in terms of length of phases, overall length and shape**.

- Fashion products have a very short life and so do high technology products because they become rapidly out-dated by new technological developments.

- **Different versions of the same product may have different life cycles**, and consumers are often aware of this. For example, the prospective buyer of a new car is more likely to purchase a recently introduced Ford than a Vauxhall that has been on the market for several years, even if there is nothing to choose in terms of quality and price.

Quality

1.16 One firm's product may be perceived to be better quality than another's, and may in some cases actually be so, if it uses sturdier materials, goes faster or does whatever it is meant to do in a 'better' way. Other things being equal, **the better quality good will be more in demand** than other versions.

Marketing

1.17 You may be familiar with the 'four Ps' of the marketing mix, all of which influence demand for a firm's goods.

(a) **Price**

(b) **Product**

(c) **Place** refers to the place where a good can be, or is likely to be, purchased.

- If a good is difficult to obtain, potential buyers will turn to substitutes.
- Some goods have no more than local appeal.

(d) **Promotion** refers to the various means by which firms draw attention to their products and services.

- A good brand name is a strong influence on demand.

- Demand can be stimulated by a variety of promotional tools, such as free gifts, money off, shop displays, direct mail and media advertising.

1.18 In recent years, **emphasis** has been placed, especially in marketing, on the importance of **non-price factors in demand**. Thus the roles of product quality, promotion, personal selling and distribution and, in overall terms, brands, have grown. While it can be relatively easy for a competitor to copy a price cut, at least in the short term, it is much **more difficult to copy a successful brand image**.

1.19 Some larger organisations go to considerable effort to estimate the demand for their products or services at differing price levels; in other words, they produce estimated demand curves. A **knowledge of demand curves can be very useful**: for example, a large transport company such as *Stagecoach* might be considering an increase in bus fares or underground fares. The effect on total revenues and profit of the fares increase could be estimated from a knowledge of the demand for transport services at different price levels. If an increase in the price per ticket caused a large fall in demand (that is, if demand were price-elastic) total revenues and profits would fall; whereas a fares increase when demand is price-inelastic would boost total revenue and since a transport authority's costs are largely fixed, would probably boost total profits too.

Markets

1.20 The price that an organisation can charge for its products will be determined to a greater or lesser degree by the market in which it operates.

> **KEY TERMS**
>
> - **Perfect competition**: many buyers and many sellers all dealing in an identical product. Neither producer nor user has any market power and both must accept the prevailing market price.
>
> - **Monopoly**: one seller who dominates many buyers. The monopolist can use his market power to set a profit-maximising price.
>
> - **Monopolistic competition**: a large number of suppliers offer similar, but not identical, products. The similarities ensure elastic demand whereas the slight differences give some monopolistic power to the supplier.
>
> - **Oligopoly**: where relatively few competitive companies dominate the market. Whilst each large firm has the ability to influence market prices the unpredictable reaction from the other giants makes the final industry price indeterminate. Cartels are often formed.

Other factors

1.21

Influence	Explanation/example
Price sensitivity	This will vary amongst purchasers. Those that can pass on the cost of purchases will be the least sensitive and will therefore respond more to other elements of perceived value. For example, the business traveller will be more concerned about the level of service and quality of food in looking for an hotel than price, provided that it fits the corporate budget. In contrast, the family on holiday are likely to be very price sensitive when choosing an overnight stay.
Price perception	This is the way customers react to prices. For example, customers may react to a price increase by buying more. This could be because they expect further price increases to follow (they are 'stocking up').
Compatibility with other products	A typical example is operating systems on computers, for which a user would like to have a wide range of compatible software available. For these types of product there is usually a **cumulative effect on demand**. The more people who buy one of the formats, the more choice there is likely to be of software for that format. This in turn is likely to influence future purchasers. The owner of the rights to the preferred format will eventually find little competition and will be able to charge a premium price for the product.
Competitors	An organisation, in setting prices, sends out signals. Competitors are likely to react to these signals in some way. In some industries (such as petrol retailing) pricing moves in unison; in others, price changes by one supplier may initiate a price war, with each supplier undercutting the others. Competition is discussed in more detail below.

Influence	Explanation/example
Competition from substitute products	These are products which could be transformed for the same use or which might become desirable to customers at particular price levels. For example, train travel comes under competition as the quality, speed and comfort of coach travel rises. Similarly, if the price of train travel rises it comes under competition from cheaper coach travel and more expensive air travel.
Suppliers	If an organisation's suppliers notice a price rise for the organisation's products, they may seek a rise in the price for their supplies to the organisation on the grounds that it is now able to pay a higher price.
Inflation	In periods of inflation the organisation may need to change prices to reflect increases in the prices of supplies and so on. Such changes may be needed to keep relative (real) prices unchanged.
Quality	In the absence of other information, customers tend to judge quality by price. Thus a price change may send signals to customers concerning the quality of the product. A price rise may indicate improvements in quality, a price reduction may signal reduced quality, for example through the use of inferior components.
Incomes	In times of rising incomes, price may become a less important marketing variable compared with product quality and convenience of access (distribution). When income levels are falling and/or unemployment levels rising, price will become a much more important marketing variable.
Ethics	Ethical considerations are a further factor, for example whether or not to exploit short-term shortages through higher prices.

Competition

1.22   In established industries dominated by a few major firms, it is generally accepted that a price initiative by one firm will be countered by a price reaction by competitors. In these circumstances, prices tend to be fairly **stable**, unless pushed upwards by inflation or strong growth in demand.

If a rival cuts its prices in the expectation of increasing its market share, a firm has several options.

(a) It will **maintain its existing prices** if the expectation is that only a small market share would be lost, so that it is more profitable to keep prices at their existing level. Eventually, the rival firm may drop out of the market or be forced to raise its prices.

(b) It may **maintain its prices but respond with a non-price counter-attack**. This is a more positive response, because the firm will be securing or justifying its current prices with a product change, advertising, or better back-up services.

(c) It may **reduce its prices**. This should protect the firm's market share so that the main beneficiary from the price reduction will be the consumer.

(d) It may **raise its prices and respond with a non-price counter-attack**. The extra revenue from the higher prices might be used to finance an advertising campaign or product design changes. A price increase would be based on a campaign to emphasise the quality difference between the firm's own product and the rival's product.

2 FULL COST-PLUS PRICING

2.1 **In practice cost is one of the most important influences on price**. Many firms base price on simple **cost-plus rules** (costs are estimated and then a profit margin is added in order to set the price). We had a brief look at cost-plus pricing when we studied job costing in Chapter 10.

> ### KEY TERM
>
> **Full cost-plus pricing** is a method of determining the sales price by calculating the full cost of the product and adding a percentage mark-up for profit.

2.2 The 'full cost' may be a fully absorbed production cost only, or it may include some absorbed administration, selling and distribution overhead.

2.3 A business might have an idea of the percentage profit margin it would like to earn, and so might **decide on an average profit mark-up** as a general guideline for pricing decisions. This would be particularly **useful for** businesses that carry out a large amount of **contract work or jobbing work**, for which individual job or contract prices must be quoted regularly to prospective customers. However, the percentage profit **mark-up does not have to be rigid and fixed**, but can be varied to suit the circumstances. In particular, the percentage mark-up can be varied to suit demand conditions in the market.

2.4 EXAMPLE: FULL COST-PLUS PRICING

Markup Ltd has begun to produce a new product, Product X, for which the following cost estimates have been made.

	£
Direct materials	27
Direct labour: 4 hrs at £5 per hour	20
Variable production overheads: machining, ½ hr at £6 per hour	3
	50

Production fixed overheads are budgeted at £300,000 per month and because of the shortage of available machining capacity, the company will be restricted to 10,000 hours of machine time per month. The absorption rate will be a direct labour rate, however, and budgeted direct labour hours are 25,000 per month. It is estimated that the company could obtain a minimum contribution of £10 per machine hour on producing items other than product X.

The direct cost estimates are not certain as to material usage rates and direct labour productivity, and it is recognised that the estimates of direct materials and direct labour costs may be subject to an error of ± 15%. Machine time estimates are similarly subject to an error of ± 10%.

The company wishes to make a profit of 20% on full production cost from product X.

Required

Ascertain the full cost-plus based price.

2.5 SOLUTION

Even for a relatively 'simple' cost-plus pricing estimate, some problems can arise, and certain assumptions must be made and stated. In this example, we can identify two problems.

- Should the opportunity cost of machine time be included in cost or not?
- What allowance, if any, should be made for the possible errors in cost estimates?

Different assumptions could be made.

(a) **Exclude machine time opportunity costs: ignore possible costing errors**

	£
Direct materials	27.00
Direct labour (4 hours)	20.00
Variable production overheads	3.00
Fixed production overheads	
(at $\dfrac{£300,000}{25,000}$ = £12 per direct labour hour)	48.00
Full production cost	98.00
Profit mark-up (20%)	19.60
Selling price per unit of product X	117.60

(b) **Include machine time opportunity costs: ignore possible costing errors**

	£
Full production cost as in (a)	98.00
Opportunity cost of machine time:	
contribution forgone (½ hr × £10)	5.00
Adjusted full cost	103.00
Profit mark-up (20%)	20.60
Selling price per unit of product X	123.60

(c) **Exclude machine time opportunity costs but make full allowance for possible under-estimates of cost**

	£	£
Direct materials	27.00	
Direct labour	20.00	
	47.00	
Possible error (15%)	7.05	
		54.05
Variable production overheads	3.00	
Possible error (10%)	0.30	
		3.30
Fixed production overheads (4 hrs × £12)	48.00	
Possible error (labour time) (15%)	7.20	
		55.20
Potential full production cost		112.55
Profit mark-up (20%)		22.51
Selling price per unit of product X		135.06

(d) **Include machine time opportunity costs and make a full allowance for possible under-estimates of cost**

	£
Potential full production cost as in (c)	112.55
Opportunity cost of machine time:	
potential contribution forgone (½ hr × £10 × 110%)	5.50
Adjusted potential full cost	118.05
Profit mark-up (20%)	23.61
Selling price per unit of product X	141.66

Using different assumptions, we could arrive at any of four different unit prices in the range £117.60 to £141.66.

Advantages and disadvantages of full cost-plus pricing

2.6 There are several disadvantages with relying on a full cost approach to pricing.

423 *BPP*

- It **fails to recognise** that since demand may be determining price, **there will be a profit-maximising combination of price and demand**.

- There may be a need to **adjust prices to market and demand conditions**.

- **Budgeted output volume** needs to be established. Output volume is a key factor in the overhead absorption rate.

- A **suitable basis for overhead absorption** must be selected, especially where a business produces more than one product.

2.7 However, it is a **quick, simple and cheap** method of pricing which can be delegated to junior managers (which is particularly important with jobbing work where many prices must be decided and quoted each day) and, since the size of the profit margin can be varied, a decision based on a price in excess of full cost should ensure that a company working at normal capacity will **cover all of its fixed costs and make a profit**.

Question 3

A company budgets to make 20,000 units which have a variable cost of production of £4 per unit. Fixed production costs are £60,000 per annum. If price is to be 40% higher than full cost, what is the price of the product using the full cost-plus method?

A   £9.80
\B   £2.80
C   £7.00
D   £5.60

Answer

Full cost per unit = variable cost + fixed cost

Variable cost = £4 per unit

Fixed cost = $\frac{£60,000}{20,000}$ = £3 per unit

Full cost per unit = £(4 + 3) = £7

∴ Price using full cost-plus pricing method = £7.00 × $\frac{140\%}{100}$

= £9.80

Option A is therefore correct.

If you selected option B, you have calculated the profit (40% × £7.00) instead of the full cost plus the profit (£7.00 + £2.80 = £9.80).

If you selected option C, you forgot to add the profit to the full cost.

If you selected option D, you have increased the variable cost by 40% only and have not included fixed costs at all.

3   MARGINAL COST-PLUS PRICING

KEY TERM

Marginal cost plus pricing/mark-up pricing is a method of determining the sales price by adding a profit margin on to either marginal cost of production or marginal cost of sales.

3.1 Whereas a full cost-plus approach to pricing draws attention to net profit and the net profit margin, a variable cost-plus approach to pricing **draws attention to gross profit** and the **gross profit margin,** or **contribution**.

Question 4

A product has the following costs.

	£
Direct materials	5
Direct labour	3
Variable overheads	7

Fixed overheads are £10,000 per month. Budgeted sales per month are 400 units to allow the product to break even.

Required

Determine the profit margin which needs to be added to *marginal* cost to allow the product to break even.

Answer

Breakeven point is when total contribution equals fixed costs.

At breakeven point, £10,000 = 400 (price − £15)
∴ £25 = price − £15
∴ £40 = price
∴ Profit margin = 40 − 15/15 × 100% = $166^2/_3$%

3.2 **The advantages of a marginal cost-plus approach to pricing**

(a) It is a **simple and easy** method to use.

(b) The **mark-up percentage can be varied,** and so mark-up pricing can be adjusted to reflect demand conditions.

(c) It **draws management attention to contribution,** and the effects of higher or lower sales volumes on profit. In this way, it helps to create a better awareness of the concepts and implications of marginal costing and cost-volume-profit analysis. For example, if a product costs £10 per unit and a mark-up of 150% is added to reach a price of £25 per unit, management should be clearly aware that every additional £1 of sales revenue would add 60 pence to contribution and profit.

(d) In practice, mark-up pricing is **used** in businesses **where there is a readily-identifiable basic variable cost**. Retail industries are the most obvious example, and it is quite common for the prices of goods in shops to be fixed by adding a mark-up (20% or 33.3%, say) to the purchase cost.

3.3 There are, of course, **disadvantages of a marginal cost-plus approach to pricing**.

(a) Although the **size** of the mark-up can be varied in accordance with demand conditions, it **does not ensure that sufficient attention is paid to demand conditions, competitors' prices and profit maximisation**.

(b) It **ignores fixed overheads** in the pricing decision, but the sales price must be sufficiently high to ensure that a profit is made after covering fixed costs.

Exam focus point

The study guide for Paper 1.2 states that you must be able to discuss the advantages and disadvantages of full cost-plus and marginal cost-plus pricing.

BPP PUBLISHING

4 OTHER PRICING POLICIES

Special orders

4.1 A special order is a **one-off** revenue earning opportunity. These may arise in the following situations.

(a) When a business has a regular source of income but also has some **spare capacity** allowing it to take on extra work if demanded. For example a brewery might have a capacity of 500,000 barrels per month but only be producing and selling 300,000 barrels per month. It could therefore consider special orders to use up some of its spare capacity.

(b) When a business has **no regular source of income** and relies exclusively on its ability to respond to demand. A building firm is a typical example as are many types of sub-contractors. In the service sector consultants often work on this basis.

The reason for making the distinction is that in the case of **(a)**, a firm would normally attempt to cover its longer-term running costs in its prices for its regular product. Pricing for special orders need therefore **take no account of unavoidable fixed costs**. This is clearly not the case for a firm in (b)'s position, where special orders are the only source of income for the foreseeable future.

4.2 The **basic approach** in both situations is to determine the **price at which the firm would break even** if it undertook the work, that is, the **minimum price** that it could afford to charge. It would have to cover the incremental costs of producing and selling the item and the opportunity costs of the resources consumed.

4.3 In today's competitive markets it is very much the **modern trend to tailor products or services to customer demand** rather than producing for stock. This suggests that 'special' **orders may become the norm** for most businesses.

New products

4.4 Suppose that Novo plc is about to launch a new product with a variable cost of £10 per unit. The company has carried out market research (at a cost of £15,000) to determine the potential demand for the product at various selling prices.

Selling price £	Demand Units
30	20,000
25	30,000
20	40,000

Its current capacity is for 20,000 units but additional capacity can be made available by using the resources of another product line. If this is done the lost contribution from the other product will be £35,000 for each additional 10,000 units of capacity.

How could we **analyse this information** for senior management in a way that helps them to **decide on the product's launch price**?

4.5 **Tabulation** is the approach to use with a problem of this type.

Selling price £	Demand Units ('000)	Variable costs £'000	Opportunity costs £'000	Total costs £'000	Sales revenue £ '000	Contribution £'000
30	20	200	-	200	600	400
25	30	300	35	335	750	415
20	40	400	70	470	800	330

4.6 The **optimum price to maximise short-term profits is £25**. However, it is quite possible that the aim will **not** be to maximise short-term profits, and a number of other strategies may be adopted, as discussed below.

4.7 The main **objections** to the approach described above are that it only **considers a limited range of prices** (what about charging £27.50?) and it **takes no account of the uncertainty of forecast demand**. However, allowance could be made for both situations by collecting more information.

4.8 A new product pricing strategy will depend largely on whether a company's product or service is the first of its kind on the market.

   (a) If the **product is the first of its kind**, there will be **no competition** yet, and the company, for a time at least, will be a **monopolist**. Monopolists have more influence over price and are able to set a price at which they think they can maximise their profits. A monopolist's price is likely to be higher, and his profits bigger, than those of a company operating in a competitive market.

   (b) If the new product being launched by a company is **following a competitor's product** onto the market, the pricing strategy will be **constrained by what the competitor** is already doing. The new product could be given a higher price if its quality is better, or it could be given a price which matches the competition. Undercutting the competitor's price might result in a price war and a fall of the general price level in the market.

Market penetration pricing

> **KEY TERM**
>
> **Market penetration pricing** is a policy of low prices when the product is first launched in order to obtain sufficient penetration into the market.

4.9 **Circumstances in which a penetration policy may be appropriate**

- If the firm wishes to **discourage new entrants** into the market

- If the firm wishes to **shorten the initial period of the product's life cycle** in order to enter the growth and maturity stages as quickly as possible

- If there are **significant economies of scale** to be achieved **from a high volume of output**, so that quick penetration into the market is desirable in order to gain unit cost reductions

- If **demand is highly elastic** and so would respond well to low prices.

4.10 Penetration prices are prices which aim to **secure a substantial share in a substantial total market**. A firm might therefore **deliberately build excess production capacity** and set its prices very low. As demand builds up the spare capacity will be used up gradually and unit costs will fall; the firm might even reduce prices further as unit costs fall. In this way, early losses will enable the firm to dominate the market and have the lowest costs.

Market skimming pricing

> ## KEY TERM
>
> **Market skimming pricing** involves charging high prices when a product is first launched and spending heavily on advertising and sales promotion to obtain sales.

4.11 As the product moves into the later stages of its life cycle, **progressively lower prices will be charged** and so the profitable 'cream' is skimmed off in stages until sales can only be sustained at lower prices.

4.12 The aim of market skimming is to **gain high unit profits early in the product's life**. High unit prices make it **more likely that competitors will enter the market** than if lower prices were to be charged.

4.13 **Circumstances in which such a policy may be appropriate**

   (a) Where the product is **new and different**, so that customers are prepared to pay high prices so as to be one up on other people who do not own it.

   (b) Where the **strength** of demand and the **sensitivity of demand** to price are **unknown**. It is better from the point of view of marketing to start by charging high prices and then reduce them if the demand for the product turns out to be price elastic than to start by charging low prices and then attempt to raise them substantially if demand appears to be insensitive to higher prices.

   (c) Where **high prices** in the early stages of a product's life might **generate high initial cash flows**. A firm with liquidity problems may prefer market-skimming for this reason.

   (d) Where the firm **can identify different market segments** for the product, each prepared to pay progressively lower prices. If **product differentiation** can be introduced, it may be possible to continue to sell at higher prices to some market segments when lower prices are charged in others. This is discussed further below.

   (e) Where products may have a **short life cycle**, and so need to recover their development costs and make a profit relatively quickly.

Premium pricing

4.14 This involves making a product **appear 'different'** through **product differentiation** so as **to justify a premium price**. The product may be different in terms of, for example, quality, reliability, durability, after sales service or extended warranties. Heavy advertising can establish brand loyalty which can help to sustain a premium and premium prices will always be paid by those customers who blindly equate high price with high quality.

Price discrimination

> ## KEY TERM
>
> **Price discrimination** is the practice of charging different prices for the same product to different groups of buyers when these prices are not reflective of cost differences.

4.15 In certain circumstances the **same product** can be sold at different prices to **different customers**. There are a number of bases on which such discriminating prices can be set.

Basis	Detail
By market segment	A cross-channel ferry company would market its services at different prices in England and France, for example. Services such as cinemas and hairdressers are often available at lower prices to old age pensioners and/or juveniles.
By product version	Many car models have **optional extras** which enable one brand to appeal to a wider cross-section of customers. The final price need not reflect the cost price of the optional extras directly: usually the top of the range model would carry a price much in excess of the cost of provision of the extras, as a prestige appeal.
By place	Theatre seats are usually sold according to their location so that patrons pay different prices for the same performance according to the seat type they occupy.
By time	This is perhaps the most popular type of price discrimination. Off-peak travel bargains, hotel prices and telephone charges are all attempts to increase sales revenue by covering variable but not necessarily average cost of provision. Railway companies are successful price discriminators, charging more to rush hour rail commuters whose demand is inelastic at certain times of the day.

4.16 Price discrimination can only be effective if a number of **conditions** hold.

(a) The market must be **segmentable** in price terms, and different sectors must show different intensities of demand. Each of the sectors must be identifiable, distinct and separate from the others, and be accessible to the firm's marketing communications.

(b) There must be little or **no** chance of a **black market** developing (this would allow those in the lower priced segment to resell to those in the higher priced segment).

(c) There must be little or **no** chance that **competitors** can and will undercut the firm's prices in the higher priced (and/or most profitable) market segments.

(d) The cost of segmenting and **administering** the arrangements should not exceed the extra revenue derived from the price discrimination strategy.

5 THE OPTIMUM PRICE/OUTPUT LEVEL

Demand curves

5.1 Some larger organisations go to considerable effort to **estimate the demand** for their products or services at differing price levels; in other words, they produce **estimated demand curves**. A knowledge of demand curves can be very useful: for example, a large transport authority such as the London Transport authority might be considering an increase in underground fares. The effect on **total revenues** and **profit** of the fares increase could be estimated from a knowledge of the demand for transport services at different price levels. If an increase in the price per ticket caused a large fall in demand (that is, if demand were price-elastic) total revenues and profits would fall; whereas a fares increase when demand is price-inelastic would boost total revenue and since a transport authority's costs are largely fixed, would probably boost total profits too.

5.2 Some businesses enjoy a **monopoly position** in their market or something akin to a monopoly position, even in a competitive market. This is because they develop a unique marketing mix, for example a unique combination of price and quality, or a monopoly in a localised area. The significance of a monopoly situation is as follows.

(a) **The business does not have to 'follow the market' on price**. It is not a 'price taker', but has more choice and flexibility in the prices it sets. Because the business has this freedom of choice in pricing, it will find that at higher prices demand for its products or services will be less. Conversely, at lower prices, demand for its products or services will be higher.

(b) **There will be an optimum price/output level at which the business can maximise its profits**. This is the price level at which the marginal cost of making an extra unit of output is equal to the marginal revenue obtained from selling it (**MC = MR**).

Deriving the demand curve

FORMULA TO LEARN

When demand is linear the equation for the **demand curve** is

$$P = a - \frac{bQ}{\Delta Q}$$

where
P = the price
Q = the quantity demanded
a = the price at which demand would be nil
b = the amount by which the price falls for each stepped change in demand
ΔQ = the stepped change in demand

The constant a is calculated as follows.

$$a = £(\text{current price}) + \left(\frac{\text{Current quantity at current price}}{\text{Change in quantity when price is changed by } £b} \times £b \right)$$

When demand is linear, an alternative equation for the **demand curve** (**linear demand function**) is

$$P = a + bQ$$

where $b = \dfrac{\Delta P}{\Delta Q} = \dfrac{\text{change in price}}{\text{change in quantity}}$

5.3 EXAMPLE: DERIVING THE DEMAND CURVE

(a) Suppose the current price of a product is £12. At this price the company sells 60 items a month. One month the company decides to raise the price to £14, but only 45 items are sold at this price. Clearly, if the company decided to go on raising its price, eventually it would sell no items at all.

(b) Assuming demand is linear, each increase of £2 in the price would result in a fall in demand of 15 units. Therefore, for demand to be nil, the price needs to rise from its current level by as many times as there are 15 units in 60 units: 60/15 = 4.

(c) The price needs to rise by £2 four times from its current level of £12 before no items at all are sold.

£12 + (4 × £2) = £20

Using the expression above, this can be shown as

$$a = £12 + \left(\frac{60}{15} \times £2 \right) = £20$$

(d) The **demand equation** can now be determined: we have all the information we need.

$$P = a - \frac{bQ}{\Delta Q}$$

$$P = 20 - \frac{2Q}{15}$$

(e) We can check this by substituting £12 and £14 for P

$$12 = 20 - 2 \times \frac{60}{15} = 20 - 8 = 12$$

$$14 = 20 - \frac{2 \times 45}{15} = 20 - 6 = 14$$

(f) The equation can also be re-arranged for Q.

$$Q = \frac{(a \times \Delta Q) - (\Delta Q \times P)}{b}$$

Alternative approach

$P_1 = £12, Q_1 = 60$

$P_2 = £14, Q_2 = 45$

$$b = \frac{\Delta P}{\Delta Q} = \frac{12 - 14}{60 - 45} = \frac{-2}{15}$$

$a = P - bQ$

$$a = 12 - (\frac{-2}{15} \times 60)$$

$a = 12 - (-8)$

$a = 20$

∴ The linear demand function is $P = 20 - \frac{2Q}{15}$ (as calculated above).

5.4 Attempt the following questions about finding an expression for a demand curve.

Question 5

The current price of a product is £30 and the producers sell 100 items a week at this price. One week the price is dropped by £3 as a special offer and the producers sell 150 items.

Find an expression for the demand curve.

Answer

$$a = \pounds 30 + \left(\frac{100}{50} \times \pounds 3 \right)$$

$$= \pounds 36$$

$$P = 36 - \frac{3Q}{50} \quad \text{or} \quad Q = \frac{1,800 - 50P}{3}$$

Check

$$27 = 36 - \frac{3Q}{50} \qquad\qquad 150 = \frac{1,800 - 50P}{3}$$

$$\frac{3Q}{50} = 9 \qquad\qquad 50P = 1,800 - 450$$

$$Q = 150 \qquad\qquad P = 27$$

Alternative approach

$P_1 = \pounds 30, Q_1 = 100$

$P_2 = \pounds 27, Q_2 = 150$

$$b = \frac{\Delta P}{\Delta Q} = \frac{30 - 27}{100 - 150} = \frac{3}{-50}$$

$$a = P - bQ$$

$$a = 30 - \left(\frac{-3 \times 100}{50} \right)$$

$$a = 30 + 6$$

$$a = 36$$

$\therefore$ An expression for the demand curve is $P = 36 - \dfrac{3Q}{50}$ or $Q = \dfrac{1,800 - 50P}{3}$

Question 6

Lynn has set up her own market stall selling terracotta pots for gardens. As an experiment she has tried two different prices, each for one week. At a price of £3 she sold 400 pots and at a price of £4 she sold 340 pots. Assuming that demand is linear, find the linear demand function for Lynn's stall.

Answer

If $P = a - \dfrac{bQ}{\Delta Q}$

$$a = \pounds 4 + \left(\frac{340 \times 1}{60} \right)$$

$$= \pounds(4 + 5.67) = \pounds 9.67$$

$$\therefore P = 9.67 - \frac{1 \times Q}{60}$$

Alternative approach

If $P = a + bQ$

$P_1 = \pounds 3, P_2 = \pounds 4$

$Q_1 = 400, Q_2 = 340$

$$\therefore b = \frac{\Delta P}{\Delta Q} = \frac{+1}{-60} = \frac{-1}{60}$$

$$a = P - bQ$$

$$a = 3 - (\frac{-1 \times 400}{60})$$

$$= 3 + 6.67$$

$$= 9.67$$

$\therefore$ The linear demand function is $P = 9.67 - \dfrac{Q}{60}$

Exam focus point

Remember to show all of your workings when performing mathematical calculations in an exam – it shows the examiner that you know exactly what you are doing even if you final answer isn't correct because you have made a simple error.

Optimum pricing in practice

5.5 There are severe problems in practice with applying the approach described above for the following reasons.

- It assumes that the demand curve and total costs can be identified with certainty. This is extremely unlikely to be so.

- It ignores the market research costs associated with acquiring knowledge of demand.

- It assumes the firm has no production constraints which could mean that the equilibrium point between supply and demand cannot be reached.

- It assumes that the organisation wishes to maximise profits. In fact it may have other objectives.

- It assumes that price is the only influence on quantity demanded. We have seen that this is far from the case.

Profit maximisation

5.6 **Profit maximisation** is assumed to be the goal of the firm in most economic and accounting textbooks. Where the entrepreneur is in full managerial control of the firm, as in the case of a small owner-managed company or partnership, this assumption would seem to be very reasonable. Even in companies owned by shareholders but run by non-shareholding managers, if the manager is serving the company's (ie the shareholders') interests, we might expect that the profit maximisation assumption should be close to the truth.

5.7 We can define **profits** as **total revenue minus total costs** at any level of output. Profits are at a maximum where the (vertical) distance between the total revenue (TR) and total cost (TC) curves is greatest. On the following graph line AB indicates where profits are at a maximum, and point M indicates the output at which profits will be maximised.

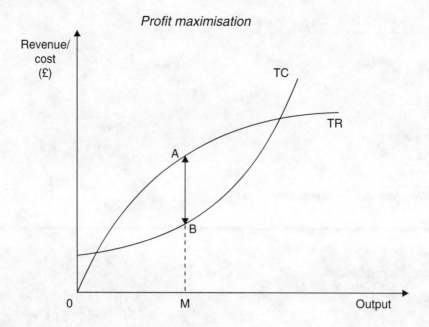

Profit maximisation

Total revenue, average revenue and marginal revenue

5.8   There are three aspects of revenue to consider.

(a) **Total revenue (TR)** is the total income obtained from selling a given quantity of output. We can think of this as quantity sold multiplied by the price per unit.

(b) **Average revenue (AR)** we can think of as the price per unit sold.

(c) **Marginal revenue (MR)** is the addition to total revenue earned from the sale of one extra unit of output.

5.9   If a firm can sell all its extra output at the same price, the AR 'curve' will be a **straight line** on a graph, **horizontal** to the x axis. The marginal revenue per unit from selling extra units at a fixed price must be the same as the average price.

5.10   Usually, though, the AR falls as more units are sold, so the MR must be less than the AR. If the price per unit must be lowered to sell more units, then the marginal revenue per unit obtained from selling the extra units will be less than the previous price per unit.

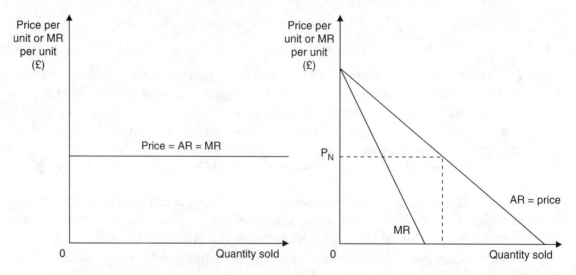

5.11   Note that all units are sold at the same price. The firm has to reduce its price to sell more, but the price must be reduced for *all* units sold, not just for the extra units. This is because we are assuming that all output is produced for a single market, where a single price will prevail.

5.12 When the price per unit has to be reduced in order to increase the firm's sales the marginal revenue can become **negative**. This happens at price P_N when a reduction in price does not increase output sufficiently to earn the same total revenue as before. In this situation, the price elasticity of demand would be inelastic.

5.13 **Revenue is maximised when MR = O** ie when the marginal revenue line shown in the graph in paragraph 5.10 cuts the x-axis. When MR = O additional units sold do not create any additional revenue, and revenue is therefore maximised at this point.

Profit maximisation: MC = MR

5.14 As a firm produces and sells more units, its total costs will increase and its total revenues will also increase (unless the price elasticity of demand is inelastic and the firm faces a downward sloping AR curve).

(a) Provided that the extra cost of making an extra unit is **less than** the extra revenue obtained from selling it, the firm will increase its profits by making and selling the extra unit.

(b) If the extra cost of making an extra unit of output **exceeds** the extra revenue obtainable from selling it, the firm's profits would be reduced by making and selling the extra unit.

(c) If the extra cost of making an extra unit of output is **exactly equal** to the extra revenue obtainable from selling it, bearing in mind that economic cost includes an amount for normal profit, it will be worth the firm's while to make and sell the extra unit. And since the extra cost of yet another unit would be higher (the law of diminishing returns applies) whereas extra revenue per unit from selling extra units is never higher, the **profit-maximising output** is reached at this point where **MC = MR**.

5.15 In other words, given the **objective of profit maximisation**:

(a) if MC is less than MR, profits will be increased by making and selling more;

(b) if MC is greater than MR, profits will fall if more units are made and sold, and a profit-maximising firm would not make the extra output.

If **MC = MR**, the profit-maximising output has been reached, and so this is the output quantity that a profit-maximising firm will decide to supply.

Question 7

A firm operates in a market where there is imperfect competition, so that to sell more units of output, it must reduce the sales price of all the units it sells. The following data is available for prices and costs.

Total output Units	Sales price per unit (AR) £	Average cost of output (AC) £ per unit
0	-	-
1	504	720
2	471	402
3	439	288
4	407	231
5	377	201
6	346	189
7	317	182
8	288	180
9	259	186
10	232	198

The total cost of zero output is £600.

At what output level and price would the firm maximise its profits, assuming that fractions of units cannot be made?

Answer

Units	Price £	Total revenue £	Marginal revenue £	Total cost £	Marginal cost £	Profit £
0	0	0	0	600	-	(600)
1	504	504	504	720	120	(216)
2	471	942	438	804	84	138
3	439	1,317	375	864	60	453
4	407	1,628	311	924	60	704
5	377	1,885	257	1,005	81	880
6	346	2,076	191	1,134	129	942
7*	317	2,219	143	1,274	140	945
8	288	2,304	85	1,440	166	864
9	259	2,331	27	1,674	234	657
10	232	2,320	-11	1,980	306	340

* Profit is maximised at 7 units of output where MR is most nearly equal to MC.

Chapter roundup

- **Price elasticity** is a measure of the extent of change in market demand for a good in response to a change in its price. If **demand is elastic** a reduction in price would lead to a rise in total sales revenue. If **demand is inelastic** a reduction in price would lead to a fall in total sales revenue.

- In **full cost-plus pricing** the sales price is determined by calculating the full cost of the product and then adding a percentage mark-up for profit. **Marginal cost-plus pricing** involves adding a profit margin to the marginal cost of production/sales. The most important criticism of full cost-plus pricing is that it fails to recognise that since sales demand may be determined by the sales price, there will be a profit-maximising combination of price and demand. A marginal costing approach is more likely to help with identifying a profit-maximising price.

- The basic approach to pricing **special orders** is **minimum pricing**.

- Three alternative pricing strategies for **new** products are **market penetration pricing, market skimming pricing** and **premium pricing**.

- **Price discrimination** may be used to make products appear to be different and segment markets so that premium prices can be justified in some markets.

- Some organisations produce estimated **demand curves** in order to ascertain how price increases will affect total revenues and profits.

- When demand is linear, the **equation for the demand curve** is as follows.

$$P = a - \frac{bQ}{\Delta Q} \text{ or } P = a + bQ$$

- The **optimum price/output level** at which a business can maximise its profits is when **MC = MR** (marginal cost = marginal revenue).

- **Revenue is maximised** when **MR = 0**, ie when additional units sold do not create any additional revenue.

Quick quiz

1 The price elasticity of demand for a particular good at the current price is 1.2. Demand for this good at this price is (1) **elastic/~~inelastic~~**. If the price of the good is reduced, total sales revenue will (2) **rise/~~fall/stay the same~~**.

2 Name the five stages of the product life cycle. *Introduction — Maturity*

3 Name one advantage, and one disadvantage of full cost-plus pricing. *Takes all costs into account / fails to recognise that sales demand may be determined by price*

4 A company knows that demand for its new product will be highly elastic. The most appropriate pricing strategy for the new product will be

Market penetration pricing — ✓

Market skimming pricing —

5 If demand is linear, and the linear demand function is P = a + bQ

P = *Price*

Q = *Quantity*

b = *Change in price / Change in quantity*

a = *Constant*

6 Profits are maximised when marginal cost is equal to marginal revenue.

True — ✓

False —

7 When are revenues maximised? *MR = AR* / *MR = 0*

Answers to quick quiz

1   (1) elastic, (2) rise

2   Introduction, growth, maturity, saturation and decline

3   Advantage = pricing rule can be delegated
     Disadvantage = takes no account of market and demand conditions

4   Market penetration pricing

5   P = price

     Q = quantity

$$b = \frac{\Delta P}{\Delta Q} = \frac{\text{change in price}}{\text{change in quantity}}$$

     a = constant

6   True. Profits are maximised when MC = MR.

7   Revenues are maximised when MR = 0.

Now try the questions below from the Exam Question Bank

Number	Level	Marks	Time
38	MCQ	n/a	n/a
39	Examination	10	18 mins

Part E
Budgeting and
performance
measurement

Chapter 22

PREPARING THE MASTER BUDGET

Topic list	Syllabus reference
1 The functions and purposes of a budget	8
2 Stages in the preparation of a budget	8
3 Operating budgets	8
4 Cash budgets	8
5 Budgeted profit and loss account and balance sheet	8

Introduction

This chapter is the first of two on a new topic, **budgeting**. It is a topic which you will meet at all stages of your examination studies so it is vital that you get a firm grasp of the basics now. The chapter begins by explaining the **reasons** why an organisation might prepare a budget and goes on to detail the **stages in the preparation of a budget**. The method of preparing and the relationship between the various **operating budgets** is then set out.

The chapter also considers the construction of **cash budgets** and **budgeted profit and loss accounts and balance sheets**, the budgeted profit and loss account and balance sheet making up what is known as a **master budget**.

In Chapter 23 we will build on the general awareness of budgeting gained in this chapter and look at more specific budgeting issues.

Study guide

Section 25 - Budgeting

- Explain the functions and purposes of budgeting
- Explain the administrative procedures required to ensure an effective budget process
- Describe the stages in the budgeting processs
- Prepare operating budgets including the identification and impact of a principal budget factor

Exam guide

Budgeting is one of the key areas of the syllabus for Paper 1.2. Look out for Section B questions which require the preparation of operating budgets and the identification of the principal budget factor.

1   THE FUNCTIONS AND PURPOSES OF A BUDGET

> **KEY TERM**
>
> A **budget** is 'A quantitative statement, for a defined period of time, which may include planned revenues, expenses, assets, liabilities and cash flows'.
>
> (CIMA *Official Terminology*)

441

1.1 A budget has four main purposes.

- To **coordinate** the activities of different departments towards a single plan
- To **communicate targets** to the managers responsible for achieving them
- To **establish a system of control** by comparing budgeted and actual results
- To **compel planning**

2 STAGES IN THE PREPARATION OF A BUDGET

2.1 Having seen why organisations prepare budgets we will turn our attention to the mechanics of budget preparation.

Budget committee

2.2 The **coordination** and **administration** of budgets is usually the responsibility of a **budget committee** (with the managing director as chairman). The budget committee is assisted by a **budget officer** who is usually an accountant. Every part of the organisation should be represented on the committee, so there should be a representative from sales, production, marketing and so on. Functions of the budget committee include the following.

- **Coordination and allocation of responsibility** for the preparation of budgets
- Issuing of the **budget manual**
- **Timetabling**
- **Provision of information** to assist in the preparation of budgets
- **Communication** of final budgets to the appropriate managers
- **Monitoring** the budgeting process by **comparing actual and budgeted results**

Responsibility for budgets

2.3 The responsibility for preparing the budgets should, ideally, lie with the managers who are responsible for implementing them. For example, the preparation of particular budgets might be allocated as follows.

(a) The **sales manager** should draft the **sales budget** and the selling overhead cost centre budgets.

(b) The **purchasing manager** should draft the **material purchases budget**.

(c) The **production manager** should draft the **direct production cost budgets**.

Question 1

Which of the following is the budget committee *not* responsible for?

A   Preparing functional budgets
B   Timetabling the budgeting operation
C   Allocating responsibility for the budget preparation
D   Monitoring the budgeting process

Answer

A is correct because it is the manager responsible for implementing the budget that must prepare it, not the budget committee.

If you don't know the answer, remember not to fall for the common pitfall of thinking, 'Well, we haven't had a D for a while, so I'll guess that'.

It is good practice to guess if you don't know the answer (never leave out a multiple choice question) but first eliminate some of the options if you can.

Since the committee is a co-ordinating body we can definitely say that they are responsible for B and D. Similarly, a co-ordinating body is more likely to allocate responsibility than to actually undertake the budget preparation, so eliminate C and select A as the correct answer.

The budget manual

> ### KEY TERM
>
> The **budget manual** is 'A detailed set of documents providing guidelines and information about the budget process'.
>
> CIMA *Official Terminology*

2.4   A budget manual may contain the following.

(a)   An explanation of the **objectives** of the budgetary process

- The purpose of budgetary planning and control
- The objectives of the various stages of the budgetary process
- The importance of budgets in the long-term planning of the business

(b)   **Organisational structures**

- An organisation chart
- A list of individuals holding budget responsibilities

(c)   An **outline of the principal budgets** and the **relationship between them**

(d)   **Administrative details of budget preparation**

- Membership and terms of reference of the budget committee
- The sequence in which budgets are to be prepared
- A timetable

(e)   **Procedural matters**

- Specimen forms and instructions for their completion
- Specimen reports
- Account codes (or a chart of accounts)
- The name of the budget officer to whom enquiries must be sent

Stages in budget preparation

2.5   The procedures for preparing a budget will differ from organisation to organisation but the stages described below will be indicative of the stages followed by many organisations. The preparation of a budget may take weeks or months and the **budget committee** may meet several times before the **master budget** (budgeted profit and loss account and budgeted balance sheet) is finally agreed. **Operating budgets** (sales budgets, production budgets, direct labour budgets and so on), which are amalgamated into the master budget, may need to be amended many times over as a consequence of discussions between departments, changes in market conditions and so on during the course of budget preparation.

Identifying the principal budget factor

> **KEY TERM**
>
> The **principal budget factor** is the factor which limits the activities of an organisation.

2.6 The first task in the budgetary process is to identify the **principal budget factor**. This is also known as the **key budget factor** or **limiting budget factor**.

2.7 The **principal budget factor** is usually **sales demand**: a company is usually restricted from making and selling more of its products because there would be no sales demand for the increased output at a price which would be acceptable/profitable to the company. The principal budget factor may also be machine capacity, distribution and selling resources, the availability of key raw materials or the availability of cash. Once this factor is defined then the remainder of the budgets can be prepared. For example, if sales are the principal budget factor then the production manager can only prepare his budget after the sales budget is complete.

2.8 Assuming that the principal budget factor has been identified as being sales, the stages involved in the preparation of a budget can be summarised as follows.

(a) The **sales budget** is prepared in units of product and sales value. The **finished goods stock budget** can be prepared at the same time. This budget decides the planned increase or decrease in finished goods stock levels.

(b) With the information from the sales and stock budgets, the **production budget** can be prepared. This is, in effect, the sales budget in units plus (or minus) the increase (or decrease) in finished goods stock. The production budget will be stated in terms of units.

(c) This leads on logically to budgeting the **resources for production**. This involves preparing a **materials usage budget, machine usage budget and a labour budget**.

(d) In addition to the materials usage budget, a **materials stock budget** will be prepared, to decide the planned increase or decrease in the level of stocks held. Once the raw materials usage requirements and the raw materials stock budget are known, the purchasing department can prepare a **raw materials purchases budget** in quantities and value for each type of material purchased.

(e) During the preparation of the sales and production budgets, the managers of the cost centres of the organisation will prepare their draft budgets for the department **overhead costs**. Such overheads will include maintenance, stores, administration, selling and research and development.

(f) From the above information a **budgeted profit and loss account** can be produced.

(g) In addition several other budgets must be prepared in order to arrive at the **budgeted balance sheet**. These are the **capital expenditure budget** (for fixed assets), the **working capital budget** (for budgeted increases or decreases in the level of debtors and creditors as well as stocks), and a **cash budget**.

3 OPERATING BUDGETS

3.1 Having seen the theory of budget preparation, let us look at **operating** (or **functional**) budget preparation.

3.2 EXAMPLE: PREPARING A MATERIALS PURCHASES BUDGET

ECO Ltd manufactures two products, S and T, which use the same raw materials, D and E. One unit of S uses 3 litres of D and 4 kilograms of E. One unit of T uses 5 litres of D and 2 kilograms of E. A litre of D is expected to cost £3 and a kilogram of E £7.

Budgeted sales for 20X2 are 8,000 units of S and 6,000 units of T; finished goods in stock at 1 January 20X2 are 1,500 units of S and 300 units of T, and the company plans to hold stocks of 600 units of each product at 31 December 20X2.

Stocks of raw material are 6,000 litres of D and 2,800 kilograms of E at 1 January and the company plans to hold 5,000 litres and 3,500 kilograms respectively at 31 December 20X2.

The warehouse and stores managers have suggested that a provision should be made for damages and deterioration of items held in store, as follows.

Product S :	loss of 50 units
Product T :	loss of 100 units
Material D :	loss of 500 litres
Material E :	loss of 200 kilograms

Required

Prepare a material purchases budget for the year 20X2.

3.3 SOLUTION

To calculate material purchases requirements it is first necessary to calculate the material usage requirements. That in turn depends on calculating the budgeted production volumes.

	Product S Units	*Product T* Units
Production required		
To meet sales demand	8,000	6,000
To provide for stock loss	50	100
For closing stock	600	600
	8,650	6,700
Less stock already in hand	1,500	300
Budgeted production volume	7,150	6,400

	Material D Litres	*Material E* Kgs
Usage requirements		
To produce 7,150 units of S	21,450	28,600
To produce 6,400 units of T	32,000	12,800
To provide for stock loss	500	200
For closing stock	5,000	3,500
	58,950	45,100
Less stock already in hand	6,000	2,800
Budgeted material purchases	52,950	42,300
Unit cost	£3	£7
Cost of material purchases	£158,850	£296,100
Total cost of material purchases		£454,950

3.4 The basics of the preparation of each operating budget are similar to those above. Work carefully through the following question which covers the preparation of a number of different types of operating budget.

Part E: Budgeting and performance measurement

Question 2

XYZ company produces three products X, Y and Z. For the coming accounting period budgets are to be prepared based on the following information.

Budgeted sales

Product X 2,000 at £100 each
Product Y 4,000 at £130 each
Product Z 3,000 at £150 each

Budgeted usage of raw material

	RM11	RM22	RM33
Product X	5	2	-
Product Y	3	2	2
Product Z	2	1	3
Cost per unit of material	£5	£3	£4

Finished stocks budget

	Product X	Product Y	Product Z
Beginning	500	800	700
End	600	1,000	800

Raw materials stock

	RM11	RM22	RM33
Beginning	21,000	10,000	16,000
End	18,000	9,000	12,000

	Product X	Product Y	Product Z
Expected hours per unit	4	6	8
Expected hourly rate (labour)	£3	£3	£3

Required

Draw up the following operating budgets.

(a) Sales budget in terms of both quantity and value
(b) Production budget
(c) Material usage budget
(d) Material purchases budget
(e) Labour budget

Answer

(a)

Sales budget

	Product X	Product Y	Product Z	Total
Sales quantity	2,000	4,000	3,000	
Sales price	£100	£130	£150	
Sales value	£200,000	£520,000	£450,000	£1,170,000

(b)

Production budget

	Product X Units	Product Y Units	Product Z Units
Sales quantity	2,000	4,000	3,000
Closing stocks	600	1,000	800
	2,600	5,000	3,800
Less opening stocks	500	800	700
Budgeted production	2,100	4,200	3,100

(c)

Material usage budget

	Production Units	RM11 Units	RM22 Units	RM33 Units
Product X	2,100	10,500	4,200	-
Product Y	4,200	12,600	8,400	8,400
Product Z	3,100	6,200	3,100	9,300
Budgeted material usage		29,300	15,700	17,700

446

(d)

	Material purchases budget		
	RM11	*RM22*	*RM33*
	Units	Units	Units
Budgeted material usage	29,300	15,700	17,700
Closing stocks	18,000	9,000	12,000
	47,300	24,700	29,700
Less opening stocks	21,000	10,000	16,000
Budgeted material purchases	26,300	14,700	13,700
Standard cost per unit	£5	£3	£4
Budgeted material purchases	£131,500	£44,100	£54,800

(e)

		Labour budget			
		Hours required	*Total*	*Rate per*	
Product	*Production*	*per unit*	*hours*	*hour*	*Cost*
	Units			£	£
X	2,100	4	8,400	3	25,200
Y	4,200	6	25,200	3	75,600
Z	3,100	8	24,800	3	74,400
Budgeted total wages					175,200

4 CASH BUDGETS

4.1 A **cash budget** is a statement in which estimated **future cash receipts and payments** are tabulated in such a way as to show the forecast cash balance of a business at defined intervals. For example, in December 20X2 an accounts department might wish to estimate the cash position of the business during the three following months, January to March 20X3. A cash budget might be drawn up in the following format.

	Jan	*Feb*	*Mar*
	£	£	£
Estimated cash receipts			
From credit customers	14,000	16,500	17,000
From cash sales	3,000	4,000	4,500
Proceeds on disposal of fixed assets		2,200	
Total cash receipts	17,000	22,700	21,500
Estimated cash payments			
To suppliers of goods	8,000	7,800	10,500
To employees (wages)	3,000	3,500	3,500
Purchase of fixed assets		16,000	
Rent and rates			1,000
Other overheads	1,200	1,200	1,200
Repayment of loan	2,500		
	14,700	28,500	16,200
Net surplus/(deficit) for month	2,300	(5,800)	5,300
Opening cash balance	1,200	3,500	(2,300)
Closing cash balance	3,500	(2,300)	3,000

4.2 In the example above (where the figures are purely for illustration) the accounts department has calculated that the cash balance at the beginning of the budget period, 1 January, will be £1,200. Estimates have been made of the cash which is likely to be received by the business (from cash and credit sales, and from a planned disposal of fixed assets in February). Similar estimates have been made of cash due to be paid out by the business (payments to suppliers and employees, payments for rent, rates and other overheads, payment for a planned purchase of fixed assets in February and a loan repayment due in January).

BPP PUBLISHING

4.3 From these estimates it is a simple step to calculate the excess of cash receipts over cash payments in each month. In some months cash payments may exceed cash receipts and there will be a **deficit** for the month; this occurs during February in the above example because of the large investment in fixed assets in that month.

4.4 The last part of the cash budget above shows how the business's estimated cash balance can then be rolled along from month to month. Starting with the opening balance of £1,200 at 1 January a cash surplus of £2,300 is generated in January. This leads to a closing January balance of £3,500 which becomes the opening balance for February. The deficit of £5,800 in February throws the business's cash position into **overdraft** and the overdrawn balance of £2,300 becomes the opening balance for March. Finally, the healthy cash surplus of £5,300 in March leaves the business with a favourable cash position of £3,000 at the end of the budget period.

The usefulness of cash budgets

4.5 The cash budget is one of the most important planning tools that an organisation can use. It shows the **cash effect of all plans made within the budgetary process** and hence its preparation can lead to a **modification of budgets** if it shows that there are insufficient cash resources to finance the planned operations.

4.6 It can also give management an indication of **potential problems** that could arise and allows them the opportunity to take action to avoid such problems. A cash budget can show **four positions**. Management will need to take appropriate action depending on the potential position.

Cash position	Appropriate management action
Short-term surplus	• Pay creditors early to obtain discount • Attempt to increase sales by increasing debtors and stocks • Make short-term investments
Short-term deficit	• Increase creditors • Reduce debtors • Arrange an overdraft
Long-term surplus	• Make long-term investments • Expand • Diversify • Replace/update fixed assets
Long-term deficit	• Raise long-term finance (such as via issue of share capital) • Consider shutdown/disinvestment opportunities

Exam focus point

A cash budgeting question in an examination could ask you to recommend appropriate action for management to take once you have prepared the cash budget. Ensure your advice takes account both of whether there is a surplus or deficit and whether the position is long or short term.

4.7 EXAMPLE: CASH BUDGET

Peter Blair has worked for some years as a sales representative, but has recently been made redundant. He intends to start up in business on his own account, using £15,000 which he currently has invested with a building society. Peter maintains a bank account showing a small credit balance, and he plans to approach his bank for the necessary additional finance. Peter asks you for advice and provides the following additional information.

(a) Arrangements have been made to purchase fixed assets costing £8,000. These will be paid for at the end of September and are expected to have a five-year life, at the end of which they will possess a nil residual value.

(b) Stocks costing £5,000 will be acquired on 28 September and subsequent monthly purchases will be at a level sufficient to replace forecast sales for the month.

(c) Forecast monthly sales are £3,000 for October, £6,000 for November and December, and £10,500 from January 20X4 onwards.

(d) Selling price is fixed at the cost of stock plus 50%.

(e) Two months' credit will be allowed to customers but only one month's credit will be received from suppliers of stock.

(f) Running expenses, including rent but excluding depreciation of fixed assets, are estimated at £1,600 per month.

(g) Blair intends to make monthly cash drawings of £1,000.

Required

Prepare a cash budget for the six months to 31 March 20X4.

4.8 SOLUTION

The opening cash balance at 1 October will consist of Peter's initial £15,000 less the £8,000 expended on fixed assets purchased in September. In other words, the opening balance is £7,000. Cash receipts from credit customers arise two months after the relevant sales.

Payments to suppliers are a little more tricky. We are told that cost of sales is 100/150 × sales. Thus for October cost of sales is 100/150 × £3,000 = £2,000. These goods will be purchased in October but not paid for until November. Similar calculations can be made for later months. The initial stock of £5,000 is purchased in September and consequently paid for in October.

Depreciation is not a cash flow and so is *not* included in a cash budget.

4.9 The cash budget can now be constructed.

CASH BUDGET FOR THE SIX MONTHS ENDING 31 MARCH 20X4

	Oct £	*Nov* £	*Dec* £	*Jan* £	*Feb* £	*Mar* £
Payments						
Suppliers	5,000	2,000	4,000	4,000	7,000	7,000
Running expenses	1,600	1,600	1,600	1,600	1,600	1,600
Drawings	1,000	1,000	1,000	1,000	1,000	1,000
	7,600	4,600	6,600	6,600	9,600	9,600
Receipts						
Debtors	-	-	3,000	6,000	6,000	10,500
Surplus/(shortfall)	(7,600)	(4,600)	(3,600)	(600)	(3,600)	900
Opening balance	7,000	(600)	(5,200)	(8,800)	(9,400)	(13,000)
Closing balance	(600)	(5,200)	(8,800)	(9,400)	(13,000)	(12,100)

Question 3

You are presented with the budgeted data shown in Annex A for the period November 20X1 to June 20X2 by your firm. It has been extracted from the other functional budgets that have been prepared.

You are also told the following.

(a) Sales are 40% cash, 60% credit. Credit sales are paid two months after the month of sale.
(b) Purchases are paid the month following purchase.
(c) 75% of wages are paid in the current month and 25% the following month.
(d) Overheads are paid the month after they are incurred.
(e) Dividends are paid three months after they are declared.
(f) Capital expenditure is paid two months after it is incurred.
(g) The opening cash balance is £15,000.

The managing director is pleased with the above figures as they show sales will have increased by more than 100% in the period under review. In order to achieve this he has arranged a bank overdraft with a ceiling of £50,000 to accommodate the increased stock levels and wage bill for overtime worked.

Annex A

	Nov X1	Dec X1	Jan X2	Feb X2	Mar X2	Apr X2	May X2	June X2
	£	£	£	£	£	£	£	£
Sales	80,000	100,000	110,000	130,000	140,000	150,000	160,000	180,000
Purchases	40,000	60,000	80,000	90,000	110,000	130,000	140,000	150,000
Wages	10,000	12,000	16,000	20,000	24,000	28,000	32,000	36,000
Overheads	10,000	10,000	15,000	15,000	15,000	20,000	20,000	20,000
Dividends		20,000						40,000
Capital Expenditure			30,000			40,000		

Required

(a) Prepare a cash budget for the 6 month period January to June 20X2.
(b) Comment upon your results in the light of your managing director's comments and offer advice.

Answer

Cash budget for January to June 20X2

(a)

	January £'000	February £'000	March £'000	April £'000	May £'000	June £'000
Receipts						
Sales revenue						
Cash	44	52	56	60	64	72
Credit	48	60	66	78	84	90
	92	112	122	138	148	162
Payments						
Purchases	60	80	90	110	130	140
Wages						
75%	12	15	18	21	24	27
25%	3	4	5	6	7	8
Overheads	10	15	15	15	20	20
Dividends			20			
Capital expenditure			30			40
	85	114	178	152	181	235
b/f	15	22	20	(36)	(50)	(83)
Net cash flow	7	(2)	(56)	(14)	(33)	(73)
c/f	22	20	(36)	(50)	(83)	(156)

(b) The overdraft arrangements are quite inadequate to service the cash needs of the business over the six month period. If the figures are realistic then action should be taken now to avoid difficulties in the near future. The following are possible courses of action.

(i) Activities could be curtailed.

(ii) Other sources of cash could be explored, for example a long-term loan to finance the capital expenditure and a factoring arrangement to provide cash due from debtors more quickly.

(iii) Efforts to increase the speed of debt collection could be made.

(iv) Payments to creditors could be delayed.

(v) The dividend payments could be postponed (the figures indicate that this is a small company, possibly owner-managed).

(vi) Staff might be persuaded to work at a lower rate in return for, say, an annual bonus or a profit-sharing agreement.

(vii) Extra staff might be taken on to reduce the amount of overtime paid.

(viii) The stockholding policy should be reviewed: it may be possible to meet demand from current production and minimise cash tied up in stocks.

---

5 BUDGETED PROFIT AND LOSS ACCOUNT AND BALANCE SHEET

5.1 As well as wishing to forecast its cash position, a business might want to estimate its profitability and its financial position for a coming period. This would involve the preparation of a budgeted profit and loss account and balance sheet, both of which form the **master budget**.

5.2 EXAMPLE: PREPARING A BUDGETED PROFIT AND LOSS ACCOUNT AND BALANCE SHEET

Using the information in Paragraph 4.7, you are required to prepare Peter Blair's budgeted profit and loss account for the six months ending on 31 March 20X4 and a budgeted balance sheet as at that date.

5.3 SOLUTION

The profit and loss account is straightforward. The first figure is sales, which can be computed very easily from the information in Paragraph 4.7(c). It is sufficient to add up the monthly sales figures given there; for the profit and loss account there is no need to worry about any closing debtor. Similarly, cost of sales is calculated directly from the information on gross margin contained in Paragraph 4.7 (d).

FORECAST TRADING AND PROFIT AND LOSS ACCOUNT
FOR THE SIX MONTHS ENDING 31 MARCH 20X4

	£	£
Sales $(3,000 + (2 \times 6,000) + (3 \times 10,500))$		46,500
Cost of sales $(^2/_3 \times £46,500)$		31,000
Gross profit		15,500
Expenses		
Running expenses $(6 \times £1,600)$	9,600	
Depreciation $(£8,000 \times 20\% \times 6/12)$	800	
		10,400
Net profit		5,100

Items will be shown in the balance sheet as follows.

(a) Stock will comprise the initial purchases of £5,000.

(b) Debtors will comprise sales made in February and March (not paid until April and May respectively).

(c) Creditors will comprise purchases made in March (not paid for until April).

(d) The bank overdraft is the closing cash figure computed in the cash budget.

FORECAST BALANCE SHEET AT 31 MARCH 20X4

	£	£
Fixed assets £(8,000 – 800)		7,200
Current assets		
Stocks	5,000	
Debtors (2 × £10,500)	21,000	
	26,000	
Current liabilities		
Bank overdraft	12,100	
Trade creditors (March purchases)	7,000	
	19,100	
Net current assets		6,900
		14,100
Proprietor's interest		
Capital introduced		15,000
Profit for the period	5,100	
Less drawings	6,000	
Deficit retained		(900)
		14,100

Chapter roundup

- The **purposes** of a budget are as follows.

  - To **coordinate** activities
  - To **communicate** targets
  - To **establish a system of control**
  - To **compel planning**

- A **budget** is a financial or quantitative plan of operations for a forthcoming accounting period.

- The **budget committee** is the **coordinating** body in the preparation and administration of budgets.

- The manager responsible for preparing each budget should ideally be the manager responsible for carrying out the budget.

- The **budget manual** is a collection of instructions governing the responsibilities of persons and the procedures, forms and records relating to the preparation and use of budgetary data.

- The sales budget is usually the first operational budget prepared because sales is usually the **principal budget factor**. The order of preparation of the remaining budgets could be finished goods stock budget, production budget, budgets for resources of production, materials stock budget, raw materials purchases budget and overhead cost budgets.

- **Cash budgets** show the expected receipts and payments during a budget period. The usefulness of cash budgets is that they enable management to make any **forward planning decisions** that may be needed, such as advising their bank of estimated overdraft requirements or strengthening their credit control procedures to ensure that debtors pay more quickly.

- The **master budget** consists of a budgeted profit and loss account and a budgeted balance sheet.

Quick quiz

1   Budgets have four main purposes. Fill in the key words which are missing from the statements below.

(a) To Coordinate. the activities of different departments towards a single plan.

(b) To Comunicate. targets to managers responsible for achieving them.

(c) To establish a system of Control. by comparing budgeted and actual results.

(d)   To compel ....Planning....

2   Which of the following is unlikely to be contained with a budget manual?

A   Organisational structures
B   Objectives of the budgetary process
C   Selling overhead budget
D   Administrative details of budget preparation

3   The factor which limits the activities of an organisation is known as:

I   The key factor budget
II   The limiting budget factor
III   The principal budget factor
IV   The main budget factor

A   I,II and IV
B   I and III
C   II and III
D   I, II and III

4   If the principal budget factor is sales demand, in which order would the following budgets be prepared?

Materials usage	Materials purchase	Production	Sales	Cash

1st   SALES
2nd   PRODUCTION
3rd   MATERIALS USAGE
4th   Material purchase
5th   CASH

5   Match the following cash positions with the appropriate management action.

Short-term surplus   Increase creditors

Long-term surplus   Replace/update fixed assets

Short-term deficit   Issue share capital

Long-term deficit   Increase debtors and stock

6   Depreciation has an effect on net profit and is therefore included in a cash budget.

True   ☐

False   ☑

7   Which of the following are included in the master budget?

I   Budgeted profit and loss account
II   Budgeted balance sheet
III   Cash budget
IV   Functional budgets

A   I and II
B   II and III
C   II, III and IV
D   IV only

Answers to quick quiz

1 (a) Coordinate
   (b) Communicate
   (c) Control
   (d) Planning

2 C

3 D

4 1st | Sales |

   2nd | Production |

   3rd | Materials usage |

   4th | Materials purchase |

   5th | Cash |

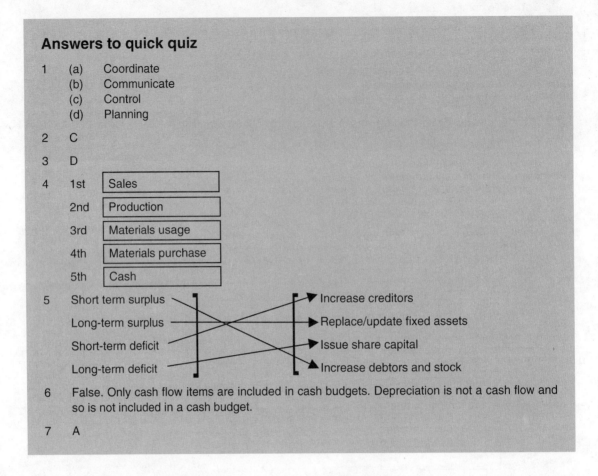

5 Short term surplus → Increase debtors and stock
   Long-term surplus → Replace/update fixed assets
   Short-term deficit → Increase creditors
   Long-term deficit → Issue share capital

6 False. Only cash flow items are included in cash budgets. Depreciation is not a cash flow and so is not included in a cash budget.

7 A

Now try the questions below from the Exam Question Bank

Number	Level	Marks	Time
40	MCQ	n/a	n/a
41	Examination	10	18 mins

Chapter 23

FURTHER ASPECTS OF BUDGETING

Topic list	Syllabus reference
1 Flexible budgets	8
2 Flexible budgets and budgetary control	8
3 Cost estimation	8

Introduction

You should now be able to **prepare operating budgets, a cash budget and a master budget** and have some idea of the **budgetary process**. This chapter takes the budgeting theme further and looks at a number of specific issues.

We begin by looking at **flexible budgets**, a vital management planning and control tool. This part of the chapter relies on your understanding of **cost behaviour** covered in Chapter 4. We then move on to methods of **estimating** the costs to be included in budgets.

This chapter ends our study of budgeting. You will, however, come across **variances** again, which are mentioned in this chapter in relation to flexible budgets, in Chapters 24 to 26, which look at a new topic and consider the use of **standard costing** and **variance analysis**.

Study guide

Section 25 - Budgeting

- Explain, prepare and evaluate fixed, flexed and flexible budgets
- Identify reasons for variances between actual and budgeted information
- Describe how the review of actual and budget could be reported to management

Exam guide

Budgeting is one of the key areas of the syllabus for Paper 1.2. Look out for Section B questions requiring you to prepare flexible budgets at various activity levels.

1   FLEXIBLE BUDGETS

> **KEY TERM**
>
> - A **fixed budget** is a budget which is set for a single activity level.
>
> - A **flexible budget** is 'A budget which, by recognising different cost behaviour patterns, is designed to change as volume of activity changes'.
>
>   (CIMA *Official Terminology*)

1.1 **Master budgets** are based on planned volumes of production and sales but do not include any provision for the event that actual volumes may differ from the budget. In this sense they may be described as **fixed budgets**.

1.2 A **flexible budget** has two advantages.

(a) At the **planning** stage, it may be helpful to know what the effects would be if the actual outcome differs from the prediction. For example, a company may budget to sell 10,000 units of its product, but may prepare flexible budgets based on sales of, say, 8,000 and 12,000 units. This would enable **contingency plans** to be drawn up if necessary.

(b) At the end of each month or year, actual results may be compared with the relevant activity level in the flexible budget as a **control** procedure.

1.3 Flexible budgeting uses the principles of marginal costing. In estimating future costs it is often necessary to begin by looking at cost behaviour in the past. For costs which are wholly fixed or wholly variable no problem arises. But you may be presented with a cost which appears to have behaved in the past as a semi-variable cost (partly fixed and partly variable). A technique for estimating the level of the cost for the future is called the high/low method. We looked at this technique in Chapter 4: attempt the following question to ensure that you can remember what to do.

Question 1

The cost of factory power has behaved as follows in past years.

	Units of output produced	Cost of factory power £
20X1	7,900	38,700
20X2	7,700	38,100
20X3	9,800	44,400
20X4	9,100	42,300

Budgeted production for 20X5 is 10,200 units. Estimate the cost of factory power which will be incurred. Ignore inflation.

Answer

	Units	£
20X3 (highest output)	9,800	44,400
20X2 (lowest output)	7,700	38,100
	2,100	6,300

The variable cost per unit is therefore £6,300/2,100 = £3.

The level of fixed cost can be calculated by looking at any output level.

	£
Total cost of factory power in 20X3	44,400
Less variable cost of factory power (9,800 × £3)	29,400
Fixed cost of factory power	15,000

An estimate of costs is 20X5 is as follows.

	£
Fixed cost	15,000
Variable cost of budgeted production (10,200 × £3)	30,600
Total budgeted cost of factory power	45,600

1.4 We can now look at a full example of preparing a flexible budget.

1.5 EXAMPLE: PREPARING A FLEXIBLE BUDGET

(a) Prepare a budget for 20X6 for the direct labour costs and overhead expenses of a production department at the activity levels of 80%, 90% and 100%, using the information listed below.

(i) The direct labour hourly rate is expected to be £3.75.

(ii) 100% activity represents 60,000 direct labour hours.

(iii) Variable costs

Indirect labour	£0.75 per direct labour hour
Consumable supplies	£0.375 per direct labour hour
Canteen and other welfare services	6% of direct and indirect labour costs

(iv) Semi-variable costs are expected to relate to the direct labour hours in the same manner as for the last five years.

Year	Direct labour hours	Semi-variable costs £
20X1	64,000	20,800
20X2	59,000	19,800
20X3	53,000	18,600
20X4	49,000	17,800
20X5	40,000 (estimate)	16,000 (estimate)

(v) *Fixed costs*

	£
Depreciation	18,000
Maintenance	10,000
Insurance	4,000
Rates	15,000
Management salaries	25,000

(vi) Inflation is to be ignored.

(b) Calculate the budget cost allowance (ie expected expenditure) for 20X6 assuming that 57,000 direct labour hours are worked.

1.6 SOLUTION

(a)

	80% level 48,000 hrs £'000	90% level 54,000 hrs £'000	100% level 60,000 hrs £'000
Direct labour	180.00	202.50	225.0
Other variable costs			
Indirect labour	36.00	40.50	45.0
Consumable supplies	18.00	20.25	22.5
Canteen etc	12.96	14.58	16.2
Total variable costs (£5.145 per hour)	246.96	277.83	308.7
Semi-variable costs (W)	17.60	18.80	20.0
Fixed costs			
Depreciation	18.00	18.00	18.0
Maintenance	10.00	10.00	10.0
Insurance	4.00	4.00	4.0
Rates	15.00	15.00	15.0
Management salaries	25.00	25.00	25.0
Budgeted costs	336.56	368.63	400.7

Working

Using the high/low method:

		£
Total cost of 64,000 hours		20,800
Total cost of 40,000 hours		16,000
Variable cost of 24,000 hours		4,800
Variable cost per hour (£4,800/24,000)		£0.20

		£
Total cost of 64,000 hours		20,800
Variable cost of 64,000 hours (× £0.20)		12,800
Fixed costs		8,000

Semi-variable costs are calculated as follows.

			£
60,000 hours	(60,000 × £0.20) + £8,000	=	20,000
54,000 hours	(54,000 × £0.20) + £8,000	=	18,800
48,000 hours	(48,000 × £0.20) + £8,000	=	17,600

(b) The budget cost allowance for 57,000 direct labour hours of work would be as follows.

		£
Variable costs	(57,000 × £5.145)	293,265
Semi-variable costs	(£8,000 + (57,000 × £0.20))	19,400
Fixed costs		72,000
		384,665

Exam focus point

You must be able to analyse the fixed and variable elements of cost to be able to produce a flexible budget.

2 FLEXIBLE BUDGETS AND BUDGETARY CONTROL

2.1 **Budgetary control** is the practice of establishing budgets which identify areas of responsibility for individual managers (for example production managers, purchasing managers and so on) and of regularly comparing actual results against expected results. The most important method of budgetary control, for the purpose of your examination, is **variance analysis**, which involves the comparison of actual results achieved during a control period (usually a month, or four weeks) with a flexible budget. The differences between actual results and expected results are called **variances** and these are used to provide a guideline for **control action** by individual managers. We will be looking at variances in some detail in Chapters 25 and 26.

2.2 The wrong approach to budgetary control is to compare actual results against a fixed budget. Consider the following example.

Windy Ltd manufactures a single product, the cloud. Budgeted results and actual results for June 20X2 are shown below.

	Budget	Actual results	Variance
Production and sales of the cloud (units)	2,000	3,000	
	£	£	£
Sales revenue (a)	20,000	30,000	10,000 (F)
Direct materials	6,000	8,500	2,500 (A)
Direct labour	4,000	4,500	500 (A)
Maintenance	1,000	1,400	400 (A)
Depreciation	2,000	2,200	200 (A)
Rent and rates	1,500	1,600	100 (A)
Other costs	3,600	5,000	1,400 (A)
Total costs (b)	18,100	23,200	5,100
Profit (a) – (b)	1,900	6,800	4,900 (F)

2.3 (a) In this example, the variances are meaningless for purposes of control. Costs were higher than budget because the **volume of output was also higher**; variable costs would be expected to increase above the budgeted costs in the fixed budget. There is no information to show whether control action is needed for any aspect of costs or revenue.

   (b) For control purposes, it is necessary to know the answers to questions such as the following.

   - Were actual costs higher than they should have been to produce and sell 3,000 clouds?

   - Was actual revenue satisfactory from the sale of 3,000 clouds?

2.4 The correct approach to budgetary control is as follows.

   - Identify fixed and variable costs.
   - Produce a flexible budget using marginal costing techniques.

2.5 In the previous example of Windy Ltd, let us suppose that we have the following estimates of cost behaviour.

   (a) Direct materials, direct labour and maintenance costs are variable.

   (b) Rent and rates and depreciation are fixed costs.

   (c) Other costs consist of fixed costs of £1,600 plus a variable cost of £1 per unit made and sold.

2.6 The budgetary control analysis should be as follows.

	Fixed budget (a)	Flexible budget (b)	Actual results (c)	Budget variance (b) - (c)
Production & sales (units)	2,000	3,000	3,000	
	£	£	£	£
Sales revenue	20,000	30,000	30,000	0
Variable costs				
Direct materials	6,000	9,000	8,500	500 (F)
Direct labour	4,000	6,000	4,500	1,500 (F)
Maintenance	1,000	1,500	1,400	100 (F)
Semi-variable costs				
Other costs	3,600	4,600	5,000	400 (A)
Fixed costs				
Depreciation	2,000	2,000	2,200	200 (A)
Rent and rates	1,500	1,500	1,600	100 (A)
Total costs	18,100	24,600	23,200	1,400 (F)
Profit	1,900	5,400	6,800	1,400 (F)

Note. (F) denotes a **favourable** variance and (A) an **adverse** or unfavourable variance. Adverse variances are sometimes denoted as (U) for 'unfavourable'.

Exam focus point

Variances are calculated by comparing actual results and the flexible budget, *not* actual results and the original budget.

2.7 We can analyse the above as follows.

(a) In selling 3,000 units the expected profit should have been, not the fixed budget profit of £1,900, but the flexible budget profit of £5,400. Instead, actual profit was £6,800 ie £1,400 more than we should have expected. The reason for this £1,400 improvement is that, given output and sales of 3,000 units, overall costs were lower than expected (and sales revenue was exactly as expected). For example the direct material cost was £500 lower than expected.

(b) Another reason for the improvement in profit above the fixed budget profit is the **sales volume**. Windy Ltd sold 3,000 clouds instead of 2,000 clouds, with the following result.

	£	£
Budgeted sales revenue increased by		10,000
Budgeted variable costs increased by:		
direct materials	3,000	
direct labour	2,000	
maintenance	500	
variable element of other costs	1,000	
Budgeted fixed costs are unchanged		6,500
Budgeted profit increased by		3,500

Budgeted profit was therefore increased by £3,500 because sales volume increased.

(c) A full variance analysis statement such as the one shown below could be used when reporting to management.

WINDY LTD
VARIANCE ANALYSIS STATEMENT
JUNE 20X2

	£	£
Fixed budget profit		1,900
Variances		
Sales volume	3,500 (F)	
Direct materials cost	500 (F)	
Direct labour cost	1,500 (F)	
Maintenance cost	100 (F)	
Other costs	400 (A)	
Depreciation	200 (A)	
Rent and rates	100 (A)	
		4,900 (F)
Actual profit		6,800

2.8 If management believes that any of these variances are large enough to justify it, they will investigate the reasons for them to see whether any corrective action is necessary.

Question 2

The budgeted variable cost per unit was £2.75. When output was 18,000 units, total expenditure was £98,000 and it was found that fixed overheads were £11,000 over budget whilst variable costs were in line with budget.

What was the amount budgeted for fixed costs?

A £37,500   B £48,500   C £49,500   D £87,000

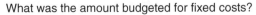

Answer

	£
Total expenditure	98,000
Budgeted variable cost (18,000 × £2.75)	49,500
Actual fixed costs incurred	48,500
Fixed overhead expenditure variance	11,000
Budgeted fixed costs	37,500

The correct answer is A.

Option D is incorrect: it is simply the £98,000 total expenditure less the £11,000 fixed overhead expenditure variance.

Option C is also incorrect, being the budgeted variable cost (£2.75 × 18,000).

Option B is incorrect: £48,000 is the actual fixed costs incurred (see working above).

---

3   COST ESTIMATION

3.1 It should be obvious that the production of a budget calls for the preparation of **cost estimates** and **sales forecasts**. In fact, budgeting could be said to be as much a test of estimating and forecasting skills than anything else. In this section we will consider the two cost estimation techniques that you need to know about for **Financial Information for Management**.

Cost estimation methods

3.2 Cost estimation involves the measurement of **historical costs** to predict **future costs**. Some estimation techniques are more sophisticated than others and are therefore likely to be more reliable but, in practice, the simple techniques are more commonly found and should give estimates that are sufficiently accurate for their purpose.

High/low method

3.3   We met the **high/low method** again earlier in this chapter. The major drawback to the high/low method is that **only two historical cost records from previous periods are used** in the cost estimation. Unless these two records are a reliable indicator of costs throughout the relevant range of output, which is unlikely, only a 'loose approximation' of fixed and variable costs will be obtained. The advantage of the method is its relative **simplicity**.

The scattergraph method

3.4   You should recall from Chapter 5 that a **graph** can be plotted of the historical costs from previous periods, and from the resulting scatter diagram, a '**line-of-best-fit**' can be drawn by visual estimation.

3.5   The advantage of the scattergraph over the high/low method is that a **greater quantity of historical data is used** in the estimation, but its disadvantage is that the cost line is drawn by visual judgement and so is a **subjective approximation**.

Chapter roundup

- A **Fixed budget** is a budget which is set for a single activity level.

- A **flexible budget** is a budget which recognises different cost behaviour patterns and is designed to change as volume of activity changes.

- **Budgetary control** is the practice of establishing budgets which identify areas of responsibility for individual managers and of regularly comparing actual results against expected results.

- **Variance analysis** involves the comparison of actual results achieved during a control period with a flexible budget. **Variances** are the differences between actual results and expected results.

- **Budget variances** are calculated by comparing the **flexible budget** with actual results. Budget variances may be divided into **expenditure** and **volume** variances.

- **(F)** denotes a **favourable** variance and **(A)** denotes an **adverse** or **unfavourable** variance.

- A prerequisite of flexible budgeting is a knowledge of **cost behaviour patterns**. The production of a budget also calls for the preparation of **cost estimation** and **sales forecasts**. Simple cost estimation techniques include the **high-low method** and the **scattergraph method**.

Quick quiz

1   What are the advantages of a flexible budget over a fixed budget? *recognises different cost beh. patterns*

2   Flexible budgets are normally prepared on a marginal costing basis.

  True   ☑

  False   ☐

3   Define budgetary control. *Identifies area of budgetary control.*

4   What is the wrong approach to budgetary control? *Comparing Budgets against actual.*

5   What is the correct approach to budgetary control? *~~Compare~~ Identify fixed + variable costs., Produce a flexible budget.*

6   In what way is the scattergraph method more reliable than the high/low method of cost estimation? *Greater quantity of data used (rather than just 2.*

7   The main weakness of the scattergraph method of cost estimation is

     A   It only uses two historical cost records
   \ B   It is a subjective approximation
     C   It is a relatively simple method
     \D   It uses vast amounts of historical data

Answers to quick quiz

1   (a)   At the planning stage, a flexible budget can show what the effects would be if the actual outcome differs from the prediction.

     (b)   At the end of each period, actual results may be compared with the relevant activity level in the flexible budget as a control procedure.

2   True

3   Budgetary control is the practice of establishing budgets which identify areas of responsibility for individual managers and of regularly comparing actual results against expected results.

4   To compare actual results against a fixed budget.

5   •   To identify fixed and variable costs
     •   To produce a flexible budget using marginal costing techniques

6   A greater quantity of historical data is used in the estimation.

7   B

Now try the questions below from the Exam Question Bank

Number	Level	Marks	Time
42	MCQ	n/a	n/a
43	Examination	10	18 mins

Chapter 24

INTRODUCTION TO STANDARD COSTING

Topic list	Syllabus reference
1 What is standard costing?	5(a), (b), 3(c)
2 Setting standards	5(a), (b), 3(c)

Introduction

Just as there are **standards** for most things in our daily lives (cleanliness in hamburger restaurants, educational achievement of nine year olds, number of trains running on time), there are standards for the costs of products and services. Moreover, just as the standards in our daily lives are not always met, the standards for the costs of products and services are not always met. We will not, however, be considering the standards of cleanliness of hamburger restaurants in this chapter but we will be looking at standards for **costs**, what they are used for and how they are set.

In the next chapter we will see how **standard costing** forms the basis of a process called **variance analysis**, a vital management control tool.

Study guide

Section 7 – Material costs 1

- Calculate the standard cost of stocks from given information

Section 12 – Marginal and absorption costing

- Establish the standard cost per unit from given data under absorption and marginal costing

Section 26 – Standard costing

- Explain the purpose of standard costing
- Establish the standard cost per unit from given data under absorption and marginal costing

1 WHAT IS STANDARD COSTING?

1.1 The building blocks of standard costing are standard costs and so before we look at standard costing in any detail you really need to know what a standard cost is.

Standard cost

1.2 The standard cost of product 1234 is set out below.

STANDARD COST CARD - PRODUCT 1234

	£	£
Direct materials		
Material X – 3 kg at £4 per kg	12	
Material Y – 9 litres at £2 per litre	18	
		30
Direct labour		
Grade A – 6 hours at £1.50 per hour	9	
Grade B – 8 hours at £2 per hour	16	
		25
Standard direct cost		55
Variable production overhead – 14 hours at £0.50 per hour		7
Standard variable cost of production		62
Fixed production overhead – 14 hours at £4.50 per hour		63
Standard full production cost		125
Administration and marketing overhead		15
Standard cost of sale		140
Standard profit		20
Standard sales price		160

KEY TERM

A **standard cost** is a planned unit cost.

1.3 Notice how the total standard cost is built up from standards for each cost element: standard quantities of materials at standard prices, standard quantities of labour time at standard rates and so on. It is therefore determined by management's estimates of the following.

- The expected prices of materials, labour and expenses
- Efficiency levels in the use of materials and labour
- Budgeted overhead costs and budgeted volumes of activity

We will see how management arrives at these estimates in Section 2.

1.4 But why should management want to prepare standard costs? Obviously to assist with standard costing, but what is the point of standard costing?

The uses of standard costing

1.5 **Standard costing** has a variety of uses but its two principal ones are as follows.

(a) To **value stocks** and **cost production** for cost accounting purposes. It is an alternative method of valuation to methods like FIFO and LIFO which we looked at in Chapter 6.

(b) To act as a **control device** by establishing standards (planned costs), highlighting (via **variance analysis** which we will cover in the next chapter) activities that are not conforming to plan and thus **alerting management** to areas which may be out of control and in need of corrective action.

Question 1

Bloggs Ltd makes one product, the joe. Two types of labour are involved in the preparation of a joe, skilled and semi-skilled. Skilled labour is paid £10 per hour and semi-skilled £5 per hour. Twice as many skilled labour hours as semi-skilled labour hours are needed to produce a joe, four semi-skilled labour hours being needed.

A joe is made up of three different direct materials. Seven kilograms of direct material A, four litres of direct material B and three metres of direct material C are needed. Direct material A costs £1 per kilogram, direct material B £2 per litre and direct material C £3 per metre.

Variable production overheads are incurred at Bloggs Ltd at the rate of £2.50 per direct labour (skilled) hour.

A system of absorption costing is in operation at Bloggs Ltd. The basis of absorption is direct labour (skilled) hours. For the forthcoming accounting period, budgeted fixed production overheads are £250,000 and budgeted production of the joe is 5,000 units.

Administration, selling and distribution overheads are added to products at the rate of £10 per unit.

A mark-up of 25% is made on the joe.

Required

Using the above information draw up a standard cost card for the joe.

Answer

STANDARD COST CARD - PRODUCT JOE

	£	£
Direct materials		
A - 7 kgs × £1	7	
B - 4 litres × £2	8	
C - 3 m × £3	9	
		24
Direct labour		
Skilled - 8 × £10	80	
Semi-skilled - 4 × £5	20	
		100
Standard direct cost		124
Variable production overhead - 8 × £2.50		20
Standard variable cost of production		144
Fixed production overhead - 8 × £6.25 (W)		50
Standard full production cost		194
Administration, selling and distribution overhead		10
Standard cost of sale		204
Standard profit (25% × 204)		51
Standard sales price		255

Working

$$\text{Overhead absorption rate} = \frac{£250,000}{5,000 \times 8} = £6.25 \text{ per skilled labour hour}$$

1.6 Although the use of standard costs to simplify the keeping of cost accounting records should not be overlooked, we will be concentrating on the **control** and **variance analysis** aspect of standard costing.

KEY TERM

Standard costing is 'A control technique which compares standard costs and revenues with actual results to obtain variances which are used to stimulate improved performance'.

CIMA *Official Terminology*

1.7 Notice that the above definition highlights the control aspects of standard costing.

Standard costing as a control technique

1.8 **Standard costing** therefore involves the following.

- The establishment of predetermined estimates of the costs of products or services
- The collection of actual costs
- The comparison of the actual costs with the predetermined estimates.

1.9 The predetermined costs are known as **standard costs** and the difference between standard and actual cost is known as a **variance**. The process by which the total difference between standard and actual results is analysed in known as **variance analysis**.

1.10 Although standard costing can be used in a variety of costing situations (batch and mass production, process manufacture, jobbing manufacture (where there is standardisation of parts) and service industries (if a realistic cost unit can be established)), the greatest benefit from its use can be gained if there is a **degree of repetition** in the production process. It is therefore most suited to **mass production** and **repetitive assembly work**.

2 SETTING STANDARDS

2.1 Standard costs may be used in both absorption costing and in marginal costing systems. We shall, however, confine our description to standard costs in absorption costing systems.

2.2 As we noted earlier, the standard cost of a product (or service) is made up of a number of different standards, one for each cost element, each of which has to be set by management. We have divided this section into two: the first part looks at setting the monetary part of each standard, whereas the second part looks at setting the resources requirement part of each standard.

Standard rates

Direct material prices

2.3 **Direct material prices** will be estimated by the purchasing department from their knowledge of the following.

- Purchase contracts already agreed
- Pricing discussions with regular suppliers
- The forecast movement of prices in the market
- The availability of bulk purchase discounts

2.4 Price inflation can cause difficulties in setting realistic standard prices. Suppose that a material costs £10 per kilogram at the moment and during the course of the next twelve months it is expected to go up in price by 20% to £12 per kilogram. What standard price should be selected?

- The current price of £10 per kilogram
- The average expected price for the year, say £11 per kilogram

2.5 Either would be possible, but neither would be entirely satisfactory.

(a) If the **current price** were used in the standard, the reported price variance will become adverse as soon as prices go up, which might be very early in the year. If prices go up gradually rather than in one big jump, it would be difficult to select an appropriate time for revising the standard.

(b) If an **estimated mid-year price** were used, price variances should be favourable in the first half of the year and adverse in the second half of the year, again assuming that prices go up gradually throughout the year. Management could only really check that in any month, the price variance did not become excessively adverse (or favourable) and that the price variance switched from being favourable to adverse around month six or seven and not sooner.

Direct labour rates

2.6 **Direct labour rates per hour** will be set by discussion with the personnel department and by reference to the payroll and to any agreements on pay rises with trade union representatives of the employees.

(a) A separate hourly rate or weekly wage will be set for each different labour grade/type of employee.

(b) An average hourly rate will be applied for each grade (even though individual rates of pay may vary according to age and experience).

2.7 Similar problems when dealing with inflation to those described for material prices can be met when setting labour standards.

Overhead absorption rates

2.8 When standard costs are fully absorbed costs, the **absorption rate** of fixed production overheads will be **predetermined**, usually each year when the budget is prepared, and based in the usual manner on budgeted fixed production overhead expenditure and budgeted production.

For selling and distribution costs, standard costs might be absorbed as a percentage of the standard selling price.

2.9 Standard costs under marginal costing will, of course, not include any element of absorbed overheads.

Standard resource requirements

2.10 To estimate the materials required to make each product (**material usage**) and also the labour hours required (**labour efficiency**), **technical specifications** must be prepared for each product by production experts (either in the production department or the work study department).

(a) The '**standard product specification**' for materials must list the quantities required per unit of each material in the product. These standard input quantities must be made known to the operators in the production department so that control action by management to deal with **excess material wastage** will be understood by them.

(b) The '**standard operation sheet**' for labour will specify the expected hours required by each grade of labour in each department to make one unit of product. These standard times must be carefully set (for example by work study) and must be understood by the labour force. Where necessary, **standard procedures** or **operating methods** should be stated.

Performance standards

2.11 The quantity of material and labour time required will depend on the level of performance required by management. There are two types of **performance standard** which might be used. Standards may be set at '**attainable levels** which assume efficient levels of operation, but which include **allowances** for normal loss, waste and machine downtime, or at **ideal levels**, which make **no allowance** for the above losses, and are only attainable under the most favourable conditions' (CIMA *Official Terminology*).

2.12 **Ideal standards** are sometimes thought to have a negative motivational impact, because employees will often feel that the goals are unattainable and not work so hard. When setting standards, managers must be aware of two requirements.

- The need to establish a useful control measure
- The need to set a standard which will have the desired motivational effect.

These two requirements are often conflicting, so that the final standard cost might be a compromise between the two.

Taking account of wastage, losses etc

2.13 If, during processing, the quantity of material input to the process is likely to reduce (due to wastage, evaporation and so on), the quantity input must be greater than the quantity in the finished product and a material standard must take account of this.

2.14 Suppose that the fresh raspberry juice content of a litre of Purple Pop is 100ml and that there is a 10% loss of raspberry juice during process due to evaporation. The standard material usage of raspberry juice per litre of Purple Pop will be:

$$100\text{ml} \times \frac{100\%}{(100-10)\%} = 100\text{ml} \times \frac{100\%}{90\%} = 111.11\text{ml}$$

Exam focus point

Make sure that you understand how to account for wastage and losses etc when calculating standard costs. Examination questions could well ask you to calculate the standard cost of a product given that there is loss due to evaporation or idle time and so on. Have a go at question 2 below.

Question 2

A unit of product X requires 24 active labour hours for completion. It is anticipated that there will be 20% idle time which is to be incorporated into the standard times for all products. If the wage rate is £10 per hour, what is the standard labour cost of one unit of product X?

A £192   B £240   C £288   D £300

Answer

The basic labour cost for 24 hours is £240. However with idle time it will be necessary to pay for more than 24 hours in order to achieve 24 hours of actual work Therefore options A and B are incorrect.

$$\text{Standard labour cost} = \text{active hours for completion} \times \frac{125}{100} \times £10$$

$$= 24 \times 1.25 \times £10 \quad = \quad \underline{£300}$$

Option D is correct.

Option C is incorrect because it results from simply adding an extra 20 per cent to the labour hours. However the idle hours are 20 per cent of the *total* hours worked, therefore we need to add 25 per cent to the required active hours, as shown in the working.

Problems in setting standards

Question 3

What sort of problems can you envisage arising when setting standards?

Answer

(a) Deciding how to incorporate **inflation** into planned unit costs

(b) Agreeing on a **performance standard** (attainable or ideal)

(c) Deciding on the **quality** of materials to be used (a better quality of material will cost more, but perhaps reduce material wastage)

(d) Estimating materials **prices** where seasonal price variations or bulk purchase discounts may be significant

(e) Finding sufficient **time** to construct accurate standards as standard setting can be a **time-consuming process**

(f) Incurring the **cost of setting up and maintaining a system** for establishing standards

(g) Dealing with possible **behavioural problems**, managers responsible for the achievement of standards possibly resisting the use of a standard costing control system for fear of being blamed for any adverse variances

2.15 Note that standard costing is most difficult in times of inflation but it is still worthwhile.

(a) **Usage** and **efficiency** variances will still be meaningful

(b) **Inflation is measurable**: there is no reason why its effects cannot be removed from the variances reported.

(c) Standard costs can be **revised** so long as this is **not done too frequently**.

The advantages of standard costing

Question 4

What do you think are the benefits to be gained from using standard costing?

Answer

The advantages for **control** in having a standard costing system in operation can be summarised as follows.

(a) Carefully planned standards are an **aid to more accurate budgeting**.

(b) Standard costs provide a **yardstick** against which actual costs can be measured.

(c) The **setting of standards** involves determining the best materials and methods which may lead to **economies**.

(d) A **target of efficiency** is set for employees to reach and **cost consciousness** is stimulated.

(e) Variances can be calculated which enable the principle of '**management by exception**' to be operated. Only the variances which exceed acceptable tolerance limits need to be investigated by management with a view to control action.

(f) Standard costs **simplify the process of bookkeeping** in cost accounting, because they are easier to use than LIFO, FIFO and weighted average costs.

(g) Standard times **simplify the process of production scheduling**.

(h) Standard performance levels might provide an **incentive for individuals** to achieve targets for themselves at work.

Chapter roundup

- A **standard cost** is a **predetermined estimated unit cost**, used for stock valuation and control.

- A **standard cost card** shows full details of the standard cost of each product.

- Differences between actual and standard cost are called **variances**.

- **Performance standards** are used to set efficiency targets. There are basically two types: **attainable and ideal**.

- A standard cost is an **average** expected unit cost. The actual cost of individual items may fluctuate around this average.

- Management should only receive information of **significant** variances. This is known as '**management by exception**'.

- There are a number of advantages and disadvantages associated with standard costing.

Quick quiz

1 A standard cost is ....

2 What are two main uses of standard costing?

3 A control technique which compares standard costs and revenues with actual results to obtain variances which are used to stimulate improves performance is known as:

    A   Standard costing
    B   Variance analysis
    C   Budgetary control
    D   Budgeting

4 Standard costs may only be used in absorption costing.

    True   ☐

    False   ☐

5 Two types of performance standard are

    (a)   ....
    (b)   ....

6 List three problems in setting standards.

7 List three advantages of using standard costing.

Answers to quick quiz

1   A planned unit cost.

2   (a) To value stocks and cost production for cost accounting purposes.

     (b) To act as a control device by establishing standards and highlighting activities that are not conforming to plan and bringing these to the attention of management.

3   A

4   False

5   (a) Attainable
     (b) Ideal

6   See answer to Question 3.

7   See answer to Question 4.

Now try the questions below from the Exam Question Bank

Number	Level	Marks	Time
44	MCQ	n/a	n/a
45	Examination	10	18 mins

Chapter 25

BASIC VARIANCE ANALYSIS

Topic list	Syllabus reference
1 Variances	1(b), (d), 5(a)
2 Direct material cost variances	1(b), (d), 5(a)
3 Direct labour cost variances	1(b), (d), 5(a)
4 Variable production overhead variances	1(b), (d), 5(a)
5 Fixed production overhead variances	1(b), (d), 5(a)
6 The reasons for cost variances	1(b), (d), 5(a)
7 The significance of cost variances	1(b), (d), 5(a)

Introduction

The actual results achieved by an organisation during a reporting period (week, month, quarter, year) will, more than likely, be different from the expected results (the expected results being the standard costs and revenues which we looked at in the previous chapter). Such differences may occur between individual items, such as the cost of labour and the volume of sales, and between the total expected profit/contribution and the total actual profit/contribution.

Management will have spent considerable time and trouble setting standards. Actual results have differed from the standards. The wise manager will consider the differences that have occurred and use the results of these considerations to assist in attempts to attain the standards. The wise manager will use **variance analysis** as a method of **control**.

This chapter examines **variance analysis** and sets out the method of calculating the following variances.

- Direct material cost variances
- Direct labour cost variances
- Variable production overhead variances
- Fixed production overhead variances

We will then go on to look at the reasons for and significance of cost variances.

Chapter 26 of this **Financial Information for Management** Study Text will build on the basics set down in this chapter by introducing **sales variances** and **operating statements**.

Study guide

Section 5 – Cost classification

- Describe the nature of control achieved through the comparison of actual costs against plan

Section 26 – Standard costing

- Explain the purpose of the following variances:

    - materials price and usage

    - labour rate, idle time and efficiency

    - variable overhead expenditure and efficiency

- fixed overhead expenditure, volume and where appropriate, efficiency and capacity

• Calculate and interpret the above variances using the appropriate costing method

Exam guide

Variance calculation is a very important part of your **Financial Information for Management** studies and it is vital that you are able to calculate all of the different types of variance included in the syllabus. Examination questions on this topic might appear in either Section A and/or Section B.

1 VARIANCES

> **KEY TERM**
>
> A **variance** is 'The difference between a planned, budgeted, or standard cost and the actual cost incurred. The same comparisons may be made for revenues.'
>
> CIMA *Official Terminology*

1.1 The process by which the **total** difference between standard and actual results is analysed is known as **variance analysis**.

> **KEY TERM**
>
> **Variance analysis** is defined as 'The evaluation of performance by means of variances, whose timely reporting should maximise the opportunity for managerial action'.
>
> CIMA *Official Terminology*

1.2 When actual results are better than expected results, we have a **favourable variance** (F). If, on the other hand, actual results are worse than expected results, we have an **adverse variance** (A).

1.3 Variances can be divided into three main groups.

• Variable cost variances
• Sales variances
• Fixed production overhead variances.

In the remainder of this chapter we will consider, in detail, variable cost variances and fixed production overhead variances.

2 DIRECT MATERIAL COST VARIANCES

> **KEY TERM**
>
> The **direct material total variance** is the difference between what the output actually cost and what it should have cost, in terms of material.

2.1 The **direct material total variance** can be divided into two sub-variances.

KEY TERMS

- The **direct material price variance**. This is the **difference between the standard cost and the actual cost for the actual quantity of material used or purchased.** In other words, it is the difference between what the material did cost and what it should have cost.

- The **direct material usage variance**. This is the **difference between the standard quantity of materials that should have been used for the number of units actually produced, and the actual quantity of materials used, valued at the standard cost per unit of material.** In other words, it is the difference between how much material should have been used and how much material was used, valued at standard cost.

2.2 EXAMPLE: DIRECT MATERIAL VARIANCES

Product X has a standard direct material cost as follows.

10 kilograms of material Y at £10 per kilogram = £100 per unit of X.

During period 4, 1,000 units of X were manufactured, using 11,700 kilograms of material Y which cost £98,600.

Required

Calculate the following variances.

(a) The direct material total variance
(b) The direct material price variance
(c) The direct material usage variance

2.3 SOLUTION

(a) **The direct material total variance**

This is the difference between what 1,000 units should have cost and what they did cost.

	£
1,000 units should have cost (× £100)	100,000
but did cost	98,600
Direct material total variance	1,400 (F)

The variance is **favourable** because the units cost less than they should have cost.

Now we can break down the direct material total variance into its two constituent parts: the direct material **price** variance and the direct material **usage** variance.

(b) **The direct material price variance**

This is the difference between what 11,700 kgs should have cost and what 11,700 kgs did cost.

	£
11,700 kgs of Y should have cost (× £10)	117,000
but did cost	98,600
Material Y price variance	18,400 (F)

The variance is **favourable** because the material cost less than it should have.

(c) **The direct material usage variance**

This is the difference between how many kilograms of Y should have been used to produce 1,000 units of X and how many kilograms were used, valued at the standard cost per kilogram.

1,000 units should have used (× 10 kgs)	10,000 kgs
but did use	11,700 kgs
Usage variance in kgs	1,700 kgs (A)
× standard cost per kilogram	× £10
Usage variance in £	£17,000 (A)

The variance is **adverse** because more material than should have been used was used.

(d) **Summary**

	£
Price variance	18,400 (F)
Usage variance	17,000 (A)
Total variance	1,400 (A)

Materials variances and opening and closing stock

2.4   Suppose that a company uses raw material P in production, and that this raw material has a standard price of £3 per metre. During one month 6,000 metres are bought for £18,600, and 5,000 metres are used in production. At the end of the month, stock will have been increased by 1,000 metres. In variance analysis, the problem is to decide the **material price variance**. Should it be calculated on the basis of **materials purchased** (6,000 metres) or on the basis of **materials used** (5,000 metres)?

2.5   The answer to this problem depends on how **closing stocks** of the raw materials will be valued.

(a)   If they are valued at **standard cost**, (1,000 units at £3 per unit) the price variance is calculated on material **purchases** in the period.

(b)   If they are valued at **actual cost** (FIFO) (1,000 units at £3.10 per unit) the price variance is calculated on materials **used in production** in the period.

2.6   A **full standard costing system** is usually in operation and therefore the price variance is usually calculated on **purchases** in the period. The variance on the full 6,000 metres will be written off to the costing profit and loss account, even though only 5,000 metres are included in the cost of production.

2.7   There are two main advantages in extracting the material price variance at the time of **receipt**.

(a)   If variances are extracted at the time of receipt they will be **brought to the attention of managers earlier** than if they are extracted as the material is used. If it is necessary to correct any variances then management action can be more timely.

(b)   Since variances are extracted at the time of receipt, **all stocks will be valued at standard price**. This is administratively easier and it means that all issues from stocks can be made at standard price. If stocks are held at actual cost it is necessary to calculate a separate price variance on each batch as it is issued. Since issues are usually made in a number of small batches this can be a time-consuming task, especially with a manual system.

2.8   The price variance would be calculated as follows.

	£
6,000 metres of material P purchased should cost (× £3)	18,000
but did cost	18,600
Price variance	600 (A)

3 DIRECT LABOUR COST VARIANCES

3.1 The calculation of **direct labour variances** is very similar to the calculation of direct material variances.

> **KEY TERMS**
>
> - The **direct labour total variance** (the difference between what the output should have cost and what it did cost, in terms of labour) can be divided into two sub-variances.
>
> - The **direct labour rate variance**. This is similar to the direct material price variance. If is the **difference between the standard cost and the actual cost for the actual number of hours paid for.**
>
>   In other words, it is the difference between what the labour did cost and what it should have cost.
>
> - The **direct labour efficiency variance**. This is similar to the direct material usage variance. It is the **difference between the hours that should have been worked for the number of units actually produced, and the actual number of hours worked, valued at the standard rate per hour.**
>
>   In other words, it is the difference between how many hours should have been worked and how many hours were worked, valued at the standard rate per hour.

3.2 EXAMPLE: DIRECT LABOUR VARIANCES

The standard direct labour cost of product X is as follows.

> 2 hours of grade Z labour at £5 per hour = £10 per unit of product X.

During period 4, 1,000 units of product X were made, and the direct labour cost of grade Z labour was £8,900 for 2,300 hours of work.

Required

Calculate the following variances.

(a) The direct labour total variance
(b) The direct labour rate variance
(c) The direct labour efficiency (productivity) variance

3.3 SOLUTION

(a) **The direct labour total variance**

This is the difference between what 1,000 units should have cost and what they did cost.

	£
1,000 units should have cost (× £10)	10,000
but did cost	8,900
Direct labour total variance	1,100 (F)

The variance is **favourable** because the units cost less than they should have done.

Again we can analyse this total variance into its two constituent parts.

(b) **The direct labour rate variance**

This is the difference between what 2,300 hours should have cost and what 2,300 hours did cost.

	£
2,300 hours of work should have cost (× £5 per hr)	11,500
but did cost	8,900
Direct labour rate variance	2,600 (F)

The variance is **favourable** because the labour cost less than it should have cost.

(c) **The direct labour efficiency variance**

1,000 units of X should have taken (× 2 hrs)	2,000 hrs
but did take	2,300 hrs
Efficiency variance in hours	300 hrs (A)
× standard rate per hour	× £5
Efficiency variance in £	£1,500 (A)

The variance is **adverse** because more hours were worked than should have been worked.

(d) **Summary**

	£
Rate variance	2,600 (F)
Efficiency variance	1,500 (A)
Total variance	1,100 (F)

Idle time variance

3.4 A company may operate a costing system in which any **idle time** is recorded. Idle time may be caused by machine breakdowns or not having work to give to employees, perhaps because of bottlenecks in production or a shortage of orders from customers. When idle time occurs, the labour force is still paid wages for time at work, but no actual work is done. Time paid for without any work being done is unproductive and therefore inefficient. In variance analysis, **idle time is always an adverse efficiency variance**.

3.5 When idle time is recorded separately, it is helpful to provide control information which identifies the cost of idle time separately, and in variance analysis, there will be an idle time variance **as a separate part of the total labour efficiency variance**. The remaining efficiency variance will then relate only to the productivity of the labour force during the hours spent **actively working**.

3.6 EXAMPLE: LABOUR VARIANCES WITH IDLE TIME

Refer to the standard cost data in Paragraph 3.2. During period 5, 1,500 units of product X were made and the cost of grade Z labour was £17,500 for 3,080 hours. During the period, however, there as a shortage of customer orders and 100 hours were recorded as idle time.

Required

Calculate the following variances.

(a) The direct labour total variance
(b) The direct labour rate variance
(c) The idle time variance
(d) The direct labour efficiency variance

3.7 SOLUTION

(a) **The direct labour total variance**

	£
1,500 units of product X should have cost (× £10)	15,000
but did cost	17,500
Direct labour total variance	2,500 (A)

Actual cost is greater than standard cost. The variance is therefore **adverse**.

(b) **The direct labour rate variance**

The rate variance is a comparison of what the hours paid should have cost and what they did cost.

	£
3,080 hours of grade Z labour should have cost (× £5)	15,400
but did cost	17,500
Direct labour rate variance	2,100 (A)

Actual cost is greater than standard cost. The variance is therefore **adverse**.

(c) **The idle time variance**

The idle time variance is the hours of idle time, valued at the standard rate per hour.

Idle time variance = 100 hours (A) × £5 = £500 (A)

Idle time is **always** an adverse variance.

(d) **The direct labour efficiency variance**

The efficiency variance considers the hours actively worked (the difference between hours paid for and idle time hours). In our example, there were (3,080 – 100) = 2,980 hours when the labour force was not idle. The variance is calculated by taking the amount of output produced (1,500 units of product X) and comparing the time it should have taken to make them, with the actual time spent **actively** making them (2,980 hours). Once again, the variance in hours is valued at the **standard rate per labour hour**.

1,500 units of product X should take (× 2hrs)	3,000 hrs
but did take (3,080 – 100)	2,980 hrs
Direct labour efficiency variance in hours	20 hrs (F)
× standard rate per hour	× £5
Direct labour efficiency variance in £	£100 (F)

(e) **Summary**

	£
Direct labour rate variance	2,100 (A)
Idle time variance	500 (A)
Direct labour efficiency variance	100 (F)
Direct labour total variance	2,500 (A)

3.8 Remember that, if idle time is recorded, the actual hours used in the efficiency variance calculation are the **hours worked and not the hours paid for**.

Question 1

Growler Ltd is planning to make 100,000 units per period of product AA. Each unit of AA should require 2 hours to produce, with labour being paid £11 per hour. Attainable work hours are less than clock hours, so 250,000 hours have been budgeted in the period.

Actual data for the period was:

Units produced	120,000
Direct labour cost	£3,200,000
Clock hours	280,000

Required

Calculate the following variances.

(a) Labour rate variance
(b) Labour efficiency variance
(c) Idle time variance

Answer

The information means that clock hours have to be multiplied by $\dfrac{200,000}{250,000}$ (80%) in order to arrive at a realistic efficiency variance.

(a) **Labour rate variance**

	£'000
280,000 hours should have cost (× £11)	3,080
but did cost	3,200
Labour rate variance	120 (A)

(b) **Labour efficiency variance**

120,000 units should have taken (× 2 hours)	240,000	Hrs
but did take (280,000 × 80%)	224,000	Hrs
	16,000	hrs (F)
	× £11	
Labour efficiency variance	£176,000	(F)

(c) **Idle time variance**

280,000 × 20%	56,000	hrs
	× £11	
	£616,000	(A)

4 VARIABLE PRODUCTION OVERHEAD VARIANCES

4.1 Suppose that the variable production overhead cost of product X is as follows.

2 hours at £1.50 = £3 per unit

During period 6, 400 units of product X were made. The labour force worked 820 hours, of which 60 hours were recorded as idle time. The variable overhead cost was £1,230.

Calculate the following variances.

(a) The variable overhead total variance
(b) The variable production overhead expenditure variance
(c) The variable production overhead efficiency variance

4.2 Since this example relates to variable production costs, the total variance is based on actual units of production. (If the overhead had been a variable selling cost, the variance would be based on sales volumes.)

	£
400 units of product X should cost (× £3)	1,200
but did cost	1,230
Variable production overhead total variance	30 (A)

4.3 In many variance reporting systems, the variance analysis goes no further, and expenditure and efficiency variances are not calculated. However, the adverse variance of £30 may be explained as the sum of two factors.

(a) The hourly rate of spending on variable production overheads was higher than it should have been, that is there is an **expenditure variance**.

(b) The labour force worked inefficiently, and took longer to make the output than it should have done. This means that spending on variable production overhead was higher than it should have been, in other words there is an **efficiency (productivity) variance**. The variable production overhead efficiency variance is exactly the same, in hours, as the direct labour efficiency variance, and occurs for the same reasons.

4.4 It is usually assumed that **variable overheads are incurred during active working hours**, but are not incurred during idle time (for example the machines are not running, therefore power is not being consumed, and no direct materials are being used). This means in our example that although the labour force was paid for 820 hours, they were actively working for only 760 of those hours and so variable production overhead spending occurred during 760 hours.

KEY TERMS

The **variable production overhead expenditure variance** is the difference between the amount of variable production overhead that should have been incurred in the actual hours actively worked, and the actual amount of variable production overhead incurred.

4.5 (a)

	£
760 hours of variable production overhead should cost (× £1.50)	1,140
but did cost	1,230
Variable production overhead expenditure variance	90 (A)

KEY TERMS

The **variable production overhead efficiency variance**. If you already know the direct labour efficiency variance, the variable production overhead efficiency variance is exactly the same in hours, but priced at the variable production overhead rate per hour.

(b) In our example, the efficiency variance would be as follows.

400 units of product X should take (× 2hrs)	800 hrs
but did take (active hours)	760 hrs
Variable production overhead efficiency variance in hours	40 hrs (F)
× standard rate per hour	× £1.50
Variable production overhead efficiency variance in £	£60 (F)

(c) **Summary**

	£
Variable production overhead expenditure variance	90 (A)
Variable production overhead efficiency variance	60 (F)
Variable production overhead total variance	30 (A)

5 FIXED PRODUCTION OVERHEAD VARIANCES

5.1 You may have noticed that the method of calculating cost variances for variable cost items is essentially the same for labour, materials and variable overheads. Fixed production overhead variances are very different. In an **absorption costing system,** they are an attempt to explain the **under- or over-absorption of fixed production overheads** in production costs. We looked at under/over absorption of fixed overheads in Chapter 8.

5.2 The fixed production overhead total variance (ie the under- or over-absorbed fixed production overhead) may be broken down into two parts as usual.

- An **expenditure** variance

- A **volume** variance. This in turn may be split into two parts

    - A **volume efficiency variance**
    - A **volume capacity variance**

5.3 You will find it easier to calculate and understand **fixed overhead variances**, if you keep in mind the whole time that you are trying to 'explain' (put a name and value to) any under- or over-absorbed overhead.

Remember that the **absorption rate** is calculated as follows.

$$\text{Overhead absorption rate } = \frac{\text{Budgeted fixed overhead}}{\text{Budgeted activity level}}$$

If either of the following are incorrect, then we will have an under- or over-absorption of overhead.

- The numerator (number on top) = Budgeted fixed overhead
- The denominator (number on bottom) = Budgeted activity level

The fixed overhead expenditure variance

5.4 The fixed overhead expenditure variance occurs if the numerator is incorrect. It measures the under- or over-absorbed overhead caused by the **actual total overhead** being different from the budgeted total overhead.

5.5 Therefore, fixed overhead expenditure variance = **Budgeted expenditure – Actual Expenditure.**

The fixed overhead volume variance

5.6 As we have already stated, the fixed overhead volume variance is made up of the following sub-variances.

- Fixed overhead efficiency variance
- Fixed overhead capacity variance

These variances arise if the denominator (ie the budgeted activity level) is incorrect.

5.7 The fixed overhead efficiency and capacity variances measure the under- or over-absorbed overhead caused by the **actual activity level** being different from the budgeted activity level used in calculating the absorption rate.

5.8 There are two reasons why the **actual activity** level may be different from the **budgeted activity level** used in calculating the absorption rate.

(a) The workforce may have worked more or less efficiently than the standard set. This deviation is measured by the **fixed overhead efficiency variance.**

(b) The hours worked by the workforce could have been different to the budgeted hours (regardless of the level of efficiency of the workforce) because of overtime and strikes etc. This deviation from the standard is measured by the **fixed overhead capacity variance.**

How to calculate the variances

5.9 In order to clarify the overhead variances which we have encountered in this section, consider the following definitions which are expressed in terms of how each overhead variance should be calculated.

> **KEY TERMS**
>
> • **Fixed overhead total variance** is the difference between fixed overhead incurred and fixed overhead absorbed. In other words, it is the under- or over-absorbed fixed overhead.
>
> • **Fixed overhead expenditure variance** is the difference between the budgeted fixed overhead expenditure and actual fixed overhead expenditure.
>
> • **Fixed overhead volume variance** is the difference between actual and budgeted volume multiplied by the standard absorption rate per *unit*.
>
> • **Fixed overhead volume efficiency variance** is the difference between the number of hours that actual production should have taken, and the number of hours actually taken (that is, worked) multiplied by the standard absorption rate per *hour*.
>
> • **Fixed overhead volume capacity variance** is the difference between budgeted hours of work and the actual hours worked, multiplied by the standard absorption rate per *hour*.

5.10 You should now be ready to work through an example to demonstrate all of the fixed overhead variances.

5.11 EXAMPLE: FIXED OVERHEAD VARIANCES

Suppose that a company budgets to produce 1,000 units of product E during August 20X3. The expected time to produce a unit of E is five hours, and the budgeted fixed overhead is £20,000. The standard fixed overhead cost per unit of product E will therefore be as follows.

5 hours at £4 per hour = £20 per unit

Actual fixed overhead expenditure in August 20X3 turns out to be £20,450. The labour force manages to produce 1,100 units of product E in 5,400 hours of work.

Task

Calculate the following variances.

(a) The fixed overhead total variance
(b) The fixed overhead expenditure variance
(c) The fixed overhead volume variance
(d) The fixed overhead volume efficiency variance
(e) The fixed overhead volume capacity variance

5.12 SOLUTION

All of the variances help to assess the under- or over-absorption of fixed overheads, some in greater detail than others.

(a) **Fixed overhead total variance**

	£
Fixed overhead incurred	20,450
Fixed overhead absorbed (1,100 units × £20 per unit)	22,000
Fixed overhead total variance	1,550 (F)
(= under-/over-absorbed overhead)	

The variance is favourable because more overheads were absorbed than budgeted.

(b) **Fixed overhead expenditure variance**

	£
Budgeted fixed overhead expenditure	20,000
Actual fixed overhead expenditure	20,450
Fixed overhead expenditure variance	450 (A)

The variance is adverse because actual expenditure was greater than budgeted expenditure.

(c) **Fixed overhead volume variance**

The production volume achieved was greater than expected. The fixed overhead volume variance measures the difference at the standard rate.

	£
Actual production at standard rate (1,100 × £20 per unit)	22,000
Budgeted production at standard rate (1,000 × £20 per unit)	20,000
Fixed overhead volume variance	2,000 (F)

The variance is **favourable** because output was greater than expected.

(i) The labour force may have worked efficiently, and produced output at a faster rate than expected. Since overheads are absorbed at the rate of £20 per unit, more will be absorbed if units are produced more quickly. This **efficiency variance** is exactly the same in hours as the direct labour efficiency variance, but is valued in £ at the standard absorption rate for fixed overhead.

(ii) The labour force may have worked longer hours than budgeted, and therefore produced more output, so there may be a **capacity variance**.

(d) **Fixed overhead volume efficiency variance**

The volume efficiency variance is calculated in the same way as the labour efficiency variance.

1,100 units of product E should take (× 5 hrs)	5,500 hrs
but did take	5,400 hrs
Fixed overhead volume efficiency variance in hours	100 hrs (F)
× standard fixed overhead absorption rate per hour	× £4
Fixed overhead volume efficiency variance in £	£400 (F)

The labour force has produced 5,500 standard hours of work in 5,400 actual hours and so output is 100 standard hours (or 20 units of product E) higher than budgeted for this reason and the variance is **favourable**.

(e) **Fixed overhead volume capacity variance**

The volume capacity variance is the difference between the budgeted hours of work and the actual active hours of work (excluding any idle time).

Budgeted hours of work	5,000 hrs
Actual hours of work	5,400 hrs
Fixed overhead volume capacity variance	400 hrs (F)
× standard fixed overhead absorption rate per hour	× £4
Fixed overhead volume capacity variance in £	£1,600 (F)

Since the labour force worked 400 hours longer than budgeted, we should expect output to be 400 standard hours (or 80 units of product E) higher than budgeted and hence the variance is **favourable**.

The variances may be summarised as follows.

Expenditure variance	450 hrs (A)
Efficiency variance	400 hrs (F)
Capacity variance	1,600 hrs (F)
Over-absorbed overhead (total variance)	£1,550 (F)

Exam focus point

In general, a favourable cost variance will arise if actual results are less than expected results. Be aware, however, of the **fixed overhead volume variance** and the **fixed overhead volume capacity variance** which give rise to favourable and adverse variances in the following situations.

- A favourable fixed overhead volume variance occurs when actual production is **greater than** budgeted production

- An adverse fixed overhead volume variance occurs when actual production is **less than budgeted** production

- A favourable fixed overhead volume capacity variance occurs when actual hours of work are **greater than** budgeted hours of work

- An adverse fixed overhead volume capacity variance occurs when actual hours of work are **less than** budgeted hours of work

---

5.13 Do not worry if you find fixed production overhead variances more difficult to grasp than the other variances we have covered. Most students do. Read over this section again and then try the following practice questions.

The following information relates to questions 2, 3 and 4

Barbados Ltd has prepared the following standard cost information for one unit of Product Zeta.

Direct materials	4kg @ £10/kg	£40.00
Direct labour	2 hours @ £4/hour	£8.00
Fixed overheads	3 hours @ £2.50	£7.50

The fixed overheads are based on a budgeted expenditure of £75,000 and budgeted activity of 30,000 hours.

Actual results for the period were recorded as follows.

Production	9,000 units
Materials – 33,600 kg	£336,000
Labour – 16,500 hours	£68,500
Fixed overheads	£320,000

Question 2

The direct material price and usage variances are:

	Material price £	Material usage £
A	-	24,000 (F)
B	-	24,000 (A)
C	24,000 (F)	-
D	24,000 (A)	-

Answer

Material price variance

	£
33,600 kg should have cost (× £10/kg)	336,000
and did cost	336,000
	-

Material usage variance

9,000 units should have used (× 4kg)	36,000 kg
but did use	33,600 kg
	2,400 kg (F)
× standard cost per kg	× £10
	24,000 (F)

The correct answer is therefore A.

Question 3

The direct labour rate and efficiency variances are:

	Labour rate £	Labour efficiency £
A	6,000 (F)	2,500 (A)
B	6,000 (A)	2,500 (F)
C	2,500 (A)	6,000 (F)
D	2,500 (F)	6,000 (A)

Answer

Direct labour rate variance

	£
16,500 hrs should have cost (× £4)	66,000
but did cost	68,500
	2,500 (A)

Direct labour efficiency variance

9,000 units should have taken (× 2 hrs)	18,000 hrs
but did take	16,500 hrs
	1,500 (F)
× standard rate per hour (× £4)	× £4
	6,000 (F)

The correct answer is therefore C.

Question 4

The total fixed production overhead variance is:

A   £5,000 (A)
B   £5,000 (F)
C   £2,500 (A)
D   £2,500 (F)

Answer

	£
Fixed production overhead absorbed (£7.50 × 9,000)	67,500
Fixed production overhead incurred	70,000
	2,500 (A)

The correct answer is therefore C.

Question 5

Brain Ltd produces and sells one product only, the Blob, the standard cost for one unit being as follows.

	£
Direct material A - 10 kilograms at £20 per kg	200
Direct wages – 5 hours at £6 per hour	30
Fixed production overhead	50
Total standard cost	280

The fixed overhead included in the standard cost is based on an expected monthly output of 900 units.

During April 20X3 the actual results were as follows.

Production	800 units
Material A	7,800 kg used, costing £159,900
Direct wages	4,200 hours worked for £24,150
Fixed production overhead	£47,000

Required

(a)   Calculate material price and usage variances.
(b)   Calculate labour rate and efficiency variances.
(c)   Calculate fixed production overhead expenditure and volume variances
(d)   Calculate fixed production overhead volume efficiency and volume capacity variances

Answer

(a)   **Material price variance**

	£
7,800 kgs should have cost (× £20)	156,000
but did cost	159,900
Price variance	3,900 (A)

Material usage variance

800 units should have used (× 10 kgs)	8,000 kgs
but did use	7,800 kgs
Usage variance in kgs	200 kgs (F)
× standard cost per kilogram	× £20
Usage variance in £	£4,000 (F)

(b)   **Labour rate variance**

	£
4,200 hours should have cost (× £6)	25,200
but did cost	24,150
Rate variance	1,050 (F)

Labour efficiency variance

800 units should have taken (× 5 hrs)	4,000 hrs
but did take	4,200 hrs
Efficiency variance in hours	200 hrs (A)
× standard rate per hour	× £6
Efficiency variance in £	£1,200 (A)

(c) **Fixed production overhead expenditure variance**

	£
Budgeted expenditure (£50 × 900)	45,000
Actual expenditure	47,000
Expenditure variance	2,000 (A)

Fixed production overhead volume variance

	£
Budgeted production at standard rate (900 × £50)	45,000
Actual production at standard rate (800 × £50)	40,000
Volume variance	5,000 (A)

(d) **Fixed production overhead volume efficiency variance**

800 units should have taken (× 5 hrs)	4,000 hrs
but did take	4,200 hrs
Volume efficiency variance in hours	200 hrs (A)
× Standard fixed overhead absorption rate per hour (£50 ÷ 5 hrs)	× £10
Volume efficiency variance in £	2,000 (A)

Fixed production overhead volume capacity variance

Budgeted hours of work (5 hours × 900 units)	4,500 hrs
Actual hours of work	4,200 hrs
Volume capacity variance in hours	300 hrs (A)
× standard fixed overhead absorption rate per hour	× £10
Volume capacity variance in £	3,000 (A)

6   THE REASONS FOR COST VARIANCES

6.1   There are many possible reasons for cost variances arising, as you will see from the following list of possible causes.

Exam focus point

This is not an exhaustive list and in an examination question you should review the information given and use your imagination and common sense to suggest possible reasons for variances.

Variance	Favourable	Adverse
(a) Material price	Unforeseen discounts received More care taken in purchasing Change in material standard	Price increase Careless purchasing Change in material standard
(b) Material usage	Material used of higher quality than standard More effective use made of material Errors in allocating material to jobs	Defective material Excessive waste Theft Stricter quality control Errors in allocating material to jobs
(c) Labour rate	Use of apprentices or other workers at a rate of pay lower than standard	Wage rate increase Use of higher grade labour
(d) Idle time	**The idle time variance is always adverse.**	Machine breakdown Non-availability of material Illness or injury to worker
(e) Labour efficiency	Output produced more quickly than expected because of work motivation, better quality of equipment or materials, or better methods Errors in allocating time to jobs	Lost time in excess of standard allowed Output lower than standard set because of deliberate restriction, lack of training, or sub-standard material used Errors in allocating time to jobs
(f) Overhead expenditure	Savings in costs incurred More economical use of services	Increase in cost of services used Excessive use of services Change in type of services used
(g) Overhead volume efficiency	Labour force working more efficiently (favourable labour efficiency variance)	Labour force working less efficiently (adverse labour efficiency variance)
(h) Overhead volume capacity	Labour force working overtime	Machine breakdown, strikes, labour shortages

7 THE SIGNIFICANCE OF COST VARIANCES

7.1 Once variances have been calculated, management have to decide whether or not to investigate their causes. It would be extremely time consuming and expensive to investigate every variance therefore managers have to decide which variances are worthy of investigation.

7.2 There are a number of factors which can be taken into account when deciding whether or not a variance should be investigated.

(a) **Materiality.** A standard cost is really only an **average** expected cost and is not a rigid specification. Small variations either side of this average are therefore bound to occur. The problem is to decide whether a variation from standard should be considered **significant** and worthy of investigation. **Tolerance limits** can be set and only variances which exceed such limits would require investigating.

(b) **Controllability.** Some types of variance may not be controllable even once their cause is discovered. For example, if there is a general worldwide increase in the price of a raw material there is nothing that can be done internally to control the effect of this. If a central decision is made to award all employees a 10% increase in salary, staff costs in division A will increase by this amount and the variance is not controllable by division A's manager. Uncontrollable variances call for a change in the plan, not an investigation into the past.

(c) **The type of standard being used.**

    (i)   The efficiency variance reported in any control period, whether for materials or labour, will depend on the **efficiency level** set. If, for example, an **ideal standard** is used, variances will always be **adverse**.

    (ii)   A similar problem arises if **average price levels** are used as standards. If inflation exists, favourable price variances are likely to be reported at the beginning of a period, to be offset by adverse price variances later in the period as inflation pushes prices up.

(d) **Interdependence between variances** . Quite possibly, individual variances should not be looked at in isolation. One variance might be inter-related with another, and much of it might have occurred only because the other, inter-related, variance occurred too. We will investigate this issue further in a moment.

(e) **Costs of investigation.** The costs of an investigation should be weighed against the benefits of correcting the cause of a variance.

Interdependence between variances

7.3   When two variances are interdependent (interrelated) one will usually be adverse and the other one favourable. Here are some examples.

Materials price and usage

7.4   It may be decided to purchase cheaper materials for a job in order to obtain a favourable price variance, possibly with the consequence that materials wastage is higher and an adverse usage variance occurs. If the cheaper materials are more difficult to handle, there might be some adverse labour efficiency variance too.

7.5   If a decision is made to purchase more expensive materials, which perhaps have a longer service life, the price variance will be adverse but the usage variance might be favourable.

Labour rate and efficiency

7.6   If employees in a workforce are paid higher rates for experience and skill, using a highly skilled team to do some work would incur an adverse rate variance, but should also obtain a favourable efficiency variance. In contrast, a favourable rate variance might indicate a larger-than-expected proportion of inexperienced workers in the workforce, which could result in an adverse labour efficiency variance, and perhaps poor materials handling and high rates of rejects too (adverse materials usage variance).

Chapter roundup

- **Variances** measure the difference between **actual results** and **expected results**.

- The direct material total variance can be subdivided into the **direct material price** variance and the **direct material usage** variance.

- Direct material price variances are usually extracted at the time of **receipt** of the materials, rather than at the time of usage.

- The direct labour total variance can be subdivided into the **direct labour rate** variance and the **direct labour efficiency** variance.

- If **idle time** arises, it is usual to calculate a separate idle time variance, and to base the calculation of the efficiency variance on **active hours** (when labour actually worked) only. It is always an **adverse** variance.

- The variable production overhead total variance can be subdivided into the variable production overhead **expenditure** variance and the variable production overhead **efficiency** variance **(based on active hours).**

- The fixed production overhead total variance can be subdivided into an **expenditure** variance and a **volume** variance. The fixed production overhead volume variance can be further subdivided into an **efficiency** and a **capacity** variance.

- Ensure that you can provide possible **reasons** for cost variances.

- Materiality, controllability, the type of standard being used, the interdependence of variances and the cost of an investigation should be taken into account when deciding whether to investigate reported variances.

Quick quiz

1   Subdivide the following variances.

(a)   Direct materials cost variance ⟨ *Materials Price Variance / Materials Usage Variance*

(b)   Direct labour cost variance ⟨ *Direct labour rate variance. / labour rate efficiency variance*

(c)   Variable production overhead variance ⟨ *Variable production o/h exp / Variable production o/h efficiency.*

2   What are the two main advantages in calculating the material price variance at the time of receipt of materials? *Diff can be spotted immediatly, easier to use.*

3   Idle time variances are always adverse.

    True   ☑

    False ☐

4   Adverse material usage variances might occur for the following reasons.

    I   Defective material
    II   Excessive waste
    III   Theft
    IV   Unforeseen discounts received

    A   I
    B   I and II
    C   I, II and III
    D   I, II, III and IV

5   List the factors which should be taken into account when deciding whether or not a variance should be investigated. *Cost, time, amount of variance, are they interrellated,*

Answers to quick quiz

1 (a) 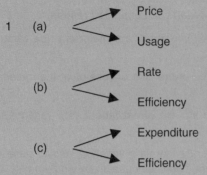 Price

Usage

(b) Rate

Efficiency

(c) Expenditure

Efficiency

2 (a) The earlier variances are extracted, the sooner they will be brought to the attention of managers.

(b) All stocks will be valued at standard price which requires less administration effort.

3 True

4 C

5 • Materiality
• Controllability
• Type of standard being used
• Interdependence between variances
• Costs of investigation

Now try the questions below from the Exam Question Bank

Number	Level	Marks	Time
46	MCQ	n/a	n/a
47	Examination	10	18 mins

Chapter 26

FURTHER VARIANCE ANALYSIS

Topic list	Syllabus reference
1 Sales variances	5(a), 3(c)
2 Operating statements	5(a), 3(c), 1(b)
3 Variances in a standard marginal costing system	5(a), 3(c)
4 Deriving actual data from standard cost details and variances	5(a), 3(c)

Introduction

The objective of cost variance analysis, which we looked at in the previous chapter, is to assist management in the **control of costs**. Costs are, however, only one factor which contribute to the achievement of planned profit. **Sales** are another important factor and sales variances can be calculated to aid management's control of their business. We will therefore begin this chapter by examining **sales variances**.

Having discussed the variances you need to know about, we will be looking in Section 2 at the **ways in which variances should be presented to management** to aid their control of the organisation.

We then consider in Section 3 how **marginal cost variances** differ from absorption cost variances and how marginal costing information should be presented.

Finally we will consider **how actual data can be derived from standard cost details and variances**.

Study guide

Section 5 – Cost classification

- Describe the nature of control achieved through the comparison of actual costs against plan

Section 26 – Standard costing

- Explain the purpose of sales volume and price variances

- Prepare operating statements to reconcile budgeted to actual profit

- Discuss the implications of the results of variance analysis for management

- Calculate and interpret sales volume and price variances using the appropriate costing method

Exam guide

Variance analysis is traditionally a very popular exam topic. Make sure that you are able to prepare operating statements and explain why calculated variances have occurred. Look out for variance analysis questions in both sections of your examination.

1 SALES VARIANCES

Selling price variance

> **KEY TERM**
>
> The **selling price variance** is a measure of the effect on expected profit of a different selling price to standard selling price. It is calculated as the **difference between what the sales revenue should have been for the actual quantity sold, and what it was.**

1.1 Suppose that the standard selling price of product X is £15. Actual sales in 20X3 were 2,000 units at £15.30 per unit. The selling price variance is calculated as follows.

	£
Sales revenue from 2,000 units should have been (× £15)	30,000
but was (× £15.30)	30,600
Selling price variance	600 (F)

1.2 The variance calculated in paragraph 1.1 is **favourable** because the price was higher than expected.

Sales volume profit variance

> **KEY TERM**
>
> The **sales volume profit variance** is the difference between the actual units sold and the budgeted quantity, valued at the standard profit per unit. In other words, it measures **the increase or decrease in standard profit as a result of the sales volume being higher or lower than budgeted.**

1.3 Suppose that a company budgets to sell 8,000 units of product J for £12 per unit. The standard full cost per unit is £7. Actual sales were 7,700 units, at £12.50 per unit.

The **sales volume profit variance** is calculated as follows.

Budgeted sales volume	8,000 units
Actual sales volume	7,700 units
Sales volume variance in units	300 units (A)
× standard profit per unit (£(12–7))	× £5
Sales volume variance	£1,500 (A)

1.4 The variance calculated in paragraph 1.3 is **adverse** because actual sales were less than budgeted.

Question 1

Jasper Ltd has the following budget and actual figures for 20X4.

	Budget	Actual
Sales units	600	620
Selling price per unit	£30	£29

Standard full cost of production = £28 per unit.

Required

Calculate the selling price variance and the sales volume profit variance.

Answer

Sales revenue for 620 units should have been (× £30)	18,600
but was (× £29)	17,980
Selling price variance	620 (A)
Budgeted sales volume	600 units
Actual sales volume	620 units
Sales volume variance in units	20 units (F)
× standard profit per unit (£(30 – 28))	× £2
Sales volume profit variance	£40 (F)

The significance of sales variances

1.5   The possible **interdependence** between sales price and sales volume variances should be obvious to you. A reduction in the sales price might stimulate bigger sales demand, so that an adverse sales price variance might be counterbalanced by a favourable sales volume variance. Similarly, a price rise would give a favourable price variance, but possibly at the cost of a fall in demand and an adverse sales volume variance.

1.6   It is therefore important in analysing an unfavourable sales variance that the overall consequence should be considered, that is, has there been a counterbalancing favourable variance as a direct result of the unfavourable one?

2   OPERATING STATEMENTS

2.1   So far, we have considered how variances are calculated without considering how they combine to reconcile the difference between budgeted profit and actual profit during a period. This reconciliation is usually presented as a report to senior management at the end of each control period. The report is called an **operating statement** or **statement of variances**.

> **KEY TERM**
>
> An **operating statement** is 'A regular report for management of actual costs, and revenues, as appropriate. Usually compares actual with budget and shows variances'.
>
> CIMA *Official Terminology*

2.2   An extensive example will now be introduced, both to revise the variance calculations already described, and also to show how to combine them into an operating statement.

2.3   EXAMPLE: VARIANCES AND OPERATING STATEMENTS

Sydney Ltd manufactures one product, and the entire product is sold as soon as it is produced. There are no opening or closing stocks and work in progress is negligible. The company operates a standard costing system and analysis of variances is made every month. The standard cost card for the product, a boomerang, is as follows.

BPP
PUBLISHING

STANDARD COST CARD - BOOMERANG

		£
Direct materials	0.5 kilos at £4 per kilo	2.00
Direct wages	2 hours at £2.00 per hour	4.00
Variable overheads	2 hours at £0.30 per hour	0.60
Fixed overhead	2 hours at £3.70 per hour	7.40
Standard cost		14.00
Standard profit		6.00
Standing selling price		20.00

Selling and administration expenses are not included in the standard cost, and are deducted from profit as a period charge.

Budgeted output for the month of June 20X7 was 5,100 units. Actual results for June 20X7 were as follows.

Production of 4,850 units was sold for £95,600.

Materials consumed in production amounted to 2,300 kgs at a total cost of £9,800.

Labour hours paid for amounted to 8,500 hours at a cost of £16,800.

Actual operating hours amounted to 8,000 hours.

Variable overheads amounted to £2,600.

Fixed overheads amounted to £42,300.

Selling and administration expenses amounted to £18,000.

Required

Calculate all variances and prepare an operating statement for the month ended 30 June 20X7.

2.4 SOLUTION

(a)

	£
2,300 kg of material should cost (× £4)	9,200
but did cost	9,800
Material price variance	600 (A)

(b)

4,850 boomerangs should use (× 0.5 kgs)	2,425 kg
but did use	2,300 kg
Material usage variance in kgs	125 kg (F)
× standard cost per kg	× £4
Material usage variance in £	£ 500 (F)

(c)

	£
8,500 hours of labour should cost (× £2)	17,000
but did cost	16,800
Labour rate variance	200 (F)

(d)

4,850 boomerangs should take (× 2 hrs)	9,700 hrs
but did take (active hours)	8,000 hrs
Labour efficiency variance in hours	1,700 hrs (F)
× standard cost per hour	× £2
Labour efficiency variance in £	£3,400 (F)

(e) Idle time variance 500 hours (A) × £2 — £1,000 (A)

(f)

	£
8,000 hours incurring variable o/hd expenditure should cost (× £0.30)	2,400
but did cost	2,600
Variable overhead expenditure variance	200 (A)

(g) Variable overhead efficiency variance in hours is the same as the
labour efficiency variance:
1,700 hours (F) × £0.30 per hour   £ 510 (F)

(h)   £
Budgeted fixed overhead (5,100 units × 2 hrs × £3.70)   37,740
Actual fixed overhead   42,300
Fixed overhead expenditure variance   4,560 (A)

(i)   £
4,850 boomerangs should take (× 2 hrs)   9,700 hrs
 but did take (active hours)   8,000 hrs
Fixed overhead volume efficiency variance in hrs   1,700 hrs (F)
× standard fixed overhead absorption rate per hour   × £3.70
Fixed overhead volume efficiency variance in £   6,290 (F)

(j)   £
Budgeted hours of work (5,100 × 2 hrs)   10,200 hrs
Actual hours of work   8,000 hrs
Fixed overhead volume capacity variance in hrs   2,200 hrs (A)
× standard fixed overhead absorption rate per hour   × £3.70
Fixed overhead volume capacity variance in £   8,140 (A)

(k)   £
Revenue from 4,850 boomerangs should be (× £20)   97,000
 but was   95,600
Selling price variance   1,400 (A)

(l)   Budgeted sales volume   5,100 units
Actual sales volume   4,850 units
Sales volume profit variance in units   250 units
× standard profit per unit   × £6 (A)
Sales volume profit variance in £   £1,500 (A)

2.5 There are several ways in which an operating statement may be presented. Perhaps the most
common format is one which **reconciles budgeted profit to actual profit**. In this example,
sales and administration costs will be introduced at the end of the statement, so that we
shall begin with 'budgeted profit before sales and administration costs'.

2.6 Sales variances are reported first, and the total of the budgeted profit and the two sales
variances results in a figure for 'actual sales minus the standard cost of sales'. The cost
variances are then reported, and an actual profit (before sales and administration costs)
calculated. Sales and administration costs are then deducted to reach the actual profit for
June 20X7.

SYDNEY LTD - OPERATING STATEMENT JUNE 20X7

			£	£
Budgeted profit before sales and administration costs				30,600
Sales variances:	price		1,400 (A)	
	volume		1,500 (A)	
				2,900 (A)
Actual sales minus the standard cost of sales				27,700

Cost variances	(F)	(A)	
	£	£	
Material price		600	
Material usage	500		
Labour rate	200		
Labour efficiency	3,400		
Labour idle time		1,000	
Variable overhead expenditure		200	
Variable overhead efficiency	510		
Fixed overhead expenditure		4,560	
Fixed overhead volume efficiency	6,290		
Fixed overhead volume capacity		8,140	
	10,900	14,500	3,600 (A)
Actual profit before sales and administration costs			24,100
Sales and administration costs			18,000
Actual profit, June 20X7			6,100

Check	£	£
Sales		95,600
Materials	9,800	
Labour	16,800	
Variable overhead	2,600	
Fixed overhead	42,300	
Sales and administration	18,000	
		89,500
Actual profit		6,100

3 VARIANCES IN A STANDARD MARGINAL COSTING SYSTEM

3.1 In all of the examples we have worked through so far, a system of standard absorption costing has been in operation. If an organisation uses **standard marginal costing** instead of standard absorption costing, there will be two differences in the way the variances are calculated.

(a) In marginal costing, fixed costs are not absorbed into product costs and so there are no fixed cost variances to explain any under or over absorption of overheads. There will, therefore, be **no fixed overhead volume variance**. There will be a fixed overhead expenditure variance which is calculated in exactly the same way as for absorption costing systems.

(b) The **sales volume variance** will be valued at **standard contribution margin** (sales price per unit minus variable costs of sale per unit), **not** standard **profit** margin.

Preparing a marginal costing operating statement

3.2 Returning once again to the example of Sydney Ltd, the variances in a system of standard marginal costing would be as follows.

(a) There is **no fixed overhead volume variance** (and therefore no fixed overhead volume efficiency and volume capacity variances).

498

(b) The standard contribution per unit of boomerang is £(20 – 6.60) = £13.40, therefore the **sales volume contribution variance** of 250 units (A) is valued at (× £13.40) = £3,350 (A).

3.3 The other variances are unchanged. However, this operating statement differs from an absorption costing operating statement in the following ways.

(a) It begins with the budgeted **contribution** (£30,600 + budgeted fixed production costs £37,740 = £68,340).

(b) The subtotal before the analysis of cost variances is actual sales (£95,600) less the standard **variable** cost of sales (£4,850 × £6.60) = £63,590.

(c) **Actual contribution** is highlighted in the statement.

(d) Budgeted fixed production overhead is adjusted by the fixed overhead expenditure variance to show the **actual** fixed production overhead expenditure.

3.4 Therefore a marginal costing operating statement might look like this.

SYDNEY LTD - OPERATING STATEMENT JUNE 20X7

	£	£	£
Budgeted contribution			68,340
Sales variances: volume		3,350 (A)	
price		1,400 (A)	
			4,750 (A)
Actual sales minus the standard variable cost of sales			63,590

	(F)	(A)	
	£	£	
Variable cost variances			
Material price		600	
Material usage	500		
Labour rate	200		
Labour efficiency	3,400		
Labour idle time		1,000	
Variable overhead expenditure		200	
Variable overhead efficiency	510		
	4,610	1,800	
			2,810 (F)
Actual contribution			66,400
Budgeted fixed production overhead		37,740	
Expenditure variance		4,560 (A)	
Actual fixed production overhead			42,300
Actual profit before sales and administration costs			24,100
Sales and administration costs			18,000
Actual profit			6,100

3.5 Notice that the actual profit is the same as the profit calculated by standard absorption costing because there were no changes in stock levels. Absorption costing and marginal costing do not always produce an identical profit figure.

Question 2

Piglet Ltd, a manufacturing firm, operates a standard marginal costing system. It makes a single product, PIG, using a single raw material LET.

Standard costs relating to PIG have been calculated as follows.

Standard cost schedule – PIG

	Per unit
	£
Direct material, LET, 100 kg at £5 per kg	500
Direct labour, 10 hours at £8 per hour	80
Variable production overhead, 10 hours at £2 per hour	20
	600

The standard selling price of a PIG is £900 and Piglet Ltd produce 1,020 units a month.

During December 20X0, 1,000 units of PIG were produced. Relevant details of this production are as follows.

Direct material LET

90,000 kgs costing £720,000 were bought and used.

Direct labour

8,200 hours were worked during the month and total wages were £63,000.

Variable production overhead

The actual cost for the month was £25,000.

Stocks of the direct material LET are valued at the standard price of £5 per kg.

Each PIG was sold for £975.

Required

Calculate the following for the month of December 20X0.

(a) Variable production cost variance
(b) Direct labour cost variance, analysed into rate and efficiency variances
(c) Direct material cost variance, analysed into price and usage variances
(d) Variable production overhead variance, analysed into expenditure and efficiency variances
(e) Selling price variance
(f) Sales volume contribution variance

Answer

(a) This is simply a 'total' variance.

	£
1,000 units should have cost (× £600)	600,000
but did cost (see working)	808,000
Variable production cost variance	208,000 (A)

(b) **Direct labour cost variances**

	£
8,200 hours should cost (× £8)	65,600
but did cost	63,000
Direct labour rate variance	2,600 (F)

1,000 units should take (× 10 hours)	10,000 hrs
but did take	8,200 hrs
Direct labour efficiency variance in hrs	1,800 hrs (F)
× standard rate per hour	× £8
Direct labour efficiency variance in £	£14,400 (F)

Summary	£
Rate	2,600 (F)
Efficiency	14,400 (F)
Total	17,000 (F)

(c) **Direct material cost variances**

	£
90,000 kg should cost (× £5)	450,000
but did cost	720,000
Direct material price variance	270,000 (A)

1,000 units should use (× 100 kg)	100,000 kg
but did use	90,000 kg
Direct material usage variance in kgs	10,000 kg (F)
× standard cost per kg	× £5
Direct material usage variance in £	£50,000 (F)

Summary	£
Price	270,000 (A)
Usage	50,000 (F)
Total	220,000 (A)

(d) **Variable production overhead variances**

	£
8,200 hours incurring o/hd should cost (× £2)	16,400
but did cost	25,000
Variable production overhead expenditure variance	8,600 (A)

Efficiency variance in hrs (from (b))	1,800 hrs (F)
× standard rate per hour	× £2
Variable production overhead efficiency variance	£3,600 (F)

Summary	£
Expenditure	8,600 (A)
Efficiency	3,600 (F)
Total	5,000 (A)

(e) **Selling price variance**

	£
Revenue from 1,000 units should have been (× £900)	900,000
but was (× £975)	975,000
Selling price variance	75,000 (F)

(f) **Sales volume contribution variance**

Budgeted sales	1,020 units
Actual sales	1,000 units
Sales volume variance in units	20 units (A)
× standard contribution margin (£(900 − 600))	× £300
Sales volume contribution variance in £	£6,000 (A)

Workings	£
Direct material	720,000
Total wages	63,000
Variable production overhead	25,000
	808,000

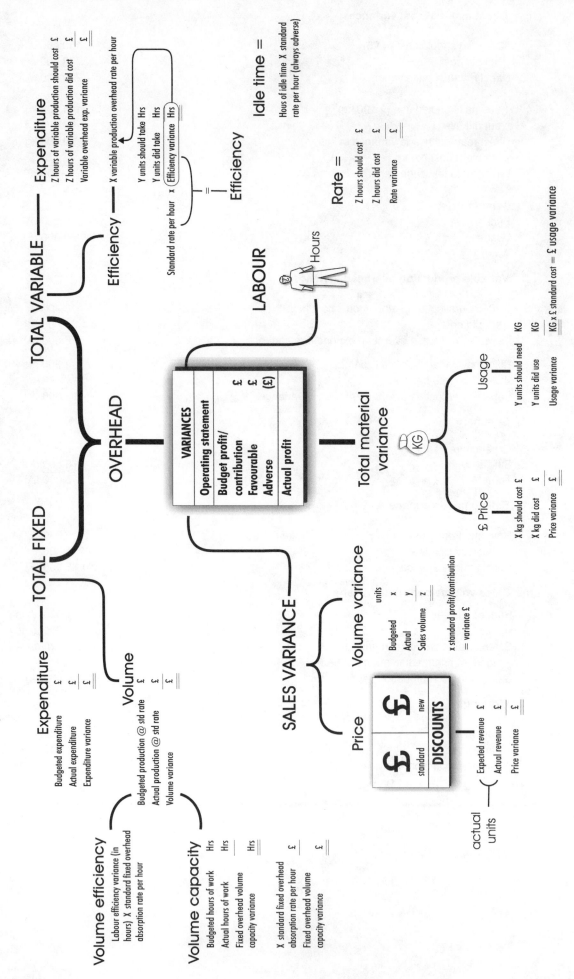

4 DERIVING ACTUAL DATA FROM STANDARD COST DETAILS AND VARIANCES

4.1 EXAMPLE: WORKING BACKWARDS

The standard cost card for the trough, one of the products made by Pig Ltd, is as follows.

	£
Direct material 16 kgs × £6 per kg	96
Direct labour 6 hours × £12 per hour	72
Fixed production overhead 6 hours × £14 per hour	84
	252

Pig Ltd reported the following variances in control period 13 in relation to the trough.

Direct material price: £18,840 favourable
Direct material usage: £480 adverse
Direct labour rate: £10,598 adverse
Direct labour efficiency: £8,478 favourable
Fixed production overhead expenditure: £14,192 adverse
Fixed production overhead volume: £11,592 favourable

Actual fixed production overhead cost £200,000 and direct wages, £171,320. Pig Ltd paid £5.50 for each kg of direct material. There was no opening or closing stocks of the material.

Required

Calculate the following.

(a) Budgeted output
(b) Actual output
(c) Actual hours worked
(d) Average actual wage rate per hour
(e) Actual number of kilograms purchased and used

4.2 SOLUTION

(a) Let budgeted output = q

Fixed production overhead expenditure variance = budgeted overhead – actual overhead = £(84q – 200,000) = £14,192 (A)

$$\therefore 84q - 200,000 = -14,192$$
$$84q = -14,192 + 200,000$$
$$q = 185,808 \div 84$$
$$\therefore q = 2,212 \text{ units}$$

(b)

	£
Total direct wages cost	171,320
Adjust for variances:	
labour rate	(10,598)
labour efficiency	8,478
Standard direct wages cost	169,200

$$\therefore \text{Actual output} = \text{Total standard cost} \div \text{unit standard cost}$$
$$= £169,200 \div £72$$
$$= 2,350 \text{ units}$$

(c)

	£
Total direct wages cost	171,320.0
Less rate variance	(10,598.0)
Standard rate for actual hours	160,722.0
÷ standard rate per hour	÷ £12.0
Actual hours worked	13,393.5 hrs

(d) Average actual wage rate per hour = actual wages/actual hours = £171,320/13,393.5 = £12.79 per hour.

(e) Number of kgs purchased and used = x

	£
x kgs should have cost (× £6)	6.0x
but did cost (× £5.50)	5.5x
Direct material price variance	0.5x

∴   £0.5x = £18,840

∴   x = 37,680 kgs

Question 3

XYZ Ltd uses standard costing. The following data relates to labour grade II.

Actual hours worked	10,400 hours
Standard allowance for actual production	8,320 hours
Standard rate per hour	£5
Rate variance (adverse)	£416

What was the actual rate of pay per hour?

A   £4.95
B   £4.96
C   £5.04
D   £5.05

Answer

Rate variance per hour worked = $\dfrac{£416}{10,400}$ = £0.04 (A)

Actual rate per hour = £(5.00 + 0.04) = £5.04.

The correct answer is C.

You should have been able to eliminate options A and B because they are both below the standard rate per hour. If the rate variance is adverse then the actual rate must be above standard.

Option D is incorrect because it results from basing the calculations on standard hours rather than actual hours.

Question 4

The standard material content of one unit of product A is 10kgs of material X which should cost £10 per kilogram. In June 20X4, 5,750 units of product A were produced and there was an adverse material usage variance of £1,500.

Required

Calculate the quantity of material X used in June 20X4.

Answer

Let the quantity of material X used = Y

5,750 units should have used (× 10kgs)	57,500 kgs
but did use	Y kgs
Usage variance in kgs	(Y – 57,500) kgs
× standard price per kg	× £10
Usage variance in £	£1,500 (A)

$$\therefore \quad 10(Y - 57,500) = 1,500$$
$$Y - 57,500 = 150$$
$$\therefore \quad Y = 57,650 \text{ kgs}$$

Exam focus point

One way that the examiner can test your understanding of variance analysis is to provide information about variances from which you have to 'work backwards' to determine the actual results.

Make sure that you understand the examples and questions covering this technique that we have provided in this section. This type of question **really** tests your understanding of the subject. If you simply memorise variance formulae you will have difficulty in answering such questions.

Chapter roundup

- The **selling price variance** measures the effect on profit of a different selling price to standard selling price.

- The **sales volume profit variance** measures the effect on profit of sales volume being different to budgeted volume.

- **Operating statements** show how the combination of variances reconcile budgeted profit and actual profit.

- There are two main differences between the variances calculated in an absorption costing system and the variances calculated in a marginal costing system.

  - In a marginal costing system **the only fixed overhead variance is an expenditure variance.**

  - The sales volume variance is **valued at standard contribution margin**, not standard profit margin.

- Variances can be used to derive actual data from standard cost details.

Quick quiz

1   What is the sales volume profit variance? *Measure effect on profit of Sales volume being diff to budget*

2   A regular report for management of actual cost, and revenue, and usually comparing actual with budget (and showing variances) is known as

   A   Bank statement
   B   Variance statement
   C   Budget statement
   D   Operating statement

3   If an organisation uses standard marginal costing instead of standard absorption costing, which two variances are calculated differently?

Fixed Cost Variance is only expenditure
Sale Volume Variance valued at Standard Contribution Margin

4   Which of the following statements is correct?

A   Sales volume variance = Sales volume expenditure variance + Sales volume efficiency variance
B   Sales volume variance = Sales volume efficiency variance – Sales volume capacity variance
C   Sales volume variance – Sales volume capacity variance = Sales volume efficiency variance
D   Sales volume variance = Sales volume expenditure variance + Sales volume capacity variance

Answers to quick quiz

1   It is a measure of the increase or decrease in standard profit as a result of the sales volume being higher or lower than budgeted.

2   D

3   (a)   In marginal costing there is no fixed overhead volume variance (because fixed costs are not absorbed into product costs).

       (b)   In marginal costing, the sales volume variance will be valued at standard contribution margin and not standard profit margin.

4   C

Now try the questions below from the Exam Question Bank

Number	Level	Marks	Time
48	MCQ	n/a	n/a
49	Examination	10	18 mins

Chapter 27

INDEX NUMBERS

Topic list	Syllabus reference
1 Basic terminology	7(d)
2 Simple indices	7(d)
3 Index relatives	7(d)
4 Time series deflation	7(d)
5 Composite index numbers	7(d)
6 Weighted index numbers	7(d)
7 Laspeyre and Paasche indices	7(d)

Introduction

Index numbers provide a **standardised way of comparing the values**, over time, of prices, wages, volume of output and so on. They are used extensively in business, government and commerce in order to **measure performance**.

No doubt you will be aware of some index numbers – the RPI, the Financial Times All Share Index and so on. This chapter will explain how to construct indices and will look at associated issues such as their relative merits.

Study guide

Section 27 – Index numbers

- Explain the purpose of index numbers, and calculate and interpret simple index numbers for one or more variables

- Deflate time related data using an index

- Construct a chained index series

- Explain the term 'average index', distinguishing between simple and weighted averages

- Calculate Laspeyre and Paasche price and quantity indices

- Discuss the relative merits of the Laspeyre and Paasche indices

Exam guide

Index numbers is not one of the key areas of the **Financial Information for Management** syllabus. However, be prepared to answer questions on this topic in both sections of your examination. Note that you might be required to use your knowledge of index numbers when answering exam questions covering other topics.

BPP PUBLISHING

1 BASIC TERMINOLOGY

Price indices and quantity indices

> **KEY TERMS**
>
> An **index** is a measure, over time, of the average changes in the values (prices or quantities) of a group of items. **An index comprises a series of index numbers** and may be a **price index** or a **quantity index**.
>
> - A **price index** measures the change in the money value of a group of items over time.
>
> - A **quantity index** (also called a volume index) measures the change in the non-monetary values of a group of items over time.

1.1 It is possible to prepare an index for a single item, but such an index would probably be unnecessary. **An index is a most useful measure of comparison when there is a group of items**.

Index points

1.2 **The term 'points' refers to the difference between the index values in two years.**

1.3 EXAMPLE: INDEX POINTS

For example, suppose that the index of food prices in 20X1 – 20X6 was as follows.

20X1	180
20X2	200
20X3	230
20X4	250
20X5	300
20X6	336

The index has risen 156 points between 20X1 and 20X6 (336 – 180). This is an increase of $(156/180) \times 100 = 86.7\%$.

Similarly, the index rose 36 points between 20X5 and 20X6 (336 – 300), a rise of 12%.

The base period, or base year

1.4 **Index numbers normally take the value for a base date as 100.** The base period is usually the starting point of the series, though this is not always the case.

2 SIMPLE INDICES

2.1 When one commodity only is under consideration, we have the following formulae.

FORMULAE TO LEARN

- **Price index** $= 100 \times \dfrac{P_1}{P_0}$

- **Quantity index** $= 100 \times \dfrac{Q_1}{Q_0}$

where P_1 = the price for the period under consideration
P_0 = the price for the base period
Q_1 = the quantity for the period under consideration
Q_0 = the quantity for the base period

2.2 EXAMPLE: SINGLE-ITEM INDICES

(a) **Price index number**

If the price of a cup of coffee was 40p in 20X0, 50p in 20X1 and 76p in 20X2, then using 20X0 as a base year the **price index numbers** for 20X1 and 20X2 would be as follows.

20X1 price index $= 100 \times \dfrac{50}{40} = 125$

20X2 price index $= 100 \times \dfrac{76}{40} = 190$

(b) **Quantity index number**

If the number of cups of coffee sold in 20X0 was 500,000, in 20X1 700,000 and in 20X2 600,000, then using 20X0 as a base year, the **quantity index numbers** for 20X1 and 20X2 would be as follows.

20X1 quantity index $= 100 \times \dfrac{700,000}{500,000} = 140$

20X2 quantity index $= 100 \times \dfrac{600,000}{500,000} = 120$

3 INDEX RELATIVES

KEY TERM

An **index relative** (sometimes just called a relative) is the name given to an index number which measures the change in a single distinct commodity.

FORMULAE TO LEARN

- A **price relative** is calculated as $100 \times P_1/P_0$
- A **quantity relative** is calculated as $100 \times Q_1/Q_0$

3.1   We calculated price and quantity relatives for cups of coffee in paragraph 2.2.

Time series of relatives

3.2   There are two ways in which index relatives can be calculated.

(a) The **fixed base method**. A base year is selected (index 100), and all subsequent changes are measured against this base. Such an approach should only be used if **the basic nature of the commodity is unchanged over time**.

(b) The **chain base method**. Changes are calculated with respect to the value of the commodity in the period immediately before. This approach can be used for any set of commodity values but must be used if **the basic nature of the commodity is changing over time**.

3.3   EXAMPLE: FIXED BASE METHOD

The price of a commodity was £2.70 in 20X0, £3.11 in 20X1, £3.42 in 20X2 and £3.83 in 20X3. Construct a **fixed base index** for the years 20X0 to 20X3 using 20X0 as the base year.

3.4   SOLUTION

Fixed base index	20X0	100	
	20X1	115	
	20X2	127	$(3.42/2.70 \times 100)$
	20X3	142	$(3.83/2.70 \times 100)$

3.5   EXAMPLE: CHAIN BASE METHOD

Using the information in Paragraph 3.3 construct a chain base index for the years 20X0 to 20X3 using 20X0 as the base year.

3.6   SOLUTION

Chain base index	20X0	100	
	20X1	115	$(3.11/2.70 \times 100)$
	20X2	110	$(3.42/3.11 \times 100)$
	20X3	112	$(3.83/3.42 \times 100)$

3.7   **The chain base relatives show the rate of change in prices from year to year, whereas the fixed base relatives show changes relative to prices in the base year.**

Changing the base of fixed base relatives

3.8   It is sometimes necessary to change the base of a time series (to **rebase**) of fixed base relatives, perhaps because the **base time point is too far in the past**. The following time series has a base date of 1970 which would probably be considered too out of date.

	1990	1991	1992	1993	1994	1995
Index (1970 = 100)	451	463	472	490	499	505

To change the base date, divide each relative by the relative corresponding to the new base time point and multiply the result by 100.

510

Question 1

Rebase the index in Paragraph 3.8 to 1993.

Answer

	1990	1991	1992	1993	1994	1995
Index (1993 = 100)	92*	94	96	100**	102***	103

* $451/490 \times 100$

** $490/490 \times 100$

*** $499/490 \times 100$

Comparing sets of fixed base relatives

3.9 You may be required to compare two sets of time series relatives. For example, an index of the annual number of advertisements placed by an organisation in the press and the index of the number of the organisation's product sold per annum might be compared. If the base years of the two indices differ, however, comparison is extremely difficult (as the illustration below shows).

	20W8	20W9	20X0	20X1	20X2	20X3	20X4
Number of advertisements Placed (20X0 = 100)	90	96	100	115	128	140	160
Volumes of sales (20W0 = 100)	340	347	355	420	472	515	572

3.10 From the figures above it is impossible to determine whether sales are increasing at a greater rate than the number of advertisements placed, or vice versa. This difficulty can be overcome by **rebasing** one set of relatives so that the **base dates are the same**. For example, we could rebase the index of volume of sales to 20X0.

	20W8	20W9	20X0	20X1	20X2	20X3	20X4
Number of advertisements Placed (20X0 = 100)	90	96	100	115	128	140	160
Volumes of sales (20X0 = 100)	96	98*	100	118	133**	145	161

* $347/355 \times 100$

** $472/355 \times 100$

3.11 The two sets of relatives are now much easier to compare. They show that volume of sales is increasing at a slightly faster rate, in general, than the number of advertisements placed.

4 TIME SERIES DEFLATION

4.1 The real value of a commodity can only be measured in terms of some '**indicator**' such as the **rate of inflation** (normally represented by the Retail Prices Index (RPI)). For example the cost of a commodity may have been £10 in 20X0 and £11 in 20X1, representing an increase of 10%. However, if we are told the prices **in general** (as measured by the RPI) increased by 12% between 20X0 and 20X1, we can argue that the **real** cost of the commodity has decreased.

4.2 EXAMPLE: DEFLATION

Mack Johnson works for Pound of Flesh Ltd. Over the last five years he has received an annual salary increase of £500. Despite his employer assuring him that £500 is a reasonable annual salary increase, Mack is unhappy because, although he agrees £500 is a lot of money, he finds it difficult to maintain the standard of living he had when he first joined the company.

Consider the figures below.

Year	(a) Wages £	(b) RPI	(c) Real wages £	(d) Real wages index
1	12,000	250	12,000	100.0
2	12,500	260	12,019	100.2
3	13,000	275	11,818	98.5
4	13,500	295	11,441	95.3
5	14,000	315	11,111	92.6

(a) This column shows Mack's wages over the five-year period.

(b) This column shows the current RPI.

(c) This column shows what Mack's wages are worth taking prices, as represented by the RPI, into account. The wages have been deflated relative to the new base period (year 1). Economists call these deflated wage figures **real wages** The real wages for years 2 and 4, for example, are calculated as follows.

Year 2:   £12,500 × 250/260 = £12,019
Year 4:   £13,500 × 250/295 = £11,441

(d) This column is calculated by dividing the entries in column (c) by £12,000:

$$\textbf{Real index} = \frac{\text{current value}}{\text{base value}} \times \frac{\text{base indicator}}{\text{current indicator}}$$

So, for example, the real wage index in year 4 $= \frac{13,500}{12,000} \times \frac{250}{295} \times 100 = 95.3$

4.3   The real wages index shows that the real value of Mack's wages has fallen by 7.4% over the five-year period. In real terms he is now earning £11,111 compared to £12,000 in year 1. He is probably justified, therefore, in being unhappy.

Question 2

The mean weekly take-home pay of the employees of Staples Ltd and a price index for the 11 years from 20X0 to 20Y0 are as follows.

Year	Weekly wage £	Price index (20X0 = 100)
20X0	150	100
20X1	161	103
20X2	168	106
20X3	179	108
20X4	185	109
20X5	191	112
20X6	197	114
20X7	203	116
20X8	207	118
20X9	213	121
20Y0	231	123

Required

Construct a time series of real wages for 20X0 to 20Y0 using a price index with 20X6 as the base year.

Answer

The index number for each year with 20X6 as the base year will be the original index number divided by 1.14, and the real wages for each year will be (money wages × 100)/index number for the year.

Year	Index	Real wage £
20X0	88	170
20X1	90	179
20X2	93	181
20X3	95	188
20X4	96	193
20X5	98	195
20X6	100	197
20X7	102	199
20X8	104	199
20X9	106	201
20Y0	108	214

5 COMPOSITE INDEX NUMBERS

5.1 Most practical indices cover more than one item and are hence termed **composite index numbers**.

5.2 Suppose that the cost of living index is calculated from only three commodities: bread, tea and caviar, and that the prices for 20X1 and 20X2 were as follows.

	20X1	*20X2*
Bread	20p a loaf	40p a loaf
Tea	25p a packet	30p a packet
Caviar	450p a jar	405p a jar

5.3 A simple index could be calculated by adding the prices for single items in 20X2 and dividing by the corresponding sum relating to 20X1 (if 20X1 is the base year). In general, if the sum of the prices in the base year is ΣP_0 and the sum of the prices in the new year is ΣP_1, the index is $100 \times \dfrac{\Sigma P_1}{\Sigma P_0}$. (The sign Σ (sigma) means sum of.) The index, known as a **simple aggregate price index**, would therefore be calculated as follows.

	P_0 *20X1* £	P_1 *20X2* £
Bread	0.20	0.40
Tea	0.25	0.30
Caviar	4.50	4.05
	$\Sigma P_0 = 4.95$	$\Sigma P_1 = 4.75$

Year	$\Sigma P_1 / \Sigma P_0$	*Simple aggregate price index*
20X1	4.95/4.95 = 1.00	100
20X2	4.75/4.95 = 0.96	96

5.4 The simple aggregate price index has a number of **disadvantages**.

(a) It ignores the **amounts** of bread, tea and caviar consumed (and hence the importance of each item).

(b) It ignores the **units** to which the prices refer. If, for example, we had been given the price of a cup of tea rather than a packet of tea, the index would have been different.

Average indices

5.5 To overcome the problem of different units we consider the changes in prices as **ratios** rather than absolutes so that all price movements, whatever their absolute values, are treated as equally important. Price changes are considered as ratios rather than absolutes by using the **average price relatives index**. Quantity changes are considered as ratios by using the **average quantity relatives index**.

> ### FORMULAE TO LEARN
>
> - **Average price relatives index** $= 100 \times \dfrac{1}{n} \times \Sigma(P_1/P_0)$
>
> - **Average quantity relatives index** $= 100 \times \dfrac{1}{n} \times \Sigma(Q_1/Q_0)$
>
> where n is the number of goods.

5.6 The price relative P_1/P_0 (so called because it gives the new price level of each item relative to the base year price) for a particular commodity will have the same value whatever the unit for which the price is quoted.

5.7 Using the information in Paragraph 5.2, we can construct the **average price relatives index** as follows.

Commodity	P_0 £	P_1 £	P_1/P_0
Bread	0.20	0.40	2.00
Tea	0.25	0.30	1.20
Caviar	4.50	4.05	0.90
			4.10

Year	$\dfrac{1}{n}\Sigma(P_1/P_0)$	Average price relatives index
20X1	$^1/_3 \times 3.00 = 1.00$	100
20X2	$^1/_3 \times 4.10 = 1.37$	137

5.8 There has therefore been an average price increase of 37% between 20X1 and 20X2.

5.9 No account has been taken of the **relative importance** of each item in this index. Bread is probably more important than caviar. To overcome both the problem of quantities in different units and the need to attach importance to each item, we can use **weighting** which reflects the **importance of each item**. To decide the weightings of different items in an index, it is necessary to obtain information, perhaps by market research, about the **relative importance** of each item. The next section of this chapter shall look at **weighted index numbers**.

6 WEIGHTED INDEX NUMBERS

6.1 There are two types of index which give different weights to different items.

- Weighted average of relatives indices
- Weighted aggregate indices

Weighted average of relatives indices

6.2 **This method of weighting involves calculating index relatives for each of the components and using the weights given to obtain a weighted average of the relatives.**

FORMULAE TO LEARN

- Weighted average of price relative index $= \dfrac{\Sigma \, W \times {}^{P_1}/_{P_0}}{\Sigma \, W}$

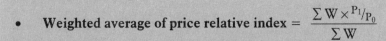

- Weighted average of quantity relative index $= \dfrac{\Sigma \, W \times {}^{Q_1}/{}_{Q_0}}{\Sigma \, W}$

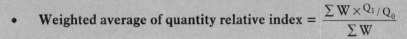

where W = the weighting factor

6.3 EXAMPLE: WEIGHTED AVERAGE OF RELATIVES INDICES

Use both the information in Paragraph 5.2 and the following details about quantities purchased by each household in a week in 20X1 to determine a weighted average of price relatives index number for 20X2 using 20X1 as the base year.

	Quantity
Bread	12
Tea	5
Caviar	3

6.4 SOLUTION

Price relatives ($^{P_1}/_{P_0}$)	Bread	40/20 =	2.00
	Tea	30/25 =	1.20
	Caviar	405/450 =	0.90
Weightings (W)	Bread		12.00
	Tea		5.00
	Caviar		3.00
	$\Sigma W =$		20.00
Index	Bread	$2 \times 12 =$	24.00
	Tea	$1.2 \times 5 =$	6.00
	Caviar	$0.9 \times 3 =$	2.70
	$\Sigma W \times {}^{P_1}/_{P_0} =$		32.70

Index number $= \dfrac{32.7}{20.0} \times 100 = \quad 163.5$

Question 3

The average prices of three commodities and the number of units used annually by a company are given below.

| | 20X1 | 20X2 | |
Commodity	*Price per unit (P_0)*	*Price per unit(P_1)*	*Quantity*
	£	£	Units
X	20	22	20
Y	40	48	2
Z	100	104	10

The price for 20X2 based on 20X1, calculated using the weighted average of relatives method is (to the nearest whole number)

A   107
B   108
C   109
D   110

Answer

Commodity	Price $\dfrac{P_1}{P_0}$	Weight (W)	Relative weight $\left(W \times \dfrac{P_1}{P_0}\right)$
X	$\dfrac{22}{20} = 1.1$	20	22.0
Y	$\dfrac{48}{40} = 1.2$	2	2.4
Z	$\dfrac{104}{100} = 1.04$	$\underline{10}$	$\underline{10.4}$
		$\Sigma W = \underline{\underline{32}}$	$\underline{\underline{34.8}}$

$$\text{Index} = \frac{34.8}{32} \times 100 = 108.75 = 109$$

The correct answer is therefore C.

7 LASPEYRE AND PAASCHE INDICES

7.1 **Laspeyre** and **Paasche** indices are special cases of **weighted aggregate indices**.

Laspeyre indices

7.2 **Laspeyre indices use weights from the base period and are therefore sometimes called base weighted indices.**

FORMULAE TO LEARN

- **Laspeyre price index** $= 100 \times \dfrac{\Sigma Q_0 P_1}{\Sigma Q_0 P_0}$

- **Laspeyre quantity index** $= 100 \times \dfrac{\Sigma Q_1 P_0}{\Sigma Q_0 P_0}$

7.3 **A Laspeyre price index uses quantities consumed in the base period as weights. A Laspeyre quantity index uses prices from the base period as weights.**

Paasche indices

7.4 **Paasche indices use current time period weights. In other words the weights are changed every time period.**

FORMULAE TO LEARN

- **Paasche price index** $= 100 \times \dfrac{\Sigma Q_1 P_1}{\Sigma Q_1 P_0}$

- **Paasche quantity index** $= 100 \times \dfrac{\Sigma Q_1 P_1}{\Sigma Q_0 P_1}$

7.5 **A Paasche price index uses quantities consumed in the current period as weights. A Paasche quantity index uses prices from the current period as weights.**

7.6 EXAMPLE: LASPEYRE AND PAASCHE PRICE INDICES

The wholesale price index in Ruritania is made up from the prices of five items. The price of each item, and the average quantities purchased by manufacturing and other companies each week were as follows, in 20X0 and 20X2.

Item	Quantity 20X0 '000 units	Price per unit 20X0 Roubles	Quantity 20X2 '000 units	Price per unit 20X2 Roubles
P	60	3	80	4
Q	30	6	40	5
R	40	5	20	8
S	100	2	150	2
T	20	7	10	10

Required

Calculate the price index in 20X2, if 20X0 is taken as the base year, using the following.

(a)   A Laspeyre index
(b)   A Paasche index

7.7 SOLUTION

Workings

Item					Laspeyre		Paasche	
	Q_o	P_o	Q_1	P_1	Q_oP_o	Q_oP_1	Q_1P_1	Q_1P_o
P	60	3	80	4	180	240	320	240
Q	30	6	40	5	180	150	200	240
R	40	5	20	8	200	320	160	100
S	100	2	150	2	200	200	300	300
T	20	7	10	10	140	200	100	70
					900	1,110	1,080	950

20X2 index numbers are as follows.

(a)   **Laspeyre index** $= 100 \times \dfrac{1,110}{900} = 123.3$

(b)   **Paasche index** $= 100 \times \dfrac{1,080}{950} = 113.7$

The Paasche index for 20X2 reflects the decline in consumption of the relatively expensive items R and T since 20X0. The Laspeyre index for 20X2 fails to reflect this change.

Question 4

A baker has listed the ingredients he used and their prices, in 20X3 and 20X4, as follows.

	Kgs used 20X3 '000s	Price per kg 20X3 £	Kgs used 20X4 '000s	Price per kg 20X4 £
Milk	3	1.20	4	1.50
Eggs	6	0.95	5	0.98
Flour	1	1.40	2	1.30
Sugar	4	1.10	3	1.14

BPP PUBLISHING

Required

Calculate the following quantity indices for 20X4 (with 20X3 as the base year).

(a)   A Laspeyre index
(b)   A Paasche index

Answer

Workings

	Q_0	P_0	Q_1	P_1	Laspeyre Q_0P_0	Laspeyre Q_1P_0	Paasche Q_1P_1	Paasche Q_0P_1
Milk	3	1.20	4	1.50	3.60	4.80	6.00	4.50
Eggs	6	0.95	5	0.98	5.70	4.75	4.90	5.88
Flour	1	1.40	2	1.30	1.40	2.80	2.60	1.30
Sugar	4	1.10	3	1.14	4.40	3.30	3.42	4.56
					15.10	15.65	16.92	16.24

Quantity index numbers for 20X4 are as follows.

(a)   Laspeyre method   = $100 \times \dfrac{15.65}{15.10}$ = 103.64

(b)   Paasche method   = $100 \times \dfrac{16.92}{16.24}$ = 104.19

Relative merits of the Laspeyre and Paasche indices

7.8   Both patterns of consumption and prices change and a decision therefore has to be made as to whether a Paasche or a Laspeyre index should be used.

7.9   The following points should be considered when deciding which type of index to use.

PAASCHE INDICES	**LASPEYRE INDICES**
(use weights from the current time period)	**(use weights from the base period)**
(a) Requires quantities to be ascertained each year which may be costly.	Requires quantities to be ascertained for base year only.
(b) The denominator has to be recalculated each year. The index cannot be calculated until the end of a period when the current prices/quantities are known.	The denominator is fixed. The index may therefore be calculated as soon as current prices/quantities are known.
(c) Because the denominator has to be recalculated each year, comparisons can only be drawn directly between the current year and the base year.	Because the denominator is fixed, the Laspeyre index numbers for several years can be directly compared.
(d) Paasche indices are updated each year.	The weights for a Laspeyre index become out of date.
(e) The effect of current year weighting means that greater importance is placed on goods that are relatively cheaper now than they were in the base year. Inflation could therefore be understated.	Assumes that whatever the price changes, the quantities purchased will remain the same. It therefore assumes that as goods become relatively more expensive, the same quantities will be purchased. Inflation could therefore be overstated.

In practice, it is common to use a Laspeyre index and revise the weights every few years. (Where appropriate, a new base year may be created when the weights are changed.)

Exam focus point

If you get confused between **Laspeyre** and **Paasche** indices remember that 'L' (for Laspeyre) comes **before** 'P' (for Paasche) in the alphabet and that Laspeyre indices use weights from the **base** year which comes **before** the **current** year (the provider of weights for Paasche indices).

Chapter roundup

- An **index** is a measure, over time, of the average changes in the value (price or quantity) of a group of items relative to the situation at some period in the past.

- An **index relative** is an index number which measures the change in a single distinct commodity.

- Index relatives can be calculated using the **fixed base method** or the **chain base method**.

- In order to compare two time series of relatives, each series should have the same base period and hence one (or both) may need **rebasing**.

- The **real value** of a commodity can only be measured in terms of some 'indicator' (such as the RPI).

- **Time series deflation** is a technique used to obtain a set of index relatives that measure the changes in the real value of some commodity with respect to some given indicator.

- **Composite indices** cover more than one item.

- **Weighting** is used to reflect the importance of each item in the index.

- **Weighted means of relatives indices** are found by calculating indices and then applying weights.

- There are two types of weighted aggregate index

  - The Laspeyre
  - The Paasche

- The **Laspeyre** index uses quantities/prices from the **base period** as weights.

- The **Paasche** index uses quantities/prices from the **current** period as weights.

Quick quiz

1. What does a price index measure? *Changes over time of the value of a group of items*

2. What does a quantity index measure? *" " " of the amount of goods used in a group of iter.*

3. Complete the following equations using the symbols in the box below.

   (a) **Price index** = $\dfrac{P_1}{P_0} \times 100$ *P/P*

P_1	P_0
Q_1	Q_0

   (b) **Quantity index** = $\dfrac{Q_1}{Q_0} \times 100$

4. An index relative is the name given to an index number which measures the change in a group of items.

   True ☑

   False ☐

BPP PUBLISHING

5

Fixed base method		Changes are measured against base period
Chain base method		Changes are measured against the previous period

6 What is a composite index number?

7 How are problems of quantities different units and the need to attach importance to each item over come? *Weighting*

8 There are two types of index which give different weights to different items.

- Weighted average of relatives indices
- Weighted aggregate indices

What is the general form of a weighted average of quantity relative index number?

9 Laspeyre indices use quantities/prices from the (1) *base* .... period as weights whilst the Paasche indices use quantities/prices from the (2) *Current* .... period as weights.

Answers to quick quiz

1 The change in the money value of a group of items over time.

2 The change in the non-monetary values of a group of items over time.

3 (a) Price index = $\dfrac{P_1}{P_0} \times 100$

(b) Quantity index = $\dfrac{Q_1}{Q_0} \times 100$

4 False. An index relative is an index number which measures the change in a **single distinct commodity.**

5
Fixed base method	⟶	Changes are measured against the base period
Chain base method	⟶	Changes are measured against the previous period

6 A composite index number is an index covering more than one item.

7 By using weightings and calculating weighted index numbers.

8 $\dfrac{\sum W \times \dfrac{Q_1}{Q_0}}{\sum W}$

Where W = the weighing factor

$\dfrac{Q_1}{Q_0}$ = the index relative

9 (1) base
(2) current

Now try the questions below from the Exam Question Bank

Number	Level	Marks	Time
50	MCQ	n/a	n/a
51	Examination	10	18 mins

Chapter 28

PERFORMANCE MEASUREMENT

Topic list	Syllabus reference
1 Performance measurement	1(a), (b), 7(a), (b), (c), (e), (f)
2 Responsibility centres	1(a), (b), 7(a), (b), (c), (e), (f)
3 Measuring profitability, productivity and activity	1(a), (b), 7(a), (b), (c), (e), (f)
4 Performance measures for manufacturing businesses	1(a), (b), 7(a), (b), (c), (e), (f)
5 Performance measures for services	1(a), (b), 7(a), (b), (c), (e), (f)
6 Performance measures for non-profit making organisations	1(a), (b), 7(a), (b), (c), (e), (f)
7 The balanced scorecard	1(a), (b), 7(a), (b), (c), (e), (f)
8 Benchmarking	1(a), (b), 7(a), (b), (c), (e), (f)
9 Management performance measures	1(a), (b), 7(a), (b), (c), (e), (f)

Introduction

Performance measurement is the final chapter in this **Financial Information for Management** Study Text. The chapter begins by introducing the term **performance measurement** and then describes the various performance measures that are used by various types of entity.

It is important that the performance of an organisation is monitored, and this is most commonly done by calculating a number of ratios. The **balanced scorecard approach** to performance measurement considers both financial (ratios) and non-financial indicators. **Benchmarking** is another type of comparison exercise through which an organisation attempts to improve performance. We shall be reviewing these two performance measurement approaches at the end of this chapter.

Finally we shall be looking at **management performance measures**. It is important that you are able to distinguish between measures of performance of **individual managers** and measures of performance of **what it is they manage**.

Study guide

Section 2 – Management information systems

- Describe the various types of responsibility centres and the impact of these on management information

Section 28 – Performance measurement

- Outline the essential features of responsibility accounting for various types of entity

- Describe the various types of responsibility centre and the impact of these on management appraisal

- Describe the range of management performance measures available for various types of entity

- Calculate and explain the concepts of return on investment and residual income

- Explain and give examples of appropriate non-monetary performance measures

- Discuss the potential conflict in the use of a measure for both business and management performance

- Analyse the application of financial performance measures including cost, profit, return on capital employed

- Assess and illustrate the measurement of profitability, activity and productivity

- Discuss the measurement of quality and service

- Identify areas of concern from information supplied and performance measures calculated

- Describe the features of benchmarking and its application to performance appraisal

Exam guide

Performance measurement is not one of the key areas of the **Financial Information for Management** syllabus. Make sure that you can calculate all of the ratios covered in this chapter – they could well be tested in Section A of your examination.

1 PERFORMANCE MEASUREMENT

1.1 **Performance measurement** aims to establish how well something or somebody is doing in relation to a planned activity. The 'thing' may be a machine, a factory, a subsidiary company or an organisation as a whole. The 'body' may be an individual employee, a manager or a group of people.

1.2 Performance measurement is a **vital part of** the **control process.**

Performance measures

1.3 Different measures are appropriate for different businesses. Factors to consider:

(a) **Measurement needs resources** - people, equipment and time to collect and analyse information. The costs and benefits of providing resources to produce a performance indicator must be carefully weighed up.

(b) **Performance must be measured in relation to something,** otherwise measurement is meaningless. Overall performance should be measured against the objectives of the organisation. If the organisation has no clear objectives, the first step in performance measurement is to set them. The second is to identify the factors that are critical to the success of those objectives.

(c) **Measures must be relevant**. This means finding out what the organisation does and how it does it so that measures reflect what actually occurs.

(d) **Measurement needs responses,** but managers will only respond to measures that they find useful. The management accountant therefore needs to adopt a modern marketing philosophy to the provision of performance measures: satisfy customer wants, not pile 'em high and sell 'em cheap.

1.4 Once suitable performance measures have been selected they must be **monitored on a regular basis** to ensure that they are providing useful information. There is little point in an organisation devoting considerable resources to measuring market share if an increase in market share is not one of the organisation's objectives.

1.5   Performance measures may be divided into two groups.

- Financial performance measures
- Non-monetary performance measures.

Financial performance measures

1.6   Financial measures (or **monetary** measures) include:

Measure	Example
Profit	**Profit** is the commonest measure of all. Profit maximisation is usually cited as the main objective of most business organisations: 'ICI increased pre-tax profits to £233m'; 'General Motors... yesterday reported better-than-expected first-quarter net income of $513 (£333m) ... Earnings improved $680m from the first quarter of last year when GM lost $167m.
Revenue	'the US businesses contributed £113.9m of total group turnover of £409m'.
Costs	'Sterling's fall benefited pre-tax profits by about £50m while savings from the cost-cutting programme instituted in 1991 were running at around £100m a quarter'; 'The group interest charge rose from £48m to £61m'.
Share price	'The group's shares rose 31p to 1,278p despite the market's fall'.
Cash flow	'Cash flow was also continuing to improve, with cash and marketable securities totalling $8.4bn on March 31, up from $8bn at December 31'.

1.7   Note that the monetary amounts stated are **only given meaning in relation to something else**. Financial results should be compared against a **yard-stick** such as:

- Budgeted **sales, costs** and **profits**
- **Standards** in a standard costing system
- The **trend** over time (last year/this year, say)
- The results of **other parts of the business**
- The results of **other businesses**
- The **economy** in general
- **Future potential** (for example the performance of a new business may be judged in terms of nearness to breaking even).

Non-monetary performance measures

Quantitative and qualitative performance measures

1.8   Quantitative information is capable of being expressed in numbers. Qualitative information is not numeric. Qualitative information can sometimes be converted into numeric through tools such as ranking scales. For example 1 = Good, 2 = Average, 3 = Poor.

- An example of a **quantitative** performance measure is 'You have been late for work **twice** this week and it's only Tuesday!'.

- An example of a **qualitative** performance measure is 'My bed is **very** comfortable'.

The first measure is likely to find its way into a **staff appraisal report**. The second would feature in a bed manufacturer's **customer satisfaction survey**. Both are indicators of whether their subjects are doing as good a job as they are required to do.

BPP PUBLISHING

1.9 **Qualitative measures** are by nature **subjective** and **judgmental** but they can still be useful. They are especially valuable when they are derived from several **different sources,** as the likelihood of an unreliable judgement is reduced.

1.10 Consider the statement.

'Seven out of ten customers think our beds are very comfortable.'

This is a **quantitative measure** of customer satisfaction (7 out of 10), as well as a **qualitative measure** of the perceived performance of the beds (very comfortable).

Non-financial indicators

1.11 Financial measures do not convey the full picture of a company's performance, especially in a **modern business environment**. In today's global environment, organisations are **competing** in terms of product quality, delivery, reliability, after-sales service and customer satisfaction. None of these variables is directly measured by a traditional accounting system.

1.12 Organisations are increasingly using quantitative and qualitative **non-financial indicators (NFIs)** such as:

- Quality rating
- Number of customer complaints
- Number of warranty claims
- Lead times
- Rework
- Delivery to time
- Non-productive hours
- System (machine) down time

1.13 Unlike traditional variance reports, measures such as these can be **provided quickly** for managers, per shift or on a daily or even hourly basis as required. They are likely to be **easy to calculate**, and **easier** for non-financial managers **to understand** and therefore to use effectively.

1.14 **Anything can be compared if it is meaningful to do so**. The measures should be **tailored to the** circumstances. For example, the number of coffee breaks per 20 pages of text might indicate to you how hard you are studying!

Exam focus point

If you are asked to suggest suitable performance measures in an exam, think about NFIs. Remember that anything can be compared if it is meaningful to do so.

Ratios

1.15 Ratios are a useful performance measurement technique.

- It is **easier to look at changes over time** by comparing ratios in one time period with the corresponding ratios for periods in the past.

- Ratios are often **easier to understand than absolute measures** of physical quantities or money values. For example, it is easier to understand that 'productivity in March was 94%' than 'there was an adverse labour efficiency variance in March of £3,600'.

- Ratios **relate one item to another, and so help to put performance into context**. For example the profit/sales ratio sets profit in the context of how much has been earned per £1 of sales, and so shows how wide or narrow profit margins are.

- Ratios can be used as **targets,** for example for productivity. Managers will then take decisions which will enable them to achieve their targets.

- Ratios provide a way of **summarising** an organisation's results, and **comparing** them with similar organisations.

Percentages

1.16 A percentage expresses one number as a proportion of another and **gives meaning to absolute numbers**. Market share, capacity levels, wastage and staff turnover are often expressed using percentages.

2 RESPONSIBILITY CENTRES

2.1 We had a brief introduction to responsibility centres (cost centres, profit centres and investment centres) in Chapter 3 when we studied cost classification. We are now going to look at these centres in more detail as we continue our study of **performance measurement.**

> **KEY TERMS**
>
> **Responsibility accounting** is a system of accounting that segregates revenue and costs into areas of personal responsibility in order to monitor and assess the performance of each part of an organisation.
>
> A **responsibility centre** is a function or department of an organisation that is headed by a manager who has direct responsibility for its performance.

2.2 If a manager is to bear responsibility for the performance of his area of the business he will need information about its performance. In essence, a manager needs to know three things.

Requirements	Examples of information
What are his resources?	Finance, stocks of raw materials, spare machine capacity, labour availability, the balance of expenditure remaining for a certain budget, target date for completion of a job.
At what rate are his resources being consumed?	How fast is his labour force working, how quickly are his raw materials being used up, how quickly are other expenses being incurred, how quickly is available finance being consumed?
How well are the resources being used?	How well are his objectives being met?

2.3 Decisions must also be made as to the level of detail that is provided and the frequency with which information is provided. Moreover the cost of providing information must be weighed against the benefit derived from it.

2.4 In a traditional system managers are given monthly reports, but there is no logical reason for this except that it ties in with financial reporting cycles and may be administratively convenient. With modern systems, however, there is a danger of **information overload**, since information technology allows the information required to be made available much more frequently.

2.5 The task of the management accountant, therefore, is to learn from the managers of responsibility centres what information they need, in what form and at what intervals, and then to design a planning and control system that enables this to be provided.

2.6 It is to this end that responsibility centres are usually divided into different categories. Here we shall describe cost centres, profit centres and investment centres.

Cost centres

> **KEY TERM**
>
> A **cost centre** is any unit of an organisation to which costs can be separately attributed.

2.7 Cost centres can be small, sometimes one person or one machine, or large, for example an entire department. An organisation might establish a **hierarchy of cost centres**. For example, within a transport department, individual vehicles might each be made a cost centre, the repairs and maintenance section might be a cost centre and there might be cost centres for expenditure items such as vehicle insurance and road tax. The transport department as a whole might be a cost centre at the top of this **hierarchy**.

2.8 **To charge actual costs to a cost centre,** each cost centre will have a **cost code**. Items of expenditure will be recorded with the appropriate cost code. When costs are eventually analysed, there may well be some apportionment of the costs of one cost centre to other cost centres. If this happens:

(a) The costs of those cost centres which receive an apportionment of shared costs should be divided into directly attributable costs (for which the cost centre manager is responsible) and shared costs (for which another cost centre is directly accountable).

(b) The **control system** should **trace shared costs back to the cost centres from which the costs have been apportioned**, so that their **managers can be made accountable** for the costs incurred.

2.9 Information about cost centres might be collected in terms of **total actual costs, total budgeted costs** and **total cost variances** (the differences between actual and budgeted costs) sub-analysed perhaps into efficiency, usage and expenditure variances. In addition, the information might be analysed in terms of **ratios**, such the following.

- Cost per unit produced (budget and actual)
- Hours per unit produced (budget and actual)
- Efficiency ratio
- Selling costs per £ of sales (budget and actual)
- Transport costs per tonne/kilometre (budget and actual)

Profit centres

> **KEY TERM**
>
> A **profit centre** is any unit of an organisation (for example, division of a company) to which both revenues and costs are assigned, so that the profitability of the unit may be measured.

2.10 Profit centres differ from cost centres in that they **account for both costs and revenues** and the **key performance measure** of a profit centre is therefore **profit**.

2.11 For profit centres to have any validity in a planning and control system based on responsibility accounting, **the manager of the profit centre must have some influence over both revenues and costs**, that is, a say in both sales and production policies.

2.12 A profit centre manager is likely to be a fairly senior person within an organisation, and a profit centre is likely to cover quite a large area of operations. A profit centre might be an entire division within the organisation, or there might be a separate profit centre for each product, product range, brand or service that the organisation sells. Information requirements will be similarly focused, as appropriate.

2.13 In the hierarchy of responsibility centres within an organisation, there are likely to be several cost centres within a profit centre.

Investment centres

> **KEY TERM**
>
> An **investment centre** is a profit centre whose performance is measured by its return on capital employed. (We shall be studying this performance measure in detail in the next section of this chapter.)

2.14 This implies that the **investment centre manager has some say in investment policy** in his area of operations as well as being responsible for costs and revenues.

2.15 Several profit centres might share the same capital items, for example the same buildings, stores or transport fleet, and so investment centres are likely to include several profit centres, and provide a basis for control at a very senior management level, like that of a subsidiary company within a group.

3 MEASURING PROFITABILITY, PRODUCTIVITY AND ACTIVITY

Profitability

Return on investment (ROI)

> **KEY TERM**
> **Return on investment (ROI)** (also called **return on capital employed (ROCE)**) is calculated as (profit/capital employed) × 100% and shows how much profit has been made in relation to the amount of resources invested.

3.1 Profits alone do not show whether the return is sufficient, in view of the value of assets committed. Thus if company A and company B have the following results, company B would have the better performance.

	A	B
	£	£
Profit	5,000	5,000
Sales	100,000	100,000
Capital employed	50,000	25,000
ROI	10%	20%

The profit of each company is the same but company B only invested £25,000 to achieve that profit whereas company A invested £50,000.

3.2 ROI may be calculated in a number of ways, but management accountants prefer to exclude from profits all revenues and expenditures not related to the core operation of the business (such as interest payable and income from trade investments). **Profit before interest and tax** is therefore often used.

3.3 Similarly **all assets of a non-operational nature** (for example trade investments and intangible assets such as goodwill) **should be excluded** from capital employed.

3.4 **Profits should be related to average capital employed**. In practice many companies calculate the ratio **using year-end assets**. This can be misleading. If a new investment is undertaken near to year end and financed, for example, by an issue of shares, the capital employed will rise by the finance raised but profits will only have a month or two of the new investment's contribution.

3.5 What does the ROI tell us? What should we be looking for? There are **two principal comparisons** that can be made.

- The change in ROI from one year to the next
- The ROI being earned by other entities

Profit margin

KEY TERM

The **profit margin** (profit to sales ratio) is calculated as (profit ÷ sales) × 100%.

3.6 The profit margin provides a simple measure of performance for management. Investigation of unsatisfactory profit margins enables control action to be taken, either by reducing excessive costs or by raising selling prices.

3.7 Profit margin is usually calculated using operating profit.

3.8 EXAMPLE: THE PROFIT TO SALES RATIO

A company compares its year 2 results with year 1 results as follows.

	Year 2	Year 1
	£	£
Sales	160,000	120,000
Cost of sales		
Direct materials	40,000	20,000
Direct labour	40,000	30,000
Production overhead	22,000	20,000
Marketing overhead	42,000	35,000
	144,000	105,000
Profit	16,000	15,000
Profit to sales ratio	10%	12½%

3.9 Ratio analysis on the above information shows that there is a decline in profitability in spite of the £1,000 increase in profit, because the profit margin is less in year 2 than year 1.

Gross profit margin

3.10 The profit to sales ratio above was based on a profit figure which included non-production overheads. The **pure trading activities of a business can be analysed** using the gross profit margin, which is calculated as (gross profit ÷ turnover) × 100%.

3.11 For the company in Paragraph 3.8 the gross profit margin would be

((16,000 + 42,000)/160,000) × 100% = 36.25% in year 2 and ((15,000 + 35,000)/120,000) × 100% = 41.67% in year 1.

Cost/sales ratios

3.12 There are three principal ratios for analysing profit and loss account information.

- Production cost of sales ÷ sales
- Distribution and marketing costs ÷ sales
- Administrative costs ÷ sales

3.13 When particular areas of weakness are found subsidiary ratios are used to examine them in greater depth. For example, for production costs the following ratios might be used.

- Material costs ÷ sales value of production
- Works labour costs ÷ sales value of production
- Production overheads ÷ sales value of production

3.14 EXAMPLE: COST/SALES RATIOS

Look back to the example in Paragraph 3.8. A more detailed analysis would show that higher direct materials are the probable cause of the decline in profitability.

	Year 2	Year 1
Material costs/sales	25%	16.7%

Other cost/sales ratios have remained the same or improved.

Productivity

3.15 This is the quantity of the product or service produced (**output**) **in relation to** the resources put in (**input**). For example so many units produced per hour, or per employee, or per tonne of material. It measures **how efficiently resources are being used**.

Activity

3.16 **Indices** can be used in order to measure activity. We studied index numbers in the previous chapter.

3.17 You will remember that indices show **how a particular variable has changed relative to a base value**. The base value is usually the level of the variable at an earlier date. The 'variable' may be just one particular item, such as material X, or several items may be incorporated, such as 'raw materials' generally.

3.18 In its simplest form an index is calculated as **(current value ÷ base value) × 100%**.

Thus if materials cost £15 per kg in 20X0 and now (20X3) cost £27 per kg the 20X0 value would be expressed in index form as 100 (15/15 × 100) and the 20X3 value as 180 (27/15 × 100). If you find it easier to think of this as a percentage, then do so.

3.19 EXAMPLE: WORK STANDARDS AND INDICES

Standards for work done in a service department could be expressed as an index. For example, suppose that in a sales department, there is a standard target for sales representatives to make 25 customer visits per month each. The budget for May might be for ten sales representatives to make 250 customer visits in total. Actual results in May might be that nine sales representatives made 234 visits in total. Performance could then be measured as:

Budget	100	(Standard = index 100)
Actual	104	(234 ÷ (9 × 25)) × 100

This shows that 'productivity' per sales representative was actually 4% over budget.

Residual income (RI)

3.20 An alternative way of measuring the performance of an investment centre, instead of using ROI, is residual income (RI). **Residual income is a measure of the centre's profits after deducting a notional or imputed interest cost**.

- The centre's profit is **after deducting depreciation** on capital equipment.

- The imputed cost of capital might be the organisation's cost of borrowing or its weighted average cost of capital.

KEY TERM

Residual income (RI) is 'Pretax profits less an imputed interest charge for invested capital. Used to assess divisional performance'. (CIMA *Official Terminology*)

Question 1

A division with capital employed of £400,000 currently earns a ROI of 22%. It can make an additional investment of £50,000 for a 5 year life with nil residual value. The average net profit from this investment would be £12,000 after depreciation. The division's cost of capital is 14%.

Required

Calculate the residual income before and after the investment.

Answer

	Before investment	After investment
	£	£
Divisional profit	88,000	100,000
Imputed interest		
(400,000 × 0.14)	56,000	
(450,000 × 0.14)		63,000
Residual income	32,000	37,000

4 PERFORMANCE MEASURES FOR MANUFACTURING BUSINESSES

Performance measures for sales

4.1 Traditionally sales performance is measured in terms of price and volume variances, and a sales mix variance. Other possible measures include revenue targets and target market share. They may be analysed in detail: by country, by region, by individual products, by salesperson and so on.

4.2 In a customer-focused organisation the basic information 'Turnover is up by 14%' can be supplemented by a host of other indicators.

(a) **Customer rejects/returns: total sales**. This ratio helps to monitor customer satisfaction, providing a check on the efficiency of quality control procedures.

(b) **Deliveries late: deliveries on schedule**. This ratio can be applied both to sales made to customers and to receipts from suppliers. When applied to customers it provides an indication of the efficiency of production and production scheduling.

(c) **Flexibility measures** indicate how well able a company is to respond to customers' requirements. Measures could be devised to measure how quickly and efficiently **new products** are launched, and how well procedures meet **customer needs**.

(d) **Number of people served and speed of service**, in a shop or a bank for example. If it takes too long to reach the point of sale, future sales are liable to be lost.

(e) **Customer satisfaction questionnaires,** for input to the organisation's management information system.

Performance measures for materials

4.3 Traditional measures are **standard costs,** and price and usage **variances**. Many traditional systems also analyse **wastage**.

4.4 Measures used in **modern manufacturing environments** include the number of **rejects** in materials supplied, and the **timing and reliability of deliveries** of materials.

Performance measures for labour

4.5 Labour costs are traditionally measured in terms of **standard performance** (ideal, attainable and so on) and rate and efficiency **variances**.

4.6 **Qualitative measures** of labour performance concentrate on matters such as **ability to communicate, interpersonal relationships** with colleagues, **customers' impressions** and **levels of skills** attained.

4.7 Managers can expect to be judged to some extent by the performance of their staff. High profitability or tight cost control are not the only indicators of managerial performance!

Performance measures for overheads

4.8 Standards for variable overheads and efficiency variances are traditional measures. Various time based measure are also available, such as:

- **Machine down time: total machine hours**. This ratio provides a measure of machine usage and efficiency.

- **Value added time: production cycle time**. Value added time is the direct production time during which the product is being made. The production cycle time includes non-value-added times such as set-up time, downtime, idle time and so on. The 'perfect' ratio is 100%, but in practice this optimum will not be achieved. A high ratio means non-value-added activities are being kept to a minimum.

Measures of performance using the standard hour

4.9   Sam Ltd manufactures plates, mugs and eggcups. Production during the first two quarters of 20X5 was as follows.

	Quarter 1	Quarter 2
Plates	1,000	800
Mugs	1,200	1,500
Eggcups	800	900

The fact that 3,000 products were produced in quarter 1 and 3,200 in quarter 2 does not tell us anything about Sam Ltd's performance over the two periods because plates, mugs and eggcups are so different. The fact that the production mix has changed is not revealed by considering the total number of units produced. The problem of how to **measure output when a number of dissimilar products are manufactured** can be overcome, however, by the **use of the standard hour**.

4.10   The standard hour (or standard minute) is the **quantity of work achievable at standard performance, expressed in terms of a standard unit of work done in a standard period of time.**

4.11   The standard time allowed to produce one unit of each of Sam Ltd's products is as follows.

	Standard time
Plate	$1/2$ hour
Mug	$1/3$ hour
Eggcup	$1/4$ hour

4.12   By measuring the standard hours of output in each quarter, a more useful output measure is obtained.

		Quarter 1		Quarter 2	
Product	Standard hours per unit	Production	Standard hours	Production	Standard hours
Plate	$1/2$	1,000	500	800	400
Mug	$1/3$	1,200	400	1,500	500
Eggcup	$1/4$	800	200	900	225
			1,100		1,125

The output level in the two quarters was therefore very similar.

Efficiency, activity and capacity ratios

4.13   Standard hours are useful in computing levels of **efficiency, activity and capacity**. Any management accounting reports involving budgets and variance analysis should incorporate control ratios. The three main control ratios are the efficiency, capacity and activity ratios.

(a)   The **capacity ratio compares actual hours worked and budgeted hours**, and measures the **extent to which planned utilisation has been achieved.**

(b)   The **activity** or **production volume ratio compares the number of standard hours equivalent to the actual work produced and budgeted hours.**

(c) **The efficiency ratio** measures the **efficiency of the labour force** by **comparing equivalent standard hours for work produced and actual hours worked.**

4.14 EXAMPLE: RATIOS AND STANDARD HOURS

Given the following information about Sam Ltd for quarter 1 of 20X5, calculate a capacity ratio, an activity ratio and an efficiency ratio and explain their meaning.

Budgeted hours	1,100 standard hours
Standard hours produced	1,125 standard hours
Actual hours worked	1,200

4.15 SOLUTION

$$\text{Capacity ratio} = \frac{\text{Actual hours worked}}{\text{Budgeted hours}} \times 100\% = \frac{1,200}{1,100} \times 100\% = 109\%$$

$$\text{Activity ratio} = \frac{\text{Standard hours produced}}{\text{Budgeted hours}} \times 100\% = \frac{1,125}{1,100} \times 100\% = 102\%$$

The overall activity or production volume for the quarter was 2% greater than forecast. This was achieved by a 9% increase in capacity.

$$\text{Efficiency ratio} = \frac{\text{Standard hours produced}}{\text{Actual hours worked}} \times 100\% = \frac{1,125}{1,200} \times 100\% = 94\%$$

The labour force worked 9% below standard levels of efficiency.

5 PERFORMANCE MEASURES FOR SERVICES

Service businesses

5.1 A service business does not produce a physical product. Instead it provides a service, for example a haircut, or insurance.

- A service is **intangible**. The actual benefit being bought can not be touched.

- The production and consumption of a service are **simultaneous,** and therefore it cannot be inspected for quality in advance.

- Services are **perishable,** that is, they cannot be stored. For example a hairdresser cannot do haircuts in advance and keep them stocked away in case of heavy demand.

- A service is **heterogeneous**. The service received will vary each time. Services are more reliant on people. People are not robots, so how the service is delivered will not be identical each time.

'Dimensions' of performance measurement

5.2 Performance measurement in service businesses is made more difficult because of the four factors listed above. However, performance measurement is possible, the key being to ensure what you are measuring has been clearly enough defined. A range of performance measures covering **six 'dimensions'** are used.

Competitive performance

5.3 **Competitive performance** focuses on factors such as sales growth, market share and ability to obtain new business.

Financial performance

5.4　Like any other business, a service business needs to plan, and its short-term plans can be drawn up in the form of a **budget**.

- There might be a **budgeted expenditure limit** for individual activities within the business.

- **Standard performance measures** (such as standard cost per unit of activity or standard quantity of 'output' per unit of resource used up (ie productivity)) can be established as targets.

Quality of service

5.5　**Service quality** is measured principally by **qualitative measures**, although some quantitative measures are used by some businesses. An equipment hire company used a 'successful hire indicator'. This was expressed as a percentage. All hires has to be classified as successful or unsuccessful (based on equipment performance) when equipment was returned.

5.6　The following table shows the measures used to assess 4 quality factors and the means of obtaining the information by British Airports Authority (BAA), a transport facility service provider.

Service quality factors	Measures	Mechanisms
Access	Walking distances Ease of finding way around	Customer survey and internal operational data
Cleanliness/tidiness	Cleanliness of environment and equipment	Customer survey and management inspection
Comfort	Crowdedness of airport	Customer survey and management inspection
Friendliness	Staff attitude and helpfulness	Customer survey and management inspection

Flexibility

5.7　Flexibility has three aspects.

(a)　**Speed of delivery** is vital in some service industries. Measures include factors such as waiting time in queues.

In other types of service it may be more a question of timeliness. Does the auditor turn up to do the annual audit during the appointed week? Is the audit done within the time anticipated by the partner or does it drag on for weeks? These aspects are all easily measurable in terms of 'days late'. Depending upon the circumstances 'days late' may also reflect on inability to cope with fluctuations in demand.

(b)　The ability of a service organisation to **respond to customers' specifications** will depend on the type of service. A professional service such as legal advice must be tailored exactly to the customer's needs. Performance is partly a matter of customer perception. Customer attitude surveys may be appropriate. Performance also depends on the diversity of skills possessed by the service organisation. This can be measured in terms of the mix of staff skills and the amount of time spent on training.

(c)　**Coping with demand** is measurable in quantitative terms. For example train companies can measure the extent of overcrowding. Customer queuing time can be for banks and retailers. Professional services can measure levels of overtime worked.

Resource utilisation measures

5.8 Resource utilisation is usually measured in terms of **productivity**. The ease with which this may be measured varies according to the service being delivered. The main input resource of a firm of accountants, for example, is the **time** of staff. The main output of an accountancy firm is **chargeable hours**. Productivity will therefore be measured as the ratio of chargeable hours to total hours.

5.9 Here are some resource utilisation ratios.

Business	Input	Output
Consulting firm	Man hours available	Chargeable hours
Hotel	Rooms available	Rooms occupied
Railway company	Train miles available	Passenger miles
Bank	Number of staff	Number of accounts

Innovation

5.10 Companies do not have to innovate to be successful, but it helps! Others will try to steal their market, and so others' innovations must at least be matched. In a modern environment in which product quality, product differentiation and continuous improvement are the order of the day, a company that can find innovative ways of satisfying customers' needs has an important **competitive advantage**.

5.11 The **innovating process can be measured** in terms of **how much it costs to develop a new service, how effective the process is** (that is, how innovative is the organisation, if at all?), and **how quickly it can develop new services**. In more concrete terms this might translate into:

(a) The **amount of spending on research and development**, and whether these costs are recovered from new service sales (and how quickly).

(b) The **proportion of new services to total services** provided.

(c) The **time between identification of the customer need for a new service and making it available**.

6 PERFORMANCE MEASURES FOR NON-PROFIT-MAKING ORGANISATIONS

Non-profit-making organisations (NPMOs)

6.1 NPMOs include private sector organisations such as charities and churches and much of the public sector. Commercial organisations generally have market competition and the profit motive to guide the process of managing resources economically, efficiently and effectively. However, NPMOs **cannot** by definition **be judged by profitability** nor do they generally have to be successful against competition, so other methods of assessing performance have to be used.

6.2 A major problem with many NPMOs, particularly government bodies, is that it is **difficult to define their objectives**.

How can performance be measured?

6.3 Performance is usually judged in terms of inputs and outputs. This ties in with the '**value for money**' criteria often used to assess NPMOs.

   (a) **Economy** (spending money frugally)

   (b) **Efficiency** (getting out as much as possible for what goes in)

   (c) **Effectiveness** (getting done, by means of (a) and (b), what was supposed to be done)

6.4 **Effectiveness** is the relationship between an organisation's outputs and its objectives, **efficiency** is the relationship between inputs and outputs, and **economy** means controlling expenditure.

6.5 The **problems** with an NPMO are:

   (a) NPMOs tend to have **multiple objectives**, so that even if they can all be clearly identified it is impossible to say which is the overriding objective.

   (b) **Outputs can seldom be measured** in a way that is generally agreed to be meaningful. (For example, are good exam results alone an adequate measure of the quality of teaching?)

6.6 Here are four possible solutions.

   • Performance can be judged in terms of **inputs**. This is very common in everyday life. If somebody tells you that their suit cost £750, you would generally conclude that it was a good quality suit. The **drawback** is that you might also conclude that the person wearing the suit had been cheated. So it is with the inputs and outputs of a NPMO. Does the output justify the input?

   • A second possibility is to accept that performance measurement must to some extent be subjective. **Judgements** can be made **by experts** in that particular non-profit-making activity **or by the persons who fund the activity**.

   • NPMOs can **compare** their performance **against each other** and **against the historical results** of their predecessors.

   • **Unit cost measurements** like 'cost per patient day' or 'cost of borrowing one library book' can be established to allow organisations to assess whether they are doing better or worse than their counterparts.

6.7 EXAMPLE: INPUTS AND OUTPUTS

Suppose that at a cost of £40,000 and 4,000 hours (**inputs**) in an average year, two policemen travel 8,000 miles and are instrumental in 200 arrests (**outputs**). A large number of **possibly meaningful measures** can be derived from these few figures, as the table below shows.

BPP
PUBLISHING

	£40,000	4,000 hours	8,000 miles	200 arrests
Cost £40,000 (£)		£40,000/4,000 = £10 per hour	£40,000/8,000 = £5 per mile	£40,000/200 = £200 per arrest
Time 4,000 (hours)	4,000/£40,000 = 6 minutes patrolling per £1 spent		4,000/8,000 = ½ hour to patrol 1 mile	4,000/200 = 20 hours per arrest
Miles 8,000	8,000/£40,000 = 0.2 of a mile per £1	8,000/4,000 = 2 miles patrolled per hour		8,000/200 = 40 miles per arrest
Arrests 200	200/£40,000 = 1 arrest per £200	200/4,000 = 1 arrest every 20 hours	200/8,000 = 1 arrest every 40 miles	

6.8 These measures do not necessarily identify cause and effect or personal responsibility and accountability. Actual performance needs to be **compared**:

- With **standards,** if there are any
- With similar **external activities**
- With similar **internal activities**
- With **targets**
- With **indices**
- Over time - **as trends**

7 THE BALANCED SCORECARD

7.1 So far in our discussion we have focussed on performance measurement and control from a financial point of view. Another approach is the use of what is called a 'balanced scorecard' consisting of a **variety of indicators both financial and non-financial.**

> **KEY TERM**
>
> The **balanced scorecard approach** is 'An approach to the provision of information to management to assist strategic policy formulation and achievement. It emphasises the need to provide the user with a set of information which addresses all relevant areas of performance in an objective and unbiased fashion. The information provided may include both financial and non-financial elements, and cover areas such as profitability, customer satisfaction, internal efficiency and innovation.' (CIMA *Official Terminology*)

7.2 The balanced scorecard focuses on **four different perspectives,** as follows.

Perspective	Question	Explanation
Customer	What do existing and new customers value from us?	Gives rise to targets that matter to customers: cost, quality, delivery, inspection, handling and so on.
Internal	What processes must we excel at to achieve our financial and customer objectives?	Aims to improve internal processes and decision making.

Perspective	Question	Explanation
Innovation and learning	Can we continue to improve and create future value?	Considers the business's capacity to maintain its competitive position through the acquisition of new skills and the development of new products.
Financial	How do we create value for our shareholders?	Covers traditional measures such as growth, profitability and shareholder value but set through talking to the shareholder or shareholders direct.

Performance targets are set once the key areas for improvement have been identified, and the balanced scorecard is the **main monthly report**.

7.3 The scorecard is 'balanced' in the sense that managers are required to **think in terms of all four perspectives**, to **prevent improvements being made in one area at the expense of** another.

7.4 The types of measure which may be monitored under each of the four perspectives include the following. The list is not exhaustive but it will give you an idea of the possible scope of a balanced scorecard approach. The measures selected, particularly within the internal perspective, will vary considerably with the type of organisation and its objectives.

Customer perspective

- New customers acquired
- Customer complaints
- On-time deliveries
- Returns

Internal perspective

- Quality control rejects
- Average set-up time
- Speed of producing management information

Innovation and learning perspective

- Labour turnover rate
- Training days per employee
- Percentage of revenue generated by new products and services
- Average time taken to develop new products and services

Financial perspective

- Return on capital employed
- Cash flow
- Revenue growth
- Earnings per share

7.5 The **important features** of this approach are as follows.

- It looks at both **internal and external matters** concerning the organisation.
- It is **related to the key elements of a company's strategy**.
- **Financial and non-financial measures** are linked together.

7.6 The balanced scorecard approach may be particularly useful for performance measurement in organisations which are unable to use simple profit as a performance measure. For example the **public sector** has long been forced to use a **wide range of performance indicators**, which can be formalised with a balanced scorecard approach.

Problems

7.7 As with all techniques, problems can arise when it is applied.

Problem	Explanation
Conflicting measures	Some measures in the scorecard such as research funding and cost reduction may naturally conflict. It is often difficult to determine the balance which will achieve the best results.
Selecting measures	Not only do appropriate measures have to be devised but the number of measures used must be agreed. Care must be taken that the impact of the results is not lost in a sea of information.
Expertise	Measurement is only useful if it initiates appropriate action. Non-financial managers may have difficulty with the usual profit measures. With more measures to consider this problem will be compounded.
Interpretation	Even a financially-trained manager may have difficulty in putting the figures into an overall perspective.

Question 2

Upon which of the following perspectives does the balanced scorecard focus?

(i)   Innovation and learning
(ii) Internal
(iii) Financial
(iv) Non-financial
(v)   External

A   (i), (ii) and (iii)
B   (i), (ii), (iii), (iv) and (v)
C   (ii) and (v) only
D   (iii) and (iv) only

Answer

A. In addition, the balanced scorecard focuses upon the customer perspective.

8 BENCHMARKING

8.1 We have seen how standard costing achieves control by the comparison of actual results with a pre-determined standard.

8.2 **Benchmarking is another type of comparison exercise through which an organisation attempts to improve performance.** The idea is to seek the best available performance against which the organisation can monitor its own performance.

> **KEY TERM**
>
> **Benchmarking** is 'The establishment, through data gathering, of targets and comparators, through whose use relative levels of performance (and particularly areas of underperformance) can be identified. By the adoption of identified best practices it is hoped that performance will improve.'
>
> CIMA *Official Terminology*

8.3 There are four types of benchmarking.

(a) **Internal benchmarking:** a method of comparing one operating unit or function with another within the same industry.

(b) **Functional benchmarking:** in which internal functions are compared with those of the best external practitioners of those functions, regardless of the industry they are in (also known as **operational** or **generic** benchmarking).

(c) **Competitive benchmarking**: in which information is gathered about direct competitors, through techniques such as reverse engineering.

(d) **Strategic benchmarking**: a type of competitive benchmarking aimed at strategic action and organisational change.

8.4 From this list you can see that a benchmarking exercise **does not necessarily have to involve the comparison of operations with those of a competitor**. Indeed, it might be difficult to persuade a direct competitor to part with any information which is useful for comparison purposes. Functional benchmarking, for example, does not always involve direct competitors. For instance a railway company may be identified as the 'best' in terms of on-board catering, and an airline company that operates on different routes could seek opportunities to improve by sharing information and comparing their own catering operations with those of the railway company.

8.5 A 1994 survey of the *The Times* Top 1,000 companies (half of which were in manufacturing) revealed that the business functions most subjected to benchmarking in the companies using the technique were **customer services, manufacturing, human resources and information services.**

Why use benchmarking?

8.6 Anna Green, in her article *The Borrowers* in the October 1996 edition of Pass magazine, explains the benefits of benchmarking.

(a) Its flexibility means that it can be used in both the public and private sector and by people at different levels of responsibility.

(b) Cross comparisons (as opposed to comparisons with similar organisations) are more likely to expose radically different ways of doing things.

(c) It is an effective method of implementing change, people being involved in identifying and seeking out different ways of doing things in their own areas.

(d) It identifies the processes to improve.

(e) It helps with cost reduction.

(f) It improves the effectiveness of operations.

(g) It delivers services to a defined standard.

(h) It provides a focus on planning.

'Most importantly benchmarking establishes a desire to achieve continuous improvement and helps develop a culture in which it is easier to admit mistakes and make changes.'

8.7 Benchmarking works, it is claimed, for the following reasons.

(a) The comparisons are carried out by the managers who have to live with any changes implemented as a result of the exercise.

(b) Benchmarking focuses on improvement in key areas and sets targets which are challenging but 'achievable'. What is *really* achievable can be discovered by examining what others have achieved: managers are thus able to accept that they are not being asked to perform miracles.

8.8 Benchmarking has other advantages: it can provide **early warning of competitive disadvantage** and should lead to a greater incidence of **teamworking** and **cross-functional learning.**

8.9 **Limitations of benchmarking exercises**

- Difficulties in deciding which activities to benchmark
- Identifying the 'best in class' for each activity
- Persuading other organisations to share information
- Successful practices in one organisation may not transfer successfully to another
- The danger of drawing incorrect conclusions from inappropriate comparisons

9 MANAGEMENT PERFORMANCE MEASURES

9.1 We have not so far **distinguished between measures of performance of individual managers** and **measures of performance of what it is they manage.**

9.2 The distinction is very important. A manager may improve performance of a poorly performing division, but the division could still rank as one of the poorest performing divisions within the organisation. If the manager is assessed purely on the division's results then he will not appear to be a good performer.

9.3 The problem is deciding which performance measures should be used to measure management performance and which should be used to measure the performance of the business.

9.4 It is difficult to devise performance measures that relate specifically to a manager to judge his or her performance **as a manager**. It is possible to calculate statistics to assess the manager as an **employee** (days absent, professional qualifications obtained, personality and so on), but this does not measure managerial performance.

9.5 It is necessary to consider a manger in relation to his or her **area of responsibility**. If we want to know how good a manager is at marketing, the marketing performance of his or her division is the **starting point**. Then we must consider to what extent the manager is able to **influence** the performance, and the performance **trend.**

9.6 It is unreasonable to assess managers' performance in relation to matters that are beyond their control. Management performance measures should therefore **only include those items that are directly controllable by the manager in question.**

Possible management performance measures

9.7 (a) **Subjective measures,** for example ranking performance on a scale of 1 to 5. This approach is imprecise but does measure managerial performance rather than divisional performance. The process must be perceived by managers to be fair. The judgement should be made by somebody impartial, but close enough to the work of each manager to appreciate the efforts he has made and the difficulties he faces.

(b) The **judgement of outsiders.** An organisation might, for example, set up a bonus scheme for directors under which they would receive a bonus if the share price outperforms the FT-SE 100 index for more than three years. This is fair in that the share price reflects many aspects of performance, but it is questionable whether they can all be influenced by the directors concerned.

(c) **Upward appraisal.** This involves staff giving their opinions on the performance of their managers. To be effective this requires healthy working relationships.

(d) **Accounting measures** can be used, but must be tailored according to what or whom is being judged.

Chapter roundup

- **Performance measurement** aims to establish how well something or somebody is doing in relation to a planned activity.

- Performance measures may be divided into two groups.
  - Financial performance measures
  - Non-monetary performance measures

- Performance measures can be **quantitative** or **qualitative**.

- **Non-financial indicators (NFIs)** are useful in a modern business environment.

- **Ratios** and **percentages** are useful performance measurement techniques.

- **Responsibility accounting** is a system of accounting that segregates revenue and costs into areas of personal responsibility in order to monitor and assess the performance of each part of an organisation.

- A **responsibility centre** is a function or department of an organisation that is headed by a manager who has direct responsibility for its performance.

- A **cost centre** is any unit of an organisation to which costs can be separately attributed.

- A **profit centre** is any unit of an organisation to which both revenues and costs are assigned, so that the profitability of the unit may be measured.

- An **investment centre** is a profit centre whose performance is measured by its return on capital employed.

- **Return on investment (ROI)** or **return on capital employed (ROCE)** shows how much profit has been made in relation to the amount of resources invested.

- The **profit margin** (profit to sales ratio) is calculated as (profit ÷ sales) × 100%.

- **Residual income (RI)** is an alternative way of measuring the performance of an investment centre. It is a measure of the centre's profits after deducting a notional or imputed interest cost.

- Performance measures for **materials** and **labour** include variances. Performance can also be measured using the **standard hour**.

- Performance measures covering the following six 'dimensions' have been suggested for service organisations.
  - Competitive performance
  - Financial performance
  - Quality of service
  - Flexibility
  - Resource utilisation
  - Innovation

- Performance of NPOs can be measured as follows.
  - In terms of inputs and outputs
  - By judgement
  - By comparison

- The **balanced scorecard** is a performance measurement which consists of a variety of indicators both **financial** and **non-financial**.

- **Benchmarking** is a type of comparison exercise through which an organisation attempts to improve performance.

- Possible management performance measures include the following.
  - Subjective measures
  - Judgement of outsiders
  - Upward appraisal
  - Accounting measures

Quick quiz

1   What is the main aim of performance measurement?

2   Give five examples of a financial performance measure.

- Profit
- Revenue
- Costs
- Share price
- Interest

3   How do quantitative and qualitative performance measures differ? *Numbers + Not.*

4   ROI = $\dfrac{A}{B}$ × 100%

A = Capital Employed

B = Profit

5   Profit margin = $\dfrac{C}{D}$ × 100%

C = Profit

D = Turnover.

6   What are traditionally-used performance measures for materials and labour? *standard hour variance.*

7   If   X = Actual hours worked
     Y = Budgeted hours
     Z = Standard hours produced

What is $\dfrac{Z}{Y}$?

A   Capacity ratio
B   Activity ratio
C   Efficiency ratio
D   Standard hours produced ratio

8   **Service quality** is measured principally by quantitative measures.

True   ☐

False   ☑

9   Match up the following correctly.

(1)   Effectiveness =   A
(2)   Efficiency =   C
(3)   Economy =   B

A =   Relationship between an organisation's outputs and its objectives
B =   Controlling expenditure
C =   Relationship between inputs and outputs

10   What are the three most important features of the balanced scorecard approach?

11   What is the main aim of benchmarking?

12   List four types of benchmarking

- Internal
- Functional
- Competitive
- Strategic

Answers to quick quiz

1   To establish how well something or somebody is doing in relation to a planned activity.

2   • Profit
    • Revenue
    • Costs
    • Share price
    • Cash flow

3   Quantitative measures are expressed in numbers whereas qualitative measures are not.

4   A = profit
    B = capital employed

5   C = profit
    D = sales

6   Variances

7   B

8   False. Service quality is measured principally by **qualitative** measures.

9   (1) A
    (2) C
    (3) B

10 • It looks at both internal and external matters concerning the organisation
    • It is related to the key elements of a company's strategy
    • Financial and non-financial measures are linked together

11 To seek the best available performance against which the organisation can monitor its own performance.

12 • Internal
    • Functional
    • Competitive
    • Strategic

Now try the questions below from the Exam Question Bank

Number	Level	Marks	Time
52	MCQ	n/a	n/a
53	Examination	10	18 mins

BPP
PUBLISHING

Appendix
Mathematical
Tables

Linear regression

$$r = \frac{n\Sigma XY - \Sigma X \Sigma Y}{\sqrt{[n\Sigma X^2 - (\Sigma X)^2][n\Sigma Y^2 - (\Sigma Y)^2]}}$$

Economic order quantity

$$EOQ = \sqrt{2C_O D/C_H}$$

Future value

$$S = P(1 + r)^n$$

Present value

$$P = \frac{S}{(1 + r)^n}$$

Annuity

$$PV\ Annuity = A \times \frac{1}{r}\left(1 - \frac{1}{(1 + r)^n}\right)$$

Perpetuity

$$PV\ Perpetuity = \frac{A}{r}$$

PRESENT VALUE TABLE

Present value of 1 ie $(1+r)^{-n}$

where   r = discount rate

n = number of periods until payment

Periods					Discount rates (r)					
(n)	1%	2%	3%	4%	5%	6%	7%	8%	9%	10%
1	0.990	0.980	0.971	0.962	0.952	0.943	0.935	0.926	0.917	0.909
2	0.980	0.961	0.943	0.925	0.907	0.890	0.873	0.857	0.842	0.826
3	0.971	0.942	0.915	0.889	0.864	0.840	0.816	0.794	0.772	0.751
4	0.961	0.924	0.888	0.855	0.823	0.792	0.763	0.735	0.708	0.683
5	0.951	0.906	0.863	0.822	0.784	0.747	0.713	0.681	0.650	0.621
6	0.942	0.888	0.837	0.790	0.746	0.705	0.666	0.630	0.596	0.564
7	0.933	0.871	0.813	0.760	0.711	0.665	0.623	0.583	0.547	0.513
8	0.923	0.853	0.789	0.731	0.677	0.627	0.582	0.540	0.502	0.467
9	0.914	0.837	0.766	0.703	0.645	0.592	0.544	0.500	0.460	0.424
10	0.905	0.820	0.744	0.676	0.614	0.558	0.508	0.463	0.422	0.386
11	0.896	0.804	0.722	0.650	0.585	0.527	0.475	0.429	0.388	0.350
12	0.887	0.788	0.701	0.625	0.557	0.497	0.444	0.397	0.356	0.319
13	0.879	0.773	0.681	0.601	0.530	0.469	0.415	0.368	0.326	0.290
14	0.870	0.758	0.661	0.577	0.505	0.442	0.388	0.340	0.299	0.263
15	0.861	0.743	0.642	0.555	0.481	0.417	0.362	0.315	0.275	0.239

Periods										
(n)	11%	12%	13%	14%	15%	16%	17%	18%	19%	20%
1	0.901	0.893	0.885	0.877	0.870	0.862	0.855	0.847	0.840	0.833
2	0.812	0.797	0.783	0.769	0.756	0.743	0.731	0.718	0.706	0.694
3	0.731	0.712	0.693	0.675	0.658	0.641	0.624	0.609	0.593	0.579
4	0.659	0.636	0.613	0.592	0.572	0.552	0.534	0.516	0.499	0.482
5	0.593	0.567	0.543	0.519	0.497	0.476	0.456	0.437	0.419	0.402
6	0.535	0.507	0.480	0.456	0.432	0.410	0.390	0.370	0.352	0.335
7	0.482	0.452	0.425	0.400	0.376	0.354	0.333	0.314	0.296	0.279
8	0.434	0.404	0.376	0.351	0.327	0.305	0.285	0.266	0.249	0.233
9	0.391	0.361	0.333	0.308	0.284	0.263	0.243	0.225	0.209	0.194
10	0.352	0.322	0.295	0.270	0.247	0.227	0.208	0.191	0.176	0.162
11	0.317	0.287	0.261	0.237	0.215	0.195	0.178	0.162	0.148	0.135
12	0.286	0.257	0.231	0.208	0.187	0.168	0.152	0.137	0.124	0.112
13	0.258	0.229	0.204	0.182	0.163	0.145	0.130	0.116	0.104	0.093
14	0.232	0.205	0.181	0.160	0.141	0.125	0.111	0.099	0.088	0.078
15	0.209	0.183	0.160	0.140	0.123	0.108	0.095	0.084	0.074	0.065

ANNUITY TABLE

Present value of annuity of 1, ie

where   r = discount rate

          n = number of periods.

Periods   **Discount rates (r)**

(n)	1%	2%	3%	4%	5%	6%	7%	8%	9%	10%
1	0.990	0.980	0.971	0.962	0.952	0.943	0.935	0.926	0.917	0.909
2	1.970	1.942	1.913	1.886	1.859	1.833	1.808	1.783	1.759	1.736
3	2.941	2.884	2.829	2.775	2.723	2.673	2.624	2.577	2.531	2.487
4	3.902	3.808	3.717	3.630	3.546	3.465	3.387	3.312	3.240	3.170
5	4.853	4.713	4.580	4.452	4.329	4.212	4.100	3.993	3.890	3.791
6	5.795	5.601	5.417	5.242	5.076	4.917	4.767	4.623	4.486	4.355
7	6.728	6.472	6.230	6.002	5.786	5.582	5.389	5.206	5.033	4.868
8	7.652	7.325	7.020	6.733	6.463	6.210	5.971	5.747	5.535	5.335
9	8.566	8.162	7.786	7.435	7.108	6.802	6.515	6.247	5.995	5.759
10	9.471	8.983	8.530	8.111	7.722	7.360	7.024	6.710	6.418	6.145
11	10.368	9.787	9.253	8.760	8.306	7.887	7.499	7.139	6.805	6.495
12	11.255	10.575	9.954	9.385	8.863	8.384	7.943	7.536	7.161	6.814
13	12.134	11.348	10.635	9.986	9.394	8.853	8.358	7.904	7.487	7.103
14	13.004	12.106	11.296	10.563	9.899	9.295	8.745	8.244	7.786	7.367
15	13.865	12.849	11.938	11.118	10.380	9.712	9.108	8.559	8.061	7.606

Periods

(n)	11%	12%	13%	14%	15%	16%	17%	18%	19%	20%
1	0.901	0.893	0.885	0.877	0.870	0.862	0.855	0.847	0.840	0.833
2	1.713	1.690	1.668	1.647	1.626	1.605	1.585	1.566	1.547	1.528
3	2.444	2.402	2.361	2.322	2.283	2.246	2.210	2.174	2.140	2.106
4	3.102	3.037	2.974	2.914	2.855	2.798	2.743	2.690	2.639	2.589
5	3.696	3.605	3.517	3.433	3.352	3.274	3.199	3.127	3.058	2.991
6	4.231	4.111	3.998	3.889	3.784	3.685	3.589	3.498	3.410	3.326
7	4.712	4.564	4.423	4.288	4.160	4.039	3.922	3.812	3.706	3.605
8	5.146	4.968	4.799	4.639	4.487	4.344	4.207	4.078	3.954	3.837
9	5.537	5.328	5.132	4.946	4.772	4.607	4.451	4.303	4.163	4.031
10	5.889	5.650	5.426	5.216	5.019	4.833	4.659	4.494	4.339	4.192
11	6.207	5.938	5.687	5.453	5.234	5.029	4.836	4.656	4.486	4.327
12	6.492	6.194	5.918	5.660	5.421	5.197	4.988	4.793	4.611	4.439
13	6.750	6.424	6.122	5.842	5.583	5.342	5.118	4.910	4.715	4.533
14	6.982	6.628	6.302	6.002	5.724	5.468	5.229	5.008	4.802	4.611
15	7.191	6.811	6.462	6.142	5.847	5.575	5.324	5.092	4.876	4.675

Exam question bank

1   **INFORMATION FOR MANAGEMENT MCQs**

    (a)   Which of the following statements is/are true?

        I   Information is the raw material for data processing

        II   External sources of information include an organisation's financial accounting records

        III   The main objective of a non-profit making organisation is usually to provide goods and services

        A   I and III only
        B   I, II and III
        C   II and III only
        D   III only

    (b)   Which of the following statements is **not** true?

        A   Management accounts detail the performance of an organisation over a defined period and the state of affairs at the end of that period

        B   There is no legal requirement to prepare management accounts

        C   The format of management accounts is entirely at management discretion

        D   Management accounts are both an historical record and a future planning tool

2   **THE ROLE OF INFORMATION TECHNOLOGY IN MANAGEMENT INFORMATION MCQs**

    (a)   Which of the following is an output device?

        A   Screen
        B   Keyboard
        C   CPU
        D   Disk

    (b)   A method of input which involves a machine that is able to read characters by using lasers to detect the shape of those characters is known as

        A   MICR
        B   OCR
        C   OMR
        D   CPU

3   **COST CLASSIFICATION MCQs**

    (a)   Which of the following items might be a suitable cost unit within the accounts payable department of a company?

        (i)   Postage cost
        (ii)   Invoice processed
        (iii)   Supplier account

        A   Item (i) only
        B   Item (ii) only
        C   Item (iii) only
        D   Items (ii) and (iii) only

    (b)   Which of the following are direct expenses?

        (i)   The cost of special designs, drawing or layouts
        (ii)   The hire of tools or equipment for a particular job
        (iii)   Salesman's wages
        (iv)   Rent, rates and insurance of a factory

        A   (i) and (ii)
        B   (i) and (iii)
        C   (i) and (iv)
        D   (iii) and (iv)

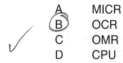

4   **COST BEHAVIOUR MCQs**

(a)   Variable costs are conventionally deemed to

A   be constant per unit of output
B   vary per unit of output as production volume changes
C   be constant in total when production volume changes
D   vary, in total, from period to period when production is constant

(b)   The following is a graph of total cost against level of activity.

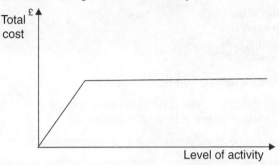

To which one of the following costs does the graph correspond?

A   Photocopier rental costs, where a fixed rental is payable up to a certain number of copies each period. If the number of copies exceeds this amount, a constant charge per copy is made for all subsequent copies during that period.

 B   Vehicle hire costs, where a constant rate is charged per mile travelled, up to a maximum monthly payment regardless of the miles travelled.

C   Supervisor salary costs, where one supervisor is needed for every five employees added to the staff.

D   The cost of direct materials, where the unit rate per kg purchased reduces when the level of purchases reaches a certain amount.

5   **COST BEHAVIOUR AGAIN**   *18 mins*

Prepare a report for the managing director of your company explaining how costs may be classified by their behaviour, with particular reference to the effects both on total and on unit costs.

Your report should:

(a)   say why it is necessary to classify costs by their behaviour; and
(b)   be illustrated by sketch graphs within the body of the report.

                                                                                    (10 marks)

6   **CORRELATION AND REGRESSION MCQs**

(a)   A company's weekly costs (£C) were plotted against production level (P) for the last 50 weeks and a regression line calculated to be C = 1,000 + 250P. Which statement about the breakdown of weekly costs is true?

A   Fixed costs are £1,000. Variable costs per unit are £5.
B   Fixed costs are £250. Variable costs per unit are £4.
C   Fixed costs are £250. Variable costs per unit are £1,000.
D   Fixed costs are £1,000. Variable costs per unit are £250.

(b)   The value of the correlation coefficient between x and y is 0.9. Which of the following is correct?

A   There is a weak relationship between x and y

B   x is 90% of y

C   If the values of x and y were plotted on a graph, the line relating them would have a slope of 0.9

D   There is a very strong relationship between x and y

7   SOUTH (PILOT PAPER)   *18 mins*

South has reported the following costs for the past four months:

Month	Activity level (units)	Total cost
1	300	£3,800
2	400	£4,000
3	150	£3,000
4	260	£3,500

Required:

(a)   Using regression analysis calculate the total cost equation.   **(6 marks)**

(b)   Calculate the total cost of the following activity levels:

  (i)   200 units
  (ii)   500 units

  and comment on the usefulness of your equation with regard to these estimates.   **(4 marks)**

                                                                              (10 marks)

8   MATERIAL COSTS MCQs

(a)   In a period of continual price inflation for material purchases

  A   the LIFO method will produce lower profits than the FIFO method, and lower closing stock values

  B   the LIFO method will produce lower profits than the FIFO method, and higher closing stock values

  C   the FIFO method will produce lower profits than the LIFO method, and lower closing stock values

  D   the FIFO method will produce lower profits than the LIFO method, and higher closing stock values

(b)   The following data relates to an item of raw material

Unit cost of raw material	£20
Usage per week	250 units
Cost of ordering material, per order	£400
Annual cost of holding stock, as a % of cost	10%
Number of weeks in a year	48

  What is the economic order quantity, to the nearest unit?

  A   316 units
  B   693 units
  C   1,549 units
  D   2,191 units

(c)   The following data relates to the stores ledger control account of Duckboard Limited, a manufacturing company, for the month of October.

	£
Opening stock	18,500
Closing stock	16,100
Deliveries from suppliers	142,000
Returns to suppliers	2,300
Cost of indirect materials issued	25,200

  The issue of direct materials would have been recorded in the cost accounts as follows.

			£	£
A	Debit	Stores ledger control account	119,200	
	Credit	Work in progress control account		119,200
B	Debit	Work in progress control account	119,200	
	Credit	Stores ledger control account		119,200
C	Debit	Stores ledger control account	116,900	
	Credit	Work in progress control account		116,900

555   *BPP*
PUBLISHING

/D   *Debit*   Work in progress control account   116,900

        Credit   Stores ledger control account   116,900

9   WIVELSFIELD (PILOT PAPER)   *18 mins*

Wivelsfield currently uses the economic order quantity (EOQ) to establish the optimal reorder levels for their main raw material. The company has been approached by an alternative supplier who would be willing to offer the following discounts.

Order level	Discount
0 - 199 units	1%
200 - 499 units	3%
500 - 699 units	5%
700 units or more	7%

Information regarding current stock costs are as follows:

Holding cost per unit per annum = 10% of purchase price
Order costs = £2 per order
Annual demand = 15,000 units
Purchase price = £15
Current EOQ = 200 units

Required:

(a)	Calculate the new optimal reorder level.	**(6 marks)**
(b)	Explain your approach with regard to each discount band.	**(4 marks)**
		(10 marks)

10   LABOUR COSTS MCQs

(a)   Gross wages incurred in department 1 in June were £54,000. The wages analysis shows the following summary breakdown of the gross pay.

	Paid to direct labour £	Paid to indirect labour £
Ordinary time	25,185	11,900
Overtime: basic pay	5,440	3,500
premium	1,360	875
Shift allowance	2,700	1,360
Sick pay	1,380	300
	36,065	17,935

What is the direct wages cost for department 1 in June?

   A   £25,185
   B   £30,625
   C   £34,685
   D   £36,065

(b)   The wages control account for A Limited for February is shown below.

WAGES CONTROL ACCOUNT

	£		£
Bank	128,400	Work in progress control	79,400
Balance c/d	12,000	Production overhead control	61,000
	140,400		140,400
		Balance b/d	12,000

Which of the following statements about wages for February is *not* correct?

   A   Wages paid during February amounted to £128,400
   B   Wages for February were prepaid by £12,000
   C   Direct wages cost incurred during February amounted to £79,400
   D   Indirect wages cost incurred during February amounted to £61,000

11 REMUNERATION SCHEMES

18 mins

The following information is available.

Normal working day	8 hours
Guaranteed rate of pay (on time basis)	£5.50 per hour
Standard time allowed to produce one unit	3 minutes
Piecework price	£0.10 per standard minute
Premium bonus	75% of time saved, in addition to hourly pay

Required:

(a) For daily production levels of 80, 120 and 210 units, calculate earnings based on the following remuneration methods.

    (i)   Piecework, where earnings are guaranteed at 80% of time-based pay

    (ii)   Premium bonus system **(7 marks)**

(b) What is idle time and how is it measured? **(3 marks)**

(10 marks)

12 OVERHEADS AND ABSORPTION COSTING MCQs

A company absorbs overheads based on labour hours. Data for the latest period are as follows.

Budgeted labour hours	8,500
Budgeted overheads	£148,750
Actual labour hours	7,928
Actual overheads	£146,200

(a) Based on the data given above, what is the labour hour overhead absorption rate?

    A   £17.20 per hour
    B   £17.50 per hour
    C   £18.44 per hour
    D   £18.76 per hour

(b) Based on the data given above, what is the amount of under-/over-absorbed overhead?

    A   £2,550 under-absorbed overhead
    B   £2,550 over-absorbed overhead
    C   £7,460 over-absorbed overhead
    D   £7,460 under-absorbed overhead

13 WARNINGLID (PILOT PAPER)

18 mins

Warninglid has two production centres and two service centres to which the following applies:

	Production departments		Service centres		
	1	2	Stores	Maintenance	Total
Floor area (m²)	5,900	1,400	400	300	8,000
Cubic capacity (m³)	18,000	5,000	1,000	1,000	25,000
Number of employees	14	6	3	2	25
Direct labour hours	2,400	1,040			
Machine hours	1,500	4,570			

The following overheads were recorded for the month just ended:

	£'000
Rent	12
Heat and light	6
Welfare costs	2
Supervisors	
Department 1	1.5
Department 2	1

The service centres work for the other centres as follows:

	1	2	Stores	Maintenance
Work done by:				
Stores	50%	40%	-	10%
Maintenance	45%	50%	5%	-

Required:

(a) What would be the overheads allocated and apportioned to each department? **(3 marks)**

(b) Calculate the total overheads included in the production departments after reapportionment using the reciprocal method. **(4 marks)**

(c) Calculate the overhead absorption rate for each production department. Justify the basis that you have used. **(3 marks)**

(10 marks)

14 MARGINAL AND ABSORPTION COSTING MCQs

(a) The overhead absorption rate for product Y is £2.50 per direct labour hour. Each unit of Y requires 3 direct labour hours. Stock of product Y at the beginning of the month was 200 units and at the end of the month was 250 units. What is the difference in the profits reported for the month using absorption costing compared with marginal costing?

- A The absorption costing profit would be £375 less
- B The absorption costing profit would be £125 greater
- C The absorption costing profit would be £375 greater
- D The absorption costing profit would be £1,875 greater

(b) Which of the following is *not* a feature of activity based costing?

I It recognises that a single factor such as machine hours cannot be the driver of all overhead costs.

II It seeks to recognise the causes of the costs of activities through the use of cost drivers.

III It allocates the costs associated with cost drivers into cost pools.

IV It uses a basis such as labour hours to incorporate overheads into product costs.

A None of the above
B All of the above
C IV only
- D II only

15 PROFIT DIFFERENCES

18 mins

The following data have been extracted from the budgets and standard costs of ABC Limited, a company which manufactures and sells a single product.

	£ per unit
Selling price	45.00
Direct materials cost	10.00
Direct wages cost	4.00
Variable overhead cost	2.50

Fixed production overhead costs are budgeted at £400,000 per annum. Normal production levels are thought to be 320,000 units per annum.

Budgeted selling and distribution costs are as follows.

Variable	£1.50 per unit sold
Fixed	£80,000 per annum

Budgeted administration costs are £120,000 per annum.

The following patterns of sales and production are expected during the first six months of 20X3.

	January - March	April - June
Sales (units)	60,000	90,000
Production (units)	70,000	100,000

There is no stock on 1 January 20X3.

Required:

Prepare profit statements for each of the two quarters, in a columnar format, using the following

(a) Marginal costing.
(b) Absorption costing.

(10 marks)

16 JOB, BATCH AND CONTRACT COSTING MCQs

(a) Ali Pali Ltd is a small jobbing company. Budgeted direct labour hours for the current year were 45,000 hours and budgeted direct wages costs were £180,000.

Job number 34679, a rush job for which overtime had to be worked by skilled employees, had the following production costs.

	£	£
Direct materials		2,000
Direct wages		
Normal rate (400 hrs)	2,000	
Overtime premium	500	
		2,500
		4,000
Production overhead		8,500

Production overhead is based on a direct labour hour rate

If production overhead had been based on a percentage of direct wages costs instead, the production cost of job number 34679 would have been:

- A £5,500
- B £9,000
- C £10,250
- D £10,750

(b) A construction company has the following data concerning one of its contracts.

	£
Contract price	2,000,000
Value certified	1,300,000
Cash received	1,200,000
Costs incurred	1,050,000
Cost of work certified	1,000,000

The profit (to the nearest £1,000) to be attributed to the contract is:

- A £150,000
- B £277,000
- C £300,000
- D £950,000

17 INDRICAR LIMITED

18 mins

Indricar Limited manufactures carpets for the hotel trade. They do not carry any stock of finished goods as they only manufacture specifically to customers' orders. They do however hold a range of raw materials in their storeroom.

At 30 November 20X8 they had two incomplete jobs in progress. The details of this work and the costs incurred up to and including the 30 November 20X8 were as follows:

	Job X123		Job X124	
Direct material	£1,250		£722	
Direct labour	£820	(164 hours)	£600	(120 hours)
Factory overhead	£1,640		£1,200	

For the period from 1 December 20X8 to 31 December 20X8 the company accepted three more jobs, X125, X126 and X127 and incurred additional costs as follows:

	Job X123	Job X124	Job X125	Job X126	Job X127
Direct material issued from stores	£420	£698	£1,900	£1,221	£516
Direct material returned to stores	(£120)	Nil	(£70)	(£217)	Nil
Direct material transfers	(£100)	Nil	£100	Nil	Nil
Direct labour hours	52	78	312	151	58

Direct labour is paid at a rate of £5.00 per hour and factory production overhead is absorbed at the rate of 200% of labour cost.

During the month of December Jobs X123, X124 and X125 were completed, but Jobs X126 and X127 would not be completed until January 20X9. On completion of a job the company adds 20% to the total factory production in order to recover its selling, distribution and administration costs. The amounts invoiced to customers during December for the completed jobs were:

Job X123	Job X124	Job X125
£6,250	£6,000	£7,900

Required:

(a) Calculate the total production cost for Jobs X123, X124, X125, X126 and X127 taking into account the recovery of selling, distribution and administration overhead as appropriate.

(8 marks)

(b) Calculate the profit or loss arising on those Jobs completed and invoiced to customers during December 20X8.

(2 marks)

(10 marks)

18 PROCESS COSTING MCQs

The following data relates to questions (a) and (b)

A chemical is manufactured in two processes, X and Y. Data for process Y for last month are as follows.

Material transferred from process X	2,000 litres @ £4 per litre
Conversion costs incurred	£12,250
Output transferred to finished goods	1,600 litres
Closing work in progress	100 litres

Normal loss is 10% of input. All losses are fully processed and have a scrap value of £4 per litre.

Closing work in progress is fully complete for material, but is only 50 per cent processed.

(a) What is the value of the completed output (to the nearest £)?

   A   £15,808
   B   £17,289
   C   £17,244
   D   £17,600

(b) What is the value of the closing work in progress (to the nearest £)?

   A   £674
   B   £728
   C   £750
   D   £1,100

19 PRODUCT XK

18 mins

A chemical producer manufactures Product XK by means of two successive processes, Process 1 and Process 2. The information provided below relates to the most recent accounting period, period 10.

	Process 1	*Process 2*
Opening work in progress	Nil	Nil
Material input during period	2,400 units - cost £5,280	2,200 units (from Process 1)
Added material		£9,460
Direct labour	£2,260	£10,560
Factory overhead	100% of labour cost	2/3 of labour cost
Transfer to Process 2	2,200 units	
Transfer to finished goods		2,200 units
Closing work in progress	200 units	Nil

Closing work in progress: 100% complete with respect to materials and 30% complete with respect to labour and production overhead.

Required:

(a) Calculate the value of the goods transferred from Process 1 to Process 2 during period 10 and the value of the closing work in progress left in Process 1 at the end of period 10. **(7 marks)**

(b) Calculate the value of the goods transferred from Process 2, to finished goods, during period 10, and the value of one unit of production. **(3 marks)**

(10 marks)

20 JOINT AND BY-PRODUCTS MCQ

SH Ltd manufactures three joint products and one by-product from a single process.

Data for May are as follows.

Opening and closing stocks	Nil
Raw materials input	£90,000
Conversion costs	£70,000

Output

	Units	*Sales price* £ per unit
Joint product J	2,500	36
K	3,500	40
L	2,000	35
By-product M	4,000	1

By-product sales revenue is credited to the process account. Joint costs are apportioned on a physical units basis.

What were the full production costs of product K in May?

A   £45,500
B   £46,667
C   £68,250
D   £70,000

21 CHEMICALS X, Y AND Z   *18 mins*

Chemicals X, Y and Z are produced from a single joint process. The information below relates to the month of November 20X8:

Input into process:	Direct materials 3,200 litres, cost £24,000
	Direct labour £48,000
	Factory overheads are absorbed at 120% of prime cost

Output from process: Scrap normally accounts for 10% of input and can be sold for £16.20 per litre. Actual scrap in November 20X8 was 10% of input. Proceeds from the sale of scrap is credited to the process account.

Chemical X -	1,440 litres
Chemical Y -	864 litres
Chemical Z -	576 litres

The selling price of the three chemicals are
Chemical X - £100 per litre
Chemical Y - £80 per litre
Chemical Z - £60 per litre

Required:

Calculate the total cost of each of Chemicals X, Y and Z using the following methods for splitting joint costs.

(a)	Relative sales value	**(5 marks)**
(b)	Volume	**(5 marks)**

All workings should be to the nearest £. **(10 marks)**

22 SERVICE COSTING MCQ

Which of the following would be appropriate cost units for a transport business?

(i)   Cost per tonne-kilometre
(ii) Fixed cost per kilometre
(iii) Maintenance cost of each vehicle per kilometre

A   (i) only
B   (i) and (ii) only
C   (i) and (iii) only
D   All of them

23 HAPPY RETURNS LTD   *18 mins*

Happy Returns Ltd operates a haulage business with three vehicles. The following estimated cost and performance data are available:

Petrol	£0.50 per kilometre on average
Repairs	£0.30 per kilometre
Depreciation	£1.00 per kilometre, plus £50 per week per vehicle
Drivers' wages	£300.00 per week per vehicle
Supervision and general expenses	£550.00 per week
Loading costs	£6.00 per tonne

During week 26 it is expected that all three vehicles will be used, 280 tonnes will be loaded and a total of 3,950 kilometres travelled (including return journeys when empty) as shown in the following table:

Journey	Tonnes carried (one way)	Kilometres (one way)
1	34	180
2	28	265
3	40	390
4	32	115
5	26	220
6	40	480
7	29	90
8	26	100
9	25	135
	280	1,975

Required:

Calculate the average cost per tonne - kilometre for week 26. **(10 marks)**

24 TIME SERIES ANALYSIS MCQs

(a)   Under which of the following circumstances would a multiplicative model be preferred to an additive model in time series analysis?

A   When a model easily understood by non-accountants is required
B   When the trend is increasing or decreasing

C   When the trend is steady
D   When accurate forecasts are required

(b) Based on the last 15 periods the underlying trend of sales is y = 345.12 – 1.35x. If the 16th period has a seasonal factor of –23.62, assuming an additive forecasting model, then the forecast for that period, in whole units, is

    A   300
    B   301
    C   324
    D   325

---

25   SUMMER SUN   *18 mins*

The managers of a company have observed recent demand patterns of a particular product line in units. The original data, which have been partially analysed, are as follows.

Year	Quarter	Data	Sums of fours	Sums of twos
20X3	2	31		
	3	18		
			94	
	4	20		190
			96	
20X4	1	25		193
			97	
	2	33		195
			98	
	3	19		197
			99	
	4	21		198
			99	
20X5	1	26		198
			99	
	2	33		199
			100	
	3	19		201
			101	
	4	22		
20X6	1	27		

You have been commissioned to undertake the following analyses *and* to provide appropriate explanations. *(Work to three decimal places.)*

(a) Calculate the underlying four-quarterly moving average trend.   **(3 Marks)**

(b) Calculate the seasonally-adjusted demand for each quarter based on the multiplicative model if the seasonal factors are as follows.

Quarter 1	1.045
Quarter 2	1.343
Quarter 3	0.765
Quarter 4	0.847

(5 Marks)

(c) Explain the difference between the multiplicative and additive models for producing seasonally-adjusted data.   **(2 Marks)**

(10 marks)

26   **BREAKEVEN ANALYSIS MCQs**

(a)   A company manufactures a single product for which cost and selling price data are as follows.

Selling price per unit   £12
Variable cost per unit   £8
Fixed costs per month   £96,000
Budgeted monthly sales   30,000 units

The margin of safety, expressed as a percentage of budgeted monthly sales, is (to the nearest whole number):

A   20%
B   25%
C   73%
D   125%

(b)

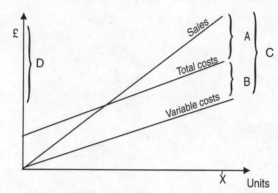

In the above breakeven chart, the contribution at level of activity x can be read as:

A   distance A
B   distance B
C   distance C
D   distance D

27   **BUILDING COMPANY**   *18 mins*

A building company constructs a standard unit which sells for £30,000. The company's costs can be readily identifiable between fixed and variable costs.

Budgeted data for the coming six months includes the following.

	Sales Units	Profit £
January	18	70,000
February	20	100,000
March	30	250,000
April	22	130,000
May	24	160,000
June	16	40,000

You are told that the fixed costs for the six months have been spread evenly over the period under review to arrive at the monthly profit projections.

Required:

Prepare a graph for total sales, costs and output for the six months under review that shows the breakeven point in units and revenue, total fixed costs, the variable cost line and the margin of safety for the total budgeted sales.   **(10 marks)**

28   **RELEVANT COSTING AND DECISION MAKING MCQs**

(a)   Sue is considering starting a new business and she has already spent £5,000 on market research and intends to spend a further £2,000.

In the assessment of the relevant costs of the decision to set up the business, market research costs are:

A   a sunk cost of £7,000
B   a sunk cost of £5,000 and an incremental cost of £2,000
C   a sunk cost of £2,000 and an incremental cost of £5,000
D   an opportunity cost of £7,000

(b) ABC Ltd is in the process of deciding whether or not to accept a special order. The order will require 100 litres of liquid X. ABC Ltd has 85 litres of liquid X in stock but no longer produces the product which required liquid X. It could therefore sell the 85 litres for £2 per litre if it rejected the special order. The liquid was purchased three years ago at a price of £8 per litre but its replacement cost is £10 per litre. What is the relevant cost of liquid X to include in the decision-making process?

A   £200
B   £320
C   £800
D   £1,000

29 ABC LTD

18 mins

ABC Ltd makes three products, all of which use the same machine which is available for 50,000 hours per period.

The standard costs of the products per unit are as follows.

	Product A	Product B	Product C
	£	£	£
Direct materials	70	40	80
Direct labour:			
Machinists (£8 per hour)	48	32	56
Assemblers (£6 per hour)	36	40	42
Total variable cost	154	112	178
Selling price per unit	£200	£158	£224
Maximum demand (units)	3,000	2,500	5,000

Fixed costs are £300,000 per period.

ABC Ltd could buy in similar quality products at the following unit prices.

A   £175
B   £140
C   £200

Required:

(a) Calculate the deficiency in machine hours for the next period.   **(2 Marks)**
(b) Determine which product(s) and quantities (if any) should be bought externally.   **(8 Marks)**

                                                    (10 marks)

30 DECISION MAKING WITH UNCERTAINTY MCQs

(a) Daily sales of product X by Y Ltd are likely to be 400 units, 500 units or 600 units. The probability of sales of 500 units is 0.5, while the probability of sales of 600 units is 0.1. What is the expected value of the daily sales volume?

A   1,500 units
B   500 units
C   710 units
D   470 units

(b)   The decision tree below relates to the cost of sales options for a company.

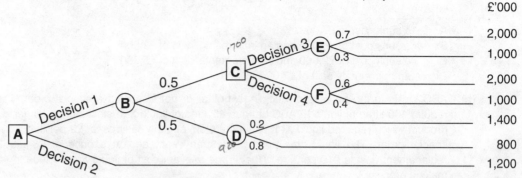

Which of the following statements are true for the above?

I   At decision point C, decision 4 would be chosen.
II   The expected value at outcome point B is £680,000.
III   Decision 2 would be chosen over decision 1.
IV   The expected value at outcome point D is £920,000.

A   I, III and IV
B   IV only
C   I and III
D   III only

31   GEOLOGICAL TESTS

18 mins

An oil company has recently acquired rights in a certain area to conduct surveys and test drillings, to lead to extracting oil where it is found in commercially exploitable quantities.

The area is already considered to have good potential for finding oil in commercial quantities. At the outset the company has the choice to conduct further geological tests or to carry out a drilling programme immediately. Given the known conditions, the company estimates that there is a 70% chance of further tests showing a 'success'.

Whether the tests show the possibility of ultimate success or not, or even if no tests are undertaken at all, the company could still pursue its drilling programme or alternatively consider selling its rights to drill in the area. Thereafter, however, if it carries out the drilling programme, the likelihood of final success or failure depends on the foregoing stages.

If 'successful' tests have been carried out, the probability of success in drilling is 80%.

If tests have indicated 'failure', then the probability of success in drilling is 20%.

If no tests have been carried out at all, the probability of success in drilling is 55%.

Costs and revenues have been estimated for all possible outcomes and the net cash flow of each is given below.

Outcome	Net cash flow £m
Success	
With prior tests	100
Without prior tests	120
Failure	
With prior tests	– 50
Without prior tests	– 40
Sales of exploitation rights	
Prior tests show 'success'	65
Prior tests show 'failure'	15
Without prior tests	45

Required:

(a)   Draw up a decision tree to represent the above information.   **(5 marks)**
(b)   Evaluate the tree in order to advise the company on its best course of action.   **(5 marks)**

(10 marks)

32 LINEAR PROGRAMMING MCQs

(a)   A company produces two types of orange juice, ordinary (X cartons per year) and premium (Y cartons per year). Which of the following inequalities represents the fact that the amount of ordinary orange juice produced must be no more than twice the amount of premium orange juice produced.

    A $X \geq 2Y$
    B $2X \geq Y$
    C $2X \leq Y$
    D $X \leq 2Y$

(b)   In a linear programming problem, the constraints are $X \leq 41$ and $Y \geq 19$. Describe the feasible region, assuming where appropriate that the axes also constitute boundaries.

    A   A rectangle to the left of $X = 41$ and below $Y = 19$
    B   An infinite rectangle to the right of $X = 41$ and below $Y = 19$
    C   An infinite region above $Y = 19$ and to the right of $X = 41$
    D   An infinite rectangle to the left of $X = 41$ and above $Y = 19$

33 CUCKFIELD (PILOT PAPER)   *18 mins*

Cuckfield manufactures two products, the D and the H, which have the following standard costs per unit:

	D £	H £
Materials		
A (at £3/kg)	9	6
N (at £7/litre)	3.50	14
Labour		
Skilled (at £10/hour)	10	14
Semi skilled (at £6/hour)	9	9
Overheads		
(at 60% of direct material cost)	5.70	13.80
	37.20	56.80
Selling price	40.00	70.00
Profit	2.80	13.20

Unfortunately there is a problem obtaining some of the raw materials for production. Only 3,000 kg of material A is available and only 1,000 litres of material N can be found for the week.

There are 45 semi-skilled workers who can only work a 40 hour week as there has been an overtime ban. Skilled workers are guaranteed a 35 hour week. There are 20 of these workers and there is no overtime ban for these employees.

The company's objective is to maximise contribution.

Required:

(a)   Formulate the constraint equations for this problem excluding the non-negativity constraint.

                                                                              (4 marks)

(b)   Plot the constraints on a graph and suggest possible points for the optimal solution.
      (Note: calculations for the optimal solution are NOT required).

                                                                              (6 marks)

                                                                              (10 marks)

34 INTEREST MCQs

(a)   A bank offers depositors a nominal 4% pa, with interest payable quarterly. What is the effective annual rate of interest?

    A   1%
    B   4%
    C   1.025%
    D   4.06%

(b) An annual rent of £1,000 is to be received for ten successive years. The first payment is due tomorrow.

Assuming the relevant interest rate to be 8%, the present value of this stream of cash flows is closest to

    A   £6,247
    B   £6,710
  \C   £7,247
    D   £7,710

35 FIXED INTEREST MORTGAGE
18 mins

A fixed-interest ten-year £100,000 mortgage is to be repaid by 40 equal quarterly payments in arrears. Interest is charged at 3% a quarter on the outstanding part of the debt.

Required:

(a) Find the sum to which an investment of £100,000 would grow after 10 years, at a quarterly compound interest rate of 3%. **(2 marks)**

(b) Using your answer to (a), or otherwise, calculate the quarterly repayments on the mortgage. **(7 marks)**

(c) Find the effective annual rate of interest on the mortgage. **(1 mark)**

The sum, S, of a geometric series of n terms, with first term A and common ratio R, is given by S =

$$\frac{A(R^n - 1)}{(R - 1)}$$ **(10 marks)**

36 INVESTMENT APPRAISAL MCQ

When the discount rate is 8%, an investment has a net present value of £18,000. At 9% its net present value is −£11,000 (*minus* eleven thousand pounds). The internal rate of return of this investment (to two decimal places) is

  A   8.62%
  B   8.38%
  C   8.5%
  D   10.57%

37 BARCOMBE (PILOT PAPER)
18 mins

Barcombe has been looking at a potential project which has the following cash inflows:

End of year	£'000
1	15
2	17
3	22
4	2

To acquire these inflows Barcombe would have to invest £36,000 in fixed assets now. The assets would be expected to be sold at the end of the project for £2,000.

Required:

(a) Calculate the net present value of the project using 10% and 20% as the discount factors. **(5 marks)**

(b) Using your results from part (a), calculate the internal rate of return for this investment to one decimal place. **(3 marks)**

(c) Comment on the use of these two net present values to estimate the internal rate of return. **(2 marks)**

(10 marks)

38   PRICING MCQ

S Limited manufactures product G, for which cost data are as follows.

	£ per unit
Direct material and labour	7
Variable overhead	2
Total variable cost	9

The following revenue functions have been established for product G.

Price = 25 − (0.2 × quantity)

Marginal revenue = 25 − (0.4 × quantity)

At what selling price per unit would profits from product G be maximised?

A   £13.50
B   £16.00
C   £17.00
D   £23.72

39   DEMAND, PRICE, REVENUE AND COSTS   *18 mins*

When the price of a product X is £48, seventy units are demanded each week. When the price is £78, only 40 units are demanded each week. The manufacturer's fixed costs are £1,710 a week and variable costs are £9 per unit.

Required:

(a)   Calculate the equation of the demand function linking price (P) to quantity demanded (X).
(b)   Calculate the equation of the revenue function linking revenue to price (P) and quantity sold (X).
(c)   Determine the equation of the total cost function.

(10 marks)

40   PREPARING THE MASTER BUDGET MCQs

(a)   What does the statement 'sales is the principal budget factor' mean?

A   Sales is the largest item in the budget
B   The level of sales will determine the level of cash at the end of the period
C   The level of sales will determine the level of profit at the end of the period
D   The company's activities are limited by the level of sales it can achieve

(b)   Budgeted sales of X for December are 18,000 units. At the end of the production process for X, 10% of production units are scrapped as defective. Opening stocks of X for December are budgeted to be 15,000 units and closing stocks will be 11,400 units. All stocks of finished goods must have successfully passed the quality control check. The production budget for X for December, in units is

A   12,960
B   14,400
C   15,840
D   16,000

41   HAROLD GODWINSSON LTD   *18 mins*

Harold Godwinsson Ltd makes two products, the Viking and the Norman, and is preparing an annual budget for 20X3.

The following information is available.

STANDARD DATA PER UNIT OF PRODUCT

Direct material	Standard price per kilo £	Viking kg	Norman kg
Athelstan	1.50	8	4
Halfdan	4.00	5	10

Direct wages	Standard rate per hour £	Hours	Hours
Thames	3.50	6	12
Serfs	1.00	10	6

Fixed production overhead is absorbed on a direct labour hour basis. There is no variable overhead. Administration, selling and distribution costs are absorbed on a budgeted basis of $16^2/3\%$ of production cost.

Gross profit on production cost is budgeted at 25% of selling price.

BUDGETED DATA: SALES FOR THE YEAR

Division	Viking £'000	Norman £'000
Danelaw	1,808	1,280
Wessex	600	1,600
Mercia	900	2,600
Kent	500	800

Finished goods stock, valued at standard production cost

	Viking	Norman
1 January 20X3	238	628
31 December 20X3	595	1,413

	Athelstan £'000	Halfdan £'000
Direct material stocks, valued at standard prices		
1 January 20X3	120	160
31 December 20X3	40	180

Fixed production overhead, per annum = £3,717,000
Direct labour hours, per annum = 1,062,000 hours

It is expected that there will be no work in progress at the beginning or end of the year.

Required:

Using the information given above, prepare the following.

(a) Production budget
(b) Direct materials cost budget
(c) Purchases budget

(10 Marks)

42   **FURTHER ASPECTS OF BUDGETING MCQs**

(a)   A flexible budget is

   A   a budget comprising variable production costs only

   B   a budget which is updated with actual costs and revenues as they occur during the budget period

   C   a budget which shows the costs and revenues at different levels of activity

   D   a budget which is prepared using a computer spreadsheet model

(b)   Leanne Ltd budgets to make 1,000 units next period and estimates that the standard labour cost of a unit will be £10. In fact 1,100 units are made at a labour cost of £11,500. For the purposes of budgetary control of the expenditure on labour cost which two figures should be compared?

	Actual	Budget
A	£1,000	£1,100
B	£11,500	£10,000
C	£11,500	£11,000
D	£11,000	£10,000

43   JAK LTD   *18 mins*

Jak Ltd is a small company which manufactures a single product, the Anori. The company's directors have just received the actual results for May 20X3 for comparison with the budget for the same period, set out below.

	Budget	Actual results
Production and sales of the Anori (units)	40,000	48,000
	£	£
Sales revenue	50,000	55,200
Direct materials	12,000	16,800
Direct labour	8,000	10,290
Variable o/hds (allocated on basis of direct labour hrs)	5,000	5,560
Fixed overheads	15,000	16,500
Total costs	40,000	49,150
Profit	10,000	6,050

Clearly the directors of the company are concerned about the results, particularly bearing in mind that the following operational changes were authorised after the budget for May 20X3 had been prepared in the belief they would increase the profitability of Jak Ltd.

(a)   The unit selling price of the Anori was cut from £1.25 to £1.15 on the 1st May 20X3 in a deliberate attempt to increase sales.

(b)   To reduce operating costs it was decided to use a cheaper but more wasteful alternative material - a 15% price reduction was obtained.

(c)   The hourly rate for direct labour was increased from £5.00 to £5.25 in order to encourage greater productivity. However, overtime had to be authorised during the month in order to meet demand.

(d)   There was a one-off sales promotion campaign costing £2,000.

Required:

Prepare a flexible budget which will be useful for management control purposes.   **(10 marks)**

44   STANDARD COSTING MCQs

(a)   Which of the following would *not* be used to estimate standard direct material prices?

    A   The availability of bulk purchase discounts
    B   Purchase contracts already agreed
    C   The forecast movement of prices in the market
    D   Performance standards in operation

(b)   JC Limited operates a bottling plant. The liquid content of a filled bottle of product T is 2 litres. During the filling process there is a 30% loss of liquid input due to spillage and evaporation. The standard price of the liquid is £1.20 per litre. The standard cost of the liquid per bottle of product T, to the nearest penny, is

    A   £2.40
    B   £2.86
    C   £3.12
    D   £3.43

45   QUESTION WITH HELP: DOODLE LTD   *18 mins*

Doodle Ltd manufactures and sells a range of products, one of which is the squiggle.

The following data relates to the expected costs of production and sale of the squiggle.

Budgeted production for the year	11,400 units
Standard details for one unit:	
direct materials	30 metres at £6.10 per metre
direct wages	
Department P	40 hours at £2.20 per hour
Department Q	36 hours at £2.50 per hour
Budgeted costs and hours per annum	
Variable production overhead (factory total)	
Department P	£525,000 : 700,000 hours
Department Q	£300,000 : 600,000 hours

Fixed overheads to be absorbed by the squiggle

Production	£1,083,000 (absorbed on a direct labour hour basis)
Administration	£125,400 (absorbed on a unit basis)
Marketing	£285,000 (absorbed on a unit basis)

Required:

(a)   Prepare a standard cost sheet for the squiggle, to include the following.

    (i)   Standard total direct cost
    (ii)   Standard variable production cost
    (iii)   Standard production cost
    (iv)   Standard full cost of sale   **(8 marks)**

(b)   Calculate the standard sales price per unit which allows for a standard profit of 10% on the sales
    price.   **(2 marks)**
                                                                                (10 marks)

46   BASIC VARIANCE ANALYSIS MCQs

(a)   The standard cost information for SC Limited's single product shows the standard direct material
    content to be 4 litres at £3 per litre.

Actual results for May were:

Production	1,270 units
Material used	5,000 litres at a cost of £16,000

All of the materials were purchased and used during the period. The direct material price and
usage variances for May are:

	Material price	*Material usage*
A	£1,000 (F)	£240 (F)
B	£1,000 (A)	£240 (F)
C	£1,000 (F)	£240 (A)
D	£1,000 (A)	£256 (F)

The following information relates to questions (b) and (c)

The standard variable production overhead cost of product B is as follows.

4 hours at £1.70 per hour = £6.80 per unit

During period 3 the production of B amounted to 400 units. The labour force worked 1,690 hours, of
which 30 hours were recorded as idle time. The variable overhead cost incurred was £2,950.

(b)   The variable production overhead expenditure variance for period 3 was

    A   £77 adverse
    B   £128 adverse
    C   £128 favourable
    D   £230 adverse

(c)   The variable production overhead efficiency variance for period 3 was

A	£102 favourable
B	£102 adverse
C	£105 adverse
D	£153 adverse

47 BRAIN LTD

18 mins

Brain Ltd produces and sells one product only, the Blob, the standard cost for one unit being as follows.

	£
Direct material A - 10 kilograms at £20 per kg	200
Direct material B - 5 litres at £6 per litre	30
Direct wages - 5 hours at £6 per hour	30
Direct expense	5
Fixed production overhead	50
Total standard cost	315

The fixed overhead included in the standard cost is based on an expected monthly output of 900 units. Fixed production overhead is absorbed on the basis of direct labour hours.

During April 20X3 the actual results were as follows.

Production	800 units
Material A	7,800 kg used, costing £159,900
Material B	4,300 units used, costing £23,650
Direct wages	4,200 hours worked for £24,150
Direct expenses	£3,750
Fixed production overhead	£47,000

Required:

(a) Calculate price and usage variances for each material.

(b) Calculate labour rate and efficiency variances.

(c) Calculate the expense variance.

(d) Calculate fixed production overhead expenditure and volume variances and then subdivide the volume variance. **(10 marks)**

48 FURTHER VARIANCE ANALYSIS MCQs

(a) W Ltd uses a standard absorption costing system. The following data relate to one of its products.

	£ per unit	£ per unit
Selling price		27.00
Variable costs	12.00	
Fixed costs	9.00	
		21.00
Profit		6.00

Budgeted sales for control period 7 were 2,400 units, but actual sales were 2,550 units. The revenue earned from these sales was £67,320.

Profit reconciliation statements are drawn up using absorption costing principles. What sales variances would be included in such a statement for period 7?

	Price	*Volume*
A	£1,530 (F)	£900 (F)
B	£1,530 (A)	£900 (F)
C	£1,530 (F)	£900 (A)
D	£1,530 (A)	£900 (A)

(b) A standard marginal costing system:

(i) calculates fixed overhead variances using the budgeted absorption rate per unit

(ii) calculate sales volume variances using the standard contribution per unit

(iii) values finished goods stock at the standard variable cost of production

Which of the above statements is/are correct?

A	(i), (ii) and (iii)	
B	(i) and (ii) only	
\ C	(ii) and (iii) only	
D	(i) and (iii) only	

49 TARDIS LTD

18 mins

Tardis Ltd manufactures three products, the Dalek, the Yeti and the Cyberman. The budget relating to period 1 is given below.

	Standard selling price per unit	*Standard cost of product per unit*	*Profit per unit*	*Budgeted sales*	*Standard mix*
	£	£	£	Units	%
Dalek	5	3	2	500	50
Yeti	7	4	3	300	30
Cyberman	10	6	4	200	20

Actual sales in period 1 were as follows.

	Sales Units	*Mix %*
Dalek	700	46.7
Yeti	300	20.0
Cyberman	500	33.3
	1,500	100.0

Required:

Calculate the sales volume variance, sales mix variance and sales quantity variance for each product.

(10 marks)

50 INDEX NUMBERS MCQs

(a) The price index for a commodity in the current year is 135 (base year = 100). The current price for the commodity is £55.35 per kg.

What was the price per kg in the base year?

A	£35	
\ B	£41	
C	£74.72	
D	£100	

(b) A country uses three items as the basis for its wholesale price index. Relevant information about the items is as follows.

Item	*Quantity purchased Year 1* '000 units	*Price per unit Year 1* francs	*Quantity purchased Year 6* '000 units	*Price per unit Year 6* francs
X	50	10	80	30
Y	90	12	110	16
Z	110	14	130	12

Year 1 is used as the basis for all price indices.

What is the Laspeyre price index for year 6 (to 1 decimal place)?

A	73.2
B	126.3
\ C	136.5
D	145.2

51 WEIGHTED INDEX

The following information relates to three products sold by a company over a five-year period.

| | Year 1 | | Year 5 | |
	'000 units sold	Selling price per unit £	'000 units sold	Selling price per unit £
Product A	76	0.60	72	0.78
Product B	52	0.75	60	1.00
Product C	28	1.10	40	1.32

Required:

(a) Calculate the percentage increase in total sales revenue over the period. **(2 marks)**

(b) Calculate the Laspeyres price index for Year 5 based on Year 1. **(3 marks)**

(c) Provide an explanation of the change in sales over the period, using the answers to (a) and (b) above. **(5 marks)**

(10 marks)

52 PERFORMANCE MEASUREMENT MCQs

(a) Manager M is the manager of profit centre P. Over which of the following is he likely to have control?

    (i)   Controllable costs
    (ii)   Transfer prices
    (iii)   Selling prices
    (iv)   Apportioned head office costs

    A   All of the above
    B   (i), (ii) and (iii)
    C   (i) and (ii)
    D   (i) and (iii)

(b) The manager of a trading division of the BM Group has complete discretion over the purchase and use of fixed assets and stock. Head office keeps a central bank account, collecting all cash from debtors and paying all creditors. The performance of the manager of the division is assessed on the basis of the division's controllable residual income. The BM Group requires a rate of return of 12% from all its divisions. The latest balance sheet and profit results for the division are as follows.

	£'000
Divisional profit	62
Head office management charges	4
Divisional net profit	58

	£'000	£'000
Divisional fixed assets		380
Divisional working capital		
Stock	18	
Debtors	41	
Creditors	(28)	
		31
		411

What is the controllable residual income for the division for the latest period?

    A   £10,240
    B   £14,240
    C   £16,400
    D   £62,000

53   PERFORMANCE MEASUREMENT   *18 mins*

(a)   Helmut runs the Western division of a large multinational company. He has prepared the following forecast for the year 20X0.

	£
Profit before depreciation	100,000
Depreciation	25,000
Net current assets at 1/1/20X0	50,000
Net book value of fixed assets at 1/1/20X0	200,000

The company's cost of capital is 10%.

He is considering selling a fixed asset with a net book value of £7,500 which, after depreciation of £600, generates a profit per annum of £3,000. The proceeds and a subsidy from head office would be used to purchase a new machine for £20,000 which would generate an annual profit of £6,000 after depreciation of £1,500.

Required:

(i)   Assuming that Helmut does not sell and replace the machine, using opening year balance sheet values calculate the following.

   (1)   The division's return on capital employed.   **(2 marks)**
   (2)   The division's residual income.   **(2 marks)**

(ii)   If Helmut does sell and replace the machine, calculate the following.

   (1)   The division's return on capital employed   **(2 marks)**
   (2)   The division's residual income   **(2 marks)**

(b)   Draw up a list of possible performance measures for a hotel. Divide the measures into those relating to financial performance, those relating to competitive performance, those relating to resource utilisation and those relating to service quality.   **(2 marks)**

                                                                             (10 marks)

Exam answer bank

1 INFORMATION FOR MANAGEMENT MCQs

(a) D **Data** is the raw material for data processing. **Information** is data that has been processed in such a way as to be meaningful to the person who receives it. Statement I is therefore incorrect.

An organisation's financial accounting records are an example of an **internal** source of information. Statement II is therefore incorrect.

The main objective of a non-profit making organisation is usually to provide goods and services. Statement III is therefore correct.

(b) A **Financial accounts** (not management accounts) detail the performance of an organisation over a defined period and the state of affairs at the end of that period. **Management accounts** are used to aid management record, plan and control the organisation's activities and to help the decision-making process.

2 THE ROLE OF INFORMATION TECHNOLOGY IN MANAGEMENT INFORMATION MCQs

(a) A A **screen** is an output device.

A **keyboard** is an input device.

The **CPU** performs the processing function.

A **disk** is a storage device.

(b) B **MICR** is the recognition of characters by a machine that reads special formatted characters printed in magnetic ink.

OMR involves marking a pre-printed source document which is then read by a device which translates the marks on the document into machine code.

CPU is the central processing unit.

Option B is therefore correct.

3 COST CLASSIFICATION MCQs

(a) D It would be appropriate to use the cost per invoice processed and the cost per supplier account for control purposes. Therefore items (ii) and (iii) are suitable cost units and the correct answer is D.

Postage cost, item (i), is an expense of the department, therefore option A is not a suitable cost unit.

If you selected option B or option C you were probably rushing ahead and not taking care to read all the options. Items (ii) and (iii) *are* suitable cost units, but neither of them are the *only* suitable suggestions.

(b) A Special designs, and the hire of tools etc for a particular job can be traced to a specific cost unit. Therefore they are direct expenses and the correct answer is A.

Item (iii) is a selling and distribution overhead and item (iv) describes production overheads.

4 COST BEHAVIOUR MCQs

(a) A Variable costs are conveniently deemed to increase or decrease in direct proportion to changes in output. Therefore the correct answer is A. Descriptions B and D imply a changing unit rate, which does not comply with this convention. Description C relates to a fixed cost.

(b) B The cost depicted begins as a linear variable cost, increasing at a constant rate in line with activity. At a certain point the cost becomes fixed regardless of the level of activity. The vehicle hire costs follow this pattern.

Graphs for the other options would look like this.

BPP PUBLISHING

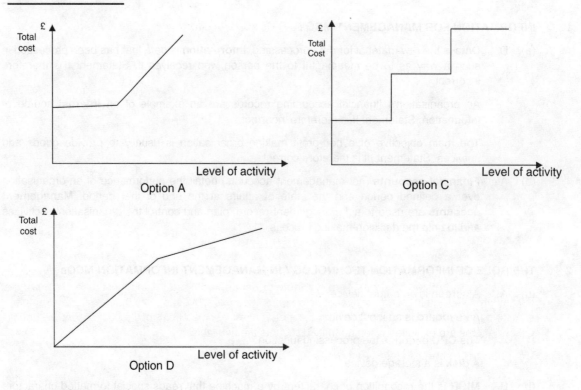

5   COST BEHAVIOUR AGAIN

REPORT

To: Managing Director
From: Chartered Certified Accountant
Subject: Cost behaviour   Date: 18 May 20X8

The classification of costs by their behaviour

Costs may be classified in many different ways, but one of the most important ways from the point of view of managing a business is classification according to how costs change in response to changes in the level of the business's activity. The main distinction is between **fixed costs** and **variable costs**.

Fixed costs are those that **do not change whatever the level of the business's activity**. The cost of rental of a business premises is a common example: this is a constant amount (at least within a stated time period) that does not vary with the level of activity conducted on the premises. Other examples are business rates, salaries, buildings insurance and so on.

A sketch graph of a fixed cost would look like this.

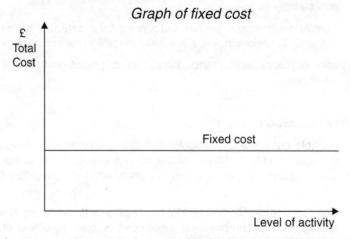

Graph of fixed cost

Variable costs, of course, are those that **do vary with the level of activity**: if a business produces two widgets, for example, it uses twice as many materials as it does for one widget. Similarly if it sells more goods, its sales administration costs like stationery and postage will vary proportionately.

A sketch graph of a variable cost would look like this.

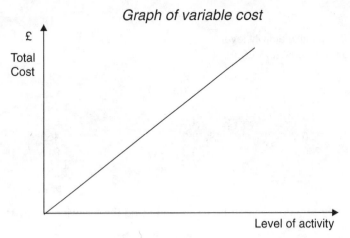

Graph of variable cost

Many costs behave in a more complicated fashion than these simple models suggest. For example a telephone bill has a fixed element (the standing charge) and a variable element (the cost of calls). These are called **mixed costs** (or **semi-variable** or **semi-fixed costs**). Other costs are **stepped**: that is, they are fixed within a certain level of activity but increase above or below that level. For example, if a second factory has to be rented to produce the required volume of output the cost of rent will double. Other patterns are exhibited when quantity discounts are available.

Cost behaviour and total and unit costs

If the variable cost of producing a widget is £5 per unit then it will remain at that cost per unit no matter how many widgets are produced. However if the business's fixed costs are £5,000 then the fixed cost per unit will decrease the more units are produced: one unit will have fixed costs of £5,000 per unit; if 2,500 are produced the fixed cost per unit will be £2; if 5,000 are produced fixed costs per unit will be only £1. Thus as the level of activity increases the total costs per unit (fixed costs plus variable costs) will decrease.

In sketch graph form this may be illustrated as follows.

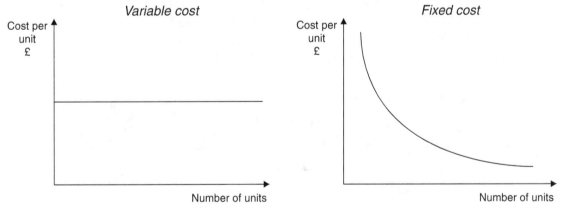

The importance of cost behaviour

The classification of costs according to behaviour serves a number of purposes.

(a)   In **planning** it is necessary to know what costs will be at various possible levels of activity so that a level appropriate to the overall resources of the business may be chosen.

(b)   To **maintain control** of the business it is necessary to compare actual results achieved to those expected and this will require adjustments depending upon actual and expected levels of activity.

(c)   When marginal costing is used, for example for **decision making**, the distinction between fixed and variable costs is fundamental to this approach.

Signed: Chartered Certified Accountant

6   **CORRELATION AND REGRESSION MCQs**

(a)   D   If C = 1,000 + 250P, then fixed costs are £1,000 and variable costs are £250 per unit.

(b)   D   The correlation coefficient of 0.9 is very close to 1 and so there is a very strong relationship between x and y.

7   **SOUTH**

(a)   Let   x = monthly activity level
         y = total cost (in £'000)

x	y	xy	x^2
units	£'000		
300	3.8	1,140	90,000
400	4.0	1,600	160,000
150	3.0	450	22,500
260	3.5	910	67,600
1,110	14.3	4,100	340,100

n = 4

The total cost equation can be calculated using the following equation which is provided in your examination.

If y = a + bx, $b = \dfrac{n\Sigma xy - \Sigma x \Sigma y}{n\Sigma x^2 - (\Sigma x)^2}$

and $a = \dfrac{\Sigma y}{n} - b\dfrac{\Sigma x}{n}$

$b = \dfrac{(4 \times 4,100) - (1,110 \times 14.3)}{(4 \times 340,100) - (1,110)^2}$

$= \dfrac{16,400 - 15,873}{1,360,400 - 1,232,100}$

$= \dfrac{527}{128,300} = 0.0041$

$a = \dfrac{14.3}{4} - 0.0041 \times \dfrac{1,110}{4}$

$= 3.575 - 1.13775$

$= 2.43725$, say 2.437 (to 3 dp)

Therefore, total cost equation (in £'000) = y

y = 2.437 + 0.0041x

where x = the monthly activity level

(Alternatively, total cost equation (in £), y, is

y = 2.437 + 4.1x.)

(b)   (i)   Using y (in £'000) = 2.437 + 0.0041x

where x = 200

y   = 2.437 + (200 × 0.0041)
    = 2.437 + 0.82
    = 3.257

Therefore, at an activity level of 200 units, total cost = £3,257

Since 200 units lies within the range of data used to calculate the total cost equation (150 – 400 units) a fair degree of reliance can be placed on this estimated cost.

(ii)   Using y (in £'000) = 2.437 + 0.0041x

where x = 500

y   = 2.437 + (500 × 0.0041)
    = 2.437 + 2.05
    = 4.487

Therefore, at an activity level of 500 units, total cost = £4,487.

Since 500 units lies outside the range of data used to calculate the total cost equation (150 – 400 units) the total cost calculated is probably not a very reliable estimation.

8   **MATERIAL COSTS MCQs**

(a)   A   With LIFO, if newer stocks cost more to buy from suppliers than older stocks, the costs of material issued and used will be higher. It follows that the cost of sales will be higher and the profit lower.

Closing stocks with LIFO will be priced at the purchase price of earlier items that were received into stock. In a period of rising prices, this means that closing stocks will be valued at old, out-of-date and low prices. Therefore the correct answer is A.

If you chose option B you were correct about the profits but your reasoning concerning the stock values was wrong.

(b)   D $EOQ = \sqrt{\dfrac{2 \times £400 \times (250 \times 48)}{£20 \times 10\%}} = 2,191$

Therefore the correct answer is D.

If you selected option A you used **weekly** usage in the calculations instead of the annual usage.

If you selected option B you did not take ten per cent of the material cost as the annual stockholding cost.

If you selected option C you omitted the 2.

(c)   D   The easiest way to solve this question is to draw up a stores ledger control account.

STORES LEDGER CONTROL ACCOUNT

	£		£
Opening stock b/f	18,500	Creditors (returns)	2,300
Creditors/cash (deliveries)	142,000	Overhead account (indirect materials)	25,200
		WIP (balancing figure)	116,900
		Closing stock c/f	16,100
	160,500		160,500

If you selected option C you determined the correct value of the direct materials issued but you **reversed the entries.**

If you selected options A or B you placed the figure for returns on the **wrong side of your account**, and in option A you **reversed the entries** for the issue of direct materials from stores.

9   **WIVELSFIELD**

(a)   New EOQ can be calculated using the following equation which is provided in your examination.

$EOQ = \sqrt{\dfrac{2 C_o D}{C_H}}$

Where   Co = £2
        D = 15,000 units
        CH = 10% × £15 = £1.50 × 0.97 = £1.455

At an order quantity of 200, there is a 3% discount, so CH will be adjusted to equal 97% × £1.50 = £1.455.

$EOQ = \sqrt{\dfrac{2 \times £2 \times 15,000}{1.455}}$

= 203 units

Order quantity Q	Purchase cost £	Order costs £	Holding costs £	Total £
203 (W1)	218,250	148	148	218,546
500 (W2)	213,750	60	356	214,166
700 (W3)	209,250	44	488	209,782

An order quantity of 700 units gives rise to the lowest total cost and therefore 700 units is the optimal order quantity.

Workings

(1)   **Purchase costs** = £15 × 0.97 × 15,000 = £218,250

   Order costs = Number of orders × £2

   Number of orders = $\dfrac{15,000}{203}$ = 73.89, say 74

   ∴ order costs = 74 × £2 = £148

   Holding costs = Costs of holding average stock

   Average stock = $\dfrac{Q}{2} = \dfrac{203}{2}$ = 102

   ∴ Holding costs = 102 × 10% × £15 × 0.97
      = £148

(2)   **Purchase costs** = £15 × 0.95 × 15,000 = £213,750

   Order costs = Number of orders × £2

   Number of orders = $\dfrac{15,000}{500}$ = 30

   ∴ Order costs = 30 × £2 = £60

   Holding costs = costs of holding average stock

   Average stock = $\dfrac{Q}{2} = \dfrac{500}{2}$ = 250

   Cost of holding one unit of stock = £15 × 0.95 × 0.1
                = £1.425

   ∴ Holding costs = 250 × £1.425
        = £356

(3)   **Purchase costs** = £15 × 0.93 × 15,000 = £209,250

   Order costs = Number of orders × £2

   Number of orders = $\dfrac{15,000}{700}$ = 21.43, say 22

   ∴ order costs = 22 × £2 = £44

   Holding costs = cost of holding average stock

   Average stock = $\dfrac{Q}{2} = \dfrac{700}{2}$ = 350

   ∴ Holding costs = 350 × 93% × £15 × 0.1
        = £488

(b)   The first discount band of 0-199 units has been excluded because this band is below the current EOQ. The new EOQ of 203 units is subject to a 3% discount and so the total costs of £203,500 and 700 units being ordered were calculated taking into account the discounts that were available at each order level.

10   LABOUR COSTS MCQs

(a)   B   The only direct costs are the wages paid to direct workers for ordinary time, plus the basic pay for overtime.

   £25,185 + £5,440 = £30,625.

   If you selected option A you forgot to include the basic pay for overtime of direct workers, which is always classified as a direct labour cost.

   If you selected option C you have included overtime premium and shift allowances, which are usually treated as indirect costs. However, if overtime and shiftwork are incurred specifically for a particular cost unit, then they are classified as direct costs of that cost unit. There is no mention of such a situation here.

Option D includes sick pay, which is classified as an indirect labour cost.

(b) B The credit balance on the wages control account indicates that the amount of wages incurred and analysed between direct wages and indirect wages was **higher** than the wages paid through the bank. Therefore there was a £12,000 balance of **wages owing** at the end of February and statement B is not correct. Therefore the correct option is B.

Statement A is correct. £128,400 of wages was paid from the bank account.

Statement C is correct. £79,400 of direct wages was transferred to the work in progress control account.

Statement D is correct. £61,000 of indirect wages was transferred to the production overhead control account.

11 REMUNERATION SCHEMES

(a) (i) **Piecework scheme**

Level of output (units)		80	120	210
Standard minutes produced ($\times 3$)		240	360	630
$\therefore$ Piecework value ($\times$ £0.1)		£24	£36	£63
$\therefore$ Earnings	(note)	£35.20	£36	£63

(*Note.* Earnings are guaranteed at 80% of time-based pay = 80% $\times$ 8 hours $\times$ £5.5 = £35.20. Since this is greater than the piecework earnings, it will be the amount paid.)

(ii) **Premium bonus system**

	80	120	210
Level of output (units)	80	120	210
Standard hours allowed ($\times$ 3/60)	4	6	10.5
Actual hours taken	8	8	8
$\therefore$ Time saved - hours	-	-	2.5
Premium bonus - 75% of time saved	-	-	1.875
$\therefore$ Hours to be paid	8	8	9.875
at £5.5 per hour = earnings	£44	£44	£54.31

(b) **Idle time** occurs when employees cannot get on with their own work, though this is through no fault of their own. Idle time occurs when machines break down and when there is a shortage of work.

Idle time can be measured by calculating an **idle time ratio.**

$$\text{Idle time ratio} = \frac{\text{Idle hours}}{\text{Total hours}} \times 100\%$$

12 OVERHEADS AND ABSORPTION COSTING MCQs

(a) B Overhead absorption rate $= \dfrac{\text{budgeted overheads}}{\text{budgeted labour hours}} = \dfrac{£148,750}{8,500} = £17.50 \text{ per hr}$

If you selected option A you divided the actual overheads by the budgeted labour hours. Option C is based on the actual overheads and actual labour hours. If you selected option D you divided the budgeted overheads by the actual hours.

(b) D

	£
Overhead absorbed = £17.50 $\times$ 7,928 =	138,740
Overhead incurred =	146,200
Under-absorbed overhead =	7,460

If you selected options A or B you calculated the difference between the budgeted and actual overheads and interpreted it as an under or over absorption. If you selected option C you performed the calculations correctly but misinterpreted the result as an over absorption.

13   WARNINGLID

(a)

	Production departments		Service centres		
	1	*2*	*Stores*	*Maintenance*	*Total*
	£	£	£	£	£
Rent (W1)	8,850	2,100	600	450	12,000
Heat and light (W2)	4,320	1,200	240	240	6,000
Welfare costs (W3)	1,120	480	240	160	2,000
Supervisors	1,500	1,000	-	-	2,500
	15,790	4,780	1,080	850	22,500

Workings

(1)   **Rent**

Rent is allocated on the basis of floor area. Total floor area = 8,000 m^2.

Production department 1 $\dfrac{5,900}{8,000} \times £12,000 = £8,850$

Production department 2 $\dfrac{1,400}{8,000} \times £12,000 = £2,100$

Stores centre $\dfrac{400}{8,000} \times £12,000 = £600$

Maintenance centre $\dfrac{300}{8,000} \times £12,000 = £450$

(2)   **Heat and light**

Heat and light costs are allocated on the basis of cubic capacity (total = 25,000 m^3).

Production department 1 $\dfrac{18,000}{25,000} \times £6,000 = £4,320$

Production department 2 $\dfrac{5,000}{25,000} \times £6,000 = £1,200$

Stores centre $\dfrac{1,000}{25,000} \times £6,000 = £240$

Maintenance centre $\dfrac{1,000}{25,000} \times £6,000 = £240$

(3)   **Welfare costs**

Welfare costs are allocated on the basis of number of employees (total = 25).

Production department 1 $\dfrac{14}{25} \times £2,000 = £1,120$

Production department 2 $\dfrac{6}{25} \times £2,000 = £480$

Stores centre $\dfrac{3}{25} \times £2,000 = £240$

Maintenance centre $\dfrac{2}{25} \times £2,000 = £160$

(b)   Reapportionment of overheads using the reciprocal method can be calculated by using algebra.

Let   S =   total stores service centre overhead for apportionment after it has been apportioned overhead from maintenance centre

M =   total of maintenance service centre overhead after it has been apportioned overhead from stores centre

S = 1,080 + 0.05M
M = 850 + 0.1S

$\therefore$ S $= 1,080 + 0.05 (850 + 0.1S)$

$= 1,080 + 42.5 + 0.005S$

$= 1,122.5 + 0.005S$

$0.995S = 1,122.5$

$S = \dfrac{1,122.5}{0.995}$

$S = 1,128$

If S $= 1,128$

M $= 850 + (0.1 \times 1,128)$
$= 850 + 112.8$
$= 962.8$
$= 963$

| | Production departments | | Service centres | | |
| | 1 | 2 | Stores | Maintenance | Total |
	£	£	£	£	£
Overhead costs	15,790	4,780	1,080	850	22,500
Apportion stores total	564	451	(1,128)	113	-
Apportion maintenance total	433	482	48	(963)	-
	16,787	5,713	-	-	22,500

(c) Production department 1 is **labour intensive** and so an overhead rate per labour hour should be calculated.

Overhead absorption rate per labour hour $= \dfrac{\text{Total overheads}}{\text{Total labour hours}}$

$= \dfrac{\text{£}16,787}{2,400}$

$= \text{£}7$

Production department 2 is **machine intensive** and so an overhead rate per machine hour should be calculated.

Overhead absorption rate per machine hour $= \dfrac{\text{Total overheads}}{\text{Total machine hours}}$

$= \dfrac{\text{£}5,713}{4,572}$

$= \text{£}1.25$

14   MARGINAL AND ABSORPTION COSTING MCQs

(a) C   Difference in profit $=$ change in stock level $\times$ fixed overhead per unit
$= (200 - 250) \times (\text{£}2.50 \times 3)$
$= \text{£}375$

The absorption costing profit will be greater because stocks have increased.

If you selected option A you calculated the correct profit difference but the absorption costing profit would be greater because fixed overheads are carried forward in the increasing stock levels.

If you selected option B you multiplied the stock difference by the direct labour-hour rate instead of by the total overhead cost per **unit**, which takes three hours.

If you selected option D you based the profit difference on the closing stock only (250 units $\times$ £2.50 $\times$ 3).

(b) C   **IV** is a feature of traditional absorption costing methods.

15 PROFIT DIFFERENCES

(a) Marginal costing profit statement

	January - March		April - June	
	£'000	£'000	£'000	£'000
Sales (W1)		2,700		4,050
Opening stock (W4)	-		165	
Variable production costs (W2)	1,155		1,650	
Closing stock (W4)	(165)		(330)	
Cost of sales		(990)		(1,485)
		1,710		2,565
Variable selling costs (W5)		(90)		(135)
Contribution		1,620		2,430
Fixed production overhead (per quarter)		(100)		(100)
Fixed selling costs (per quarter)		(20)		(20)
Administration costs (per quarter)		(30)		(30)
Budgeted profit	-	1,470		2,280

(b) Absorption costing profit statement

	January - March		April - June	
	£'000	£'000	£'000	£'000
Sales		2,700.0		4,050.0
Opening stock (W4)	-		177.5	
Production costs (W2)	1,242.5		1,775.0	
Closing stock (W4)	(177.5)		(355.0)	
Cost of sales		1,065.0		1,597.5
		1,635.0		2,452.5
(Under-)/over-absorbed overheads (W6)		(12.5)		25.0
		1,622.5		2,477.5
Variable selling costs (W5)		(90.0)		(135.0)
Fixed selling costs (per quarter)		(20.0)		(20.0)
Administration costs (per quarter)		(30.0)		(30.0)
Budgeted profit		1,482.5		2,292.5

Workings

1   Sales are 60,000 or 90,000 × £45

2   Production costs are calculated as follows.

	Per unit	70,000 units	100,000 units
	£	£'000	£'000
Direct materials	10.00		
Direct wages	4.00		
Variable overhead	2.50		
Variable production cost	16.50	1,155.00	1,650
Variable production cost	16.50	1,155.00	1,650
Fixed production overhead (W3)	1.25	87.50	125
Total production cost	17.75	1,242.50	1,775

3   Fixed production overhead per unit

$$\frac{\text{Total cost}}{\text{Total absorption basis}} = \frac{£400,000}{320,000 \text{ units}} = £1.25$$

Fixed production overheads are absorbed on a per unit basis in the absence of alternative instructions.

4   Closing stock

January - March	Units	Marginal costing £'000	Absorption costing £'000
Opening stock	-	-	-
Production (Jan-March)	70,000		
Sales	60,000		
Closing stock - March (W2)	10,000	165	177.5
Production (April-June)	100,000		
	110,000		
Sales	90,000		
Closing stock - June (W2)	20,000	330	355

5   Variable selling costs

	January - March £'000	April - June £'000
60,000 × £1.50	90	
90,000 × £1.50		135

6   (Under-)/over-absorbed fixed production overheads

Budgeted production per quarter = 320,000 ÷ 4 = 80,000 units

		£
January - March	(70,000 – 80,000) × £1.25 (W3)	(12,500)
April - June	(100,000 – 80,000) × £1.25 (W3)	25,000

Note. If overheads are underabsorbed, too little overhead is charged to profit and vice versa. The profit statement must be adjusted accordingly. The effect of the adjustment is to make **total** production costs equal whether marginal costing or absorption costing is used.

	Marginal costing £'000	£'000		Absorption costing £'000	£'000
Variable cost	(1,155)	(1,650)	Production cost	(1,242.5)	(1,775.0)
Fixed cost	(100)	(100)	Under-/over-absorbed	(12.5)	25.0
	(1,255)	(1,750)		(1,255.0)	(1,750.0)

16   JOB, BATCH AND CONTRACT COSTING MCQs

(a)   D

Hours for job 34679	= 400 hours
Production overhead cost	£4,000
∴ Overhead absorption rate (£4,000 ÷ 400)	£10 per direct labour hour
Budgeted direct labour hours	45,000
∴ Total budgeted production overheads	£450,000
Budgeted direct wages cost	£180,000
∴ Absorption rate as % of wages cost	= £450,000/£180,000 × 100%
	= 250%

Cost of job 34679

	£
Direct materials	2,000
Direct labour, including overtime premium *	2,500
Overhead (250% × £2,500)	6,250
Total production cost	10,750

* The overtime premium is a direct labour cost because the overtime was worked specifically for this job.

If you selected option A you got your calculation of the overhead absorption rate 'upside down' and derived a percentage rate of 40 per cent in error. If you selected option B you did not include the overtime premium and the corresponding overhead. If you selected option C you did not include the overtime premium in the direct labour costs.

(b) B   Since we are given no profit restriction and because the project is 65% complete (1,300/2,000) we use the following formula.

$$\text{Profit} = \text{notional profit} \times \frac{\text{Cash received on account}}{\text{Value of work certified}}$$

$$\text{Profit} = \pounds\left[(1,300,000 - 1,000,000) \times \frac{1,200,000}{1,300,000}\right]$$

Profit = £276,923 or £277,000 to the nearest £'000.

Option A is the difference between the cash received and the costs incurred, but this makes **no allowance for the retention monies and the cost of work certified.** Option C is the notional profit to date, but it is generally accepted that this **should be reduced where the contractee withholds a retention.** Option D uses the final contract price, but **the contract is not yet complete.**

17   INDRICAR LIMITED

(a)

		Job X123 £	Job X124 £	Job X125 £	Job X126 £	Job X127 £
Direct material:	to 30.11.X8	1,250	722	-	-	-
	December X8	420	698	1,900	1,221	516
	returns	(120)	-	(70)	(217)	-
	transfers	(100)	-	100	-	-
		1,450	1,420	1,930	1,004	516
Direct labour:	to 30.11.X8	820	600	-	-	-
	December X8	260	390	1,560	755	290
Total direct cost		2,530	2,410	3,490	1,759	806
Factory production overhead (W1)		2,160	1,980	3,120	1,510	580
Total factory production cost		4,690	4,390	6,610	3,269	1,386
Selling, distn and admin cost (20%)		938	878	1,322		
Total cost		5,628	5,268	7,932		

Working

		Job X123 £	Job X124 £	Job X125 £	Job X126 £	Job X127 £
1	Direct labour cost	1,080	990	1,560	755	290
	Factory production overhead (200%)	2,160	1,980	3,120	1,510	580

(b)

Tutor's hint. Profits or losses arising on jobs = Amounts invoiced to customers – total cost of job.

	Job X123 £	Job X124 £	Job X125 £
Amounts invoiced to customer	6,250	6,000	7,900
Total cost (from (a))	5,628	5,268	7,932
Profit/(loss) on job	622	732	(32)

18   PROCESS COSTING MCQs

(a) D   *Step 1.* **Determine output and losses**

Input Units	Output	Total Units	Equivalent units of production			
			Process X		Conversion costs	
			Units	%	Units	%
2,000	Finished units	1,600	1,600	100	1,600	100
	Normal loss	200				
	Abnormal loss (balance)	100	100	100	100	100
	Closing stock	100	100	100	50	50
2,000		2,000	1,800		1,750	

Step 2. Calculate cost per unit of output, losses and WIP

Input	Cost	Equivalent units	Cost per equivalent unit
	£		£
Process X material (£8,000 – 800)	7,200	1,800	4
Conversion costs	12,250	1,750	7
			11

Step 3. Calculate total cost of output

Cost of completed production = £11 × 1,600 litres = £17,600

If you selected option A you included the normal loss in your equivalent units calculation, but these units do not carry any of the process costs. If you selected option B you did not allow for the fact that the work in progress units were incomplete as regards conversion costs. If you selected option C you reduced the process costs by the scrap value of all lost units, instead of the normal loss units only.

(b) C   Using the unit rates from answer (a) step 2, we can proceed again to step 3.

Calculate the total cost of work in progress

	Cost element	Number of equivalent units	Cost per equivalent unit	Total
			£	£
Work in progress	Process X material	100	4	400
	Conversion costs	50	7	350
				750

If you selected option A you included the normal loss in your equivalent units calculation. If you selected option B you reduced the process costs by the scrap value of all lost units, instead of the normal loss units only. Option D does not allow for the fact that the work in progress (WIP) is incomplete when calculating the total cost of WIP.

19   PRODUCT XK

(a)   Remember that when closing WIP is partly completed, it is necessary to construct a **statement of equivalent units** in order to apportion costs fairly and proportionately.

STATEMENT OF EQUIVALENT UNITS

Input Units	Output	Total Units	Process 1 material	Labour	Overheads
2,400	Completed production (transfer to Process 2)	2,200	2,200 (100%)	2,200 (10%)	2,200
	Closing work in progress	200	200 (100%)	60 (30%)	60 (30%)
2,400		2,400	2,400	2,260	2,260

STATEMENT OF COST PER EQUIVALENT UNIT

Input	Cost	Cost	Equivalent units produced	Cost per unit
	£	£		£
Process 1 materials		5,280	2,400	2.20
Labour	2,260			
Overhead	2,260	4,520	2,260	2.00
		9,800		4.20

STATEMENT OF EVALUATION

Output	Number of equivalent units	Cost per unit	Value £	£
Transfers to Process 2	2,200	4.20		9,240
Closing work in progress				
Process 1 materials	200	2.20	440	
Labour and overhead	60	2.00	120	
				560
				9,800

PROCESS 1 ACCOUNT

	Units	£		Units	£
Process 1	2,400	5,280	Transfers to Process 2	2,200	9,240
Labour and overheads		4,520	Closing WIP	200	560
	2,400	9,800		2,400	9,800

Therefore, value of goods transferred from Process 1 to Process 2 during period 10 was £9,240 and the value of the closing work in progress left in Process 1 at the end of period 10 was £560.

(b)   STATEMENT OF EQUIVALENT UNITS

Input Units	Output	Total	Materials	Labour and overhead
2,200	Transferred from Process 1	2,200	2,200 (100%)	2,200 (100%)
2,200		2,200	2,200	2,200

NB. No opening or closing WIP in Process 2.

STATEMENT OF COST PER EQUIVALENT UNIT

Input	Cost £	£	Equivalent units produced	Cost per unit
Transfers from Process 1		9,240	2,200	4.20
Added materials		9,460	2,200	4.30
Labour	10,560			
Overhead	7,040	17,600	2,200	8.00
Value of one unit of production =				16.50

Value of goods transferred from Process 2 to finished goods = 2,200 units × £16.50 = £36,300.

20   JOINT AND BY-PRODUCTS MCQ

C   **Net process costs**

	£
Raw materials	90,000
Conversion costs	70,000
Less by-product revenue	(4,000)
Net process costs	156,000

Apportionment of net process costs

		Units	£	Apportioned costs £
Product	J	2,500	£156,000 × (2,500/8,000)	48,750
	K	3,500	£156,000 × (3,500/8,000)	68,250
	L	2,000	£156,000 × (2,000/8,000)	39,000
		8,000		156,000

If you selected option A or B you apportioned a share of the process costs to the by-product, and with option B or D you did not deduct the by-product revenue from the process costs.

21 CHEMICALS X, Y AND Z

Initial assumption: prime cost is calculated, for the purposes of absorbing overhead, before the deduction of scrap value.

Common process costs

	£
Direct materials	24,000
Direct labour	48,000
Prime cost	72,000
Factory overheads 120%	86,400
Total production cost	158,400
Less: Scrap proceeds (3,200 litres × 10% × £16.20)	(5,184)
Total common costs	153,216

(a) **Apportioning costs according to sales value**

Chemical	Output litres	£ per litre	Sales value £		Total cost £
X	1,440	100	144,000	(144,000/247,680 × £153,216)	89,079
Y	864	80	69,120	(69,120/247,680 × £153,216)	42,758
Z	576	60	34,560	(34,560/247,680 × £153,216)	21,379
			247,680		153,216

(b) **Apportioning costs according to volume**

Chemical	Output litres		Total cost £
X	1,440	(1,440/2,880 × £153,216)	76,608
Y	864	(864/2,880 × £153,216)	45,965
Z	576	(576/2,880 × £153,216)	30,643
	2,880		153,216

22 SERVICE COSTING MCQ

C   Cost per tonne - kilometre (i) is appropriate for cost control purposes because it **combines** the distance travelled and the load carried, **both of which affect cost.**

The fixed cost per kilometre (ii) is not particularly useful for control purposes because it **varies with the number of kilometres travelled.**

The maintenance cost of each vehicle per kilometre (iii) can be useful for control purposes because it **focuses on a particular aspect** of the cost of operating each vehicle. Therefore the correct answer is C.

23 HAPPY RETURNS LTD

Calculation of tonne km

Journey	Tonnes	Km	Tonne km
1	34	180	6,120
2	28	265	7,420
3	40	390	15,600
4	32	115	3,680
5	26	220	5,720
6	40	480	19,200
7	29	90	2,610
8	26	100	2,600
9	25	135	3,375
	280	1,975	66,325

Distance travelled   1,975 × 2 = 3,950 km

Calculation of costs

Variable costs	£	£
Petrol (£0.50 × 3,950)		1,975
Repairs (£0.30 × 3,950)		1,185
Deprecation (£1.00 × 3,950)		3,950
Loading costs (£6.00 × 280)		1,680
Total variable costs		8,790
Fixed costs		
Deprecation (£50 × 3)	150	
Drivers' wages (£300 × 3)	900	
Supervision and general expenses	550	
Total fixed costs		1,600
Total costs		10,390

Average cost per tonne km $= \dfrac{10,390}{66,325}$

$= £0.1567$ per tonne km

24 TIME SERIES ANALYSIS MCQs

(a) B   When the trend is increasing or decreasing, additive seasonal components change in their importance relative to the trend whereas multiplicative components remain in the same proportion to the trend. Option B is therefore a circumstance in which the multiplicative model would be preferred to the additive model.

It would generally be agreed that non-numerate people find the multiplicative model more difficult to understand than the additive model, perhaps due to problems with percentages. Option A does not apply in this instance.

When the trend is steady an additive model is acceptable but when it is increasing or decreasing it is important to use the multiplicative model so that the seasonal components remain the same proportion of the trend. Option C does not apply in this instance.

Provided the additive model is appropriate, as it is when the trend is steady, it will give forecasts as accurate as those given by the multiplicative model. Option D does not apply in this instance.

(b) A   If x = 16, y = 345.12 − (1.35 × 16) = 323.52

Forecast = trend + seasonal component = 323.52 − 23.62 = 299.9 = 300 (to nearest unit)

If you selected option B, you calculated the forecast for the fifteenth period and deducted the seasonal component of the sixteenth period.

If you selected option C, you correctly forecast the trend for the sixteenth period but forgot to deduct the seasonal component.

If you selected option D, you simply calculated the trend for the fifteenth period instead of the sixteenth period.

25 SUMMER SUN

(a)

Year	Quarter	Sum of twos	Trend*
20X3	2		
	3		
	4	190	23.750
20X4	1	193	24.125
	2	195	24.375
	3	197	24.625
	4	198	24.750
20X5	1	198	24.750
	2	199	24.875
	3	201	25.125
	4		
20X6	1		

*The trend is calculated as (figure for 'sum of twos' ÷ 8), where 8 relates to the 8 quarters' figures which make the 'sum of twos' figure. For example, the figure of 190 incorporates the actual values from the following quarters.

20X3	Q2, Q3, Q4 and 20X4 Q1 - which total to	94
20X3	Q3, Q4 and 20X4 Q1, Q2 - which total to	96
		190

(b) The **multiplicative model is Y = T × S × I**

where Y = the actual time series (original data)
T = the trend series
S = the seasonal component
I = the random irregular component

Assuming the irregular component is relatively small, and hence negligible, we have Y = T × S.

∴ Seasonally-adjusted data (for meaning see (d)) = Y/S = original data ÷ seasonal factor

Year	Quarter	Original data (Y)	Seasonal factor (S)	Seasonally-adjusted demand (Y/S)
20X3	2	31	1.343	23.083
	3	18	0.765	23.529
	4	20	0.847	23.613
20X4	1	25	1.045	23.923
	2	33	1.343	24.572
	3	19	0.765	24.837
	4	21	0.847	24.793
20X5	1	26	1.045	24.880
	2	33	1.343	24.572
	3	19	0.765	24.837
	4	22	0.847	25.974
20X6	1	27	1.045	25.837

(c) The **additive model** assumes that the components of a time series are **independent of each other**, so that the size of a seasonal variation is **independent of the trend value**. The **additive model therefore adds (or deducts) absolute and unchanging seasonal variations to (from) actual data to produce seasonally-adjusted data**. If the trend were increasing, for example, it would lessen the impact of any seasonal effect (and would increase the impact of the seasonal effect if the trend were decreasing). **The multiplicative model, on the other hand, by dividing data values by a constant seasonal variation factor, takes account of seasonal variations that vary in line with the trend**; if the trend is increasing, the absolute value of seasonal variations is also likely to increase rather than remain a fixed amount. The multiplicative model could therefore be said to provide a **more realistic model** of what actually happens.

26 BREAKEVEN ANALYSIS MCQs

(a) A $\text{Breakeven point} = \dfrac{\text{Fixed costs}}{\text{Contribution per unit}} = \dfrac{£96,000}{£(12-8)} =$ 24,000 units

Budgeted sales	30,000 units
Margin of safety	6,000 units

Expressed % of budget = $\dfrac{6,000}{30,000} \times 100\% = 20\%$

If you selected option B you calculated the correct margin of safety in units, but you then expressed this as a percentage of the breakeven point. If you selected option C you divided the fixed cost by the selling price to determine the breakeven point, but the selling price also has to cover the variable cost. You should have been able to eliminate option D; the margin of safety expressed as a percentage must always be less than 100 per cent.

(b) C   Contribution at level of activity x = sales value less variable costs, which is indicated by distance C. Distance A indicates the profit at activity x, B indicates the fixed costs and D indicates the margin of safety in terms of sales value.

27 BUILDING COMPANY

First we need to calculate the fixed costs for the period using the high-low method.

	Units	Profit
		£'000
High - March	30	250
Low - June	16	40
	14	210

Variable cost per unit (£210,000/14)	£15,000

Taking March as an example	£'000
Sales (30 × £30,000)	900
Profit	250
Total costs	650
Variable costs (30 × £15,000)	450
Fixed costs	200

Fixed costs for the six months = 6 × £200,000 = £1,200,000.

We now need to calculate the breakeven point as follows.

Per unit	£'000
Selling price	30
Variable cost	15
Contribution	15

Breakeven point is where total contribution = fixed costs. Breakeven point is therefore where £15,000N – £1,200,000, where N is the breakeven quantity of units.

N = £(1,200,000/15,000) = 80 units

Breakeven sales revenue = 80 × £30,000 = £2,400,000

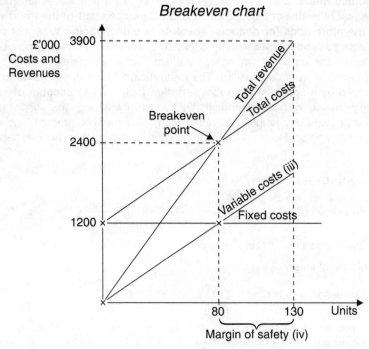

Breakeven chart

Note that at 80 units, the variable cost is 80 × £15,000 = £1,200,000.

28 RELEVANT COSTING AND DECISION MAKING MCQs

(a) **B** £5,000 has been spent on market research already and is therefore a **sunk cost** and irrelevant to the decision. The further £2,000 will only be spent if Sue continues with the project, therefore it is an **incremental (relevant) cost** of the decision to go ahead.

The cost is not an opportunity cost (option D) because Sue has not forgone an alternative use for the resources.

(b) **B** The relevant cost of the material in stock is the **opportunity cost of £2 per litre**, because the material would be sold if the order was rejected. The remainder of the required material **must be purchased at £10 per litre**.

Relevant cost is therefore (85 × £2)+ (15 × £10) = £320.

If you selected option A you valued all of the 100 litres required at £2 per litre, but this opportunity cost only applies to the 85 litres in stock. Option C values the stock items at their original cost of £8 per litre, but this is a **sunk cost** which is not relevant to decisions about the future use of the material. Option D values all the material at replacement cost, but the items in stock will not be replaced by ABC Limited.

29 ABC LTD

(a)

	Product A	Product B	Product C	Total
Machine hours required per unit	6	4	7	
Maximum demand (units)	3,000	2,500	5,000	
Total machine hours required	18,000	10,000	35,000	63,000
Machine hours available				50,000
Deficiency in machine hours for next period				13,000

(b)

	Product A	Product B	Product C
	£ per unit	£ per unit	£ per unit
External purchase price	175	140	200
Variable cost of internal manufacture	154	112	178
Saving through internal manufacture	21	28	22
Machine hours per unit	6	4	7
Saving per machine hour	£3.50	£7.00	£3.14
Priority ranking for internal manufacture	2	1	3

Since all products can be sold for more than their bought-in cost, unsatisfied demand should be met through external purchases. Purchases should be made in the reverse order of the above ranking, until the deficiency in machine hours (13,000) has been covered.

Some units of Product C should therefore be purchased from the external supplier.

$$\text{Number of units of C to be purchased} = \frac{13,000 \text{ hours}}{7} \text{ (from (a))}$$

$$= \textbf{1,858 units}$$

30 DECISION MAKING WITH UNCERTAINTY MCQs

(a) **D** EV = (500 × 0.5) + (600 × 0.1) + (400 × (1 − 0.5 − 0.1)) = 470

If you chose **option A**, you appear to have simply totalled the three possible sales levels.

If you chose **option B,** you appear to have taken the average daily sales level.

If you chose **option C,** you have calculated the EV as (500 × 0.5) + (600 × 0.1) + 400.

(b) **A** **Statement I:** The EV at E is £1,700,000, whereas the EV at F is £1,600,000. Cost of sales should be minimised, so Decision 4 would be chosen.

Statement II: The EV at C would be £1,600,000 (the *lower* of £1,700,000 and £1,600,000) while the EV at D is £920,000 and so the EV at B is (£1,600,000 × 0.5) + (£920,000 × 0.5) = £1,260,000.

Statement III: The EV of decision 1 is £1,260,000, whereas the known value of decision 2 is £1,200,000. The lower figure is taken because the figures relate to cost of sales.

Statement IV: The EV at D = (£1,400,000 × 0.2) + (£800,000 × 0.8) = £920,000

31   GEOLOGICAL TESTS

(a)

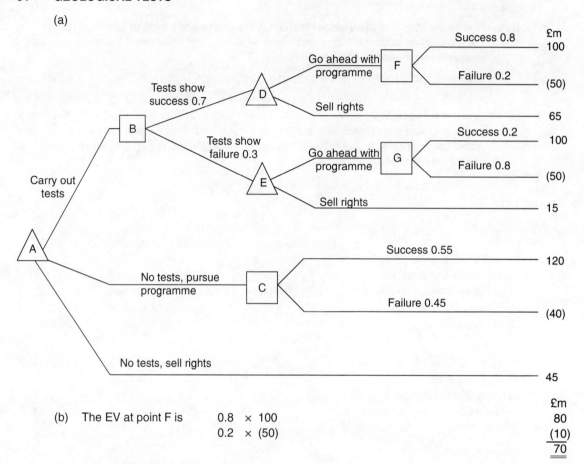

(b)   The EV at point F is

		£m
0.8	× 100	80
0.2	× (50)	(10)
		70

The decision at point D will be to pursue the programme rather than sell the rights for £65,000,000, and the EV at point D is therefore £70,000,000.

The EV at point G is

		£m
0.2	× 100	20
0.8	× (50)	(40)
		(20)

The decision at point E will be to sell the rights rather than pursue the programme, and the EV at point E is £15,000,000.

The EV at point C is

		£m
0.55	× 120	66
0.45	× (40)	(18)
		48

The EV at point B is

		£m
0.7	× 70	49.0
0.3	× 15	4.5
		53.5

The decision at point A is between

(i)	conducting tests	EV	£53,500,000
(ii)	not conducting tests and pursuing the programme	EV	£48,000,000
(iii)	not conducting tests and selling the rights	EV	£45,000,000

The EV at point A, choosing option (i) with the highest EV, is £53,500,000.

32   LINEAR PROGRAMMING MCQs

(a)   D   This inequality states that X must be at most 2Y, as required.

The inequality in **option A** states that X must be at least 2Y, whereas 2Y is meant to be the very maximum value of X.

The inequality in **option B** states that Y must be at most 2X, whereas X is meant to be at most 2Y.

The inequality in **option C** states that Y must be at least 2X, whereas X is meant to be at most 2Y.

(b)   D   The region to the left of X = 41 satisfies X ≤ 41 while that above Y = 19 satisfies Y ≥ 19.

Option A is incorrect because the region you have described is bounded by X ≤ 41, but Y ≤ 19 instead of Y ≥ 19.

Option B is incorrect because the region you have described is bounded by X ≥ 41 and Y ≤ 19 instead of by X ≤ 41 and Y ≥ 19.

Option C is incorrect because the region you have described is bounded by Y ≥ 19 but by X ≥ 41 instead of X ≤ 41.

33   CUCKFIELD

(a)   Let the number of units of product D made be D
Let the number of units of product H made be H

The constraints are therefore as follows.

Material A	(1) $3D + 2H \le 3,000$	
Material N	(2) $0.5D + 2H \le 1,000$	
Semi-skilled labour	(3) $1.5D + 1.5H \le 1,800$	(W1)
Skilled labour	(4) $D + 1.4H \ge 700$	(W2)

Workings

(1)   Semi-skilled workers can only work a 40-hour week. There are 45 semi-skilled workers. 45 × 40 hours = 1,800 hours.

(2)   Skilled labour workers are guaranteed a 35-hour week. Therefore, the number of skilled hours worked must be **greater than or equal to** 700 (20 × 35 hours).

(b)

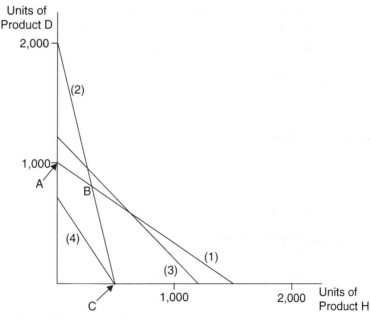

The optimal solution will be either A, B or C as shown on the graph above.

Workings

(1)   3D + 2H ≤ 3,000

        If D = 0, H = 1,500   (3,000/2)
        If H = 0, D = 1,000   (3,000/3)

(2)   0.5D + 2H ≤ 1,000

        If D = 0, H = 500   (1,000/2)
        If H = 0, D = 2,000   (1,000/0.5)

(3)   1.5D + 1.5H ≤ 1,800

        If D = 0, H = 1,200   (1,800/1.5)
        If H = 0, D = 1,200   (1,800/1.5)

(4)   D + 1.4H ≥ 700

        If D = 0, H = 500   (700/1.4)
        If H = 0, D = 700   (700/1)

34   INTEREST MCQs

(a)   D   Effective quarterly rate   = 1% (4% ÷ 4)

                Effective annual rate   = $[(1.01)^4 - 1]$
                                             = 0.0406 = 4.06% pa

        Remember that the formula for calculating the effective annual rate is not provided in your examination.

        You should have been able to eliminate options A and B immediately. 1% is simply 4% ÷ 4 = 1%. 4% is the nominal rate and is therefore not the effective annual rate of interest.

(b)   C   There are ten flows but one is at time 0. We therefore need to look up the present value of £1 per annum received at the end of **nine** years at an interest rate of 8% in cumulative present value tables = 6.247.

                Present value of cash flows   = £1,000 × (1 + 6.247)*
                                               = £1,000 × 7.247
                                               = £7,247

        * We need to add 1 to the annuity factor for years 1-9 since the first rent is to be paid **now**.

        Option A is incorrect since it represents the present value of the cashflows in years 1-9 only (and excludes the first payment that is made now). £1,000 × 6.247 = £6,247.

        Option B is incorrect because it represents the ten rental payments starting in one year's time for ten years, ie £1,000 × 6.710 = £6,710.

        Option D represents the present value of 11 payments, the first payment now followed by 10 further payments = £1,000 × (1 + 6.710) = £1,000 × 7.710 = £7,710. Remember that if there are ten payments and the first one is made now, there will only be nine further payments (not ten).

35   FIXED INTEREST MORTGAGE

(a) $S = P(1 + r)^n$
        $S = £100,000(1 + 0.03)^{40}$
        $S = £326,203.78$

(b)   At the end of quarter 1, the value of the repayment   = x
        At the end of quarter 2, the value of the repayments   = x(1 + 0.03) + x
        At the end of quarter 3, the value of the repayments   = $x(1 + 0.03)^2$ +
                                                                    x(1 + 0.03) + x
        At the end of quarter 40, the value of the repayments   = $x(1 + 0.03)^{39}$ + ... + x

        This is a geometric progression with   A = x
                                               R = (1 + 0.03)
                                               n = 40

and so using the formula for the sum of a geometric series of n terms with first term A and common ratio R, the total value of the repayments, S =

$$\frac{A(R^n - 1)}{(R-1)} = \frac{x((1 + 0.03)^{40} - 1)}{(1 + 0.03 - 1)} = \frac{x(1.03^{40} - 1)}{0.03}$$

The initial loan will have increased to

£326,203.78 (from (i))

For the loan to be paid off, the two amounts must be equal.

$$326,203.78 = \frac{x(1.03^{40} - 1)}{0.03}$$

$$\frac{326,203.78 \times 0.03}{(1.03^{40} - 1)} = x$$

£4,326.24 = x

(c) Effective annual rate = $[(1 + 0.03)^4 - 1] = 12.55\%$

36 INVESTMENT APPRAISAL MCQ

A $IRR = a\% + \left[\frac{A}{A - B} \times (b - a)\right]\%$

Where   a = one interest rate = 8%
        b = other interest rate = 9%
        A = NPV at rate A = £18,000
        B = NPV at rate B = −£11,000

IRR $= 8\% + \left[\frac{£18,000}{£18,000 - (-£11,000)} \times (9 - 8)\right]\%$

      = 8% + 0.62%
      = 8.62%

If you selected option B, you used A = NPV at rate B and B = NPV at rate A and therefore divided the range from 8% to 9% in the ratio 11:18 instead of 18:11.

If you selected option C, you have simply taken the midpoint [(8 + 9) ÷ 2 = 8.5%]. The IRR is the discount rate where NPV = 0.

If you selected option D, you have not accounted for the fact that the NPV at 9% is **negative**.

37 BARCOMBE

(a)

Year	Cashflow	Discount factor 10%	20%	Present value 10%	20%
	£			£	£
0	(36,000)	1	1	(36,000)	(36,000)
1	15,000	0.909	0.833	13,635	12,495
2	17,000	0.826	0.694	14,042	11,798
3	22,000	0.751	0.579	16,522	12,738
4	4,000*	0.683	0.482	2,732	1,928
		Net present values		10,931	2,959

* £2,000 (cash inflow) + £2,000 (sale of fixed assets at end of the project)

(b) The internal rate of return (IRR) can be calculated using the following formula.

$IRR = a\% + \left[\frac{A}{A - B} \times (b - a)\right]\%$ where

a = one interest rate (10%)
b = the other interest rate (20%)
A = the NPV at rate a (£10,931)
B = the NPV at rate b (£2,959)

Therefore, IRR $= 10\% + \left[\dfrac{10{,}931}{10{,}931 - 2{,}959} \times (20 - 10)\right]\%$

$= 10\% + \left[\dfrac{10{,}931}{7{,}972} \times 10\right]\%$

$= 10\% + 13.7\%$

$= 23.7\%$

(c) The IRR formula works when A and B are both positive or both negative NPVs and even if the discount rates a and b are a long way from the true IRR. The IRR formula, however, will give more accurate results if the different discount factors had given one positive NPV and one negative NPV.

38 PRICING MCQ

C Profit is maximised when marginal cost $=$ marginal revenue
$9 = 25 - (0.4 \times \text{quantity})$
$(0.4 \times \text{quantity}) = 16$
$\text{quantity} = 40$

Substituting in the equation for price:
$\text{price} = 25 - (0.2 \times 40)$
$= £17.00$

If you selected option A or B you used only the variable overhead and the direct cost respectively as the marginal cost per unit.

39 DEMAND, PRICE, REVENUE AND COSTS

(a) $P = a - \dfrac{bQ}{\Delta Q}$

$a = £48 + \dfrac{70}{-30} \times -£30$

$= 118$

$P = 118 - \dfrac{30X}{30}$

$P = 118 - X$

Alternative approach

$P = a + bQ$

where $b = \dfrac{\Delta P}{\Delta Q}$

$b = \dfrac{48 - 78}{70 - 40} = \dfrac{-30}{30} = -1$

$\therefore \quad a = P - bX$

If P = 48, b = −1 and Q = 70, then
$a = 48 - (-1 \times 70)$
$= 48 + 70$
$= 118$

$\therefore$ The demand function is $\underline{P = 118 - X}$

(b) Revenue (R) = price × quantity sold
= PX
= (118 − X)X
= 118 X − X^2

(c)   Total costs   = fixed costs + variable costs
                      = 1,710 + 9X

40   PREPARING THE MASTER BUDGET MCQs

(a)   D   The **principal budget factor** is the factor which limits the activities of an organisation.

Although cash and profit are affected by the level of sales (options B and C), sales is not the only factor which determines the level of cash and profit.

(b)   D

	Units
Budgeted sales	18,000
Budgeted reduction in finished goods	(3,600)
Budgeted production of completed units	14,400
Allowance for defective units (10% of output = 1/9 of input)	1,600
Production budget	16,000

If you selected option A you deducted a ten per cent allowance for defective units, instead of adding it, and option B makes no allowance for defective units at all. If you selected option C you added ten per cent to the required completed units to allow for the defective units, but the ten per cent **should be based on the total number of units output**, ie ten per cent of 16,000 = 1,600 units.

41   HAROLD GODWINSSON LTD

Workings

Budgeted production overhead	£3,717,000
Budgeted labour hours	1,062,000 hrs
Absorption rate per direct labour hour	£3.50

This is applied to Vikings at the rate of £(3.50 × 16)	=	£56 per unit
and to Normans at the rate of £(3.50 × 18)	=	£63 per unit

Standard costs

	Viking £	Norman £
Direct material		
Athelstan	12	6
Halfdan	20	40
Direct wages		
Thanes	21	42
Serfs	10	6
Production overhead	56	63
Standard production cost	119	157

	Viking	Norman
Budgeted opening stocks	£238,000	£628,0000
ie	2,000 units	4,000 units
Budgeted closing stocks	£595,000	£1,413,000
ie	5,000 units	9,000 units

Budgeted sales

	£'000	£'000
Danelaw	1,808	1,280
Wessex	600	1,600
Mercia	900	2,600
Kent	500	800
Total	3,808	6,280
at production cost (75%)	£2,856,0000	£4,710,000
ie	24,000 units	30,000 units

(a) **Production budget**

	Viking Units	Norman Units
Closing stock, finished goods	5,000	9,000
Less opening stock	2,000	4,000
Stock increase, finished goods	3,000	5,000
Sales	24,000	30,000
Production requirement	27,000	35,000

(b) **Direct materials cost budget**

	Athelstan £ per unit	Athelstan £'000	Halfdan £ per unit	Halfdan £'000	Total £'000
Vikings (27,000 units)	12	324	20	540	864
Normans (35,000 units)	6	210	40	1,400	1,610
		534		1,940	2,474

(c) **Purchases budget**

	Athelstan £'000	Halfdan £'000	Total £'000
Closing stock	40	180	
Opening stock	120	160	
Increase/(decrease) in stock	(80)	20	
Production requirements	534	1,940	
Purchase requirements	454	1,960	2,414

42 FURTHER ASPECTS OF BUDGETING MCQs

(a) C A flexible budget **recognises different cost behaviour patterns** and is designed to change as the volume of activity changes.

A flexible budget includes both fixed and variable costs, and identifies them separately. Therefore option A is not correct. Any budget can be prepared using a spreadsheet model therefore option D is not correct.

(b) C The actual labour cost (£11,500) should be compared with the **budget cost allowance for the actual production** $(1,100 \times £10 = £11,000)$.

Option A includes the figures for output volume. Option B is incorrect because it compares the actual expenditure with the original budget. This would not be useful for the control of expenditure because **it is not possible to identify how much of the extra expenditure is due to the change in activity**.

43 JAK LTD

Comparison of budget and actual results for May 20X3

	Budget	Flexed budget	Actual results	Variance
Production and sales of the Anori (units)	40,000	48,000	48,000	
	£	£	£	
Sales	50,000	60,000	55,200	(4,800)
Direct materials	12,000	14,400	16,800	(2,400)
Direct labour	8,000	9,600	10,290	(690)
Variable overheads	5,000	6,000	5,560	440
Fixed overheads	15,000	15,000	16,500	(1,500)
Total costs	40,000	45,000	49,150	(4,150)
Profit	10,000	15,000	6,050	(8,950)

44   STANDARD COSTING MCQs

(a)   D   Performance standards would be taken into account when estimating **material usage**, they would not have a direct effect on material price. Therefore the correct answer is D.

All of the other factors would be used to estimate standard material prices for a forthcoming period.

(b)   D   Required liquid input = 2 litres $\times \dfrac{100}{70}$ = 2.86 litres

Standard cost of liquid input = 2.86 × £1.20 = £3.43 (to the nearest penny)

If you selected option A you made no allowance for spillage and evaporation. Option B is the figure for the quantity of material input, not its cost. If you selected option C you simply added an extra 30 per cent to the finished volume. However, the wastage is 30 per cent of the liquid **input**, not 30 per cent of output.

45   DOODLE LTD

Workings

The **budgeted direct labour hours** = 11,400 × (40 + 36) = 866,400 direct labour hours.

The **fixed production overhead absorption rate** = £1.25 per hour (£1,083,000 ÷ 866,400 hours).

The **variable production overhead rate** (both for costs incurred and absorbed) is:

department P :   75 pence per hour
department Q :   50 pence per hour

Administration overhead = £125,400 ÷ 11,400 = £11 per unit

Marketing overhead = £285,000 ÷ 11,400 = £25 per unit

STANDARD COST SHEET - THE SQUIGGLE		
	£	£
Direct materials: 30 metres at £6.10		183
Direct wages		
Department P: 40 hours at £2.20	88	
Department Q: 36 hours at £2.50	90	
		178
(a) (i) Standard total direct cost		361
Variable production overhead		
Department P: 40 hours at £0.75	30	
Department Q: 36 hours at £0.50	18	
		48
(ii) Standard variable production cost		409
Fixed production overhead: 76 hours at £1.25		95
(iii) Standard production cost		504
Administration overhead (note 1)		11
Marketing overhead (note 2)		25
(iv) Standard cost of sale		540
Standard profit (10% of sales price)		60
(b) Standard sales price		600

BPP
PUBLISHING

46   BASIC VARIANCE ANALYSIS MCQs

(a)   B

		£
Material price variance		
5,000 litres did cost		16,000
But should have cost (× £3)		15,000
		1,000 (A)

Material usage variance		
1,270 units did use		5,000 litres
But should have used (× 4 litres)		5,080 litres
Usage variance in litres		80 (F)
× standard cost per litre		£3
		240 (F)

If you selected options A or C you calculated the money values of the variances correctly but misinterpreted their direction.

If you selected option D you valued the usage variance in litres at the actual cost per litre instead of the standard cost per litre.

(b)   B

	£
1,660 hours of variable production overhead should cost (× £1.70)	2,822
But did cost	2,950
	128 (A)

If you selected option A you based your expenditure allowance on all of the labour hours worked. However, it is usually assumed that **variable overheads are incurred during active working hours**, but are not incurred during idle time.

If you selected option C you calculated the correct money value of the variance but you misinterpreted its direction.

Option D is the variable production overhead total variance.

(c)   B

400 units of Product B should take (× 4 hours)	1,600 hours
But did take (active hours)	1,660 hours
Efficiency variance in hours	60 hours (A)
× standard rate per hour	× £1.70
	102 (A)

If you selected option A you calculated the correct money value of the variance but you misinterpreted its direction.

If you selected option C you valued the efficiency variance in hours at the actual variable production overhead rate per hour. Option D bases the calculation on all of the hours worked, instead of only the **active hours**.

47   BRAIN LTD

(a)   **Price variance - A**

	£
7,800 kgs should have cost (× £20)	156,000
but did cost	159,900
Price variance	3,900 (A)

Usage variance - A

800 units should have used (× 10 kgs)	8,000 kgs
but did use	7,800 kgs
Usage variance in kgs	200 kgs (F)
× standard cost per kilogram	× £20
Usage variance in £	£4,000 (F)

Price variance - B

	£
4,300 units should have cost (× £6)	25,800
but did cost	23,650
Price variance	2,150 (F)

Usage variance - B

800 units should have used (× 5 l)	4,000 l
but did use	4,300 l
Usage variance in litres	300 (A)
× standard cost per litre	× £6
Usage variance in £	£1,800 (A)

(b) **Labour rate variance**

	£
4,200 hours should have cost (× £6)	25,200
but did cost	24,150
Rate variance	1,050 (F)

Labour efficiency variance

800 units should have taken (× 5 hrs)	4,000 hrs
but did take	4,200 hrs
Efficiency variance in hours	200 hrs (A)
× standard rate per hour	× £6
Efficiency variance in £	£1,200 (A)

(c) **Expense variance**

	£
Expense for 800 units should have been (× £5)	4,000
but was	3,750
Expense variance	250 (F)

(d) **Fixed overhead expenditure variance**

	£
Budgeted expenditure (£50 × 900)	45,000
Actual expenditure	47,000
Expenditure variance	2,000 (A)

Fixed overhead volume variance

	£
Budgeted production at standard rate (900 × £50)	45,000
Actual production at standard rate (800 × £50)	40,000
Volume variance	5,000 (A)

Fixed overhead volume efficiency variance

	£
800 units should have taken (× 5 hrs)	4,000 hrs
but did take	4,200 hrs
Volume efficiency variance in hours	200 hrs
× standard absorption rate per hour	× £10
Volume efficiency variance	£2,000 (A)

Fixed overhead volume capacity variance

Budgeted hours	4,500 hrs
Actual hours	4,200 hrs
Volume capacity variance in hours	300 hrs (A)
× standard absorption rate per hour (£50 ÷ 5)	× £10
	£3,000 (A)

48 FURTHER VARIANCE ANALYSIS MCQs

(a) B

Actual sales	2,550 units
Budgeted sales	2,400 units
Variance in units	150 units (F)
x standard profit per unit (£(27 − 12))	× £6
Sales volume variance in £	£900 (F)

	£
Revenue from 2,550 units should have been (× £27)	68,850
but was	67,320
Sales price variance	1,530 (A)

If you selected option A, C or D, you calculated the monetary values of the variances correctly, but misinterpreted their direction.

(b)   C   Statement (i) is not correct. Fixed overhead is not absorbed into production costs in a marginal costing system.

Statement (ii) is correct. Sales volume variances are calculated using the standard contribution per unit (and not the standard profit per unit which is used in standard absorption costing systems).

Statement (iii) is correct. As stated above, fixed overhead is not absorbed into production costs in a marginal costing system.

49   TARDIS LTD

Sales volume variance

	Dalek	Yeti	Cyberman
Budgeted sales	500	300	200
Actual sales	700	300	500
Sales volume variance in units	200 (F)	-	300 (F)
× standard profit per unit	× £2	× £3	× £4
Sales volume variance in £	£400 (F)	-	£1,200 (F)

Total sales volume variance   £1,600 (F)

Sales mix variance

	Dalek	Yeti	Cyberman
Mix should have been (1,500 × 50%/30%/20%)	750	450	300
but was	700	300	500
Mix variance in units	50 (A)	150 (A)	200 (F)
× standard profit per unit	× £2	× £3	× £4
Sales mix variance in £	£100 (A)	£450 (A)	£800 (F)

Total sales mix variance   £250 (F)

Sales quantity variance

	Dalek	Yeti	Cyberman
Actual sales in budgeted mix	750	450	300
Budgeted sales	500	300	200
Sales quantity variance n units	250 (F)	150 (F)	100 (F)
× standard profit per unit	× £2	× £3	× £4
Sales quantity variance in £	£500 (F)	£450 (F)	£400 (F)

Total sales quantity variance   £1,350 (F)

50   INDEX NUMBERS MCQs

(a)   B $100 \times P_1/P_0 = 135$

$P_1 = £55.35$

$\therefore \dfrac{100 \times £55.35}{P_0} = 135$

$\therefore \dfrac{100 \times £55.35}{135} = P_0 = £41$

If you selected option C you interchanged P_0 and P_1 in the above formula. If you selected option D you have mistakenly taken the base year index of 100 as being the commodity price per kg.

(b)   C   The formula for the Laspeyre price index is $\dfrac{\Sigma p_1 q_0}{\Sigma p_0 q_0} \times 100$

	p_1	q_0	p_0	p_1q_0	p_0q_0
X	30	50	10	1,500	500
Y	16	90	12	1,440	1,080
Z	12	110	14	1,320	1,540
				4,260	3,120

Laspeyre price index for year 6 $= \dfrac{4,260}{3,120} \times 100$

$= 136.5$

If you selected option A your formula was upside down!

Option B is the **Laspeyre quantity index** and option D is the **Paasche price index** for this data.

51 WEIGHTED INDEX

(a)

		Year 1			Year 2	
	'000 units	Selling price	Total	'000 units	Selling price	Total
Product	sold	per unit	revenue	sold	per unit	revenue
		£	£'000		£	£'000
A	76	0.60	45.6	72	0.78	56.16
B	52	0.75	39.0	60	1.00	60.00
C	28	1.10	30.8	40	1.32	52.80
			115.4			168.96

% increase $= \dfrac{168.96 - 115.4}{115.4} \times 100\% = 46.41\%$

(b) **Laspeyre price index for Year 5 based on Year 1**

$= \dfrac{\Sigma p_n q_0}{\Sigma p_0 q_0} \times 100$

where p_0, q_0 = prices/quantities in Year 1 and p_n = prices in Year 5.

$\Sigma p_0 q_0$ = total revenue for Year 1 = £115,400 (from (i) above)

$\Sigma p_n q_0 = (£0.78 \times 76,000) + (£1.00 \times 52,000) + (£1.32 \times 28,000) = £148,240$

∴ Laspeyre price index for Year 5 based on Year 1

$= \dfrac{148,240}{115,400} \times 100 = 128.46$

(Alternatively your answer could be given as 1.2846)

(c) Price increases in the five-year period caused total sales revenue to increase by 28.46%. The remaining increase (46.41% − 28.46% = 17.95%) is due to changes in sales volume and sales mix. The volume of total units sold increased by 10.26% (((172,000 − 156,000)/156,000) × 100) and the proportion of the mix comprising the two highest priced products increased (the proportion comprising the lowest priced product obviously decreasing).

52 PERFORMANCE MEASUREMENT MCQs

(a) B   Apportioned head office costs are uncontrollable by the manager of a profit centre, but controllable costs are within his control. He also has control over revenue, whether from sales within the organisation (transfer prices) or from sales external to the organisation (selling prices).

(b) B   **Divisional residual income**

	£
Divisional return	62,000
Imputed interest (380 + 18) × 12%	47,760
Divisional residual income	14,240

If you selected option A you did not add back the head office management charges to the divisional net profit. These costs are **not controllable** by the divisional manager.

If you selected option C you based the imputed interest charge on the fixed assets only, but the manager also has **complete discretion over the purchase and use of stock**.

Option D is the controllable divisional profit, but the **imputed interest** must be deducted from this to derive the **controllable residual income**.

53 PERFORMANCE MEASUREMENT

(a) (i) (1) Operating profit = £100,000 − £25,000 = £75,000

Divisional capital employed = £50,000 + £200,000 = £250,000

$$\text{ROCE} = \frac{£75,000}{£250,000} = 30\%$$

(2)

	£
Operating profit (per (i))	75,000
Imputed interest = 10% × £250,000 =	25,000
∴ Residual income	50,000

(ii) The investment will alter the profit and capital employed

	Operating profit	*Capital employed*
	£	*£*
Per (a)	75,000	250,000
Machine sold	(3,000)	(7,500)
Machine bought	6,000	20,000
	78,000	262,500

(1) $\text{ROCE} = \dfrac{£78,000}{£262,500} = 29.7\%$

(2)

	£
Operating profit	78,000
Imputed interest (10% × £262,500)	(26,250)
Residual income	51,750

(b) **Financial performance**

Profit/loss per department
Variance analysis

Competitive performance

Market share (rooms occupied as a percentage of rooms available locally)
Competitor occupancy
Repeat bookings

Resource utilisation

Rooms occupied/rooms available

Service quality

Complaints

List of key
terms and index

Note: **Key Terms** and their references are given in **bold**

BPP
PUBLISHING

BPP
PUBLISHING

BPP PUBLISHING

REVIEW FORM & FREE PRIZE DRAW

All original review forms from the entire BPP range, completed with genuine comments, will be entered into a draw on 31 January 2002 and 31 July 2002. The names on the first four forms picked out will be sent a cheque for £50.

Name: _____   **Address:** _____

_____

How have you used this Text?
(Tick one box only)

☐ Home study (book only)

☐ On a course: college _____

☐ With 'correspondence' package

☐ Other _____

Why did you decide to purchase this Text?
(Tick one box only)

☐ Have used complementary Study Text

☐ Have used BPP Texts in the past

☐ Recommendation by friend/colleague

☐ Recommendation by a lecturer at college

☐ Saw advertising

☐ Other _____

During the past six months do you recall seeing/receiving any of the following?
(Tick as many boxes as are relevant)

☐ Our advertisement in *ACCA Students' Newsletter*

☐ Our advertisement in *Pass*

☐ Our brochure with a letter through the post

Which (if any) aspects of our advertising do you find useful?
(Tick as many boxes as are relevant)

☐ Prices and publication dates of new editions

☐ Information on Text content

☐ Facility to order books off-the-page

☐ None of the above

Have you used the companion Kit/Passcard/Video/Tape * for this subject?   ☐ Yes   ☐ No
(* Please circle)

Your ratings, comments and suggestions would be appreciated on the following areas

	Very useful	Useful	Not useful
Introductory section (Key study steps, personal study)	☐	☐	☐
Chapter introductions	☐	☐	☐
Key terms	☐	☐	☐
Quality of explanations	☐	☐	☐
Case examples and other examples	☐	☐	☐
Questions and answers in each chapter	☐	☐	☐
Chapter roundups	☐	☐	☐
Qucik quizzes	☐	☐	☐
Exam focus points	☐	☐	☐
Question bank	☐	☐	☐
Answer bank	☐	☐	☐
List of key terms and index	☐	☐	☐
Icons	☐	☐	☐
Mind maps	☐	☐	☐

	Excellent	Good	Adequate	Poor
Overall opinion of this Text	☐	☐	☐	☐

Do you intend to continue using BPP Products?   ☐ Yes   ☐ No

Please note any further comments and suggestions/errors on the reverse of this page. The BPP author of this edition can be e-mailed at: lynnwatkins@bpp.com

Please return to: Katy Hibbert, ACCA Range Manager, BPP Publishing Ltd, FREEPOST, London, W12 8BR

REVIEW FORM & FREE PRIZE DRAW (continued)

Please note any further comments and suggestions/errors below

FREE PRIZE DRAW RULES

1   Closing date for 31 July 2002 draw is 30 June 2002. Closing date for 31 January 2002 draw is 31 December 2001.

2   No purchase necessary. Entry forms are available upon request from BPP Publishing. No more than one entry per title, per person. Draw restricted to persons aged 16 and over.

3   Winners will be notified by post and receive their cheques not later than 6 weeks after the draw date.

4   The decision of the promoter in all matters is final and binding. No correspondence will be entered into.

See overleaf for information on other
BPP products and how to order

Mr/Mrs/Ms (Full name)

Daytime delivery address

Postcode

Date of exam (month/year)

Daytime Tel

	2/01 Texts	9/01 Kits	9/01 Psscrds	MCQ cards	Tapes	Videos
PART 1						
1.1 Preparing Financial Statements	£19.95	£10.95	£5.95	£5.95	£12.95	£25.00
1.2 Financial Information for Management	£19.95	£10.95	£5.95	£5.95	£12.95	£25.00
1.3 Managing People	£19.95	£10.95	£5.95		£12.95	£25.00
PART 2						
2.1 Information Systems	£19.95	£10.95	£5.95		£12.95	£25.00
2.2 Corporate and Business Law (6/01)	£19.95	£10.95	£5.95		£12.95	£25.00
2.3 Business Taxation FA 2000 (for 12/01 exam)	£19.95	£10.95 (4/01)	£5.95 (4/01)		£12.95	£25.00
2.4 Financial Management and Control	£19.95	£10.95	£5.95		£12.95	£25.00
2.5 Financial Reporting (6/01)	£19.95	£10.95	£5.95		£12.95	£25.00
2.6 Audit and Internal Review (6/01)	£19.95	£10.95	£5.95		£12.95	£25.00
PART 3						
3.1 Audit and Assurance Services (6/01)	£20.95	£10.95	£5.95		£12.95	£25.00
3.2 Advanced Taxation FA 2000 (for 12/01 exam)	£20.95	£10.95 (4/01)	£5.95 (4/01)		£12.95	£25.00
3.3 Performance Management	£20.95	£10.95	£5.95		£12.95	£25.00
3.4 Business Information Management	£20.95	£10.95	£5.95		£12.95	£25.00
3.5 Strategic Business Planning and Development	£20.95	£10.95	£5.95		£12.95	£25.00
3.6 Advanced Corporate Reporting (6/01)	£20.95	£10.95	£5.95		£12.95	£25.00
3.7 Strategic Financial Management	£20.95	£10.95	£5.95		£12.95	£25.00
INTERNATIONAL STREAM						
1.1 Preparing Financial Statements	£19.95	£10.95	£5.95	£5.95		
2.5 Financial Reporting (6/01)	£19.95	£10.95	£5.95			
2.6 Audit and Internval Review (6/01)	£19.95	£10.95	£5.95			
3.1 Audit and Assurance services (6/01)	£20.95	£10.95	£5.95			
3.6 Advanced Corporate Reporting (6/01)	£20.95	£10.95	£5.95			
SUCCESS IN YOUR RESEARCH AND ANALYSIS PROJECT						
Tutorial Text (9/00)	£19.95					

SUBTOTAL £

POSTAGE & PACKING

Study Texts

	First	Each extra	
UK	£3.00	£2.00	£
Europe*	£5.00	£4.00	£
Rest of world	£20.00	£10.00	£

Kits/Passcards/Success Tapes/MCQ cards

	First	Each extra	
UK	£2.00	£1.00	£
Europe*	£2.50	£1.00	£
Rest of world	£15.00	£8.00	£

Breakthrough Videos

	First	Each extra	
UK	£2.00	£2.00	£
Europe*	£2.00	£2.00	£
Rest of world	£20.00	£10.00	£

Grand Total (Cheques to *BPP Publishing*) I enclose

a cheque for (incl. Postage) **£**

Or charge to Access/Visa/Switch

Card Number

Expiry date   Start Date

Issue Number (Switch Only)

Signature

We aim to deliver to all UK addresses inside 5 working days; a signature will be required. Orders to all EU addresses should be delivered within 6 working days. All other orders to overseas addresses should be delivered within 8 working days. * Europe includes the Republic of Ireland and the Channel Islands.